T0237386

Pro PHP XML and Web Services

Robert Richards

Apress®

Pro PHP XML and Web Services

Copyright © 2006 by Robert Richards

Softcover re-print of the Hardcover 1st edition 2006
All rights reserved. No part of this work may be reproduced or transmitted in any form or by any means, electronic or mechanical, including photocopying, recording, or by any information storage or retrieval system, without the prior written permission of the copyright owner and the publisher.

ISBN-13: 978-1-4842-2015-3

ISBN-10: 1-4842-2015-3

DOI 10.1007/978-1-4302-0139-7

Library of Congress Cataloging-in-Publication data is available upon request.

Trademarked names may appear in this book. Rather than use a trademark symbol with every occurrence of a trademarked name, we use the names only in an editorial fashion and to the benefit of the trademark owner, with no intention of infringement of the trademark.

Lead Editor: Matt Wade
Technical Reviewers: Christian Stocker, Adam Trachtenberg
Editorial Board: Steve Anglin, Dan Appleman, Ewan Buckingham, Gary Cornell, Jason Gilmore,
    Jonathan Hassell, James Huddleston, Chris Mills, Matthew Moodie, Dominic Shakeshaft,
    Jim Sumser, Matt Wade
Project Manager: Kylie Johnston
Copy Edit Manager: Nicole LeClerc
Copy Editor: Kim Wimpsett
Assistant Production Director: Kari Brooks-Copony
Production Editor: Kelly Gunther
Compositor: Linda Weidemann, Wolf Creek Press
Proofreader: Nancy Sixsmith
Indexer: Jan Wright
Artist: Kinetic Publishing Services, LLC
Cover Designer: Kurt Krames
Manufacturing Director: Tom Debolski

Distributed to the book trade worldwide by Springer-Verlag New York, Inc., 233 Spring Street, 6th Floor, New York, NY 10013. Phone 1-800-SPRINGER, fax 201-348-4505, e-mail orders-ny@springer-sbm.com, or visit http://www.springeronline.com.

For information on translations, please contact Apress directly at 2560 Ninth Street, Suite 219, Berkeley, CA 94710. Phone 510-549-5930, fax 510-549-5939, e-mail info@apress.com, or visit http://www.apress.com.

The information in this book is distributed on an "as is" basis, without warranty. Although every precaution has been taken in the preparation of this work, neither the author(s) nor Apress shall have any liability to any person or entity with respect to any loss or damage caused or alleged to be caused directly or indirectly by the information contained in this work.

The source code for this book is available to readers at http://www.apress.com in the Source Code section.

This book is dedicated to my wife and best friend, Julie.
Thank you for your patience, support, and encouragement
at the times I most needed it.

Contents

About the Author

 **ROB RICHARDS**, currently an independent contractor, has worked in various fields including medical information, telecommunications, media, and e-learning. Having been exposed to XML since its inception, he has used the technology for various projects throughout his career; his most extensive work with XML was within the e-learning space. He helped create a proprietary XML-based application server that used XML for data publishing, defining application business logic, and data querying. He was also the lead engineer for the company's involvement in the Shareable Content Object Reference Model (SCORM), which is used for Web-based learning and was established by the Department of Defense through its Advanced Distributed Learning (ADL) initiative.

After becoming the latest casualty of the dot-com implosion in 2001, Rob got his first taste of PHP and began contributing code to the domxml extension in 2002. Since then, he has become one of the authors of the DOM extension for PHP 5; he also contributes to the other XML-based extensions and authored the XMLReader and XMLWriter extensions. Also, on occasion, he contributes bug fixes to the libxml2 project for bugs found during the development of these extensions.

About the Technical Reviewers

CHRISTIAN STOCKER is one of the developers of numerous XML extensions in PHP and has been involved in developing PHP since version 4.1.

In addition, he has been a speaker for many international conferences (ApacheCon, PHP Conference, and OSCOM) and actively takes part in the open source community. He's also the author of the German book *PHP de Luxe*, recently republished in its second edition.

In his day job, he is the CEO of Bitflux GmbH, a Web development company specializing in XML/XSLT, PHP, and Ajax and based in Zurich, Switzerland.

ADAM TRACHTENBERG is the senior manager of platform evangelism at eBay, where he preaches the gospel of the eBay platform to developers and businesspeople around the globe. Before eBay, Adam cofounded and served as vice president for development at two companies, Student.com and TVGrid.com. At both firms, he led the front- and middle-end Web site design and development. Adam began using PHP in 1997; he is the author of *Upgrading to PHP 5* (O'Reilly, 2004) and the coauthor of *PHP Cookbook* (O'Reilly, 2002). He lives in San Francisco, blogs at `http://www.trachtenberg.com`, and has a bachelor's degree and a master's degree from Columbia University.

Acknowledgments

I would like to thank both Christian Stocker and Adam Trachtenberg for taking time out of their busy schedules to perform technical reviews of this book. The comments and feedback were invaluable to its completion. I also cannot forget to mention all the contributions from all the PHP developers who wrote and contributed to the various XML extensions in PHP 5, as well as Daniel Veillard and the maintainers of the libxml2 and libxslt libraries. Without all the hard work of these people, it is uncertain what the state of XML would be in PHP. I would also like to thank Matt Wade, Kylie Johnston, Kim Wimpsett, and the rest of the staff at Apress for making this book possible.

On a more personal note, a special thanks goes out to my family: my parents, Brian and Lillian; my wife, Julie; and her parents, Tony and Val. You all encouraged me during the entire book process and kept me going when things got difficult.

Introduction

XML and its associated technologies have been around for many years. Although some support has been available, it has not always been easy to work with XML using PHP. This all changed with the release of PHP 5. The inclusion of a variety of XML processors provides a developer with an arsenal of tools to tackle virtually any type of challenge involving XML. PHP 5 also went the extra step with the creation of the SOAP extension, providing native SOAP client and server support and allowing a developer to quickly and easily consume or create Web services.

With all these tools now available, PHP has become a more viable solution to implement applications that involve XML and Web services. The problem is that it is often difficult for a developer to understand how to begin using any of these tools. Not only do you need to understand the APIs of these extensions, but you also need to know which extension to use. On top of all this, you also need to understand the specifications for the different XML technologies.

This book takes a different approach than most on this subject. *Pro PHP XML and Web Services* provides an in-depth and comprehensive look at not only the tools available with PHP but also the specifications for a variety of XML-based tools. An understanding of the specifications is often critical when developing an XML-based application. After all, a tool is only good as your understanding of what you can do with it. However, the problem with the specifications is that they tend to be overly complex. For this reason, I will explain them in easy-to-understand language and include complete examples. Specifically, I take the concepts from the technical specifications and show how to adapt them to real-world use in PHP by covering the APIs and areas of functionality and showing examples of their usage.

Regardless of whether you are a novice or a more advanced developer in the area of XML, the material presented in this book will get you developing XML-based applications in PHP faster, and it will demonstrate how to maximize your usage of the XML tools now supported in PHP.

Who This Book Is For

This book is for developers of all skill levels looking to use XML in PHP. I explain the XML technologies and PHP extensions in easy-to-understand terms and examples. This will allow developers new to XML or Web services to start coding right away instead of spending countless hours deciphering the often-cryptic specifications and documentation. Developers already proficient in XML will find techniques and information about interoperability, optimization, and undocumented features of some of the XML-based extensions in order to maximize the effectiveness of an XML or Web service–based application they may be writing.

How This Book Is Structured

For you to get the most out of XML and Web services in PHP, this book is really grouped into three sections. The first section contains terminology and technical information about XML. This includes the concepts and structure of an XML document, validation, and other XML technologies commonly used. The chapters covering this information are based on various specifications. These specifications often use cryptic language and are difficult to understand, so I distill the information in clear terms.

The next group of chapters covers how to parse and manipulate XML documents using some of the extensions in PHP. I explain each extension and its API in detail with real-world examples to help reenforce the concepts covered. I also compare and contrast the extensions, providing you with some insight about where a particular extension excels and how it may not be the correct one to use in a particular situation.

The last group of chapters covers Web services. Although only a single native Web service extension exists in PHP (SOAP), I will provide in-depth coverage of additional technologies using the extensions from earlier chapters. In addition, I will cover how to integrate with the Yahoo, Google, Amazon, and eBay Web services.

Specifically, the chapters break down as follows:

Chapter 1, "Introduction to XML and Web Services": This chapter provides some background information about XML and Web services. In addition, the chapter defines what these terms mean, explains the history of how they came about, and shows some examples of how XML is used in the real world.

Chapter 2, "XML Structure": The XML 1.0 specification defines what XML is and the structure of documents but uses language that is not always so straightforward. This chapter explains the structure of an XML document in simple terms and provides some lucid examples. In addition, this chapter introduces some terminology used throughout the book.

Chapter 3, "Validation": This chapter explains the use of validation in XML using Document Type Definitions (DTDs), XML Schemas, and RELAX NG.

Chapter 4, "XPath, XPointer, XInclude, and the Future": The focus of this chapter is explaining how to write XPath expressions to query an XML document. You can use XPath with a few of the PHP extensions, and XPath serves as the foundation for XSLT in Chapter 10. The chapter also explains both XPointer and XInclude, which allow for more advanced XML processing.

Chapter 5, "PHP and XML": This chapter introduces the new XML support in PHP 5. It explains much of the functionality shared by the XML-based extensions, such as parser options, error handling, PHP streams, and document encoding.

Chapter 6, "Document Object Model (DOM)": This chapter provides an in-depth look at using the DOM extension and shows how it is used to manipulate an XML document.

Chapter 7, "SimpleXML": The SimpleXML extension provides a simple interface for working with XML documents. This chapter explains how to use the extension to access virtually any type of XML document, including more complex ones that use namespaces.

Chapter 8, "Simple API for XML (SAX)": This chapter explains how to work with the xml extension and covers issues you may encounter when migrating an application that uses this extension from PHP 4 to PHP 5.

Chapter 9, "XMLReader": The XMLReader extension is a lightweight parser and an alternative to the xml extension covered in Chapter 8. This chapter explains and demonstrates how to process an XML document using this extension.

Chapter 10, "Extensible Stylesheet Language Transformation (XSLT)": You can transform XML documents using XSLT. This chapter begins by explaining the XSLT specification in easy-to-understand terms. Then, this chapter shows how to use the XSL extension in PHP to perform transformations.

Chapter 11, "Effective and Efficient Processing": With a number of different extensions that can be used to work with XML in PHP, it is often difficult to decide which one to use. This chapter explains the differences between the extensions and continues with tips and tricks that can be used to optimally work with XML in PHP.

Chapter 12, "XML Security": Data integrity and data security are topics that every developer must be concerned with when writing applications. In this chapter, you will learn how to work with digital signatures and encryption as they pertain to XML.

Chapter 13, "PEAR and XML": The PHP Extension and Application Repository (PEAR) is a collection of software that can be used when writing an application. This chapter introduces PEAR and explores some of the XML packages it provides.

Chapter 14, "Content Syndication: RSS and Atom": Content syndication has become popular with the explosion of weblogs (blogs). This chapter examines the three formats that are used to syndicate data and shows how to create and consume syndicated feeds using the PHP extensions.

Chapter 15, "Web Distributed Data Exchange (WDDX)": This chapter explains what WDDX is and how you can use the wddx extension to exchange data between systems.

Chapter 16, "XML-RPC": This chapter examines the structure and exchange of XML-RPC documents. You will then learn about the xmlrpc extension and how you can use it to communicate with remote systems.

Chapter 17, "Representational State Transfer (REST)": Representational State Transfer (REST) is a simple method to create and consume Web services. I demonstrate how to create and consume REST-based services. In particular, you will see how to consume some real services from both Yahoo and Amazon.

Chapter 18, "SOAP": SOAP allows for the creation of complex Web services. The specifications involved are also quite complex. In this chapter, I show examples of both the Web Services Description Language (WSDL) specification and the SOAP specification. Using this knowledge, you will see how to use the SOAP extension in PHP using real-world examples from eBay and Google.

Chapter 19, "Universal Description, Discovery, and Integration (UDDI)": UDDI is a technology meant to make working with Web services easier. This chapter shows how you can use PHP to access and maintain records in a UDDI registry.

Chapter 20, "PEAR and Web Services": Chapter 13 introduces PEAR and its XML packages; this chapter introduces you to some packages that you can use to create and consume a variety of Web services.

Chapter 21, "Other XML Technologies and Extensions": There are too many XML-based technologies to cover in a single book. In this chapter, I will introduce you to the XML-Writer and SDO XML Data Access Service extensions as well as show how to work with Ajax and Wireless Application Protocol (WAP) using PHP.

Prerequisites

Although the general information about XML and the different specifications pertain to any version of PHP, the tools and extensions covered in this book require PHP 5 or higher. For the greatest functionality, it is highly suggested that you use PHP 5.1 or higher because of the many enhancements and additional functionality in this release.

Downloading the Code

All the code featured in this book is available for download at the book's Web page, which you can find in the Source Code section at http://www.apress.com.

Contacting the Authors

You can contact the author at rrichards@php.net.

CHAPTER 1

■ ■ ■

Introduction to XML and Web Services

The Extensible Markup Language (XML) is a simple, platform-independent standard for describing data within a structured format. XML is not a language but instead a metalanguage that allows you to create markup languages. In layman's terms, it allows data to be tagged using descriptive names so both humans and computer applications can understand the meaning of different pieces of data.

For example, reading the following structure, it is easy to understand what this data means:

```
<state>
    <name>Maine</name>
    <capitol>Augusta</capitol>
    <animal>Moose</animal>
    <bird>Chickadee</bird>
    <tree>White Pine</tree>
</state>
```

The state capitol of Maine is Augusta. The state animal is the moose, the state bird is the chickadee, and the state tree is the white pine. Although no officially named standard markup language was used for this example, it is still a well-formed XML document. XML offers the freedom of defining your own language to describe your data as needed.

With these new languages, the number of applications (ranging from document publishing applications to distributed applications) and the number of people and businesses adopting XML continue to grow. One of the most visible XML-based technologies today is the Web service technology, where Web-based applications are able to communicate in a standardized, platform-neutral way over the Internet. As you may have guessed, this is a big reason why *XML* and *Web services* have become buzzwords. With almost 30 years of history leading up to its creation, XML may just be what the original pioneers behind generalized markup envisioned.

This chapter will cover XML and Web services, beginning with the history of XML and including the introduction of Web services. By the end of this chapter, you should have an idea of the problems XML was initially meant to solve and how it has evolved to what it is today.

■**Note** Throughout this chapter, you may encounter terms and technologies you don't know. I don't explain these terms in detail here because you can find more detailed information in the later, relevant chapters.

Exploring the History of XML

Regardless of your personal opinion of XML, everyone has at least heard of it. Not everyone, however, knows the origins of XML, and it is helpful to understand at least the basics of its evolution. Imagine you're attending a company party, and someone from management (it's even worse when they're not from the information technology [IT] group) decides to ask you about XML because they have been hearing all about it in meetings. After covering the history of XML, you'll be certain to be left alone the rest of the night. Seriously, though, understanding how and why XML was conceived will provide an understanding of the problems it was origi-nally meant to solve, which ultimately can aid in determining whether you should use it and how you can use it to solve current problems.

Generalized Markup Language

XML can trace its roots all the way back to 1969. Charles F. Goldfarb, previously a practicing attorney, accepted a position at IBM that involved integrating information systems with legal practices. The project involved integrating text editing, information retrieving, and document rendering. The problem at hand was that each application required different markup. Gold-farb, along with Ed Mosher and Ray Lorie, began what was to be eventually known as the Generalized Markup Language (GML). The name was actually created based on the initials of Goldfarb, Mosher, and Lorie, and from here the term *markup language* was coined.

The purpose of GML was to describe the structure of a document using *tags*, allowing for the retrieval of different parts of the text while separating document formatting from its content. This way the same document could easily be used amongst different applications and systems. These different systems would then use their own processing commands based upon the tags encountered within the document. Another important aspect was the introduction of Docu-ment Type Definitions (DTDs). GML was officially named in 1973.

Standard Generalized Markup Language

In 1978, Goldfarb joined the American National Standards Institute (ANSI) and worked on a project based on GML to be known as the Standard Generalized Markup Language (SGML). While GML was a proprietary IBM format, SGML was developed by many people and groups and aimed to standardize textual representation and manipulation in documents in a plat-form- and vendor-neutral, open format. SGML is not really a language in the sense most people think of languages but rather defines how to create a markup language, so it is really a *metalanguage*.

The first working draft of SGML was published in 1980 and continued to evolve, being released as a recommendation for an industry standard in 1983. In 1986, the International Organization for Standardization (ISO) published it as an international standard.

Although adopted by some large organizations, such as the U.S. Department of Defense (DOD), the U.S. Internal Revenue Service (IRS), and the Association of American Publishers (AAP), SGML was extremely complex, which ultimately prevented its widespread adoption. Most companies did not have the time or resources to leverage SGML in their business activi-ties. However, some people say using SGML reduces a product's time to market, because in the long run less time is spent on application integration and day-to-day editing. This may be true, but the upfront cost in time is typically too great for smaller companies that cannot afford to dedicate enough resources to this.

The complexity of SGML and the time-to-market paradigm of using it play significant roles in the history of XML and ultimately led to its creation. The following are a few notable concepts of SGML that are relevant in the evolution of XML (and are further elaborated on later in the book):

- A document is defined structurally by a DTD.

- Named elements, also referred to as *markup tags*, defined within the DTD comprise the document.

- *Entities*, which are named parts of the document and consist of a name and a value, can perform substitutions within the document.

Hypertext Markup Language

Many of you may not remember the Internet before the World Wide Web was created. In those days, Gopher was a common technology used to access documents on the Internet. It was extremely primitive compared to what everyone uses today, but back then it allowed people to access documents and in most cases search for documents from all over the globe.

In 1989, while working at CERN, the European Particle Physics Laboratory, Tim Berners-Lee came up with an idea that would allow documents on the Internet to cross-reference each other. In basic terms, a document could link to other documents, including specific text within the documents. The language used to create these documents was Hypertext Markup Language (HTML). In 1990, the Web was born with the first live HTML document on the Internet.

HTML was based on SGML and added some features such as hyperlinking and anchors. Specifically created for the Internet, HTML featured a small set of tags and was designed for displaying content, causing it and the Web to quickly gain widespread adoption. Its features, however, were also its major limitations. Because it is simple, its tag set is not extendable. The tags also have no meaning to anything other than the application, such as a browser, that renders the document.

Extensible Markup Language

The technology started to come full circle in 1996. With SGML being considered too complicated and HTML too limited, the next logical step was taken. The World Wide Web Consortium (W3C) formed a committee to combine the flexibility and power of SGML with the simplicity and ease of use of HTML, which resulted in XML. Finally in February 1998, XML 1.0 was released as a W3C recommendation. Again, it was originally intended for electronic publishing, but little did they anticipate the reaching effects XML would have. The design goals were as follows:

- XML shall be straightforwardly usable over the Internet.

- XML shall support a wide variety of applications.

- XML shall be compatible with SGML.

- It shall be easy to write programs that process XML documents.

- The number of optional features in XML is to be kept to the absolute minimum, ideally zero.

- XML documents should be human legible and reasonably clear.

- The XML design should be prepared quickly.

- The design of XML shall be formal and concise.

- XML documents shall be easy to create.

- Terseness in XML markup is of minimal importance.

To understand how simple XML can be, consider that an example of a complete well-formed XML document can be as simple as `<mydocument/>`. (I'll cover the syntax and structure of XML in Chapter 2.)

Using XML in the Real World

Once hitting the streets, XML became the flavor of the day. Its use started spreading like wild-fire. Personally, I attribute this to its timing. It was the age of the "dot-com," where companies were popping up like weeds and XML was being applied to everything. Although this may be grossly overstated because many companies—especially the larger, well-founded ones—were using XML sparingly and judicially, the vast majority of these start-up companies tried apply-ing XML to virtually every situation. My opinions on this matter not only originate from personal experience but also from acquaintances who experienced the same situation.

I can remember, while working at one company, word came down from management that we had to incorporate XML into our development. XML didn't particularly fit and better tech-nologies existed, but it was out of our control, so we did it. To this day, I can only speculate on why we received this mandate. It could have been that everyone was talking about the tech-nology, and someone in management questioned why it wasn't being used or thought it would make sense to use the technology so that, when the company was discussed amongst poten-tial venture capitalists, management could throw out the *XML* word to sound more attractive. In any event, XML is a useful technology, when used correctly. Everyone needs to remember XML is not the Holy Grail but is just another technology that can get the job done. In fact, this is important to remember when dealing with any technology!

Once the Internet bubble started deflating and companies, at least ones that survived, began re-evaluating their business and technology, it appears they also began using technology more prudently. You will always encounter the XML zealots who have to use XML for everything and claim it can replace most other technologies; you will also encounter those on the other end of the spectrum who contend XML is just a fad and will soon die. Reality, however, paints a different picture. XML is alive and doing well, just no longer plastered everywhere and being touted as the second coming. Before you start mumbling something about Web services under your breath (I'll address them shortly), let's focus on some of the areas XML has some real use, because this is the heart of the matter at hand. I'll break the discussion down into four general areas:

- Standardized data description

- Publishing

- Data storage and retrieval

- Distributed computing

In most cases, the same XML data is used within more than one of these areas, which is one of its original design goals as well as why it became so popular.

Standardized Data Description

Standardized data description is not technically an application of XML but rather its heart and soul. It is the backbone of XML-based applications. Take, for example, the following document:

```
<RobR>
    <Rob>Hello World</Rob>
</RobR>
```

This is a well-formed XML document in a language I just created; however, it is pretty much useless to anyone but myself, which is fine as long as I am the only one who needs to use the data. It does not work this way in the real world, however.

Companies, organizations, and even industries formally define languages as standards, meaning everyone must use the set of defined rules without deviation. This ensures data can be shared and easily understood by any human or machine that uses the defined language. If you were to search the Web for *GML*, trying to locate information about the Generalized Markup Language, you may be surprised at the results. You will get an abundance of information covering the Geography Markup Language and Geotech-XML, and if you are lucky, you might find several sites that actually concern the Generalized Markup Language. In fact, try a search on *ML* prefixed by almost any random character or two, and odds are you will find some sort of XML-based markup language. The following are just a few examples of publicly defined standardized languages.

Mathematical Markup Language

Mathematical Markup Language (MathML) is a standard, developed by the W3C, that defines a universally consistent manner to describe mathematics for use on the Web. It actually has two parts, consisting of presentation tags and content tags. The presentation tags in Listing 1-1, obviously, are for presentation in a browser, and the content tags in Listing 1-2 describe the meaning of an expression, which can then also be used in automated processes.

Listing 1-1. *Presentation Tags Expressing 1+2*

```
<math xmlns="http://www.w3.org/1998/Math/MathML" >
    <mi>1</mi>
    <mo>+</mo>
    <mi>2</mi>
</math>
```

Listing 1-2. *Content Tags Expressing 1+2*

```
<math xmlns="http://www.w3.org/1998/Math/MathML" >
    <apply>
        <plus/>
        <cn>1</cn>
        <cn>2</cn>
    </apply>
</math>
```

Extensible Business Reporting Language

Extensible Business Reporting Language (XBRL) is an open and international standard for describing business and financial data. This language is not as simple and short as MathML, so you can find real examples of this at Reuters (http://www.reuters.com) and Microsoft (http://www.microsoft.com). Each of these companies offers financial reports, available to the public, in XBRL format. It is also noteworthy that the Committee of European Banking Supervisors (CEBS), the U.S. Securities and Exchange Commission, and the United Kingdom are among some of the early adopters of this technology.

Publishing

Publishing is an obvious application of XML. Looking at XML's history, this was the primary factor driving the development of generalized markup languages. Publishing involves taking the data content and transforming it for presentation. The presentation may take any form understandable to a user or program, such as Portable Document Format (PDF), HTML, or even another markup language.

Publishing to Different Formats

XML offers the flexibility to present the same content in multiple formats. Envision an application where the data needs to be sent to a Web browser in HTML format as well as to a wireless device understanding the Wireless Markup Language (WML). The same data content can be transformed into each of these markup languages using Extensible Stylesheet Language Transformations (XSLT), which is covered in depth in Chapter 10.

Content Syndication

You might remember Microsoft's Active Channels from many years ago. The Channel Definition Format (CFD) was the first Web syndication technology based on the *push method*. (The push method basically meant the server was pushing this content down your throat.) If you are lucky enough to not have been online during the Microsoft/Netscape technology wars back then, you are probably more familiar with the current-day RSS or ATOM (these acronyms will be explained in Chapter 14). These are much more friendly because the client machine pulls the data if and when you want it. This data is then loaded into some type of parser, which then processes the data, usually for display.

Content Management Systems

A content management system (CMS) is a system used for creating, editing, organizing, searching, and publishing content. You can put XML to good use within a CMS (though it is not required, and many CMS systems you may encounter do not use any XML at all). For those that do employ XML, its use may fall into a few of the previously mentioned areas. Using a CMS for a Web site as an example, the minimal it would do is transform the XML content into HTML. As the site design changes or the business focus changes, you would have no need to modify the content. You might need to make some changes to style sheets for output, but you could leave the core content alone. Compare this to having content just embedded within an HTML page. Although you could use Cascading Style Sheets (CSS) for some design changes, moving content around within the layout would require some large cut-and-paste operations. This leads right into content-editing issues.

Even for small companies and organizations, copy changes to HTML-only pages are not all that simple. Normally the changes are coming from those who are not involved in the technical aspects of the Web site. This leads to the request for changes having to go through the proper channels until a designer actually makes the changes. In addition, the changes, after being made to the HTML, usually have to be double-checked and approved before they can move into the production system. While this may not seem all that difficult, imagine the implications when dealing on a larger scale, such as in big corporations or global organizations. Basically, it becomes a management nightmare. As you may infer from this, not only is the publishing of the data playing a role in the problem but the editing of the content is also contributing to the problem.

The final content used in the output typically consists of many smaller pieces of content, with some content even referencing and possibly including other chunks of content. Systems dealing with this often have a built-in editor where each person or group is in control of their own pieces of content, which are managed by the CMS. When dealing with XML-based content, the editor will help ensure valid syntax is used so the user does not require knowledge of XML. As content is added or edited, no longer is a large process needed to publish any of the changes. The content may still need to go through an approval process, but the ones involved would include only those who specifically deal with the site content. The CMS would take care of publishing these changes, again by processing all the content involved, which may include adding any referenced subcontent pieces and transforming the content into the appropriate layout. This would effectively take an IT department out of the process, because the IT team would no longer be needed to manually update copy, resulting in an increase in productivity.

Data Storage and Retrieval

The data storage, search, and retrieval area is another where XML is used. For simplicity's sake, as well as that it aids in the understanding of this area, I will break this topic down into two distinct areas. On a small scale, you can use an XML document as a cross-platform database. Looking at the much larger picture, systems dealing with large amounts of XML content need ways to store this data so it can easily be searched, modified, and retrieved. Though related in some small way, the applications of these two examples differ significantly.

An XML Document As a Database

Many instances exist where data needs to be stored and retrieved, but conventional databases are overkill or simply cannot be used. For example, desktop applications need to load and save user settings. In many cases, simple text files (or in the case of some Windows applications, the registry) are used for storing the data. Typical text files use a layout consisting of a section identifier followed by name/value pairs that correspond to specific settings within the application. Listing 1-3 shows an example of this.

Listing 1-3. *Configuration File Example (Text File Format)*

```
[General]
Version=1.0
Country=United States

[Menu]
Background=212 226 217
FontColor=0 0 0
```

An application would read this file and set its internal parameters accordingly. An alternate approach would be to use XML for this, as shown in Listing 1-4.

Listing 1-4. *Configuration File Example (XML Format)*

```
<Application>
    <General>
        <Version>1.0</Version>
        <Country>United States</Country>
    </General>
    <Menu>
        <Background>212 226 217</Background>
        <FontColor>0 0 0</FontColor>
    </Menu>
</Application>
```

Using XML in this manner is mainly a personal preference. As demonstrated in the example, it is a bit more verbose than a simple text file, but in certain cases it can also add some benefit. A large configuration file could easily be broken up into smaller files, with the possibility of certain files residing on a network. An application could use an XML parser to load the main configuration file, reassemble the entire configuration file, and load the settings into the application. Sharing a configuration file amongst applications is also easier. Common settings could live within one level of the document, and application-specific settings could live within their own respective levels in the hierarchy. Again, this is just an alternative way to handle configuration files but can be found in some applications on the market today.

Native XML Databases

Recently, native XML databases have begun to gain traction in the marketplace. A native XML database (NXD) specializes in XML storage, focuses on document storage, and uses XPath to query data. Historically, XML has been stored in relational databases in a few ways. A binary large object (BLOB) field could store the entire document in the field. Documents could also be stored on the file system with the database used to locate the documents. A document could also be mapped to a database, where an element could be represented by a table and attributes, and nested elements could be represented by fields within the table.

Take, for example, Microsoft's SQL Server 2000. The database could be queried using the following hypothetical Structured Query Language (SQL), which would output the record in XML format:

```
Select user_id AS ID, user_name AS NAME from Users User where user_id=1 FOR XML AUTO
```

```
<Users>
    <User ID="1" NAME="Rob" />
</Users>
```

As demonstrated, the fields are returned as attributes of the User element within the document. Inserts and updates to the table, however, are still accomplished using standard INSERT and UPDATE SQL commands with field name/value pairs. An NXD, on the other hand, uses XML technologies such as XPath and the Document Object Model (DOM) to create and manipulate documents within the database. For systems and companies utilizing XML-based content, NXDs may make sense because they offer common XML syntax for data access and deal with documents in their native formats. Relational databases, however, have also made strides in this area; many are beginning to include advanced XML features. These "XML-enabled" databases still provide their core relational model but also add many of the features of an NXD, such as native XML storage, which will preserve the infoset and XPath or XQuery querying. It is yet to be seen, however, whether these new XML-enabled databases will make native XML databases obsolete or just position the native ones to target XML-focused organizations with no real needs for relational data.

Distributed Computing

Distributed computing is not a new technology. Ever since computers were hooked into networks, systems have been working together and sharing tasks with other systems. With the introduction of the Internet came a much larger distributed network that could be leveraged. XML brings a common technology that can easily be used by all systems to take advantage of this area. The next section focuses on Web services and goes into greater detail on this matter.

Introducing Service Oriented Architecture and Web Services

Systems integration is one thing that virtually every IT department has had to deal with, from management down to the single developer. Whether a common platform was required or the same tool sets were needed, integration was never a simple task in the past and was usually costly in both time and money. Service Oriented Architecture (SOA) is a concept where none of these issues matters. It takes the approach that interacting systems should not be tightly bound to each other, thus promoting independence and reusability of services.

Using object-oriented programming in PHP 5 as an example, say you build an application using objects. The classes for the objects were well thought out, so each performs operations for specific areas of functionality. Another area of the company is working on a separate application and ends up needing to access functionality from the first application. On top of that, this new application isn't even written using PHP so cannot reuse any code natively. The brute-force method would be to have this new application duplicate the logic the PHP application does. This, however, presents problems if the logic were to change in the PHP application. The other application would need to also change its logic or face the problem that it no longer works correctly, which could lead to a variety of problems within the company, including data corruption.

Using SOA, the PHP application can expose the functionality of its classes via a service. Through a common protocol and descriptive messaging, the other application can access the functionality of the PHP application. For example, a *daemon*, which is a process waiting for invocation to perform a task, is written in PHP and run via the PHP command-line interpreter (CLI). The daemon accepts connections via Transmission Control Protocol/Internet Protocol (TCP/IP) and processes requests based on the messages it receives, which are written in some company-standardized text language. This text language describes the class to access, the function to call, the arguments, and their values needed by the function. The outside application then connects to the daemon, sends its message, and receives some response. Because the task was an external process, the calling application does not care how it was done, just that it was performed.

Although generic in its description and not going into specifics, the previous scenario should give you some sense of what SOA is. The inception of the Web service technology, which is a specific implementation of SOA, has brought new steam to the SOA concept. XML as a common message format using standard Internet protocols, such as Hypertext Transfer Protocol (HTTP) and HTTP Secure (HTTPS), has sparked new interest in this type of architecture, because using these standards is simple, is universally supported, and does not require anyone to reinvent the wheel.

The term *Web services* has to be one of the most confusing and controversial terms ever. In extremely general terms, Web services are a form of distributed computing using XML in their communications. Shortly, it will become clearer why I've left this so vague. Before attempting to define Web services, some background of how they came about is in order.

Evolution of Web Services

Tracing the roots of Web services, it seems XML-RPC—which is Remote Procedure Call (RPC) over HTTP via XML—is the obvious starting point. XML-RPC was a fork of the early, still in development, SOAP specification. A general misconception was that XML-RPC was the origin of SOAP and that SOAP was actually built upon XML-RPC. According to Dave Winer, "Before folklore becomes reality, XML-RPC was originally, privately called SOAP, when Don Box and I were working with Bob Atkinson and Mohsen Al-Ghosein at Microsoft, in early 1998." It sounds like Microsoft was taking too long with internal politics so XML-RPC split from SOAP and was released to the masses.

These technologies, XML-RPC and SOAP, are just another form of distributed computing and use XML for the encoding, which allows for greater interoperability. You may have heard the Web service technology is a replacement for distributed object technologies, such as Distributed Component Object Model (DCOM), Common Object Request Broker Architecture (CORBA), or Remote Method Invocation (RMI). You can probably find arguments both for and against this. The Web service technology, however, is *not* a replacement for these technologies and isn't even the same as them. Similarities do exist, but XML is just another tool to build distributed systems.

The Definition of Web Services

If you asked ten people to define the term *Web services*, you are likely to get ten different answers. This term has no single definition. Even the standards authorities cannot agree on what this term means. Before presenting you with what I consider to be a Web service, let's first examine some definitions you may encounter.

The W3C created the Web Services Architecture Working Group to advise and create architectural documents in the area of Web services. After a bit of searching to find out what happened to this group, I found that it appears the group could not even agree on the definition of a *Web service*, ultimately spelling the end of this group over some time. The closest definition I could find is from the latest Working Group Note dated February 11, 2004:

> *A Web service is a software system designed to support interoperable machine-to-machine interaction over a network. It has an interface described in a machine-processable format (specifically WSDL). Other systems interact with the Web service in a manner prescribed by its description using SOAP messages, typically conveyed using HTTP with an XML serialization in conjunction with other Web-related standards.*

> W3C Web Services Architecture Working Group

In addition, the Web Services Interoperability Organization (WS-I) conveniently does not state any definition for Web services; rather, the group defines requirements for the interoperability of Web services, which must be adhered to for an application to be granted conformance. (The WS-I is not a standards body but a collection of the larger corporations considered "leaders" in the Web service arena.) A definition that can be inferred from reading the specifications is that a Web service consists of Web Services Description Language (WSDL), SOAP, and Universal Description, Discovery, and Integration (UDDI). This is pretty much in line with what you would be told if you were to ask a Web service purist to define *Web service*.

Personally, I do not agree with such strict definitions of the term. I prefer to define a Web service as an application that is accessed across the Internet using standard Internet protocols and that uses XML as its messaging format. It would be one thing if the term were defined from the beginning, but in my opinion, it is too late for an industry or organization to come up with any formal, standard definition that places limits on what a Web service is or what it comprises.

▦ Note Throughout this book, the term *Web service* will refer to any application that is accessed across the Internet using standard Internet protocols and that uses XML as its messaging format.

The companies pushing WSDL, SOAP, and UDDI as the backbone of Web services are the same ones that have invested heavily in these technologies over the years. It is in their best interests to push these as standards to at least recoup some of the cost they have incurred. Based on those strict guidelines, Representational State Transfer (REST) is not even considered a Web service, although most people think of REST-based services as such. You almost get the feeling that unless you are using WSDL, SOAP, and UDDI, you are doing it wrong. <SARCASM>As developers, we all know there is only ever a single solution to a problem, and everything else is just plain wrong </SARCASM >. See, I told you basic XML was not difficult. I bet those of you who have never even seen XML before fully understood that.

Web Services in the Real World

It may be easier to come to some understanding of the term *Web services* by looking at a few places it is currently used on the Internet. Some big Internet companies, which you are probably already familiar with, offer Web services so you can tie your application into their systems. A few of the services, which are also covered within this book through examples, are Yahoo, Google, Amazon, and eBay.

Yahoo Web Services

The Yahoo Web service, which uses REST, provides an application to use Yahoo's search engine to find images, businesses, news, and video on the Internet. You must register for the service to obtain an application ID that is used in the requests. You can obtain this ID via http:// developer.yahoo.net/; its use is limited to the terms of service on the Yahoo Web site. (The following example does not require registration because it is just using the demo mode.)

Consider a hypothetical application that needs to search on terms and display the results it finds on the Internet to a user. Prior to these public Web services, many people would have their application perform a request to the search engine the same way a browser would do it. The result would be that the application would receive a nice HTML page, which then the developer would have to somehow parse to gather the correct information. This was not all that easy, and if the resulting HTML layout changed or if the content the application expected to be there for identification purposes changed, the application would need to be modified to work again. This is considered *screen scraping*, and some Web sites frown upon this method.

Using the Yahoo application programming interface (API), a search for the term *XML* is now very simple, and the results are easy to integrate into an application. Using a browser, enter the following location: http://api.search.yahoo.com/WebSearchService/V1/ webSearch?appid=YahooDemo&query=xml&results=2. The result should be an XML document that is easily parsed and contains two results. Compare that with what is normally returned when searching from a browser: http://search.yahoo.com/search?p=xml&sm=Yahoo%21+ Search&fr=FP-tab-web-t&toggle=1.

The first two results from the normal browser search are the same as the results returned from the Web service. The format is completely different. The Web service returns the information in XML, which allows for easy application integration, and the normal browser search is returned in HTML for presentation.

You can find working examples of using the Yahoo Web service and using REST in Chapter 17.

Google Web APIs

Google also offers a wide range of Web services, including searches as well as integration with many of their other services such as AdWords and Blogger. You can find a complete list of the services at http://www.google.com/apis/index.html. Registration is required to obtain a license key and access the Web services. Accessing the Web Search API is different from the previous Yahoo Web service example. Google uses SOAP rather than REST, though the concept is the same as Yahoo. XML is used in communications so an application can be easily integrated. You can find examples of integrating with Google via SOAP in Chapter 18.

A more advanced Web service is the AdWords API. AdWords is Google's cost-per-click advertising service. Using the API, an application can hook directly into the AdWords server, allowing for remote management of accounts and campaigns. For example, the application can manage the keywords, ad text, and the Uniform Resource Locator (URL) of a running advertisement.

Amazon E-commerce Service (ECS)

Amazon provides access to its products and to its e-commerce functionality through its E-commerce Service (ECS). The service is accessible using either REST or SOAP, which offers more flexibility to developers because they can use the technology they're most comfortable using. Registration is required to obtain a subscription ID for accessing the service. You will need to navigate to the Web service page from http://www.amazon.com for more information.

The service provides access to product information, including descriptions, images, and customer reviews, as well as search capabilities such as wish list searches. On top of the normal functionality you would expect, you can also access remote shopping carts. Putting all these services together, a site dedicated to some specific topic—for example, dogs—could dynamically add products from Amazon involving dogs to their site and offer the ability to add items to the cart that is eventually sent to Amazon for the checkout process. Prior to this capability, it was common to see a product on a Web site linked directly to Amazon for purchase. Using the service, the user could remain on the developer's site and continue adding products until they are ready to check out.

Refer to Chapter 17 for examples of accessing the Amazon services using REST.

eBay

eBay offers a developer program, at http://developer.ebay.com/, allowing an application to tap into its platform using eBay's XML API, REST, or SOAP. Registration is required, and a free individual license is available. The REST API is quite limited in functionality compared to the other two APIs. Using REST, only publicly available information is available to be accessed so is currently limited to searching listings. The other APIs, however, offer an extensive collection of functionality. Virtually anything you can do via a browser can now be automated through an application. For example, an application could integrate with a current inventory and sales system. This not only reduces the amount of time spent manually handling transactions and keying them into a system and offers a seamless user interface (UI) for a sales system, but it also allows eBay transactions to be integrated with an inventory system to maintain a real-time inventory.

For more information regarding the SOAP API and an example usage, refer to Chapter 18, which covers SOAP.

Defining Common Terms and Acronyms

XML is one of those technologies where you just cannot escape acronyms, and throughout this book, you will encounter many. Table 1-1 is a quick guide to some of the more commonly used terms and acronyms.

Table 1-1. *XML-Related Terms*

Term	Definition
URI	Uniform Resource Identifier. An address to locate a resource on a network (for example, `http://www.example.com`).
URL	Uniform Resource Locator. URLs are subsets of URIs but today are considered synonymous with URIs.
W3C	World Wide Web Consortium (`http://www.w3.org/`). An international consortium developing Web standards.
OASIS	Organization for the Advancement of Structured Information Standards (`http://www.oasis-open.org/`). An international consortium developing various standards.
ANSI	American National Standards Institute (`http://www.ansi.org/`). A private organization that creates standards for the computer and communications industries.
ISO	International Organization for Standardization (`http://www.iso.org/`). An international standards organization consisting of national standards bodies from around the world.
DTD	Document Type Definition. This is used within an XML document primarily for validation.
Parser	A processor that reads and breaks up XML documents. Validating parser can validate documents based on at least DTDs.
DOM	Document Object Model. See Chapter 6 for more information.
SAX	Simple API for XML. See Chapter 8 for more information.
XSLT	Extensible Stylesheet Language Transformations. See Chapter 10 for more information.
XPath	A language for addressing parts of an XML document.
REST	Representational State Transfer. See Chapter 17 for more information.
SOAP	This once stood for Simple Object Access Protocol. As of SOAP 1.2, though, this is no longer considered an acronym. See Chapter 18 for more information.

Conclusion

XML is a flexible tool that can solve a wide range of problems. It is not meant to replace all your existing technology practices. Looking at the history of XML, it clearly indicates that XML came about to solve a particular problem. This is something to always remember when considering using XML. That being said, XML does offer many possibilities, which were difficult and cumbersome to develop and deploy in the past. The Web service technology is one of those things.

Now that you have a basic idea of what things are and where they came from, an understanding of XML documents is the next step needed to begin developing your own XML applications and services. The next chapter will explain document structure and basic syntax so you can begin creating your own XML documents.

CHAPTER 2

XML Structure

Reading and understanding the W3C specifications can be a difficult and daunting task. This chapter explains XML structures in an easy-to-understand way. This information is based on the third edition of the WC3's XML 1.0 specification. I did not use the XML 1.1 specification as a basis for this chapter in order to ensure the greatest compatibility amongst parsers and applications. In other words, the XML 1.0 specification is compatible with XML 1.1, but the reverse is not true.

This chapter will cover the basics for understanding and building an XML document. It begins with some fundamental concepts of XML; using these concepts, I'll break down the structure of a document and explain the syntax for document composition. Once you have a basic understanding of document structure, I'll introduce additional features such as namespaces and IDs. By the end of this chapter, you should be armed with enough knowledge not only to build XML documents but also to at least understand some of the more complex documents you may encounter. Although I'll present some information about DTDs, Chapter 3 provides more in-depth coverage.

Introducing Characters

XML uses most of the characters within the Unicode character set. The specification actually refers to the ISO 10646 character set, but usually you will find these two used interchangeably, because the two character sets are kept in sync. Unicode, a 32-bit character set, provides a standard and universal character set by assigning a unique number to every character. This way, by using Unicode, data is the same without regard to language or country. The two Unicode formats, which all parsers must accept, are UTF-8 and UTF-16, although you can use other character encodings as long as they comply with Unicode.

Character References

Characters cannot always be represented in their literal formats. Also, sometimes certain characters in their literal forms are invalid to use because they violate the XML specification, which depends upon the type of markup being used at the time. Character references represent the literal forms using their numeric equivalents. You can express character references in two ways: using decimal notation or hexadecimal notation. For example:

- The character *A* in decimal format is A.

- The character *A* in hexadecimal format is &x41;.

The only constraint for the character to be considered well-formed is that it conforms to the rules for valid characters, which are expressed in hexadecimal format and include the following range of characters:

```
#x9 | #xA | #xD | [#x20-#xD7FF] | [#xE000-#xFFFD] | [#x10000-#x10FFFF]
```

Whitespace

Throughout this chapter, you will encounter the term *whitespace*. Whitespace, as used within XML, consists of one or more of the following characters (expressed in hexadecimal): #x20 (space), #x9 (tab), #xD (carriage return), or #xA (line feed). By default, whitespace is significant within an XML document. In *most* cases, it is up to the application to determine how it wants to handle whitespace. As you will see later in this chapter in the section "Using xml:space and xml:lang," xml:space is a way to force an application to preserve whitespace.

Names

The term *name*, as used within this chapter for explaining XML syntax, defines the valid sequence of characters that you can use. A name begins with an alphabetical character, an underscore, or a colon and is followed by any combination of alphanumeric characters, periods, hyphens, underscores, and colons, as well as a few additional characters defined by CombiningChar and Extender within the XML specification.

Names beginning with the case-insensitive xml are also reserved by the current and future XML specifications. For example, names already in use include xmlns and xml. Basically, it is not wise to use a name beginning with those three letters. It is also not good practice to use colons in names. Although you will find people using them, especially when using the DOM and not using namespace-aware functionality, using colons can lead to problems when not used for namespace purposes. Table 2-1 shows some example names.

Table 2-1. *Example Names*

Valid Names	Invalid Names
automobile1	1automobile
_automobile	+automobile
:automobile	(automobile
my.automobile	.automobile
my:_automobile	@automobile

Character Data

Markup consists of XML declarations, document type declarations, elements, entity references, character references, comments, processing instructions (PIs), CDATA section delimiters, text declarations, and any whitespace outside the document element and not contained within other markup. An example of whitespace that is considered markup is the line feed used between the prolog and the body. Character data, simply, is everything else that is not markup. It is the actual content of the document, which is being described and structured by the markup.

A few characters require special attention:

- Less-than sign (<)

- Ampersand (&)

- Greater-than sign (>)

- Double quote (")

- Single quote (')

Except when used for markup delimiters or within a comment, PI, or CDATA section, & and < can never be used directly. The > character must never be used when creating a string containing]]> within content and not being used at that time to close a CDATA section. The double and single quote characters must never be used in literal form within an attribute value. Attribute values may be enclosed within either double or single quotes, so to avoid potential conflicts, those characters are not allowed within the value. All these characters, according to their particular rule sets, must be represented using either the numeric character references or the entity references, as shown in Table 2-2.

Note The entity references for these special characters do not need to be defined in a DTD because they are automatically built into the parser.

Table 2-2. *Special Character Representations*

Character	Character Reference (Decimal)	Character Reference (Hexadecimal)	Entity Reference
<	&#60;	&#x3C;	&lt;
&	&#38;	&#x26;	&amp;
>	&#62;	&#x3E;	&gt;
"	&#60;	&#x3C;	&lt;
'	&#39;	&#x27;	&apos;

Case Sensitivity

XML is case-sensitive. You must be careful when writing markup to ensure that you use case correctly. An element that has a start tag in all lowercase must have an end tag that is also in all lowercase. This also is important to remember when using attributes. The attribute a is not the same as the attribute A. It is a good idea to be consistent with case within a document. All attributes should use the same case; lowercase is commonly used for attributes. Element names should also be consistent. The common methods for case in elements names are using all lowercase, using all uppercase, or using uppercase for the first letter of a word and using lowercase for the rest of the word. For example:

```
<document>
    <MyElement>content here</MyElement>
    <MYELEMENT>content here</MYELEMENT>
    <myelement a="1" b="2" />
    <!-- The following is well-formed,
         but it is not good to mix attribute cases -->
    <myelement a="1" A="2" />
    <!-- The following is invalid because of mismatching start and end tags -->
    <MYELEMENT>content here </myelement>
</document>
```

Understanding Basic Layout

An XML document describes content and must be well-formed, as defined in the WC3's XML specifications. The bare minimum for a well-formed document is a single element that is properly started and terminated. This element is called the *root* or *document element*. It serves as the container for any content. A document's layout consists of an optional prolog; a document body, which consists of the document element and everything it contains; and an optional epilog.

Prolog

A *prolog* provides information about the document. A prolog may consist of the following (in this order): an XML declaration; any number of comments, PIs, or whitespace; a document type declaration; and then again any number of comments, PIs, or whitespace. Though not required, an XML declaration is highly recommended. You can find information about comments and PIs in the section "Understanding Basic Syntax." Listing 2-1 shows an example prolog.

Listing 2-1. *Example Prolog*

```
<?xml version="1.0"?>
<!--The previous line contains the XML declaration -->
<!--The following document type declaration contains no subsets -->
<!DOCTYPE foo [
]>
<!--This is the end of the prolog -->
```

The prolog in Listing 2-1 takes the form of an XML declaration, two comments, a document type declaration, and another comment.

XML Declaration

The *XML declaration*, the first line in Listing 2-1, provides information about the version of the XML specification used for document construction, the encoding of the document, and whether the document is self-contained or requires an external DTD. The basic rules for composition of the declaration are that it must begin with <?xml, it must contain the version, and it must end with ?>. Documents containing no XML declaration are treated as if the version were specified as 1.0. When using an XML declaration, it must be the first line of the document. No whitespace is allowed before the XML declaration. Listing 2-2 shows an example XML declaration.

Listing 2-2. *Example XML Declaration*

```
<?xml version="1.0" encoding="UTF-8" standalone="yes"?>
```

Version

The version information (version), which is mandatory when using an XML declaration, indicates to which XML specification the document conforms. The major difference between the two specifications, XML 1.0 and XML 1.1, is the allowed characters. XML 1.1 allows flexibility and supports the changes to the Unicode standards. The rationale behind creating a new version rather than modifying the XML 1.0 specification was to avoid breaking existing XML parsers. Parsers that support XML 1.0 are not required to support XML 1.1, but those that support XML 1.1 *are* required to support XML 1.0. With respect to the XML declaration, the version either can be 1.0, as in version="1.0" (as shown in Listing 2-2), or can be 1.1, as in version="1.1".

Encoding

The encoding declaration (encoding), which is not required in the XML declaration, indicates the character encoding used within the document. Encodings include, but are not limited to, UTF-8, UTF-16, ISO-8859-1, and ISO-2022-JP. It is recommended that the character sets used are ones registered with the Internet Assigned Numbers Authority (IANA). When encoding is omitted and not specified by other means, such as byte order mark (BOM) or external protocol, the XML document must use either UTF-8 or UTF-16 encoding. Although Listing 2-2 explicitly sets the encoding to UTF-8, this is not needed because UTF-8 is supported by default.

Stand-alone

The stand-alone declaration (standalone), also not required within the XML declaration, indicates whether the document requires outside resources, such as an external DTD. The value yes means the document is self-contained, and the value no indicates that external resources may be required. Documents that do not include a stand-alone declaration within the XML declaration, yet do include external resources, automatically assume the value of no.

Document Type Declaration

The *document type declaration* (DOCTYPE) provides the DTD for the document. It may include an internal subset, which means declarations would be declared directly within the DOCTYPE, and/or include an external subset, which means it could include declarations from an external source. The internal and external subsets collectively are the DTD for the document. Chapter 3 covers DTDs in detail. Listing 2-3, Listing 2-4, and Listing 2-5 show some example DTDs.

Listing 2-3. *Document Type Declaration with External Subset*

```
<!DOCTYPE foo SYSTEM "foo.dtd">
```

Listing 2-4. *Document Type Declaration with Internal Subset*

```
<!DOCTYPE foo [
    <!ELEMENT foo (#PCDATA)>
]>
```

Listing 2-5. *Document Type Declaration with Internal and External Subset*

```
<!DOCTYPE foo SYSTEM "foo.dtd" [
    <!ELEMENT foo (#PCDATA)>
]>
```

Body

The *body* of an XML document consists of the document element and its content. In the simplest case, the body can be a single, empty element. You may have heard the term *document tree* before; this term is synonymous with the body. The document element is the base of the tree and branches out through elements contained within the document element. The section "Understanding Basic Syntax" covers the basic building blocks of the body. Listing 2-6 shows an example of a document body.

Listing 2-6. *Example of an XML Document Body*

```
<root>
    <element1>Some Content</element1>
    <element2 attr1="attribute value">More Content</element2>
</root>
```

Epilog

If you are referring to the XML specifications, you will not find a reference to the *epilog*. Within the XML specifications, the epilog is equivalent to the Misc* portion of the document definition as defined using the Extended Backus-Naur Form (EBNF) notation. For example:

```
document   ::=   prolog element Misc*
```

The epilog refers to the markup following the close of the body. It can contain comments, PIs, and whitespace. Epilogs are not mandatory and, other than possibly containing whitespace, are not very common. Many parsers will not even parse past the closing tag of the document element. Because of this limitation, a possible use for the epilog is to add some comments for someone reading the XML document. This type of usage of an epilog causes no problems if a parser does not read it.

Understanding Basic Syntax

XML syntax is actually pretty simple. Many people get away with documents consisting of only elements and text content. These documents tend to have a simple structure with simple data, but isn't that the whole point of XML in the first place? Once you begin working with more complex documents, such as those involving namespaces and content that is not just valid plain text, you may start to get a little intimidated. I know the first time I ever encountered a schema, I felt a little overwhelmed.

After reading the following sections, you should understand at least the basics of XML documents and be able to understand documents used in some XML techniques such as validation using schemas, SOAP, and RELAX NG. Some documents may seem impossible to ever understand, but armed with the basic knowledge in this chapter, you should be able to find your way.

Elements

Elements are the foundation of a document, and at least one is required for a well-formed document. An element consists of a start tag, an end tag, and content, which is everything between the start and end tags. Elements with no content are the exception to this rule because the element may consist of a single empty-element tag.

Start Tags

Start tags consist of <, the name, any number of attributes, and then >. *Name* refers to a valid, legal name as explained within the "Characters" section.

This shows an element start tag named MyNode having one attribute:

```
<MyNode att1="first attribute">
```

End Tags

End tags take the form of </", Name, ">, where Name is the same as the starting tag. The end tag for the previous example would be as follows:

```
</MyNode>
```

Element Content

Content may consist of character data, elements, references, CDATA sections, PIs, and comments. Everything contained within the element's start and end tags is considered to be an element's content. For example:

```
<myElement>
    <nestedElement>content of nestedElement</nestedElement>
</myElement>
```

Breaking this document down, the element name nestedElement contains a string of character data. The document element myElement contains content consisting of whitespace (a line feed and then a tab), followed the element nestedElement and its content, followed by more whitespace (line feed).

Empty-Element Tags

Elements without content can appear in the form of a start tag directly followed by an end tag (as well as without any whitespace). To simplify expressing this, you can use an *empty-element tag*. Empty-element tags take the form of <", Name, "/>. For example:

```
<!-- start and end tags without content -->
<myElement></myElement>

<!-- empty-element tag -->
<myElement/>

<!-- start and end tags WITH content -->
<myElement> </myElement>
```

Notice that the last example does contain content. Even though it's only a single space, the element contains content. Every character, including whitespace, is considered content.

Element Hierarchy

The most important point to remember when dealing with XML is that it must be well-formed. This may be redundant information, but if you are coming from the HTML world, it can be easy to forget. It's easy to get away with malformed documents when writing HTML, especially because not all tags are required to be closed. Take the HTML document shown in Listing 2-7, for example.

Listing 2-7. *HTML Example*

```
<HTML><BODY>
    <P>This is all in <I>Italics and this is <B>Bold</I></B><BR>
    New line here</P>
    <form name="myform" method="post" action="mypage.php">
        <table width="100%" border="0">
            <tr valign="top">
                <td>Name: <input type="text" name="name" value=""></td>
            </tr>
            <tr>
                <td><input type="submit" name="submit" value="Submit">
                    </form>
                </td>
            </tr>
        </table>
</BODY></HTML>
```

The document in Listing 2-7 is not well-formed at all. The simplest piece to identify is that the BR tag is opened and never closed. Within the P tag, the hierarchy is completely broken. Beginning with the I tag, you'll see some text followed by an opening B tag. Using XML rules, you would expect the B tag to be closed prior to the I tag, but as illustrated, the I tag is actually closed first and then the B tag is closed. If you have ever wondered why XML tends to be illustrated in an indented format, well, the answer might be much clearer now. Not only is the document easier for human readability, it also is easier to find problems in malformed documents.

The hierarchy of tags is completely invalid in Listing 2-7. Not only is there a problem with the B and I tags, but also the opening and closing form and table tags do not nest correctly. When writing HTML, it's all about presentation in the browser. A problem many UI designers ran into years ago, before the days of CSS, was related to forms and tables. Depending upon the placement of the form and table tags, additional whitespace would appear in the rendered page within a Web browser. To remove the additional whitespace, designers would open forms prior to the table tag and close them before closing the table. Web browsers, being forgiving, would render the output correctly without the extra whitespace even though the syntax of the document was not actually correct. As far as XML is concerned, that type of document is not well-formed and will not parse. Elements must be properly nested, which means they must be opened and closed within the same scope. In Listing 2-7, the table tag is opened within the scope of the form tag but closed after the form tag has been closed. Even though it may render when viewed in a browser, the structure is broken and flawed because the form tag should not be closed until all tags residing within its scope have been properly terminated.

Each time an element tag (start, end, or empty element) is encountered, you should insert a line feed and a certain number of indents. Typically for each level of the tree you descend (each time you encounter an element start tag), you should indent one more time than you did the previous time. When ascending the tree (each time an element's end tag is encountered), you should index one less time than previously. Because an empty-element tag serves both purposes, it can be ignored. If you tried to do this with the example from Listing 2-7, you just could not do it. Using whitespace for formatting also makes it pretty easy to spot where it is broken as well:

```
<HTML>
    <BODY>
        <P>This is in
            <I>Italics and this is
                <B>Bold
                </I>
            </B>
            <BR>New Line here
        </P>
        <form name="myform" method="post" action="mypage.php">
            <table width="100%" border="0">
                <tr valign="top">
                    <td>Name:
                        <input type="text" name="name" value="">
                        </td>
                    </tr>
                    <tr>
                        <td>
                            <input type="submit" name="submit" value="Submit">
                            </form>
                        </td>
                    </tr>
                </table>
    </BODY>
</HTML>
```

Although this document has several issues, the most obvious problem should jump out at you. The indenting is completely off between the closing table tag and the closing BODY tag.

This clearly indicates something is wrong with the document. The document in Listing 2-8 applies the rules for XML elements to the document from Listing 2-7 to produce a well-formed XML document.

Listing 2-8. *HTML Example Using Well-Formed XML*

```
<HTML>
    <BODY>
        <P>This is in
            <I>Italics and this is
                <B>Bold</B>
            </I>
            <BR/>
        </P>
        <form name="myform" method="post" action="mypage.php">
            <table width="100%" border="0">
                <tr valign="top">
                    <td>Name:
                        <input type="text" name="name" value="" />
                    </td>
                </tr>
                <tr>
                    <td>
                        <input type="submit" name="submit" value="Submit" />
                    </td>
                </tr>
            </table>
        </form>
    </BODY>
</HTML>
```

This might also give you an inclination of why Extensible HTML (XHTML) was created. XHTML is a stricter version of HTML that not only can be processed by a browser but, because it is XML compliant, can also be processed by applications.

Attributes

You can think of *attributes* as properties of an element, similar to properties of an object. You might be shaking your head right now completely disagreeing with me. You are 100 percent correct, but for a simple document and to give at least a basic idea of what they are, I will use that analogy for now. Attributes can exist within element start tags and empty-element tags. In no case may they appear in an element end tag. Attributes take the form of name/value pairs using the following syntax: `Name="Value"` or `Name='Value'`. You can surround values with either double or single quotes. However, you must use the same type of quotes to encapsulate the attribute's value. It also is perfectly acceptable to use one style of quotes for one attribute and another style for a different attribute. The attribute name must conform to the constraints defined by the term *name* earlier in this chapter. Also, attributes within an element must be uniquely named, meaning an element cannot contain more than one attribute with the same name. Listing 2-9 shows an invalid attribute usage.

Listing 2-9. *Invalid Attribute Usage*

```
</Car color="black">
<Car color="black" color='white' />
```

Attributes also have no specified order within the element, so the following two examples are identical, even though the order and quoting are different:

```
<Car make="Ford" color="black" />
<Car color="black" make='Ford' />
```

Attribute Values

Attributes must also have a *value*, even if the value is empty. Again, referring to HTML, you may be accustomed to seeing lone attribute names such as `<HR size="5" `**`noshade`**`>` or `<frame name="xxx" scrolling="NO" `**`noresize`**`>`. Notice that `noshade` and `noresize` have no defined values. These are not well-formed XML and to be made conformant must be written as `<HR size="5" noshade="noshade">` and `<frame name="xxx" scrolling="NO" noresize="noresize">`, which now makes them XHTML and XML compliant. In cases where an attribute value is empty and there are no rules for any default values, such as those for converting HTML to XHTML, you would write an attribute as such: `attrname=""`.

Attribute values can also not contain unescaped < or & characters. Also, you should use escaped characters for double and single quotes. Although it might be OK to use a literal single quote character within an attribute value that is encapsulated by double quotes (though in this case double quote characters must be escaped), it is not good practice and highly discouraged.

Suppose you wanted to add some attributes to the element `Car` with the following name/value pairs:

- `color`: Black and white

- `owner`: Rob's

- `score`: Less than 5

You would write this as follows:

```
<Car color="black &amp; white" owner="Rob&apos;s" score="&lt; 5" />
```

Attribute Use

The use of attributes, unless specifically required such as through a DTD, is really a choice left to the document author. You will find opinions on attribute use running the full spectrum, with some saying you should never use attributes. When considering whether you should use an attribute or whether it should be a child element, you have a few facts to consider. If you can answer "yes" to any of the following questions, then you should use an element rather than an attribute:

- Could multiple values apply to an element?

- Is a DTD requiring the attribute being used?

- Is the data essential to the document and not just an instruction for an application?

- Is the value complex data or difficult to understand?

- Does the value need to be extensible for potential future use?

If the questions aren't applicable, then it comes down to personal preference. One point to always remember is that the document should end up being easily understood by a human and not just meant for electronic processing. With this in mind, you have to ask yourself which of the following is easier to understand. This is the first choice:

```
<Car make='Ford' color='black' year='1990' model='Escort' />
```

and this is the second choice:

```
<Car>
    <make>Ford</make>
    <color>black</color>
    <year>1990</year>
    <model>Escort</model>
</Car>
```

CDATA

CDATA sections allow the use of all valid Unicode characters in their literal forms. The CDATA contents bypass parsing so are great to use when trying to include content containing markup that should be taken in its literal form and not processed as part of the document. CDATA sections begin with `<![CDATA[`, which is followed by your content, and end with `]]>`, like so:

```
<![CDATA[ ..content here ..]]>
```

The only invalid content in this example is the literal string `]]>`. As you may have guessed, using `]]>` indicates the close of the CDATA section. To represent this string, you would need to use `]]&gt;`.

For example, if you were writing an article about using XML and were using XML as the document structure, CDATA sections would allow you to embed your examples without requiring any character escaping. Listing 2-10 shows an example without a CDATA section, and Listing 2-11 shows an example with one.

Listing 2-10. *Example Without a CDATA Section*

```
<document>
    <title>Example of an XML</title>
    <example>
        &lt;xml version="1.0"?&gt;
        &lt;document&gt;
        this &amp;amp; that
        &lt;/document&gt;
    </example>
</document>
```

Listing 2-11. *Example Using CDATA Section*

```
<document>
    <title>Example of an XML</title>
    <example><![CDATA[
        <xml version="1.0">
        <document>
            this & that
        </document>
    ]]></example>
</document>
```

Clearly, the document in Listing 2-11 is much easier to read than the one in Listing 2-10. If editing a document by hand, it is also easier to write because you don't need to be concerned with figuring out what the correct entities to use are.

Because of the flexibility of CDATA sections, you may have heard or read somewhere that CDATA is great to use for binary data. In its native form, this is not true. You have no guarantee that the binary data will not contain the characters]]>. For this reason, binary data that must be encoded should use a format such as Base64. Now, if Base64 is used for encoding, a CDATA section is not even necessary, and it could be embedded directly as an element's content. This is because Base64 does not use any of the characters that would be deemed illegal for element content.

Comments

You can use *comments* to add notes to a document. This is comparable to a developer adding comments to source code. They do not affect the document but can be used to add some notes or information for someone reading it. For this reason, parsers are not required to parse comments, although most will allow access to the content. This is what a comment looks like:

```
<!-- This is a comment -->
```

Comments consist of the initial <!--, the actual text for the comment, and finally the closing -->. Be aware of the following stipulations when using comments:

- The content for a comment must not contain --.

- A comment may not end with -.

Other than those conditions, comments can contain any other characters.

Comments may also occur anywhere after the XML declaration as long as they are not contained within markup. Listing 2-12 shows some valid comments, and Listing 2-13 shows some invalid ones.

Listing 2-12. *Valid Comments*

```
<!-- The <Car> elements do not contain all known automobiles -->
<!-- This is valid as a whitespace follows the last "-" character - -->
<!-- Don't forget to escape the & character when used as element content -->
```

Listing 2-13. *Invalid Comments*

```
<!-- Comments take the form of <!-- This is a comment --> within a document -->
<!-- This comment is invalid as it ends with three "-" characters. --->
<Car <!-- Invalid because it resides within the element start tag -->>
```

Processing Instructions

XML is purely concerned with document content. A PI allows application-specific instructions to be passed with the document to indicate to the application how it should be processed. The PI takes the form of <?, which is followed by the target (which must be a valid name) and white-space, then takes the actual instruction, and closes with ?>, like so:

```
<?target instructions ?>
```

The target indicates the application that the instruction targets. You might already be familiar with this syntax from PHP:

```
<?php echo "Hello World"; ?>
```

This syntax is a PI. The PI target is php, and the instruction is echo "Hello World";. If you were creating an XHTML document and embedding PHP code, this would constitute a well-formed XML document.

Another case you may have already encountered is the association of style sheets with an XML document. Many XML editors will add the following PI so they can easily perform XSL transformations on the XML you may be editing:

```
<?xml-stylesheet type="text/xsl" href="mystylesheet.xsl"?>
```

Entity References

You have already encountered some of the built-in entity references (&, <, >, ', and ") throughout this chapter. Just as characters can be represented using numeric character references, entity references are used to reference strings, which are defined in the DTD. They take the form of &, which is followed by a legal name, and they terminate with a semicolon. You are probably familiar with the concept from HTML:

```
<P> Copyright &copy; 2002</P>
```

The entity reference © is defined in the HTML DTD and represents the copyright symbol. Entity references cannot just be used blindly, however. The document must pro-vide a meaning to an entity reference. For instance, if you were looking at a document that contained <p>&myref;<p>, the entity reference &myref; has absolutely no meaning to you or may mean something completely different to you than to me. You can use DTDs to define an entity reference. It is mandatory that any entity reference, other than those that are built in, must be defined. Looking at an HTML page, you may notice the DOCTYPE tag at the top of the page. The contents depend upon the type of HTML you are writing. For instance, -//W3C//DTD HTML 4.01 Transitional//EN refers to the DTD http://www.w3.org/TR/html4/loose.dtd. This file contains a reference to http://www.w3.org/TR/html4/HTMLlat1.ent. If you looked at the contents of this file, you will notice that the entity copy is defined as <!ENTITY copy   CDATA © -- copyright sign, U+00A9 ISOnum -->.

The entity reference, when used within the document, then is able to take its "meaning" from the definition. This is further explained in Chapter 3.

General Entity Declaration

Entity declarations may be either general or parameter entity declarations. Entity declarations will be covered in more depth in Chapter 3, though general entities have some bearing to this discussion with respect to entity references. The common use of general entities is to declare the text replacement value for entity references. General entities are commonly referred to as *entities* unless used in a context where that name would be ambiguous; therefore, for the sake of this section, *entities* will refer to general entities.

Entities are defined within the DTD, which is part of the prolog. Suppose you had the string "This is replacement text", which you want to use many times within the document. You could create an entity with a legal name, in this case "replaceit":

```
<?xml version="1.0"?>
<!DOCTYPE foo [
    <!ENTITY replaceit "This is replacement text">
]>
<foo>&replaceit;</foo>
```

If this document were loaded into a parser that was substituting entities, which means it is replacing the entity reference (&replaceit;) with the text string defined in the entity declaration, the results would look something like this:

```
<?xml version="1.0"?>
<!DOCTYPE foo [
    <!ENTITY replaceit "This is replacement text">
]>
<foo>This is replacement text</foo>
```

Using Namespaces

Documents can become quite complex. They can consist of your own XML as well as XML from outside sources. Element and attribute names can start overlapping, which then makes the names ambiguous. How do you determine whether the name comes from your data or from an outside source? Looking at the document, you would have to guess what the elements and attributes mean depending on the context. Unfortunately, applications processing the XML typically don't understand context, so the document would no longer have the correct meaning. *Namespaces* solve this potential problem.

Namespaces are collections of names identified by URIs. They are not part of the XML specification but have their own specification that applies to XML. Through the use of namespaces, names within a document are able to retain their original meanings even when combined with another document that contains some of the same names with completely different meanings.

Assume you are building a document that includes customer information as well as items they have ordered, and assume your customer records look like the following:

```
<Customer>
     <Name>John Smith</Name>
     <Number>12345</Number>
</Customer>
```

The items ordered by the customer take the form of the following structure:

```
<Items>
     <Item>
          <Name>Book</Name>
          <Number>11111</Number>
     </Item>
</Items>
```

Combining these into a single document would result in the following:

```
<Order>
     <Customer>
          <Name>John Smith</Name>
          <Number>12345</Number>
     </Customer>
     <Items>
          <Item>
               <Name>Book</Name>
               <Number>11111</Number>
          </Item>
     </Items>
</Order>
```

Unless you read the pieces of the document in context, the elements Name and Number are ambiguous. Does Number refer to the customer number or an item number? Right now the only way you can tell is that if you are within an item, then Number must refer to an item number; otherwise, it refers to a customer number. This is just a simple case, but it does get worse, such as when elements appear within the same scope. In any event, using namespaces uniquely identifies the elements and attributes, so there is no need for guesswork or trying to figure out the context. Take the following document, for instance. Separate namespaces have been created for Customer and Item data. Just by looking at the element names, you can easily distinguish to what the data refers.

```
<Order xmlns:cus="http://www.example.com/Customer"
       xmlns:item="http://www.example.com/Item">
     <cus:Customer>
     <cus:Name>John Smith</cus:Name>
          <cus:Number>12345</cus:Number>
     </cus:Customer>
     <item:Items>
          <item:Item>
               <item:Name>Book</item:Name>
               <item:Number>11111</item:Number>
          </item:Item>
     </item:Items>
</Order>
```

Defining Namespaces

Looking at the previous example, you may have already determined that `xmlns:cus="http://www.example.com/Customer"` is a namespace definition. Usually, and I stress *usually*, this is not the case; namespaces are created using a special prefixed attribute name and a URI, like so:

```
xmlns:prefix="URI"
```

Based on this definition, `prefix` refers to the namespace prefix you want to use throughout your document to associate certain elements and attributes to a namespace name (`URI`). In this example, the `Number` element within the `Customer` element becomes `cus:Number`, and the `Number` element within the `Item` element becomes `item:Number`. Now, the XML clearly distinguishes between the meanings of these two elements. You have removed any ambiguity from the document.

These new names being used in the elements are called *qualified names*, also referred to as *QNames*. They can be broken down into two parts, separated by a colon: the prefix and the local name. When using namespaced elements, the start and end tags now must contain the qualified name. Again, an exception to this exists, which you will come to in the "Default Namespace" section.

The significant portion of the namespace declaration is the URI (the namespace name). Once bound to a node or element, this will never change. The prefix, however, is not guaranteed. By manipulating the tree, such as moving elements around using the DOM, it is possible a namespace collision may occur. This frequently happens when a namespace defined lower in the tree declares a namespace and uses a prefix, which was used in one of its ancestors. By moving some element as a child of this other element, the prefixes would collide because they refer to two different URIs. It is perfectly valid for the prefix to automatically be changed to one that would not conflict. This is covered in more detail in the section "Namespace Scope."

Elements containing the namespace definition are not part of the namespace unless prefixed. Listing 2-14 shows the `Order` element within a namespace, because it is prefixed with `ord`, as specified in the namespace definition. The `Order` element in Listing 2-15 is not in any namespace even though a namespace is being defined.

Listing 2-14. *Element Order Within the* `http://www.example.com/Order` *Namespace*

```
<ord:Order xmlns:ord="http://www.example.com/Order" />
```

Listing 2-15. *Element Order Not Within the* `http://www.example.com/Order` *Namespace*

```
<Order xmlns:ord="http://www.example.com/Order" />
```

Namespaces are not required for every element and attribute within a document. You need to remember that namespaces remove ambiguity when there are, or there could be, overlapping names. Looking at the example, the only two elements that require namespacing are `Name` and `Number`. It would have been perfectly valid to not put all other elements into namespaces.

Namespaces can also apply to attributes as well:

```
<cus:Customer cus:cid="12345" />
```

The attribute `cid`, with the `cus` prefix, falls within the `http://www.example.com/Customer` namespace.

Default Namespaces

All rules have exceptions. If you remember from the previous section that namespaces take the form of `prefix:name`, well here is the exception: default namespaces allow a namespace to be defined that causes all elements, unless explicitly set to a namespace, to automatically be assigned to the default namespace, like so:

```
<Order xmlns="http://www.example.com/Order" />
```

You may think that the `Order` element is not associated with any namespace. This, however, is wrong. Default namespaces apply to the element they are defined on as well as to all elements, but not to attributes contained in the defining element, unless already associated with a namespace using the QName approach.

Caution Default namespaces do not affect attributes. Unless explicitly set to a namespace with a prefix, attributes do not belong to any namespace. This is extremely important to remember when working with many of the XML technologies, not just the ones within PHP. This knowledge may save you many hours and days of trying to debug an XML-based project.

Let's return to a simplified version of the order structure:

```
<Order xmlns="http://www.example.com/Order"
       xmlns:item="http://www.example.com/Item">
    <Items>
        <Item itid="12345">
            <item:Name>Book</item:Name>
            <item:Number>11111</item:Number>
        </Item>
    </Items>
</Order>
```

This structure contains two namespaces. One is `http://www.example.com/Item`, which is referenced by the prefix `item`, and the other, `http://www.example.com/Order`, is a default namespace. Based on the structure, the elements `Name` and `Number` belong to the `http://www.example.com/Item` namespace because they are using QNames with the `item` prefix. The elements `Order`, `Items`, and `Item` all belong to the `http://www.example.com/Order` namespace, because they are not explicitly set to any namespace so inherit the default namespace. Lastly, the attribute `itid` does not belong to any namespace. It is not explicitly set and hence doesn't use a QName, and as you remember, attributes do not inherit the default namespace.

If possible, I recommend avoiding default namespaces and using QNames with namespaces. As documents become more complex, they become much more difficult to read and understand. Default namespaces do not easily stand out, and when adding namespace scope to the equation, they can become quite confusing to follow. Using qualified names also will help avoid the confusion that sometimes happens with attributes; many people have been bitten by the fact that attributes do not inherit the default namespace and have spent a great deal of time trying to find the bugs in their XML.

Reserved Prefixes and Namespace Names

By default, XML processors are required to define two namespaces with associated prefixes by default:

- The prefix xml is bound to http://www.w3.org/XML/1998/namespace. You can use this namespace to define things such as ID attributes (xml:id) and languages (xml:lang).

- The prefix xmlns is bound to http://www.w3.org/2000/xmlns/. You can use this namespace to declare XML namespaces.

These namespaces may not be bound by using any other prefix except those defined. Within a document, the prefix xmlns must never be declared. The xml prefix, on the other hand, may be declared, although it's not necessary. If declared, though, it must be bound to the http://www.w3.org/XML/1998/namespace namespace.

Prefixes should also not begin with the characters xml. Prefixes that begin with these characters are reserved for future specifications. However, a processor will not treat the use of these as a fatal error, but documents that do use prefixes with these characters may possibly not be valid in the future if a specific prefix ends up being used in any currently undefined specifications.

Namespace Scope

Up until now, you have looked only at namespaces defined in the document element. You can declare namespaces by using any element in the document. So what happens when you encounter additional namespaces? Consider the following document:

```
<Order xmlns:cus="http://www.example.com/Customer"
     xmlns:item="http://www.example.com/Item"
     xmlns="http://www.example.com/Order">
    <cus:Customers>
        <Customer xmlns:cus="http://www.example.com/GENERIC_Customer">
            <cus:Name>John Smith</cus:Name>
            <cus:Number>12345</cus:Number>
        </Customer>
        <cus:Count>1</cus:Count>
    </cus:Customers>
    <item:Items>
        <item1:Item xmlns:item1="http://www.example.com/GENERIC_Item">
            <item1:Name>Book</item1:Name>
            <item1:Number>11111</item1:Number>
        </item1:Item>
        <Item xmlns:item="http://www.example.com/GENERIC_Item">
            <item:Name>Software</item:Name>
            <item:Number>22222</item:Number>
        </Item>
    </item:Items>
    <GeneralInfo xmlns="http://www.example.com/General">
        <Name>General Information</Name>
        <Number>33333</Number>
    </GeneralInfo>
</Order>
```

It's time to play the "Which namespace am I in?" game. You may have been curious why I suggested avoiding using default namespaces if possible. This document is not highly complex because it is quite small and has only a few levels, but it takes namespace use to the extreme—almost to the level of abuse. It should help you to not only understand namespace scoping but also to understand why default namespaces can cause a document to become confusing to read.

What namespace is the `item:Name` element in?

At first glance, you might say `http://www.example.com/Item` because that is the namespace defined on the `Order` element using the `item` prefix. This, however, is wrong. The element is actually in the `http://www.example.com/GENERIC_Item` namespace.

To fully understand how the namespace/element associations are made, you should walk through the document tree and examine the elements. Beginning with the document element, three namespaces are defined:

- `cus` is associated with `http://www.example.com/Customer`.

- `item` is associated with `http://www.example.com/Item`.

- `http://www.example.com/Order` is a default namespace.

The element `cus:Customers` is in the `http://www.example.com/Customer` namespace. This should be obvious, as you have encountered no other namespace definitions. Descending into the content, you encounter the `Customer` element. This element belongs to the `http://www.example.com/Order` namespace. Because it has no prefix and is not defining a default namespace, it inherits the current in-scope default namespace. The element does, however, define a new namespace, `http://www.example.com/GENERIC_Customer`, and it associates the prefix `cus` with it. This prefix used to be associated with `http://www.example.com/Customer`, but for any elements or attributes using this prefix within the contents of the `Customer` element, it now refers to `http://www.example.com/GENERIC_Customer`. This means `cus:Name` and `cus:Number`, which are children of `Customer`, are both in the `http://www.example.com/GENERIC_Customer` namespace.

As you exit from the `Customer` element, the `http://www.example.com/GENERIC_Customer` namespace associated with the `cus` prefix goes out of scope. These were defined on the `Customer` element, which is now closed, so the definition ceases to exist. However, `cus` is now in scope from its definition on the `Order` element. When you encounter the next element, `cus:Count`, it belongs to the `http://www.example.com/Customer` namespace because of the scoping rules. Moving back up the tree, you can safely ignore the `cus:Customers` closing element. Because the element did not define any namespaces, it does not alter anything.

The `item:Items` element is the next element encountered. No changes exist in namespace, so it is bound to the `http://www.example.com/Item` namespace as defined on the `Order` element. Its child element, `item1:Item`, defines the `http://www.example.com/GENERIC_Item` namespace with the `item1` prefix. As this element is also prefixed with `item1`, it ends up in the `http://www.example.com/Item/1` namespace, which it is defining. Both of its children, `item1:Name` and `item1:Number`, will belong to the same `http://www.example.com/GENERIC_Item` namespace defined on their parent.

Entering the second `Item` element, the namespace `http://www.example.com/GENERIC_Item` is once again defined but associated with the `item` prefix. This changes the scope of the prefix so that all the elements contained within `Item` and using the prefix `item` will now be bound to `http://www.example.com/GENERIC_Item` rather than to the one defined on the `Order` element.

The Item element itself has no prefix so is bound to the default namespace, which currently is http://www.example.com/Order. With the newly defined item prefix, both the children elements, item:Name and item:Number, belong to http://www.example.com/GENERIC_Item. Upon leaving the last Item element, the item prefix loses scope, but since it was defined before in an ancestor element (Order), item again refers to the http://www.example.com/Item namespace.

The next element hit is the GeneralInfo element. This demonstrates how it might be confusing to use default namespaces. This element resides in the default namespace. It, however, is also defining a default namespace. The question now arises—to which default namespace does it belong?

Remember the section "Default Namespaces"? Elements defining a default namespace, and not bound to any namespace, will be bound to the default namespace they're defining. To answer the original question then, GeneralInfo is bound to http://www.example.com/General. This also means all elements contained within GeneralInfo will now use http://www.example.com/General as the default namespace. So with that information, there is no way to trick you by asking you what the namespace for the child Name and Number elements are. Of course, they are bound to http://www.example.com/General. When a parser encounters the GeneralInfo closing tag, the default namespace defined on that element falls out of scope, and http://www.example.com/Order comes back into scope as the default namespace of the document.

It's a good thing this was a simple document. Just imagine how hard it would have been to explain a large and complex document. Here are a few tips for writing XML documents:

- If you don't need namespaces, don't use them.

- If you have the choice, use QNames rather than default namespaces.

- Attributes are not bound to default namespaces.

- DTDs and namespaces are not all that compatible and can lead to invalid documents.

Namespaces and Attribute Uniqueness

Back in the "Attributes" section, you learned attributes must be unique for an element. Namespaces add a little twist to this. Attributes names must still be unique, where the name consists of the prefix and local name for a namespaced attribute, but they must also not have the same local name and prefixes that are bound to the same namespace.

In the following example, although the attribute names, a1:z and a2:z, are unique, they are both bound to the same namespace, http://www.example.com/a, which means this is an invalid document:

```
<x xmlns:a1="http://www.example.com/a" xmlns:a2="http://www.example.com/a">
    <y a1:z="1" a2:z="2" />
</x>
```

The following attributes are perfectly legal. The attribute a1:z is bound to http://www.example.com/a1, and a2:z is bound to http://www.example.com/a2.

```
<x xmlns:a1="http://www.example.com/a1" xmlns:a2="http://www.example.com/a2">
    <y a1:z="1" a2:z="2" />
</x>
```

The following example may throw you a bit. Default namespaces do not apply to attributes, so these attributes are unique. Their names are unique because the qualified names are used for comparison, and no duplicate namespace exists. Attribute a:z is bound to http://www.example.com/a, and attribute a is not in any namespace.

```
<x xmlns:a="http://www.example.com/a" xmlns="http://www.example.com/a">
    <y a:z="1" z="2" />
</x>
```

Note The remainder of the examples in this chapter that use DTDs are well-formed documents but are not valid. If loading them into a parser, make sure you disable validation; otherwise, validation errors will occur. For more information, see Chapter 3.

Using IDs, IDREF/IDREFS, and xml:id

When dealing with documents, it is often useful to be able to uniquely identify elements and be able to easily locate them. Attribute IDs serve this same purpose. When applied to an element, which can have at most a single ID (though this is not the case when using xml:id), the value of the attribute on the element serves as the unique identifier for the element. An IDREF, on the other hand, allows elements to reference these unique elements.

At first glance, you may be wondering what purpose the ID and IDREF instances actually serve. Of course, they uniquely identify an element, but what advantage does that offer to you? Before answering that question, I'll cover how you construct them. You can create an attribute ID in two ways. The first is through an attribute declaration (ATTLIST) in a DTD. (Chapter 3 covers DTDs in depth; in this chapter, I'll explain ATTLIST and its makeup in regard to IDs.) On February 8, 2004, the W3C released the xml:id specification as a candidate recommendation. This provides a mechanism to define IDs without requiring a DTD. Since this is relatively new, I will begin with the ATTLIST method and then return to xml:id.

Defining IDs Using a DTD

Earlier, when discussing the prolog of the document, I touched upon the document type declaration and where it is defined. Similar to Listing 2-4, you can use an internal subset to declare the attribute. Defining attributes takes the following form:

```
<!ATTLIST element_name attribute_name attribute_type attribute_default >
```

In this case, attribute_type is the ID. Attribute types, as well as the entire ATTLIST definition, are fully explained in Chapter 3, so for now, just take this at face value. You also, for now, will use #REQUIRED for attribute_default. This just means every element with the name element_name is required to have the ID attribute named attribute_name defined.

Consider the XML document in Listing 2-16, which could serve as a course list for a school.

Listing 2-16. *Course Listing*

```
<Courses>
    <Course id="1">
        <Title>Spanish I</Title>
        <Description>Introduction to Spanish</Description>
    </Course>
    <Course id="2">
        <Title>French I</Title>
        <Description>Introduction to French</Description>
    </Course>
    <Course id="3">
        <Title>French II</Title>
        <Description>Intermediate French</Description>
    </Course>
</Courses>
```

Does this document contain IDs used to uniquely identify elements and for ID lookups?

The answer is no. However, it may appear to do so; since the attribute name is id and the values of the attributes are unique, the attributes within the document are just plain, everyday attributes. This is a problem many people frequently encounter, and I have fielded many bug reports claiming that IDs are not working properly in a document. The fact is, just creating an attribute with the name ID does not make it an ID. IDs can actually be named anything you like, assuming it is a legal XML name. The document must somehow be told that the attribute is of type ID. There is also a caveat about the allowed values for attribute IDs. The values must follow the rules for legal XML names. So within the previous example, the value 1 is invalid because names cannot begin with a number.

■**Caution** An attribute with the name ID is not automatically an ID. You must make the document aware that an attribute is of type ID. Once identified, the values of the attribute IDs must conform to the rules defined by legal XML names and so may not begin with a number.

Listing 2-17 shows how to rewrite the document so it can use IDs.

Listing 2-17. *New Course Listing*

```
<!DOCTYPE Courses [
    <!ATTLIST Course cid ID #REQUIRED>
]>
<Courses>
    <Course cid="c1">
        <Title>Spanish I</Title>
        <Description>Introduction to Spanish</Description>
    </Course>
```

```
    <Course cid="c2">
        <Title>French I</Title>
        <Description>Introduction to French</Description>
    </Course>
    <Course cid="c3">
        <Title>French II</Title>
        <Description>Intermediate French</Description>
    </Course>
</Courses>
```

Comparing the documents from Listing 2-16 and Listing 2-17, you will notice that I added a document type declaration and I named the attributes cid. I changed the name to illustrate that you can use any valid names for IDs and not just id. I added the ATTLIST declaration to define the attributes named cid when applied to elements named Course of type ID and to define that the attribute is required for all Course elements. You may also notice that the values for the attributes have changed. With respect to the rules surrounding the attribute value, I prefixed the numeric values with the letter *c* so they conform to the rules for legal XML names.

After the document in Listing 2-17 has been parsed, you will end up with two Course elements that are uniquely identified by the value of the cid attribute. Now I can answer the original question of what purpose they serve. The answer really depends upon what you are doing. For instance, if you were to load the document under the DOM, using the DOM Document object, you could retrieve specific elements by calling the getElementById() method. Passing in the unique value as the parameter to the method, such as c2, the Course element that contains information on French I would be returned. Distinct elements could also be returned using XPath queries, such as those used in XSL. IDs can also be referenced within a document, which brings us to IDREF.

IDREF

An IDREF is a method that allows an element to reference another element. It is basically a pointer from one element to another. Taking the course list in Listing 2-17, how could you expand it to add course prerequisite information? One way to do this would be to duplicate the course information for the prerequisites, as shown in Listing 2-18.

Listing 2-18. *Course Listing with Prerequisites*

```
<!DOCTYPE Courses [
    <!ATTLIST Course cid ID #REQUIRED>
]>
<Courses>
    <Course cid="c2">
        <Title>French I</Title>
        <Description>Introduction to French</Description>
    </Course>
    <Course cid="c3">
        <Title>French II</Title>
        <Description>Intermediate French</Description>
        <pre-requisite>
```

```
        <Pcourse>
            <Title>French I</Title>
            <Description>Introduction to French</Description>
        </Pcourse>
    </pre-requisite>
  </Course>
</Courses>
```

This is not an efficient way of handling data. The element name Course could not be used for the prerequisite. Course elements require the ID attribute cid, but for this document, the prerequisites should not be IDs. This could be handled by changing the attribute_type in the ATTLIST, covered in Chapter 3, but this still requires duplicating the content for the French I course. No correlation within the document exists that says the Course element containing French I in the prerequisites is the same as the Course element identified by c2.

Modifying the document in Listing 2-18, you can add an IDREF, as shown in Listing 2-19. For now, the document continues to use Pcourse for the element name.

Listing 2-19. *Course Listing with Prerequisites Using* IDREF

```
<!DOCTYPE Courses [
    <!ATTLIST Course cid ID #REQUIRED>
    <!ATTLIST Pcourse cref IDREF #REQUIRED>
]>
<Courses>
    <Course cid="c2">
        <Title>French I</Title>
        <Description>Introduction to French</Description>
    </Course>
    <Course cid="c3">
        <Title>French II</Title>
        <Description>Intermediate French</Description>
        <pre-requisite>
            <Pcourse cref="c2" />
        </pre-requisite>
    </Course>
</Courses>
```

Pcourse no longer contains all the additional baggage and redundant data. The IDREF, cref, now refers to the Course element identified by c2. The document no longer contains redundant data, making it more compact as well as easier to read. In addition, you can reuse the content. Imagine how long the document would be if you created an entire school course list, along with all prerequisites, without using IDs and IDREF.

IDREFS

Sometimes an element will need to reference more than one ID of the same element type. For example, in Listing 2-19, it would be much easier if the pre-requisite element could reference the courses directly, rather than adding child elements for the courses. Multiple attributes of the same name are not allowed for an element, so you must use IDREFS to perform this feat, as shown in Listing 2-20.

Listing 2-20. *Course Listing with Prerequisites Using* IDREFS

```
<!DOCTYPE Courses [
    <!ATTLIST Course cid ID #REQUIRED>
    <!ATTLIST pre-requisite cref IDREFS #REQUIRED>
]>
<Courses>
    <Course cid="c1">
        <Title>Basic Languages</Title>
        <Description>Introduction to Languages</Description>
    </Course>
    <Course cid="c2">
        <Title>French I</Title>
        <Description>Introduction to French</Description>
    </Course>
    <Course cid="c3">
        <Title>French II</Title>
        <Description>Intermediate French</Description>
        <pre-requisite cref="c1 c2" />
    </Course>
</Courses>
```

You will notice that the element pre-requisite now contains a single attribute, cref, with the value c1 c2. The value of the IDREFS attribute is a whitespace-delimited list of IDREF. This means cref is a pointer to *both* the Course element identified by c1 and the Course element identified by c2.

Using xml:id

In 2004, the W3C released the xml:id specification as a recommendation. Using xml:id within a document allows you to create IDs without requiring a DTD. This is a much easier method than creating attribute declarations, though the two have a few differences:

- The values for xml:id *must* conform to legal namespace names. This is almost identical to regular IDs, except a colon is not a valid character for the value.

- When defined in a DTD, though not a requirement to do so, xml:id *must* be defined as an ID. The attribute type for xml:id cannot be modified to another type.

Re-creating the course list from Listing 2-17, using xml:id rather than declaring attributes of type ID, the document would look as follows:

```
<Courses>
    <Course xml:id="c1">
        <Title>Spanish I</Title>
        <Description>Introduction to Spanish</Description>
    </Course>
```

```
    <Course xml:id="c2">
        <Title>French I</Title>
        <Description>Introduction to French</Description>
    </Course>
    <Course xml:id="c3">
        <Title>French II</Title>
        <Description>Intermediate French</Description>
    </Course>
</Courses>
```

To use an IDREF, however, the IDREF still must be declared in the DTD. So, re-creating the document in Listing 2-18 using xml:id and IDREF, the document would take this form:

```
<!DOCTYPE Courses [
    <!ATTLIST Pcourse cref IDREF #REQUIRED>
]>
<Courses>
    <Course xml:id="c2">
        <Title>French I</Title>
        <Description>Introduction to French</Description>
    </Course>
    <Course xml:id="c3">
        <Title>French II</Title>
        <Description>Intermediate French</Description>
        <pre-requisite>
            <Pcourse cref="c2" />
        </pre-requisite>
    </Course>
</Courses>
```

You don't need to do anything else to handle IDs using xml:id. As I said before, it is simple to use and is great when you don't want to deal with DTDs. One less thing to complicate the document is always better!

Using xml:space and xml:lang

Two special attributes that are part of the XML specification can provide additional information to a document about how certain things should be processed: xml:space and xml:lang. These are not like PIs, which are application specific. These attributes, being part of the XML specification, are meant to be handled by any application. When using these attributes within a document to be validated, you must define attribute declarations for these attributes within the DTD; otherwise, validation errors may occur.

xml:space

This attribute specifies to an application how it should handle whitespace. The valid values are preserve and default. When set to default, the application handles whitespace as it normally does. A value of preserve instructs the application that it must preserve all whitespace within the context of the element on which the attribute is set. For example:

```
<Description xml:space="preserve">
<a>This</a>
    <b>is</b>
        <c>the</c>
            <d>description</d>
</Description>
```

The value of preserve should instruct the application to preserve the whitespace within the description content. If this were set to default, the application may or may not preserve whitespace. It would depend upon its default behavior.

xml:lang

The xml:lang attribute can specify the language used for the content within an element. The values can come from the ISO standard 639, denoted by the IANA prefix i-, or from private sources, denoted by the prefix x-. For example:

```
<docu xml:lang="en">
    <p xml:lang="fr">Bonjour monde en français </p>
    <p xml:lang="de">Hallo Welt auf Deutsch<p>
    <p>Hello World in English</p>
</docu>
```

The document illustrates "Hello World" in French (xml:lang="fr"), German (xml:lang="de"), and English. The p tag for English has no xml:lang attribute because it is in the scope of the docu element, which is set to xml:lang="en". Therefore, unless overridden, the default content of the docu element is in English.

Understanding XML Base

Unlike xml:space and xml:lang, XML Base is not part of the XML specification. It has its own specification from the W3C. The xml:base attribute specifies a base URI on an element, which is used to resolve relative URIs used within the scope of the element. The use of xml:base may also be stacked. By this I mean that within the scope of an element defining an xml:base, an element may define a relative URI as its xml:base. This would effectively set the base URI within the context of this subelement as the path of this new base, relative to the ancestor base URI.

XML Base is primarily used for XLink to describe linking between resources. You may also see it used in other contexts, such as with XInclude and XSLT. The following is a document that uses XInclude to illustrate how xml:base can define base URIs for the XInclude documents:

```
<example xmlns:xi="http://www.w3.org/2001/XInclude">
    <para xml:base="http://www.example.com/">
        <xi:include href="example.xml" />
        <p2 xml:base="examples/">
            <xi:include href="example1.xml" />
        </p2>
        <p3>
            <xi:include href="examples/example1.xml" />
        </p3>
    </para>
</example>
```

Within the para element, the base URI is set to http://www.example.com/. Everything within the scope of this element will now use this URI as the base for any relative URI. As you descend into the child elements, the first xi:include points to example.xml. This will resolve to http://www.example.com/example.xml when included in the document.

Moving to the p2 element, xml:base is set to examples/. This is a relative URI, so for all practicality, it inherits the base of the encapsulating element's URI (http://www.example.com/) and sets the base relative to this. The base is now http://www.example.com/examples/ for the p2 element and everything within its scope. When the xi:xinclude element is reached within this element, the file example1.xml will resolve to http://www.example.com/examples/example1.xml when included.

Continuing to navigate the document, you reach the end of p2. The base that was set falls out of scope, which means the base set by the para element, http://www.example.com/, becomes the active base again. Upon reaching the xi:include within the p3 element, the file examples/example1.xml, being relative, uses the base URI from para and resolves to http://www.example.com/examples/example1.xml when included. This is the same file that p2 had included, just using relative pathing a little differently based upon the scope of xml:base within the document.

Conclusion

This chapter covered the basic structure, syntax, and a few other areas of XML that will help you understand documents, regardless of their complexity. Although a few more complex aspects of XML exist, you should be well on your way to creating well-formed XML documents with the basics presented here. The next chapter will introduce you to validating with DTDs, XML Schemas, and RELAX NG. What you have learned in this chapter will be invaluable to you throughout the rest of this book.

CHAPTER 3

■ ■ ■

Validation

By now, you have most likely heard that all XML documents must be well-formed but that documents are not required to be valid. This chapter will explain what it means for a document to be valid and will show how to create valid documents. I will cover DTDs, XML Schemas, and Relax NG in depth and discuss the differences between them.

Introducing Validation

A *well-formed* document is one that is written using legal XML syntax and structure according to the XML specification. A *valid* document is one that is well-formed and conforms to a structure outlined in a DTD or schema. You can think of this as a database schema. A table definition defines the fields and their data types, lengths, and defaults. Using primary and foreign keys, you can also define a database structure. If someone tries to insert data that does not fit the model, they'll get an error.

Validation in XML works in almost the same way. The schema defines how an XML document must look. It can define the order of elements in the document, what child elements are valid for particular elements, and what type of content particular elements can have. You can apply similar constraints to other pieces of an XML document.

If you were receiving XML from some undefined source and were expecting a document that looked like the following one, you would use validation to ensure the document conforms to your expectations. The system you are processing the documents with must have the document in this format; otherwise, it will cause an error. Therefore, validating the document prior to processing is essential in this case.

```
<question number="1">
   <query>Is this XML?</query>
   <answer>true</answer>
</question>
```

Validation allows you to describe a document in generic terms. You know that this example's document element must be the element question. The question element must have a number attribute that can have an integer for its value. Here you don't care what the specific value is, just that the value is an integer. The question element must also contain two elements, query and answer, in that order. No other content is allowed for the question element. The query element cannot have any attributes and can have only text content. You don't care what the text is, just that there is text and no XML markup. The answer element cannot have any attributes and must contain true or false. Validation allows you to take this verbal description of the constraints placed on a document, write the description in a schema using the schema's *grammar* (the language it uses to describe a document), and then perform automated validation of the document. You will be able to determine whether the document conforms to your expectations before actually sending the document to be processed.

Introducing Document Type Definitions

Chapter 2 briefly touched on DTDs in respect to `ID`, `IDREF`, and `IDREFS`. These are just a small aspect of DTDs. The main purpose of a DTD is to perform document validation. Although other methods to perform document validation exist, DTDs are part of the XML 1.0 specification so have been around for some time now. Before getting under the hood of a DTD, though, you need to back up and re-examine document type declarations, mentioned in Chapter 2.

Document Type Declarations

The document type declaration is *not* a DTD but is the declaration to declare a DTD. It can include an internal subset, an external subset, or both. These subsets together make up the document's DTD. The difference between an internal and external subset is, as their names imply, that an external subset is a subset that is not defined within the document. The document must access the subset from an external resource, such as from the file system or the network. An internal subset is defined directly within the document. You may be wondering why two different subsets exist. External subsets allow documents to share common DTDs. If you were working at a large company, for example, you might have a standard DTD for documents created within the company. Rather than having to define the same DTD within each document, documents can reference a common standard DTD via an external subset. As mentioned in Chapter 2, a declaration looks like the following:

```
<!DOCTYPE document_element definitions>
```

The `document_element` is the root, or document element, of the body of the XML document, and `definitions` is the internal and/or external subsets. The document type declaration must contain the `document_element` and at least an internal or external subset declaring the element; otherwise, the document type declaration is not written properly and has no DTD to validate against. In the following sections, you'll examine external subsets and how they are declared.

External Subsets

External subsets are accessed through external IDs. The external ID includes a system identifier and possibly a public identifier, which serve to locate the external subset. The system literal is a URI that provides the specific location of the subset. Note that the URI cannot be a fragment (which is a URI using the # character to point to a specific portion of a document). You may be more familiar with this when using anchors in HTML. Public identifiers allow the use of some other identifier, which your parser would then translate to a URI. When using public identifiers, a system identifier is also required in the event the parser is unable to resolve the public identifier.

Listing 3-1 illustrates how to use both system and public identifiers. You denote system identifiers, when not used with a public identifier, by using the keyword `SYSTEM`. You denote a public identifier by using the PUBLIC keyword. Normally, unless the document is used internally, public identifiers are rarely used. This is because anyone outside your organization would not understand what the public identifier was referring to or even how to resolve it.

Listing 3-1. *System and Public Identifiers*

```
<!-- Using System Identifier -->
<!DOCTYPE courses SYSTEM "http://www.example.com/courses.dtd">
<!-- Using Public Identifier -->
<!DOCTYPE courses PUBLIC "-//Example//Courses DTD//EN"
                        "http://www.example.com/courses.dtd">
```

The external subset contains the markup that makes up the DTD. It consists of an optional text declaration followed by the external subset declarations. Chapter 2 didn't cover text declarations, as they pertain only to external entities; I'll cover them next.

Text Declaration

You are already familiar with the syntax for *text declarations*. They are similar to XML declarations of documents; however, the standalone declaration is not valid, version is optional, and encoding is required. It is also recommended that you use a text declaration for external entities. A text declaration primarily indicates the encoding of the external entity, which is necessary when the entity uses a different encoding than the main XML document. The examples in Listing 3-2 illustrate the two possible structures of a text declaration, where the only difference is the use of the optional version attribute.

Listing 3-2. *Text Declaration*

```
<!-- Text declaration without version -->
<?xml encoding="ISO-8859-1" ?>

<!-- Text declaration with version -->
<?xml version="1.0" encoding="ISO-8859-1" ?>
```

External Subset Declaration

The *external subset declaration* is where the actual grammar for the DTD resides. It consists of one or many markup declarations, conditional sections, and declaration separators. I'll cover all these in depth in upcoming sections; markup declarations and declaration separators, which are explained later in the chapter in the "Parameter Entities" section, are common to both external and internal subsets, and conditional sections are specific to external subsets and external parameter entities. Listing 3-3 shows an example, which is explained in more detail throughout this chapter, for the courses.dtd file from Listing 3-1.

Listing 3-3. *External Subset*

```
<?xml encoding="ISO-8859-1"?>
<!ELEMENT courses (course+)>
<!ELEMENT course (title, description, pre-requisite*)>
<!ATTLIST course cid ID #REQUIRED>
<!ELEMENT title (#PCDATA)>
<!ELEMENT description (#PCDATA)>
<!ELEMENT pre-requisite EMPTY>
<!ATTLIST pre-requisite cref IDREFS #REQUIRED>
```

If you refer to the previous chapter, this external subset looks fairly similar to describing the structure of the document body. Note that the case has changed on the elements—they are now all lowercase. If you lowercased all the elements in the IDREF example, you could use this external subset as the DTD for courses.dtd.

Internal Subset

An *internal subset* consists of the grammar for the DTD defined directly within the document. Within the document type declaration, the internal subset is enclosed within the characters [and]. When used with an external subset, the internal subset is defined right after the external subset. Although defined last, any declarations defined in the internal subset take precedence over definitions from the external subset. Basically, you can use an internal subset to override an external subset.

If you refer to the external subset declaration section in Listing 3-3—specifically to the markup used to define the contents of the course.dtd file as well as Listing 3-1—you could rewrite the document type using an internal subset as follows:

```
<!DOCTYPE courses [
    <!ELEMENT courses (course+)>
    <!ELEMENT course (title, description, pre-requisite*)>
    <!ATTLIST course cid ID #REQUIRED>
    <!ELEMENT title (#PCDATA)>
    <!ELEMENT description (#PCDATA)>
    <!ELEMENT pre-requisite EMPTY>
    <!ATTLIST pre-requisite cref IDREFS #REQUIRED>
]>
```

But, as previously mentioned, using internal subsets is restrictive because they cannot be shared. It's best to use an external subset. According to this DTD, pre-requisite elements contain attributes but must be empty. What happens, however, if this document will contain content within the pre-requisite element but the external subset is being used for the document? This is where the internal subset really comes in handy. Using the external subset in Listing 3-3, you can override the element declaration for the pre-requisite element in an internal subset, as shown in Listing 3-4.

Listing 3-4. *Overriding Prerequisite Declaration Using Internal Subset*

```
<!DOCTYPE courses SYSTEM "http://www.example.com/courses.dtd" [
    <!ELEMENT pre-requisite (#PCDATA)>
]>
```

If you notice the bold code in Listing 3-4, the definition of the pre-requisite element now allows data. This differs from Listing 3-3, where it is defined as EMPTY in the external subset. The declaration within the internal subset takes precedence in definitions, so a document written according to this new DTD (Listing 3-4) would allow certain content within the pre-requisite element.

Markup Declarations

So far you have seen how to declare internal and external subsets as well as what they look like, but now it's time to look at all the markup they contain. Markup declarations declare elements types, attribute lists, entities, and notations. They can also take the form of PIs and comments; although these do not actually declare anything for the document, they can be used for application instructions or author notes, as described in Chapter 2. When writing declarations, you will encounter a few wildcards, which can be used in your grammar. Before examining element declarations, you'll learn more about the wildcards.

Wildcards

A grammar, within a declaration, is written through expressions. Wildcards determine grouping as well as the number of matches. This is similar to using wildcards when writing regular expressions. For those of you unfamiliar with regular expressions, they are a syntax used to write rules and perform pattern matches against strings. Just as you could write the expression [A-Z]+ in a regular expression, which would match one or more characters in the range of A–Z, you could use similar functionality when writing declaration rules. Within the declaration, an expression can be an element type or element name. The following list shows some of the basic wildcards that can be used, where expression could be as simple as an element name:

- ?: The expression is optional (expression?).

- expression1 expression2: Matches an expression1 followed by expression2.

- |: Matches either expression (expression1 | expression2).

- -: Matches the first expression but not the second (expression1 - expression2).

- +: Matches one or more occurrences of the expression (expression+).

- *: Matches zero or more occurrences of the expression (expression*).

- (expression): The expression within the parentheses is treated as a single unit.

For example, if you wanted to match on the logic that element1 must be followed by one or more element2 *or* that it should match on zero or more element3 elements or a single element4, the expression would look like this:

```
(element1 element2+) | (element3* | element4)
```

Notice that element1 and element2 are within parentheses and so are element3 and element4. The parentheses will take each of the two expressions as a whole and match on either one of them, because of the | character.

You will see more examples of writing expressions and what they translate to as you take a closer look at the declarations within a DTD.

Element Type Declaration

In this chapter, you have encountered examples of element type declarations many times. These have been the markup that begins with <!ELEMENT followed by whitespace. They define an element and what is valid for its content. Element type declarations take the following form:

```
<!ELEMENT element_name contentspec>
```

The element_name is exactly what it implies. It is the name of the element you are defining. The contentspec defines what type of content, if any, is valid for the element. It can take the value EMPTY or ANY or may be a content model of the type mixed or child. EMPTY simply implies the element cannot contain content. Within the document, the element must be an empty-element tag or must be a start and end tag with nothing in between, not even whitespace. ANY implies that any type of content, including none at all, is allowed. You can use this when you have no specific rules for an element. It doesn't matter if there are child elements or what their names are, and it doesn't matter what other content may appear, as long as the content follows the rules for allowable content in the XML specification. Using the pre-requisite element as an example, in the external subset it is empty; and in the internal subset, you want to allow any type of content, so it takes the following forms:

```
<!-- declaration from external subset requiring the element to be empty -->
<!ELEMENT pre-requisite EMPTY>
<!-- declaration from internal subset allowing any content for element -->
<!ELEMENT pre-requisite ANY>
```

Mixed and child content model types are not as simple, as these are user-written rules to which the element content must conform.

Child Content Model

An element that can contain only child elements and no other content, excluding insignificant whitespace, follows the child content model. As mentioned in Chapter 2, whitespace is typically significant and consists of spaces, tabs, carriage returns, and line feeds. When dealing with validation, this whitespace is considered insignificant when it's not used with any other text. This means you can't use any other type of text besides these whitespace characters directly within the element's content. When thinking of element content in these terms, the text content would include text, which is in the immediate scope of the element being defined. Text contained within any of the child elements of this element would be validated according to the declarations of the child elements. An element following this model would look like the following:

```
<course>
    <title>French II</title>
    <description>Intermediate French</description>
    <pre-requisite>
        ... some type of content
    </pre-requisite>
</course>
```

You may remember this structure from Chapter 2. It is a fragment from the courses document. Notice that the course element contains no text, other than the insignificant whitespace, but has three child elements. Also, the pre-requisite element is not a required element because not all courses have prerequisites. You could now write the element declaration for the course element as follows:

```
<!ELEMENT course (title, description, pre-requisite*)>
```

The content specification, which defines the data content, for this declaration is (title, description, pre-requisite*). This is a *sequence list*, denoted by the list of elements separated by commas. A sequence list accepts other types than just elements, but in this case, under the child content model, no other types are allowed. Using a list means that each of the types used must appear in a document in the exact order they are specified in the sequence list. Based upon the wildcard used in the expression, the content specification would translate to a course element that may contain only the child element's title, description, and any number, including zero pre-requisite elements. These elements must appear in this order within a course element. Therefore, the following fragment would not be valid according to this declaration:

```
<course>
    <description>Intermediate French</description>
    <title>French II</title>
</course>
```

This document has no pre-requisite element, but that is perfectly fine. The definition indicates that zero or more pre-requisite elements are considered valid, denoted by pre-requisite* in the declaration. The problem with this document is that according to the declaration, title must come before the description element, which is not the case here. To allow both ordering schemes, the declaration would need to define the two cases as follows:

```
<!ELEMENT course (((title, description) | (description, title)), pre-requisite*)>
```

Notice the use of parentheses. Following the order of precedence, the course element must contain either title followed by description *or* description followed by title. Either of these variants then must be followed by zero or more pre-requisite elements.

Expanding upon the course element, you can add some new information to a course, which will provide more information on the course being offered. It can take the form of a URL or embedded text, but not both. Say you decide to add two more possible elements, course_url and course_info, to the course element. The document could look like any of the following:

```
<!-- course without course_info and course_url -->
<course>
    <description>Intermediate French</description>
    <title>French II</title>
</course>
<!-- course with course_url -->
<course>
    <title>French II</title>
    <description>Intermediate French</description>
    <course_url>http://www.example.com/french.html</course_url>
</course>
<!-- course with course_info -->
<course>
    <title>French II</title>
    <description>Intermediate French</description>
    <course_info>This is miscellaneous info on French II</course_info>
</course>
```

Although the pre-requisite element does not appear in any of these fragments, it is still valid (it was omitted for brevity). Enforcement of element order has also been reinstituted, so description must follow title. Listing 3-5 shows how you would write the new declaration.

Listing 3-5. *New* course *Element Declaration*

```
<!ELEMENT course (title, description, (course_url | course_info)?, pre-requisite*)>
```

Breaking down this grammar, course must contain title followed by description. The description element then can be followed by a single, optional course_url *or* course_info element, but not both. Regardless of whether one of these elements exists as a child, the last element in the order would be zero or more pre-requisite elements. Based on these rules, the following fragment is invalid:

```
<course>
    <title>French II</title>
    <description>Intermediate French</description>
    <course_info>This is miscellaneous info on French II</course_info>
    <course_url>http://www.example.com/french.html</course_url>
</course>
```

The course element *cannot*, according to the declaration, contain both the course_info and course_url elements.

So far, you have looked at child elements only as an element's content. Using what you've learned up to now, you'll see content that can include a mix of text and other element types.

Mixed Content Model

Many times the child content model is too strict for a document. You might want to add comments, PIs, or even text within an element's content. Depending upon your expression, mixed content allows for PCDATA, which stands for *parsed character data*, and possibly child elements.

Recall from Chapter 2 that you must escape special characters such as < and & when using them within parsed text sections. PCDATA is such a section. It can, however, contain nonparsed character sections, such as comments, CDATA, and PIs. The simplest form of mixed content is text-only content.

Text-only content means that an element contains no child elements, and its content is pure text, including comments, CDATA, and PI sections. Examining the course element in this chapter, examples of elements containing pure text are the title, description, and course_info elements. Referring to Listing 3-3, the external subset, you will notice that title and description have been declared as follows:

```
<!ELEMENT title (#PCDATA)>
<!ELEMENT description (#PCDATA)>
```

Declaring the course_info is the same. The following element will have no child elements, but CDATA content may be desired:

```
<!-- Declaration of course info -->
<!ELEMENT course_info (#PCDATA)>
<!-- example of course_info content allowed based on declaration -->
<course_info><![CDATA[
    Trip available to Corsica & Ile-de-France.
    GPA < 3.0 requires instructor permission.
    ]]>
    Trip coordinators will be Mr. Smith &amp; Mr. Jones.
    <!-- Need to check scheduling -->
</course_info>
```

Pure text content may suffice for a majority of the elements within a document, but sometimes you'll need both text and child elements. In cases like these, you'll need to mix PCDATA with the child elements.

In Listing 3-4, pre-requisite has been defined as #PCDATA. This is so that you can add comments to the content. However, when writing this document, this definition ends up being too restrictive. Sometimes not only are some courses required, but also instructor approval is required. To indicate whether prior approval is required before being able to take the course, you need to add an optional element, instructor_approval, as a child element to the pre-requisite element. It has also been determined that when this new element is missing, no prior approval is required. With this new element, however, the pre-requisite element may now look like this:

```
<pre-requisite cref="1">
    <!-- This prerequisite may not be required next semester -->
    <instructor_approval>Y</instructor_approval>
</pre-requisite>
```

The new declaration for pre-requisite is as follows:

```
<!ELEMENT pre-requisite (#PCDATA | instructor_approval)*>
```

Notice that when mixing content, you use the | character as well as the * character. These are required per the specifications, which means you are unable to use strict element ordering in mixed content. For example, if you added a child element to the `pre-requisite` element—say you were adding an element for the required next semester flag called `req_next_sem`—you would just add it as part of the `OR` expression.

This means that the `pre-requisite` element may contain zero or more #PCDATA (text content), `instructor_approval` elements, and/or `req_next_sem` elements and may appear in any order. For example:

```
<!ELEMENT pre-requisite (#PCDATA | instructor_approval | req_next_sem)*>
```

As you may infer from the translation, mixed content may not be a good idea to use when validation is a major concern for a document. Using the declaration, you could end up with a `pre-requisite` element that has multiple `instructor_approval` elements or multiple `req_next_sem` elements that may even contain conflicting values. Consider the `pre-requisite` element in Listing 3-6; it is valid according to the declaration but is *not* what is intended to be valid.

Listing 3-6. *Valid* `pre-requisite` *Element and Conflicting Data*

```
<pre-requisite cref="c1" >
    <!-- This prerequisite may not be required next semester -->
    <req_next_sem>N</req_next_sem>
    <instructor_approval>Y</instructor_approval>
    <instructor_approval>N</instructor_approval>
    <req_next_sem>Y</req_next_sem>
</pre-requisite>
```

■**Caution** Although it is much easier to declare elements using the mixed content model, you must be careful when using it. You lose much of the stricter control that you get when using child content, which can lead to documents that are valid according to the DTD but contain conflicting content that is not valid for processes you may be using the document with.

Entity Declaration

Before moving to declaring attributes, which is the next logical step, it is important to understand *entities*. Entities are not only declared but can also be used within other declarations. Although an area more difficult than most of the others, the following sections cover entities, including the different types and how they are declared. As you read this chapter, you will encounter entity usage within other declarations, so I will now help clarify questions that may arise from their usage.

Entities are simply references to data regardless of whether the data is a simple string or from an external location. Rather than having to include the same block of data repetitively throughout a document, you can use a simple entity instead. They can reduce the overall physical size of a document, and you can use them to quickly change data and have the changes reflected throughout a document. You will encounter two types of entities: general entities and parameter entities. Before examining the declarations of entities, a brief refresher on entity references is in order.

Entity References

As mentioned in Chapter 2, entity references reference the content of a declared entity. They can reference general entities or parameter entities, both of which are examined in the following sections. A parsed general entity reference, usually just called an *entity reference*, takes the form of &name;, and a parameter entity reference takes the form of %name;. The name in each case is the name of an entity declared in the DTD. You have already encountered some of the built-in ones, such as & and <, which refer to & and <, respectively. Unparsed general entities, used with the ENTITY attribute type (which is the only place they can be used), take no special form and are referenced directly by name.

General Entities

General entities come in three flavors: internal parsed entities, external parsed entities, and unparsed entities, which are always external. Parsed entities define replacement text. Unparsed entities, being external to the document, are resources containing data. The data can be of any type such as text, including non-XML text and binary text.

Parsed Entities As previously mentioned, you use parsed entities for replacing text within a document. They can be either internal, which are declared within the internal subset, or external, which point to an external subset. The easiest one to start with is an internal parsed entity.

You can declare an internal parsed entity in an internal subset in the following manner:

```
<!ENTITY name "replacement">
```

The name must be a legal name as defined in Chapter 2. The replacement must be well-formed XML. This means replacement can include entity references, character references, and parameter entity references. When using references within the value, circular references are not legal. It is incorrect to include an entity reference pointing to the entity being defined, as well as to include an entity reference pointing to an entity that may include the entity being defined in its replacement. All the entity declarations within Listing 3-7 are invalid because of circular references.

Listing 3-7. *Circular Entity References*

```
<!-- Entity references cannot be circular -->
<!ENTITY myentity "Some replacement text &secondentity;">
<!ENTITY secondentity "Expanded with &myentity;">
```

You may think that the entities declared in Listing 3-7 are not valid because the myentity declaration is using the &secondentity; reference before secondentity has been declared. However, this is perfectly legal. The only time the ordering of an entity declaration is important is when using an entity reference within the value of an attribute-list declaration. In this case, the entity *must* be declared before the attribute-list declaration. The reason these declarations are invalid is that they are circular. The myentity declaration is using an entity reference to secondentity, and secondentity is using an entity reference right back to myentity. This ends up in an infinite loop scenario.

Caution The ordering of a general entity declaration is significant when using the entity reference as a default value within an attribute-list declaration. You must declare the entity declaration before the attribute-list declaration. In all other cases, you can declare entities in any order.

Listing 3-8 illustrates the proper usage of entity references within content.

Listing 3-8. *Valid Entity Reference Usage Within Content*

```
<!ENTITY myentity "Some replacement text">
<!-- Entity defined using references within content -->
<!ENTITY secondentity "Expanded with &myentity; &amp; char A: &#65;">
<!-- Entity Reference Usage -->
<myelement>&secondentity;</myelement>
```

When the &secondentity; reference is expanded within the myelement element, it would look like this:

```
<myelement>Expanded with Some replacement text &amp; char A: A</myelement>
```

Content can also come from external resources rather than from text included directly within the DTD. In this case, you must use an external parsed entity.

You declare external parsed entities similarly to how you declare the external subset on the DOCTYPE:

```
<!ENTITY name SYSTEM "URI">
<!ENTITY name PUBLIC "publicID" "URI">
```

name is the same as name for an internal parsed entity and follows the same rules. Taking the myentity from Listing 3-8 and changing it to an external parsed entity, the text "Some replacement text" would reside within a file, called foo.txt. The resulting declarations would now look like this:

```
<!ENTITY myentity SYSTEM "foo.txt">
<!-- Entity defined using references within content -->
<!ENTITY secondentity "Expanded with &myentity; &amp; char A: &#65;">
<!-- Entity Reference Usage -->
<myelement>&secondentity;</myelement>
```

Once &secondentity; is expanded, the myelement element would again look like this:

```
<myelement>Expanded with Some replacement text &amp; char A: A</myelement>
```

One thing to remember about the foo.txt file is that it should contain a text declaration like in Listing 3-2. This sets the encoding of the content within this external file.

Unparsed Entities Unparsed entities are external entities that can contain any type of data. The data need not be XML, and it doesn't even need to be text. These entities are used for attributes of type ENTITY or ENTITIES. Earlier, an entity named myimage was defined and referenced a GIF image file. You can declare unparsed entities in one of two ways:

```
<!ENTITY name SYSTEM "URI" NDATA notation>
<!ENTITY name PUBLIC "publicID" "URI" NDATA notation>
```

These are quite similar to the declarations of external parsed entities. The name is used for the same purpose and follows the same rules. The difference comes from the use of the last two parameters. The NDATA keyword indicates that this entity is an unparsed entity. The last parameter, notation, is a reference to a notation declared in the DTD and must match the notation name it is referencing. Refer to the section "ENTITY/ENTITIES" later in this chapter for an example of how an unparsed entity is used and its relationship to NOTATION and ATTLIST.

Parameter Entities

Parameter entities are similar to general entities in the respect that they are also used for replacement. Parameter entities, however, are used only within a DTD. They allow for the replacement of grammar. The caveat is that parameter entities, although they can be declared within external and internal subsets, cannot be referenced within markup in the internal subset. I will return to this point in a moment. These entities may also be internal or external, with their declarations taking the following form:

```
<!ENTITY % name "entity_value">
<!ENTITY % name SYSTEM "URI">
<!ENTITY % name PUBLIC "publicID" "URI">
```

Because these may appear in markup only in an external subset, first look at the grammar within the foo.dtd file, as shown in Listing 3-9.

Listing 3-9. *External Subset Defined in File* foo.dtd

```
<?xml encoding="ISO-8859-1"?>
<!ENTITY % pc "(#PCDATA)">
<!ELEMENT courses (course+)>
<!ELEMENT course (title, description, pre-requisite*)>
<!ATTLIST course cid ID #REQUIRED>
<!ELEMENT title %pc;>
<!ELEMENT description %pc;>
<!ELEMENT pre-requisite EMPTY>
<!ATTLIST pre-requisite cref IDREFS #REQUIRED>
```

You will notice the first declaration after the text declaration is the parameter entity pc. The replacement text is (PCDATA). The element declarations for title and description both use the parameter entity reference %pc; where the contentspec would go. Based on the substitution, it is equivalent to writing them as follows:

```
<!ELEMENT title (#PCDATA)>
<!ELEMENT description (#PCDATA)>
```

As long as you're using the parameter entity references within an external subset, you can use them as text replacements for any of the grammar. You can also modify the cref attribute-list declaration to use a parameter entity reference, like so:

```
<!ENTITY % IDREFREQ "IDREFS #REQUIRED">
<!ATTLIST pre-requisite cref %IDREFREQ;>
```

Using parameter entities in these cases really depends upon how often you might need to repeat the same grammar as well as how readable you would like the document to be. Using short names to save some keystrokes may also cause the document to be hard to decipher. And this would just get worse as the document became more complex.

You can also use parameter entities within the internal subset. Although I said you couldn't use it within markup in the internal subset, you won't use it in that way. Consider the possibility that you write a document that includes a shared external subset; in fact, say you're using the one from Listing 3-9 called foo.dtd. Then, say you need to include another external subset, the file foo2.dtd in Listing 3-10, to be part of the DTD; however, you cannot modify foo.dtd and just copy the declarations into the file, because it is shared.

Listing 3-10. *External Subset from File* foo2.dtd

```
<?xml encoding="ISO-8859-1"?>
<!ELEMENT instructor_approval (#PCDATA)>
<!ELEMENT req_next_sem (#PCDATA)>
```

This is a scenario where it is possible to use a parameter entity reference within the internal subset. For example:

```
<!DOCTYPE courses SYSTEM "foo.dtd" [
    <!ENTITY % foo2 SYSTEM "foo2.dtd">
    %foo2;
]>
```

The parameter entity foo2 refers to the external subset foo2.dtd. The parameter entity reference %foo2; is not within any markup so is perfectly valid. This is equivalent to writing the following:

```
<!DOCTYPE courses SYSTEM "dtddef.dtd" [
    <!ENTITY % foo2 SYSTEM "dtddef2.dtd">
    <!ELEMENT instructor_approval (#PCDATA)>
    <!ELEMENT req_next_sem (#PCDATA)>
]>
```

The only issue you may run into is that by having used the parameter entity reference within the internal subset, everything declared within the external subset referenced by the parameter entity is now considered part of the internal subset. This may cause problems if you are overriding some declarations. In this case, ordering within the internal subset is important; another way is to use a general external subset file for the DOCTYPE and use parameter entities and references within the general file to include the other external subsets, `foo.dtd` and `foo2.dtd`. In this case, you may end up with a file such as `general.dtd` that looks like this:

```
<!ENTITY % foo SYSTEM "dtddef.dtd">
%foo;
<!ENTITY % foo2 SYSTEM "dtddef2.dtd">
%foo2;
```

You could then modify the `DOCTYPE` to the following:

```
<!DOCTYPE courses SYSTEM "general.dtd">
```

This would allow you to keep all external subsets truly external and leave the internal subset for your own personal declarations.

Parameter entity references, when used in this fashion outside of markup, are called *declaration separators*.

Attribute-List Declaration

You have already encountered attribute-list declarations when using `ID`/`IDREF`/`IDREFS` in Chapter 2. Those cases are just a small piece of functionality provided by using attribute-list declarations. Within the scope of validation, the declarations specify the name, type, and any default value for attributes associated with an element. A declaration takes the following form:

```
<!ATTLIST element_name att_definition*>
```

This is similar to the declaration of an element, although two names are required. The `element_name` is the name of the element to which this attribute-list declaration applies. The `att_definition` includes the name of the attribute being defined as well as the rules for the attribute.

Note the * in the definition. You can define multiple attributes within a single attribute-list declaration. If the same attribute is defined multiple times within the declaration, the first definition encountered is the binding one, and the rest are ignored. Depending upon the options used for the parser, which you will see in later chapters when using the PHP extensions, sometimes you'll get warnings. Defining an attribute multiple times for an element is not an error though may result in a warning from the parser. Declaring multiple attribute-list declarations for an element is also not an error, because you may prefer to define one attribute per attribute-list declaration for an element, though that may also result in a warning for a parser. Just keep in mind that these are warnings and not errors and can be controlled by the parser.

The `att_definition` is the grammar for defining the rules for an attribute. It can be broken down into `Name AttType DefaultDecl`, where `Name` is the name of the attribute being defined, `AttType` is the type of attribute, and `DefaultDecl` is the rule for the default value. Referring to Listing 2-17 from Chapter 2, when the notion of an `ID` was introduced, you may recall the declaration `<!ATTLIST Course cid ID #REQUIRED>`. Breaking this declaration down now makes much more sense. `Course` refers to the attribute `element_name`, `cid` refers to the attribute `Name`, `ID` is the attribute `AttType`, and `#REQUIRED` is the attribute `DefaultDecl`. Let's take a closer look at the `AttType` and `DefaultDecl` attributes.

Attribute Defaults

The attribute default (DefaultDecl) indicates any default value for an attribute as well as whether an attribute is required and how it should be handled if it's not. DefaultDecl may take one of four forms: #REQUIRED, #IMPLIED, #FIXED plus a default value, or just a default value. During the course of examining attribute defaults, you'll see the attribute type (AttType) set to CDATA. I'll explain this in more detail in the "Attribute Types" section, but for now using the CDATA type means that the attribute is a character type; therefore, its value must be a literal string. For example, within the fragment in Listing 3-11, the attribute make has the string value "Ford".

Listing 3-11. *Example Element with the* make *Attribute*

```
<Car make='Ford' />
```

#REQUIRED Attributes with the #REQUIRED default are exactly that. The attribute is required for every element within a document for which the attribute is defined. In the case of the Car element in Listing 3-11, you could define the attribute-list declaration as follows:

```
<!ATTLIST Car make CDATA #REQUIRED>
```

Based on this declaration, the fragments in Listing 3-12 illustrate both valid and invalid structures, though the elements themselves are well-formed.

Listing 3-12. *Examples of Valid and Invalid Attributes Defined As* #REQUIRED

```
<!-- Valid attribute because it exists and contains a string value -->
<Car make='Ford' />

<!-- Valid attribute because it exists and contains empty string value -->
<Car make='' />

<!-- Invalid attribute because it does not exist on the Car element -->
<Car />
```

#IMPLIED Attributes with the #IMPLIED default means no default value is specified and the attribute is optional on the element for which it is defined. Returning to the Car element in Listing 3-11, you can change the attribute-list declaration so that make is an optional attribute, as illustrated in Listing 3-13.

Listing 3-13. *Attribute-List Declaration Using the* #IMPLIED *Default*

```
<!ATTLIST Car make CDATA #IMPLIED>
```

Comparing the elements from Listing 3-12 to those in Listing 3-14, you will notice that by declaring the attribute as #IMPLIED, all fragments are now valid.

Listing 3-14. *Examples of Valid Attributes Defined As* #IMPLIED

```
<!-- Valid attribute because it exists and contains a string value -->
<Car make='Ford' />

<!-- Valid attribute because it exists and contains empty string value -->
<Car make='' />

<!-- Valid attribute even though it does not exist on the Car element -->
<Car />
```

#FIXED Attributes with the #FIXED default require a default value within the attribute-list declaration. These types of attributes have values that must be identical to the value specified by the default value. The good thing, though, is that it is optional to add the attribute to the element. When the attribute is not specifically added, the parser will automatically provide the default value specified in the declaration.

Using the Car element from Listing 3-11 and building upon the ATTLIST attribute from Listing 3-13, you may also want to limit the scope to automobiles manufactured in 2002, where the attribute year indicates the manufacturing year for the auto. To enforce this rule, you can write the attribute-list declaration as demonstrated in Listing 3-15.

Listing 3-15. *Combined Attribute-List Declaration for the* make *and* year *Attributes*

```
<!ATTLIST Car
    make CDATA #IMPLIED
    year CDATA #FIXED "2002">
```

This declaration combines the rule for the make attribute with the new rule for the year attribute into a single declaration. You could also write the declaration like so:

```
<!ATTLIST Car make CDATA #IMPLIED>
<!ATTLIST Car year CDATA #FIXED "2002">
```

Based upon the declaration in Listing 3-15, the following illustrates some valid and invalid fragments:

```
<!-- Valid with unspecified attribute year defaulting to fixed value of "2002" -->
<Car make='Ford' />

<!-- Valid as attribute year is "2002" which is the same as the fixed value -->
<Car make='Ford' year="2002" />

<!-- Invalid as year is "2003" which IS NOT the same as the fixed value -->
<Car make='Ford' year="2003" />
```

Default Value So far, you have looked at requiring attributes, making them optional, and restricting attributes. The last case offers a bit more flexibility because it allows for optional attributes, such as using #IMPLIED, but also adds default values, similar to using #FIXED, when attributes are not specified. Unlike using #FIXED, however, the attribute is not restricted to the default value. The default value is used *only* when the attribute is missing from the element. Taking the declaration from Listing 3-15 and changing the year to default to "2002" but not restricting it to that value, you would have this new declaration:

```
<!ATTLIST Car
    make CDATA #IMPLIED
    year CDATA "2002">
```

With this new declaration, you can update the valid and invalid fragment list:

```
<!-- Valid with unspecified attribute year defaulting to value of "2002" -->
<Car make='Ford' />

<!-- Valid with value of year being "2002"-->
<Car make='Ford' year="2002" />

<!-- Valid with value of year being "2003" -->
<Car make='Ford' year="2003" />
```

Now that you understand an attribute's default types, you can examine the attribute types in some detail.

Attribute Types

Attribute types (AttType) simply define the type of attribute. An attribute can be a string type (CDATA), enumerated type, or tokenized type. The easiest to begin with is the string type, which was used within the previous "Attributes Defaults" section.

CDATA Type The CDATA type simply means the attribute has character data content. The vast majority of attributes fall into this type. As mentioned in Chapter 2, you must escape the characters < and & when using them literally. Character and entity references are also valid content for an attribute default value, although unless using the built-in entity references, such as < and &, the entity (which was covered earlier in this chapter) cannot be an external entity reference. In simple terms, if the attribute-list declaration is within the internal subset, then the entity must be declared within the internal subset; otherwise, the entity may be declared in the internal subset or the same external subset as the attribute-list declaration. From reading Chapter 2 and from seeing the earlier examples in this chapter, which used the CDATA type, you should have a basic understanding of how to use character data with attributes. Here, however, I will demonstrate how to use entity references when declaring attribute lists. The following listings, Listing 3-16 and Listing 3-17, are examples of how attribute-list declarations interact with entity declarations.

Listing 3-16. *External Subset Defining* coursedata *Entity Using* ext.dtd *Filename*

```
<?xml version="1.0" ?>
<!ENTITY coursedata "Some Course Data">
<!ENTITY moredata "More Course Data">
<!-- ATTLIST IS valid as moredata is declared in this subset -->
<!ATTLIST courses mcdata CDATA "&moredata;">
<!-- ATTLIST IS valid as evenmoredata is declared in internal subset -->
<!ATTLIST courses emcdata CDATA "&evenmoredata;">
```

Listing 3-17. *Invalid* ATTLIST *Declaration in Internal Subset Referencing External Entity*

```
<!DOCTYPE courses SYSTEM "ext.dtd" [
<!ELEMENT courses ANY>
<!-- ATTLIST is invalid as it references the external entity from Listing 3-16 -->
<!ATTLIST courses somedata CDATA "&coursedata;">
<!ENTITY evenmoredata "More Course Data">
<!-- ATTLIST IS valid as evenmoredata is declared in this subset -->
<!ATTLIST courses evenmcdata CDATA "&evenmoredata;">
]>
```

The CDATA type is probably the easiest and most often used attribute type. The only real complexity may come when using entities, which are covered later in this chapter in the "ENTITY/ENTITIES" section. For now, though, you will examine the attribute's enumerated type.

Enumerated Type   Enumerated types allows you to define certain values that are valid for an attribute. Any value set for the attribute, which is not in the defined list within the declaration, is considered invalid. Returning to the course element from the courses document, you can add an attribute named iscurrent. This attribute indicates whether the content has been updated. Say the values Y and N are the only acceptable values you want for the attribute value. Therefore, you could write a declaration as follows:

```
<!ATTLIST course iscurrent (Y | N) #REQUIRED>
```

By this definition, iscurrent is required and must have the value Y or N, so the following illustrates how to use the iscurrent attribute with the course element:

```
<course iscurrent="Y" />
<course iscurrent="N" />

<!-- The following are invalid because XML is case-sensitive -->
<course iscurrent="y" />
<course iscurrent="n" />
```

This might be fine if you wrote the DTD before you had some data, but in this case, you already have course data in XML format. Someone could manually fix all the course elements within the document, but a much easier approach is to just use a default value based on one of the listed values. Since this attribute is new to the document, you can assume that the default will be N, indicating that any course element without this attribute is to be considered as not having been updated. For example:

```
<!ATTLIST course iscurrent (Y | N) "N">
```

Based on this new declaration, the following are all valid:

```
<course iscurrent="Y" />
<course iscurrent="N" />
<!-- following course element uses default value of "N" for iscurrent attribute -->
<course />
```

▒Caution XML is case-sensitive. When using an enumerated type, you must be careful, because the attribute value must match one of the values defined within the attribute type. For example, the value Y is *not* the same as the value y.

Notations, which are covered later in this chapter in the section "Notation Declaration," are also of the enumerated type. An attribute of this type must match one of the notations listed, and the mutation must have been declared in the DTD. This is an example of the declaration:

```
<!ATTLIST image type NOTATION (gif|jpg) "gif">
```

An image attribute within a document using this declaration could have the value gif or jpg, where the default value, if not set on the image element, is gif. Furthermore, gif and jpg must also be declared as notations within the DTD. Please refer to the "Notation Declaration" section for information about notations.

ID/IDREF/IDREFS Chapter 2 covered these types in detail, along with examples. You should note, however, attributes of type ID must use the #REQUIRED or #IMPLIED default within their declarations (because of the nature of attribute IDs). To summarize their functionality, an ID uniquely identifies an element, and IDREF and IDREFS reference an element identified by an attribute of the ID type. Their declarations, from Chapter 2, take the following form:

```
<!ATTLIST Course cid ID #REQUIRED>
<!ATTLIST Pcourse cref IDREF #REQUIRED>
<!ATTLIST pre-requisite cref IDREFS #REQUIRED>
```

NMTOKEN/NMTOKENS Up until now, you have seen that the CDATA type allows virtually any value for an attribute, assuming the value is legal for an attribute. Enumerated types restrict attribute values to one of a given list. An NMTOKEN offers a little more restriction than CDATA and much less than an enumeration. The value for an NMTOKEN is restricted to the characters that make up a name, as defined in Chapter 2. You have no restriction, however, on the first character like you have with a name. To put it simply, an NMTOKEN is similar to CDATA, except values containing whitespace, certain punctuation, character references, and entity references are not valid. The use of whitespace has an exception. The value of an attribute is first normalized before validity checks are performed on it. Leading and trailing whitespace is removed during normalization, so att=" value " would validate the same for an NMTOKEN as att="value". Attributes of this type are defined as follows:

```
<!ATTLIST course code NMTOKEN "default_value">
```

This declaration defines the attribute code on the course element with a default value of default_value. Based on this declaration, Listing 3-18 illustrates valid and invalid usage.

Listing 3-18. *Valid and Invalid* NMTOKEN *Type Usage*

```
<!-- Valid NMTOKEN type usage -->
<course code=" 123 " />
<course code="123" />


<!-- Invalid NMTOKEN usage -->
<course code=" 1 2 3 " />
<!-- The / character is not valid for NMTOKEN -->
<course code="1/2/3" />
<!-- The character references are not valid for NMTOKEN -->
<course code="1#x20" />
<!-- Entity references (&amp;) are not valid for NMTOKEN -->
<courses code=" 1&amp;2&amp;3 " />
```

If the attribute had been declared a CDATA type, all examples would have been valid.

An NMTOKEN allows for the value of an attribute to contain more than one NMTOKEN separated by whitespace. This, in simple terms, just means that by defining an attribute as an NMTOKEN type, whitespace characters become valid within the attribute value. In reality, the attribute value consists of multiple NMTOKEN values. By changing the declaration used for Listing 3-18 to the following:

```
<!ATTLIST course code NMTOKENS "default_value">
```

the example <course code=" 1 2 3 " /> is now valid.

ENTITY/ENTITIES The last tokenized attribute types are ENTITY and ENTITIES. These types reference unparsed entities within a document. You have already been introduced to entities in the "Entity Declaration" section, but a quick synopsis of an unparsed entity is that an unparsed entity is an external entity, such as a remote file, that contains non-XML data.

Consider what is involved in adding an image to an XML document. The first thing that may come to mind is using a CDATA section. This has issues, however. The binary data may contain invalid characters such as]]>. You may then decide to Base64 encode the image and use the encoded data as content. This would work; however, not only does the size of your document increase, but you would also need to include information for the image, such as how it should be handled. Another option would be to use an attribute of type ENTITY to refer-ence the image, such as declared in Listing 3-19.

Listing 3-19. *Attribute Type* ENTITY *Declaration*

```
<!NOTATION GIF SYSTEM "image/gif">
<!ENTITY myimage SYSTEM "mypicture.gif" NDATA GIF>
<!ATTLIST image imgsrc ENTITY #REQUIRED>
```

To use an ENTITY type, you must declare the entity, myimage; also, because it is an unparsed entity, you must declare a NOTATION, GIF, and associate it with the entity. Based on these decla-rations, Listing 3-20 illustrates the usage of the unparsed entity.

Listing 3-20. *Usage of Unparsed Entity Reference*

```
<image imgsrc="myimage" />
```

The attribute value *must* be one of the unparsed entities defined in the DTD. In this case, this uses myimage, which refers to the file mypicture.gif.

The attribute type ENTITIES is just a whitespace-separated list of entities. It is similar to the NMTOKEN/NMTOKENS relationship. For example:

```
<!NOTATION GIF SYSTEM "image/gif">
<!ENTITY myimage SYSTEM "mypicture.gif" NDATA GIF>
<!ENTITY yourimage SYSTEM "yourpicture.gif" NDATA GIF>
<!ATTLIST courses imgsrc ENTITIES #REQUIRED>
```

An example for the ENTITIES type based on these declarations is as follows:

```
<image imgsrc="myimage yourimage" />
```

Before you get too excited and think you can change all your image references to use this format, you need to understand the ramifications. Using attribute entities in this manner works well for traditional publishing. Everything is within a controlled environment. On the Web, however, you have little control over the client side. The actual MIME type for a file is usually determined by the Web server and sent to the client. If you were to call the file mypicture.gif, the file could actually be a JPG, and the Web server might send you MIME type information for a JPG rather than a GIF. Based on the declarations you have here, however, you are setting the handling of the unparsed entity within the notation declaration. So, in short, most people find using attribute entities and notations in a Web environment not a good idea, but in reality, it really depends upon how you are using and what you are using them to do.

Notation Declaration

A *notation* indicates how data should be processed. Typically, notations identify the format of unparsed entities and elements bearing a NOTATION type attribute. You can use the provided external identifier to provide the location of a helper application that is able to process the noted data. Do you remember the use of the NOTATION type for an attribute? The notation pro-vided an identifier of image/gif. Based on this MIME type, an application could call the program associated with the image/gif MIME type to handle the image data. You declare notations as you would declare the external subset on the DOCTYPE:

```
<!NOTATION name SYSTEM "URI">
<!NOTATION name PUBLIC "publicID">
<!NOTATION name PUBLIC "publicID" "URI">
```

The name portion of the notation declaration must be a valid name as defined in Chapter 2. Using the previous declaration, <!NOTATION GIF SYSTEM "image/gif">, you have declared a notation named GIF with a system identifier of image/gif. In a controlled environment, you might rather want to specifically identify an application to handle the data. Suppose all desktops in an organization were clones of each other and locked down to prevent modification, and an application called GIFProcessor existed in /usr/local/bin on all systems. You could then modify the notation to <!NOTATION GIF SYSTEM "/usr/local/bin/GIFProcessor">. If the image/gif MIME type were associated with this program, then these two declarations would be equivalent. If the MIME type were set to something else, then using a specified application rather than a MIME type would ensure that the data was handled correctly.

Now that you have a better idea of what a notation is, you need to revisit the NOTATION type within an attribute-list declaration. Remember, the notation type is an enumerated type. Enumerated types mean that the allowed values for attributes must be specified within the attribute-list declaration. When used in this case, the notation provides information for the element. For example, suppose an image is embedded directly within an XML document. It has been Base64 encoded so that it can live within the content of an element. Using a notation attribute, you can associate a handler for the element contents with the element. For example:

```
<!NOTATION BASE64 SYSTEM "location of base64 handler">
<!ATTLIST embededdata enctype NOTATION (BASE64) #REQUIRED>

<!-- example of enctype attribute on embededdata element -->
<embededdata enctype="BASE64">Some Base64 embedded data</embededdata>
```

Because this is an enumerated type, you could use multiple notations for the attribute-list declaration. You will now add a handler for UUencode:

```
<!NOTATION BASE64 SYSTEM "location of base64 handler">
<!NOTATION UUENCODE SYSTEM "location of UUencode handler">
<!ATTLIST embededdata enctype NOTATION (BASE64 | UUENCODE) #REQUIRED>

<!-- example of enctype attribute on embededdata element -->
<embededdata enctype="BASE64">Some Base64 embedded data</embededdata>
<embededdata enctype="UUENCODE">Some UUencoded embedded data</embededdata>
```

As illustrated, the enctype attribute may now use either BASE64 or UUENCODE notations for its value. Any other value, as well as not associating the attribute with the embededdata element, is deemed invalid because of the #REQUIRED default.

Notations are also required when using unparsed entities. Please refer to the ENTITY attribute type and the section "Unparsed Entities" within this chapter for more information. Notations are declared as described in this section, and their usage is similar to the NOTATION attribute type. The only difference is the applicable XML structure.

Conditional Sections

You use conditional sections to selectively include and exclude sections of a DTD; you can use them only within an external subset. You may be wondering why you would need such functionality. You may need this functionality for several reasons. Consider publishing from the traditional sense.

A document may be a draft, or it may be the finalized version. When it is still a draft, additional information, such as user notes and comments attached to paragraphs, may be considered valid for the document. Certainly when the document is ready to be published in its finalized state, these must not appear in the final version. Of course, you could always define two completely separate DTDs for the document, but then each must be managed, and the document must be altered to reference the correct one depending upon the state. A much simpler way would to use the same external subset with conditional sections encapsulating the appropriate sections for the current state of the document.

Another possible scenario is working on a shared external subset that is currently in production. If you have had to debug applications in a live environment before, then this is a similar case. The original code must be left unaltered because it is currently running, but you need to alter and test code at the same time. You possibly can use if/else blocks based on your terminal ID (yes, terminals still do exist, as I know from experience) or IP address, assuming you have a dedicated IP addresses at your workstation and are not behind a firewall. Using conditional sections will allow the subset to continue working for everyone else except you, giving you the time you need to fix or alter it without disrupting anyone else's productivity.

This should give you a basic idea on why you might need conditional sections, and by now you are probably on the edge of your seat, waiting in anticipation on how to use these sections. You can define conditional sections in one of two ways, depending upon whether you want a section included or ignored:

```
<![ IGNORE [
    declarations
]]>
```

```
<![ INCLUDE [
    declarations
]]>
```

Within the INCLUDE and IGNORE blocks, declarations refers to any declaration you want included or suppressed. So you might have a subset list the one in Listing 3-21.

Listing 3-21. *Example Using Conditional Sections in* course.dtd

```
<?xml encoding="ISO-8859-1"?>
<!ELEMENT courses (course+)>
<!ELEMENT course (title, description, pre-requisite*)>
<!ATTLIST course cid ID #REQUIRED>
<!ELEMENT title (#PCDATA)>
<!ELEMENT description (#PCDATA)>
<!ELEMENT pre-requisite ANY>
```

```
<![ INCLUDE [
    <!ATTLIST pre-requisite cref IDREFS #REQUIRED>
    <!ELEMENT instructor_approval EMPTY>
    <!ELEMENT req_next_sem (#PCDATA)>
]]>
<![ IGNORE [
    <!ATTLIST pre-requisite cref CDATA #IMPLIED>
    <!ELEMENT instructor_approval ANY>
    <!ELEMENT req_next_sem ANY>
]]>
```

This may not look very useful because INCLUDE and IGNORE are both hard-coded into the subset, but it should give you the basic idea. Everything within the INCLUDE section will be used for validation, and everything within the IGNORE section is ignored. When using conditional sections, parameter entities are your friends. Remember that you can use them within the DTD to replace a grammar. You can modify the course.dtd file to use parameter entities, as shown in Listing 3-22.

Listing 3-22. *Conditional Sections in* course.dtd *Using Parameter Entities in* course.dtd

```
<?xml encoding="ISO-8859-1"?>
<!ENTITY % livedata "INCLUDE">
<!ENTITY % debugdata "IGNORE">
<!ELEMENT courses (course+)>
<!ELEMENT course (title, description, pre-requisite*)>
<!ATTLIST course cid ID #REQUIRED>
<!ELEMENT title (#PCDATA)>
<!ELEMENT description (#PCDATA)>
<!ELEMENT pre-requisite ANY>
<![ %livedata; [
    <!ATTLIST pre-requisite cref IDREFS #REQUIRED>
    <!ELEMENT instructor_approval EMPTY>
    <!ELEMENT req_next_sem (#PCDATA)>
]]>
<![ %debugdata; [
    <!ATTLIST pre-requisite cref CDATA #IMPLIED>
    <!ELEMENT instructor_approval ANY>
    <!ELEMENT req_next_sem ANY>
]]>
```

This code adds the parameter entities livedata and debugdata to the subset. The previously hard-coded text INCLUDE and IGNORE have also been removed and replaced with the parameter entity references for these new entities. Anyone now using this subset will be using the declarations in Listing 3-23.

Listing 3-23. *Declarations Used by Default Within* `course.dtd`

```
<!ATTLIST pre-requisite cref IDREFS #REQUIRED>
<!ELEMENT instructor_approval EMPTY>
<!ELEMENT req_next_sem (#PCDATA)>
```

Within the working document, you can override the `livedata` and `debugdata` entity declarations within the internal subset:

```
<!DOCTYPE courses SYSTEM "course.dtd" [
    <!ENTITY % livedata "IGNORE">
    <!ENTITY % debugdata "INCLUDE">
]>
```

While everyone else uses the declarations listed in Listing 3-23, this document will be using this:

```
<!ATTLIST pre-requisite cref CDATA #IMPLIED>
<!ELEMENT instructor_approval ANY>
<!ELEMENT req_next_sem ANY>
```

The last point to discuss on the topic of conditional sections is nesting. It is perfectly valid to nest sections within each other. Everything within an IGNORE section is completely ignored. Basically, once the parser sees an IGNORE, it skips to the closing marker for that particular section. For INCLUDE sections, everything is included *except* any IGNORE sections. A section written like this:

```
<![ INCLUDE [
    <!ATTLIST pre-requisite cref IDREFS #REQUIRED>
    <![ IGNORE [
        <!ELEMENT instructor_approval EMPTY>
    ]]>
    <!ELEMENT req_next_sem (#PCDATA)>
]]>
```

could have just as well been written like this:

```
<![ INCLUDE [
    <!ATTLIST pre-requisite cref IDREFS #REQUIRED>
    <!ELEMENT req_next_sem (#PCDATA)>
]]>
```

Though basic, this should give you the idea of how nesting works. Through the use of parameter entities, it can get quite complex.

You should now be well on your way to validating documents using a DTD. This is just one of the possible ways to perform validation. The next section will cover XML Schemas and their role in validation.

Using XML Schemas

You probably have realized by now that although DTDs can be useful to validate a document, they also have limitations. Take, for instance, text content. You can declare an element allowing PCDATA, such as `<!ELEMENT element (#PCDATA)>`, but you can't enforce what the acceptable content is. Other than the element name and possibly using attributes, you can't determine the exact type of text content that exists within the element. XML Schemas were developed to overcome many of the shortcomings of DTDs. They are designed to be extensible, to support data types, to be easy to write using XML syntax, to support namespaces, and to allow for user-derived data types. XML Schemas are a standard from the W3C so are widely available. The following sections will cover XML Schemas including their construction and how to write them. Because of the extensive amount of information on XML Schemas, not everything will be covered, but after reading the following sections, you should have enough information to at least understand an XML Schema and begin building your own.

Introducing XML Schemas

You may have looked at some tutorials or even the specifications for XML Schemas, and you may still be completely confused about how to use them. If, on the other hand, you are already familiar with XML Schemas and are able to build at least basic ones, then this section may not contain any information new to you. Advanced features of schemas are out of the scope of this section. My primary goal is to offer you a simple breakdown of structure and syntax as well as basic concepts surrounding schemas. With this in mind, I'll show you how to build your first schema.

Using slightly modified data, you will compose a schema for the courses document in Listing 3-24. The approach is not going to be top-down, but rather inside-out. You will understand the reasoning as you build it. Schemas are usually located in an external file with the `.xsd` extension. Unless otherwise indicated, it is safe to assume that the schema I'm showing how to build is in a file called `courses.xsd`.

■**Note** Unless otherwise indicated, the schema being built will be residing in a file called `course.xsd`. The term *schema* used in this section refers to a schema being built using XML Schemas unless otherwise noted.

Listing 3-24. *Courses Document*

```
<courses>
    <course cid="c1">
        <title>Basic Languages</title>
        <description>Introduction to Languages</description>
        <credits>1.5</credits>
        <lastmodified>2004-09-01T11:13:01</lastmodified>
    </course>
```

```
    <course cid="c2">
        <title>French I</title>
        <description>Introduction to French</description>
        <credits>3.0</credits>
        <lastmodified>2005-06-01T14:21:37</lastmodified>
    </course>
    <course cid="c3">
        <title>French II</title>
        <description>Intermediate French</description>
        <credits>3.0</credits>
        <lastmodified>2005-03-12T15:45:44</lastmodified>
        <pre-requisite cref="c1" req_next_sem="true">
            <instructor_approval>false</instructor_approval>
        </pre-requisite>
        <pre-requisite cref="c2" req_next_sem="false">
            <instructor_approval>true</instructor_approval>
        </pre-requisite>
    </course>
</courses>
```

Schema Elements

The beginning of every schema is the schema element. The courses document is not using namespaces, which will be explained later, so the basic structure begins as follows:

```
<xsd:schema xmlns:xsd="http://www.w3.org/2001/XMLSchema">
</xsd:schema>
```

The schema element is the root of the document. The prefix xsd will denote the namespace http://www.w3.org/2001/XMLSchema. This prefix indicates that the XML within the schema is from the W3C XML Schemas namespace. You can use any prefix you like, though xsd is the most common. Additional attributes are available for the schema element, but for now, you will use the most basic structure.

■**Note** Throughout the discussion of XML Schemas, the xsd prefix refers to the http://www.w3.org/2001/XMLSchema namespace.

Simple Types

Simple types are components that contain only text. They cannot be broken down any further. Elements without attributes and children elements, as well as attributes, are composed of simple types. An attribute cannot be broken down any further than its value, which is text content. An element that had child elements would be able to be broken down further into its child elements so would not be defined by a simple type, but rather a complex type.

Let's start building a schema based on some of the simple type elements: title, description, credits, and datelastmodified. You could declare these elements, in their simplest forms, as follows:

```
<xsd:element name="title" type="xsd:string"/>
<xsd:element name="description"  type="xsd:string"/>
<xsd:element name="credits" type="xsd:decimal"/>
<xsd:element name="datelastmodified" type="xsd:dateTime"/>
```

Breaking the first one of these down, the element name element comes from the XML Schema namespace, because it is used to declare an element. If you recall, you associated the sd prefix with that name, so element is prefixed with xsd. The value of the name attribute, in this case title, is the name of the element you are declaring. The value of the type attribute is the data type for the element. In this case, the title element is to hold a string. You will notice that every type attribute is coming from the XML Schema namespace, noted by the xsd prefix. Because you are starting simple, you are using built-in types.

Built-in types are data types defined within the XML Schema specification. These types are either primitive types, meaning they exist on their own and are not derivatives of other data types, or derived types, which means they are built from another data type. Other user-derived types are data types derived by the schema author. This means the author can create their own data type, which is based on other existing data types. Continuing to build the schema, you know that attributes are also composed of simple types. For example:

```
<xsd:attribute name="cid" type="xsd:ID"/>
<xsd:attribute name="cref" type="xsd:IDREF"/>
<xsd:attribute name="req_next_sem" type="xsd:boolean" />
```

The declaration for attributes, in this current case, is the same as the element declarations. The element name attribute indicates an attribute is being declared and is prefixed by xsd because it comes from the XML Schema namespace. The value of the name attribute is the name of the attribute you are declaring, and the type is the data type. Notice the declarations for the cid and cref attributes.

The data types, ID and IDREF, are both built-in derived types. The base type for a derived type is the data type from which the derived type was derived. Sound confusing? Well, it's really not. The base type for ID and IDREF is NCName, because they both are derived from the NCName type. This type is also a derived type having a base type of name. The name type in turn is derived from the token type, which in turn is derived from the normalizedString type. You finally get down to the primitive type; the base type for normalizedString is string, which, being a primitive type, is the lowest denominator.

You now have all the simple types for the document declared, so how do you build the rest of the schema? Looking at the document in Listing 3-24, the remainder of the document contains everything you have declared to this point. As they can be broken down, they are declared with complex types. You can find a list of all built-in data types in Appendix A.

Complex Types

Within the document in Listing 3-24, you have elements containing child elements as well as elements with attributes. These cannot be declared with a simple type. Take, for example, the pre-requisite element. This element contains two attributes, cref and req_next_sem, as well as the child element instructor_approval. Listing 3-25 shows the declaration for this element.

Listing 3-25. *Element Declaration for* pre-requisite

```
<xsd:element name="pre-requisite" minOccurs="0" maxOccurs="unbounded">
    <xsd:complexType>
        <xsd:sequence>
            <xsd:element name="instructor_approval" type="xsd:boolean"/>
        </xsd:sequence>
        <xsd:attribute name="cref" type="xsd:IDREF"/>
        <xsd:attribute name="req_next_sem" type="xsd:boolean"/>
    </xsd:complexType>
</xsd:element>
```

Let's examine the element declaration. You will notice two new attributes, minOccurs and maxOccurs. These attributes control the number of times this element may occur within its parent element. The element pre-requisite is not required to be a child element of the course element, so its minOccurs is set to 0. On the other end of the spectrum, there can be any number of these elements within the course element. Since you do not have an exact number, the value unbounded translates to unspecified. This gives you an unlimited number of times this element may occur within a course element. These attributes must be either a non-negative integer or the value unbounded. When the attribute is not present on the element, it defaults to the value 1.

You should also notice that this element does not have a type attribute. It is not a simple type, and you are not using named types, which allow the reuse of content models. The type is defined within the context of the declaration. The child element xsd:complexType indicates this element is a complex type, and the rules are encapsulated within the child elements on the xsd:complexType element.

The next child element encountered is xsd:sequence. This element indicates the elements declared within the scope of this element must appear in the order in which they are declared. Even though there is only a single child element, it still must be present. You could have used other indicators, such as <choice />, but I'll discuss those later in the section. Within the xsd:sequence element, you come to the instructor_approval element, which you should already be familiar with because it was defined in the "Simple Types" section.

Upon exiting the xsd:sequence element, you hit the attribute declarations, which were also declared in the "Simple Types" section. The ordering here is important. All attribute declarations must come last within a complexType element. I'll discuss this in further detail later in the "Attributes" section, but for now it is important to at least understand a basic schema.

Now that the pre-requisite element is declared, you can learn how to declare the course element. You have already declared all elements contained within this element, either as simple types or a complex type, so you are slowing making your way up the tree:

```
<xsd:element name="course" minOccurs="0" maxOccurs="unbounded">
    <xsd:complexType>
        <xsd:sequence>
            <xsd:element name="title" type="xsd:string"/>
            <xsd:element name="description" type="xsd:string"/>
```

```
            <xsd:element name="credits" type="xsd:decimal"/>
            <xsd:element name="lastmodified" type="xsd:dateTime"/>
            <!-- declaration for pre-requisite in Listing 3-25 goes here -->
        </xsd:sequence>
        <xsd:attribute name="cid" type="xsd:ID"/>
    </xsd:complexType>
</xsd:element>
```

Just like the `pre-requisite` declaration in Listing 3-25, the `course` declaration is following the same rules, including the number of times this element may appear as a child element within the `course` element. Again, this is a complex type, noted by the `xsd:complexType` element, and is defined within the scope of the declaration. This time, however, multiple elements reside within the `xsd:sequence` element. The elements, when appearing within the XML document, must follow the order `title`, `description`, `credits`, `lastmodified`, and `pre-requisite`. Note that the declaration for `pre-requisite` in Listing 3-25 was left out for brevity. When you finish constructing the schema, it will be laid out for you in its entirety. For now the missing declaration is noted by an XML comment.

If you recall the rules regarding `minOccurs` and `maxOccurs`, they default to 1 when not present on an element. By omission, each of the element declarations within the `xsd:sequence` element must appear exactly one time in the order specified. The only exception is the `pre-requisite` element. Although it still must obey the element ordering, it is not required to appear as a child element because those attributes were explicitly set on its declaration.

The final piece is to build the declaration for the `courses` element, which is the root of the XML document. If you have been following along, you should have no problem with the last piece of the puzzle. Listing 3-26 shows the entire schema, including the `courses` element declaration, which would constitute the contents of the `courses.xsd` file. With this schema, the `course` document from Listing 3-24 is perfectly valid.

Listing 3-26. *XML Schema for the Courses Document*

```
<?xml version="1.0"?>
<xsd:schema xmlns:xsd="http://www.w3.org/2001/XMLSchema">
    <xsd:element name="courses">
        <xsd:complexType>
            <xsd:sequence>
                <xsd:element name="course" minOccurs="0" maxOccurs="unbounded">
                    <xsd:complexType>
                        <xsd:sequence>
                            <xsd:element name="title" type="xsd:string"/>
                            <xsd:element name="description" type="xsd:string"/>
                            <xsd:element name="credits" type="xsd:decimal"/>
                            <xsd:element name="lastmodified" type="xsd:dateTime"/>
                            <xsd:element name="pre-requisite" minOccurs="0"
                                        maxOccurs="unbounded">
                                <xsd:complexType>
                                    <xsd:sequence>
                                        <xsd:element name="instructor_approval"
                                                    type="xsd:boolean"/>
```

```
          </xsd:sequence>
          <xsd:attribute name="cref" type="xsd:IDREF"/>
          <xsd:attribute name="req_next_sem" type="xsd:boolean"/>
        </xsd:complexType>
      </xsd:element>
    </xsd:sequence>
    <xsd:attribute name="cid" type="xsd:ID"/>
  </xsd:complexType>
  </xsd:element>
  </xsd:sequence>
  </xsd:complexType>
  </xsd:element>
</xsd:schema>
```

You probably now understand why you took the inside-out approach rather than a top-down approach for this introduction to XML Schemas. Up to this point, I have not covered all the basic syntax and functionality, but you should now have a good working knowledge to start taking a more in-depth look at them.

Understanding the Structure

So far I've only touched on XML Schema structures a bit. An interesting aspect of schemas is that virtually all XML Schema elements (meaning the elements in general such as xsd:attribute, xsd:element, and xsd:complexType) will accept any attributes outside the XML Schema namespace. For example, if you have a namespace declared as xmlns:foo="http://www.example.com/foo" within the schema, you can add arbitrary attributes to schema elements. (I'll cover namespaces in detail later in the "Namespaces" section.) For example:

```
<xsd:attribute name="att1" type="xsd:string" foo:myatt="this is my attribute" />
```

It is perfectly valid to add a foo:myatt attribute. Though not affecting validation, you may want some additional information within your schema for some other reason. You cannot, however, add attributes from the xsd namespace that do not belong on an element. For example:

```
<!-- The following is an ILLEGAL use of xsd:boolean as an attribute -->
<xsd:attribute name="att1" type="xsd:string" xsd:boolean="invalid" />
```

Elements

You can perform other tasks with elements than just those shown earlier in the chapter. Elements may have default content or NULL values. This may be substituted and may be grouped.

Default Content

Recall the attribute-list declaration in a DTD. Attributes can specify default as well as fixed values. Using XML Schemas, you can do the same to elements. The defaulted or fixed content is a string, so the data type for an element must support this type of content. For example:

```
<xsd:element name="myelement" default="some text" />
<xsd:element name="secondelement" fixed="fixed text" />
```

When the element myelement is used in a document and is empty, the content is auto-matically set to some text. The element secondelement behaves the same way, but if it already contains content, the content must match the string set by the fixed attribute; otherwise, it is not valid. Elements may use either default or fixed, but not both.

NULL Value

Comparing XML data to data from a database, you can't easily distinguish between an empty string and a NULL value. You could devise your own XML structure to add support for this, or you could do it through an XML Schema. Element declarations include the attribute nillable. It is a Boolean, with a default value of false, used to indicate whether an empty element is NULL. For example:

```
<element name="mydata" nillable="true" />
```

Using this attribute also requires the use of the http://www.w3.org/2001/XMLSchema-instance namespace in the XML document. Assuming the prefix xsi was set for this namespace within the XML document, the element mydata could appear as follows:

```
<mydata xsi:nill="true"></mydata>
```

Element Substitution

Schemas allow for element name substitutions. Take the case where a company has an office in the United States and one in France. The office in the United States creates most of their XML documents in English, and the office in France uses French for theirs. A shared schema could allow element names from either language:

```
<xsd:element name="street" type="xsd:string" />
<xsd:element name="rue" substitutionGroup="street" >

<xs:element name="name" type="xs:string"/>
<xs:element name="nom" substitutionGroup="name"/>

<xsd:complexType name="infoType">
    <xsd:sequence>
        <xsd:element ref="name"/>
        <xsd:element ref="street"/>
    </xsd:sequence>
</xsd:complexType>

<xs:element name="address" type="infoType"/>
<xs:element name="adresse" substitutionGroup="address"/>
```

Notice the elements with the substitutionGroup attribute. These element declarations are not defining anything other than a name and a substitionGroup, which refers to another element declaration. This allows element names to be used interchangeably and mean the same thing. For instance, the element rue is the same as the element street. Based on these declarations, the following two documents are both valid:

```
<address>
    <name />
    <street />
</address>

<adresse>
    <nom />
    <rue />
</adresse>
```

Element Groups

The sequence element you have seen used earlier in the chapter, such as within Listing 3-26, is a form of grouping. It is an unnamed local group. Groups may also be choice or all. A sequence, as you already know, means the elements must appear in that exact sequence. A choice means that a certain number determined by the maxOccurs and minOccurs attributes, which both default to 1, may be selected. Using all allows the elements to appear in any order, although all the elements must be present within the content of a parent element. When you create named groups, you can share them so you don't need to define local groups. You can just reference the named group. Take the case of an address. A document may have a shipping address as well as a billing address. In most cases, the elements required are the same. You could create a named group and share between the two, as follows:

```
<xsd:group name="Address">
    <xsd:sequence>
        <xsd:element name="street" />
        <xsd:element name="city" />
        <xsd:element name="state" />
        <xsd:element name="zipcode" />
    </xsd:sequence>
</xsd:group>

<xsd:element name="BillingAddress">
    <xsd:sequence>
        <xsd:group ref="Address" />
    </xsd:sequence>
</xsd:element>

<xsd:element name="ShippingAddress">
    <xsd:sequence>
        <xsd:element name="attention" type="xsd:string" />
        <xsd:group ref="Address" />
    </xsd:sequence>
</xsd:element>
```

The xsd:group element is laid out similarly to the xsd:element elements. Notice within the xsd:sequence elements for the element declarations that the xsd:group element does not include a name attribute, but rather a ref attribute. This attribute instructs the XML Schema to reference the group named Address. The ShippingAddress declaration also shows how you can use a group as well as declare additional elements.

Attributes

I've shown only simple attribute declarations up until this point. You can set additional pieces of information when declaring attributes, such as attribute defaults used in a DTD. You can also group and reference attributes when declaring an element. Groupings make it simple to define a set of attributes common to many different elements.

Attribute Declaration

An attribute declaration has three attributes that handle setting these values. The default attribute takes a string value to set a default value for an attribute if the attribute is not set on an element. The fixed attribute sets a fixed string value for an attribute. The last attribute, use, determines how to use the attribute. The possible values for the use attribute are optional, which is also the default; required; and prohibited. The prohibited value is one you probably don't know. It does not have a corresponding counterpart in a DTD. This value means that the attribute cannot be used. For example:

```
<xsd:attribute name="att1" type="xsd:integer" default="1" use="required" />
<xsd:attribute name="att2" type="xsd:string" fixed="fixed val" use="optional" />
<xsd:attribute name="att3" type="xsd:string" use="optional" />
```

You must never use the attributes fixed and default at the same time. These conflict with each other and will cause an error in the schema.

Attribute Groups

You can group attributes just as you can group elements. You may run into cases where you have a set of attributes applicable to a few difference elements. You may also want to group attributes just to make the schema easier to read. You group attributes by using the attributeGroup element:

```
<xsd:attributeGroup name="moveattributes">
    <xsd:attribute name="moveID" type="xsd:ID" use="required" />
    <xsd:attribute name="stars" type="xsd:integer" />
    <xsd:attribute name="rating" type="xsd:string" use="required" />
</xsd:attributeGroup>

<xsd:element name="Movie">
    <xsd:complexType>
        <xsd:attributeGroup ref="movieattributes" />
    </xsd:complexType>
</xsd:element>
```

You can use the attributeGroup element in the same way as you used a group element for elements. The attribute ref references the xsd:attributeGroup element named movieattributes.

User-Derived Types

So far, you have seen how to use some built-in simple types. XML Schemas are extensible, which allows you to define your own data types by deriving a type from a simple type. Take, for example, the declaration for the credits element in Listing 3-26. It is a decimal data type, so the values it can take are pretty much endless. Say you want to limit the possible values to 0, 0.5, 1.0, 1.5, 2.0, 2.5, 3.0, 3.5, and 4. You can't use a built-in type directly, so you must create your own that will be derived from the decimal data type, as shown in Listing 3-27.

Listing 3-27. *Enumeration Facet for* CreditType

```
<xsd:simpleType name="CreditType">
    <xsd:restriction base="xsd:decimal">
        <xsd:enumeration value="0" />
        <xsd:enumeration value="0.5" />
        <xsd:enumeration value="1.0" />
        <xsd:enumeration value="1.5" />
        <xsd:enumeration value="2.0" />
        <xsd:enumeration value="2.5" />
        <xsd:enumeration value="3.0" />
        <xsd:enumeration value="3.5" />
        <xsd:enumeration value="4.0" />
    </xsd:restriction>
</xsd:simpleType>
```

The xsd:simpleType element has been given a name, CreditType, this time. Rather than being contained within an element declaration, this definition can live as a child of the schema element and be referenced directly by the type attribute of the element that wants to use this data type. The xsd:restriction element is how user-derived types are defined. These types are created through restrictions on existing types. In this case, the existing type is xsd:decimal, as indicated by the base attribute. The restriction being placed on it is an enumeration of acceptable values, as indicated by the use of the xsd:enumeration elements. The value of the value attribute sets an acceptable value for the content when used in an XML document. Based on this definition, you can modify the credits element to use this new data type:

```
<xsd:element name="credits" type="CreditType"/>
```

The value for the type attribute is CreditType, which is the name of the derived type you created. It is not prefixed by xsd because this type is not part of the XML Schema specification. Rather, this definition is a user-derived type, so the schema knows to not look within its built-in types. You could use this type with an attribute declaration, such as <xsd:attribute name="foo" type="CreditType"/>.

enumeration is just one of the constraining facets that is available. *Constraining facet* just means it can be used to restrict values for a data type. The availability of constraining facets is determined by the data type being derived. Not all facets are applicable to every data type. You can use 11 other facets.

length/minLength/maxLength

All three of these can limit the length of a data type. Using length restricts data to be exactly the number of units set, and minLength and maxLength restrict data to be at least minLength and/or no more than maxLength. The term units is used as the base data type and determines what constitutes a unit. For instance, a string type consists of characters, so a unit is a character. List types, which you haven't come to yet, consist of items, so a unit in that case is an item. Suppose data for the title element of a course is coming from a database. The field is set to VARCHAR(255), and the application handling the data enforces that it must have at least five characters. You can create a type that would also enforce this within the XML document:

```
<xsd:simpleType name="TitleType">
    <xsd:restriction base="xsd:string">
        <xsd:minLength value="5" />
        <xsd:maxLength value="255" />
    </xsd:restriction>
</xsd:simpleType>
```

The new declaration for the title element would be as follows:

```
<xsd:element name="title" type="TitleType"/>
```

If, for some reason, the data were corrupted and a title came in as <title>Bas</title>, it would be caught when validated against the schema.

pattern

pattern restricts a value to one matching a regular expression. A simple case for this would be validating an email address:

```
<xsd:simpleType name="EmailType">
    <xsd:restriction base="xsd:string">
    <xsd:pattern
  value="([_a-z0-9-]+)(\.[_a-z0-9-]+)*@([a-z0-9-]+)(\.[a-z0-9-]+)*(\.[a-z]{2,4})" />
    </xsd:restriction>
</xsd:simpleType>
```

The xsd:pattern element is wrapping within the example. You have to deal with some whitespace issues when physically inserting a line feed and then trying to match against a value.

whiteSpace

A whiteSpace element is used in a similar manner as xml:space from Chapter 2, though it provides functionality. Using the whiteSpace facet, the values can be preserve, replace, or collapse. Values preserving whitespace leaves it intact. Values replacing whitespace will convert #x9 (tab), #xA (line feed), and #xD (carriage return) into #x20 (spaces). Values collapsing whitespace will first process the value using replace and then convert all contiguous sequences of #x20 (spaces) into a single #x20. Leading and trailing spaces are also removed from the value. The following example is defined within the context of an element declaration to illustrate that these definitions need not be named:

```
<xsd:element name="description">
    <xsd:simpleType>
        <xsd:restriction base="xsd:string">
            <xsd:whiteSpace value="collapse" />
        </xsd:restriction>
    </xsd:simpleType>
</xsd:element>
```

minInclusive /maxInclusive/minExclusive/maxExclusive

These facets set either inclusive or exclusive bounds for values. inclusive means the value must belong within the range, and exclusive means the value must belong outside the range. Though not required to do so, normally the minInclusive and maxInclusive facets are used together to define a range. You could define a range from 1 to 10, as in Listing 3-28.

Listing 3-28. *Defining Ranges*

```
<xsd:simpleType name="oneToTen">
  <xsd:restriction base="xsd:integer">
    <xsd:minInclusive value="1"/>
    <xsd:maxInclusive value="10"/>
  </xsd:restriction>
</xsd:simpleType>
```

You could also represent this with the following:

```
<xsd:simpleType name="oneToTenII">
  <xsd:restriction base="xsd:integer">
    <xsd:minExclusive value="0"/>
    <xsd:maxExclusive value="11"/>
  </xsd:restriction>
</xsd:simpleType>
```

You could also define a type for integers greater than ten:

```
<xsd:simpleType name="greaterThanTen">
  <xsd:restriction base="xsd:integer">
    <xsd:minExclusive value="10"/>
  </xsd:restriction>
</xsd:simpleType>
```

totalDigits/fractionDigits

These allow you to set the number of digits allowed. The totalDigits facet indicates the maximum total number of digits, and fractionDigits indicates the maximum number of decimal places. When used together, fractionDigits can never have a value greater than the number of totalDigits. Also, if defining a type with a base type that includes these, the values may not be greater than defined in the base type. For example:

```
<xsd:simpleType name="Digits">
  <xsd:restriction base="xsd:decimal">
    <xsd:totalDigits value="3"/>
     <xsd:fractionDigits value="2"/>
  </xsd:restriction>
</xsd:simpleType>
```

This definition would allow numbers such as 1.11, 1.0, 1.1, and 1. The total number of digits never exceeds three, and the number of decimal places never exceeds two.

More Simple Types

So far, you have seen how to use some built-in simple types as well as create user-derived types. XML Schemas offer two additional varieties of simple types. They are the list and union data types.

List Type

A list type is similar to NMTOKENS as used in a DTD for an attribute declaration. The value contains tokens separated by whitespace. In fact, NMTOKENS is a built-in derived data type for schemas. List types are more restrictive than NMTOKENS, though. The tokens are restricted to certain values that you define. Using the CreditType definition created in Listing 3-27, you can create a data type that will accept multiple values that conform to the CreditType definition and be separated by whitespace:

```
<xsd:simpleType name="Credits">
  <xsd:list itemType="CreditType" />
</xsd:simpleType>
```

The xsd:list element takes the attribute itemType, which names the data type that defined the acceptable values. Based on this definition and an element named creditlist, which is declared with this type, it could take the following form:

```
<creditlist>1.0 1.5 2.0</creditlist>
```

Union Type

Union types enable values to be provided from multiple data types rather than just a single data type. If you were to define a type that was restricted to a single alpha character (A though Z) such as this:

```
<xsd:simpleType name="AtoZ">
  <xsd:restriction base="xsd:string">
    <xsd:pattern value="[A-Z]"/>
  </xsd:restriction>
</xsd:simpleType>
```

then you could join this via a union with the oneToTen type defined in Listing 3-28:

```
<xsd:simpleType name="MyUnion">
  <xsd:union memberTypes="AtoZ oneToTen" />
</xsd:simpleType>
```

The xsd:union element takes the attribute memberTypes, which is a whitespace-delimited list of data types to combine. In this case, you are using the AtoZ and oneToTen types. An element declared with this type—for instance, myunionvals—could look like the following:

```
<myunionvals>A 1 I 9</myunionvals>
```

Complex Types and Content

Within the earlier discussion of XML Schemas, you saw how to use a complex type when declaring elements. You have yet to look at complex content as well as the built-in complex data type within the XML Schema specification. This is the anyType data type.

Any/Empty

As mentioned earlier, ANY and EMPTY either allow anything as element content (ANY) or allow nothing for element content (EMPTY). The equivalent data type using XML Schemas for ANY is the anyType data type:

```
<xsd:element name="description" type="xsd:anyType" />
```

By this declaration, the element description is completely unrestrained. It can consist of any type of content and any type of child elements. The elements any and anyAttribute also exist, which you can use to provide similar functionality in a more limited scope:

```
<xsd:element name="myelement">
    <xsd:complexType>
        <xsd:sequence>
            <xsd:element name="definedelement" type="xsd:string"/>
            <xsd:any minOccurs="0"/>
        </xsd:sequence>
        <xsd:anyAttribute processContents="skip" />
    </xsd:complexType>
</xsd:element>
```

This syntax should look familiar to you. It is a declaration for the myelement element containing child elements, as noted by the xsd:sequence element. The new element within the sequence, xsd:any, indicates that after a definedelement element any element may appear. The element need not even be declared within the schema. The minOccurs attribute indicates there could be zero or one element. The maximum value is from the default value for maxOccurs, which was not explicitly set.

The xsd:anyAttribute element allows any number of attributes for the element without restricting which ones are allowable. The attribute processContents does allow for some level of control over attribute availability. The value skip, as used in the declaration, allows for any attribute, even ones that have not been defined in the schema. A value of strict, which is also the default value if processContents is omitted, will allow only those attributes that have been declared in the schema. The third possible value is lax. This value means that if an attribute is used and has been declared in the schema, then it must be valid according to its declaration. If the attribute has not been declared, then you just allow it and continue.

Empty elements are not as easily defined as the anyType ones. There is no built-in data type, so you must create one:

```
<xsd:element name="myemptyelement">
    <xsd:complexType />
</xsd:element>
```

This declaration is extremely restrictive. Absolutely no content or attributes are allowed. You can expand upon this to allow some attributes and use a little more formal syntax in the process:

```
<xsd:element name="myemptyelement">
    <xsd:complexType>
        <xsd:complexContent>
            <xsd:restriction base="xsd:anyType">
                <xsd:attribute name="myattribute" type="xsd:string" />
            </xsd:restriction>
        </xsd:complexContent>
    </xsd:complexType>
</xsd:element>
```

This declaration is a bit more formal. You should notice the xsd:complexContent element as well as its restrictions. I wanted to throw this out there because I will be covering complex, or *mixed*, content next. You could just as easily have written this as follows:

```
<xsd:element name="myemptyelement">
    <xsd:complexType>
        <xsd:attribute name="myattribute" type="xsd:string" />
    </xsd:complexType>
</xsd:element>
```

Mixed Content

You may run into cases where you need to allow mixed content within an element. For example:

```
<note>A meeting is scheduled on <meetingdate>2005-06-03</meetingdate> at
<meetingtime>15:00:00</meetingtime>.</note>
```

The note element contains a mixture of text and child elements. Listing 3-29 illustrates a possible definition for this.

Listing 3-29. *Using Mixed Content*

```
<xsd:complexType name="meetingNote" mixed="true">
    <xsd:all>
        <xsd:element name="meetingdate" type="xsd:date"/>
        <xsd:element name="meetingtime" type="xsd:time"/>
    </xsd:all>
```

```
    <xsd:attribute name="enabled" type="xsd:boolean" default="true" />
</xsd:complexType>
<xsd:element name="note" type="meetingNote" />
```

The attribute mixed is a Boolean, defaulting to false, which specifies whether text is allowed within the content. To this point, the attribute has not appeared on any of the complexType definitions; thus, the elements using the complex data type have allowed only element and/or attributes. The attribute pertains only to the element using the type. It does not affect elements declared within the element's content. For example, the declaration of the meetingNote element is of mixed content, mixed="true". The elements declared as child elements, such as meetingdate, base their allowable content on the data type specified in their own declaration. In the case of meetingdate, the type is xsd:date, so text content is allowed.

You may also have noticed the use of the xsd:all element. This is an anonymous element group since it is local to the meetingNote definition and has no name. A sequence would not have been a good option to use in this case because the ordering of the meetingdate and meetingtime elements could not be determined ahead of time. It was a better decision to use xsd:all, which enforces that the elements must appear within the note content but in no specified order.

Complex Content

Complex content allows you to restrict or extend a complex type. You have already seen how restrictions work, so now I will show how to use complexContent to extend a complex type. Suppose you wanted to extend the meetingNote definition in Listing 3-29 and allow an additional element for the location, called meetingLocation. Unfortunately, you can't do this. The base type meetingNote is using xsd:all. This element will not allow you to extend the type and add another element to the mix. You would either have to rewrite the definition and force sequencing or create a new data type. In this case, this is how you would rewrite the definition using sequence:

```
<xsd:complexType name="meetingNote" mixed="true">
    <xsd:sequence>
        <xsd:element name="meetingdate" type="xsd:date"/>
        <xsd:element name="meetingtime" type="xsd:time"/>
    </xsd:sequence>
    <xsd:attribute name="enabled" type="xsd:boolean" value="true" />
</xsd:complexType>
```

The xsd:all element has been removed and replaced with xsd:sequence. These elements must not show up in the exact order though may be intermixed with text content because of the mixed="true" attribute. An attribute named enabled has also been declared as a Boolean with a default value of true. You can now extend this definition:

```
<xsd:element name="extendedNote">
    <xsd:complexType>
        <xsd:complexContent mixed="true">
            <xsd:extension base="meetingNote">
                <xsd:sequence>
                    <xsd:element name="meetingLocation" type="xsd:string" />
```

```
            </xsd:sequence>
         </xsd:extension>
      </xsd:complexContent>
   </xsd:complexType>
</xsd:element>
```

An element extendedNote has been declared with a complex type that is extending the meetingNote definition. It is required to set the mixed attribute on the xsd:complexContent element; otherwise, it would default to false and override the setting from the meetingNote definition.

The xsd:extension element is where the extension begins. As with user-derived types, the base attribute sets the base type you are using. All you want to do is add an element to the definition, which is handled the same way elements are declared as children. You use the normal xsd:sequence followed by the element declaration. Because this is an extension, this new type, which again is anonymous and being defined within the scope of the extendedNote declaration, inherits the definition of the meetingNote. The new element meetingLocation is added to the end of the sequence group. Based on this definition, you could write an extendedNote as follows:

```
<extendedNote enabled="false">
    A meeting is scheduled on <meetingdate>2005-06-03</meetingdate> at
    <meetingtime>15:00:00</meetingtime>
    in the <meetingLocation>Green Room</meetingLocation>.
 </extendedNote>
```

The enabled attribute was explicitly set just to illustrate that all the previous declarations set for meetingNote still apply to the complex data type set within extendedNote. If the value for the attribute were set to anything other than a Boolean value, validation would fail.

Notations

Notation elements within schemas are the same as notation declarations within a DTD. They are helpers to indicate how data should be processed. Their declarations are also similar to those in a DTD. Take a look at the following as a comparison:

```
<!-- Notations declared in DTD -->
<!NOTATION GIF SYSTEM "gifviewer.exe">
<!NOTATION GIF PUBLIC "image/gif" "gifviewer.exe">

<!-- Notations in XML Schemas. GIF only lowercased for consistency in schema -->
<xsd:notation name="gif" system="gifviewer.exe">
<xsd:notation name="gif" public=" image/gif " system="gifviewer.exe">
```

Using one of the notation declarations for an XML Schema, you could declare an element with the attribute imagetype, which is a notation type but limited to gif or jpeg:

```
<xsd:element name="image">
    <xsd:complexType>
        <xsd:simpleContent>
            <xsd:extension base="xsd:hexBinary">
```

```
                    <xsd:attribute name="imagetype">
                        <xsd:simpleType>
                            <xsd:restriction base="xsd:NOTATION">
                                <xsd:enumeration value="jpeg"/>
                                <xsd:enumeration value="gif"/>
                            </xsd:restriction>
                        </xsd:simpleType>
                    </xsd:attribute>
                </xsd:extension>
            </xsd:simpleContent>
        </xsd:complexType>
</xsd:element>
```

The image element would take the following form:

```
<image imagetype="gif">
    <!-- content here in hexBinary as defined in schema -->
</image>
```

Annotations

Annotations are notes and instructions within a schema. They have no effect on document validity and are used to supply either some documentation for the schema or some information for computer processing:

```
<xsd:annotation></xsd:annotation>
```

How an annotation element is used within a schema is determined by the child elements. It may contain documentation elements, which are used to provide schema documentation, and/or appinfo elements, which can provide computer-processing information. For example:

```
<!-- simple documentation -->
<xsd:annotation>
    <xsd:documentation>This is our master schema</xsd:documentation>
</xsd:annotation>

<!-- Processing information with supplied documentation -->
<xsd:annotation>
    <xsd:documentation>Process the function here</xsd:documentation>
    <xsd:appinfo>
        $user->update(userID, name);
    </xsd:appinfo>
</xsd:annotation>
```

The appinfo element does nothing magical. It does not automatically call the function but is only an indicator with instructions contained within the content—much like a PI. The burden still falls on you to perform any processing, if you want.

Global and Local Scope

When using a DTD, the root element is declared in the DOCTYPE declaration to specify the start-ing element of the document. XML Schemas do not have this concept. Schemas have the concept of global and local scope. All definitions and declarations, which are direct child ele-ments of the schema element, are in the global scope. Elements in this respect refer to XML elements in general and *not* to xsd:elements. The rest of the declarations and definitions are local to whichever element contains them. All elements, referring to the xsd:element elements within the schema, declared within the global scope can be used as a root element. Unlike a DTD, XML Schemas have the ability to validate multiple documents since any globally scoped element declaration can be used as the root.

The schema in Listing 3-26 contains one element in the global scope. The declaration for the courses element is the only piece of the schema in the global scope because it is the only child of the xsd:schema element. Listing 3-30 illustrates a modified version of the schema in Listing 3-26. Most of the course child element declarations have been omitted for brevity.

Listing 3-30. *Element Declarations in Global Scope*

```
<?xml version="1.0"?>
<xsd:schema xmlns:xsd="http://www.w3.org/2001/XMLSchema">

   <xsd:element name="courses">
      <xsd:complexType>
         <xsd:sequence>
            <xsd:element ref="course" minOccurs="0" maxOccurs="unbounded" />
         </xsd:sequence>
      </xsd:complexType>
   </xsd:element>

   <xsd:element name="course">
      <xsd:complexType>
         <xsd:sequence>
            <xsd:element name="title" type="xsd:string"/>
         </xsd:sequence>
         <xsd:attribute name="cid" type="xsd:ID"/>
      </xsd:complexType>
   </xsd:element>

</xsd:schema>
```

The schema in Listing 3-30 has two elements, courses and course, that have been declared in the global scope. The courses element may have a course child element, but in this case, instead of course being declared within the courses scope, it is declared in the global scope. The minOccurs and maxOccurs attributes have been removed from the declaration. These attributes have no meaning unless used within a local scope. As a result, the courses declaration contains a reference to the course declaration: <xsd:element ref="course" minOccurs="0" maxOccurs="unbounded" />. The value of the ref attribute is the name of the declaration, where the referred declaration lives in the global scope. In this case, the value is course, so the schema knows to look in the global scope for the declaration. It is also on this element that the minOccurs and maxOccurs attributes are relevant because they fall within the local scope of complexType definition for the courses declaration.

Documents to be validated using the schema in Listing 3-30 may now have either courses or course as the root element. The following are a few documents that will validate against the schema:

```
<!-- Document with a an empty courses element as root -->
<course />

<!-- Document with a course element as root -->
<course>
    <title>French I</title>
</course>

<!-- Document with a courses element as root and a course child element -->
<courses>
    <course>
        <title>Spanish I</title>
    </course>
</courses>
```

XML Schemas offer much more flexibility than a DTD in this respect. A single schema may possibly be able to replace multiple external subsets. All declarations, not just element declarations, may be declared in global scope and used in this manner. It would be perfectly legal to declare an attribute in global scope and reference the global declaration when attaching an attribute to an element.

Contrary to the courses and course declarations, title has been declared in the local scope of the course declaration. It cannot be reused; thus, it would be illegal to have a declaration containing ref="title".

Scope is also not limited to just declarations. DTDs are also affected by their scope. This is why definitions, such as those created through by using a complexType, can have names. Named definitions live in the global scope so they can be shared throughout the schema. Definitions in a local scope are not shared and thus do not require a name, as the name is pretty much meaningless.

Examples you have seen so far containing named complexType definitions are actually defining these in the global scope. The examples have been only small code snippets, so you may not even have been aware of this. So what exactly does a full schema look like when sharing definitions? Listing 3-31 builds on Listing 3-30 to define a complex data type named courseType.

Listing 3-31. complexType *Defined in Global Scope*

```
<?xml version="1.0"?>
<xsd:schema xmlns:xsd="http://www.w3.org/2001/XMLSchema">
```

```
<xsd:element name="courses">
    <xsd:complexType>
        <xsd:sequence>
            <xsd:element ref="course" minOccurs="0" maxOccurs="unbounded" />
        </xsd:sequence>
    </xsd:complexType>
</xsd:element>

<xsd:element name="course" type="courseType"/>

<xsd:complexType name="courseType">
    <xsd:sequence>
        <xsd:element name="title" type="xsd:string" minOccurs="1" maxOccurs="1"/>
    </xsd:sequence>
    <xsd:attribute name="cid" type="xsd:ID"/>
</xsd:complexType>

</xsd:schema>
```

The complexType definition, which was defined in the local scope in Listing 3-30, has been given the name courseType and moved into the global scope in Listing 3-31. The attributes minOccurs and maxOccurs have also been added to the title declaration. These are not needed, as the values set are the default values already, but have been added to illustrate how to use the attributes when within a local scope on an xsd:element and when not referencing a global element declaration. Definitions are not like declarations, because a definition becomes a data type within the schema and is used the same way as built-in data types. Notice the declaration for the course element in Listing 3-31. It now contains a type attribute with a courseType value. When a course element is validated within a document, it will validate according to the definition of courseType defined in the global scope.

Include

Schemas can become quite large in size, which makes them difficult to read. Many different groups may also manage different sections of a schema. XML documents can contain aggregated data, such as one group handling data related to courses with another group handling data related to instructors. In a case like this, the group managing course data would want to control the sections of the schema pertaining to course data, and the other group would want to control the section pertaining to instructor data. Within a DTD, you would accomplish this with external subsets. You could combine the subsets to form a single DTD. One method of doing this with XML Schemas is by using the include element.

You can use include elements to create a single schema from multiple schemas within a single namespace. You will use the import element when working across namespaces. You will learn more about namespaces in schemas and about using import in the next sections. For now let's look at the schemas in Listings 3-32, 3-33, and 3-34. The first two, Listings 3-32 and 3-33, are stand-alone schemas used to validate a course element and an instructor element. Suppose you need to create a document combining data and would like to reuse these existing schemas. Listing 3-34 illustrates a schema created from the course.xsd and instructor.xsd schemas.

Listing 3-32. *Course Schema* course.xsd

```
<?xml version="1.0"?>
<xsd:schema xmlns:xsd="http://www.w3.org/2001/XMLSchema">

    <xsd:element name="course">
        <xsd:complexType>
            <xsd:sequence>
                <xsd:element name="title" type="xsd:string"/>
                <xsd:element name="description" type="xsd:string"/>
                <xsd:element name="credits" type="xsd:decimal"/>
                <xsd:element name="lastmodified" type="xsd:dateTime"/>
            </xsd:sequence>
            <xsd:attribute name="cid" type="xsd:ID"/>
        </xsd:complexType>
    </xsd:element>

</xsd:schema>
```

Listing 3-33. *Instructor Schema* instructor.xsd

```
<?xml version="1.0"?>
<xsd:schema xmlns:xsd="http://www.w3.org/2001/XMLSchema">

    <xsd:element name="title" type="xsd:string" />

    <xsd:element name="instructor">
        <xsd:complexType>
            <xsd:sequence>
                <xsd:element name="name" type="xsd:string" />
                <xsd:element ref="title" />
            </xsd:sequence>
        </xsd:complexType>
    </xsd:element>

</xsd:schema>
```

Listing 3-34. *Courses and Instructors Schema Using an Include*

```
<?xml version="1.0"?>
<xsd:schema xmlns:xsd="http://www.w3.org/2001/XMLSchema">
    <xsd:include schemaLocation="course.xsd" />
    <xsd:include schemaLocation="instructor.xsd" />
```

```
<xsd:element name="courses">
   <xsd:complexType>
      <xsd:sequence>
         <xsd:element ref="course" minOccurs="0" maxOccurs="unbounded" />
      </xsd:sequence>
   </xsd:complexType>
</xsd:element>

<xsd:element name="instructors">
   <xsd:complexType>
      <xsd:sequence>
         <xsd:element ref="instructor" minOccurs="0" maxOccurs="unbounded" />
      </xsd:sequence>
   </xsd:complexType>
</xsd:element>

<xsd:element name="list">
   <xsd:complexType>
      <xsd:sequence>
         <xsd:element ref="courses" minOccurs="0" maxOccurs="unbounded" />
         <xsd:element ref="instructors" minOccurs="0" maxOccurs="unbounded" />
      </xsd:sequence>
   </xsd:complexType>
</xsd:element>

</xsd:schema>
```

The value of the schemaLocation attribute on the two xsd:include elements in Listing 3-34 is the URI for the schema to be included. The first element includes course.xsd and refers to the code in Listing 3-32. The second include pulls the schema from the instructor.xsd file, which refers to the code in Listing 3-33. Using include elements, your main schema may pull declarations and definitions from remote files, just as if those files were part of your main schema. You can see examples of using the remote files through the element declarations within the xsd:sequence elements. The element is referring to, through use of the ref attribute, declarations from both the included schemas. You may also notice the additional title element declaration in Listing 3-33. This element is declared in the global scope but is not used even though the course element declaration uses a title element. The title element declared within the course element is in local scope and thus takes precedence over a global scoped declaration. The title declaration in global scope was just a demonstration to show that including schemas does not change the scoping rules of declarations and definitions.

Note XML Schema *includes* are used when all schemas do not use namespaces or are all in the same single namespace. To use schemas in different namespaces, you must use the import element.

Namespaces

You now know how to combine schemas into a single schema. One thing I haven't addressed, however, is what happens if the same globally named definition or declaration appears in multiple schemas. During the development of XML Schemas, this limitation in DTDs was addressed by namespaces. XML Schemas support namespaces that can get around this problem. This section will show how to use namespaces in schemas and will introduce some new attributes in the process.

Listing 3-32 shows the schemas for the course data. If you were in charge of managing the course data and its schema, you may want to ensure that your schema, if combined into another schema, remains intact and that your declarations and definitions never conflict with other schemas. Listing 3-35 is a modified version of the course schema in that it introduces namespaces into the schema. The local complex type definition for the course element has also been broken out and defined as a named type in the global scope.

Listing 3-35. *Namespaced Course Schema* course.xsd

```
<?xml version="1.0"?>
<xsd:schema xmlns:xsd="http://www.w3.org/2001/XMLSchema"
            xmlns:cs="http://www.example.com/Course"
            targetNamespace="http://www.example.com/Course"
            elementFormDefault="unqualified"
            attributeFormDefault="unqualified">

    <xsd:complexType name="courseType">
        <xsd:sequence>
            <xsd:element name="title" type="xsd:string"/>
            <xsd:element name="description" type="xsd:string"/>
            <xsd:element name="credits" type="xsd:decimal"/>
            <xsd:element name="lastmodified" type="xsd:dateTime"/>
        </xsd:sequence>
        <xsd:attribute name="cid" type="xsd:ID"/>
    </xsd:complexType>

    <xsd:element name="course" type="cs:courseType" />

</xsd:schema>
```

Notice the new schema element. Three new attributes have been added as well as a new namespace declaration.

Unqualified Locals The value of the targetNamespace attribute indicates the namespace in which the global declarations and definitions reside. In this case, the courseType definition and the course element declaration reside in the http://www.example.com/Course namespace. A namespace declaration was also added to associate the prefix cs with this namespace. This prefix within the schema indicates the specific data type or declaration to use. You may not have realized this, but you have been working with namespaced data types all along. Every time you have used one of the built-in data types, they have been prefixed with xsd. According to the namespace declaration on the schema element, this prefix refers to the XML Schema (http://www.w3.org/2001/XMLSchema). Looking at the course element declaration in Listing 3-35, the type is cs:courseType. This informs the schema to look for the courseType definition within the http://www.example.com/Course namespace. This definition is found within the schema that has the targetNamespace of http://www.example.com/Course. In its current form and usage, this may not look very useful. You own this schema and are not including any other schemas, so you shouldn't have any problems. Namespaces become useful, however, when others begin to use your schemas, which will be demonstrated later in the "Import" section.

Elements and attributes used within the XML document that have declarations in the global scope must reside in the targetNamespace of the schema so that when the document is validated, the schema knows where to look for the rules for the element. Again, this is only for global declarations. The remaining two attributes you have not seen handle the local elements and attributes. The elementFormDefault and attributeFormDefault attributes affect the qualification of local elements and attributes within the XML document that uses this schema. The values, in Listing 3-35, are both set to unqualified. This is already the default value for both of the attributes so could have been left out in a real-world situation. This value informs the schema that local elements and attributes do not have to be qualified. That is, they do not have to be within a namespace in the XML document. Let's take a look at a document that uses the schema from Listing 3-35:

```
<?xml version="1.0"?>
<c:course xmlns:c="http://www.example.com/Course" cid="c3">
    <title>French II</title>
    <description>Intermediate French</description>
    <credits>3.0</credits>
    <lastmodified>2005-03-12T15:45:44</lastmodified>
</c:course>
```

The course element associates the prefix c with the namespace http://www.example.com/Course. This namespace is the same as the targetNamespace of the schema. The element, being the document element, must come from the global scope of a schema, and because the schema is using namespaces, the course element must reside in this namespace. For this reason, it is written as c:course. The local elements and attributes do not reside in any namespace, which is perfectly legal. The schemas set the elementFormDefault and attributeFormDefault attributes to unqualified, so none is needed. In case you are wondering why the root must be within a namespace but local elements and attributes do not, I will explain this.

When a document is being validated, it must know where to look for the declaration. The root element must be a declared in the global scope of a document; otherwise, the schema will not know where to find it. The declaration of the root element resides in the targetNamespace, so within the document, it must be in the same namespace. As long as child elements and attributes are declared within the scope of the root element declaration, and not declared in the global scope and just referenced, the schema does not have to search for the declarations, and namespaces are not needed for them.

Qualified Locals Using the value of qualified for the elementFormDefault and/or attributeFormDefault attributes requires the XML document to place elements and attributes within the targetNamespace of the schema in order to be valid. For example:

```
<?xml version="1.0"?>
<xsd:schema xmlns:xsd="http://www.w3.org/2001/XMLSchema"
            xmlns:cs="http://www.example.com/Course"
            targetNamespace="http://www.example.com/Course"
            elementFormDefault="qualified"
            attributeFormDefault="qualified">

    <xsd:complexType name="courseType">
        <xsd:sequence>
            <xsd:element name="title" type="xsd:string"/>
            <xsd:element name="description" type="xsd:string"/>
            <xsd:element name="credits" type="xsd:decimal"/>
            <xsd:element name="lastmodified" type="xsd:dateTime"/>
        </xsd:sequence>
        <xsd:attribute name="cid" type="xsd:ID"/>
    </xsd:complexType>

    <xsd:element name="course" type="cs:courseType" />

</xsd:schema>
```

Based on this new schema, the document validated against Listing 3-35 will no longer validate. Elements and attributes must be qualified. The new document would look like this:

```
<?xml version="1.0"?>
<c:course xmlns:c="http://www.example.com/Course" c:cid="c3">
    <c:title>French II</c:title>
    <c:description>Intermediate French</c:description>
    <c:credits>3.0</c:credits>
    <c:lastmodified>2005-03-12T15:45:44</c:lastmodified>
</c:course>
```

The http://www.example.com/Course namespace must be prefixed because of the attribute. Default namespaces do not apply to attributes. You can override the elementFormDefault and attributeFormDefault, which would allow the use of a default namespace, by using a local form attribute.

You can use the form attribute on element and attribute declarations to override the default settings in the schema element. Using this on the declaration of the cid attribute, the XML document could use a default namespace and eliminate the need for prefixes:

```
<?xml version="1.0"?>
<xsd:schema xmlns:xsd="http://www.w3.org/2001/XMLSchema"
            xmlns:cs="http://www.example.com/Course"
            targetNamespace="http://www.example.com/Course"
            elementFormDefault="qualified"
            attributeFormDefault="qualified">
```

```xml
<xsd:complexType name="courseType">
   <xsd:sequence>
      <xsd:element name="title" type="xsd:string"/>
      <xsd:element name="description" type="xsd:string"/>
      <xsd:element name="credits" type="xsd:decimal"/>
      <xsd:element name="lastmodified" type="xsd:dateTime"/>
   </xsd:sequence>
   <xsd:attribute name="cid" type="xsd:ID" form="unqualified"/>
</xsd:complexType>

<xsd:element name="course" type="cs:courseType" />

</xsd:schema>
```

Note that the attribute declaration for cid sets an additional attribute, form, to unqualified. This overrides the attributeFormDefault attribute, set to qualified, for this declaration only. Using this schema, you could now use a default namespace such as the following:

```xml
<?xml version="1.0"?>
<course xmlns="http://www.example.com/Course" cid="c3">
    <title>French II</title>
    <description>Intermediate French</description>
    <credits>3.0</credits>
    <lastmodified>2005-03-12T15:45:44</lastmodified>
</course>
```

All elements fall under the default namespace, including the document element, and the cid attribute may be unqualified, making this document valid according to the schema.

Import

You now know how to work with a namespace schema, as well as that the include element cannot be used with multiple namespaced schemas. The import element instructs the schema that referenced schemas are using namespaces. Listing 3-36 contains a modified instructor schema based on the schema in Listing 3-33. It is using unqualified elements and attributes because the elementFormDefault and attributeFormDefault attributes are not specified and because unqualified is the default value.

Listing 3-36. *Namespaced Instructor Schema* instructor.xsd

```xml
<?xml version="1.0"?>
<xsd:schema xmlns:xsd="http://www.w3.org/2001/XMLSchema"
            xmlns:ins="http://www.example.com/Instructor"
            targetNamespace="http://www.example.com/Instructor">

   <xsd:element name="title" type="xsd:string" />
```

```
<xsd:element name="instructor">
    <xsd:complexType>
        <xsd:sequence>
            <xsd:element name="name" type="xsd:string" />
            <xsd:element ref="ins:title" />
        </xsd:sequence>
    </xsd:complexType>
</xsd:element>

</xsd:schema>
```

Listing 3-37 is a schema modified from the one in Listing 3-34 to use new namespaced schemas. The reference to the course.xsd file is the one from Listing 3-35.

Listing 3-37. *Courses and Instructors Schema Using Import*

```
<?xml version="1.0"?>
<xsd:schema xmlns:xsd="http://www.w3.org/2001/XMLSchema"
            xmlns:c="http://www.example.com/Course"
            xmlns:in="http://www.example.com/Instructor">

    <xsd:import namespace="http://www.example.com/Course"
                schemaLocation="course.xsd" />
    <xsd:import namespace="http://www.example.com/Instructor"
                schemaLocation="instructor.xsd" />

    <xsd:element name="courses">
        <xsd:complexType>
            <xsd:sequence>
                <xsd:element ref="c:course" minOccurs="0" maxOccurs="unbounded" />
            </xsd:sequence>
        </xsd:complexType>
    </xsd:element>

    <xsd:element name="instructors">
        <xsd:complexType>
            <xsd:sequence>
                <xsd:element ref="in:instructor" minOccurs="0" maxOccurs="unbounded" />
            </xsd:sequence>
        </xsd:complexType>
    </xsd:element>
```

```
<xsd:element name="list">
    <xsd:complexType>
        <xsd:sequence>
            <xsd:element ref="courses" minOccurs="0" maxOccurs="unbounded" />
            <xsd:element ref="instructors" minOccurs="0" maxOccurs="unbounded" />
        </xsd:sequence>
    </xsd:complexType>
</xsd:element>

</xsd:schema>
```

The only changes you will notice are the addition of two namespace declarations on the schema element, the change from include elements to import elements, and the use of qualified element references.

The namespace declarations have been added so you can associate prefixes with namespaces to be used for the elements referred to in the value of the ref attributes. A targetNamespace has not been added to this schema, although one could be. Adding a targetNamespace to this schema could affect the import elements, which will be explained shortly.

The import elements, in Listing 3-37, have two attributes. You are familiar with the schemaLocation attribute because this was used for the import element. This attribute is not required but is usually provided. It indicates the location of the schema to import. When not included, it is up to the processor to be able to determine the location of the schema. The namespace attribute indicates the namespace of the schema being imported.

A few rules surround the use of this attribute. If the main schema file has a targetNamespace, then the value of the namespace attribute cannot be the same namespace. When import elements do not have a namespace attribute, you must specify a targetNamespace on the schema element of the schema doing the importing. In the case of Listing 3-37, the schema does not contain a targetNamespace attribute, so there is no limitation in this regard to the namespace attribute. Additional rules do, however, apply to the namespace attribute in respect to the schema being imported.

The namespace attribute must match the targetNamespace of the schema being imported. If the namespace attribute is not present, then the schema being imported must not have a targetNamespace. In Listing 3-37, the course.xsd and instructor.xsd files are being imported. The namespace for the course.xsd import is http://www.example.com/Course, which matches the targetNamespace in Listing 3-35. The namespace for the instructor.xsd import is http://www.example.com/Instructor, which matches the targetNamespace in Listing 3-36. Based on the rules just explained, the schema in Listing 3-37 is correct in the usage of the namespace attributes.

Putting namespaces and import all together, the following illustrates a document written according to the schema in Listing 3-37:

```
<list xmlns:c="http://www.example.com/Course"
      xmlns:ins="http://www.example.com/Instructor">
    <courses>
        <c:course cid="c3">
            <title>French II</title>
            <description>Intermediate French</description>
```

```
            <credits>3.0</credits>
            <lastmodified>2005-03-12T15:45:44</lastmodified>
        </c:course>
    </courses>
    <instructors>
        <ins:instructor>
            <name>John Smith</name>
            <ins:title>Professor</ins:title>
        </ins:instructor>
    </instructors>
</list>
```

The list, courses, and instructors elements require no namespacing. There is no targetNamespace for the master schema. The course element resides in the http:// www.example.com/Course namespace, but its children require no namespaces. According to the courses.xsd schema, the elements and attributes may be unqualified. Only the course element is required to be namespaced because the element declaration resides in the global namespace. The instructor element, as well as its child title element, is namespaced. Both of these elements are declared within the global scope of the instructor.xsd file, but the name element is not. Lastly, the namespaces attached to elements, which are namespaced, match the targetNamespace of the schema from which the element declaration was made.

As you have seen so far, schemas can get complex. You have many different aspects to take into account, such as scope, namespaces, include, and import. All these factors, although contributing to the complexity, also open the door to great possibilities in flexibility and granularity when defining a document's structure. XML Schemas have great extensibility—not only using user-derived data types but also from the nested include and import possibilities. XML Schemas are just one alternative to using a DTD.

In the next section, you'll look at Relax NG and how to utilize it for validation.

Using RELAX NG

RELAX NG is another alternative to DTDs and XML Schemas. It is a schema specification by OASIS that offers the extensibility of XML Schemas but is simple to use. RELAX NG can be written in compact syntax or XML syntax. Compact syntax is out of the scope of this book, as it is not currently supported in any of the PHP extensions. The following sections will deal strictly with the XML syntax used to create RELAX NG schemas per the OASIS Committee Specification dated December 3, 2001 (http://relaxng.org/spec-20011203.html).

Note Unless explicitly noted, the term *schema* in this section refers to a RELAX NG schema and not an XML Schema.

RELAX NG is based on patterns. In terms of an XML Schema, an element declaration is a form of pattern. It defines an element with a given name. When written in RELAX NG grammar, this particular element in an XML document, when encountered, would match the pattern in the RELAX NG schema. This may sound a little confusing at first but is simple in reality.

Introducing RELAX NG

Just as was done with XML Schemas, I'll show first how to build a schema with RELAX NG and then explain the process in more detail. I'll use the document in Listing 3-24 to show how to build a RELAX NG schema. The schema will be written to the file course.rng. This time, rather than an inside-out approach, it will be top-down. These schemas, as they are pattern-based, take a descriptive approach. Analyzing the document in Listing 3-24, you will start with the document element, courses, as it is the first element in the tree. Thinking about it descriptively, you can say you have an element named courses:

```
<?xml version="1.0" encoding="utf-8" ?>
<element name="courses" xmlns="http://relaxng.org/ns/structure/1.0">
</element>
```

This looks similar to XML Schemas in a way. The namespace http://relaxng.org/ns/structure/1.0 is the namespace for RELAX NG schemas. It works the same way as setting the namespace for XML Schemas in the schema element. In this case, however, it is not prefixed. It is perfectly valid to associate a prefix with the namespace, but make sure if you do that all elements are set to that namespace. RELAX NG handles namespaces differently than XML Schemas, so more often than not you will see the RELAX NG namespace set as a default namespace rather than with an associating prefix. This element ends up as the root of the schema, which also is different from XML Schemas (which require the schema element).

Moving to the courses child elements, you come to the course element. You know that text, other than the insignificant whitespace, is not allowed as direct content of the courses element. The only allowable content is zero or more course elements. So, following this description, you can continue writing the schema:

```
<?xml version="1.0" encoding="utf-8" ?>
<element name="courses" xmlns="http://relaxng.org/ns/structure/1.0">
    <zeroOrMore>
        <element name="course">
            <empty/>
        </element>
    </zeroOrMore>
</element>
```

The element named courses can have zero or more, zeroOrMore, child elements named course. The element pattern for course contains an additional child. This is so the schema will be valid. Element patterns cannot be empty, so <element name="course" /> is not correct. The empty element means a course element must be empty and may not contain text or child elements. This will be removed shortly, so for now it is just a placeholder while keeping the schema correct.

Continuing through the document, you must first address the cid attribute, which is required for the course element:

```
<?xml version="1.0" encoding="utf-8" ?>
<element name="courses" xmlns="http://relaxng.org/ns/structure/1.0">
   <zeroOrMore>
      <element name="course"
              datatypeLibrary="http://www.w3.org/2001/XMLSchema-datatypes">
         <attribute name="cid">
            <data type="ID"/>
         </attribute>
         <empty/>
      </element>
   </zeroOrMore>
</element>
```

You are probably thinking this is a lot of code just to add an attribute of type ID; you may also be wondering why there is a reference to XML Schemas. I'll explain data types throughout this section as well as their relation to patterns, but for now I will say that RELAX NG has two built-in data types, which are string and token. It does allow you to use externally defined data types, such as the ones from XML Schemas. You do this by using the datatypeLibrary attribute. This attribute could have been specified on the attribute element for cid, but rather, it was defined on the element for course. RELAX NG will use whatever datatypeLibrary is in scope, which means if one is not set on the current element, it will search in the hierarchy of the element patterns. Once a datatypeLibrary is in scope, the data type is set using the data element. The type attribute specifies the ID data type from the XML Schema data types, which is http://www.w3.org/2001/XMLSchema-datatypes. This effectively sets the attribute named cid to type ID. Now you can start dealing with the child elements of the course element and remove the empty element being used as a placeholder.

Moving along, you come to the title element. You define this just like the other element, except in this case it contains text content. The same holds true for the description element, so you will add the pattern for this at the same time:

```
<?xml version="1.0" encoding="utf-8" ?>
<element name="courses" xmlns="http://relaxng.org/ns/structure/1.0">
   <zeroOrMore>
      <element name="course"
              datatypeLibrary="http://www.w3.org/2001/XMLSchema-datatypes">
         <attribute name="cid">
            <data type="ID"/>
         </attribute>
         <element name="title">
            <text/>
         </element>
         <element name="description">
            <text/>
         </element>
      </element>
   </zeroOrMore>
</element>
```

In this example, the title and description definitions both use the text pattern. As long as the content of the elements is empty or text (which includes comments, CDATA, and PIs), the element is valid. You could have also used the string data type here, but I recommend the text pattern in this case. I'll discuss the differences between the two later in this section.

The next elements are credits and lastmodified. Using XML Schemas, their data types are decimal and dateTime. The decimal data type ensures the content of credits is always and only a decimal, and dateTime ensures the content of lastmodified conforms to the dateTime data type. You define their patterns in the same way you define the pattern for the attribute cid:

```
<element name="credits">
  <data type="decimal"/>
</element>
<element name="lastmodified">
  <data type="dateTime"/>
</element>
```

The entire schema was not included here, as you should have an idea of where these pieces should go. They are required elements in an ordered list of elements and go directly after the description element.

Moving to the element following lastmodified, you come to the pre-requisite element. This element is not required but may appear zero or more times. You write the definition the same way you added the course definition. You need to use the zeroOrMore pattern. Defining the rest of the contents for the pre-requisite element should now be fairly easy to figure out yourself, so the entire RELAX NG schema, for the courses document in Listing 3-24, is presented in Listing 3-38.

Listing 3-38. *RELAX NG Schema for Courses Document*

```
<?xml version="1.0" encoding="utf-8" ?>
<element name="courses" xmlns="http://relaxng.org/ns/structure/1.0">
  <zeroOrMore>
    <element name="course"
             datatypeLibrary="http://www.w3.org/2001/XMLSchema-datatypes">
      <attribute name="cid">
        <data type="ID"/>
      </attribute>
      <element name="title">
        <text/>
      </element>
      <element name="description">
        <text/>
      </element>
      <element name="credits">
        <data type="decimal"/>
      </element>
      <element name="lastmodified">
        <data type="dateTime"/>
      </element>
```

```
<zeroOrMore>
    <element name="pre-requisite">
        <attribute name="cref">
            <data type="IDREF"/>
        </attribute>
        <attribute name="req_next_sem">
            <data type="boolean"/>
        </attribute>
        <element name="instructor_approval">
            <data type="boolean"/>
        </element>
    </element>
</zeroOrMore>
    </element>
</zeroOrMore>
</element>
```

Although the ability to use XML Schema data types, which you learned about in the previous section, helped make this section much shorter than when building an XML Schema for the same set of data, you must admit the syntax for RELAX NG is also much simpler. Reading the schema in Listing 3-38, you'll see it's straightforward. The majority of the grammar is element-based with few or no attributes. The next section will take a more in-depth look at RELAX NG, its patterns, and its grammar.

Understanding the Structure

Now that you have some familiarity with a RELAX NG schema, you can take a more in-depth look at using patterns and creating more complex schemas. I'll touch on many new concepts. The first pattern I will cover is a nameClass. It may not make total sense to you initially but will become much clearer as you see how it is used within this section.

Note All RELAX NG examples are assumed to be in the http://relaxng.org/ns/structure/1.0 namespace if not explicitly set within the example.

---

nameClass/exceptNameClass

A nameClass is a pattern that matches a name, where the name may be the name of an element or attribute. The exceptNameClass is not really its own pattern but a case for the except pattern. You can use the pattern in conjunction with the nameClass pattern, so I'll discuss it in that context here. You have seen so far that you can define an element using the grammar <element name="ename">. This would cause RELAX NG to match on the element named ename in the XML document. Using a nameClass, you could also write it as follows:

```
<element>
    <name>ename</name>
    <empty/>
</element>
```

This syntax also applies to attributes. In most cases, it is much simpler to just use the name attribute on the element. Sometimes, however, using the nameClass can be useful. The empty element has been added as a placeholder because no pattern for content has been defined.

The XML Schema has the any element to allow any element as a child element. RELAX NG uses anyName within an element or attribute pattern. It translates to match the element or attribute on any name value. So, for example, to allow any element to be matched, you could write the following:

```
<element>
    <anyName />
    <empty/>
</element>
```

You can use exceptNameClass with anyName to explicitly disallow certain elements from matching. To match any element except the element's named title, you could write it as follows:

```
<element>
    <anyName>
        <except>
            <name>title</name>
        </except>
    </anyName>
    <empty/>
</element>
```

The except pattern is used here within the content of the anyName element. When used within a nameClass, it is called exceptNameClass. It functions exactly as it is named. It defines the exceptions for the current pattern. In this case, you are matching on any element name and would like to exclude elements named title from the match. To add an element that should be excluded from the match, you add a name element as a child element of the except element. The exceptNameClass also pertains to namespaces, which I'll discuss later in the section "Namespaces."

Another nameClass, which is also used within patterns, is choice. You can use choice to allow for one of the choices to be matched on, like so:

```
<element>
    <choice>
        <name>title</name>
        <name>description</name>
    </choice>
    <empty/>
</element>
```

Based on this pattern, a match would be made against a title element or a description element, but not both.

Patterns

The majority of RELAX NG patterns use more patterns as their content. Looking at the previous example, the content of the element pattern is the choice pattern and the empty pattern. The empty pattern does not have content, but the choice pattern contains two name patterns, which in this case are the nameClass patterns. The following sections will examine many of the patterns used to write a RELAX NG schema.

Choice

The choice pattern allows for any one of the patterns within the choice element content. You have seen this used within the nameClass to allow an element to match against one of the two nameClass patterns listed. This pattern has much greater use than just nameClass. For example:

```
<element name="food">
    <attribute name="group">
        <choice>
            <value>meat</value>
            <value>fruit</value>
            <value>dairy</value>
            <value>grain</value>
        </choice>
    </attribute>
    <text/>
</element>
```

Here, the valid value for the group attribute may be meat, fruit, dairy, or grain. Anything else is not valid for this attribute.

You can use this pattern anywhere you would like to allow a match based on one of any number of patterns. In the previous example, you were within the context of an attribute definition, so choice was set to allow for matching on one of the specified attribute values. You could have easily used it to match on a selection of attributes, elements, or content as well. The thing to remember is that the choice pattern contains any number of patterns where one must be matched.

Optional

The optional pattern indicates the pattern it contains is optional. This means it either must match the pattern or must not exist. If something exists that doesn't match the indicated pattern, then the document is not valid. For example:

```
<element name="course">
    <optional>
        <element name="pre-requisite">
            <text/>
        </element>
    </optional>
</element>
```

This pattern allows the course element to either have a pre-requisite child element or have empty content. You could have written this as follows:

```
<element name="course">
    <choice>
        <element name="pre-requisite">
            <text/>
        </element>
        <empty/>
    </choice>
</element>
```

Using the optional pattern not only reduces the schema by a line because the empty pattern is not needed, but you can also use it with virtually any pattern.

Group

The power and simplicity of patterns should be fairly obvious by now. One question you may have at this point is when building definitions, how can a group of patterns be considered a single pattern for matching? The answer is simple. Use the group pattern. This pattern allows you to add as many patterns within the group element. These patterns together constitute a single pattern when using the group element. Take, for example, the choice pattern. You would like the content of an element to match both the elements title and description, in that order, or just plain-text content. For example:

```
<element name="course">
    <choice>
        <group>
            <element name="title">
                <text/>
            </element>
            <element name="description">
                <text/>
            </element>
        </group>
        <text/>
    </choice>
</element>
```

You can see that the content for choice is the group pattern and the text pattern. Using the rules for choice, it must match one of these two patterns. The group pattern is a more complex pattern, though. Its pattern translates to matching both a title element with text content followed a description element with text content. These two patterns are taken as a single unit when matching on the choice pattern.

Mixed

Earlier I showed how to mix text and child elements within content. That mixing, however, was an ordered mix. It was done using the text pattern and the element pattern. Although in many cases the ordering of elements is known, the placement of text is not. You could always add a text pattern between every single element pattern, but that gets cumbersome. You can use the mixed pattern to simplify this:

```
<element name="course">
   <mixed>
      <element name="title">
         <text/>
      </element>
      <element name="description">
         <text/>
      </element>
   </mixed>
</element>
```

Using the mixed pattern, this code defines a title and a description element, which must appear in that order. The mixed pattern allows text content to appear before and after each one of the elements. The XML document could look like the following:

```
<course>
   some text
   <title/>
   more text
   <description/>
   even more text
</course>
```

Because of its nature, the mixed pattern is used only for element content. It is not valid to have mixed content anywhere else in an XML document.

Interleave

The closest you have come so far to variable ordering has been the mixed pattern. That pattern involves the ordering of text content only, which is not useful when dealing with nontext patterns. The interleave pattern is the pattern to use when ordering should not be taken into account:

```
<element name="course">
   <interleave>
      <element name="title">
         <text/>
      </element>
      <element name="description">
         <text/>
      </element>
      <text/>
   </interleave>
</element>
```

This example probably looks familiar to you. The mixed example has been changed to use the interleave pattern. The text pattern has been added as a child of the interleave element so that the content may contain any number of text blocks interspersed with a title element and a description element. These two elements may also appear in any order. There still must be one and only one title element and one and only one description element. The XML document could now look like this:

```
<course>
   some text
   <description/>
   even more text
   <title/>
   more text
</course>
```

ZeroOrMore/oneOrMore

When a pattern must be matched at least zero or one times and may be repeated any number of times, you can use the zeroOrMore and oneOrMore patterns. The content of the courses element, from Listing 3-38, can be empty or contain any number of course elements:

```
<element name="courses" xmlns="http://relaxng.org/ns/structure/1.0">
   <zeroOrMore>
      <element name="course">
         <text/>
      </element>
   </zeroOrMore>
</element>
```

If at least one course element were required, you would use the oneOrMore pattern. Consider a document that consisted of a document element named document that could contain any number of title and author elements. These elements may also appear in any order. From the previous pattern, you know you must use the interleave pattern so elements can appear in any order. Both elements are not required in the document, but at least one of them must appear as a child element of the document element. One way to accomplish this is using the choice pattern. The choice will make sure that at least one of the element patterns match. This still leaves you with only a single element. You must apply the oneOrMore pattern so that multiple choices may be selected. For example:

```
<element name="document" xmlns="http://relaxng.org/ns/structure/1.0">
   <oneOrMore>
      <interleave>
         <mixed>
            <choice>
               <element name="title">
                  <text/>
               </element>
               <element name="author">
                  <text/>
               </element>
            </choice>
         </mixed>
      </interleave>
   </oneOrMore>
</element>
```

Even though this may seem like a complicated pattern, it is actually simple. Reading the definition from top-down, you know that the element named document can have content containing one or more, in any order, title elements and/or author elements, which may also be mixed with text content. The mixed pattern was added within the interleave, and the text pattern was removed from the choice pattern to ensure that at least one element is required while still allowing for text content to be mixed in the document content.

List

The list pattern is similar to the NMTOKENS data type. It will match the patterns defined as its contents where the tokens are separated by whitespace:

```
<element name="course" xmlns="http://relaxng.org/ns/structure/1.0"
        datatypeLibrary="http://www.w3.org/2001/XMLSchema-datatypes">
    <attribute name="code">
        <list>
            <data type="integer" />
            <data type="integer" />
            <data type="integer" />
        </list>
    </attribute>
    <empty/>
</element>
```

This schema defines the value of the code attribute to consist of exactly three integers separated by whitespace. A document based on this schema could look like this:

```
<course code=" 1 2 3 4" />
```

Lists are used with patterns that can provide a distinct value, such as a data type or attribute value:

```
<element name="food" xmlns="http://relaxng.org/ns/structure/1.0">
    <attribute name="group">
        <list>
            <oneOrMore>
                <choice>
                    <value>meat</value>
                    <value>fruit</value>
                    <value>dairy</value>
                    <value>grain</value>
                </choice>
            </oneOrMore>
        </list>
    </attribute>
    <text/>
</element>
```

The element food must have a group attribute with a value consisting of one or more of the possible values separated by whitespace. A document validating against this schema could be as follows:

```
<food group="dairy grain">Milk and Bread</food>
```

Elements

You have seen two ways to define an element. One uses the name attribute, and the other uses a nameClass. In both cases, the actual content of the element, when instantiated in an XML document, must also be defined as a pattern. The nameClass section used the empty pattern, which means the content of the element must be empty. You have also seen that the text pattern indicates that the element can contain only text. I mentioned that you could also use the string data type, so let's take a look at the differences.

Text Pattern vs. String Data Type Specifying an element with content matching the text pattern and defining the element to be of the string data type may seem like they function in the same way. In their simplest forms they do. The following examples are pretty much equivalent:

```
<!-- element using text pattern -->
<element>
    <anyName/>
    <text/>
</element>

<!-- element using string data type -->
<element>
    <anyName/>
    <data type="string" />
</element>
```

In this case, the two definitions allow the same content. It is preferable to use the text pattern, because it's a native RELAX NG pattern.

The type of schema you are writing helps drive the decision for which to use as well. If, in the future, you need to expand the element to allow for mixed content, you could easily do it using the text pattern with other patterns. By setting the data type to string, the content is fixed to only text content. If the schema being designed were to be used to validate data that is coming from a database, string is probably the better choice. Using the data type, you could explicitly set the minimum and maximum lengths so that it would match the constraints you use for the data in the database.

```
<element>
    <anyName />
    <data type="string">
        <param name="maxLength">25</param>
    </data>
</element>
```

A param element has been added as a child of the data element. The param set is the maxLength attribute for the string data type from XML Schemas. This would enforce the text content to be no more than 25 characters in length. The text pattern does not have this notion. It just cares that the content contains only text.

On the flip side, the string data type now introduces limitations that prevent further extensibility. The element needs to allow for either text content or a child element. With a data type, you are stuck. You need to rewrite the definition. If you have used the text pattern, then you could just extend it:

```
<element>
    <anyName />
    <choice>
        <text/>
        <element>
            <anyName/>
            <empty/>
        </element>
    </choice>
</element>
```

In this case, a choice was added, allowing the content to be either text or any empty element. When deciding which method to use, you should consider what the schema needs to validate. If you need strong data typing, such as in the case of enforcing data from a database, then you should probably use the string data type. If the text were just content, then the text pattern would be the best choice. In most cases, the text pattern is more commonly used over a string data type.

Content Content for an element must be defined, even if the element must be empty. Empty content when pattern matching means the element has no content *and* no attributes. Elements that have no content but do have attributes are able to get around having to define content. When the attribute pattern is included within the element pattern, unless otherwise set, the content for an element is considered to match the empty pattern. For example:

```
<element name="course">
    <empty />
</element>

<element name="course">
    <attribute name="cid" />
</element>
```

This is all legal syntax. The first case explicitly sets the content to empty so would match a course element that has no attributes and is empty. The second case assumes the content is empty but not required to be stated in the definition because an attribute has been defined. This would match on a course element with the attribute cid and empty content.

Although the text pattern does not offer much in limiting the textual content of an element, the value pattern can define allowable content. Take an element named number, where the content is text and must be a number from 1 to 3:

```
<element name="number">
   <choice>
      <value>1</value>
      <value>2</value>
      <value>3</value>
   </choice>
</element>
```

A valid element for this would be <number>2</number>; <number>5</number> would not be valid.

Throughout the RELAX NG section, you have encountered many ways to define the content of an element. The important point to remember is that element content is defined by patterns. To finish off the section on content, I will leave you with a different version of the 1 to 3 content:

```
<element name="number" xmlns="http://relaxng.org/ns/structure/1.0"
         datatypeLibrary="http://www.w3.org/2001/XMLSchema-datatypes">
   <data type="integer">
      <param name="minInclusive">1</param>
      <param name="maxInclusive">3</param>
   </data>
</element>
```

Attributes

Using the attribute pattern is similar to using the element pattern. The differences are allowable content and ordering. When defining an attribute, the content must use patterns that result in a concrete value. Patterns such as zeroOrMore and oneOrMore, unless used with a list pattern, will not work with the value pattern. Attributes cannot have multiple values. Using a list is an exception because a list consists of multiple values combined by whitespace separators to make a single value in the instantiated document. Ordering is also not important when using attribute patterns. Elements match based on the order of their definitions, so the interleave pattern needs to be used to allow random ordering. You can define attributes, on the other hand, in any order and validate them in any order.

Default Type When defining an attribute that has text content with no further constraints, you can define the attribute simply with just the name attribute:

```
<attribute name="attname" />
```

Unlike the element pattern, the attribute pattern defaults to the text pattern for its content. An equivalent, but unnecessary, way to write the definition is as follows:

```
<attribute name="attname">
   <text/>
</attribute>
```

It is much easier to just write a single line and save some typing.

Value Pattern The value pattern offers the ability to provide more control over attribute values than using the text pattern. Using this pattern, not only can specific values be matched upon, but also the type of the acceptable value can also be enforced. Suppose you had an attribute called priority, which should have only the values 1 through 3. You can set the acceptable values using the value pattern for the attribute definition:

```
<attribute name="priority">
    <choice>
        <value type="integer">1</value>
        <value type="integer">2</value>
        <value type="integer">3</value>
    </choice>
</attribute>
```

You use the choice pattern so that the attribute value can match against one of the contained value patterns. The value pattern provides an acceptable value for the instantiated attribute's value, so based on the patterns, the attribute value must match the value 1, 2, or 3. The type attribute, which may be omitted because it's not really necessary, is just enforcing that the values specified are integer types.

Data Types You can also specify attribute values by data types without specifying a specific value. This is something you have become acquainted with already throughout the RELAX NG section. Data types allow the use of the built-in data types from XML Schemas to be used to validate attributes. If the priority attribute from the previous example could be any integer number, it would be written using the data pattern rather than using the value pattern. For example:

```
<attribute name="priority">
    <data type="integer" />
</attribute>
```

You can limit the value the attribute can have to 1, 2, and 3 by leveraging XML Schema components applicable to the data type being used. In this case, the integer data type may indicate the minInclusive and maxInclusive values. These are passed using the param element within the data element content:

```
<attribute name="priority">
    <data type="integer">
        <param name="minInclusive">1</param>
        <param name="maxInclusive">3</param>
    </data>
</attribute>
```

Just as is the case with elements, attributes and their values are matched with patterns. If you can write a pattern that will ultimately result in a legal value for an attribute, then the pattern should work, no matter how complicated it may seem.

Namespaces

Namespaces are handled much differently in RELAX NG than in XML Schemas. In RELAX NG, namespaces are handled by using an ns attribute. Using real namespaces in the schema, those defined by xmlns provide a way to add information in the schema, which is ignored by RELAX NG. All elements and attributes within the schema (which are not in the RELAX NG namespace, http://relaxng.org/ns/structure/1.0), are ignored:

```
<element name="course" xmlns="http://relaxng.org/ns/structure/1.0"
        xmlns:priv="http://www.example.com/Private>
   <zeroOrMore>
      <element name="title" priv:myattribute="I am ignored">
         <text/>
      </element>
      <!-- The following element is ignored -->
      <priv:element name="title">
         <!-- this looks like a dupe but this element is ignored -->
         <!-- ignore name attribute - attributes dono' inherit default namespace -->
      </priv:element>
   </zeroOrMore>
</element>
```

By specifying a namespace outside the RELAX NG namespace, you can add any type of content to the schema. From user notes to custom elements and attributes that you can use in other ways, such as processing the schema as straight XML, they are all ignored when being processed by the RELAX NG processor.

Now that you know that normal namespace usage is not how validation with namespaces is done, you will look at how to handle validation with namespaced documents.

Unqualified Names

Validating namespaced documents is quite easy. The element and attribute patterns can use the ns attribute to specify the namespace that an element or attribute must reside in:

```
<element name="course" ns="http://www.example.com/course">
   <text/>
</element>
```

Based on this definition, matches will be made against these elements:

```
<course xmlns="http://www.example.com/course" />
<c:course xmlns:c="http://www.example.com/course" />
```

but not these elements:

```
<course />
<course xmlns="http://www.example.com/other" />
```

Setting the ns value to an empty string is the same as not including the ns attribute at all. `<element name="course" ns="">` is equivalent to `<element name="course">`.

The namespace set by the ns value on an element definition is inherited by all child elements. You don't need to add an ns attribute to every element within the scope of the defining element. It may be overridden by a child element, which would set the namespace to the new value within the scope of the element providing the new definition. This is one reason to use the ns attribute with an empty string. When in a namespace scope, you may need to change the namespace including using no namespace:

```
<element name="course" ns="http://www.example.com/course">
   <element name="pre-requisite">
      <attribute name="req_next_sem" ns="http://www.example.com/course">
         <data type="boolean"/>
      </attribute>
      <empty/>
   </element>
   <element name="instructor_approval" ns="">
      <data type="boolean"/>
   </element>
</element>
```

The definition for the course element will match a course element within the http://www.example.com/course namespace. The namespace matching is inherited by the pre-requisite element, so in the XML document a pre-requisite element must also reside in this namespace. You will notice that the namespace had to be added to the attribute definition as well. If you recall, attributes do not inherit default namespaces, so in order to match against the attribute req_next_sum within the namespace, it must be explicitly defined on the attribute definition. The instructor_approval definition is not in a namespace in the XML document, so for the definition, you must remove the namespace match by setting the ns value to the empty string. It will not work just leaving off the ns attribute as you saw with the pre-requisite element, because the namespace would be inherited from the course definition. An XML document conforming to this schema would look like this:

```
<c:course xmlns:c="http://www.example.com/course">
   <c:pre-requisite c:req_next_sem="true">
   <instructor_approval>true</instructor_approval>
</c:course>
```

Qualified Names

Using qualified names makes it much easier to write schemas for namespaced documents. This is the one case where the true use of namespaces is not ignored by the RELAX NG processor. Rewriting the definition using qualified names rather than ns attributes, the schema would look like this:

```
<element name="c:course" xmlns:c="http://www.example.com/course">
   <element name="c:pre-requisite">
      <attribute name="c:req_next_sem">
         <data type="boolean"/>
      </attribute>
```

```
      <empty/>
   </element>
   <element name="instructor_approval">
      <data type="boolean"/>
   </element>
</element>
```

This code associates the namespace http://www.example.com/course with the prefix c. Within the element and attribute definitions, the value for the name attribute has been prefixed with c. The processor will now match on the name being in the namespace associated with the prefix c. Also notice that the definition for the instructor_approval element no longer needs to set the ns attribute. There is no namespace in scope, because the ns attribute has not been used within the schema, so it effectively will match only against an instructor_approval element that is not in any namespace.

If using both unqualified and qualified names, the qualified name takes precedence over the namespace that is in scope from an ns attribute value. A qualified name would be similar to setting an explicit ns attribute for that element *except* using the qualified name does not affect namespace scope. Whichever namespace may be in scope before using a qualified name continues to stay in scope for children on the definition using the qualified name.

Defines and Grammar

Defines in RELAX NG are like using user-derived named types in XML Schemas. Using a define, you can give a pattern a name that then can be referred to within your schema. For simple schemas, this may not offer much advantage but simplifies things when using a complex pattern that needs to be used in many places.

To name a pattern, the schema changes structure a bit from what you have come accustomed to so far. A grammar element is needed that encapsulates the schema. You may think of this as having to use the schema element in an XML Schema. Within the grammar element, a start element is used, which indicates the start pattern to match an XML document against. The content of the start element would be the top of the schemas you have been exploring earlier in this chapter. If you take the original schema from Listing 3-38 and place it within a grammar element, it would look like this:

```
<?xml version="1.0" encoding="utf-8" ?>
<grammar xmlns="http://relaxng.org/ns/structure/1.0">
   <start>
      <element name="courses">
         <zeroOrMore>
            <element name="course"
                     datatypeLibrary="http://www.w3.org/2001/XMLSchema-datatypes">
               <attribute name="cid">
                  <data type="ID"/>
               </attribute>
               <element name="title">
                  <text/>
               </element>
```

```
                    <element name="description">
                        <text/>
                    </element>
                    <element name="credits">
                        <data type="decimal"/>
                    </element>
                    <element name="lastmodified">
                        <data type="dateTime"/>
                    </element>
                    <zeroOrMore>
                        <element name="pre-requisite">
                            <attribute name="cref">
                                <data type="IDREF"/>
                            </attribute>
                            <attribute name="req_next_sem">
                                <data type="boolean"/>
                            </attribute>
                            <element name="instructor_approval">
                                <data type="boolean"/>
                            </element>
                        </element>
                    </zeroOrMore>
                </element>
            </zeroOrMore>
        </element>
    </start>
</grammar>
```

All you had to do was place the entire schema within the `<grammar><start></start>` `</grammar>` tags and move the RELAX NG namespace to the `grammar` element. Remember that RELAX NG ignores everything not in its namespace, so if the namespace declaration is not moved, the entire schema is ignored.

Although no repetitive patterns in reality exist that would make sense moving to a define, I will show how to create a named pattern for the patterns contained within the `course` definition. This would allow future use in the event a new type of `course` element were introduced that was not an extension of `course` but instead a distinct type of `course` that had the same internal definition:

```
<?xml version="1.0" encoding="utf-8" ?>
<grammar xmlns="http://relaxng.org/ns/structure/1.0">
    <start>
        <element name="courses">
            <zeroOrMore>
                <element name="course">
                    <ref name="courseContent" />
                </element>
            </zeroOrMore>
        </element>
    </start>
```

```
<define name="courseContent"
        datatypeLibrary="http://www.w3.org/2001/XMLSchema-datatypes">
    <attribute name="cid">
       <data type="ID"/>
    </attribute>
    <element name="title">
       <text/>
    </element>
    <element name="description">
       <text/>
    </element>
    <element name="credits">
       <data type="decimal"/>
    </element>
    <element name="lastmodified">
       <data type="dateTime"/>
    </element>
    <zeroOrMore>
       <element name="pre-requisite">
          <attribute name="cref">
             <data type="IDREF"/>
          </attribute>
          <attribute name="req_next_sem">
             <data type="boolean"/>
          </attribute>
          <element name="instructor_approval">
             <data type="boolean"/>
          </element>
       </element>
    </zeroOrMore>
  </define>

</grammar>
```

The start element now contains only a small piece of the actual pattern to match against. The bulk has been moved to the define element named courseContent. The definition of the course element now just has to use a ref element to refer to the pattern named courseContent. You probably notice that the datatypeLibrary attribute no longer resides on the course definition. No data types are used within the scope of the element anymore, just a ref element. The data types are now in the scope of the define element, so the attribute needs to be moved there. It also would have been perfectly fine to move the datatypeLibrary attribute to the grammar element as well. Since the define attribute is within the scope of the grammar element, it would inherit the library.

External Patterns

The last piece of RELAX NG I will cover deals with accessing external patterns. You have seen how to do similar things with DTDs, using external references, as well as with XML Schemas, using include and import. Relax NG uses an externalRef element to accomplish this:

```
<externalRef href="URI" />
```

This element takes a single href attribute. The value of this element is a URI pointing to the location of the RELAX NG grammar file to use. The file being referenced *must* begin with the grammar tag and indicate the start of the pattern within a start tag. You could take the previous example using the define and move the define into its own file. The main schema would be short and simple:

```
<?xml version="1.0" encoding="utf-8" ?>
<grammar xmlns="http://relaxng.org/ns/structure/1.0">
    <start>
        <element name="courses">
            <zeroOrMore>
                <element name="course">
                    <externalRef href="coursecontent.rng" />
                </element>
            </zeroOrMore>
        </element>
    </start>
</grammar>
```

The ref element has been changed to an externalRef element with the href pointing to the file coursecontent.rng. The contents of the coursecontent.rng file would contain the following:

```
<?xml version="1.0" encoding="utf-8" ?>
<grammar xmlns="http://relaxng.org/ns/structure/1.0">
    <start>
        <ref name="courseContent" />
    </start>

    <define name="courseContent"
            datatypeLibrary="http://www.w3.org/2001/XMLSchema-datatypes">
        <attribute name="cid">
            <data type="ID"/>
        </attribute>
        <element name="title">
            <text/>
        </element>
        <!-- Additional patterns omitted for brevity -->
    </define>

</grammar>
```

The define in the coursecontent.rng file was left intact and a start tag was added, which instructs RELAX NG to begin with the named define courseContent. The define could have also been removed and the contents placed directly within a group tag, which in turn could then be placed within the start tag, but this was written in this manner to illustrate using a ref element within the start tag. A group element would have been needed had this been done because a `start` element may contain only a single element. The `group` element would be used to take the patterns as a whole. This also would mean that the `datatypeLibrary` would have to have been moved to the `group` element so that all the contained patterns would have access to it.

Caution A start element can have only a single element. If your patterns are not contained with a single element, you must either use a named `define` or use a `group` element to encapsulate them.

RELAX NG Summary

Although I've provided a lot of information about RELAX NG (which should be plenty to get you started using it for validation), I have not covered certain areas. Some are not applicable to using RELAX NG in PHP 5, and others are just out of the scope of this book. For further information on RELAX NG, you can find the full specifications and a tutorial at `http://www.relaxing.org/`.

Conclusion

This chapter covered how to validate documents using DTDs, XML Schemas, and RELAX NG. You should now know what validation is and be comfortable with analyzing and writing at least basic schemas after reading this chapter for the first time. It may take longer, and some practice, for you to write more complex schemas, but the information presented in this chapter should be enough to get you through the majority of them.

The next chapter will cover XPath, XPointer, XInclude, and some additional emerging querying technologies.

CHAPTER 4

■ ■ ■

XPath, XPointer, XInclude, and the Future

Examining and constructing XML documents should be simple for you by now. Retrieving information from these documents is one of the biggest steps I haven't covered yet. Chapters 5 and 6 will demonstrate how to navigate XML documents, how to retrieve information from documents, and how to transform documents for presentation. This chapter will introduce you to some of the foundations and concepts that will help you later. The technologies covered here include querying XML using XPath and XPointer and reusing and processing external content through XInclude. I'll also cover some upcoming technologies, such as XQuery and XPath 2.0, that may eventually supercede some of the current technologies.

Introducing XPath

XPath is a language used to locate and retrieve information from an XML tree using expressions. The language not only can be used by itself, but it also plays a role when using XSLT and XPointer. The following sections will introduce you to XPath as well as cover how to write XPath expressions. This coverage will also serve as a foundation for the concepts in the "Introducing XPointer" section and in Chapter 10, which will cover XSLT. The information in this chapter pertains to the XPath 1.0 specification from the W3C (http://www.w3.org/TR/xpath).

Concepts

Before jumping right into working with XPath expressions, you need to understand some basic concepts. This coverage will serve as the foundation for understanding and building expressions. Specifically, I'll cover the data model and location paths, and throughout the upcoming sections, I'll use the document in Listing 4-1 as reference. This document may look familiar from previous chapters. I have added the namespace http://www.example.com/title and associated it with the prefix t to illustrate some of the namespace features of XPath.

Listing 4-1. *Course Document*

```
<!DOCTYPE courses [
    <!ATTLIST course cid ID #REQUIRED>
    <!ATTLIST pre-requisite cref IDREF #REQUIRED>
]>
<!-- A small course document -->
<courses xmlns:t="http://www.example.com/title">
    <course cid="c1">
        <t:title>Basic Languages</t:title>
        <description>Introduction to Languages</description>
    </course>
    <course cid="c2">
        <t:title>French I</t:title>
        <description>Introduction to French</description>
    </course>
    <course cid="c3">
        <t:title>French II</t:title>
        <description>Intermediate French</description>
        <pre-requisite cref="c2" />
        <?php print "Hello World"; ?>
        <?phpx Another PI Node ?>
    </course>
</courses>
```

Data Model

XPath views an XML document as an XML tree. The tree is broken down into nodes consisting of a root node, element nodes, attribute nodes, text nodes, namespace nodes, comment nodes, and PI nodes. When using XPath, the xml declaration and document type declaration are completely ignored. In other words, they are not considered part of the tree. This includes all comment and PI nodes that may occur within the document type declaration. XPath doesn't contain any references, because all entity references are expanded and all character references are resolved.

Every node has a string value that may be part of the node or may be computed based on the string values of the descendant nodes. Some nodes also have an *expanded name*, which consists of the local name and the namespace URI. As you remember from Chapter 2, namespaces are applicable to elements and attributes. Namespace nodes fall into the same category as attributes, so you could reason that the element nodes, attribute nodes, and namespace nodes would have expanded names, and the rest of the nodes would not. When comparing expanded names from two nodes, the prefix does not matter. Expanded names are equal as long as the local name and the namespace URI are the same. Nodes with the same name and not residing in any namespace would then be considered as having the same expanded name. The local names are the same, and both have empty namespace URIs.

XPath also follows document ordering. This means most nodes are ordered as they appear within the hierarchy of the tree. The exceptions are attribute and namespace nodes. Namespace nodes always come before attribute nodes, and within their subgroups, the namespace nodes and attributes nodes can appear in any order. The namespace and attributes nodes, however, come before the children of the element.

Every node also has a parent node, except the root node. It is impossible for the root node to have a parent, because it is the start of the tree. The parent for element, comment, and PI nodes are either the root node or an element node, depending upon where the node exists within the tree. The rest of the nodes will have an element node as parents because these remaining nodes cannot live outside the document element. Although every node, except the root node, has exactly one parent, element nodes can have a number of descendants. Descendant nodes are nodes other than attribute and namespace nodes that live within the scope of the element.

Root Node

Conceptually, you can consider the *root node* to be the encompassing document. Do not confuse this with the document element, which is the top-level element of the document. The root node is the base of the tree, with branches that can consist of comments, PIs, and the document element. Because the XML must be well-formed, you will have, at a minimum, the document element. Comments and PIs can live on the same level as the document element, so without a root node, you would have no way to access those nodes.

This node has no expanded name. The root node, being a conceptual node in the tree, cannot be assigned a name or namespace and thus cannot have an expanded name. Its string value, on the other hand, consists of a concatenation of all the text nodes' descendants as they appear in the document order. Thinking of the text node parents and document order, the value consists of the concatenation of the values of all text nodes, because they appear in the hierarchy within the document element.

Element Nodes

Every element within the document has an *element node*, and every document must have at least one element, the document element. The expanded name of an element node consists of its local name and its namespace URI. The string value for this node is a concatenation of all descendant text nodes. In the case of the document element, the string value will be the same as the string value of the root node. Unique IDs also come into play with element nodes, as you will see later in the "Expressions and Predicates" section. You can also find more information on IDs in Chapter 2.

Attribute Nodes

Attribute nodes are associated with element nodes. The element node is the parent of the attribute node, but the attribute node *is not* a child of the element node. The location of an attribute node is determined by where it has been explicitly defined or is automatically defaulted from a DTD. Attributes that are inherited, such as `xml:lang` and `xml:space`, are considered attributes only from the element that defined these attributes, even though the attribute may affect children of the element.

The expanded name of an attribute contains the same pieces as an element. It is a combination of the local name and the namespace URI. The string value, however, is different from an element. For an attribute node, the string value is the normalized value of the attribute. Take, for example, the following element: `<element att1=" 1 " />`. The string value for the att1 attribute node is 1. The value has been normalized, so the leading and trailing spaces have been removed.

As you will see in the "Namespace Nodes" section, attributes that declare namespaces are not attribute nodes. These nodes are actually namespace nodes and are handled differently than attribute nodes.

In the following example, the attribute p is not an attribute node, but rather a namespace node, because it is declaring the namespace http://www.example.com:

```
<element xmlns:p="http://www.example.com" />
```

Text Nodes

Text nodes are groups of character data (or blocks of text content). Do not confuse text content in XPath terms with what you have read in previous chapters. Comments and PIs are their own node types in XPath, and text nodes consist of CDATA and pure string text content. When using CDATA, text nodes contain only the values of the CDATA. The markup tags <![CDATA[and]]> are not included in a text node, so the string value of <![CDATA[Hello World]]> is Hello World. If you are reading the XPath specification, you may notice that it says text nodes never have other text nodes as siblings. In the pure sense of XPath, this is correct, but when used with PHP 5 extensions, such as the DOM extension or the SimpleXML extension, you may run into cases where text nodes have other text nodes as siblings. This is perfectly legal because this is based on using DOM XPath. It should also be obvious that text nodes are children of element nodes and do not have expanded names. Namespaces do not apply to text content, and text nodes are not given names.

Namespace Nodes

Namespace nodes are associated with elements and consist of all namespaces that are in scope for an element. This is important to remember. This includes not just namespaces declared on the element but all namespaces in scope for the element. Another important point is that the xml prefix is implicitly declared for a document, so a document not declaring any namespaces will still have at least one namespace. For example:

```
<mydoc xmlns:p="http://www.example.com/mydoc">
    <myelement />
</mydoc>
```

In this example, within the context of the mydoc element, you have two namespace nodes: the implicit one for the xml prefix and the one declared with the prefix p. Because the prefix p is defining a namespace, it is a namespace node and not an attribute. Although the element itself is not in the http://www.example.com/mydoc namespace, this namespace was still declared within the context of the element. Looking at the myelement element, you may guess that it has zero namespace nodes, or maybe you remembered that it is in the scope of the implicit xml prefix and guessed that it has one namespace node. Either way, you are incorrect. The myelement element, even though it is not in a namespace, is not only in the scope of the xml prefix but also in the scope of the http://www.example.com/mydoc namespace. So within the context of the myelement element, you have two namespace nodes.

Namespace nodes have expanded names. The local part is the prefix for the element, and the namespace URI is always NULL. You may be curious why this has a NULL namespace URI. The URI is actually the string value of a namespace node.

Comment Nodes

Every comment within a document has a corresponding *comment node*, excluding comments within the document type declaration (because this is ignored). Comment nodes do not have an expanded name and are children of either the root node or the element nodes. The string value of a comment node is the text value, which consists of all the characters between the `<!--` and `-->` markup. For example, the string value of `<!-- This is a comment -->` is `This is a comment.`

Processing Instruction Nodes

Similar to comment nodes, every PI, except those in the document type declaration, has a corresponding *processing instruction node*. PI nodes do have an expanded name, however. The expanded name consists of a NULL namespace and the target as the local part. The string value of a processing instruction node is the text value following the target and excluding the closing `?>` markup. For example, the string value of `<?php print "Hello World";?>` is `print "Hello World";`.

Location Paths

Location paths are paths used to locate a single node or group of nodes, called a *node set*, within a given XML document. Locations can be absolute or relative. Absolute paths begin with /, indicating that the path is beginning at the root node, and are followed by a relative path. Relative paths are relative to the current context, which is the current location you are at in the document. This is comparable to working on a file system. Consider a directory structure such as `/usr/local/lib`. This is an absolute path, because / indicates the top level of the file system. The next directory, usr, is a relative path, because it is relative to the current position, which is the top of the file system. You would now be positioned in the usr directory, so local, the next location, is relative to usr. If you were already located within the usr dir, you could use a relative path, `local/lib`, to move to the lib directory. XPath location paths work in a similar fashion. Relative paths in XPath are broken into steps separated by /. Compared to the absolute path for the file system example, you would have three steps: usr, local, and lib. This is just an analogy, but the concept is similar.

Each XPath step consists of three parts: axes, node tests, and zero or more predicates. The syntax is `axis::node_test[predicates]`. The combination of axis and node_test results in an initial node set that is further filtered by any predicates in the order they appear. You'll now examine the three parts to see how you can find nodes within an XML document.

Axes

An *axis* specifies the relationship between the context node, which is the current location in the tree, and the nodes to be selected. The location of the nodes to be selected, in the specified step, is determined by the axis relative to the context node. You can specify 13 axes, as shown in Table 4-1.

Table 4-1. *XPath Axes*

Axis	Description
ancestor	Selects the ancestors of the context node. The parent of the current node and all nodes higher in the tree, such as grandparents and their parents, will be selected.
ancestor-or-self	Selects the ancestors of the context node as well as the current node.
attribute	Selects the attributes of the context node, which, unless the current node is an element, will be empty.
child	Selects the immediate children of the context node.
descendant	Selects all nodes within the scope of the context node, such as child nodes and grandchildren. Attributes and namespace nodes are not included in the node set.
descendant-or-self	Selects the descendant nodes as well as the context node.
following	Selects all nodes, except attribute and namespace nodes, following the context node in document order while excluding the descendants of the context node.
following-sibling	Selects all sibling nodes that follow the context node. If the current node is an attribute or namespace node, no nodes are selected.
namespace	Selects all namespaces of the context node, which, unless the current node is an element node, will be empty.
parent	Selects the parent of the context node.
preceding	Selects all nodes that precede the context node, excluding ancestors, attributes, and namespace nodes. This axis basically selects all the nodes of the preceding siblings and their descendants.
preceding-sibling	Selects all preceding siblings of the context node. If this context node is an attribute or namespace node, then no nodes are selected.
self	Selects only the context node.

An axis alone is not enough to define a step, as the actual nodes to be selected still have not been indicated. It does define a principal node type indicating the type of nodes that can be contained. For example, the attribute axis has a principal node type of attribute. This axis will contain attribute nodes. The namespace axis has a principal node type of namespace, because it will contain namespace nodes. The other axes have principal node types of element. Although they can contain other types, such as comment nodes or PI nodes, the primary type is element. This means unless explicitly indicated through the node test, the node set will consist of elements.

Node Tests

A *node test* identifies the actual nodes to be selected from the specified axis. It can be either a name test or a node type test.

Name Tests   A *name test* identifies nodes by name that are of the primary node types of the axis. A name test has three forms. It can be a QName, the special character *, or NCName:*.

A QName selects nodes of the primary node type that have expanded names equal to the expanded name of the QName. Using Listing 4-1 as an example, you can select all the description nodes with the following path:

```
/child::courses/descendant::description
```

Examining this path, you can see it begins with /. This means the location is absolute and starts at the root node. The first step in the path is `child::courses`. The current context at this point is the root node. Within this context, the axis is `child`, and the node test is a name test with a QName of `courses`. The document contains two child nodes, the comment and the `courses` node. As you recall, XPath ignores the document type declaration. A name test is being used, so only nodes of the primary node type, which is an element when using the `child` axis, will be tested. The expanded name of the `courses` element, which is `courses`, is tested against that of the supplied QName, which is also `courses`. Being that they are equal, the first step in the path results in the document element, `courses`.

The next step in the path is `descendant::description`. At this point, the `courses` element is the context node from the previous step. Breaking up this step, the selected nodes will come from the descendants of the `courses` node that match the `description` QName. From Table 4-1, you can see that the `descendant` axis will select all the nodes within the scope of the context node. The results of the full XPath expression will be a node set containing the three `description` elements from the document:

```
<description>Introduction to Languages</description>
<description>Introduction to French</description>
<description>Intermediate French</description>
```

An easier way to write this would be `/descendant::description`. There really was no need for the first step in the original path other than for illustration purposes. To select the `title` elements, you need to take into account the namespace. The QName for the `title` elements is `t:title`. To match these, the path could be something along the lines of `/descendant::t:title`.

You also must take namespace scope into account. When using the prefix in the name test, the prefix refers to the prefix associated with the namespace that is in scope of the context node. If one of the `course` elements looked like the following:

```
<course cid="c2" xmlns:q="http://www.example.com/title">
   <q:title>French IV</q:title>
   <description>Advanced French</description>
</course>
```

then the `title` element contained here would also be returned from the `/descendant::t:title` path. The prefix t defined on the document element is associated with the same namespace as the prefix q defined on this local `course` element. Changing the prefix association will also affect the selected results. Listing 4-2 shows the new `course` element.

Listing 4-2. *New* course *Element*

```
<course cid="c2" xmlns:t="http://www.example.com/DIFFERENT">
   <t:title>French IV</t:title>
   <description>Advanced French</description>
</course>
```

The `title` element in Listing 4-2 is no longer in the `http://www.example.com/title` namespace. The path `/descendant::t:title` is really selecting all `title` elements that reside in the `http://www.example.com/title` namespace. The `title` element in Listing 4-2, although having the same prefix, resides in the `http://www.example.com/DIFFERENT` namespace so would not be selected from the XPath query.

A names test can also be the * character. This wildcard can match any QName of the primary node type. This time, select all attributes from all the `course` elements, like so:

```
/descendant::course/attribute::*
```

The first step in this path selects every `course` element in the document. Using the `descendant` axis in the context of the root node selects every element node, because an element is the primary node type of `descendant` that matches the QName `course`. The last step uses the `course` elements as the context and selects every attribute node. Because the match is based on *, there are no restrictions of the QName from the attribute nodes.

The last name test takes the form of `NCName:*`. This test is a combination of the QName and * tests. It allows nodes to be selected based on namespace only. `NCName` is the prefix of a namespace in scope at the current context, and * indicates to match all local names. In Listing 4-1, all the elements within the `http://www.example.com/title` namespace could be returned by the path `/child::courses/descendant::t:*`. Every `title` element in the document would be selected, because these are the only elements within the specified namespace. The element from Listing 4-2 would not match, because the `title` element in that case is not in the namespace on which you are searching.

Node Type Test A *node type test* selects specific node types from the axis. The primary node type of the axis is not taken into account. As long as the node type is valid for the axis, then the nodes will be selected. For example, valid child nodes for the root node are comments, elements, and processing instructions. Valid child nodes for an element, however, are comments, elements, processing instructions, and text. Valid node type tests are `comment()`, `text()`, `processing-instruction()`, `processing-instruction('name')`, and `node()`. No specific element node test exists. The reason for this is that an element is already the primary node type for an axis from which an element node can be selected. For this reason, the * character for the test serves the same purpose.

Using the document in Listing 4-1, you could select the comment node using the path `/child:comment()`. You can select all the children, including text nodes (which is the insignificant whitespace), of the `courses` element using `/child::courses/child::node()`. This path will select seven nodes (consisting of four text nodes, line feeds, and tabs) that are intermixed with the three `course` element nodes.

Selecting PIs works the same way. The path `/child::courses/descendant::➡ processing-instruction()` will select both PIs within the last `course` element, and the path `/child::courses/descendant::processing-instruction('php')` will select only the PI with the target `php`.

Predicates

Predicates filter the node set from the combined axis and node test. They are expressions that are evaluated for each node in the node set and return a Boolean. Each node in the node set that evaluates to `TRUE` from the expression is included in the node set; those that evaluate to `FALSE` are excluded. More than a single predicate is allowed, and you can combine them using Boolean operators. I'll explain predicates in more detail later in this chapter in the section "Expressions and Predicates."

Abbreviated Syntax

Some abbreviated syntax is available for a few of the axis and node test combinations. (I'll explain the abbreviated syntax for some predicates in the "Expressions and Predicates" section.) Table 4-2 lists some of the syntax available within XPath.

Table 4-2. *Abbreviated Syntax*

Axis and Node Test	Abbreviated Syntax
`attribute::QName`	`@QName`
`attribute::*`	`@*`
`child::QName`	`QName`
`child::*`	`*`
`child::nodetype()`	`nodetype()`
`descendant-or-self::node()/`	`//` (This would be an empty step in the path.)
`parent::node()`	`..`
`self::node()`	`.`

Taking all the paths you have encountered so far in this chapter, you can write their equivalents using abbreviated syntax. Listing 4-3 shows the comparable paths. The first path uses full syntax, and its corresponding abbreviated path follows it on the next line.

Listing 4-3. *Full Paths and Corresponding Abbreviated Paths*

```
/child::courses/descendant::description
/courses//description

/descendant::description
//description

/descendant::t:title
//t:title

/descendant::course/attribute::*
//course/@*

/child::courses/descendant::t:*
/courses//t:*

/child:comment()
/comment()

/child::courses/child::node()
/courses/node()
```

```
/child::courses/descendant::processing-instruction()
/courses//processing-instruction()

/child::courses/descendant::processing-instruction('php')
/courses//processing-instruction('php')
```

Even with these simple paths, the abbreviated syntax is useful. It is even handier once you begin writing complex paths and expressions.

Expressions and Predicates

Expressions open up the full power of XPath to you. Up to this point, you have worked with just location paths, which can also be used as expressions, containing only axes and node tests. Expressions allow you to create fine-tuned, complex filters via predicates, as well as to retrieve data other than just node sets from XML documents. When writing expressions, you can use some XPath operators, as listed in Table 4-3.

Table 4-3. *XPath Operators*

Operator	Description
+	Addition
-	Subtraction
*	Multiplication
div	Division
mod	Modulus
=	Equal
!=	Not equal
<	Less than
<=	Less than or equal to
>	Greater than
>=	Greater than or equal to
and	Boolean "and"
or	Boolean "or"
|	Union

The XML document in Listing 4-4 contains a listing of produce broken down into fruits and vegetables. I will use this document throughout the following sections to illustrate how to use expressions in XPath.

Listing 4-4. *Produce Document*

```
<?xml version="1.0"?>
<produce>
   <vegetables>
      <vegetable unit="pound">
         <name>tomatoes</name>
         <price>2.99</price>
      </vegetable>
      <vegetable unit="pound">
         <name>string beans</name>
         <price>3.99</price>
      </vegetable>
      <vegetable unit="each" specials="discount">
         <name>lettuce</name>
         <price>0.99</price>
      </vegetable>
   </vegetables>
   <fruits>
      <fruit unit="pound" specials="sale">
         <name>apples</name>
         <price>1.99</price>
      </fruit>
      <fruit unit="pound">
         <name>bananas</name>
         <price>3.99</price>
      </fruit>
      <fruit unit="pint">
         <name>strawberries</name>
         <price>4.99</price>
         <time>seasonal</time>
      </fruit>
   </fruits>
</produce>
```

Basic Filtering

Simple node sets and value comparisons are the easiest place to begin understanding expressions. Since you should be comfortable with the basics of location paths and node selections at this point, you will now look at how you can use node sets as expressions within a predicate.

Node Sets

Based on the document in Listing 4-4, you can select the elements containing the attribute specials with the following expression:

```
//*[@specials]
```

The path, excluding the predicate, selects all elements within the document. The predicate filters these nodes based on the criteria of having an attribute named specials. @specials evaluates to TRUE if the attribute node exists and FALSE if it doesn't. This is how the evaluation of node sets as expressions work. If the node set within the expression contains at least one node, then it is TRUE. If you think of this in terms of a SQL query, it would be similar to saying, "Select all elements from the document where the element contains the attribute named specials." The equivalent method to writing the expression using the full syntax is /descendant-or-self::node()/*[attribute::specials].

The node set used for filtering is not limited to just using attribute nodes. For example, how could you select the elements containing a child element named time? Looking at the document, you know only one element, fruit, has a child element named time. Although you know what the document currently looks like, assume that any of the elements might contain this attribute. The first step is to write a location path that selects all the elements:

//*

Now that every element is to be selected, each node in the node set needs to be tested for having a child element named time:

//*[time]

This is similar to filtering based on an attribute. In this case, however, you don't need an axis within the predicate. The location path //* is the abbreviated syntax for /descendant-or-self::node()/*. Based on this path and the last *, the primary node type is element. Within the predicate, you just give the element name time, which is the abbreviation for child::time. The equivalent full syntax is /descendant-or-self::node()/*[child::time]. Each of these expressions will ultimately select the single fruit element in the document containing the time element.

The expression does not need to be just a simple axis and node test. You can also use location paths. In this case, you must take into account the context of the node being tested. Searching for time elements that have a parent element named fruit requires filtering based on the name of a relative node. In this case, you must test the parent node. The first step, as always, is to write the location path for the nodes to select:

//time

The next step is to filter this node set using a predicate. Nodes must be filtered on the condition that they have a parent node named fruit:

//time[../self::fruit]

The predicate here uses the relative location .., which means "move to the parent of the context node." The context node, remember, is the node currently being tested at the time. Each node in the node set would be tested, so each node would be in context at some point or another while applying the predicate. The next step in the path selects self, which points to the parent of a time element from the original node set and matches against the name fruit. In simple terms, the expression breaks down to select all time elements that have a parent, and the parent (the self in the predicate) has the name fruit. And in case you are wondering, you could have written this much more simply by just using the following:

//time[parent::fruit]

This, however, wouldn't have been as fun to explain.

Value Comparisons

In many cases, node selection isn't dependant upon the structure of the document but upon values within the document. When comparing node sets to numbers, the string value of the node is converted to a number and compared to the number. A string comparison is performed using the string value of the node against the string. These conversions are automatic, but you can also call functions, which I'll explain later in the "XPath Functions" section, to do the conversion.

String Comparisons

The first example for expressions using node sets selected all the elements that contained the specials attribute. If this attribute could have only a single value and was not present when it did not pertain to the element, the expression would be fine. In Listing 4-4, two elements contain the specials attribute, and the value is different for each of them. Refining the node selection, only elements containing the attribute specials and having the value sale should be selected:

```
//*[@specials="sale"]
```

This will select a single fruit element:

```
<fruit unit="pound" specials="sale">
    <name>apples</name>
    <price>1.99</price>
</fruit>
```

You can achieve the same results by selecting all elements containing a specials attribute node that has a value not equal to discount:

```
//*[@specials != "discount"]
```

You can also perform comparisons on elements. The string value of an element is the content of the text nodes of all descendants concatenated together. You must be careful when performing comparisons with element nodes, because you must be sure you have taken this into account. This example selects elements that contain the child element name containing the text lettuce:

```
//*[name="lettuce"]
```

The predicate used to filter the node set in this case is name="lettuce". As you probably recall from earlier examples, you do not need an axis in this predicate. The primary node type is an element node, and the child axis is already implied. This expression is the same as writing //*[child::name="lettuce"]. The comparison taking place within the predicate is against the node set containing the child element name with the string lettuce. The element node is converted to a string, and in Listing 4-4, all name elements have only text content. It is the text content that is compared to the string lettuce. This expression results in the selection of a single vegetable element:

```
<vegetable unit="each" specials="discount">
    <name>lettuce</name>
    <price>0.99</price>
</vegetable>
```

Numeric Comparisons

Numeric comparisons are similar to string comparisons, except in this instance the value of the element or attribute is converted to a number rather than a string. Within the document, each one of the fruit and vegetable elements contains the child element price. When writing expressions, say you would like to test price numerically rather than textually. For this example, all fruit and vegetable elements that have a price greater than 1.99 will be selected:

```
//*[price > 1.99]
```

This expression selects the two vegetable elements and the two fruit elements having prices greater than 1.99. Similarly, you can select the elements with a price less than or equal to 1.99:

```
//*[price <= 1.99]
```

Advanced Filtering

With the basic concepts of filtering behind you, you can start diving into the fun stuff. The expressions to this point have been basic and unoptimized. The following sections will show more complex expressions as well as explain ways to optimize them. Optimization is important, because it helps reduce the amount of processing that needs to take place, which in turn results in faster execution time. Before getting to that, though, I'll touch on XPath built-in functions, which can be useful when writing expressions.

XPath Functions

XPath implements a core library of functions you can use to evaluate expressions. The functions are broken up into specific areas. These areas include node set, string, Boolean, and number functions. Tables 4-4, 4-5, 4-6, and 4-7 describe the functions for each area.

■**Note** In the following tables, optional parameters are enclosed in brackets, []. A parameter that is not required, yet can be repeated any number of times, is followed by *. An object parameter can be a node set, Boolean, number, or string.

Table 4-4. *XPath Node Set Functions*

Function	Description
last()	Returns the number of items in the node set.
position()	Returns the one-based index of the context node.
count(node-set)	Returns the number of nodes in the node set.
id(object)	Selects elements based on their IDs. If object is a node set, then each of the string values of the nodes are supplied as arguments to the id function. A string parameter may be a whitespace-separated list of strings.

Function	Description
local-name([*node-set*])	Returns the local-name portion of the expanded name for the first node of the *node-set* in document order. If *node-set* is empty or the first node does not have an expanded name, an empty string is returned. If *node-set* is omitted, the context node is used as the parameter value.
namespace-uri([*node-set*])	Returns the namespace URI of the expanded name for the first node of the *node-set* in document order. If *node-set* is empty or the first node does not have an expanded name, an empty string is returned. If *node-set* is omitted, the context node is used as the parameter value.
name([*node-set*])	Returns the QName for the first node of the *node-set* in document order. If *node-set* is empty or the first node does not have an expanded name, an empty string is returned. If *node-set* is omitted, the context node is used as the parameter value.

Table 4-5. *XPath String Functions*

Function	Description
string([*object*])	Converts *object* to a string. If *object* is omitted, the context node is used as the parameter value.
concat(*string, string, string**)	Returns the concatenation of the *string* parameters.
starts-with(*string1, string2*)	Returns Boolean TRUE if *string1* starts with *string2* and otherwise FALSE.
contains(*string1, string2*)	Returns Boolean TRUE if *string1* contains *string2* and otherwise FALSE.
substring-before(*string1, string2*)	Returns string from *string1* that precedes the beginning of the substring, *string2*, found in *string1*. If not found, an empty string is returned.
substring-after(*string1, string2*)	Returns string from *string1* that follows the end of the first substring, *string2*, found in *string1*. If not found, an empty string is returned.
substring(*string, start* [,*length*])	Returns the substring found in *string* beginning at the one-based position *start* with a length of *length*. If *length* is not supplied, all characters to the end of string are returned.
string-length([*string*])	Returns the number of characters in *string*. If *string* is not supplied, the string value of the context node is used as the argument.
normalize-space([*string*])	Returns the normalized string of *string*. If *string* is not supplied, the string value of the context node is used as the argument.
translate(*string1, string2, string3*)	Translates the characters in *string1* matching those in *string2* into characters from *string3*. For example, translate('abcdefgh', 'aceg', 'ACE') results in AbCdEfh. The g is removed because it is a character to match and because a corresponding character in *string3* does not exist.

Table 4-6. *XPath Boolean Functions*

Function	Description
boolean(*object*)	Returns the Boolean value of objects. A number is TRUE unless it is a positive zero, a negative zero, or NaN. Node sets are TRUE unless empty. Strings are TRUE unless empty.
not(*boolean*)	Returns the opposite of the Boolean passed in. TRUE becomes FALSE, and FALSE becomes TRUE.
true()	Returns TRUE.
false()	Returns FALSE.
lang(*string*)	Returns a Boolean indicating whether the specified xml:lang identified by the lang parameter is within the scope of the context node.

Table 4-7. *XPath Number Functions*

Function	Description
number(*object*)	Converts *object* to a number. Boolean TRUE is converted to 1 and FALSE to 0. A string having a numeric value (all numeric) will convert to a numeric; otherwise, it will convert to NaN. A node set is converted to a string, which is then converted to a number.
sum(*node-set*)	Returns the sum of each node, converted to a number, in the *node-set*.
floor(*number*)	Returns the largest integer not greater than *number*.
ceiling(*number*)	Returns the smallest integer not less than *number*.
round(*number*)	Returns the closest integer to *number*.

Throughout this chapter, I'll use many of the functions in Tables 4-4, 4-5, 4-6, and 4-7 within the examples because it is easier to understand their use and functionality within some context. With everything that has been covered up to now, you can begin looking at more complex expressions and optimization.

XPath Optimization

Some people consider optimization to be an art form. XPath can require a lot of processor power depending upon the size of the document, its structure, and the expressions you write. XPath works on a document loaded into memory, so when the document is large, not only do you have the overhead of this large document in memory but you must also consider the processing involved to select the nodes for which you are looking. Pretty much every query, meaning the location paths and expressions, written to this point have searched all the nodes in a document. They have used the // notation, which means they are searching the root node and all its descendants, and have filtered the node sets from there.

The document in Listing 4-5 is a condensed document that in theory would have many book, magazine, and cd elements along with much more content for these elements. I will use this document to illustrate some basic optimization throughout this chapter as you encounter more and more advanced documents.

Listing 4-5. *Abbreviated Store Document*

```
<store>
   <books>
      <book>
         <name>Cannery Row</name>
      </book>
      <!-- Many book elements -->
   </books>
   <magazines>
      <magazine>
         <title>fdsfsd</title>
      </magazine>
      <!-- Many magazine elements -->
   </magazines>
   <cds>
      <!-- cd elements -->
   </cds>
</store>
```

If you wanted to select all the book elements in the document, you might first just write the following expression:

```
//book
```

The problem with this expression is that the node set to be filtered contains every element in the document. This is a big waste of resources, because the name of every element in the document will have to be tested against book. This includes all the magazine and cd elements as well. You have an idea of the structure of the document and know that book elements reside within the books element, so specifying a more precise path can cut down processing significantly.

This is a much more precise query:

```
/store/books/book
```

Using this query, the expression first filters all books elements that are children of the root element. Additional filtering from this resulting set then takes place by matching all the child elements of the resulting books elements that are named book. Because you have already excluded the magazines and cds subtrees with the second step in the path, you have cut the processing down by two-thirds. The amount of time and processing saved really depends upon how many magazine and cd elements exist in the document, but you may have just saved yourself a good deal of time because you can use your system resources for other tasks. You will encounter more optimizations as you read about complex expressions and functions next.

Complex Expressions and Documents

You can now start putting all the topics in this chapter together. The following sections will cover everything you have encountered to create complex queries. I'll use the document in Listing 4-6 as the document from which to make selections.

Listing 4-6. *Expanded Store Document*

```
<store xmlns="http://www.example.com/store" xmlns:bk="http://www.example.com/book"
       xmlns:mag="http://www.example.com/magazine">
    <books>
        <rare>
            <bk:book qty="4">
                <bk:name>Cannery Row</bk:name>
                <bk:price>400.00</bk:price>
                <bk:pubdate>1945-01-01</bk:pubdate>
                <bk:authors>
                    <bk:author>Steinbeck, John</bk:author>
                </bk:authors>
                <bk:edition>1</bk:edition>
                <bk:signed>true</bk:signed>
            </bk:book>
            <bk:book qty="1">
                <bk:name>The Raven and Other Poems</bk:name>
                <bk:price>100000.00</bk:price>
                <bk:pubdate>1845-01-01</bk:pubdate>
                <bk:authors>
                    <bk:author>Poe, Edgar Allan</bk:author>
                </bk:authors>
                <bk:edition>1</bk:edition>
                <bk:signed>true</bk:signed>
            </bk:book>
        </rare>
        <classics>
            <bk:book qty="25">
                <bk:name>Grapes of Wrath</bk:name>
                <bk:price>12.99</bk:price>
                <bk:pubdate>2002-01-01</bk:pubdate>
                <bk:authors>
                    <bk:author>Steinbeck, John</bk:author>
                </bk:authors>
            </bk:book>
            <bk:book qty="25" xmlns:bk="http://www.example.com/classicbook">
                <bk:name>Of Mice and Men</bk:name>
                <bk:price>9.99</bk:price>
                <bk:pubdate>1993-09-01</bk:pubdate>
                <bk:authors>
                    <bk:author>Steinbeck, John</bk:author>
                </bk:authors>
            </bk:book>
        </classics>
```

```
    <classics xmlns="http://www.example.com/ExteralClassics">
        <book qty="33">
            <name>To Kill a Mockingbird</name>
            <price>10.99</price>
            <pubdate>2002-03-01</pubdate>
            <author>Lee, Harper</author>
        </book>
    </classics>
  </books>
  <magazines>
    <mag:magazine qty="75">
        <mag:title>fdsfsd</mag:title>
        <mag:issue>2005-11-01</mag:issue>
        <mag:price>2.99</mag:price>
        <mag:publisher>fsdfdsfsd</mag:publisher>
    </mag:magazine>
    <mag:magazine qty="5">
        <mag:title>fdsfsd</mag:title>
        <mag:issue>2002-10-01</mag:issue>
        <mag:price>2.99</mag:price>
        <mag:publisher>fsdfdsfsd</mag:publisher>
    </mag:magazine>
  </magazines>
  <cds>
    <!-- CD elements go here -->
  </cds>
</store>
```

Dealing with Namespaces As before, you will start by selecting all book elements, using an unoptimized query, from the document. Even if you remembered that this document is using namespaces, you might be tempted to write this:

```
//bk:book
```

This has a few things wrong with it. The first is that the resulting node set will be missing two book elements. Look closely at the last two book elements. The first one redefines the bk prefix association, so this element is no longer in the http://www.example.com/book namespace. The last one is using the default namespace from its parent classics element that defines the namespace http://www.example.com/ExteralClassics. If you recall, node selection by name is by the QName, so you must take into account the namespace of the element. To ensure only book elements are retrieved and you don't have to worry about the namespace, you should write the expression as follows:

```
//*[local-name() = "book"]
```

The expression now checks only the local name of the element, matches against book, and returns all five book elements. This still has another issue, though. Based on how this is written, the node set to be filtered contains every element in the document. This is a big waste of resources, because the local name of every element in the document will have to be tested against book. This includes all the magazine elements as well. You have an idea of the structure of the document and know that book elements reside within the books element, so you can optimize this query.

You might be tempted to write the following query:

```
/store/books/*[local-name() = "book"]
```

Don't be surprised when your results come up empty. The unprefixed elements in the document fall under the default namespace http://www.example.com/store. So, how can you write optimized queries that get around the issue that you have no prefix to use? Most technologies employing XPath offer ways to register namespaces and associated prefixes. You can then use these prefixes for matching QNames. You will see how to do this with regard to the DOM extension in Chapter 6, with regard to the SimpleXML extension in Chapter 7, and with regard to the XSL extension in Chapter 10. For now, I will just show how to write queries that can perform selections without external help.

Note Defaulted namespaces are not as easily dealt with in XPath as those using prefixes. Most XML technologies employing XPath offer ways to associate prefixes with namespaces that then can be used to query XML documents. You will see how to use this technique with regard to the DOM extension in Chapter 6, with regard to the SimpleXML extension in Chapter 7, and with regard to the XSL extension in Chapter 10.

The first step to take is to break the path up and think about how you could find the store element. The immediate idea that may come to mind is to use the same technique you used to filter for the book elements:

```
/*[local-name() = "store"]
```

This would work but can be written much simpler and not require the additional filtering step:

```
/*
```

As mentioned with axes as well as with default node types, * is the abbreviation for child::*, and the default node type is an element node. XML documents can contain only a single document element, and the current location is the root node. Deductively, you can reason that matching every child element of the root node is the same as selecting the document element.

The next step in the path is to select the books element, which is also in the default namespace. In this case, it is perfectly fine to use the local name test, /*/*[local-name() = "books"]. If you know the exact structure of the document, you can also specify the books element by location:

```
/*/*[position()=1]
/*/*[position() < 2]
/*/*[1]
```

All these queries are equivalent. The predicate is filtering based on the position of the node within the node set returned from /*/*. If you can be certain, usually from a DTD or schema, that the first child element of the store element is the books element, then each of the expressions filters for the node that is the first node in document order in the node set. The last expression uses the single numeric 1. A single numeric as an expression is the abbreviation for writing position()=[number].

■**Tip** You can abbreviate the expression [position()=x] as simply [x]. Using a number alone is equivalent to calling the position() function.

Within the books element, the books are contained within parent elements that describe the types. At this point, the types are of no concern, so this step will take the form of *. The last step is to select the book elements. I have already presented the expression for this; you use a check on the local name. Combining all the steps, you could write queries of the following forms:

```
/*/*[local-name() = "books"]/*/*[local-name()="book"]
/*/*[position()=1]/*/*[local-name()="book"]
/*/*[position() < 2]/*/*[local-name()="book"]
/*/*[1]/*/*[local-name()="book"]
```

Each of these queries will result in the selection of the five book elements.

This raises an interesting question. You may know the structure of the document, but how could you select only book elements within the http://www.example.com/classicbook namespace? In Listing 4-6, the book element within this namespace has redefined the bk prefix, so using the QName with a prefix of bk is not an option. The prefix bk will be associated with the http://www.example.com/book namespace because of scoping. You aren't using any technologies at this point that allow you to register a namespace and prefix, so that is also not viable. One way to accomplish this is to test the actual namespace on the element:

```
/*/*[1]/*/*[namespace-uri()="http://www.example.com/classicbook"]
```

Rather than testing for the local name of the element, you can test the actual URI of the namespace. This example assumes no other elements on the same document level as the book elements exist and reside in the same namespace. If this is a possibility, the predicate can include the check of the local name:

```
[local-name()="book" and namespace-uri()="http://www.example.com/classicbook"]
```

In this case, it first makes sure the element has a local name of book and, if that is TRUE, checks whether the namespace URI is http://www.example.com/classicbook. You can also optimize this expression. Once an expression returns FALSE, no further filtering takes place for the current node. In the case of the books element, you can safely assume that the majority of the child elements are book elements. Most of them, however, would not be in the namespace being searched. Checking the namespace URI first would eliminate almost every check for the local name of the node. So, an optimized predicate would be as follows:

```
[namespace-uri()="http://www.example.com/classicbook" and local-name()="book"]
```

Comparisons I demonstrated simple comparisons earlier in this chapter, but that was before the introduction of functions. This section will provide a more in-depth look at expressions performing comparisons as well as calculations. I'll continue to use the document in Listing 4-6 as the document being queried.

Performing a search based on a date may seem like a daunting task. Within the document, the element pubdate is using the format YYYY-MM-DD, which also conforms to the XML Schema date type. Unfortunately, XPath does not offer any date functions, so these values are treated as strings. However, string functions are available that can be manipulated to accomplish the task at hand. So, how do you go about selecting all books and magazines published in 2002?

You will need substring functions to split the date apart. It is a given, because the dates conform to the XML Schema date type, that the first four characters are the year, so using the substring function, the starting position is 1 and the length is 4:

```
/*/*[1]/*/*[*[local-name()="pubdate" and substring(., 1, 4)="2002"]]
```

No, you are not going cross-eyed. This is really a valid XPath query. The initial path should look familiar to you. The path /*/*[1]/*/* is within the books subtree because you are using the first position, and it selects all element nodes on the level at which the book elements reside. Within the document, this selects all book elements, because no other types of elements are on this level within the books subtree. The predicate is where you may get a little bug-eyed.

Breaking the predicate, [*[local-name()="pubdate" and substring(., 1, 4)="2002"]], into pieces, the first * indicates that the filter takes place on all child elements of the current node set. The current node set, in this case, consists of all the book elements. That leaves another predicate: [local-name()="pubdate" and substring(., 1, 4)="2002"]. This predicate is performed on all the child elements of the current node set. The first test is to see whether the local name matches pubdate. If this returns TRUE, then you know the current node being run against this filter is a pubdate element. You can then check the string value of this element using the substring function to see whether the first four characters match 2002. The reason the first parameter is . (a period) is that the context node itself or the current node is being passed as an argument to the function. You can also write the substring function as substring(self::*, 1, 4) or substring(child::text(), 1, 4). An element has a string value that consists of all text nodes within its contents and the contents of its children. Passing in the context node, which must be a pubdate element since it passed the first check, will effectively pass in the text containing the date being searched. This query may have looked complicated but, once broken out, should be easy to understand.

Well, you have selected all the book elements, but the query is supposed to also return all the magazine elements published in 2002. You face a few problems: the elements do not live on the same level within the document, the names of the elements being returned are not the same, the element names containing the dates are not the same, and they also live in different subtrees. For starters, the magazine elements that have an issue date in 2002 will be selected:

```
/*/*[2]/*[*[local-name()="issue" and substring(., 1, 4)="2002"]]
```

This query is almost the same as the query for the book elements. The differences here are that the magazine subtree is being traversed (indicated by the /*/*[2] portion of the path), the steps are not as deep (notice there is a /* removed from the path), and the local name test is now performed against the string issue. The query is broken down the same way the previous book selection was broken down.

This still hasn't selected all the nodes you originally wanted. The node set is supposed to contain both book and magazine elements. Right now, you have two distinct queries. One selects the book elements, and the other selects the magazine elements. An easy way at this point to get the desired results is to use the union operator. This operator joins node sets together. If you thought the previous queries were overwhelming, take a look at how to use a union with the two queries:

```
/*/*[1]/*/*[*[local-name()="pubdate" and substring(., 1, 4)="2002"]] |
/*/*[2]/*[*[local-name()="issue" and substring(., 1, 4)="2002"]]
```

This query is actually a single line. It joins the first query, selecting the book elements, with the second query, selecting the magazine elements using |, which is the union operator.

If you're using XML, you probably tend to be more on the daring side. You must be able to write a query without using the union operator that will select all the elements in one shot, right? A simplified way is to write this:

```
//*[*[(local-name()="pubdate" or local-name()="issue") and
    substring(., 1, 4)="2002"]]
```

This again doesn't fit on a single line, but in the XML world you can ignore insignificant whitespace. This query checks every element in the document to see whether it has a child element with the local name pubdate or issue. If either of these is TRUE, then it checks the substring of the string value for that child element:

```
/*/*[local-name()="books" or local-name()="magazines"]
//*[*[(local-name()="pubdate" or local-name()="issue")
    and substring(., 1, 4)="2002"]]
```

This is another one-liner broken into multiple lines. This is an optimized version of the previous query. The previous query selected every element in the document. In this revised version, it specifies to select only from the books or magazine subtree. The document in Listing 4-6 has a cds tree, which could contain any number of cd elements. Rather than checking those, because only book and magazine elements are to be returned, the two subtrees are explicitly set in the path. Within those subtrees, on the other hand, every element is checked. You will notice the use of // after the predicate for the books and magazines elements. That again is the abbreviation for descendants-or-self::node(), where node() is the element because of the axis.

The following queries are alternative ways to write this query. Each is specific to the document in Listing 4-6. If you added types, such as dvds elements, they may not work.

```
/* Using position of element */
/*/*[position() < 3]//*[*[(local-name()="pubdate" or local-name()="issue")
    and substring(., 1, 4)="2002"]]
```

```
/* Checking for != cds */
/*/*[local-name() != "cds"]//*[*[(local-name()="pubdate" or local-name()="issue")
    and substring(., 1, 4)="2002"]]
```

These queries all select the same node sets. Since I've already covered everything you need to break these queries down, I will leave it up to you to figure out how they work.

Calculations Using functions within XPath allows some calculations to be performed. Calculations and functions are typically reserved for use in a predicate. It is possible, though, for XPath to return results other than node sets.

Using Listing 4-6, you can obtain the sum of all `price` elements. For these examples, brevity over optimization will be the factor for writing the expressions. For example:

```
sum(//*[local-name()="price"])
```

This will return the value 100439.95. This will also retrieve the total number of `price` elements, indicating the number of items in the store:

```
count(//*[local-name()="price"])
```

This returns the value 7. Using these two results, you can obtain the average item price, which will be rounded:

```
round(sum(//*[local-name()="price"]) / count(//*[local-name()="price"]))
```

The resulting value for the rounded average price is 14349.

Using calculations to return non-node sets in XPath is pretty limited. For example, you simply cannot calculate the worth of inventory on hand. This involves taking the `sum` of (`price * qty`) for each item. The `sum` function takes a node set as an argument, so you have no way to perform this mathematically.

You can also perform calculations within the predicate. For some strange reason, your workflow requires that every other `book` element needs to be selected for processing:

```
//*[local-name()="book" and position() mod 2 = 1]
```

The position of the `book` element is tested to find out whether it is odd or even. You can do this through the `position() mod 2` piece of the predicate. The operator `mod` returns the remainder from a truncating division, so the value 1 means the position is odd. This query returns every other `book` element in the document starting with the first one encountered.

XPath Summary

You can use XPath locate and retrieve information from a document. As you have seen, it is simple to use yet offers the ability for advanced and complex querying. In Chapters 6, 7, and 10, which cover the PHP 5 XML extensions, you will be exposed to more XPath techniques. You will not only use it through the extensions but also as the foundation of XSLT.

Introducing XPointer

XPointer is a W3C specification, though still a working draft, used for fragment identification for URI references. It is an extension of XPath so uses the same syntax to address the internal structure of an XML document using a URI. You must perform character escaping for XPointer expressions depending upon the content of the expression. This means that if XPointer is used within a URI, it must follow the same escaping rules a URI follows; for instance, you must escape a space to %20. When used within an XML document, it must follow the escaping rules for XML. For example, XPath uses quotes around string values. XPointer, when embedded within a document, must have the quotes escaped, such as using ".

XPointer and XPath Expressions

XPointer, being an extension of XPath, uses the XPath syntax. This section will not attempt to cover the full XPath syntax, because I explained this earlier. I will use the document in Listing 4-4 to show how to reimplement the XPath expressions here using XPointer. There is little new information in this section because writing XPointer expressions is a simple as this:

```
xpointer(xpath_expression)
```

Taking a few of the example XPath expressions, the equivalent versions in XPointer are as follows:

```
/* Select all elements containing the attribute names specials */
xpointer(//*[@specials])

/* Select all time elements having a parent named fruit */
xpointer(//time[../self::fruit])

/* Select all elements with a child element named price having a value > 1.99 */
xpointer(//*[price > 1.99])
```

XPointer is really as easy as that.

When used with a URI, the `xpointer` part is the document fragment portion of the URI. For example, suppose the produce document from Listing 4-4 was a file located at `http://www.example.com/produce.xml`. The desired result is to retrieve all elements that contain the `specials` attribute, which was the first example listed previously. For example:

```
http://www.example.com/produce.xml#xpointer(//*[@specials])
```

The URL is broken down into two components: the base URL, which is `http://www.example.com/produce.xml`, and the document fragment, `xpointer(//*[@specials])`. In essence, the full URL is equivalent to saying, "Using the `produce.xml` file located at `http://www.example.com`, return all elements containing a `specials` attribute from the document."

As you will see in later sections of this chapter, you don't always need full URLs because you can imply them by other means; therefore, simply using the `xpointer(xpath_expression)` syntax may be enough. It is also worthy to note that XPointer is most often used when employing XInclude, which will be covered in the "Introducing XInclude" section, and XSL, which will be covered in Chapter 10. You will also see XPointer used in conjunction with XLink. I have included a brief introduction to XLink, but this technology is really out of the scope of this book. Currently, XLink is not supported by libxml2, the underlying XML library used within PHP 5, and no future plans exist to support it.

Stacking XPointer Expressions

Another nice feature of XPointer is the ability to stack expressions. If the first expression fails, then the following expression runs. You can add expressions to be processed only if the preceding expression has failed. Continuing to use the data from Listing 4-4, XPointer will first attempt to retrieve all elements with the attribute `specials` having the value `BADVALUE`. This document doesn't have any of these attributes with that value, so the expression fails, and the second expression is processed:

```
xpointer(//*[@specials="BADVALUE"])xpointer(//*[@specials])
```

The results of this will be all elements containing the attribute specials because of the failure of the first expression.

The following example returns the same results as the previous example. The expression xpointer(//*[@specials]) resulted in returning data, so the last expression, xpointer(//*), is never executed.

```
xpointer(//*[@specials="BADVALUE"])xpointer(//*[@specials])xpointer(//*)
```

XPointer and Namespaces

When I discussed namespaces with regard to XPath, one of problems encountered was dealing with default namespaces in documents. I mentioned that some technologies offer ways to register namespaces and prefixes to be used within the XPath queries. XPointer is one of the technologies providing functionality for this. For example:

```
<produce xmlns="http://www.example.com/produce">
   <vegetable>tomato</vegetable>
   <vegetable>lettuce</vegetable>
   <fruit>apple</fruit>
</produce>
```

Given this document containing a default namespace of http://www.example.com/produce, all vegetable elements need to be retrieved. Using XPath, you would need to test either the local names of the elements or the namespace uri for the elements:

```
/*/*[@local-name()="vegetable"]
```

XPointer adds the ability to register namespaces to be used for the XPointer expressions in the following form:

```
xmlns(prefix=URI)
```

prefix is the prefix to associate with the namespace URI identified by URI. Using this notation, the XPointer expression would be as follows:

```
xmlns(veg=http://www.example.com/produce)xpointer(//veg:vegetable)
```

Just as the XPointer expressions can be stacked, so can the namespace registrations (the following code has been split over two lines because of length):

```
xmlns(veg=http://www.example.com)xmlns(fr="http://www.example.com/fruit)
xpointer(//veg:vegetable)
```

In the event the same prefix is defined multiple times, the rightmost definition is the one used. An example of this is when you define the prefix veg multiple times. For example:

```
xmlns(veg=http://www.example.com)xmlns(veg="http://www.example.com/fruit)
```

This causes veg to be associated with the namespace http://www.example.com/fruit.

XPointer Extending XPath

At first glance, it may seem that XPointer is just an XPointer function taking an XPath expression as an argument. For the most part it is, but it also extends XPath to offer some additional functionality. XPath introduces some additional concepts such as locations, location types, location sets, points, and ranges. It adds some functions that can be used under XPointer. The following sections are not a complete, in-depth examination of XPointer and its extended functionality. At the current time, XPointer is still a working draft, and not all functionality is implemented in libxml. All XPath topics covered to this point are fully supported, however.

Location, Location Types, and Location Sets

The basic unit within XPath is the node, and a document is a tree of nodes. XPointer generalizes this and uses the concept of a *location*. A location not only includes nodes, from the XPath point of view, but also includes points and ranges, which I will explain shortly. A *location type* is a node type, point type, or range type. *Location sets* are generalized node sets. They not only include nodes, but they also include points and ranges.

Points and Ranges

Points and ranges represent non-node locations, but they are considered to be two additional node types that can be used when writing expressions. A *point* can represent the position preceding or following an element node as well as a location preceding any individual character within a text node, comment, attribute value, or PI. It is defined by a container node and an index, which is a non-negative integer. The index, unlike an XPath position, is zero-based. Points do not have expanded names and have empty string values.

A *range*, defined by starting and ending points, contains all the XML structure in between. Just as a point is just some position within a document, a range can contain partial pieces of nodes. Ranges for nodes—other than element, text, and root nodes—must have the same container node for the starting and ending points. For example, a range with a starting point inside a comment node must have an ending point within the comment node. The ending point cannot extend past the comment node.

Functions

XPointer adds some new functions to those already available from XPath. You can use these functions to deal with ranges, location sets, and pointers, which are not part of XPath.

range-to

This is the syntax for range-to:

```
location-set range-to(location-set)
```

This function returns a range consisting of a starting point from the context and an ending point determined from the location set passed in as the parameter.

The following example would return a range from the starting point for the element identified by the ID chap1 to the ending point of the element identified by the ID chap2:

```
xpointer(id("chap1")/range-to(id("chap2")))
```

Given the following document:

```
<book>
    <chapter xml:id="chap1">
        <!-- chapter data -->
    </chapter>
    <chapter xml:id="chap2">
        <!-- chapter data -->
    </chapter>
</book>
```

everything between the opening `chapter` tag with the `xml:id="chap1"` and the closing `chapter` tag with the `xml:id="chap2"` would be selected.

string-range

This is the syntax for `string-range`:

```
location-set string-range(location-set, string, position?, length?)
```

This function returns a set of ranges where the string value of the `location-set` matches the `string` parameter:

The `position` parameter is optional and indicates the starting point of the range being returned relative to the matched string. The default value, when not specified, is 1, meaning that the starting point of the range will be the point preceding the character of the matched string.

This finds all occurrences of the string `Joe` in `name` elements:

```
xpointer(string-range(//name,"Joe"))
```

This selects the character e from the first occurrence of the string `Joe`:

```
xpointer(string-range(/,"Joe",2,1)[position()=1])
```

range

This is the syntax for `range`:

```
location-set range(location-set)
```

This function returns a location set composed of the ranges for each location of the `location-set` input parameter:

range-inside

This is the syntax for `range-inside`:

```
location-set range-inside(location-set)
```

This function returns a location set composed of the ranges contained within each location of the `location-set` input parameter. A location, which is a range, returns the range itself. Other locations use the location as the container node and return the range within the container.

start-point

This is the syntax for start-point:

location-set start-point(*location-set*)

This function returns a location set composed of all the starting points for each location of the location-set input parameter. For example, start-point(//chapter) would return a set of points immediately following the opening tag of a chapter element, and start-point(chapter[1]) would return a single point located after the opening tag of the first chapter element.

end-point

This is the syntax for end-point:

location-set end-point(*location-set*)

This function returns a location set composed of all the ending points for each location of the location-set input parameter:

here

This is the syntax for here:

location-set here()

This function is valid only when being interpreted within an XML document or external parsed parameter. It returns a location-set composed of a single member, which is the node that contains the expression being evaluated. For a text node within an element node, the element node is returned.

origin

This is the syntax for origin:

location-set origin()

This function is applicable only when using XLink. It returns a location-set that locates the element from where the traversal began:

XPointer Summary

XPointer has not yet achieved recommendation status from the W3C. It has actually been broken up into several specifications. Using XPath syntax should be safe without having to anticipate any changes. This syntax is fully supported in libxml and the PHP 5 extensions where XPointer is applicable. The extended functionality presented here may change over time, and currently the extended functionality is not fully supported in libxml.

Introducing XInclude

XInclude is a W3C specification for including external documents, fragments, and other content within an XML document. This technology differs from the use of external entities in many ways. External entities are processed while a document is parsing. XInclude is independent of parsing. It occurs when instructed by the user of the document, which can occur while parsing, after the fact, or even not at all. External entities also must be defined in a DTD. XInclude does not require a DTD to work within a document. This allows it to work independently of valida- tion. Failure to load an external entity normally results in a failure to load the base document. XInclude, on the other hand, offers the ability to provide alternatives in the event the remote data cannot be loaded. Using a fallback mechanism allows the base document to load success- fully even though a remote source may be unavailable. The following sections will explain the syntax used to employ XInclude as well as how you can use it within an XML document.

XInclude defines the namespace http://www.w3.org/2001/XInclude. Although you can associate any prefix with this namespace, the typical prefix used is xi. This namespace contains two elements, include and fallback. Within the following sections, the xi prefix will refer to the http://www.w3.org/2001/XInclude namespace, so the elements will appear as xi:include and xi:fallback. Listing 4-7 is a small portion of the courses XML document. This document resides in the file courses.xml, and I will use it in the following sections for illustration.

Listing 4-7. *Small XML Course Document for the File* courses.xml

```
<?xml version="1.0" ?>
<courses>
    <course xml:id="c1">
        <title>Basic Languages</title>
        <description>Introduction to Languages</description>
    </course>
    <course xml:id="c2">
        <title>French I</title>
        <description>Introduction to French</description>
    </course>
</courses>
```

xi:include

The xi:include element defines the location of the entity to include as well as any additional information that may be needed to parse the entity when including. This element takes the following form:

```
<xi:include href="URI" parser="value" xpointer="xpointerexp" encoding="EncName"
            accept="value" accept-language="value" />
```

xi:include attributes

Although the attributes are optional, many of the requirements for attributes are dependant upon each other.

href

The value of the href attribute specifies the URI of the resource to include. This is an optional attribute. When omitted or set to an empty string (href=""), the location references the same document.

parser

The parser attribute specifies how the included resource should be parsed. The possible values are xml and text. When omitted, the default value of xml is used to parse the include. The value xml indicates that the resource should be included as parsed XML and merged into the document. The value text indicates that the resource should be included as text content. When including text, escaping will be performed on the contents of the resource to ensure proper text content. For instance, if an XML document were included using text parsing, characters such as < and > would be included using their escaped values, < and >.

xpointer

This attribute specifies an XPointer expression to be evaluated on the included document. This will allow the include to limit or specify portions of the external xml resource to include. The xpointer attribute is valid only when the parser attribute value is xml, either through omission or explicitly set. Using the xpointer attribute when the parser value is text will result in an error. When the xpointer attribute is omitted, the href attribute must be present.

encoding

The encoding attribute specifies the encoding of a text resource. It is applicable only when the parse attribute is set to text. When parsing XML, the encoding is handled through the normal XML encoding methods. There is no built-in mechanism to specify encoding on non-XML resources, so you can set an encoding name, as defined by the acceptable XML encoding names, as the value of this attribute for this purpose.

accept

The accept attribute is used for content negotiation while retrieving the resource. When fetching a resource through HTTP, the value of this attribute is added to the HTTP request as an Accept header.

accept-language

This attribute is also used for content negotiation. Similar to the accept attribute, the value of the accept-language attribute is added to the HTTP request as an Accept-Language header.

Using xi:include

The xi:include element is easy to add to a document. Using the external file courses.xml in Listing 4-7, you can construct a document that can include the contents of that file just as if the remote document were contained within the base document:

```
<?xml version="1.0" ?>
<academic xmlns:xi="http://www.w3.org/2001/XInclude">
   <xi:include href="courses.xml" parse="xml" />
</academic>
```

Processing the XInclude within this document results in the following output:

```
<?xml version="1.0"?>
<academic xmlns:xi="http://www.w3.org/2001/XInclude">
    <courses>
        <course xml:id="c1">
            <title>Basic Languages</title>
            <description>Introduction to Languages</description>
        </course>
        <course xml:id="c2">
            <title>French I</title>
            <description>Introduction to French</description>
        </course>
    </courses>
</academic>
```

I used the value xml for the parse attribute in this case, so the resource was processed and included as XML. You could also include the resource as text, which will not parse but will escape characters:

```
<?xml version="1.0"?>
<academic xmlns:xi="http://www.w3.org/2001/XInclude">
    <xi:include href="xi.xml" parse="text" />
</academic>.
```

Processing the XInclude this time produces something along these lines:

```
<?xml version="1.0"?>
<academic xmlns:xi="http://www.w3.org/2001/XInclude">
    &lt;?xml version="1.0" ?&gt;&#xD;
&lt;courses&gt;&#xD;
    &lt;course xml:id="c1"&gt;&#xD;
        &lt;title&gt;Basic Languages&lt;/title&gt;&#xD;
        &lt;description&gt;Introduction to Languages&lt;/description&gt;&#xD;
    &lt;/course&gt;&#xD;
    &lt;course xml:id="c2"&gt;&#xD;
        &lt;title&gt;French I&lt;/title&gt;&#xD;
        &lt;description&gt;Introduction to French&lt;/description&gt;&#xD;
    &lt;/course&gt;&#xD;
&lt;/courses&gt;&#xD;
</academic>
```

Even the XML declaration from the courses.xml file is included this time. XInclude was instructed by the parse attribute not to process the resource as XML but to include it as text. The XML declaration has no meaning as plain text and is added to the document. You most likely have noticed that all characters have also been escaped, including much of the whitespace.

If you notice the attributes within the courses.xml file for the course elements, they are defined as xml:id attributes, which automatically convert the attributes to type ID. Using the xpointer attribute with the xi:include element, you can select a single course with the ID of the element:

```
<?xml version="1.0" ?>
<academic xmlns:xi="http://www.w3.org/2001/XInclude">
    <xi:include href="courses.xml" parse="xml" xpointer="xpointer(id('c1'))"/>
</academic>
```

The function id() takes a string argument, which must be surrounded by quotes. This appears within an attribute whose value is enclosed in double quotes. For this reason, I used single quotes to encapsulate the string c1. When the attribute value is enclosed by single quotes, the string needs to be encapsulated by double quotes, like xpointer='xpointer(id("c1"))'. This returns the course element identified by the ID c1 from the courses.xml document. When included, the resulting document looks like this:

```
<?xml version="1.0"?>
<academic xmlns:xi="http://www.w3.org/2001/XInclude">
    <course xml:id="c1">
        <title>Basic Languages</title>
        <description>Introduction to Languages</description>
    </course>
</academic>
```

Including documents, text, and fragments is a straightforward and simple process. All that is required is the addition of an include element, which resides in the http://www.w3.org/2001/XInclude namespace, and the location of the resource to be included. Within this section you have come to know this as the xi:include element. XInclude also offers a form of error handling, which is covered next, in the event you encounter a problem with the xinclude.

xi:fallback

Sometimes an XInclude may fail. It could be because of a problem accessing the remote resource or a possibly invalid selection of data. Normally this would cause an error in processing. XInclude offers a way to handle this and use other functionality in the event of an error. You do this using the xi:fallback element.

The fallback element is referenced here using xi:fallback. It falls under the same rules as the xi:include element in respect to the namespace. It must reside within the http://www.w3.org/2001/XInclude namespace, which for this chapter has been associated with the xi prefix. This element lives as a child of the xi:include element and has no attributes. When an error occurs from the xi:include element, the contents of the xi:fallback element are used for replacement.

Sometimes a network may be unavailable, or an Internet connection goes down. It is also possible that the filename of the remote resource was mistyped in the xi:xinclude href attribute. Each of these would cause the include to fail. Take the case of an invalid href:

```
<?xml version="1.0" ?>
<academic xmlns:xi="http://www.w3.org/2001/XInclude">
    <xi:include href="coursesBAD.xml" parse="xml" />
</academic>
```

This href is pointing to coursesBAD.xml, which is a file that does not exist. Processing the xinclude will result in at a minimum a parser warning and possibly an unrecoverable parser error. To prevent this from happening, the document could add an xi:fallback element to handle an unexpected case:

```
<?xml version="1.0" ?>
<academic xmlns:xi="http://www.w3.org/2001/XInclude">
   <xi:include href="coursesBAD.xml" parse="xml">
      <xi:fallback>
         External Resource Problem
      </xi:fallback>
   </xi:include>
</academic>
```

Processing this document results in the following:

```
<?xml version="1.0"?>
<academic xmlns:xi="http://www.w3.org/2001/XInclude">

      External Resource Problem

</academic>
```

The contents of xi:fallback were added to the document including the whitespace, such as the line feeds. It is also possible to replace an error condition with no content. You do this simply using an empty xi:fallback element:

```
<?xml version="1.0" ?>
<academic xmlns:xi="http://www.w3.org/2001/XInclude">
   <xi:include href="coursesBAD.xml" parse="xml">
      <xi:fallback />
   </xi:include>
</academic>
```

The resulting document in this case is as follows:

```
<?xml version="1.0"?>
<academic xmlns:xi="http://www.w3.org/2001/XInclude">

</academic>
```

The academic element still contains the insignificant whitespace from the base document, which is why a blank line appears in the output.

You can also perform error handling in cases where an XPointer expression may fail. Using the xpointer attribute, the course element identified by the ID c6 is to be selected from the document. Looking at the document in Listing 4-7, you already know that no element with this ID exists and expect it to fail:

```
<?xml version="1.0"?>
<academic xmlns:xi="http://www.w3.org/2001/XInclude">
   <xi:include href="courses.xml" parse="xml" xpointer="xpointer(id('c6'))"/>
      <xi:fallback>Element not found</xi:fallback>
   </xi:include>
</academic>
```

As expected, the element is not found, resulting in an error and the following document:

```
<?xml version="1.0"?>
<academic xmlns:xi="http://www.w3.org/2001/XInclude">
   Element not found
</academic>
```

XInclude Summary

XInclude can be a useful technology to employ. Documents can be smaller in size as well as reused. You can overcome many of the issues with external entities using this method as well as the added ability to fall back to another case in the event of a failure. You can now handle fatal errors, preventing the complete stoppage of processing. In addition, you don't have to load external resources during initial parsing. If the resources are not needed at the time, the xincludes do not need to be processed, which not only keeps the document smaller but also reduces the processing time.

Examining the Future of XML

Some new technologies are on the horizon in the XML realm. Though not yet standards, these technologies are already being used in many commercialized products. The following sections cover these technologies; I'll also provide an overview of XLink, which although not a new technology is one that does not have as widespread use or support as the technologies already covered.

Introducing XLink

Although XLink has been a W3C standard for many years now—since June 2001 (http://www.w3.org/TR/xlink)—this chapter will not provide an in-depth examination of this technology. It is primarily a UI-based technology, and currently neither PHP nor libxml has native support for XLink. You can create documents containing XLink elements by using extensions such as the DOM extension (which will be covered in Chapter 6), but no XLink processing abilities are offered. You may find some newer browsers beginning to support XLink, but unless you are within a controlled environment, it is not recommended to use XLink for a public site.

XLink is for creating and describing links between resources. In terms of HTML, it would be the equivalent to the anchor tag, `<a href="…"></a>`, on steroids. XLink lives within the http://www.w3.org/1999/xlink namespace. For the purposes of this section, the prefix xlink will be associated with this namespace. XLink allows any element to become a link. This is a big difference from HTML, where the only link is the anchor element. Listing 4-8 illustrates a sample document using XLink.

Listing 4-8. *XML Document Using XLink*

```
<?xml version="1.0" encoding="ISO-8859-1"?>
<resources xmlns:xlink="http://www.w3.org/1999/xlink">
    <resource>
        <description xlink:type="simple"
                     xlink:href="http://www.w3.org/TR/xpath/" xlink:show="new">
            XPath 1.0 Specification
        </description>
    </resource>
    <resource>
        <description xlink:type="simple"
                     xlink:href="http://www.w3.org/TR/xlink/" xlink:show="replace">
            XLink Specification
        </description>
    </resource>
</resources>
```

Within the document, you should first notice the declaration of the XLink namespace associated with the xlink prefix. The description elements within this document are using xlink attributes, which define link behavior. Many more XLink attributes exist than the ones used here, but those are out of the scope of this book. The following sections will only briefly cover the type, href, and show attributes.

type Attribute

The type attribute specifies the type of link the element represents. This attribute is mandatory for an element using xlink. The possible values for this attribute are simple, extended, locator, arc, resource, title, and none. The only two values I'll explain here are simple and none, because the remaining values require much more in-depth knowledge of XLink than that provided in this chapter. Using the value none, the element has no XLink meaning. All xlink attributes are skipped, and the element is processed as a normal XML element. The value simple represents a simple link similar to an HTML anchor tag. The remaining values offer more extended functionality.

href Attribute

The href attribute provides the location for an XLink application to find the remote resource. Its value is a URI, and it works similarly to an href tag on an HTML anchor element.

show Attribute

The show attribute indicates where the link should be opened for presentation. Its value may be one of new, replace, embed, other, or none. This attribute is similar to the target attribute for an anchor tag but provides some additional values. The value of new will open the resource in a new window or frame. This is equivalent to a target attribute with the value _blank. The value replace, which is also the default value when not set, will replace the current window or frame with the content. Its HTML target equivalent is _self. The value embed will embed the contents of the resource within the document. This value is similar to using an image tag, IMG, in HTML.

The value other does not offer any direction for presenting the resource content but indicates to an XLink application that it should look for other markup for possible instructions. The last value, none, is similar to other. It offers no direction for presenting the resource and means that no other markup may exist to offer direction for an application.

XLink Summary

This has been an extremely brief look at the XLink technology. It has been around for quite a while, and some people think it will revolutionize Internet browsing. XLink has been a recommended specification for more than four years now, and I don't know about you, but I personally don't have a browser that supports it yet. As far as applications using XLink, I haven't yet come across any, although they must exist. If you are interested in further information on XLink and features not covered here, I suggest you read the specification at http://www.w3.org/TR/xlink/.

Introducing XQuery, XPath 2.0, and XSLT 2.0

XPath 2.0 is the new generation of XPath. It serves as the foundation for XQuery and XSLT 2.0. These technologies are still in the working draft phase from the W3C. You can find the specifications at http://www.w3.org/TR/xpath20/, http://www.w3.org/XML/Query, and http://www.w3.org/TR/xslt20/.

This section will introduce you to XPath 2.0. XQuery is almost synonymous with XPath 2.0 at this point, but XSLT 2.0 is out of the scope of this book. Although some of the larger database vendors support XQuery, PHP 5 and libxml do not support these technologies natively at this time (and there is currently no planned support). You may find, however, third-party extensions providing support for these technologies, possibly an extension for a database. For these reasons, I'll present only a brief introduction to XPath 2.0.

Like XPath 1.0, XPath 2.0 serves to address nodes within an XML tree. It is meant to be used within a host language, such as XQuery and XSLT 2.0, and not as a stand-alone language. A background on XPath 2.0 should suffice in the event you ever encounter XQuery or XSLT 2.0.

XPath 2.0 contains the same node types as 1.0, though the terminology for a root node has changed to *document node*. XPath 2.0 uses the concept of a *sequence*. Everything is a sequence, including numbers and strings. For example, a single number would be a sequence with a single number, and a string would be considered a sequence with a single string. A node would be a sequence containing one node. In terms of XPath 1.0, a node set would be a sequence of nodes. Listing 4-9 shows a simplified version of the store document from Listing 4-6.

Listing 4-9. *Simplified Store Document*

```
<store>
    <book qty="25">
        <name>Grapes of Wrath</name>
        <price>12.99</price>
    </book>
    <magazine qty="75">
        <title>fdsfsd</title>
        <issue>2005-11-01</issue>
        <price>2.99</price>
    </magazine>
```

```
      <book qty="25">
         <name>Of Mice and Men</name>
         <price>9.99</price>
      </book>
      <magazine qty="5">
         <title>fdsfsd</title>
         <issue>2002-10-01</issue>
         <price>2.99</price>
      </magazine>
</store>
```

Using XPath 1.0, you can retrieve all book and magazine elements with the following:

```
/store/*[self::book or self::magazine]
```

This query would return all the book and magazine elements in document order, which means you would have a node set that contained a book element, a magazine element, a book element, and finally a magazine element.

Under XPath 2.0, you could modify the query to retrieve all book elements followed by all magazine elements, followed again by all book elements. This type of query is not possible under XPath 1.0, because a node set could never contain the same element more than once. For example:

```
(/store/book, /store/magazine, /store/book)
```

This expression is a sequence, where a comma separates each query. The first query retrieves all book elements, the second query retrieves all magazine elements, and the last query retrieves all book elements again. The result would be a sequence containing the nodes in the order just detailed.

As you saw when performing calculations using XPath 1.0, you had no way to generate the total value of inventory on hand. This is now possible using XPath 2.0. Sequences are iterable. It is similar to being able to perform a foreach in PHP:

```
for $x in /store/* return $x/@qty * $x/price
```

This expression, after every iteration has been performed, will return a sequence containing the value of qty*price for each element in the store. The sequence returned would be (324.75, 224.25, 249.75, 14.95). You could then use this sequence within the sum function. The sum function in XPath 2.0 takes a sequence, not a node set:

```
sum(for $x in /store/* return $x/@qty * $x/price)
```

The end result would be 833.7, which is the value of the inventory on hand within the store.

Another nice addition is if/then/else. The specification's example looks like this:

```
if ($widget1/unit-cost < $widget2/unit-cost)
   then $widget1
   else $widget2
```

If my interpretation is correct, then you could calculate the total value on hand for items with a quantity greater than 25 with the following:

```
sum(for $x in /store/* return if($x/@qty > 25) then $x/@qty * $x/price else 0)
```

You could, of course, have performed this in a much simpler manner:

```
sum(for $x in /store/*[@qty > 25] return $x/@qty * $x/price)
```

The last portion of XPath 2.0 I will cover is quantified expressions. These expressions allow a test against a sequence and return TRUE or FALSE depending upon the quantifier used and whether every item in the sequence evaluates to TRUE or only some do. For example, to test whether *every* item in the store has a price of 12.99, you could use the following expression:

```
every $x in /store/*/price satisfies $x = 12.99
```

This expression returns FALSE. The price for the items varies, and only one item has a price of 12.99. You could modify the expression using the some quantifier, which returns TRUE if *any* of the price elements have a value of 12.99:

```
some $x in /store/*/price satisfies $x = 12.99
```

This expression returns TRUE, because a book element exists that has a price equal to 12.99.

As you can see, XPath 2.0 is extremely more powerful than XPath 1.0. This brief introduction has only touched the surface of what is contained within XPath 2.0. Many additional functions and keywords perform tasks such as casting, instance-of checking, and schema data typing.

In time, these technologies may be available for use with libxml and PHP, but as I have mentioned, there is currently no planned support. By the time you are reading this, things may have changed, but unless the specifications become recommendations soon, I highly doubt it.

Conclusion

The primary focus of this chapter was on XPath 1.0, XPointer, and XInclude. The material presented should give you enough information about the concepts and actual use of these technologies to utilize them in PHP. Future chapters will build upon what you have learned here and provide you with ways to use this information in the PHP 5 programming environment. You also learned about XPath 2.0 in this chapter. Although PHP doesn't support XPath 2.0, XQuery, or XSLT 2.0, you may encounter an extension at a future date that uses one of these technologies.

Using everything you have learned to this point, it is time to begin exploring how to use XML in PHP 5. The next chapter will introduce you to some functionality that is common to the XML-based extensions in PHP.

■ ■ ■

CHAPTER 5

PHP and XML

The latest version of PHP, PHP 5, introduces several new features and enhancements to the PHP language. PHP 5 introduced a new object model, exceptions, and new database support such as MySQLi and SQLite, and it makes major strides in the areas of XML and Web services. This chapter will introduce you to the new XML-based extensions, their founding library, and the basic functionality common to the PHP 5 XML extensions.

Introducing XML in PHP 5

Native XML support in PHP 4 was limited to certain basic technologies. The xml extension supported SAX, the domxml extension provided tree support as well as some XSLT support, and the xslt extension also provided XSLT support. With respect to Web services and data exchange, the wddx extension supported distributed data exchange, and xmlrpc supported XML-based remote procedure calls. Although this seems like a decent list of technologies, a fundamental problem was that each was its own distinct extension using its own underlying library. The extensions just did not work together, and to use all the extensions, you had to install all the necessary libraries.

The shortcomings of XML in PHP 4 caused much frustration for those using it. All this XML technology was available, but it would not work together. So, while PHP 5 was still in its early stages of development, a discussion began that would ultimately shape the future of XML in PHP 5. The developers decided to rework and rewrite the XML-based extensions to provide the greatest functionality and flexibility as possible.

libxml2 in PHP 5

The central library decided upon for the core of the XML extensions is libxml2, which you can find at http://www.xmlsoft.org. This library supports many of XML-related standards, including the XML, Namespaces, XML Schemas, Relax NG, XPath, and XInclude specifications—just to name a few. It was chosen for its vast XML support, which means additional technologies can be implemented in PHP, and it is one of the fastest parsers; also, it is actively maintained and widely used. Its sibling, the libxslt library, which is dependent upon libxml2 and also located at http://www.xmlsoft.org, handles XSL within PHP 5.

Both of these libraries, being actively maintained, continue to evolve by providing fixes to bugs and enhanced feature sets. To provide the best XML support possible, it is sometimes necessary to require newer versions of these two libraries in order to build PHP. Such is the case with PHP 5.1. The current minimum requirements for libxml2 and libxslt within PHP are libxml2 2.5.10 and libxslt 1.0.18 under PHP 5.0.*x* and libxml2 2.6.11 and libxslt 1.0.18 under PHP 5.1.*x*. Although minimum requirements for these libraries have been established, it is always a good idea to keep your libraries current. The bugs fixed in the latest versions alone will enhance and ensure proper XML support within the PHP extensions. Some extensions also provide new or additional functionality available only with newer libxml2 libraries.

Tip Keeping your libxml2 and libxslt libraries current ensures you have the latest bug fixes, but it also means, for some PHP 5 extensions, you'll get additional functionality not found in earlier versions. Keep in mind that this does not mean your application will behave exactly as it did before an upgrade. Both libraries follow the XML specifications, so a fix in either library to conform to specifications may adversely affect any expected output. In cases such as this, it is advantageous to correct the problem in the application rather than rely on old library behavior that might not have been correct in the first place.

Core XML Extensions

Many XML extensions and packages exist for PHP, which will be mentioned later in this book. If you are a PHP Extension and Application Repository (PEAR) fan, you have not been forgotten. I have intentionally omitted discussing PEAR at this point because Chapter 13 is dedicated to PEAR and XML. I will limit the current scope of this chapter to an introduction of the extensions bundled with core PHP 5.

Tree-Based Parsers

Tree-based parsers allow you to construct or load existing XML documents so you can navigate or modify them. To do this, the entire XML document is created or loaded into memory as a tree. Given that the entire document must reside in memory, you need to consider your memory constraints when using these technologies. These parsers also tend to initially be slower for this same reason. Once in memory, however, these parsers offer the fastest access to data within a document compared to other types of parsers.

Under PHP 4, domxml was the only native tree-based parser available. PHP 5 introduced the new parsers DOM and SimpleXML. If you are unfamiliar with these parsers, then you may be wondering why you need two. You will get an idea from the following descriptions; and after reading Chapters 6, 7, and 11, you will have the full picture.

SimpleXML Extension

Using the new functionality offered by PHP 5, SimpleXML provides an extremely simple and lightweight tool to manipulate XML documents. Compared to the DOM extension, SimpleXML has an easy-to-learn API because you can view the document as a tree of objects, where objects are synonymous with element nodes. Accessing a child element is as simple as using the child element's name as a property of an object. You can access attributes similarly to how you access an array. To a limited extent, SimpleXML also allows for content editing. You can find further information about SimpleXML in Chapter 7, which details this extension and offers examples on usage.

DOM Extension

The DOM extension is the PHP 5 replacement for domxml, which is now supported only under PHP 4. The DOM extension was created to address many of the shortcomings of domxml while also adhering to the W3C DOM specifications. Unlike SimpleXML, it has a large and complex API. This, however, is the price you pay for functionality. The DOM extension allows you to access all node types, allows you to create and modify complex documents, and gives you advanced navigation and functionality. An advantage to this extension, if you are coming from another language that incorporates a DOM-compliant parser, is that the API should already be familiar to you and easy to begin using under PHP. The next chapter covers this extension in detail.

Streaming Parsers

Unlike a tree-based parser, a streams-based parser does not load the entire document into memory, so memory usage and requirements remain at a minimum. Only small pieces of the document are available for processing at a time. PHP 5 offers both a push parser via the xml extension and a pull parser via the XMLReader extension. These parsers do not allow for document editing and offer little to no navigational capabilities, because they are forward-only streams. The minor exception to this is XMLReader.

xml Extension

The xml extension is the familiar SAX-based tool from PHP 4. Within PHP 5, a libxml compatibility layer has been added as the default library, eliminating the need for expat, although it may still be built using expat. SAX offers event-based parsing. Functions, known as *handlers*, are assigned to events, such as when the beginning or end of an element is encountered, and data is sent to the functions for processing. This is known as a *push parser* because you are not in control of the data sent to your functions. Upon the commencement of parsing, reading of the XML document begins. As events are triggered, your handler is executed with the data whether or not you are interested in the actual data. This continues until you halt the parser, a fatal error occurs, or it reaches the end of the document. Chapter 8 covers the xml extension API and offers examples.

XMLReader Extension

The XMLReader extension takes a different approach than the xml extension. It works as a forward-only cursor on the XML document, stopping at each node in the document. The user controls the progress through the document as well as decides whether any information should be retrieved from the current node pointed at by the cursor. It is for these reasons XMLReader is called a *pull parser*. The ease of use, because of a small API, gives it some advantages over the xml extension; in addition, XMLReader offers faster processing without an increase in memory usage, offers streaming validation using DTDs or RELAX NG, offers support for namespaces, offers support for xml:base and xml:id, and provides interoperability with the other PHP extensions. Chapter 9 gives you an in-depth look at XMLReader and its usage.

Note XMLReader is available for PHP 5.0 as a PHP Extension Community Library (PECL) extension. As of PHP 5.1, XMLReader is available as a core extension.

XSL Extension

XSL is an XML-based style sheet language and the language used to transform XML documents into other XML documents. Chapter 10 covers XSLT in more depth, but a quick example is when you take an XML document and create an XHTML document from select data within the original XML document.

Just as the XSLT support from the domxml extension has been removed in PHP 5, so has the xslt extension. Along with the new DOM extension, PHP 5 offers a new XSL extension to work alongside it. This time, the DOM and XSL extensions not integrated into a single extension, but XSL is its own entity (though still dependant upon DOM). A new feature, present in the XSL extension, is the ability to execute PHP and use the resulting data within the transformation.

Data Exchange and Web Services

Using XML for exchanging data and integrating systems has become a hot topic of conversation. PHP 5 includes three native extensions in this area: wddx, xmlrpc, and SOAP. While both the wddx and xmlrpc extensions have been around since the PHP 4 days, the new native SOAP extension was created exclusively for PHP 5.

wddx Extension

Web Distributed Data Exchange (WDDX) offers the ability to serialize data and their native types into platform-neutral XML. This XML can then be transmitted to another system that can unserialize the data into its own native data types. No specific transport agent is defined for this technology, because you can use any Internet protocol. WDDX is strictly for serializing and unserializing data. Unlike the XML-RPC or SOAP technologies, WDDX doesn't attempt to define methods for calling remote functions. The wddx extension, which will be covered in Chapter 15, is the tool for utilizing the WDDX technology.

xmlrpc Extension

As you read in Chapter 1, XML-RPC was one of the early Web services. It is similar to WDDX in that data and their types are serialized and unserialized into/from XML, but it goes beyond this. XML-RPC defines HTTP as its transport agent and includes the mechanism for calling remote functions, which are also transported via an XML document. The xmlrpc extension, which will be covered in Chapter 15, is the extension supporting XML-RPC in PHP 5.

SOAP Extension

Native SOAP support in PHP 5 was a major advancement for the XML-based technologies. Prior to its inception, the alternatives were implementations written in PHP, such as PEAR::SOAP and NuSOAP. Although those are viable alternatives, the biggest advantage to native support written in C is the great improvement in speed as well as the extension being considered the standard SOAP implementation for PHP. You can find detailed information about the SOAP extension and its usage in Chapter 18.

libxml Extension

The libxml extension in PHP 5 is not your typical extension. It does not offer any type of specific XML technology. This extension serves as the center of common functionality shared across all XML-based extensions and uses libxml2 as its backend. This includes functionality exposed to PHP developers as well as those developing extensions using libxml2 as their library. Within PHP 5.0.*x*, the only user functionality you could control was stream contexts. You may ask why this is important. Later in the "Introducing PHP Streams" section, I will explain the relationship of PHP streams and XML. After PHP 5.0 was originally rolled out, one of the biggest issues developers brought up about using the extensions concerned the way error handling was implemented in XML. PHP 5.1 introduced new error handling that could be controlled and accessed through the libxml extension. I'll also discuss error handling for both PHP 5.0 and 5.1 later in the "Performing Error Handling" section.

Configuring libxml Support

By default the libxml extension is enabled. Using Windows, libxml2 is built into PHP. You do not need to worry about the `libxml2.dll` file as you did under PHP 4. Disabling this extension causes all extensions based on libxml to be disabled as well. You disable this and the other extensions simply by adding the following directive to your `configure` directive:

```
--disable-libxml
```

Because you are reading this book on PHP 5 and XML, I highly doubt this is something you would want to do. But it may be possible you still want the extensions coming from PHP 4 so you can continue to use expat. You can do this using the following:

```
--with-libexpat-dir= /path_to_libexpat
```

This directive takes priority over the `configure` directive for libxml, and if used, the extensions xml, wddx, and xmlrpc will be built using expat support rather than libxml2 support.

Note Unless you are encountering problems using the libxml2 library with the xml, wddx, and/or xmlrpc extensions, using libxml2 is highly recommended. Not only does it offer a performance boost, but it also has a greater number of active developers who can provide support in the event of any problems with extensions.

The libxml extension is enabled by default, but if it is disabled (because running some packaged version has changed the code shipped from the `http://www.php.net` site), you can enable it with this:

```
--enable-libxml
```

You can specify the location of the libxml2 libraries through a configuration directive. If you cannot determine the location by running `configure`, or if you would like to specify a different location such as testing a different version of libxml2, you can set the path using the following:

```
--with-libxml-dir=/path_to_libxml_config
```

This directive looks for the file /path_to_libxml_config/bin/xml2-config.

In many cases, you will not have to worry about changing or including any directives for libxml. The default configure included with PHP 5 works right out of the box for most systems, but this will depend upon your operating system. You can find installation help in the PHP manual as well as many places on the Internet. Now that you have your system up and running with libxml support, it's time to look at what libxml extension and libxml2 support means with respect to using any of the XML-based extensions.

Introducing Encoding

Internationalization is something encountered frequently when dealing with XML and when working on the Internet in general. Those new to XML often run into problems when dealing with documents not based on the ANSI encoding or the UTF-8 encoding. Basic knowledge of Unicode is highly suggested, because you will need to understand what it means for a string to be encoded and why it is important to know what encoding is used.

Parsers are required to support UTF-8 and UTF-16 at a minimum. The libxml2 library supports a few additional encodings natively, and when built with iconv support (http://www.gnu.org/software/libiconv/), it can support all encodings supported by iconv. The iconv library provides functionality for conversions between different encodings. You may already be familiar with this through the PHP iconv extension. Table 5-1 lists the base encodings supported by the libxml2 library. This is not an exhaustive list of available encoding names because many encodings are aliases to many of these character sets.

Table 5-1. *Base Default Encodings Supported in libxml2*

Character Set	Encoding
UTF-8	UTF-8
UTF-16	UTF-16
UTF-16 Big Endian	UTF-16BE
UTF-16 Little Endian	UTF-16LE
ISO-8859-1	ISO-8859-1
ASCII	ASCII
US_ASCII	US_ASCII
HTML	HTML

The last character set listed, HTML, is a special encoding within libxml2. It is used for output only and includes predefined HTML entities. For regular XML use, you should ignore this encoding; Chapter 10 will demonstrate its use.

Encoding Detection

As you have seen in earlier chapters, you specify the document encoding in the XML declaration. For documents without a specified encoding, libxml2 attempts to detect the encoding based on the first few characters of the document or a byte order mark (BOM). A BOM is a sequence of bytes at the beginning of a data stream and can indicate the encoding form used. Table 5-2 lists the byte sequences and their corresponding encodings.

Table 5-2. *Byte Order Mark and Encodings*

Byte	Encoding
FE FF	UTF-16BE
FF FE	UTF-16LE
EF BB BF	UTF-8

Documents without a specified encoding or BOM in the data stream can also have their encoding detected based on the first few characters of the XML or test declaration. The encoding will be able to be detected only if a declaration exists. Table 5-3 lists the sequence of characters by their hexadecimal values and the corresponding encodings.

Table 5-3. *No BOM and Corresponding Encodings*

Character	Encoding
00 00 00 3C	ISO-10646-UCS-4
3C 00 00 00	ISO-10646-UCS-4
00 00 3C 00	ISO-10646-UCS-4
00 3C 00 00	ISO-10646-UCS-4
3C 3F 78 6D	UTF-8
4C 6F A7 94	EBCDIC
3C 00 3F 00	UTF-16LE
00 3C 00 3F	UTF-16BE

It may be evident now why XML declarations are recommended. Specifying an encoding not only eliminates the need for a parser to attempt to autodetect the encoding of the document, but it also makes it evident to someone looking at the document. In the event the encoding is not present in the declaration and is unable to be detected, libxml2 will use UTF-8 for the encoding, which is also the encoding it stores documents as internally. For instance, Listing 5-1 uses French characters and ISO-8859-1 encoding, although not explicitly specified.

Listing 5-1. *XML Document with French with No Encoding Defined*

```
<doc>
    <élément>contenu d'élément</élément>
</doc>
```

In this example, I didn't add any BOMs to the data stream, and no XML declaration exists. The parser cannot determine encoding, so it uses UTF-8 as a fallback. This presents a problem. The document is not proper UTF-8 encoding and thus fails when the parser attempts to load it. Trying to actually load this document results in the following libxml2 error:

```
Input is not proper UTF-8, indicate encoding !
```

Now that you know this fails, you can try using an XML declaration, as demonstrated in Listing 5-2, but still not specify encoding. This will at least give libxml2 a chance to try to auto-detect the encoding used.

Listing 5-2. *XML Document with French and XML Declaration but No Encoding*

```
<?xml version="1.0"?>
<doc>
    <élément>contenu d'élément</élément>
</doc>
```

This isn't surprising—the parser encounters the same error. The parser detected the XML declaration but detected it as UTF-8. So, the parser used the same encoding regardless of whether you specified the XML declaration. If you saved the document in Listing 5-2 as a file in UTF-16 format, the autodetection would have at least noticed this and tried loading it using UTF-16 as the encoding.

For the last try to get this document to load properly, set the encoding attribute on the XML declaration, as illustrated in Listing 5-3.

Listing 5-3. *XML Document with French and Encoding Specified*

```
<?xml version="1.0" encoding="ISO-8859-1"?>
<doc>
    <élément>contenu d'élément</élément>
</doc>
```

This time it finally loads without an error. The encoding you needed in this case was ISO-8859-1, which allows the use of the French characters within the document. If you now instructed the parser to dump the document to the standard console, you might not expect to see what it outputs:

```
<?xml version="1.0" encoding="ISO-8859-1"?>
<doc>
    <´l´ment>contenu d'´l´ment</´l´ment>
</doc>
```

You need to remember that your console may not be able to display all characters correctly. This output is from a console that doesn't support the ISO-8859-1 character set. The output is actually correct; it just doesn't look correct. The document was sent to a file, rather than to the standard output, so the contents of the file should be identical to the document in Listing 5-3. This leads to the next topic of discussion, internal storage of an XML document within libxml2.

Internal Encoding

Regardless of the encoding specified for a document, the encoding is stored internally within libxml2 in UTF-8 format. You may be wondering why you need to care about how internal data is encoded. This is actually important to understand when using any of the XML-based extensions within PHP 5. The information contained within this section may save you count-less hours of beating your head against the wall.

Once a document is loaded into the parser, you should completely ignore that an encoding may have been specified for the document. The document is stored and processed using UTF-8 encoding. Virtually all interaction with a parser or data from the parser must be performed using UTF-8 encoded data. Note that in a few instances this does not hold true, and as you read the later chapters covering the specific extensions, you will learn about the specific cases.

■**Caution** Documents are internally stored using UTF-8 encoding. Interaction with XML data in these cases must be performed using UTF-8 data. You may need to perform encoding conversions using an extension such as iconv or mbstring in order to avoid a corruption of data.

The iconv and mbstring extensions in PHP are your friends. When dealing with data that is not UTF-8 compliant, you need to perform conversions. These extensions allow you to convert data to and from UTF-8 based on virtually any encoding you need to use. Say you need to add a new element with the content contenu d'élément to a document. Although you haven't gotten there yet, this example will use the DOM extension. Listing 5-4 illustrates how to use iconv and mbstring in order to perform encoding conversions. Because I have not covered the DOM extension yet, I have omitted the bulk of the code needed for processing.

Listing 5-4. *Encoding and Decoding Using iconv and mbstring*

```php
<?php
$isostring = "contenu d'élément";

/* Conversions from ISO-8859-1 to UTF-8 */
$utf8string = iconv("ISO-8859-1", "UTF-8", $isostring);
$uft8string2 = mb_convert_encoding($isostring, "UTF-8", "ISO-8859-1");

/* Additional DOM code here */
$newelement = new DOMElement('newelement', $ utf8string);
$newelement2 = new DOMElement('newelement2', $ utf8string2);
/* Additional DOM code here */

/* Retrieve the content from newelement set above */
$value = $newelement->nodeValue;

/* Conversions from UTF-8 to ISO-8859-1 */
$isostring1 = iconv("UTF-8", "ISO-8859-1", $value);
$isostring2 = mb_convert_encoding($value, "ISO-8859-1", "UTF-8");
?>
```

The original data you began with, contenu d'élément, is stored in the variable $isostring. This data is in ISO-8859-1 encoding, but in order to interact with the DOM extension, which is based on libxml2, you need to convert $isostring to UTF-8. The code in Listing 5-4 illustrates how to perform this conversion using both iconv and mbstring (but you need to use only one). Be aware of the ordering of arguments for the functions. From the PHP manual, the prototypes for these functions are as follows:

```
string mb_convert_encoding (string str, string to_encoding [, mixed from_encoding])
string iconv (string in_charset, string out_charset, string str)
```

After performing the conversions, the strings using UTF-8 encoding, $utf8string and $utf8string2, are then used as values for the content of the DOMElement objects. Naturally these elements are added to the document within the omitted code. When reading the content of these objects, the reverse conversions are performed and stored in $isostring1 and $isostring2. These strings will contain the same string as the original $isostring variable.

Whether you need to worry about internal encoding depends upon the character set of the data you are using. In many cases, you will be using the UTF-8 and ASCII character sets, and in these cases you do not need any conversions. When working with documents containing language-specific data or when working with internationalization and XML, you must deal with encoding properly.

Figuring Out the libxml2 Version

In some cases, the version of libxml2 used determines whether you can use certain functionality within an extension. For example, namespace support within the xml extension is functional only when running libxml2 2.6.*x*. Although 2.6.0 is the minimum version for PHP 5.1, PHP 5.0 can use XML functionality with at least 2.5.10. Attempting to use namespace support through the xml_parser_create_ns function when running PHP 5.0 with a 2.5.*x* version of libxml2 results in an error message, "Please upgrade to libxml2 2.6." You may also find that other extensions require other minimum versions to utilize certain functionality and methods.

This can make writing software difficult, because it is impossible to guess what version someone else may be running. Luckily, you can retrieve the version of libxml2 and use it programmatically. The libxml extension offers two constants for this purpose: LIBXML_VERSION and LIBXML_DOTTED_VERSION. LIBXML_VERSION is a numeric value indicating the major, minor, and micro version. LIBXML_DOTTED_VERSION indicates the same information but in dotted notation. Using these notations, libxml2 version 2.6.19 would result in the following:

```
/* 2.6.19 using LIBXML_VERSION */
20619

/* 2.6.19 using LIBXML_DOTTED_VERSION */
2.6.19
```

Using this programmatically with the xml_parser_create_ns function as an example, you could test whether the functionality is supported and provide an alternative in the event it is not:

```php
<?php
if (LIBXML_VERSION >= 20600) {
    $xml = xml_parser_create_ns(…);
} else {
    $xml = xml_parser_create(…);
}
?>
```

Introducing Parser Options

As of PHP 5.1, the libxml extension contains new constraints that you can use in the DOM and SimpleXML extensions to control parser behavior. The parser uses these constants, listed in Table 5-4, at the time of document load to offer finer control over how the parser loads and parses the document.

Table 5-4. *Parser Option Constants*

Constant	Description
LIBXML_NOENT	Substitutes entities found within the document with their replacement content.
LIBXML_DTDLOAD	Loads any external subsets but does not perform validation. This flag also ensures that IDs set in a DTD are created within the document.
LIBXML_DTDATTR	Creates attributes within the document for any attributes defaulted through a DTD.
LIBXML_DTDVALID	Loads subsets and validates a document while parsing.
LIBXML_NOERROR	Suppresses errors from libxml2 that may occur while parsing.
LIBXML_NOWARNING	Surprises warnings from libxml2 that may occur while parsing.
LIBXML_NOBLANKS	Removes all insignificant whitespace within the document.
LIBXML_XINCLUDE	Performs all XIncludes found within the document.
LIBXML_NSCLEAN	Removes redundant namespace declarations found while parsing the document.
LIBXML_NOCDATA	Merges CDATA nodes into text nodes. A document using CDATA sections will be created with no CDATA nodes, because these will now be converted into plain-text nodes. This flag is useful when loading a document to be used for an XSL transformation.
LIBXML_NONET	Disables network access when loading documents. You can use this flag to increase security from untrusted documents so resources cannot be fetched from the network.

You can combine flags when parsing. For example, you can load a document that validates and suppresses all warnings while parsing using the following options:

```
LIBXML_DTDVALID | LIBXML_NOWARNING
```

These options would be passed as a single parameter to the function or method accepting a libxml parser option. I will demonstrate how to use these flags within the specific extensions in their respective chapters. Note the use of flags when working with XSL. CDATA sections often make working in XSL difficult; specifically, certain XSL functions do not work correctly when a document contains CDATA sections, because the functions are specific to text nodes. Entities are also typically substituted within the XML document being transformed.

Tip When parsing a document to be used within an XSL transformation, it is recommended that you use the flags LIBXML_NOENT and LIBXML _NOCDATA to avoid any potential problems with calls made upon the XML document from the XSL style sheet.

If you are still using PHP 5.0.*x*, these options are not available. Under this version, the DOM extension does provide a few properties that can be used for controlling the parser, but they do not include all the options listed in Table 5-4. SimpleXML, on the other hand, does not offer any additional functionality to control the parser during document loading. The interoperability within PHP 5 may be useful in this case, assuming the DOM extension has been built, because you can load a document via the DOM extension and manipulate it using SimpleXML.

Tip Under PHP 5.0.*x*, limited parser options are available, even when manipulating the tree using SimpleXML. Documents can be loaded using the DOM extension and a few of the document properties that control the parser; and through the interoperability of the extensions, you can manipulate the resulting tree using SimpleXML.

Introducing PHP Streams

Resource input/output (I/O) for XML has completely changed with PHP 5. Under PHP 4, XML-based extensions used their native I/O mechanisms for the input and output of resources. If you recall from the domxml extension, the only protocols available would be specified as file, http, and, as an input-only protocol, ftp. The old xslt extension would allow support for additional I/O handlers, but it was not all that easy to accomplish because programmers had to deal with setting handlers and adding the functionality to make this work.

PHP 5 is much different. Built-in PHP streams support now serves as the foundation for I/O handling within the XML-based extensions. The advantages of this are numerous for both developers and system administrators. The advantages include the following:

- Built-in support for numerous protocols as well as user-defined streams

- Consistent I/O handling

- Support for PHP file security checks

Protocols

PHP includes many protocols, and the XML extensions by default have access to them all. No longer are the extensions limited to the protocols defined within their base libraries. Files can now be accessed not only from the file system but also via `http`, `https`, `ftp`, `ftps`, PHP I/O streams, `zlib`, `compress.zlib`, and `compress.bzip2`. Prior to using PHP streams, unsupported protocols needed to have the file loaded into a string using PHP functions and that data sent to the extension to be processed as an in-memory string. This could get quite cumbersome for large documents. Not only did you have the overhead of the entire document loaded into memory for a tree parser, but the document was loaded in its string representation as well. You ended up getting penalized twice this way.

XML extensions can now take advantage of user-defined streams. If you are familiar with the streams functionality within PHP, you probably know that user-defined streams can be registered and used natively through the functions supporting stream usage. So, if you would like to define your own protocol—for example, `xyz://`—that uses your own defined I/O functionality, once registered, the XML extensions would have direct access to it.

Consistent I/O Handling

Using domxml in the past created a pathing issue. Depending upon whether PHP was run via the command line or an Apache module, as well as depending upon the operating system it was executing under, the base directory for files that an XML document accessed was not the same. For example, if your XML document contained relative paths for external entities or even for the location of XIncludes, the base directory did not always end up being the directory you assumed it would be. This problem even manifested itself depending upon the version of Apache being used. For instance, using Apache 2 under Windows, the base directory for an XML file sometimes ended up being the directory where the Apache binary lived.

This problem caused many headaches. It was difficult for developers to write cross-platform code. The domxml extension was eventually was fixed in some regard through workarounds, but it still exhibits some differences between operating systems. The move to PHP stream-based I/O now removes this problem. Pathing using streams is universal. The base directory will not change if your code is run from the command line or as a module under Apache—or even under a different operating system.

PHP File Security Support

Another advantage to using PHP streams comes from the built-in support for Safe Mode, which includes the `open_basedir` and `allow_url_fopen php.ini` options. These settings are typically employed in a shared server setting. Through the `php.ini` settings, a system administrator can control different aspects of file access. Prior to PHP 5, XML-based extensions used their internal I/O functionality based upon their base libraries. These libraries, having no concept of PHP streams, bypassed all the security settings.

By default, Safe Mode checks the user ID of the running script against the user ID of the file to be accessed. You can also relax the check using `safe_mode_gid` to compare group IDs as well. If the checks failed, access to the file would be denied. Accessing files using any of the XML extensions now follows the same rules, thus adding security checks when the extensions are accessible on the server.

The `open_basedir` setting allows directories to be set, limiting file access to only those within the specified directories and their subdirectories. The value for the setting is actually a prefix and not a directory. For example, a setting with the value `/usr/inc` would also match the directory `/usr/include`. To limit access to only the `/usr/inc` directory, the value would need to include the trailing slash using /usr/inc/. This setting, independent from the Safe Mode settings, also will affect how files can be accessed using the extensions.

The last setting, allow_url_fopen, can be used to limit network access. When this setting is disabled, the XML parsers will not be allowed to open or save to any remote resource using protocols such as HTTP, HTTPS, and FTP. The local file system is still available for access, but those network resources are denied. Used in conjunction with the Safe Mode and open_basedir settings, access to resources can be locked down quite effectively.

Stream Context

Stream contexts are parameters and options that can modify the behavior of a stream. Many of the stream-enabled functions within PHP accept a stream context as a parameter. The XML functions are not included in this because stream usage is almost invisible from an API perspective. The libxml extension includes the function libxml_set_streams_context that you can use for this purpose.

You can create a context with the regular PHP Streams API. You can find full documentation for this API in the PHP user manual. You then set the context using libxml_set_streams_context; the context remains active for the entire duration of the script. Consider accessing a remote XML resource, located at http://www.example.com/test.xml, while sitting behind a proxy server located at http://www.example.net:4444. Listing 5-5 illustrates the contents of the remote documents.

Listing 5-5. *Contents of* test.xml *and* testxinclude.xml

```
/* Contents of test.xml */
<test xmlns:xi="http://www.w3.org/2001/XInclude">
   <xi:include href="testxinclude.xml" parse="xml" />
</test>

/* Contents of testxinclude.xml */
<testinclude>Included Content</testinclude>
```

The first task you must perform is to create the stream context:

```
<?php
$opts = array(
   'http'=>array(
   'proxy'=>"tcp://www.example.net:4444",
   'request_fulluri'=>TRUE
   )
);

$context = stream_context_create($opts);
?>
```

In this case, the proxy server is requiring a full URI to serve the request, which requires the additional request_fulluri option set to TRUE. The next steps require setting the context with the libxml extension:

```
libxml_set_streams_context($context);
```

With the context set, the parser can now request the XML resource as it normally would. This example uses the DOM extension:

```
$dom = DOMDocument::load('http://www.example.com/test.xml');
```

The parser pulls the XML resource using the proxy set by the context. Notice that the document contains an XInclude using a relative path. It should retrieve this resource from http://www.example.xom/testinclude.xml. When the XInclude operation is performed via the DOM extension, the proxy continues to service the requests.

Performing Error Handling

With the first release of PHP 5, many people were excited about the addition of advanced XML functionality. The largest complaint was in regard to error handling using the XML functions. Errors using XML not only are issued from PHP for user errors but also from libxml2 itself to indicate XML errors, such as when a malformed document is being parsed. Errors from libxml2 range from simple warnings, which in many cases can be safely ignored, to fatal errors, which may cause a PHP error to also be issued if the operation completely fails.

Both the SOAP and DOM extensions offer exceptions, but at least in the DOM extension's case the exceptions were limited to those defined in the specifications. Errors deriving directly from libxml2 were issued as E_WARNINGS and E_NOTICES depending upon the severity of the error. Typically developers did not care about these errors. They just cared whether the operation failed or succeeded. For those who did care about the errors, they had no way to determine that the errors were XML-specific. So, adding a user error handler might be fine, but it still did not indicate that the error was XML-specific.

To get around this problem, many developers started suppressing the errors and just checking return values. For example, you can load a document using SimpleXML from a string using the simplexml_load_string function:

```
$sxe = simplexml_load_string('<root>');
print $sxe->asXML();
```

Loading a malformed document results in an error. This is an invalid document because it contains a single start element with no end element. A typical error from PHP 5 would be an E_WARNING containing the message "Entity: line 1: parser error: Premature end of data in tag root line 1," followed by an error indicating that the developer was trying to call a member function from a nonobject. The load failed, and $sxe was never created. To avoid this error, the code was often changed to this:

```
if ($sxe = @simplexml_load_string('<root>')) {
    print $sxe->asXML();
}
```

The error has been suppressed, and the print statement is executed only if $sxe exists. This is all well and good, but all errors indicating the reason of failure have now been lost.

The complaints from developers did not go unnoticed. Things changed with PHP 5.1. For backward compatibility reasons, the error-handling behavior was left intact and is the default behavior. Additional error handling was added that allows XML errors to be suppressed while also providing a mechanism for them to be accessed after the fact. The additional functions available from the libxml extensions that can access the new error-handling functionality include the following:

```
bool libxml_use_internal_errors ([bool use_errors])
void libxml_clear_errors ( void )
LibXMLError libxml_get_last_error ( void )
array libxml_get_errors ( void )
```

The function libxml_use_internal_errors is the central function, which turns on and off the new internal error handler. The optional use_errors parameter, which defaults to FALSE, indicates whether you should enable the internal error handler. The return value from the function contains the old value prior to calling the function. When in use, the libxml_clear_errors function, which takes no parameters and does not return a value, will clear all stored errors.

Errors issued from the libxml2 library are stored internally on a first-in, first-out (FIFO) basis. This means the first error in will be the first error out and will be accessed through a LibXMLError object. A LibXMLError object has no methods and has only the properties listed in Table 5-5.

Table 5-5. LibXMLError *Object Properties*

Property	Type	Description
level	int	Indicates the severity of the error. It is one of the levels defined by the libxml extension that includes LIBXML_ERR_NONE, LIBXML_ERR_WARNING, LIBXML_ERR_ERROR, and LIBXML_ERR_FATAL.
code	int	The error code from libxml2.
column	int	The column number if available from within the document the error occurred.
line	int	The line number if available from within the document the error occurred.
message	string	The textual representation of the error.
file	string	The filename, if available, of the XML document containing the error.

Not every property will be populated within a LibXMLError object. Certain values cannot always be determined, such as file when parsing a string containing an XML document.

You can access the errors through the libxml_get_last_error and libxml_get_errors functions. The libxml_get_last_error function returns the last LibXMLError object reported. This function is useful only if the last reported error is desired. One thing to note is that even when the new internal error handling is not enabled, this function is still available to access the last error issued from libxml2. The libxml_get_errors function returns an array of LibXMLError objects, starting with the first error issued and ending with the latest error. Modifying the SimpleXML code previously used, you can now suppress the error output while still having access to the XML errors:

```
libxml_use_internal_errors (TRUE);
if ($sxe = simplexml_load_string('<root>')) {
    print $sxe->asXML();
}
/* Was an error produced? */
if ($lasterror = libxml_get_last_error()) {
    /* Dump the last error reported */
    var_dump($lasterror);

    /* Get all errors as an array, loop through them, and dump the output */
    $arerrors = libxml_get_errors();
    foreach ($arerrors as $error) {
        var_dump($error);
    }

    /* Clear out the internal errors since they are no longer needed */
    libxml_clear_errors();
}
```

The code represented here assumes that this is the entire script or, if not, that internal errors have already been cleared. The test for errors was simply done using the libxml_get_last_error function. If anything was returned, then you know some type of error condition occurred. The check was not done using libxml_get_errors, because this function will always return an array, even when empty. If you used this function, you would need to execute the count function to find out whether there was at least one error in the array.

Conclusion

This chapter provided some background on the XML-related extensions in general, including the underlying libxml2 library. More important, however, is the common functionality from the libxml extension covered in this chapter. This functionality is not exclusive to any single extension but comes with any extension based on the libxml2 library. The libxml extension is a required extension, built statically within PHP, when using any of the XML extensions built with libxml2. libxml2 provides constants for use when parsing and provides access to the streams context when needed, and as of PHP 5.1, it handles and provides access to the new XML error-handling functionality.

With the knowledge of XML, many of its technologies, and the core libxml extension behind you, it is time to start looking at the parsers available in PHP 5. The first of these parsers is the tree-based DOM extension.

CHAPTER 6

■■■

Document Object Model (DOM)

This chapter is the starting point to put everything covered to this point to practical usage. You will be introduced to the DOM and its implementation in PHP 5. By the end of this chapter, you should have an understanding of what the DOM is and how to write code using the DOM extension. The examples within this chapter will build upon each other and form the foundation for the examples toward the end of this chapter.

Introducing the DOM

The DOM is a set of interfaces for accessing and modifying documents. It is a standard, but it's actually broken down into many different specifications. The W3C governs the specifications, which are located at http://www.w3.org/DOM/. The core functionality of the DOM is broken down into Level 1, Level 2, and Level 3; each level offers increased functionality, which in turn increases each API's size.

Note The material in this chapter assumes a basic knowledge of object-oriented programming (OOP). You can find information about OOP in articles and documentation published by Zend Technology (http://www.zend.com), which is the company that created the engine behind PHP 5 and the PHP manual.

Understanding the DOM Tree

Under the DOM, a document is manipulated as a tree broken down into nodes. This means the entire document is loaded or is built in memory, where the tree is broken down into smaller units all derived from a node. Nodes are the primary data type, and all other node types are derived from nodes. This breakdown is similar to how you view a document using XPath, although the DOM has a greater number of node types. The following are the node types in the DOM:

- Attr: Attribute node

- CDATASection: CDATA section node

- Comment: Comment node

- DocumentFragment: Document fragment node

- Document: Document node

- DocumentType: Document type node

- Element: Element node

- Entity: Entity node

- EntityReference: Entity reference node

- Notation: Notation node

- ProcessingInstruction: PI node

- Text: Text node

Each node type corresponds to a DOM object. In addition to these DOM objects, objects exist that do not inherit from a node object, such as NodeList, NameNodeMap, DOMImplementation, DOMException, and CharacterData. CharacterData is a special type of object in this list. It actually inherits from a node object but is not a direct DOM object. It provides some additional functionality from which a text node inherits. In addition to the objects and interfaces listed previously, the DOM provides some other interfaces, especially in Core Level 3, but I will not cover them because they have no bearing on the DOM implementation in PHP 5.

The document, represented as a tree, allows for traversal in all directions. Every type of node can be accessed, and the functionality available depends upon the type of node. Because every node type inherits from the base Node interface, all functionality derived from the node base type is accessible, although certain functionality applies only to certain node types. For example, the Node interface includes a read-only nodeValue property that returns the value of the node. Document and entity reference nodes are at least two types of nodes that have no value and that return NULL for this property.

The following is a simple XML document:

```
<?xml version="1.0" ?>
<root>
    <child att1="Att1 value">Child Contents</child>
    <!-- This is a comment -->
</root>
```

Once loaded into the DOM extension, the XML document now is represented through DOM objects, as illustrated in Figure 6-1.

Remember, when loaded, unless otherwise instructed, insignificant whitespaces such as line feeds and tabs are also included in the DOM tree as text nodes. The reason why this bit of information is important is that these additional text nodes will affect how you navigate the tree. For instance, the children of the root node include these text nodes. Those new to XML and the DOM extension often overlook this little fact; however, assuming that the children of the root element in this example contain only the element child and the comment is incorrect.

■**Note** Insignificant whitespaces within a document are created as text nodes and, unless otherwise instructed, must be taken into account when navigating and manipulating the document tree.

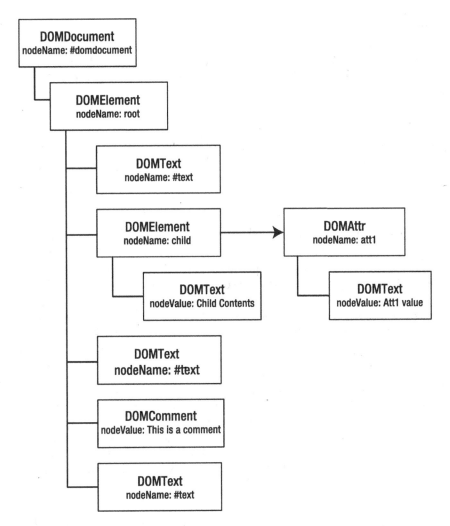

Figure 6-1. *DOM object view of a document tree*

Node Objects

Node objects are just representations of the XML structure you are already familiar with from Chapter 2. They are considered to be the node objects that make up the actual structure of the document. The objects allow the structure to be navigated and manipulated. For instance, an element within a document is accessed via the Element interface. This interface offers properties and methods that allow the underlying element node to be read from, written to, and moved. You can also use these interfaces to create new nodes and insert them into a document. This will become much more clearer to you once you reach the "Using the DOM Extension" section.

Additional Objects

Other interfaces within DOM provide additional functionality that relates to the nodes but does not have a direct correlation to a specific node type. The objects that fall under this category are CharacterData, NodeList, NameNodeMap, DOMImplementation, and DOMException.

CharacterData

The CharacterData interface extends from the Node interface but does not correspond directly to any specific node type within the document. This interface actually is used as the base type for text and comment nodes in order to provide some additional functionality for dealing with textual content.

NodeList

A NodeList is a collection of ordered nodes accessed by index starting at position 0. An object of this type is often returned from DOM methods that can return more than a single node. It is important to know that these objects are *live*. In simple terms, modifications within the document tree are reflected in these objects. For example, if you had an instance of a NodeList object containing the children of a certain element, all changes to the children would be reflected in the instantiated NodeList object. If a child were removed, then it would no longer be contained within the NodeList, and this would also affect the indexing of the NodeList. You will encounter examples and issues related to this in the "Using the DOM Extension" section.

NameNodeMap

A NameNodeMap is similar to a NodeList, except in that the collection can be accessed via item name as well as via index. The difference in the indexing is that these objects have no specific ordering for the objects they contain because the most important aspects of the contained objects are the names. These collections are also live, so the same issues surrounding a NodeList are applicable to a NameNodeMap. You will see plenty of examples of this throughout this chapter.

■**Caution** NodeList and NameNodeMap objects are live collections. Modifications made to the document tree are reflected within these collections and may affect iterating and indexing when using any of these object types.

DOMException

As you read in the previous chapter, error handling takes place in a few ways; this depends upon the version of PHP 5 you are running. The DOM extension is only one of the exceptions to the norm. Certain cases and methods within the DOM extension throw a DOMException when an error is encountered.

DOMImplementation

A `DOMImplementation` object is used to perform functionality independently of a document. Within PHP 5, its primary use is to create a `DOMDocumentType` node or a new document containing a `DOMDocumentType` node.

Understanding the DOM Extension in PHP 5

The domxml extension in PHP 4 has been plagued with issues for quite some time. An ever-changing API (which has finally been stabilized), an inefficient use of memory, and threading problems eventually led to the creation of a new DOM extension for PHP 5. Creating a stable and efficient parser, as well as learning from the problems of the domxml extension in order not to make the same ones again, were the initial goals.

Birth of the DOM Extension

From the start, the new extension was developed according to the DOM specifications, and it adhered to the proper naming conventions. This allowed the creation of a stable API right from the beginning that will not be consistently changing (though may be added to in the event of future changes to the DOM specifications). Using the features of the new engine within PHP 5, the DOM extension was created as an object-oriented API and was able to implement an improved memory-handling scheme; this allowed for better memory management and control of documents and related objects. The new DOM extension has also addressed the problems the domxml extension had with threading. The threading problems typically were encountered when running in a Windows environment using the Internet Server API (ISAPI) under the Internet Information Services (IIS) web server.

I'll cover memory management in the DOM extension in more detail later in this chapter when dealing with the DOM classes and objects in the "Using the DOM Extension" section. A brief overview of this change, however, relates to the use of reference counters. Within PHP 4, domxml would not release any memory for a document until a script was complete. A `free()` function was added toward the later part of PHP 4 to domxml, but it has to be used carefully because it cannot handle all cases. Under PHP 5, a reference counter is maintained for a document. As long as objects related to this document have not been destroyed, either by going out of scope or by manually calling `unset()` on them, the XML document remains in memory. Once all objects referencing the document have been destroyed, the XML document is automatically released from memory. When working with many documents or repeatedly loading documents to perform operations on, memory is handled in a much cleaner fashion than under domxml in PHP 4 and uses system resources better. Although this feature arose from requests in domxml, it finally can be taken advantage of in the DOM under PHP 5.

General Information on the API

The DOM extension in PHP 5 implements almost the entire API for Core Level 2 as well as much functionality from Core Level 3. Some additional functionality extending the specifications has also been added for the convenience of PHP developers. The DOM interfaces defined within the DOM specifications are implemented as classes by the DOM extension. Table 6-1 lists the classes implemented by the DOM extension in PHP 5. The Class column refers to the class name used within the DOM extension. The Base Class column refers to the base class from which this class is derived. The DOM Interface column indicates the inter-face from the W3C DOM specification used for this class.

Table 6-1. *Classes Implemented in the DOM Extension*

Class	Base Class	DOM Interface	Description
DOMException		DOMException	Certain methods within the DOM API not only issue PHP errors and those related to general XML issues from libxml2, but in certain cases a DOMException is thrown. I'll illustrate some cases within this chapter, and Appendix B documents all cases within the API.
DOMImplementation		DOMImplementation	This is generally used when creating a doc-ument from scratch with a DocumentType.
DOMNode		Node	This serves as the base class for most of the classes in the DOM API and provides com-mon functionality. It cannot be used as a stand-alone class.
DOMNameSpaceNode			This class is not defined in the DOM speci-fications. Namespace declarations are not handled as ordinary nodes in the DOM extension. When a namespace declaration is returned as a node, such as when accessed using XPath, a DOMNameSpaceNode is returned. This class implements a subset of the DOMNode functionality.
DOMDocumentFragment	DOMNode	DOMFragment	This is used to extract a portion of the tree or create lightweight documents. It can consist of nodes that by themselves would not be well-formed XML. A document frag-ment is useful when wanting to move portions of the tree around or even append some new XML into a tree.
DOMDocument	DOMNode	Document	This class represents the entire XML or HTML document. It serves as the root node for the tree, which means the tree begins with this and only this node. Everything within the document is contained within this node.
DOMNodeList		NodeList	As previously mentioned, it is a container for ordered nodes accessed by a zero-based index. This collection is live.
DOMNamedNodeMap		NameNodeMap	This class is a container for unordered nodes generally accessed by name but may also be accessed by a zero-based index. This collection is live.
DOMCharacterData	DOMNode	CharacterData	This class adds some functionality for accessing character data. It serves as a base class for other classes and is useless if instantiated directly.

Class	Base Class	DOM Interface	Description
DOMAttr	DOMNode	Attr	This class represents an attribute node. The DOM extension does not consider attributes to be part of the tree because they are not child nodes. They are treated as properties of elements.
DOMComment	DOMCharacterData	Comment	This class represents comments within a document.
DOMElement	DOMNode	Element	This class represents an element node.
DOMText	DOMCharacterData	Text	This class represents a text node.
DOMCDATASection	DOMText	CDATASection	This class represents a CDATA node.
DOMDocumentType	DOMNode	DocumentType	This class represents the DocumentType for the document. Objects of this type are read-only.
DOMNotation	DOMNode	Notation	This class represents a notation declared in the DTD. Objects of this type are read-only.
DOMEntity	DOMNode	Entity	This class represents an entity in the document. Objects of this type are read-only.
DOMEntityReference	DOMNode	EntityReference	This class represents entity references within the document. Objects of this type are read-only.
DOMProcessingInstruction	DOMNode	ProcessingInstruction	This class represents a PI within the document.
DOMXPath			This class is an add-on to the DOM extension. It is used to provide XPath functionality within the DOM extension.

You can instantiate objects within PHP 5 using the keyword new. The specifications suggest using factory methods for object creation of node-type objects, because nodes must be associated with documents. These methods live within the DOMDocument class and are used to create nodes associated with the document, such as the method createElement. Although the DOM extension does follow this through the implementation of the factory methods, it also implements constructors for the node type classes, which allows for the direct creation of these objects. Objects of this type, until associated with a document, are limited in functionality. For example, an element created using $element = new DOMElement('myelement'); may not have children appended to it until it is associated with a document. Any attempts to perform an action such as $node = $element->appendChild(…) will result in a DOMException indicating the node is read-only. As you read this chapter, you will encounter both the use of the factory methods and the use of constructors, as well as why one is sometimes preferable over the other and the merits of each method.

You must be aware of encoding. As you read in the previous chapter, the tree is internally stored as UTF-8. You must interact with the tree using data that is UTF-8–compatible. Data that cannot be handled via native UTF-8 encoding must be converted using one of the string conversion functions available in PHP 5. This applies for both reading and writing data. In certain special cases, the DOM extension can automatically detect encoding and handle the data appropriately, such as when loading or saving a document. In all other cases, you must take care to encode and decode data properly when manipulating the tree.

Caution When manipulating data within a tree, you must ensure that the data is properly encoded and decoded. All data is stored internally in UTF-8 format, and the DOM extension does not typically perform automatic conversion. You can find more information on encoding in Chapter 5.

Using the DOM Extension

The DOM extension is a large API. This chapter will cover the concepts and much of its functionality. You can find information about the entire API in Appendix B. The initial step when dealing with the DOM extension is to create or load a document. The document is the core for XML because it serves as the root of the tree for the DOM extension.

Understanding the Document

The DOMDocument class is the starting point for all applications using the DOM extension. This class not only serves to create, load, and save XML documents but also contains the factory methods for creating other node type objects. The constructor for this object takes the following form:

```
__construct([string version], [string encoding])
```

Both the version and encoding parameters are optional and serve to indicate the version of the XML specification used for the document and to indicate the encoding used for the document itself. You can instantiate an empty document using the new keyword:

```
$dom = new DOMDocument('1.0');
```

This creates an empty DOMDocument object, $dom, using the XML 1.0 specification and no specified encoding. This is equivalent to the following XML declaration:

```
<?xml version="1.0"?>
```

The version parameter, unlike the encoding parameter, has a default value of 1.0, so this parameter could realistically have been omitted from the object instantiation call. Likewise, an encoding value may also be passed as an argument, such as ISO-8859-1. When using the encoding parameter, the use of the version parameter is required. The code $dom = new DOMDocument('1.0', 'ISO-8859-1'); would result in an XML declaration of <?xml version="1.0" encoding="ISO-8859-1"?>.

In both cases, the result is the same. The object $dom has been instantiated from the DOMDocument class as an empty document. Using this object, a tree can either be manually created using the DOM API or be loaded from an XML document. You can load a document from a string containing the XML or from a remote resource. No matter which method is used to load the data, loading is one of the special cases where data does not necessarily need to be converted to UTF-8. Using one of the methods from Chapter 5, such as using an encoding parameter in the XML, using a BOM, or even detecting the first few characters, the DOM extension usually can detect the encoding of the document and load it appropriately. In the event that none of the methods is in use or autodetection fails, the data must be converted to UTF-8 prior to loading. Typically, the encoding is set within an XML declaration, especially when using non-ASCII characters, so you rarely will need to convert it manually. This is also the reason why using XML and text declarations is highly recommended and in some cases required.

Using the instantiated object, $dom, you can build the tree using load() to load from a string and using loadXML() to load from a resource. Depending upon which method you use, you need either a string containing the XML document or a URI pointing to the resource for the first parameter. When using PHP 5.1 and higher, both methods also accept a second optional parameter containing any parser options (covered in Chapter 5) that provide instructions to the parser about how the tree should be built. For example:

```
$xmldata = '<?xml version="1.0"?>
<root>
    <child>contents</child>
</root>';

$dom->loadXML($xmldata, LIBXML_NOBLANKS);
```

Given an already instantiated DOMDocument and the string $xmldata containing the XML document to load, the loadXML() method populates the tree while also removing all blanks, which are the insignificant whitespaces. This would have been the equivalent of setting $xmldata to the string <?xml version="1.0"?><root><child>contents</child></root> and loading the string without any parser options. The differences between the two strings are the line feeds, tabs, and spaces, which are removed in the first case because of the use of the parser option LIBXML_NOBLANKS, and their positions within the document.

The load() method works in the same way as the loadXML() method, except a URI is passed as the first parameter. As you probably recall from Chapter 5, you use PHP streams when loading URIs, allowing for more than the typical file and http protocols to be used. If the contents of the $xmldata string from the previous example were contained within the file xmldata.xml, you could build the tree in the following ways depending upon where the file was located:

```
/* File located in current script directory */
$dom->load('xmldata.xml', LIBXML_NOBLANKS);

/* File loaded using absolute path */
$dom->load('file:///tmp/xmldata.xml', LIBXML_NOBLANKS);

/* File loaded from http://www.example.com/xmldata.xml */
$dom->load('http://www.example.com/xmldata.xml', LIBXML_NOBLANKS);
```

A DOMDocument object does not always need to be instantiated to load a tree. These methods may also be called statically, which will load data into a tree and return the newly created DOMDocument object at the same time. The following examples illustrate how to use the methods statically, which results in the same tree structure for the $dom objects as previously shown. (I've removed the XML declaration for brevity.)

```
/* Load from string */
$dom = DOMDocument::loadXML('<root><child>contents</child></root>');

/* Load from URI */
$dom = DOMDocument::load('xmldata.xml', LIBXML_NOBLANKS);
```

You may be wondering why you wouldn't always use the static methods, because instantiating the object first requires an additional step just to load data. The primary reason for this is when using the DOM extension under PHP 5.0, the parser options are not available to be passed as a second argument to these functions. A small subset of the parser options, however, is also available as properties of a DOMDocument object. When you use these properties, you must set them prior to calling the load functions, which require an already instantiated object. For example, the equivalent to the LIBXML_NOBLANKS option is the preserveWhiteSpace property:

```
/* Removing blanks under PHP 5.0 */
$dom = new DOMDocument();
$dom->preserveWhiteSpace = FALSE;
$dom->load('xmldata.xml');
```

When you use both properties and parser options, the parser options take precedence over the properties. This means in any instance where a property is set and a parser option conflicting with a set property is passed, the parser will follow the instructions from the parser option. For example:

```
$dom = new DOMDocument();
$dom->preserveWhiteSpace = TRUE;
$dom->load('xmldata.xml', LIBXML_NOBLANKS);
```

In this case, the $dom object will load the file, with LIBXML_NOBLANKS taking precedence over the preserveWhiteSpace property, stripping out the line feeds just as if the preserveWhiteSpace property were never set.

The DOMDocument class is not limited to loading just XML data. Unless you are writing Web pages using XHTML (HTML typically does not conform to the XML constraints), errors will result if trying to load one of these documents using the XML load methods. Two corresponding load functions do exist, however, that allow HTML documents to be loaded into a tree, which can then be manipulated the same way as an XML-based tree. The methods are loadHTML() and loadHTMLFile(). Each of these methods takes exactly one parameter, either the string containing the HTML or a URI used to locate and load the HTML. Unlike their XML equivalents, these methods do not accept parser options as a second parameter. For example:

```
/* Load the file http://www.example.com/index.html */
$dom = new DOMDocument();
$dom->loadHTMLFile('http://www.example.com/index.html');

/* Loading statically */
$dom = DOMDocument::loadHTMLFile('http://www.example.com/index.html');
```

Now that you have a document containing a tree, you will see how to output the contents of the tree. The output may be as a string or to a URI, such as a file. The methods are similar to those used to load the data. To output as XML, you'll use the function saveXML() to output the contents to a string and the function save() to output to a URI.

The saveXML() method accepts one optional node parameter. The node parameter must be an object derived from the DOMNode class and must be from the same document as the DOMDocument object from which the method is being called. When this parameter is not present, the entire document is serialized to a string. Using the $dom object created when loading a document with the LIBXML_NOBLANKS option, you can serialize the document. For example:

```
$output = $dom->saveXML();
```

This would set $output to a string containing <root><child>contents</child></root>. If a DOMElement object existed called $child that represented the element child in the document, this object could be passed as a parameter to the method to output just the element. For example:

```
$output = $dom->saveXML($child);
```

This would result in the string <child>contents</child>.

The save() method also accepts a single parameter. This parameter sets the URI to which the document is to be serialized. The return value for this method is the number of bytes written to the URI. Unlike the saveXML method, a single node cannot be serialized to a URI:

```
$bytes = $dom->save('output.xml);
```

This snippet of code saves the document to the file output.xml and returns the number of bytes written to the variable $bytes. Running this code, you might be surprised to see $bytes equal to 58. Whether a document was loaded with an XML declaration or the version and encoding parameters were passed when creating a document, an XML declaration is present when serializing the document with at least the version parameter, defaulting to 1.0, set.

Documents manually created or loaded with the LIBXML_NOBLANKS option typically do not contain text nodes containing whitespace. When serialized, the output generated is not easily human readable because the output is all strung together. You can use the formatProperty on the DOMDocument class to "prettify" the output. Setting this property to TRUE prior to serialization causes the parser to add line feeds and indentations where appropriate. For example:

```
$dom->formatOutput = TRUE;
print $dom->saveXML();
```

This code results in the following output:

```
<?xml version="1.0"?>
<root>
  <child>content</child>
</root>
```

Just as with the load functionality, you can also save a document in HTML format. The methods saveHTML() and saveHTMLFile() perform this operation. The method saveHTML() takes no parameters and returns the output as a string. The saveHTMLFile() method takes a single parameter, the URI, and returns the number of bytes written. The output is normally not XML-compliant because it is true HTML and *not* XHTML. Assuming the object $htmldoc contains a tree to be serialized into HTML, the following examples illustrate how to use the methods to serialize HTML:

```
/* Serialize document to a string in HTML format */
$html = $htmldoc->saveHTML();


/* Serialize document to file index.html in HTML format */
$bytes = $htmldoc->saveHTMLFile('index.html');
```

You have spent much time examining the simple operations of instantiating, loading, and saving DOMDocument objects. Understanding the basic operations of the DOMDocument class is important because this class serves as the foundation for all operations within the DOM extension. Nearly everything in the DOM extension is derived from and associated with a document, as you will further examine when exploring the other aspects of the DOM extension throughout this chapter. With these basic concepts of the DOMDocument behind you, you can learn about navigating an existing tree.

Navigating the Tree

Compared to other tree-based parsers (in PHP 5, the SimpleXML extension is the only other native tree-based extension), one of the DOM extension's strengths is its rich navigation support. This strength can also be a weakness because this rich support results in a large number of methods and properties; this leads to a large API to learn and understand. The document in Listing 6-1 is in DocBook format. DocBook is a system for writing documentation in XML format. I will use the example document in Listing 6-1 throughout the following sections to illustrate how to navigate a document tree.

Listing 6-1. *Example Document Using* DocBook *Format*

```
<?xml version="1.0" encoding="UTF-8"?>
<!DOCTYPE book PUBLIC "-//OASIS//DTD DocBook XML V4.1.2//EN"
                      "http://www.oasis-open.org/docbook/xml/4.1.2/docbookx.dtd">
<book lang="en">
   <bookinfo>
      <title>DOM in PHP 5</title>
```

```
      <author>
         <firstname>Rob</firstname>
         <surname>Richards</surname>
      </author>
      <copyright>
         <year>2005</year>
         <holder>Rob Richards</holder>
      </copyright>
   </bookinfo>
   <preface>
      <title>The DOM Tree</title>
      <para>An example DOM Tree using DocBook.</para>
   </preface>
   <chapter id="navigation">
      <title>Navigating The Tree</title>
      <para>The document element is accessed from the
<emphasis>documentElement</emphasis> property, which is available from any class
derived from DOMNode</para>
      <para>The document node is also accessible using the
<emphasis>ownerDocument</emphasis> property, also derived from the DOMNode
class.</para>
   </chapter>
</book>
```

This first step you need to take is to load the document into a DOMDocument object. I will show how to load the document in Listing 6-1 from the file mydocbook.xml. For now, the document will be loaded with the default options. This means the DTD is *not* loaded and the id attribute within the document is a regular attribute and *not* an ID type. For example:

```
$dom = new DOMDocument();
$dom->load('mydocbook.xml');
```

Navigation all begins with a DOMDocument object. These objects have no attributes; they have only child nodes. At a minimum, all XML documents must have a document element, but as mentioned in previous chapters, a document can also have a DTD and any number of comment and PI nodes. You can access these nodes using any of the many child properties and methods available from the base DOMNode class. The body of the document is the most commonly accessed and modified portion of the tree. Before examining how to access child nodes, which will be covered later in the "Moving Within the Tree" section, you will first see how to easily access the body.

Understanding the Document Element

The document element, like the document node, is a focal point in an XML document. Being the root of the body for the document, it is a node with a fixed position—the entry point for the body and universally accessible. Objects derived from the DOMNode class are able to access the documentElement property, which returns the document element as a DOMElement to also navigate back to the document element.

The document element from Listing 6-1 is the book element. Using the DOMDocument object, $dom, you can retrieve the book element with the documentElement property:

```
$root = $dom->documentElement;
```

This call returns a DOMElement object, which is the book element node, and sets it to the variable $root. Armed with the document element, you can now explore the rest of the body.

Accessing Basic Node Information

Before going too much further, it is useful to take a brief look at how to access basic node information. Three of the most basic pieces of information often used within the DOM extension are the type of node, the name of the node, and the value of the node. Knowing the structure of a document is not a requirement when using the DOM extension, so many times you will need these pieces of information when writing applications in PHP. The properties within the next sections are all from the base DOMNode class. Although all classes derived from the DOMNode class may call these properties, not all properties return useful information for all types of nodes. In some cases, the return value may even be NULL when the called property is not applicable for the node.

Node Type

In many cases when using the DOM extension, a node will be returned but you won't know what type of node it is. In these instances, you can check the type of node using the nodeType property. This property returns an integer corresponding to one of the built-in constants for node types:

```
$type = $root->nodeType;
print $type;
```

This code prints the number 1, which corresponds to the XML_ELEMENT_NODE constant. You can find the complete list of node type constants in Appendix B, and in a moment you will be introduced to a few more.

Node Name

The name of a node is generally applicable to element and attribute nodes. All nodes have names, but unlike elements and attributes that actually have specific names, most other nodes have generalized names corresponding to the type of node. The property used to access the node name is nodeName:

```
print $dom->nodeName."\n";
print $root->nodeName."\n";
```

This code illustrates the difference of the node name for a document node and an element node. The document node, $dom, returns the value #document. The element node, $root, on the other hand, returns the tag name for the element, book. If this returned the node name of a text node, the value would be #text. As you can see, the node name for the text node is nondescriptive and offers no additional information that could have just as easily been obtained from the node type. A few additional node types exist that do have specific names, such as entities, entity references, notations, document type definitions, and PIs. Although a few of these may be useful to you, elements and attributes are still the most commonly used nodes with this property.

Node Value

The property nodeValue offers access to the contents of certain nodes. Nodes having values are attributes, CDATA sections, comments, PIs, and text. This is according to the specification. For convenience, the DOM implementation in PHP 5 allows you to access this property by element node as well:

```
print $dom->nodeValue."\n";
print $root->nodeValue."\n";
```

In the first call, the node value for the document node is accessed. The property is not valid for document nodes, and NULL is returned with only a line feed printed. In the second call, the nodeValue of the document element is printed. As mentioned, this property is not valid according to the DOM specifications. To make things a little easier, the DOM extension in PHP 5 does allow this property for an element and returns a concatenation of all text nodes within the scope of the element. The output is a bit long, but the abbreviated output looks like the following:

```
        DOM in PHP 5


            Rob
            Richards



            2005
/* Rest of Output Omitted for Brevity */
```

When the document was initially loaded, whitespaces were not removed from the document. These whitespaces, being text nodes, are also concatenated and included as part of the output, resulting in the previous formatting.

Using the Properties Together

The nodeType, nodeName, and nodeValue properties are often useful and used together when writing code where logic is conditional based on the specifics of the node being tested. Consider the following code, which can be used as a function. A node, referenced by $node, is tested; based on criteria of these properties, certain actions are taken.

```
switch ($node->nodeType) {
    case XML_ELEMENT_NODE:
        print "Element Tag Name: ".$node->nodeName;
        if ($node->nodeName == "book") {
            /* We may want the lang attribute */
        }
```

```
        break;
    case XML_ATTRIBUTE_NODE:
        print "Attribute Name: ".$node->nodeName."\n";
        print "Attribute Value: ".$node->nodeValue."\n";
        if ($node->nodeName == "lang") {
            /* Do something with the language */
        }
        break;
    case XML_TEXT_NODE:
    case XML_CDATA_SECTION_NODE:
        print "Content: ".$node->nodeValue."\n";
        break;
    default:
        print "Other Node Names: ".$node->nodeName."\n";
}
```

This code uses a `switch` statement to perform certain actions based on the node type of the node passed in. Depending upon the type, actions then take place based on the name and possible value of the node. This is a simplified case but should give you an idea of how these properties can be useful. As you become more familiar with other aspects of tree navigation, you will revisit and modify this code.

Moving Within the Tree

At this point, you are still situated on the document element with the $root object. You can navigate to most other node types by accessing children. Attribute nodes are an exception to this. These are treated as properties of element nodes, which will be covered in the "Accessing Attributes" section. Movement, however, is not restricted to descending into the tree. As you will see, accessing siblings, accessing parents, and even directly accessing the document node are all possible.

Accessing Children

Child nodes are those that are direct descendants of the current node. Simply put, all nodes living exactly one level beneath the current node are children. For example, an element node may have mixed content consisting of, but not limited to, a comment, a text node, and some additional element nodes. An attribute node contains a single child node, which is a text node holding the value for the attribute. Document nodes can contain comment nodes, PIs, a document type, and a single element node as children. The type of children possible depends upon the type of the current node. You can perform a quick check to see whether a node has child nodes with the `hasChildNodes()` method, which returns a Boolean indicating whether child nodes are present on the current node.

All child nodes can be returned as a `DOMNodeList` using the `childNodes` property. An object of the `DOMNodeList` class is an iterable object. You can access it using the `item` property to retrieve a specific node from the list or even the iterator functions in PHP, such as `foreach`:

```
if ($root->hasChildNodes()) {
   $children = $root->childNodes;
   foreach($children as $node) {
      print $node->nodeName."\n";
   }
}
```

This code retrieves the children of the document element, iterating through the resulting DOMNodeList object using foreach, and prints the name of each node. The output from this is as follows:

```
#text
bookinfo
#text
preface
#text
chapter
#text
```

The book element contains three child elements but also is interspersed with whitespace. This whitespace was not removed when the document was loaded, resulting in the previous text nodes being created in the tree. Using this property, you can see why the nodeType property can come in handy. Unless you need to take some specific action with the whitespace, more often than not you will ignore it when navigating the tree. For example:

```
foreach($children as $node) {
   if ($node->nodeType != XML_TEXT_NODE) {
      print $node->nodeName."\n";
   }
}
```

Here the text nodes have been skipped, resulting in the following output:

```
bookinfo
preface
chapter
```

You can also access a subtree directly using the firstChild and lastChild properties. Rather than having to retrieve the entire collection of children, these properties are quick ways to access the start or end of the subtree:

```
$first = $root->firstChild;
$last = $root->lastChild;
```

The variable $first contains the DOMText object that is the first child beneath the book element and prior to the bookinfo element. The variable $last contains the DOMText object that is the last child of book and that contains the line feed after the closing chapter tag. Currently being whitespace, these nodes can be ignored for now. So where does this get you? you may ask. You can also move laterally by accessing node siblings, which you will learn about now.

Accessing Siblings

Sibling nodes are those residing on the same level as the current node. For example, all nodes within the $children DOMNodeList object are siblings of each other. They all live on the same level and have the same parent. You move laterally within a subtree using the nextSibling and previousSibling properties.

Using the $first object created in the previous section, you can access the sibling nodes using the nextSibling property:

```
$node = $first;
while($node) {
    if ($node->nodeType == XML_ELEMENT_NODE) {
        print $node->nodeName."\n";
    }
    $node = $node->nextSibling;
}
```

This gives you the same results as when iterating $children and printing only element tag names:

```
bookinfo
preface
chapter
```

The previousSibling property allows navigation to be performed in reverse:

```
$node = $last;
while($node) {
    if ($node->nodeType == XML_ELEMENT_NODE) {
        print $node->nodeName."\n";
    }
    $node = $node->previousSibling;
}
```

The output this time is as follows:

```
chapter
preface
bookinfo
```

Accessing Parents and Using ownerDocument

Nodes can also perform ascending movement within a tree. Every node within a document has a parent with the exception of the document node. A parent is the direct ancestor of the current node; hence, a document node cannot have a parent node because it is the root node for the entire document. You can access the parent using the parentNode property:

```
do {
    $node = $first;
    while($node) {
        if (! $node->parentNode->isSameNode($root)) {
            print "ERROR: Parent Node Test FAILED";
            break 2;
        }
        $node = $node->nextSibling;
    }
    print "All parent node tests PASSED";
} while(0);
```

Using the code from the nextSibling example, the parentNode for each of the nodes, including the text nodes, is returned and tested against the document element, $root, using the isSameNode() method. This example uses object dereferencing features from PHP 5 and is equivalent to writing the following:

```
$parent = $node->parentNode;
if (! $parent->isSameNode($root)) {
...
```

The isSameNode() method tests the current node against the node passed as an argument to determine whether they are the same node. By "same node," I mean the nodes must be the same node within the document. This is not the same as saying the nodes are equivalent; equivalent nodes must just have the same names and content but do not have to be the same node with the same position in the document. As you can see from the resulting All parent node tests PASSED message, the parent node for these is the document element, $root.

Nodes have direct access to their associated document through the ownerDocument property. Although the body is accessible using the documentElement property, the document node is still an important node even when not needing or using a DTD. Later in this chapter, in the "Document Nodes" section, you will learn how to use the document node object for factory methods. This node provides much of the functionality used when creating and editing documents and is accessed frequently in applications. For example:

```
$node = $root->ownerDocument;
print $node->nodeName."\n";
```

The code prints the value #document, because the document node is returned from the property. To verify this, you can execute the following code using the isSameNode() method:

```
if ($dom->isSameNode($node))
    print "TRUE";
```

Accessing Specific Elements

You can also access specific elements by tag names. When you need to access specific elements within the scope of the current node, you can use the methods getElementsByTagName() and getElementsByTagNameNS(). Element nodes can be contained only within document nodes and element nodes; thus, these methods are available only when the current node is based on a DOMDocument or DOMElement class. For example, from the document node, $dom, you can retrieve all title elements within the document using the getElementsByTagName() method:

```
$elements = $dom->getElementsByTagName("title");
$length = $elements->length;
for ($x=0;$x < $length;$x++) {
    print "Element Value: ".$elements->item($x)->nodeValue."\n";
}
```

This code retrieves a DOMNodeList object, $elements, containing all title elements within the scope of the document node, $dom. Being the document node, this returns all elements named title within the entire document. The collection is iterated using a for loop based on length, indicating the number of nodes within the collection. length is the total number of elements, and the collection uses a zero-based index, so no items are at an index equal to or greater than the length. Using dereferencing (available in PHP 5), the element at the current index, $x, is retrieved, and the nodeValue for the node is printed. The output from this operation is as follows:

```
Element Value: DOM in PHP 5
Element Value: The DOM Tree
Element Value: Navigating The Tree
```

You can pass the special value * for the tag name argument. This is a wildcard used to match any element name. For example:

```
$preface = $root->getElementsByTagName("preface");
$elements = $preface->item(0)->getElementsByTagName("*");
$length = $elements->length;
for ($x=0;$x < $length;$x++) {
    print "Element Name: ".$elements->item($x)->nodeName."\n";
    print "Element Value: ".$elements->item($x)->nodeValue."\n";
}
```

From the document element, $root, all preface elements within its scope are retrieved as a DOMNodeList object, $preface. No length test is performed, because you already know that an element exists in the document (although it is a good habit to test the return values prior to using them). Again, dereferencing is used; the first element in the DOMNodeList is retrieved, and immediately in the same line of code, getElementsByTageName("*") is called on the node. All elements within the scope of the preface element are returned and set to the $elements variable. You can access this collection the same way as before: by using a for loop. This time the node name is also printed with its value, because you have no way to know exactly what elements are returned when using the wildcard. The resulting output is as follows:

```
Element Name: title
Element Value: The DOM Tree
Element Name: para
Element Value: An example DOM Tree using DocBook.
```

When working with namespaced documents, the getElementsByTagNameNS() method allows elements in specified namespaces to be returned. The example document in this chapter does not contain namespaces, so I cannot give a specific example at this time. The method differs from the non-namespaced method in that it takes two arguments. The first is the namespace URI, and the second is the local name of the element, which is the same as the tag name for the previous method. Just like the name parameter, the namespace URI parameter also accepts the * wildcard. Using the wildcard results in retrieving all elements in any namespace, but they must be in a namespace with the name determined from the second parameter, which can also be a wildcard. For example:

```
$result = $dom->getElementsByTagNameNS("*", "*");
```

The resulting DOMNodeList, $result, will contain every element in the document that is within any namespace.

Accessing Attributes

Attributes inherit the same methods and properties from the DOMNode class as other node types, but they are not accessed in the same manner as other nodes in a document. As you have seen so far, nodes are traversed through children of nodes. Attributes are different because they are not children of elements, which is the only node type from which attributes may reside; rather, attributes, conceptually, are properties of elements. You access them through their own set of properties and methods.

Collections of Attributes

Just like you can check and access children, you can check attributes with the hasAttributes() method and access them with the attributes property. Both of these are defined on the DOMNode class and are safe to use with all node types, although an object of DOMElement will be the only class type that can return useful data:

```
if ($root->hasAttributes()) {
    $attributes = $root->attributes;
    foreach($attributes as $attr) {
        print "Attribute Name: ".$attr->nodeName."\n";
        print "Attribute Value: ".$attr->nodeValue."\n";
    }
}
```

If attributes exist on the $root object, tested using the hasAttributes() method, a DOMNamedNodeMap object, $attributes, is returned from the attributes property. This object is iterated in the same way the DOMNodeList is iterated. The resulting output for this code is as follows:

```
Attribute Name: lang
Attribute Value: en
```

One of the differences with the node map is that attributes can be accessed directly by name rather than just a position. For example:

```
$attr = $attributes->getNamedItem("lang");
print "Attribute Name: ".$attr->nodeName."\n";
print "Attribute Value: ".$attr->nodeValue."\n";
```

The document element contains only a single element, so the previous code returns the same results as the code iterating the attributes. This time, the lang attribute was accessed directly from the node map rather than iterating the entire map. Just like a DOMNodeList, the position could also have been used to access the attribute. Using a DOMNamedNodeMap, however, the items are unordered, so you have no guarantee that an item at a certain position is the item for which you are looking. For example:

```
if ($attributes->length > 0) {
    $attr = $attributes->item(0);
    print "Attribute Name: ".$attr->nodeName."\n";
    print "Attribute Value: ".$attr->nodeValue."\n";
}
```

This code outputs the same results as before. The difference here is the test for the length of the DOMNamedNodeMap, which returns the number of items in the collection, and the use of the item() method to access the item at the zero-based index. Passing in the value of 0 for the argument returns the first item in the list, which is the lang attribute.

Individual Attributes

Attributes do not have to be accessed through a DOMNamedNodeMap. The DOMElement class offers attribute-specific methods that you can use to access specific attributes. The method used depends upon whether just the value of the attribute or the entire attribute node needs to be returned. It also depends upon whether namespaces are in use. You can access attributes using the getAttribute(), getAttributeNode(), getAttributeNS(), and getAttributeNodeNS() methods. For example:

```
/* Access lang attribute value directly */
print "Attribute Value: ".$root->getAttribute("lang")."\n";

/* Return the lang attribute node and access the returned attribute node */
$attr = $root->getAttributeNode("lang");
print "Attribute Value: ".$attr->nodeValue."\n";
```

The previous two pieces of code print the same results but perform the operations differently. The first snippet returns the value of the named attribute, lang, and prints the value. The second block of code retrieves the attribute node named lang and prints the value from the returned node.

Although the document in Listing 6-1 is not using namespaces, the namespace-aware methods can be used:

```
print "Attribute Value: ".$root->getAttributeNS(NULL, "lang")."\n";
$attr = $root->getAttributeNodeNS(NULL, "lang");
print "Attribute Value: ".$attr->nodeValue."\n";
```

The first argument for these methods is the namespace URI for the attribute being accessed. Your attributes do not live in any namespaces, so by passing NULL, you access the attributes normally. It is the same as accessing attributes that do not live in any namespace. If the attributes were associated with a namespace, the results from the methods would be empty unless the appropriate namespace URI were passed as the first parameter.

Declaring Namespaces

Namespace declarations are handled as attributes within the DOM extension and as such are created using the namespace's attribute methods. The prefix xmlns is bound to the http:// www.w3.org/2000/xmlns/ namespace as defined in the XML 1.1 specification from the W3C (http://www.w3.org/TR/xml-names11/). For example:

```
$doc = DOMDocument::loadXML('<root/>');
$root = $doc->documentElement;

$root->setAttributeNS('http://www.w3.org/2000/xmlns/',
                    'xmlns:exa','http://www.example.com/example');
$root->appendChild(new DOMElement('exa:child', 'content',
                                'http://www.example.com/example'));
$doc->formatOutput = TRUE;
print $doc->saveXML();
```

Using the setAttributeNS() method, a namespace that contains the prefix exa and is bound to http://www.example.com/example is declared. The namespace for the xmlns prefix is used as the namespace URI in this method, and the value of the attribute is the namespace that will be created. To declare a namespace, it is mandatory that the namespace URI parameter be the value http://www.w3.org/200/xmlns/; otherwise, the DOM extension will not know that a namespace is supposed to be created and a normal attribute will result. The following line illustrates how to append a new element bound to this newly created namespace, which results in the following document upon serialization:

```
<?xml version="1.0"?>
<root xmlns:exa="http://www.example.com/example">
  <exa:child>content</exa:child>
</root>
```

Creating and Editing a Tree

The DOM extension's biggest strength comes from its functionality for creating and editing trees. As you will see with the other XML technologies, none comes close to the capabilities the DOM extension offers in this respect. Unless you are a hard-core XML developer or integrator, you may end up using only a quarter of the offered functionality yet still encounter no shortcomings with the small subset of functionality used. Within the following sections, you will begin by creating the document in Listing 6-1 from scratch and then work on editing the result.

Document Nodes

Earlier in this chapter, you saw many different methods for creating a DOMDocument object. The document being created contains a document type declaration, so you will use the DOMImplementation class to create the DOMDocument object; this allows you to create a

DOMDocType object that can be passed as a parameter to create a document with a subset. This class allows static method calls, so in this case, you have no need to instantiate an object. For example:

```
$doctype = DOMImplementation:: createDocumentType("book",
        "-//OASIS//DTD DocBook XML V4.1.2//EN",
        "http://www.oasis-open.org/docbook/xml/4.1.2/docbookx.dtd");
$dom = DOMImplementation:: createDocument(NULL, "book", $doctype);
```

The first step is creating a DOMDoctType object, because it is needed when creating the document. You do this using the createDocumentType() method and passing the name for the document declaration, which, as you recall from Chapter 2, must match the name of the document element, the public identifier, and finally the system identifier. If the declaration is a system identifier, you pass NULL for the public identifier argument. The final step is to create the document using the createDocument() method. The first argument is the namespace for the document element. In this case, the document is not using namespaces, and you use NULL. The remaining parameters are the name of the document element, which will be created when the method returns, and the DOMDocType object, $doctype, that was created in the previous line. Upon executing this code, the DOMDocument object, $dom, will contain the document node with a DTD and the document element created.

At this point, if the tree were output using a method such as saveXML(), you would notice that the encoding is missing. Using the DOMImplementation class to create the document does not offer a way to set the version or encoding. The version at least defaults to 1.0. You can set the encoding using the encoding property of the document:

```
$dom->encoding = "UTF-8";
```

This property does not affect how you create the document. Data that is not conformant to the internal UTF-8 encoding of the tree still needs to be converted to UTF-8. Upon output of the tree, however, the data is converted to the proper encoding set by this property.

Element Nodes

You can create, insert, and remove element nodes from a tree, but you cannot (unlike with most other nodes) edit their contents. Whether they are just text or combinations of other nodes, in order to edit them, you must access the child nodes or attributes. The next sections will take you through how to create, insert, and remove element nodes in a document.

Creating Elements

You have two ways to create element nodes. One is to use the factory methods from the DOMDocument object, and the other is direct instantiation. According to the specification, nodes must be associated with a document. The factory methods follow this rule. As you will see following the factory methods, the DOM extension allows direct instantiation of DOMElement objects, which results in element nodes with no tree association. This exists not only for convenience during development, but as discussed later in this chapter, it also allows for limited functionality of extending the DOM classes.

As previously mentioned, the DOMDocument object is a focal object when using the DOM extension. You can create a new element associated to the current document using the factory methods createElement() and createElementNS(). The document that has been created to this point contains a DTD and the document element node book. Ignoring the attribute for now, the next node to be created is the bookinfo element, which is the first child element of book. For example:

```
$bookinfo = $dom->createElement("bookinfo");
```

This piece of code returns a DOMElement object, $bookinfo, with the name bookinfo. The createElement method takes one mandatory parameter and one optional parameter. The first parameter is the qualified name of the element to be created, which in this case is bookinfo. The second optional parameter is the value of the element. In the event the element node will contain text content, you can do this at the same time the element is created. In actuality, a text node is created and appended as a child of the element being created. For instance, the first child of the bookinfo element is a title element, consisting of only text:

```
$bititle = $dom->createElement("title", "DOM in PHP 5");
```

With these two lines of code, you have created two new objects. The variable $bookinfo holds the DOMElement object for the bookinfo node, and the variable $bititle holds the DOMElement object for a title node. This $bititle node also has a child text node, with the contents DOM in PHP 5. For now they exist as stand-alone nodes. They are associated with the current document but are not within the tree at this point. Before inserting these nodes, it is helpful to look at other ways to create element nodes.

You can also create elements within a namespace. The document being created here does not use namespaces, but you could still use the createElementNS() method:

```
$biauthor = $dom->createElementNS(NULL, "author");
```

This method requires two mandatory parameters and accepts a third parameter, which is an optional value parameter. The first parameter is the namespace URI. In this case, nodes are not within any namespace, so NULL is passed. The second parameter is the qualified name of the element. As you probably recall, this consists of the prefix and the local name. For example, you could create an element named trash in the http://www.example.com/trash namespace. The prefix tr will also be associated with this element:

```
$trash = $dom->createElementNS("http://www.example.com/trash", "tr:trash");
```

When the $trash object is inserted into a tree, the element will be associated with the prefix, and if needed, the namespace declaration will be created within the document. If possible, however, an existing namespace declaration within scope at the insertion point will be used. This may result in a change to the prefix, which is not incorrect, because the namespace itself is the important aspect here and not the prefix. I will illustrate how to do this in the examples in the "Building an XSL Template" example toward the end of this chapter.

You can also directly instantiate elements using the new keyword. The firstname and surname elements, which will be the children of the bookinfo element, will be created using the new keyword. The constructor for the DOMElement class takes the same parameters as the createElement() method. The first required parameter is the name of the elements, and the second is an optional value for the element:

```
$firstname = new DOMElement("firstname", "Rob");
$surname = new DOMElement("surname", "Richards");
```

These two new elements, unlike the previous created elements, are not associated with a document and are read-only. Until they are associated with a document, they can be inserted into a tree, but no children, other than any text nodes that may have been created during instantiation, can be appended to these elements.

When creating elements, you have a possibility of a DOMException being thrown. The name of the element is checked to ensure that it is valid. In the event the check fails, the object is not created and a DOMException indicating that invalid characters were used may be thrown. For example, the name 123 is used when trying to instantiate a DOMElement object:

```
try {
    $test = new DOMElement("123");
} catch (DOMException $e) {
    var_dump($e);
}
```

According to the XML specification, names cannot start with a numeric, which results in a DOMException being thrown.

As previously mentioned, the constructor can take a third parameter indicating the URI for the namespace of the element. When this is passed, the first argument, being a qualified name, will split the name parameter into any prefix and local name values. Without the third parameter being used, the name passed is used as the local name even if it contains a colon:

```
$nsElement = new DOMElement("nse:myelement", NULL, "http://www.example.com/ns");
```

This instantiates a DOMElement object with the myelement element prefixed with nse and living in the http://www.example.com/ns namespace. A value can be passed for the content, but in this case, NULL is passed, and the element is created without any children.

Inserting Elements

With a few elements currently created, they need to be inserted into the tree. The methods for appending and inserting nodes come from the DOMNode class and thus are not specific to element nodes; in other words, they can be called from other node types as well. Currently, the document contains only a single document element. Using the document node, $dom, the document element will be retrieved and the bookinfo element appended:

```
$dom->documentElement->appendChild($bookinfo);
```

The appendChild() method takes a node to be appended as a child of the current node for a parameter and returns the node appended. The node is appended as the last child of the current node's children. In this case, the book element currently has no children, so the bookinfo is added as the first child. Also, you already have a handle on the node being inserted, so you have no need to capture the return value.

This method, like the other insertion methods, may throw a DOMException. The possible cases for an exception are a hierarchy error, when the node being appended already exists in the tree and is a parent of the current node; a wrong document error, when the node being appended is associated with a document other than the current nodes document; and lastly a "no modification allowed" error, when the current node is read-only. One point to note about a hierarchy error is that it is not considered an error to append a node without an associated document to a node with a document because the appended node will become part of the tree and automatically be associated with the document. In cases where the current node is not associated with a document, a "no modification allowed" error is issued, because these nodes are read-only.

Before appending the author element, $biauthor, into the tree, you can append the firstname and surname nodes to the author element. Remember, $biauthor was created with an association to the document, so the firstname and surname elements, once appended, will inherit this association:

```
$biauthor->appendChild($surname);
$biauthor->insertBefore($firstname, $surname);
```

The first line should look familiar because it was used to append the bookinfo element. The second line uses a new method, insertBefore(). It works similarly to appendChild(), but the second argument, which must be a child node of the current node, is used as a reference point to insert the new node before. This code is the same as writing the following:

```
$biauthor->appendChild($firstname);
$biauthor->appendChild($surname);
```

You will typically use insertBefore() when trying to insert elements in the middle of a list of child nodes, but it's used in the example to show how it works. With the author element complete with content, you can now insert it into the document:

```
$bookinfo->appendChild($biauthor);
```

If you look at the output now, you will see the document beginning to take shape. The document may look odd because it is all strung together without any line feeds, so you can beautify the output using the formatOutput property:

```
$dom->formatOutput = TRUE;
print $dom->saveXML();
```

Well, it looks like the title element was omitted and needs to be inserted. In this case, insertBefore() is definitely appropriate. The title node is supposed to come before the author element, which is already in the tree:

```
$bookinfo->insertBefore($bititle, $biauthor);
```

You can deal with the remainder of the elements for the tree later because you already have enough information to create them. For now, you'll move on to dealing with attribute nodes.

Attribute Nodes

You can handle attribute nodes, as well as specific attribute functionality from the DOMElement class, in a similar fashion to element nodes. You can create them using factory methods from the DOMDocument class by directly instantiating them, and you can create them using methods from a DOMElement object. You can also insert and remove them using the methods from the DOMNode class as well as methods from a DOMElement object.

Equivalent methods for attribute creation exist for a DOMDocument object as for element creation. Currently (though this may change in future version of PHP), you cannot create attributes with values using the factory methods. The only parameter is a name (or in the case of using namespaces, a namespace URI and a name):

```
/* Equivalent methods for creation of lang attribute */
$lang = $dom->createAttribute("lang");
$lang = $dom->createAttributeNS(NULL, "lang");
```

Both of these lines of code result in the creation of a DOMAttr object named lang. Using these methods, you need to specify a value, which you can do using the nodeValue property from the DOMNode class or using the value property from the DOMAttr class:

```
/* Equivalent calls to set the value for the lang attribute to "en" */
$lang->nodeValue = "en";
$lang->value = "en";
```

You can also create attributes with values at the same time using the new keyword. Again, these nodes will not be associated with a document:

```
$lang = new DOMAttr("lang", "en");
```

Using any of these methods to create an attribute requires the attribute to be inserted into the tree. Using methods already covered, you could add it doing this:

```
/* Equivalent methods for inserting an attribute */
$bookinfo->appendChild($lang);
$bookinfo->insertBefore($lang, NULL);
```

The last method uses insertBefore() with the reference node parameter being NULL. When NULL is passed as the reference node, the function works in the same way as appendChild(). The node is inserted as the last node.

Note Attributes are not children of element nodes. When using the appending child functions, such as appendChild(), the attribute is not appended as a child but instead appended in the attribute property list of the element.

You can also add attribute nodes using the setAttributeNode() and setAttributeNodeNS() methods from the DOMElement class. These methods take a single DOMAttr object as a parameter. These methods will first check whether an attribute with the same name—and in the case of setAttributeNodeNS(), the same name and namespace—exists. Then, if it exists, these methods remove the attribute and replace it with the new attribute. These methods return NULL if no attribute was replaced or return the replaced attribute. For example:

```
/* Equivalent calls for this document as no namespaces are being used */
$oldlang = $bookinfo->setAttributeNode($lang);
$oldlang = $bookinfo->setAttributeNodeNS($lang);
```

You can also create attributes without ever having to directly create a DOMAttr object. The DOMElement class includes the methods setAttribute() and setAttributeNS(). These methods are the counterparts to the getAttribute() and getAttributeNS() methods you encountered earlier when navigating the tree. Both of the set methods create an attribute based on the name and value, passed as parameters, and return the newly created DOMAttr object. Just like all the other namespace functions, getAttributeNS() accepts a namespace URI as a parameter and uses a qualified name as an argument:

```
/* Equivalent calls to create the lang attribute with value "en" */
$bookinfo->setAttribute("lang", "en");
$bookinfo->setAttributeNS(NULL, "lang", "en");
```

■**Caution** When creating an attribute with an entity reference as a value, you must create a DOMAttr object and set the value manually. The value argument for the constructor of a DOMAttr and for the setAttribute() and setAttributeNS() methods is simple text that is not parsed and treated as literal text.

Text Nodes

Text nodes are simple nodes, because they cannot have child nodes or attributes. In other words, they simply contain text content. This does not mean they offer little functionality, though. You can use the text nodes to set content as well as perform string functions. You create and insert them in the same manner as element nodes. You can create them either using a factory method from a DOMDocument object or using the new keyword. You can insert them using the normal appendChild() and insertBefore() methods.

Creating and Inserting Text Nodes

You use a DOMDocument object to create a text node with the createTextNode() method. A data parameter is required that specifies the content, or value, for the text node. Instantiating a DOMText object with the new keyword does not require a value, because the default is to create a text node with empty content. For example:

```
/* Equivalent creation of DOMText objects */
$yeartxt = $dom->createTextNode("2005");
$yeartxt = new DOMText("2005");
```

The text node created, whichever method you decide to use, will be used as the content for the yet-to-be-created year element, which will be the child of a yet-to-be-created copyright element. While inserting these nodes, this also creates the holder element. For example:

```
/* Create and Append a copyright element */
$copyright = $bookinfo->appendChild(new DOMElement("copyright"));
```

In one line, a new copyright element is instantiated using the new keyword and is appended to the bookinfo element. You might have wondered why the return values mattered before because all examples previously used instantiated objects when appending nodes. In this case, the $copyright variable, upon the method returning, will contain the newly created DOMElement object that contains the copyright element. For example:

```
/* Create year element */
$year = $dom->createElement("year");

/* Append text node to set content */
$year->appendChild($yeartxt);
$copyright->appendChild($year);
```

After creating the year element, the DOMText object, previously created, is appended as content. Once this is done, the year element is appended to the copyright element. For example:

```
/* Append a newly created holder element with content "Rob Richards" */
$copyright->appendChild(new DOMElement("holder", "Rob Richards"));
```

Again, a single line of code performs multiple operations. A new DOMElement object is created with the name holder and the value Rob Richards. This element is appended to the copyright element.

Manipulating Text

The DOMText class derives from the DOMCharacterData class. Methods exist in both classes that can manipulate text on DOMText objects. For example, take the following piece of code, which includes the appropriate output that will print after the colon in each of the comments:

```
/* If content is not whitespace then ... */
if (! $yeartxt->isElementContentWhitespace()) {
    /* Print substring at offset 1 and length 2: 00 */
    print $yeartxt->substringData(1,2)."\n";

    /* Append the string -2006 to the content and print output: 2005-2006 */
    $yeartxt->appendData("-2006");
    print $yeartxt->nodeValue."\n";

    /* Delete content at offset 4 with length of 5 and print output: 2005 */
    $yeartxt->deleteData(4,5);
    print $yeartxt->nodeValue."\n";

    /* Insert string "ABC" at offset 1 and print output: 2ABC005 */
    $yeartxt->insertData(1, "ABC");
    print $yeartxt->nodeValue."\n";

    /* Replace content at ofset 1 with length of 3 with an empty string: 2005 */
    $yeartxt->replaceData(1, 3, "");
    print $yeartxt->nodeValue."\n";
}
```

At this point the tree is really starting to take shape. The output at this point—using formatting, of course—looks like this:

```
<?xml version="1.0" encoding="UTF-8"?>
<!DOCTYPE book PUBLIC "-//OASIS//DTD DocBook XML V4.1.2//EN"
                     "http://www.oasis-open.org/docbook/xml/4.1.2/docbookx.dtd">
<book>
  <bookinfo lang="en">
    <title>DOM in PHP 5</title>
    <author>
      <firstname>Rob</firstname>
      <surname>Richards</surname>
    </author>
    <copyright>
      <year>2005</year>
      <holder>Rob Richards</holder>
    </copyright>
  </bookinfo>
</book>
```

The serialized tree looks almost exactly like the tree in Listing 6-1. This is good because that is the goal you are working toward. The only missing pieces are the preface and chapter subtrees. This will be left as an exercise for you to finish because I have already covered everything you need to complete the tree.

Other Node Types

The node types covered to this point are the most frequently used, which is why I have given them much greater emphasis. You can create and insert the remaining node types in the same manner as the previous nodes. Because the complete API is included in Appendix B, I will show how to create the remaining nodes through code:

```
/* Create a DOMDocumentFragment */
$frag = $dom->createDocumentFragment();
$frag = new DOMDocumentFragment();

/* Create DOMComment */
$comment = $dom->createComment("this is a comment");
$comment = new DOMComment("this is a comment");
/* Results in <!-- this is a comment --> */

/* Create DOMCDATASection */
$cdata = $dom->createCDATASection("<html></html>");
$cdata = new DOMCDATASection("<html></html>");
/* Results in <![CDATA[<html></html>]]> */

/* Create DOMProcessingInstruction */
$pi = $dom->createProcessingInstruction("php", "echo 'Hello World';");
$pi = new DOMProcessingInstruction("php", "echo 'Hello World';");
/* Results in <?php echo 'Hello World';?> */
```

```
/* Create DOMEntityReference */
$entityref = $dom->createEntityReference("lt");
$entityref = new DOMEntityReference("lt");
/* Results in &lt; */
```

Outside the methods inherited from the DOMNode class, the DOMDocumentFragment class is the only class with additional functionality. This functionality is only a single method and available only in PHP 5.1 and higher. Rather than having to build a fragment manually by appending nodes, you can use the method appendXML() to create a fragment from string data. Take the case of building a fragment manually versus building it from a string:

```
$frag = $dom->createDocumentFragment();
$frag->appendChild(new DOMElement("node1", "node1 value"));
$frag->appendChild(new DOMElement("node2", "node2 value"));
```

It would have been so much easier to append the data as a string. You had no need to manually create the DOMElement objects because the appropriate nodes are automatically created through the appendXML() method:

```
$frag = $dom->createDocumentFragment();
$frag->appendXML("<node1>node1 value</node1><node2>node2 value</node2>");
```

Note When appending a DOMDocumentFragment object into a tree, only the children on the fragment are added. The DOMDocumentFragment object that is left after an append will be empty because the nodes have been removed and inserted into the tree.

Removing and Replacing Nodes

The last piece of editing a document is removing and replacing nodes in a tree. Some of the methods encountered so far will perform this type of functionality. Take, for instance, the setAttributeNode() method. When a node with the same name exists on the element, the old attribute is removed and replaced with the new attribute node, and the old attribute is returned. The same functionality can happen with other node types using the replaceChild() method. Sometimes, however, you want just to remove a node. In this case, you can use the removeChild() method.

Given the following document loaded into a DOMDocument object:

```
$doc = DOMDocument::loadXML('<?xml version="1.0"?>
<root>
    <child1>child1 content</child1>
    <child2>child2 content</child2>
    <child3>child3 content</child3>
</root>');
```

the element child2 needs to be removed from this document, and child3 needs to be replaced with the element newchild. The first step is to get access to each of these nodes. To reduce the number of steps, I will show how to retrieve the elements using the getElementsByTagName() method:

```
$root = $doc->documentElement;
$child2 = $root->getElementsByTagName("child2")->item(0);
$child3 = $root->getElementsByTagName("child3")->item(0);
```

The first step is to remove the $child object:

```
$root->removeChild($child2);
```

If you look at the serialized tree now, you would see this:

```
<?xml version="1.0"?>
<root>
    <child1>child1 content</child1>

    <child3>child3 content</child3>
</root>
```

The whitespaces are left in the document, causing the blank line in the output. The $child3 object is still in scope so can now be replaced with a new element. This also will be condensed using the new keyword for the new element:

```
$oldchild = $root->replaceChild(new DOMElement("newchild", "new content"), $child3);
```

In this case, the new element is being created inline. Unfortunately, using the new keyword here does not give direct access to the newly created node. This method returns the node being removed from the tree. The resulting serialized tree is as follows:

```
<?xml version="1.0"?>
<root>
    <child1>child1 content</child1>

    <newchild>new content</newchild>
</root>
```

Wrapping up this section, you might want to remove those whitespaces within the root element children. I have already covered everything you need to know in order to do this. One way is to use the following piece of code:

```
$children = $root->childNodes;
for ($x=$children->length; $x--; $x>=0) {
    $node = $children->item($x);
    if ($node->nodeType == XML_TEXT_NODE && $node-> isElementContentWhitespace()) {
        $root->removeChild($node);
    }
}
```

You have many ways to accomplish this task. One question you may have is why the iteration was performed from last to first. Based on how this code was written, DOMNodeList objects are being used. These are live collections resulting in changes of indexes when nodes are added or removed. For now, I will let you think about this and possibly come up with the answer. Have no worries if you are unsure of why the code was written in this manner, because I answer this question in depth in the section "Common Questions, Misconceptions, and Problems."

Performing Validation

Chapter 3 covered three methods of validating XML documents. You can use each of these methods with the DOM extension to perform validation. As shown in the previous chapter, you can invoke and perform validation using DTDs during parsing by using the LIBXML_DTDVALID constant with either of the load options. It is not always the case that a document would need to be validated at the time of being parsed, and the bigger issue is that only DTDs can currently be used, leaving XML Schemas and RELAX NG unaccounted for. The DOMDocument class implements the accessor methods to perform validation after an XML document has been loaded.

Validating with DTDs

You must load DTDs prior to trying to validate against them within the DOM extension. Loading a document with the LIBXML_DTDLOAD parser option will load an external DTD but not perform validation at parse time. With a DOMDocument object instantiated and containing a loaded DTD, validation is as simple as calling the validate() method.

This method returns TRUE or FALSE, indicating the validity state of the document. Errors and warnings from libxml can be issued from this method call and should be handled appropriately, either by using a user error handler, allowing the printing of the errors; by using error suppression; or by using the new error handling available in PHP 5.1.

```
$dom = DOMDocument::loadXML('<?xml version="1.0"?>
<!DOCTYPE courses [
    <!ELEMENT courses (course+)>
    <!ELEMENT course (title)>
    <!ELEMENT title (#PCDATA)>
]>
<courses>
    <course>
        <title>Algebra</title>
    </course>
</courses>');
```

The variable $dom, after running this code, is a DOMDocument object containing an internal subset. Internal subsets do not require any parameters instructing a DTD to be loaded because they are internal. It has not been validated, because the parser was not instructed to validate it. At this point, you may want to find out whether the document is valid, and you can easily do this with the validate() method:

```
$isvalid = $dom->validate();
var_dump($isvalid);
```

The result of this is bool(true), which indicates the document is valid.

It becomes more difficult when building a document manually containing a DTD and performing validation. Internal subsets cannot be created with the DOM extension manually. You can create external subsets using methods from the DOMImplementation class, but these still are not loaded into memory. In these instances, a document should be serialized, reloaded, and then validated in order for validation to work properly.

Validating with XML Schemas

Validation with XML Schemas is a bit different than working with DTDs. The schema is not loaded at parse time like internal and external subsets are. Associating an XML schema with an XML document is not even performed until validation is ready to be performed. An advantage of this is that it removes the need for any type of document serialization.

You can specify XML Schemas either through a string containing the schema or through a URI pointing to the location of the schema. The DOMDocument class implements the methods schemaValidate() and schemaValidateSource() to load a schema and validate it against the current document at the same time. Each takes a single parameter. The method schemaValidate() accepts a string containing the URI of the schema; schemaValidateSource() takes a string containing the XML of the schema itself. These methods return the same results as validating against a DTD. A Boolean is returned, and errors from libxml are possible. Each must be handled appropriately. For example:

```
$dom = DOMDocument::loadXML('<?xml version="1.0"?>
<courses>
   <course>
      <title>Algebra</title>
   </course>
</courses>');

$schema = '<?xml version="1.0"?>
<xsd:schema xmlns:xsd="http://www.w3.org/2001/XMLSchema">
   <xsd:element name="courses">
      <xsd:complexType>
         <xsd:sequence>
            <xsd:element name="course" minOccurs="0" maxOccurs="unbounded">
               <xsd:complexType>
                  <xsd:sequence>
                     <xsd:element name="title" type="xsd:string"/>
                  </xsd:sequence>
               </xsd:complexType>
            </xsd:element>
         </xsd:sequence>
      </xsd:complexType>
   </xsd:element>
</xsd:schema>';

$isvalid = $dom->schemaValidateSource($schema);
var_dump($isvalid);
```

This example loads a scaled-down XML Schema from Chapter 3 into the string $schema. The method schemaValidateSource() is called on the DOMDocument object, $dom, to be validated. In this case, the document validates and returns the Boolean, TRUE, identified by the $isvalid variable.

Validating with RELAX NG

Validation using RELAX NG works in the same manner as validating with an XML Schema. It offers the same advantage in that the schema is associated at the time of validation, and document serialization is not required. Other than using RELAX NG for the schema and a minor difference in method names, the parameters, return values, and error issuance is the same as when using XML Schemas. The methods used with RELAX NG validation are relaxNGValidate() and relaxNGValidateSource(). The first method takes a URI, and the latter takes a string containing the XML for the RELAX NG schema. For example:

```
$schema = '<?xml version="1.0" encoding="utf-8" ?>
<element name="courses" xmlns="http://relaxng.org/ns/structure/1.0">
   <zeroOrMore>
      <element name="course">
         <element name="title">
            <text/>
         </element>
      </element>
   </zeroOrMore>
</element>';

$isvalid = $dom->relaxNGValidateSource($schema);
var_dump($isvalid);
```

Using the DOMDocument object, $dom, from the XML Schema example, the RELAX NG schema (in serialized form and set to the $schema variable) is validated against the document using the relaxNGValidateSource() method. Just like the other validation methods, this document successfully validates and returns the Boolean TRUE to the $isvalid variable.

Using XPath

The DOMXPath class in the DOM extension offers access to the underlying tree using XPath expressions, as examined in Chapter 4. This class is simple to use because it has minimal methods yet allows for complex expression. When running under PHP 5.0, a DOMNodeList containing nodes is the only return type available using the query() method. For PHP 5.1 and higher, the evaluate() method allows for a greater number of return types.

Instantiating DOMXPath

No factory methods exist for creating a DOMXPath object. DOMXPath is not part of the core DOM specification and exists solely to provide XPath support with the DOM extension. You can create a DOMXPath object using the new keyword, passing the DOMDocument object to be used with

XPath as the sole parameter. Using the DOMDocument object $dom, created from the document in Listing 6-1, you can instantiate a DOMXPath object:

```
$domxpath = new DOMXPath($dom);
```

This object has no built-in properties and, depending upon the version of PHP, implements at most three methods.

Using the query() Method

The query() method is available in all versions of PHP 5. It retrieves nodes from a tree using XPath expressions. No matter what expression is used, even those that return no nodes, a DOMNodelist object is returned. In the event the expression returns no nodes, as either a result of no matching nodes or a different return type, the resulting DOMNodelist is empty. This method takes one required parameter, the XPath expression as a string, and an optional second parameter, an object derived from the DOMNode class, which would be used as the context for the XPath expression. For example, you can query for the author node in the document with the expression /book/bookinfo/author:

```
$list = $domxpath->query("/book/bookinfo/author");
$author = $list->item(0);
```

Examining the $author variable, you will see it refers to the author element in the document. You could then use this node as the context parameter to access the surname node:

```
$list = $domxpath->query("surname", $author);
$surname = $list->item(0);
```

If you tried to return the contents of the surname element as a string via an XPath expression, you will see that a DOMNodeList object is returned but is empty:

```
$list = $domxpath->query("string('/book/bookinfo/author/surname')");
var_dump($list);
print "Number of Nodes Returned: ".$list->length."\n";
```

The var_dump of the $list variable clearly shows that the object is a DOMNodeList. The list after that illustrates that the number of nodes contained, from the length property, is 0.

Using the evaluate() Method

PHP 5.1 added a method, evaluate(), so that additional types supported by XPath could be returned. This method takes the same parameters as the query method(): an object derived from a DOMNode class followed by an optional context parameter. Using this method, you would write the same expression to return the contents of the surname element as a string, as follows:

```
$list = $domxpath->evaluate("string(/book/bookinfo/author/surname)");
var_dump($list);
```

The output for the var_dump in this case is much different. A DOMNodeList is not returned in this case. Instead a string is returned:

```
string(8) "Richards"
```

With this new method, return values can be of type Boolean, Integer, String, Null, or DOMNodeList. It all depends upon the expression used. For instance, an expression could perform a calculation on the year element, such as adding one year and returning the numeric value:

```
$newyear = $domxpath->evaluate("number(/book/bookinfo/copyright/year) + 1");
var_dump($newyear);
```

You can use this method, also being able to return a DOMNodeList, as a replacement for the query() method. For backward compatibility, query() was left untouched, returning only a DOMNodeList, with support for new additional types added to the evaluate() method:

```
$list = $domxpath->evaluate("/book/bookinfo/author");
$author = $list->item(0);
print $author->nodeName."\n";
```

This code is almost identical to the code using the query() method, but it uses the evaluate() method. Examining the $author variable, you will see it is identical to the $author variable previously returned from the query() method.

Using XPath and Namespaces

In Chapter 4, I showed the functionality for dealing with namespaces in XPath. I also pointed out the problem with default namespaces. Without prefixes, it is harder to differentiate or write expressions based on namespaces. You can use the helper method, registerNamespace(), on a DOMXPath object to associate a prefix with a namespace, which can then be used in an expression. In Chapter 4, you saw a document containing many different book elements—some in no namespace, some prefixed and within a namespace, and some in a default namespace. One such book element within the default namespace looks like this:

```
<classics xmlns="http://www.example.com/ExternalClassics">
    <book qty="33">
        <name>To Kill a Mockingbird</name>
        <price>10.99</price>
        <pubdate>2002-03-01</pubdate>
        <author>Lee, Harper</author>
    </book>
</classics>
```

It tends to be easier when writing expressions to be able to use a prefix when dealing with namespaced nodes. In this case, you can use the registerNamespace() method:

```
$domxpath->registerNamespace("ec", " http://www.example.com/ExternalClassics");
```

Prior to executing an expression, if the namespace http://www.example.com/ ExternalClassics and the prefix ec are registered with the DOMXPath class, you can use the prefix within an expression to access namespaced nodes.

It is important to understand that when performing a query or evaluation with an XPath object, some automatic namespace registration takes place. Prefixed namespaces within the scope of the context node are automatically registered and can be used within an expression. When a context node is not supplied, prefixed namespaces on the document element are automatically registered. For example, had the namespace from the classics node been associated with a prefix and no context node supplied when performing a query, its prefix would automatically be available to be used in an expression. However, had any namespaces been declared within the children of the element, they would not have been registered because the context node, the classics element, is not within the scope of those namespaces and would need to be manually registered. It is also important to understand that when namespaces are automatically registered, the prefixes closest to the context take precedence over the same prefixes declared higher up in the tree. It is all about scope here.

If you loaded the previous snippet into a DOMDocument object, $xd, and treated it as a complete document, rather than just a piece of the document from Chapter 4, you could then access the price element with the newly registered namespace:

```
$xp = new DOMXPath($xd);
$xp->registerNamespace("ec", "http://www.example.com/ExternalClassics");
$list = $xp->evaluate("/ec:classics/ec:book/ec:price");
var_dump($list->item(0)->nodeName);
```

Namespaces are not dependant upon the prefix. The important aspect is the actual namespace. When registering a prefix to use with a namespace, it is crucial to choose unique names. A prefix that is automatically registered will take priority over one manually registered on the DOMXPath object. Scope comes into play in this case. To avoid potential conflicts, it is best to use prefixes that are guaranteed not to be used within a document.

Extending Classes

One of the nice features of the DOM extension is the ability to extend the core classes. Under PHP 4 and the domxml extension, this functionality was impossible to achieve. With the capabilities from the new Zend Engine in PHP 5, this has finally become a reality in DOM. This feature has its limits, which will be explained within this section.

You can extend one of the DOM classes in the same manner as extending any other class within PHP 5. You define a class using the extends keyword:

```
class customDoc extends DOMDocument {}

$mydoc = new customDoc();
print $mydoc->saveXML();
```

In this case, other than creating a new class type extending the DOMDocument class, you have not defined any custom constructor or additional methods and properties. The methods and properties from the DOMDocument class, though, are inherited and, as shown by the last print statement, are invoked just as if you were using a DOMDocument object.

You can also override the constructor and methods as well as add custom methods and properties. You must remember a few points when extending the DOM classes:

- Overriding the constructor requires the parent constructor to be called.

- Properties built into the DOM classes cannot be overridden.

- Methods built into the DOM classes can be overridden.

- The life span of an extended object is that of the object itself.

Other than these points, extended DOM classes work in the same manner as regular objects and extended objects.

Overriding the Constructor

A subclass can override the constructor of a base class by defining its own constructor. When using the DOM classes, you must invoke the parent constructor within the extended class's constructor, or an instantiated object will not be usable with the DOM extension. For example:

```
class customDoc extends DOMDocument {
    function __construct($rootName, $rootValue = "") {
        parent::__construct();
        if (! empty($rootName)) {
            $element = $this->appendChild(new DOMElement($rootName, $rootValue));
        }
    }
}

$myc = new customDoc("root", "content");
print $myc->saveXML();
```

The class customDoc is defined and extends the DOMDocument class. A constructor for this class is also defined that accepts the variables $rootName for the document element and $rootValue, which is passed when text content is to be created for the document element when this class is instantiated.

When an object of the customDoc type is instantiated, this new constructor is used. The first thing that takes place is the constructor for the parent class, DOMDocument, is called. This parent constructor *must* be called prior to using any of the DOM functionality with this class; otherwise, $this will not have been properly initialized, and the DOM methods will fail. Once this is completed, you can use the appendChild() method to set the document element within the tree. The output of this code results in the following:

```
<?xml version="1.0"?>
<root>content</root>
```

Understanding That Properties Cannot Be Overridden

Properties of a base DOM class *cannot* be overridden. They can be defined in the subclass definition but are silently ignored, and the built-in properties are used. This is a big difference between the constructor and the methods defined in DOM, because those can both be overridden. For example:

```
class customDoc extends DOMDocument {
    public $nodeName = "customDoc";
}

$myc = new customDoc();
print $myc->nodeName;
```

This piece of code defines the property nodeName within the customDoc definition. The nodeName property is also defined in the DOMNode class, which is inherited by the DOMDocument class. Looking at the code, you might expect customDoc to be printed, but in actuality #document is printed. Some people may consider this behavior to be an issue, but it has worked this way from the beginning, will not be changing, and can easily be worked around by using different property names.

Overriding Built-in Methods

You can override DOM class methods, unlike the properties, through user-implemented methods. PHP is a typeless language and does not allow casting an object to a specific class. The method createElement() from the DOMDocument class returns only an object that is a DOMElement class type. Of course, you can instantiate different classes that extend a DOMElement using the new keyword; you might want the createElement() method to return some other class type as well. For example:

```
class customElement extends DOMElement { }

class customDoc extends DOMDocument {
    function createElement($name, $value) {
        $custom = new customElement($name, $value);
        return $custom;
    }
}

$myc = new customDoc();
$myelement = $myc->createElement("myname", "myvalue");
if ($myelement instanceof customElement) {
    print "This is a customElement";
}
```

This code implements a custom createElement() method that returns an element of the customElement class type rather than a DOMElement class. It works well in that the test using the instanceof operator results in the text This is a customElement being printed. The only issue with this code is that the new element is not associated with a document, which occurs through the use of the native createElement() method. Eventually the adoptNode() method will be implemented, allowing the node to be associated with a document, but until that time, the node exists without a document associated until inserted into a tree.

Understanding Object Lifetime and Scope

Scope and object lifetime are features many people struggle with when using extended classes within the DOM extension. It is important to understand that DOM objects are not nodes within the tree. This is confusing because accessing the object directly affects the underlying node in the tree, but the object is just an "accessor" to the underlying node. This being said, when an object is instantiated, either by using new or by accessing a node within a tree, the object itself is not part of any tree or subtree, just the internal node.

Just as in most other languages, objects have a lifetime and are eventually destroyed. Once an object goes out of scope and no references to this object exist, it is destroyed. The same rules pertain to objects from the DOM extension. This is where much confusion comes into play. When no object is currently referencing an underlying node and the node is accessed, a new object is created based on the pertinent built-in DOM class. By "pertinent," I mean that the DOM class type that pertains to the specific node type is instantiated.

You may be wondering why all this matters. Using subclasses with the DOM extension does not guarantee that the original class used to create a node will be the type of class of the object returned when the node is accessed later in a script. Consider the effects of using the unset() function on an instantiated subclassed object:

```
class customElement extends DOMElement { }

$doc = new DOMDocument();

$myelement = $doc->appendChild(new customElement("custom", "element"));
print get_class($myelement)."\n";

unset($myelement);

$myelement = $doc->documentElement;
print get_class($myelement)."\n";
```

This code initially defines the class customElement that does not override anything from the DOMElement class. A DOMDocument object is instantiated, and a new customElement is appended. This new element is returned as a customElement object and set to the $myelement variable. The output of the first get_class() function is customElement and clearly shows that the object associated with this node is of the customElement type.

Unset() is then called on the $myelement variable; because no other references exist for this object, the object is destroyed. The element node that was previously appended as the document element is then accessed with the documentElement property, and the resulting object is set to the $myelement variable. Examining the output of the last get_class() function call reveals that this object is of the DOMElement class and *not* the customElement class.

Caution Objects based on extended DOM classes have a life span and once destroyed no longer associate the extended class type with the underlying XML node in the tree. Accessing a node after the object has been destroyed results in an object based on a DOM built-in class type and not the extended class type.

This is the limitation I previously mentioned about extending DOM classes. How your code is written will determine whether an object based on an extended class will be returned or whether it will be based on a built-in DOM class when accessing a node. You must think about scope carefully when using extended classes. For example:

```
class customElement extends DOMElement { }

class customDoc extends DOMDocument {
    function addRoot($name, $value) {
        if (! $this->documentElement) {
            $custom = new customElement($name, $value);
            return $this->appendChild($custom);
        }
        return NULL;
    }
}

$dom = new customDoc();
$dom->addRoot("root", "content");
$myelement = $dom->documentElement;
print get_class($myelement)."\n";
```

This piece of code creates a `customDoc` object and adds a document element using the `addRoot()` method. The method returns the newly created object or `NULL` if a document element already exists. Within the script, however, the return value is not captured, and when the `get_class()` is called on the `$myelement` object, `DOMElement` is printed.

You can make a slight change to the code and capture the return value:

```
$myelement = $dom->addRoot("root", "content");
$myelement = $dom->documentElement;
print get_class($myelement)."\n";
```

In this case, `get_class()` returns `customElement`. Upon returning from the `addRoot()` method, the object is captured and set to the `$myelement` variable. Previously, even though the resulting element was being returned, it was not captured, and the `customElement` object created was immediately destroyed. With this object destroyed, accessing the `documentElement` property resulted in a new object associated with the node being created. This new object, being created automatically from a node access, ends up being based on the `DOMElement` class. The updated code keeps the `$myelement` object in scope, so when the `documentElement` property is accessed, it returns the object already associated with the node, which is of the `customElement` class.

Common Questions, Misconceptions, and Problems

The DOM specification is quite lengthy and not always easy to interpret. It is common to expect a certain result just to find out that the actual result is not even close to your expectation. This also holds true even with DOM interaction within PHP. The following sections will explore many of the common questions, misconceptions, and problems people encounter using the DOM extension and will provide some insight into methods you can employ to achieve your desired results.

DOM Objects and PHP Sessions

The most frequently encountered "problem" developers have when using the DOM extension concerns storing DOM objects in session. Let me just say that DOM objects *cannot* be natively stored in session. This doesn't mean it is impossible to store an XML document in session, just that some additional coding is required to perform this action.

Storing data in session requires serialization. DOM objects natively cannot be serialized using PHP functions such as serialize() or the automatic serialization that is performed when storing data to a session without losing data. This is because of the reliance on the underlying libxml2 library and because the DOM classes do not implement the magic sleep() and wakeup() methods. Your first reaction to this might be the question, why aren't those methods implemented? The answer is simple. You have two ways to serialize a document: to a string or to a file. Because of the size of XML documents, in many cases they are stored on the file system rather than as a string in memory, so these specific methods were never implemented and left to the user to handle in whatever manner they like.

Working around this is not all that difficult; in fact, you can deal with this in a couple of ways. The first method is extremely simple and can be performed in the same number of lines of code as you would need when storing or fetching a DOM object from a session:

```
$_SESSION['domobj'] = $dom->saveXML();
```

Rather than storing the DOMDocument object, $dom, in session, the tree is serialized by the saveXML() method, which is then stored in session. For example:

```
$dom = DOMDocument::loadXML($_SESSION['domobj']);
```

When the DOM object needs to the restored from session, a new DOMDocument is created from the serialized tree in session.

Another method you can use is to extend the DOMDocument class and implement the sleep() and wakeup() methods:

```
class customDoc extends DOMDocument() {
    private $serializedDoc = NULL;

    function __sleep() {
        $this->serializedDoc = $this->saveXML();
        return array("serializedDoc");
    }

    function __wakeup() {
        if (! empty($this->serializedDoc)) {
            $this->loadXML($this->serializedDoc);
            $this->serializedDoc = NULL;
        }
    }
}
```

The customDoc class extends the DOMDocument class and implements the magic methods. Once instantiated (in this case $doc will be used), the object can be easily stored and retrieved from session as a normal object:

```
/* Store in session */
$_SESSION['domobj'] = $doc;

/* Retrieve from session */
$doc = $_SESSION['domobj'];
```

Using an extended class in this case allows for the object to be serialized and stored as desired. For instance, rather than storing the document as a string in memory, it could be saved as a file in the sleep() method and restored during wakeup().

Removing Nodes While Iterating Skips Nodes

Another issue often arises when iterating through a DOMNodeList or DOMNamedNodeMap and removing nodes. Nodes are often skipped during such operation. For example, when trying to remove all children from an element, the first thing someone may think of is to grab all children, iterate through the DOMNodeList, and remove the node from the document. For example:

```
$children = $element->childNodes;
foreach($children as $node) {
    $element->removeChild($node);
}
```

This code does not work as expected, and child nodes are still left within $element. Both DOMNodeList and DOMNamedNodeMap are live collections. Additions and subtractions of nodes within a tree can directly affect the nodes contained with the collections as well as their indexes within the collection. In the previous code snippet, once a node is removed, all nodes that follow it within the collection automatically have their index reduced by 1. The results of this code would end up removing every other node in the collection, starting with the first node.

You can work around this issue by removing nodes in reverse order or performing a loop while $element still has children:

```
/* Removal Based on Index */
$length = $children->length;
for($x=$length-1; $x >= 0; $x--) {
    $element->removeChild($children->item($x));
}

/* Removal based on children */
while ($element->hasChildNodes()) {
    $element->removeChild($element->firstChild);
}
```

You can use many different techniques to do this. The first method illustrated shows how you can perform the iteration without regard to the type of node within the collection. It is possible that you have to change the actual code used for removal, because the code used here is specific to removing child nodes. The second example performs the same task as the first example, but instead no collections are used. As long as $element has children, the loop will be processed and continue to remove the first child of $element.

The XML Tree Contains Garbled Characters

No matter how much encodings are stressed, people often forget that data is internally stored in UTF-8 encoding. Other than during the loading and saving of an XML document, data that is not compatible with UTF-8 must be encoded or decoded when accessing or modifying content. Chapter 5 explains this in detail as well as covers the methods you can employ to handle data correctly when interacting with the XML-based extensions in PHP 5.

Extended Class Not Being Returned When Accessing Node

This has to be the most often encountered issue when using extended classes, which is why it is mentioned here even though it has already been covered in this chapter. If you run into this issue, refer to the "Object Lifetime and Scope Within the Extending Classes" section for an in-depth examination of the topic. To reiterate, though, objects refer to nodes within a tree and have a lifetime completely separate from the node. Object destruction follows the same rules as all other objects in PHP 5:

```
class customElement extends DOMElement{}
function addElement($doc, $name) {
    $doc->appendChild(new customElement($name));
}
$doc = new DOMDocument();
addElement($doc, "root");
$element = $doc->documentElement;
print get_class($element)."\n";
```

This results in DOMElement being printed for output. If a node is referenced by an object subclassed from a built-in DOM class and is destroyed, subsequent access to the node will return an object based on the corresponding DOM class for the node. The extended class will not be used for new object creation. The object of the customElement type is appended into the tree but never returned, so it is destroyed. Accessing the documentElement property ends up returning a DOMElement object, because the node no longer has an associated object. You must take object scope and lifetime into account when extending DOM objects.

Unable to Retrieve Elements by ID

The method getElementById() will return NULL when an element with the specific ID is not found. Even though you might think the ID is valid in the document and that a DOMElement should be returned, a common misconception may result in NULL being returned.

Attributes for elements are using the name ID but are not recognized as ID attributes. The name ID is not special in XML. Just because an attribute uses this name does not automatically turn it into an ID attribute. To create IDs, you must define attributes in a DTD as IDs. The DTD, if external, must also be processed while loading the document. Once the DTD has been loaded and the document processed, elements will then be able to be accessed by their IDs.

In a couple of special cases, this does not hold true. The qualified attribute name xml:id is one of these cases. Attributes with this name are handled as ID attributes and do not require a DTD. Currently, these attributes are recognized and set up as IDs only when a document is loaded. Work is taking place within the libxml2 library to support appending attributes with this name that also automatically result in IDs, but as of libxml2 2.6.20, this has yet to be implemented.

Another special case is the `setIdAttribute()` methods. These methods have not yet been implemented at the time of writing but are on the to-do list for the DOM extension so may or may not be available by the time you read this. These methods will allow already existing attributes to be set and unset as ID attributes without needing a DTD or schema.

Loading Document Issues Entity Errors

By definition, an XML document must be well-formed. Entity errors and warnings are issued when a document uses entity references and the entities are not defined in a DTD. The most common problem encountered deals with the use of the & character:

```
<root>this & that</root>
```

This, contrary to what many believe, is *not* a legal XML document. Unless & is contained within a CDATA section, it cannot be used alone for text content. Within text content, it must be escaped and can be written as this:

```
<root>this &amp; that </root>
```

When trying to load a document containing a stand-alone & within text content, you have two options. You can either convert it to the appropriate entity reference or completely disregard the document. The problem with the latter is that for some reason, this issue gets reported as a bug because the document being loaded is coming from a remote source, such as an RSS feed. In a case like that, your best bet is to contact the owner of the document and let them know their XML is not legal.

Added DTD Not Recognized

A DTD manually added to a document using append and insert operations is not handled by the document as a regular DTD. DTDs are parsed and set up appropriately while a document is being parsed. Adding one later, unless creating the DTD and document using the `DOMImplementation` methods, requires the document to be serialized and reloaded in order for the DTD to be read correctly.

Unable to Access Elements in Default Namespace Using XPath

One of the biggest issues encountered when using XPath concerns selecting elements in the default namespace. No prefixes are associated with the namespace, and the elements cannot be selected just by using their names. Although you can hack together an expression to get access to these elements, the easiest method is to manually register the default namespace with some prefix. This then allows you to call the elements using the newly associated prefix and element name. Refer to the "Using XPath and Namespaces" section in this chapter for additional information.

Migrating from domxml to the DOM Extension

As long as the code from domxml is not from an extremely old version of PHP 4, migrating from code written for domxml to the DOM extension is not difficult. The reason for the problems from older PHP 4 versions is because of the changes made within the domxml extension. Around the time PHP 4.3 was rolled out, domxml was updated to implement most of the functionality using W3C-compliant methods according to the specifications, and the older functionality was depreciated. This section will show how to migrate from the PHP 4.3–compliant implementation of domxml because prior versions will need a complete review and many code changes to work with the DOM extension in PHP 5.

Compliance with the specifications makes migration a much easier task. The first task is to identify any classes created using the new keyword. Although many of the classes use the same name in the DOM extension, a few differ. Table 6-2 lists the classes from domxml that have different names or are not implemented in the DOM extension.

Table 6-2. *Class Equivalents in the domxml and DOM Extensions*

domxml Class Name	DOM Class Name
DOMAttribute	DOMAttr
DOMCdata	DOMCdataSection
DOMEntityRef	DOMEntityReference
DOMPi	DOMProcessingInstruction
DOMParser	

All other classes in domxml map directly to the same class names in the DOM extension. If you have read the source code, you might also wonder about the domdtd and domnamespacenode classes. These are no longer relevant within domxml and have been intentionally omitted from Table 6-2.

The next step in the process is to modify method names used with the objects. In the majority of the cases, all that is required is capitalizing the first character after an underscore and removing the underscore from the method name. Take, for example, the method get_elements_by_tagname(), which is from the DOMElement class in domxml. Following the rules just defined, the corresponding method within the DOM extension is getElementsByTagName().

With the methods converted, the next step is to look at the methods that are implemented differently in the DOM extension as well as methods in domxml that are now true properties in DOM. Table 6-3 lists many, but not all, methods within domxml that are now properties in the DOM extension.

Table 6-3. *Methods in domxml and the Corresponding DOM Extension Properties*

domxml Method	DOM Property
DOMAttribute->name()	DOMAttr->name
DOMAttribute->value()	DOMAttr->value
DOMAttribute->set_value()	DOMAttr->value
DOMDocument->doctype()	DOMDocument->doctype
DOMDocument->document_element()	DOMDocument->documentElement
DOMNode->node_name()	DOMNode->nodeName
DOMNode->node_value()	DOMNode->nodeValue

Many additional methods must be converted, but similarly to converting methods, all that is required for most methods is changing some character cases and removing the underscores and parentheses. In some instances, such as set_value(), you must do a little more because the method is writing data, but the number of cases this affects is much smaller than the number of writable properties in DOM.

The most difficult step in the process is converting methods existing in domxml that have completely different names or implementations in DOM. Two that you will definitely encounter deal with loading and saving data:

```
/* Opening a file under domxml in PHP 4 */
$doc = domxml_open_file('filename.xml');

/* Opening a file under DOM in PHP 5 */
$doc = DOMDocument->load('filename.xml');
```

The implementations are completely different in both of these cases. The same thing occurs when saving data. Consider the case when outputting data with a specified encoding in domxml and the difference when performing the same operation using the DOM extension:

```
/* Output data with ISO-8859-1 encoding using domxml */
print $doc->dump_mem(TRUE, "ISO-8859-1");

/* Output data with ISO-8859-1 encoding using DOM */
$doc->formatOutput = TRUE;
$doc->encoding = "ISO-8859-1";
print $doc->saveXML();
```

You must modify some other methods to work correctly under the DOM extension in PHP 5, but the load and save methods are two of the most commonly ones encountered.

Without having to completely recode applications using domxml yet run them under PHP 5, you can use wrapper code. Such code already exists, such as that found at http://alexandre.alapetite.net/doc-alex/domxml-php4-php5/. Personally, I have not used this code; instead, I found it quick and easy to simply modify existing code using the domxml extension to code using the new DOM extension. If you do not have the time or are still leery about changing code, this may be a viable option.

The last option for migration is to recode applications using domxml to use code that is compliant with the DOM extension in PHP 5. I expect you may have a quizzical look on your face right now. You can write wrapper classes in PHP that mimic the behavior of the DOM extension in PHP 5 but are built using the functionality in the domxml extension to ease eventual migration. This way when the upgrade to PHP 5 happens, your code would need no modification. Well, it might need a little. Unfortunately, code for this no longer exists so must be written from scratch. A few years ago, during the initial development stages of the DOM extension, some code surfaced on the Internet that did just this. At the time it was not 100 percent functional, but was a good start. The site that offered this code is no longer reachable; it may have just been lost in the black void somewhere.

Seeing Some DOM Examples

The DOM extension is a large API, and finding an example using the entire API is not very realistic. I have demonstrated many of the features and concepts in small code snippets throughout this chapter. The following sections introduce two different examples that show some of the more frequently used functionality within the API. The first example will create a template XML document, based on an XML document describing its structure, that will be used in a SimpleXML example in Chapter 7. The second example will demonstrate how to create an XSL template using namespaces; you could use this template to process a document with the XSL extension, which will be covered in Chapter 10. You can find additional examples, as well as demonstrations of advanced functionality, in later chapters within this book.

Building a Portable Application Description Template

The Portable Application Description (PAD) is a specification designed by the Association of Shareware Professionals (ASP); you can find it at http://www.asp-shareware.org/pad/. It is a standard format allowing authors of shareware software to provide information such as company and contact information, support information, software information, and licensing in a common format that can be leveraged not only by end users looking for more information about a piece of software but also by online libraries building content and search engines. You can find more information about this topic in Chapter 7.

This example will create an XML template that is used in Chapter 7 to create the actual PAD document for an application. The structure of a PAD document is defined by another XML document, http://www.padspec.org/pad_spec.xml. I will show how to use the DOM extension to dynamically build the template document for SimpleXML from this PAD specification file:

```php
<?php
/* Path to PAD specification File */
$location = "http://www.padspec.org/pad_spec.xml";
/* Default PAD version - Version is read from Spec File */
$padVersion = "2.01";
```

```php
function setPADInfo($doc, $version) {
    $node = $doc->documentElement;
    $node = $node->appendChild(new DOMElement("MASTER_PAD_VERSION_INFO"));
    $node->appendChild(new DOMElement("MASTER_PAD_VERSION", $version));
    $node->appendChild(new DOMElement("MASTER_PAD_EDITOR", "PHP"));
    $node->appendChild(new DOMElement("MASTER_PAD_INFO", "http://www.padspec.org/"));
}

function createField($doc, $node, $name) {
    if ($node == NULL) {
        $node = $doc->documentElement;
        if (! $node) {
            $node = $doc->appendChild(new DOMElement($name));
        }
        return $node;
    }
    foreach ($node->childNodes AS $child) {
        if ($child->nodeName == $name) {
            return $child;
        }
    }
    return $node->appendChild(new DOMElement($name));
}

if ($dom = DOMDocument::load($location)) {
    $padSet = FALSE;
    /* Create the new template output tree */
    $template = new DOMDocument("1.0", "UTF-8");

    $xpath = new DOMXPath($dom);
    /* Find PAD Version element */
    $verNode = $xpath->query("PAD_Spec_Version");
    if ($verNode && $verNode->length == 1) {
        /* Retrieve template version */
        $padVersion = $verNode->item(0)->nodeValue;
    }

    /* Query and loop through all elements named Field */
    $fields = $xpath->query("//Field");
    foreach ($fields as $field) {
        /* Retrieve element named Path within current Field element */
        $path = $xpath->query("Path", $field);

        if ($path->length == 1) {
            $node = NULL;
```

```
        /* Get value of Path element */
        $xmlnodes = trim($path->item(0)->nodeValue);

        /* Split Path by / separator */
        $arPath = explode("/", $xmlnodes);

        /* Loop through path to create specified element
           Parent elements are created as needed based on Path */
        foreach ($arPath AS $key=>$value) {
            /* IF PAD information not set and Field refers to
               PAD information then create it */
            if (! $padSet && $value == "MASTER_PAD_VERSION_INFO") {
                setPADInfo($template, $padVersion);
                $padSet = TRUE;
                break;
            }

            /* Path begins with parent so returned $node is
               parent for next node within local foreach loop */
            $node=createField($template, $node, $value);
        }
    }
}

/* Save the generated XML Tree to padtemplate.xml file */
$template->formatOutput = TRUE;
print $template->save("padtemplate.xml");
}
?>
```

The script initially initializes two variables: $location, which points to the location of the PAD XML definition file, and $padVersion, which sets the version of the definition file in the unlikely event it cannot be obtained from the definition file. Rather than a hard-coded location, the definition file can be retrieved and stored locally, in which case the location should be updated to the localized path. Skipping over the two functions for now, the definition file is loaded into a DOMDocument, $dom. This tree reads the definition from which the PAD template is dynamically created.

Take a look at the actual definition file, in particular the Company_Name element; it is defined as follows:

```
<PAD_Spec>
    <PAD_Spec_Version>2.01</PAD_Spec_Version>
        <Fields>
            <Field>
                <Name>Company_Name</Name>
                <Path>XML_DIZ_INFO/Company_Info/Company_Name</Path>
                <Title>Company name</Title>
```

```
            <ShortDescription>Company name or, if no company name, author
                            name</ShortDescription>
            <RegExDocumentation>Text string 2-40 characters</RegExDocumentation>
            <RegEx>^[^&lt;\x09]{2,40}\Z</RegEx>
         </Field>
      </Fields>
   </PAD_Spec_Version>
</PAD_Spec>
```

Each PAD element is defined in such a manner within a `Field` element in the definition file. The child elements define the different aspects of the particular field. For example:

- `Name`: The name of PAD element within XML document

- `Path`: The location of the element within the tree

- `Title`: A descriptive title for the element

- `ShortDescription`: A short description of the element

- `RegExDocumentation`: A description of the regular expression

- `RegEx`: The regular expression used to validate the contents of the element

Most of these fields are self-explanatory. The `Path` element may give rise to some questions, though. This field defines the location of the specified element within the tree. Using the `Path` for the `Company_Name` element, `XML_DIZ_INFO/Company_Info/Company_Name`, the element within the document is as follows:

```
<XML_DIZ_INFO>
   <Company_Info>
      <Company_Name/>
   </Company_Info>
</XML_DIZ_INFO>
```

With the definition file loaded, a new document, `$template`, is created that will hold the created PAD template. It is initially created as an empty document using `new DOMDocument()`. The first step is to retrieve the PAD version from the definition file. Here, XPath is used. Rather than trying to walk through the tree and manually locate the element, the document is queried for the `PAD_Spec_Version` element. Queries return `DOMNodeList` objects even when empty, unless an error has occurred. As long as one is returned and it contains a node, `$padVersion` is set from the contents of the node, overriding the default initially set up at the beginning of the script. At this point, all initialization steps have been completed, and the actual building of the PAD XML template can commence.

Each `Field` element represents an element within the PAD document template, so building the template begins with retrieving a `DOMNodeList` containing all `Field` elements using XPath. Again, it is much faster and easier to manage getting these using XPath rather than manually walking the tree. Using the `DOMNodeList`, `$fields`, the script can iterate through each of the contained `Field` elements and process them within the `foreach` loop.

The Path element is then retrieved using XPath and the current Field element, $field, as the context. This will give you the full location of the element within the PAD template document. The Path is then split into an array based on the separator, /, resulting in an array, $arPath, containing the entire tree hierarchy for the current element. The array is then iterated to create the structure within the template.

One exception applies when building the template, and that deals with the versioning information for the PAD file. The MASTER_PAD_VERSION_INFO element within the template contains the version number of the definition file and some additional information concerning how the file is created. When encountered, the setPADInfo() function is called, creating this information as an element and its children beneath the document element. This function is straightforward because it appends and then encapsulates the MASTER_PAD_VERSION_INFO element, and finally it continues to append the additional elements to this newly created node. The real work is performed for the rest of the Field elements from the specification document using the createField() function.

Notice that for each iteration of the DOMNodeList containing the Field elements, $fields, $node is set to NULL. During the iteration of the array, $arPath, containing the broken up path, $node is not only passed in as an argument to createField() but also receives the returned value from the function. This function takes three parameters: $doc, which is the DOMDocument being built and corresponds to $template in this case; $node, which is the parent node for the element being created; and finally $name, which is the name of the element being created.

When the parent node, $node, is passed as NULL, it signals the top of the tree. The function grabs the document element from the document and creates it if it doesn't exist. The method appendChild() is used to append a nonexistent node. This method also returns the newly appended node, which gets set to $node. In either instance, $node is returned to the script pointing to the document element.

Within the foreach of $arPath, $node is updated with the return value from createField(). The next iteration then passes the previous $node to the createField() function, forcing it to append any element created to this node. Assuming $node is not NULL in this case, the function first checks to make sure the element has not already been created and appended. If it has, it returns the existing element; otherwise, it creates, appends, and returns the new element. The check simply takes place by iterating through the child nodes of the passed-in parent, $node, and testing the node name against the name of the element to be created, $name.

The script processes each of the Field elements from the specification file this way. Upon completion, the DOMDocument object, $template, contains an XML tree conforming to the PAD specifications. The last step is to save the template to some location so that it can be used in the next chapter. The formatting performed by $template->formatOutput = TRUE; is not necessary but makes the final output much more readable through indenting and adding line feeds.

Note Note the location of the final output document. It is used in the example for SimpleXML as the input document and is required to execute the example in the next chapter.

Building an XSL Template

As you will see in Chapter 10, the XSL extension works with and requires the DOM extension. XSL loads both the style sheet and the document through the use of a DOMDocument object. In many cases, the style sheet is a file loaded into a DOMDocument object, but it is possible to create a properly namespaced style sheet manually using the DOM API. This example will cover the process of building a simple style sheet that can be used by the XSL processor. An XML document containing sites and URLs needs to be transformed and displayed in an HTML page. The document containing the data looks like the following:

```
<sites>
    <site>
        <name>Libxml</name>
        <url>http://www.xmlsoft.org</url>
    </site>
    <site>
        <name>W3C DOM Level 3 Specifications</name>
        <url>www.w3.org/TR/DOM-Level-3-Core/</url>
    </site>
</sites>
```

Without going into the details of the XSLT language, which is covered in Chapter 10, I will show how to build a template using the DOM extension. XSL templates depend upon proper namespacing. Normally templates are loaded into a DOM document from a file and processed by XSL. Elements within the tree, assuming the template is written correctly, are already properly namespaced internally. Building a tree manually, on the other hand, requires elements to be properly namespaced, or the template will not work properly when passed to XSL. The namespace used within XSL and the example is http://www.w3.org/1999/XSL/Transform. To make this more manageable to code with, the namespace is set to the variable $xslns in the following code, and $xslns is used when the namespace is needed:

```php
<?php
/* Set the xsl namespace url for re-use */
$xslns = "http://www.w3.org/1999/XSL/Transform";

/* Create the document for the style sheet */
$stylesheet = new domDocument;

/* Create the stylesheet node */
$root = $stylesheet->createElementNS($xslns, "xsl:stylesheet");
$stylesheet->appendChild($root);
$root->setAttribute("version", "1.0");

/* Create the output method node */
$output = $stylesheet->createElementNS($xslns, "xsl:output");
$output->setAttribute("method", "html");
$root->appendChild($output);
```

```
/* Create the main template that matches on the document element */
$template= $stylesheet->createElementNS($xslns, "xsl:template");
$template->setAttribute("match", "/");
$root->appendChild($template);

$html = $template->appendChild(new domElement("html"));
$body = $html->appendChild(new domElement("body"));

/* Call another template matching on /sites/site elements */
$subtemplate = $stylesheet->createElementNS($xslns, "xsl:apply-templates");
$body->appendChild($subtemplate);
$subtemplate->setAttribute("select", "/sites/site");

/* Create the template for matching /sites/site elements */
$template= $stylesheet->createElementNS($xslns, "xsl:template");
$template->setAttribute("match", "/sites/site");
$root->appendChild($template);

$paragraph = $template->appendChild(new domElement("p"));

/* Get the value of the name */
$xslvalueof = $stylesheet->createElementNS($xslns, "xsl:value-of");
$xslvalueof->setAttribute("select", "./name");
$paragraph->appendChild($xslvalueof);

/* Add a colon in the final output separating name and url */
$paragraph->appendChild(new domText(" : "));

/* Get the value of the url */
$xslvalueof = $stylesheet->createElementNS($xslns, "xsl:value-of");
$xslvalueof->setAttribute("select", "./url");
$paragraph->appendChild($xslvalueof);

/* Output the stylesheet using formatting */
$stylesheet->formatOutput = TRUE;
print $stylesheet->saveXML();
?>
```

Other than the XSL syntax, the example is straightforward. The XSL-specific language is created using elements prefixed with xsl and within the XSL namespace. Generic output is created using non-namespaced DOM functionality. Upon executing this script, the newly created style sheet is printed to output:

```
<?xml version="1.0"?>
<xsl:stylesheet xmlns:xsl="http://www.w3.org/1999/XSL/Transform" version="1.0">
  <xsl:output method="html"/>
  <xsl:template match="/">
    <html>
      <body>
        <xsl:apply-templates select="/sites/site"/>
      </body>
    </html>
  </xsl:template>
  <xsl:template match="/sites/site">
    <p><xsl:value-of select="./name"/> : <xsl:value-of select="./url"/></p>
  </xsl:template>
</xsl:stylesheet>
```

This document does not look like anything special. Elements have qualified names, and a namespace is defined on the xsl:stylesheet element. Internally, however, because the namespace functionality was used when creating the elements, they are properly associated with the namespace correctly.

Try creating the stylesheet node using the createElement() method:

```
$root = $stylesheet->createElement("xsl:stylesheet");
```

This method is not namespace-aware and creates the element with the local name xsl:stylesheet. The output of the script looks the same as when createElementNS() was used, but internally it is *very* different. If the final style sheet, $stylesheet, is directly passed to the XSL processor in the same script, it will result in an error. The element xsl:stylesheet will not be within the XSL namespace and thus have no meaning to the XSL processor. On the other hand, if the style sheet is first serialized and then reloaded, it will work correctly. During the loading of the serialized style sheet, the namespaces will be correctly associated internally to the elements.

■**Caution** When working with documents in memory, documents built manually may differ while being built from their serialized version. Namespace-aware methods properly associate namespaces to elements and attributes while in memory. Using non-namespace aware methods may result in the same output when serialized, but until the document is serialized and reloaded, the namespaces are not properly associated with elements or attributes.

Conclusion

The DOM extension is the implementation of the DOM specification, defined by the W3C, in PHP 5. It is the heavyweight XML processor in that it allows virtually complete access to read, create, and modify an XML document. This functionality does come at a cost, however. It has a large API and is memory-hungry. Being based upon specifications, the API will not be changing, unlike its predecessor domxml, and many resources are available to understand the DOM extension. Memory usage completely depends upon the size of the document, because the DOM extension is tree-based and the tree must reside in memory.

This chapter introduced you to the DOM extension by providing some background, some explanations of many of the features found within the API, and some common issues encountered using the extension. The material presented here is more than enough for even those unfamiliar with this technology to begin using this extension.

The next chapter deals with the other tree-based parser in PHP 5, SimpleXML. Though not as feature-rich with regard to tree access and modifications, the simplicity SimpleXML offers more than makes up for this pitfall. And because of the interoperability in PHP 5, you have the best of both worlds available to you because you can use the two extensions together. One can pick up the slack for the other.

CHAPTER 7

■ ■ ■

SimpleXML

The SimpleXML extension is another tree-based parser available in PHP 5. The previous chapter introduced the DOM extension, which had an extensive API and allowed for complete control and manipulation of an XML document. SimpleXML takes a different approach to handling the tree; it has a much smaller API and handles elements and attributes more intuitively. This chapter will cover SimpleXML and explain why you need this second tree parser, how you use it, and what you can do with it.

Introducing SimpleXML

The SimpleXML extension was created to provide an easy, intuitive way to process XML documents. After reading the previous chapter, you might be overwhelmed by the size of the DOM extension's API and all the different aspects you need to understand. You might be saying, there has to be an easier way to deal with XML! SimpleXML is the answer to your pleas.

In many cases, documents are not overly complex and all you care about are the elements, attributes, and text content of nodes. Documents such as these tend to be configuration or data files not consisting of mixed content. (You can find an explanation of mixed content in Chapter 3.) You might view the rest of the nodes in the document as excess baggage. Therefore, using the DOM extension's API may be overkill with all its different class types and its slew of methods that you will never use. By contrast, the SimpleXML extension has a single class type, three functions, and six class methods. Compare that to the uncountable number of classes and methods within the DOM extension, and you might get an idea of why this is called SimpleXML.

Using SimpleXML

The SimpleXMLElement class is the central class for all operations within this extension. You can create an object of this class by using the new keyword, by using the simplexml_load_file() function, or by using the simplexml_load_string() function. (I will cover a fourth method for creating a SimpleXMLElement object that involves importing DOM objects later in the "Using DOM Interoperability" section.) I will use the document in Listing 7-1 to illustrate much of the functionality of SimpleXML throughout this chapter. I will refer to this XML document as sxml.xml.

Listing 7-1. *Example Document Using* DocBook *Format: Filename* sxml.xml

```
<?xml version="1.0" encoding="UTF-8"?>
<!DOCTYPE book PUBLIC "-//OASIS//DTD DocBook XML V4.1.2//EN"
                      "http://www.oasis-open.org/docbook/xml/4.1.2/docbookx.dtd">
<book lang="en">
   <bookinfo>
       <title>SimpleXML in PHP 5</title>
       <author>
          <firstname>Rob</firstname>
          <surname>Richards</surname>
       </author>
       <copyright>
          <year>2005</year>
          <holder>Rob Richards</holder>
       </copyright>
   </bookinfo>
   <preface>
       <title>Using SimpleXML</title>
       <para>An example DOM Tree using DocBook.</para>
   </preface>
   <chapter id="navigation">
       <title>Accessing Elements</title>
       <para>Elements are accessed as properties</para>
       <para>
          <![CDATA[
             <?php
             $data = '<?xml version="1.0"?>
             <root>content</root>';

             $sxe = simplexml_load_string($data);
             var_dump($sxe);
             ?>
          ]]>
       </para>
   </chapter>
</book>
```

Creating a SimpleXMLElement Object

The new keyword allows a SimpleXMLElement to be directly instantiated using an XML document within a string as its data source:

```
$xml = "<root><node1>content</node1></root>";
$sxe = new SimpleXMLElement($xml);
```

You can obtain the same results using simplexml_load_string():

```
$xml = "<root><node1>content</node1></root>";
$sxe = simplexml_load_string($xml);
```

So, why do you need both methods? The function `simplexml_load_string()` offers more functionality than illustrated, such as the ability to control parser options. When this additional functionality is not needed, it comes down to personal preference. Before going into more details, let's instantiate an object using `simplexml_load_file()`:

```
$sxe = simplexml_load_file("filename.xml");
```

Both the `simplexml_load_string()` and `simplexml_load_file()` functions take one mandatory parameter, either a string containing the data or a URI locating the data (as already shown), as well as optional parameters. The prototype for `simplexml_load_file`, which is the same for `simplexml_load_string` other than the first parameter, is as follows:

```
/* Prototype for PHP 5.0 */
simplexml_load_file(string data [, string class_name])

/* Prototype for PHP 5.1 */
simplexml_load_file(string data [, string class_name [, int options]])
```

I will cover the parameter `class_name` in the later section "Extending the SimpleXMLElement Class." PHP 5.1 has a third, optional parameter that allows parser options, which control the parsing of the tree. Chapter 5 covered these parser options, and Chapter 6 also mentioned them when covering how to load DOM documents. I will demonstrate how to use these parameters throughout this chapter.

Saving XML Data

Just like the DOM extension, SimpleXML offers a method to output XML content. Using the `asXML()` method, you can output a document or subtree to a string or a file. The actual output depends upon the node from which this method is called. When called from the document element, which is the element returned from the initial load functions, the entire document is output. This includes the XML declaration, the prolog, the body, and any epilog the document may contain. When called from any other node within the tree, the entire node and any subtree are output. For example:

```
$xml = "<root><node1>content</node1></root>";
$sxe = new SimpleXMLElement($xml);
print $sxe->asXML();
```

```
<?xml version="1.0"?>
<root><node1>content</node1></root>
```

In this instance, the `asXML()` method is called from the document element, $sxe. When no parameter is passed to this method, the results are returned as a string. Optionally, you can pass a filename, which causes SimpleXML to save the XML to the named file:

```
$xml = "<root><node1>content</node1></root>";
$sxe = new SimpleXMLElement($xml);
$sxe->asXML('filename.xml');
```

Because you have yet to learn about navigating the tree, I will not explain how to call this method using a node from within the tree for now. You can find examples of its usage throughout this chapter.

Accessing Element Nodes

Unlike under the DOM extension, where you needed to check child elements to find a specific one, SimpleXML offers direct access to specified elements by name. Not only will this save time coding, but also it can boost performance. Consider navigating a large document using a structure already known to you. Using the DOM extension—unless you use XPath, that is—you need to loop through children and check node names to find certain nodes. Finding certain nodes using SimpleXML is as easy as accessing a parent element using the node name—it requires just one line of code compared to many.

Accessing Elements

The document element is the object returned when a document is first loaded into SimpleXML. You access all other elements of the tree by element name as properties of `SimpleXMLElement` objects. The following example uses the document `sxml.xml` from Listing 7-1 for its data:

```php
<?php
$book = simplexml_load_file('sxml.xml');

/* Access the bookinfo child element of the book element */
$bookinfo = $book->bookinfo;

/* Access the title child element from the bookinfo element */
$title = $bookinfo->title;
?>
```

As you can see from this piece of code, the objects refer to the elements within the document. Accessing a child element is as simple as returning the object from the parent object by using the name of the child element you would like to access. Compare this code to what you would need to write using the DOM extension. Without using XPath, your code may be similar to the following:

```php
$dom = new DOMDocument();
$dom->->load('sxml.xml');
$book = $dom->documentElement;
foreach($book->childNodes as $node) {
    if ($node->nodeName == "bookinfo") {
        foreach($node->childNodes as $child) {
            if ($child->nodeName == "title") {
                $node = $child;
                break 2;
            }
        }
    }
}
```

```
if ($node) {
    $title = $node;
}
```

What took only three lines of code, excluding the comments and blank lines, takes 15 lines of code using the DOM extension. And all that the code needs to do is navigate to the title element, so imagine how much additional code you would need to deal with an entire document.

Accessing Content

From the previous section, you know that accessing elements returns SimpleXMLElement objects. You can use these same objects to access the content. It all depends upon how you use the objects. For example:

```php
<?php
$book = simplexml_load_file('sxml.xml');
$bookinfo = $book->bookinfo;
$title = $bookinfo->title;

/* Object examined with var_dump */
var_dump($title);

/* Using print with element containing text-only content */
print "Title: ".$title."\n";

$author = $bookinfo->author;

/* Object examined with var_dump */
var_dump($author);

/* Using print with element containing child elements */
print "Author: ".$author."\n";
?>
```

This accesses and examines two SimpleXMLElement objects, $author and $title. The difference between the two is that the author element contains child elements while the title element contains only a text node. When this script runs, the output looks like the following:

```
object(SimpleXMLElement)#4 (1) {
  [0]=>
  string(18) "SimpleXML in PHP 5"
}
Title: SimpleXML in PHP 5
```

```
object(SimpleXMLElement)#6 (2) {
  ["firstname"]=>
  string(3) "Rob"
  ["surname"]=>
  string(8) "Richards"
}
Author:
```

Examining the output from the var_dump() function of the $title variable, you can see it is a SimpleXMLElement whose text content is SimpleXML in PHP 5. The 0 index, in this case, denotes the text content of the element. This is because the element has no child elements and only text content. As a result of this, when the print statement is used with the object, the text content is returned as a string.

The next element broken out is the author element. The output in this case is very different. The author element contains two child elements. Looking at the output of the var_dump() method, you will see these elements shown as properties, firstname and surname, of the object. The values of these properties are the content contained by each element. However, when this object is used with the print statement, a string containing spaces and line feeds is returned.

This exercise has taught you a few features of how SimpleXML behaves:

- You can use SimpleXMLElement objects containing text-only content—that is, the current element has no child elements—as a string to access the text. In most cases, the cast is performed automatically, but in other cases an explicit cast must be performed. For example, using the title element, a string can be returned via $titlecontent = (string) $title.

- SimpleXMLElement objects having child elements return a concatenation of all immediate child text nodes but not the content of any child elements. An examination of the string returned by the author element, var_dump((string)$author);, shows a string 27 characters in length that contains spaces and line feeds. Neither of the child elements, firstname or surname, nor their content is returned in the string.

To understand the last point, take a look at the following code:

```
$doc = new SimpleXMLElement('<root>some<child1>subtext</child1>thing</root>');
print $doc;
```

The document element, root, contains mixed content. The first child is a text node containing the text some. The next child is the child1 element that has only the text content subtext. The last child node is another text node with the content thing. The result of the print statement is the text something. The child1 element and its content were completely skipped. Also, notice that the output does not contain any spaces or line feeds. The previous example using the author element did contain these because the element contained whitespace within its content, which could have been removed when the document was being parsed using the LIBXML_NOBLANKS parser option.

Using Iterable Objects

The elements presented to this point have been straightforward. No element has been repeated within the children of any of the accessed elements. Looking closely at the document in Listing 7-1, you might have noticed that the chapter element contains two para elements, and you might be wondering how to access these elements. The answer is simple. In most cases, SimpleXMLElement objects are iterable.

When accessing an element using the name of the element as a property, the object is not really a single node accessor. The object is really a collection of all child nodes with the name supplied through the property. The collection is seamless, as you may have noticed, because accessing the object directly actually means you are accessing the first element node in the collection. Up to now the collections have contained only a single node, so you would not even notice that the object could be iterated or accessed as a collection unless you already were aware of this.

Using the material just presented, let's access the para elements and print the contents:

```
$book = simplexml_load_file('sxml.xml');
$para = $book->chapter->para;
print $para."\n";

foreach($para AS $node) {
   print $node."\n";
}
```

Rather than requiring multiple lines of code to gain access to the para elements, everything takes place in a single line using overloading. The variable $para now contains the collection of para elements. As you can see from the results of the print statement, which prints Elements are accessed as properties, using the object works off the first element in the collection. To prove that this object is really a collection and the object can be iterated, look at the output from the foreach loop. Each para element is accessed in document order and its contents printed. The resulting output of the foreach loop is as follows:

```
Elements are accessed as properties


                <?php
                $data = '<?xml version="1.0"?>
                <root>content</root>';

                $sxe = simplexml_load_string($data);
                var_dump($sxe);
                ?>
```

The content of the CDATA node from the second para element is treated as plain-text content. All the insignificant whitespace is included in the text.

Having to loop through all the elements is not always practical. In many cases, you may be interested only in a specific element in the collection. The good news is that you can do this. You can access the collection through a zero-based index to retrieve a specific element in the collection. For instance, the first para element is easily accessed because, being the first element in the collection, it is the default element accessed when not performing iteration and not locating a specific element in the collection. However, in this case, that element doesn't contain anything useful because you need the content of the CDATA node contained within the second para element. Rather than wasting cycles looping through the collection and having to manually count the elements in order to stop at the second one, you can access the second para element directly using the index 1. For example:

```
$book = simplexml_load_file('sxml.xml');
$para = $book->chapter->para[1];
print "Content: ".$para."\n";

foreach($para AS $node) {
    print "Iter Content: ".$node."\n";
}
```

Notice the change in the second line. The para object is accessed with [1]. This indicates that the second element, because it is zero-based, should be returned. The result of the print statement on this object verifies that the second para element was retrieved successfully:

```
Content:
```

```php
<?php
$data = '<?xml version="1.0"?>
<root>content</root>';

$sxe = simplexml_load_string($data);
var_dump($sxe);
?>
```

The failure of the foreach loop to print any output may have you a little confused. Earlier I mentioned that in most cases SimpleXMLElement objects are iterable. This is a case where they are not. Because of the element being retrieved using an index, SimpleXML knows you are looking for one specific element and not a collection of elements. The returned object in this case cannot be iterated.

Caution Accessing a SimpleXMLElement object using an index results in an object that cannot be iterated because it represents a single element and not a collection of possible elements.

Accessing Unknown Elements

Knowing the structure of a document is helpful when using SimpleXML. You can navigate to elements just using the element names as properties. However, this has one problem I have not addressed yet. What happens when you do not know the structure of a document ahead of time?

Because it is not a given that you already know the structure, the SimpleXMLElement class implements the children() method that returns an iterable SimpleXMLElement object, which allows you to iterate through all the child elements of an element. This object works the same as the other objects you have seen so far, except the elements in the collection are not limited to specific named elements, but rather include all immediate child elements. For example:

```
$book = simplexml_load_file('sxml.xml');
$author = $book->bookinfo->author;
$children = $author->children();

foreach($children AS $child) {
    print $child."\n";
}
```

Taking the author element, consider the possibility that the elements in Listing 7-1 are not required and that any element can be added on the fly. You have no guarantee that the name of the child elements will be known ahead of time. The previous code accesses the $author object using the children() method and returns the SimpleXMLElement object to the $children variable. The resulting output from the print statement in the foreach loop is as follows:

```
Rob
Richards
```

The text Rob is from the firstname element, and the text Richards is from the surname element. In this case, though, you did not need to know the element names. You could also access the children by index. The code print $children[1]; would print just Richards.

This presents an interesting issue. You can access elements without knowing their names, but how can you determine the name of an element? Unfortunately, you cannot do this using SimpleXML alone. Let's take a look at possible ways to get this missing information.

Understanding PHP Object Functions

Properties of a SimpleXMLElement object are dynamic. That is, the properties depend upon the instance of the object and not the class itself. Within PHP, it is possible to retrieve object properties using the get_object_vars() function. Rather than using the children() method on the $author object, you can return an array of the properties and values instead:

```
$props = get_object_vars($author);
foreach ($props AS $name=>$value) {
    print $name.": ".$value."\n";
}
```

The output is similar to that when using the children() method, except in this case the name of the element is also available:

```
firstname: Rob
surname: Richards
```

This was a simple case. The child elements contained text content only, so the array contained the property names and strings for the values. When used on an element containing child elements, on the other hand, the values will be SimpleXMLElement objects:

```
$props = get_object_vars($book->bookinfo);
var_dump($props);
```

The results from using the get_object_vars() function of the bookinfo element is much different from the previous array returned:

```
array(3) {
  ["title"]=>
  string(18) "SimpleXML in PHP 5"
  ["author"]=>
  object(SimpleXMLElement)#6 (2) {
    ["firstname"]=>
    string(3) "Rob"
    ["surname"]=>
    string(8) "Richards"
  }
  ["copyright"]=>
  object(SimpleXMLElement)#7 (2) {
    ["year"]=>
    string(4) "2005"
    ["holder"]=>
    string(12) "Rob Richards"
  }
}
```

The array contains not only string values but also SimpleXMLElement objects, as shown with the author and copyright properties:

```
function processValue($name, $value, $level) {
    if (is_object($value)) {
        print str_repeat (" ", $level);
        print $name."\n";
        processSXEObject($value, $level + 1);
    } else if (is_array($value)) {
        foreach($value as $node) {
            processValue($name, $node, $level);
        }
    } else {
        print str_repeat (" ", $level);
        print $name.": ".$value."\n";
    }
}
```

```php
function processSXEObject($sxe, $level) {
   $props = get_object_vars($sxe);
   if (count($props) == 0) {
      print str_repeat (" ", $level);
      print "Special Content: ".$sxe."\n";
      return;
   }
   foreach ($props AS $name=>$value) {
      processValue($name, $value, $level);
   }
}


$book = simplexml_load_file('sxml.xml');
processSXEObject($book, 0);
```

Other than calling the load function and using the special handling of strings in SimpleXML, you do not need any additional methods from SimpleXML to process the tree in Listing 7-1. The code shown prints every element name, indenting using spaces for the level within the tree, and prints any text content the elements may have. It doesn't handle mixed content, which I will leave as an exercise for you to implement if you like. The output of this code is as follows:

```
bookinfo
 title: SimpleXML in PHP 5
 author
  firstname: Rob
  surname: Richards
 copyright
  year: 2005
  holder: Rob Richards
preface
 title: Using SimpleXML
 para: An example DOM Tree using DocBook.
chapter
 title: Acessing Elements
 para: Elements are accessed as properties
 para
  Special Content:

            <?php
            $data = '<?xml version="1.0"?>
            <root>content</root>';

            $sxe = simplexml_load_string($data);
            var_dump($sxe);
            ?>
```

The case for special content was added to handle the CDATA node. Currently an element containing a CDATA child is not handled the same way as an element containing just text node children. This functionality may change in future versions of PHP; however, as of PHP 5.1, just be aware of this.

Using DOM Interoperability

Another method of handling unknown elements is to use DOM interoperability. You can import nodes into the DOM extension and access them using DOM properties and methods. Returning to the original code accessing the author element using the children() method, you can easily extract the name of the node using the DOM extension:

```
$book = simplexml_load_file('sxml.xml');
$author = $book->bookinfo->author;
$children = $author->children();

foreach($children AS $child) {
    /* Import node into DOM, and get nodeName */
    $element = dom_import_simplexml($child);
    $name = $element->nodeName;
    print $name.": ".$child."\n";
}
```

As you can clearly see, this is much cleaner and easier to deal with than using the get_object_vars() function. Importing nodes into the DOM extension does not result in copies of nodes but direct access to the node imported. Not only does this allow the use of DOM functionality with SimpleXMLElement objects, but it also doesn't impose any performance penalty either. The drawback of this is that the DOM extension must be available to take advantage of this feature. (Even though it is enabled by default, it is possible to disable the DOM extension.)

Modifying Content

Just like navigation is easy to work with in SimpleXML, so is content modification. Using SimpleXML, you cannot add new elements to the tree, but you can change and remove existing ones. To add a new element, the interoperability with the DOM extension comes into play:

```
$xml = "<root><node1>content</node1></root>";
$sxe = new SimpleXMLElement($xml);
$dom = dom_import_simplexml($sxe);
$dom->appendChild(new DOMElement("node2", "content2"));
print $sxe->asXML();
```

```
<?xml version="1.0"?>
<root><node1>content</node1><node2>content2</node2></root>
```

Editing Content

You can edit nodes and content natively using SimpleXML. When working with elements that exist multiple times as a child of another element, you must ensure you are modifying the correct element. When indexes are not used to indicate a specific element to edit and when multiple elements with the name exist, a warning is issued indicating that the multiple elements exist and the modification cannot be performed.

Elements with Text Content

The following example attempts to modify the content of a para element within the document. The problem is that multiple para elements exist, and SimpleXML does not know which one of them should be modified.

```
$book = simplexml_load_file('sxml.xml');
/* Modify an unspecified para element where multiple para elements exist */
$book->chapter->para = "Removed CDATA";
```

```
Warning: main() [/phpmanual/function.main.html]: Cannot assign to an array of nodes
(duplicate subnodes or attr detected)
```

You must specify the index of the para element to be edited:

```
$book = simplexml_load_file('sxml.xml');
$book->chapter->para[1] = "Removed CDATA";
print $book->chapter->asXML();
```

```
<chapter id="navigation">
    <title>Acessing Elements</title>
    <para>Elements are accessed as properties</para>
    <para>Removed CDATA</para>
  </chapter>
```

In this case, the content of the second para element is changed to Removed CDATA. The method asXML() is used in this case from the chapter object. When used from an element that is not the document element, only the element and its subtree are returned.

Indexes are not required when a single element with the name exists. In the following code, the content of the title element is changed, as well as the second para element:

```
$book = simplexml_load_file('sxml.xml');
$book->chapter->title = "New Title";
$book->chapter->para[1] = "Removed CDATA";
print $book->chapter->asXML();
```

```
<chapter id="navigation">
    <title>New Title</title>
    <para>Elements are accessed as properties</para>
    <para>Removed CDATA</para>
  </chapter>
```

Unless you are absolutely sure about the structure of the document, using indexes to modify elements is highly suggested. It is much safer to modify the title element using the code $book->chapter->title[0] = "New Title";, because the first title element is specifically identified by the use of [0].

Elements with Subtrees You can edit elements containing subtrees, or child elements, in the same manner as those with text content. The subtree, however, is removed from the document and replaced with the text content. Not only will any objects pointing to elements within the subtree become invalid, but as you recall from earlier in the chapter, you cannot add elements using SimpleXML natively. The string containing the content to be used for replacement, even if it contains XML, will be escaped and used as strictly text content. Let's look at two cases of replacing the content of the chapter element with different data and the results of any objects pointing to child elements:

```
$book = simplexml_load_file('sxml.xml');
$cholder = $book->bookinfo->copyright->holder;
print $cholder->asXML()."\n";
$book->bookinfo = "No Book Info";
print $book->bookinfo->asXML()."\n";
print $cholder->asXML()."\n";
```

```
<holder>Rob Richards</holder>
<bookinfo>No Book Info</bookinfo>

Warning: SimpleXMLElement::asXML() [/phpmanual/function.asXML.html]: Node no
longer exists in N:\CVS Projects\php5\Debug_TS\booksxe.php on line 7
```

Initially, the holder element is retrieved from the document and set to the $cholder variable. The XML for this element is printed and shown in the first line of the results. The bookinfo element contains a subtree that includes the title, author, and copyright elements. The content of this element is then changed to the simple text string No Book Info. When printed, the child elements have clearly been removed and the content replaced with the text, which is shown in the second line of the results. Upon trying to access the $cholder variable again to print its XML content, a warning is issued. This variable is still a SimpleXMLElement object, but the underlying node from the tree was destroyed when the content was changed for the bookinfo element.

The next case will use XML data for the replacement text. The content for the copyright element will be replaced with the string <title>SimpleXML in PHP 5</title>, like so:

```
$book = simplexml_load_file('sxml.xml');
$book->bookinfo = "<title>SimpleXML in PHP 5</title>";
print $book->bookinfo->asXML()."\n";
```

You may be surprised by the output. If you thought all child elements for bookinfo would be removed and a new title element created as a child of bookinfo, you would be mistaken.

```
<bookinfo>&lt;title&gt;SimpleXML in PHP ·5&lt;/title&gt;</bookinfo>
```

The child elements are removed from the bookinfo element, but the XML data is escaped and set as text-only content.

Tip Remember, SimpleXML will not add elements to a tree. Using the interoperability of the XML-related extensions in PHP 5, you must use the DOM extension to create and append new elements to a tree being accessed by SimpleXML.

To replace the subtree with another subtree, you can use the DOM extension:

```
$book = simplexml_load_file('sxml.xml');
$bookinfo = dom_import_simplexml($book->bookinfo);

/* Remove all child elements of the bookinfo element */
while ($bookinfo->firstChild) {
    $bookinfo->removeChild($bookinfo->firstChild);
}
$bookinfo->appendChild(new DOMElement("title", "SimpleXML in PHP 5"));
print $book->bookinfo->asXML()."\n";
```

```
<bookinfo>
  <title>SimpleXML in PHP 5</title>
</bookinfo>
```

Removing Elements

You can remove elements from a tree using SimpleXML. You do this using the unset() function built into PHP. The argument for unset() must be an overloaded SimpleXMLElement, accessing the element to remove by the property. For example, removing the title element from the chapter node takes place through the following code:

```
$book = simplexml_load_file('sxml.xml');
$book->chapter->para[1] = "Removed CDATA";
unset($book->chapter->title);
print $book->chapter->asXML();
```

The second para element was modified just to shorten the final output because it originally contained the CDATA node from Listing 7-1. Notice the third line using the unset() function. The parameter passed is $book->chapter->title. It is important that title is used as a property when making this call; otherwise, the node will not be removed:

```
<chapter id="navigation">

    <para>Elements are accessed as properties</para>
    <para>Removed CDATA</para>
  </chapter>
```

Compare these results with those using unset() on a lone SimpleXMLElement object that refers to the title element:

```php
$book = simplexml_load_file('sxml.xml');
$book->chapter->para[1] = "Removed CDATA";
$title = $book->chapter->title;
unset($title);
print $book->chapter->asXML();
```

```xml
<chapter id="navigation">
    <title>Acessing Elements</title>
    <para>Elements are accessed as properties</para>
    <para>Removed CDATA</para>
  </chapter>
```

The title element was not removed. All unset() did in this case was unset the variable $title and not actually remove the title element from the tree.

An issue to be aware of when removing elements is that specific elements cannot be identified for removal. This at least is the current behavior in PHP 5.0 and 5.1. Using an index will *not* result in the removal of the element:

```php
$book = simplexml_load_file('sxml.xml');
$book->chapter->para[1] = "Removed CDATA";
unset($book->chapter->title[0]);
print $book->chapter->asXML();
```

```xml
<chapter id="navigation">
    <title>Acessing Elements</title>
    <para>Elements are accessed as properties</para>
    <para>Removed CDATA</para>
  </chapter>
```

This causes a little problem. What happens when you need to remove the para elements? If all para child elements of the chapter element are to be removed, then you do not have a problem. The unset() function will remove all elements matching the property name:

```php
$book = simplexml_load_file('sxml.xml');
unset($book->chapter->para);
print $book->chapter->asXML();
```

```xml
<chapter id="navigation">
    <title>Acessing Elements</title>


  </chapter>
```

The para elements have been removed from the tree, but that still leaves an issue when only one of the para elements needs to be removed. Again, it's back to interoperability with the DOM extension:

```
$book = simplexml_load_file('sxml.xml');
$chapter = dom_import_simplexml($book->chapter);
$node = $chapter->lastChild;
while($node) {
    if ($node->nodeName == "para") {
        $chapter->removeChild($node);
        $node = NULL;
        break;
    }
    $node = $node->previousSibling;
}
print $book->chapter->asXML();
```

```
<chapter id="navigation">
    <title>Acessing Elements</title>
    <para>Elements are accessed as properties</para>

</chapter>
```

Although the current version DOM must be used in this case, the behavior of unset() with SimpleXML may change in future versions to allow indexes to be used. This will make coding with SimpleXML a bit easier, and it will remove another reliance on the DOM extension when performing modifications on a document using SimpleXML.

Accessing Attributes

Accessing an attribute is similar to accessing a specific element in a document. Rather than using a numeric index to specify an element, you use the name of the attribute for the index. Attributes are uniquely named, meaning that any element having two or more elements with the same name is not well-formed XML. I will cover this a bit more in the "Namespaces in SimpleXML" section because it is possible to have two attributes with the same local name as long as they live in different namespaces. The information covered in the following sections, though, deals only with accessing non-namespaced attributes.

Reading Attributes

The following code prints the value for the lang attribute that resides on the document element, book. In this case, you do not need to worry about identifying the correct element since the document can contain only a single document element.

```
$book = simplexml_load_file('sxml.xml');
print $book['lang'];
```

The following piece of code uses the numeric index to specifically identify a chapter element, even though only one exists. It is not really needed here but illustrates how you would deal with multiple elements and attribute access. It then prints the value of the id attribute on this node, which results in navigation.

```
$book = simplexml_load_file('sxml.xml');
print $book->chapter[0]['id'];
```

You can also access attributes when you don't know the attribute names. The method attributes() works just like the children() method, except in this case it returns an iterable object containing the attributes for an element:

```
$book = simplexml_load_file('sxml.xml');
foreach($book->chapter->attributes() AS $attribute) {
    print $attribute."\n";
}
```

The foreach loops through all attributes of the chapter element, with each attribute set to the variable $attribute as the loop is executed. The chapter element contains only a single attribute, id, so the loop is executed only once and the value navigation is printed. You can obtain additional information using DOM functionality, just as when using elements:

```
$book = simplexml_load_file('sxml.xml');
foreach($book->chapter->attributes() AS $attribute) {
    $att = dom_import_simplexml($attribute);
    print $att->nodeName."\n";
    print $attribute."\n";
}
```

```
id
navigation
```

Writing to Attributes

Modifying the content of an attribute works the same way as modifying an element. You just set the attribute to a string, which in turn changes the attribute value:

```
$book = simplexml_load_file('sxml.xml');
$book['lang'] = "es";
print $book['lang'];
```

The lang attribute is changed from en to es, as shown in the results from the print statement.

A difference with writing to attributes and writing to elements is that new attributes *can* be created using SimpleXML:

```
$book = simplexml_load_file('sxml.xml');
$book->bookinfo->author->firstname["prefix"] = "Mr.";
print $book->bookinfo->author->asXML();
```

```
<author>
        <firstname prefix="Mr.">Rob</firstname>
        <surname>Richards</surname>
    </author>
```

When an attribute is being written to and does not exist on the element, the attribute is automatically created with the content specified by the string to which it is being set. In this instance, the firstname element originally contained no attributes. Writing the string Mr. to an attribute named prefix, the prefix attribute was created on the firstname element and its value set to the value of the supplied string.

Removing Attributes

Again, you can use the function unset() to remove attributes from elements, just as you remove elements from the tree:

```
$book = simplexml_load_file('sxml.xml');
$book->bookinfo->author->firstname["prefix"] = "Mr.";
print $book->bookinfo->author->firstname->asXML()."\n\n";

unset($book->bookinfo->author->firstname["prefix"]);
print $book->bookinfo->author->firstname->asXML();
```

```
<firstname prefix="Mr.">Rob</firstname>

<firstname>Rob</firstname>
```

After adding the prefix attribute and printing the XML data from the firstname element, the code continues, removes this newly added attribute, and again prints the updated XML data from the firstname element.

Extending the SimpleXMLElement Class

You can extend the SimpleXMLElement class just as you would any other class:

```
class mySXE extends SimpleXMLElement {
    function appendChild($name, $content) {
        $dom = dom_import_simplexml($this);
        $dom->appendChild($dom->ownerDocument->createElement($name, $content));
    }
}
```

A big difference with extended classes in SimpleXML from those in the DOM extension is that once an object using the extended class has been instantiated, all objects returned from the SimpleXML methods will use the extended class type.

Looking at the class definition, you can see that the method appendChild() has been added. This allows for an easy way to append child nodes in SimpleXML:

```
$sxe = new mySXE("<root><node1></node1></root>");
$sxe->node1->appendChild("node2", "content");
print $sxe->asXML();
```

```
<?xml version="1.0"?>
<root><node1><node2>content</node2></node1></root>
```

The initial $sxe object was created using the new keyword with the extended class. As shown in the second line, the object returned from the node1 property was created using the extended class. Once the initial object based on a SimpleXMLElement class is created, all objects will be created using the same class.

The new keyword is nice to use when working with XML contained in a string, but it doesn't help much when the data resides in a file. As mentioned in the earlier "Creating a SimpleXMLElement Object" section, the load functions take an optional class_name parameter. This parameter indicates the class to use for creating the initial object. Using the mySXE class, you can load data from either a string or a file and have the ability to use the custom appendChild() method:

```
$sxe = simplexml_load_string("<root><node1></node1></root>", "mySXE");
$sxe->node1->appendChild("node2", "content");
print $sxe->asXML();
```

The result of this is the same as the results using the new keyword.

Using Namespaces in SimpleXML

Dealing with namespaced documents using SimpleXML is a bit different from handling documents without namespaces. Listing 7-2 contains the document from Listing 7-1 modified to use namespaces.

Listing 7-2. *Modified Document Using Namespaces: Filename* sxmlns.xml

```
<?xml version="1.0" encoding="UTF-8"?>
<book ns2:lang="en" xmlns:ns1="http://www.example.com/ns1"
                     xmlns:ns2="http://www.example.com/ns2">
    <ns1:bookinfo>
        <title>SimpleXML in PHP 5</title>
        <ns1:author>
            <ns1:firstname>Rob</ns1:firstname>
            <surname>Richards</surname>
        </ns1:author>
        <copyright>
            <year>2005</year>
            <holder>Rob Richards</holder>
        </copyright>
    </ns1:bookinfo>
</book>
```

If you tried to access this document using the normal methods for accessing elements and attributes, you would find out that nothing works. For example:

```
$book = simplexml_load_file('sxmlns.xml');
print $book["lang"]."\n";
print $book->bookinfo->title."\n";
```

This code prints nothing but two blank lines.

To initially access namespaced nodes, you must use the methods `children()` and `attributes()`. Not only are these methods used to access nodes without using their names, but these methods also accept a namespace URI as a parameter, which must be supplied to retrieve namespaced nodes from these methods. I have good news. Once a `SimpleXMLElement` object is returned from either of these methods, you can then access the elements and attributes residing in the supplied namespace as normal elements and attributes. For example, you can rewrite the previous piece of code to print valid output:

```
$book = simplexml_load_file('sxmlns.xml');
/* Retrieve all attributes in the http://www.example.com/ns2 namespace */
$bookatts = $book->attributes("http://www.example.com/ns2");

print $bookatts["lang"]."\n";

/* Retrieve all elements in the http://www.example.com/ns1 namespace */
$bookns = $book->children("http://www.example.com/ns1");
$bookinfo = $bookns->bookinfo;

/* Reset namespace to access non-namespaced elements */
$nonsbkinfo = $bookinfo->children();
print $nonsbkinfo->title."\n";
```

The `children()` and `attributes()` methods basically act as filters. When no parameter or `NULL` is passed as the parameter, nodes residing in no namespace are retrieved; otherwise, nodes that reside in the specified namespace are retrieved. Until reset, the specified namespace remains in effect and is inherited by the child nodes. For instance, using the `$bookinfo` object, which has been set to the `http://www.example.com/ns1` namespace, the `firstname` from the `author` element can be printed by `print $bookinfo->author->firstname`. All elements reside in the same namespace, so you have no need to alter the namespace set by the `children()` method when creating the `$bookinfo` object.

Default namespaces work differently than prefixed namespaces do. The document in Listing 7-3 is a modified version of the document from Listing 7-2. All prefixed namespaces have been removed, and only a single default namespace, `http://www.example.com/ns1`, has been added.

Listing 7-3. *Modified Document Using Default Namespace: Filename* `sxmlns2.xml`

```
<?xml version="1.0" encoding="UTF-8"?>
<book lang="en">
    <bookinfo xmlns="http://www.example.com/ns1">
        <title>SimpleXML in PHP 5</title>
        <author>
            <firstname>Rob</firstname>
            <surname>Richards</surname>
        </author>
```

```
      <copyright>
         <year>2005</year>
         <holder>Rob Richards</holder>
      </copyright>
   </bookinfo>
</book>
```

After playing around with namespaces using the document from Listing 7-2, you proba-bly are trying the same code used with the last document. The only change you made most likely is removing the use of the attributes() method since the attribute in this document is not in a namespace. The results are also what you probably expected. It works correctly, and the content of the title element was printed.

Now for the kicker: all that code is not necessary to print the title element. In fact, you can do it using the code first tried in the namespace section that did not work with prefixed namespaces:

```
$book = simplexml_load_file('sxmlns2.xml');
print $book["lang"]."\n";
print $book->bookinfo->title."\n";
```

Elements in the default namespace work the same as elements not in any namespace. In fact, they can also work the same as elements that are in prefixed namespaces. Does this sound a little strange? I am not exactly sure how this came to be. It may have been by design or left over from the changes made to namespace handling in SimpleXML prior to the initial PHP 5.0 launch, but in any event, you can write code in either fashion, for non-namespaced docu-ments or for namespaced documents, when elements reside in a default namespace.

Using XPath

XPath in SimpleXML is easy to use but is limited to returning elements and attributes. Because of how SimpleXML works, queries that normally return text nodes return the text node's parent node. You can use the xpath() method to query a document and return an array containing all relevant nodes from the XPath query:

```
$book = simplexml_load_file('sxml.xml');
$arAuthor = $book->xpath("/book/bookinfo/author/*");
foreach($arAuthor AS $node) {
    print $node."\n";
}
```

```
Rob
Richards
```

Using the document in Listing 7-1, the child elements of the author element are queried and returned as an array to the $arAuthor variable. This query results in the array returning the firstname and surname elements, which are printed as you move through the array in the foreach loop.

The next example will query for the text node, which will be the content, of the `firstname` element:

```
$book = simplexml_load_file('sxml.xml');
$arAuthor = $book->xpath("/book/bookinfo/author/firstname/child::text()");
foreach($arAuthor AS $node) {
   print $node."\n";
}
```

Of course, the result from the `print` statement is `Rob`. There is only a single text node after all. The $node object, however, is really the `firstname` element. You can check this by either importing it to the DOM extension or checking the class type of the object, which will be `SimpleXMLElement`.

If you have read Chapter 4 and Chapter 6, you already know there is an issue when dealing with documents using default namespaces and XPath. Just like the DOM extension, SimpleXML offers a method to register namespaces and associated prefixes: `registerXPathNamespace()`. This method works the same way and even takes the same parameters as the method in the DOM extension. The first parameter is the prefix, and the second parameter is the namespace URI.

Caution The method `registerXPathNamespace` is available only in PHP 5.1+. To perform XPath queries dealing with default namespaces in PHP 5.0.*x*, you will need to leverage the XPath functionality in the DOM extension or write XPath queries in such a way that the qualifiers bypass any namespace checks. Refer to Chapters 4 and 6 for additional information.

Using the document in Listing 7-3, retrieving the `firstname` element requires the use of namespaces. The namespaced elements reside in a default namespace, so the `registerXPathNamespace()` method will be used to register a prefix that can be used in the XPath expression:

```
$book = simplexml_load_file('sxmlns2.xml');
$book->registerXPathNamespace("sxe", "http://www.example.com/ns1");
if ($arAuthor = $book->xpath("/book/sxe:bookinfo/sxe:author/sxe:firstname")) {
   foreach($arAuthor AS $node) {
      print $node."\n";
   }
}
```

The prefix `sxe` is registered and associated with the namespace `http://www.example.com/ns1`. The query is executed, and the resulting variable is tested to make sure that nodes were returned. In the event no nodes result from the query, the method `xpath()` returns `FALSE` rather than an array. In some cases, an empty array is returned and occurs when nodes are returned, but they are not a valid type under SimpleXML. For instance, a query that results in a PI node is valid in XPath, but the node type is not supported in SimpleXML. In this case, an empty array is returned, indicating that the query was successful but no usable nodes are available.

Seeing Some Examples in Action

Throughout this chapter you have seen how to work with SimpleXML using known documents and have seen a few ways of even dealing with unknown document structures. You can find additional examples of using SimpleXML in later chapters such as Chapter 14, which covers RSS, and Chapter 17, which covers REST. For a different type of example, I will show how to generate a PAD XML file.

PAD is a specification designed by the ASP; you can find it at http://www.asp-shareware.org/ pad/. It is a standard format allowing authors of shareware software to provide information such as company and contact information, support information, software information, and licensing in a common format that may be leveraged not only by users looking for more information about a piece of software but also by online libraries building content and search engines.

Applications to generate PAD files already exist, but in this case, you will build your own Web-based generator using PHP and SimpleXML. As you have read in this chapter, SimpleXML does not provide the capability to create documents. I will show how to use a template for the PAD document that was created in Chapter 6 with the DOM extension. Using the generated template and the PAD specification file, located at http://www.padspec.org/pad_spec.xml, you will see how to use SimpleXML to build not only the final PAD document but also a good portion of the input portion of the UI for this application.

What sets this example apart from those you have already seen is that other than the base information, consisting of three fields, the entire application will be built dynamically—with no knowledge of the PAD structure—using the XML-based PAD specification. This does have a few drawbacks. The UI is not clean as field lengths, and required fields and lookups are not easily determined. The specification does include regular expressions for each field that this application uses to validate input, so although no attempt has been made to use them because creating the UI is out of scope for this example, it may be possible to leverage them when building the UI. With the background and explanation of what is being built out of the way, it's time to create the application.

Note This example requires the PAD template generated by the DOM extension in the examples from Chapter 6. No validation other than specific field checks using the regular expression provided by the PAD specification is taking place. In its raw state, it is not secure and should be used only in a controlled environment.

Listing 7-4 contains the entire code used to build the application. Much of the general PHP usage in this example could be coded in many different ways, but for the sake of this example the most important areas are those dealing with SimpleXML usage. This application has been designed to work under a Web server running PHP.

Listing 7-4. *PAD Generator Application*

```php
<html>
<body>
<?php
/* BEGINNGING OF USER VARIABLES */
/* Location of PAD Specification File */
$padspec = "http://www.padspec.org/pad_spec.xml";

/* Location of PAD Template Generated by DOM */
$padtemplate = "padtemplate.xml";

/* Name of PAD File to Save Results to */
$savefile = "padout.xml";
/* END OF USER VARIABLES */


/* Output field name/values for input and preview based on state of $bPreview */
function printDisplay($sxe, $sxetemplate, $bPreview) {
   $section = "";
   /* Loop through the Field nodes of the specification */
   foreach ($sxe->Fields->Field as $field) {
      /* Get the node path used in the template */
      $arPath = explode("/", trim($field->Path));
      array_shift($arPath);
      /* Skip MASTER_PAD_VERSION_INFO nodes.
         Values for these are set by template generator */
      if ($arPath[0] != "MASTER_PAD_VERSION_INFO") {
         if ($arPath[0] != $section) {
            $section = $arPath[0];
            print "<p>".str_replace("_"," ", $section)."</p>";
         }
         $input_value = getStoredValue($sxetemplate, $arPath);
         array_shift($arPath);
         print "\n".$field->Title.': ';
         if ($bPreview) {
            print $input_value."<br>";
         } else {
            $input_name = $section;
            /* Generate the field name using named-based keys for an array */
            foreach ($arPath AS $key=>$value) {
               $input_name .= "[$value]";
            }
            print '<input type="text" name="'.$input_name.
                  '" value="'.$input_value.'"><br>';
         }
      }
   }
}
```

```
/* Retrieve text content for node from working template */
function getStoredValue($sxe, $arPath) {
  if ($sxe) {
      /* Loop through node path to find SimpleXML element from working template */
      foreach($arPath AS $key=>$value) {
         $sxe = $sxe->$value;
      }
      return (string)$sxe;
  }
  return "";
}


/* Set the text content for a node from working template */
function setValue($sxe, $field, $value) {
  if (is_array($value)) {
      /* Loop through node path to find SimpleXML element from working template */
      foreach ($value AS $fieldname=>$fieldvalue) {
         setValue($sxe->$field, $fieldname, $fieldvalue);
      }
  } else {
      /* Encode the value to ensure content will be valid XML */
      $sxe->$field = htmlentities($value);
  }
}


/* Validate fields in working template using the RegEx defined in specification */
function validatePAD($spec, $template) {
  $arRet = array();
  foreach ($spec->Fields->Field as $field) {
      $arPath = explode("/", trim($field->Path));
      array_shift($arPath);
      if ($arPath[0] != "MASTER_PAD_VERSION_INFO") {
         $sxe = $template;
         $regex = "/".trim($field->RegEx)."/";
         foreach($arPath AS $key=>$value) {
            $sxe = $sxe->$value;
            if (! $sxe) {
               break;
            }
         }
         if ($sxe) {
            $value = (string)$sxe;
            if (! preg_match($regex, $value)) {
               /* Capture fields failing validation for later display */
               $arRet[] = array($field->Title, $field->RegExDocumentation);
```

```
                }
            }
        }
    }
    /* Return array containing any captured errors */
    return $arRet;
}

/* Initial states for application variables */
$sxetemplate = NULL;
$bPreview = FALSE;
$bError = FALSE;
$bSave = FALSE;

/* BEGIN ACTUAL PROCESSING */
if ($sxe = simplexml_load_file($padspec)) {
    if (isset($_POST['Save']) || isset($_POST['Preview']) || isset($_POST['Edit'])) {
        /* Working template in hidden field is Base64 encoded and must be decoded */
        $sxetemplate = new SimpleXMLElement(base64_decode($_POST['ptemplate']));
        /* Loop through $_POST vars. vars that are arrays are PAD fields to be set */
        foreach($_POST AS $name=>$value) {
            if (is_array($value)) {
                setValue($sxetemplate, $name, $value);
            }
        }
        if (isset($_POST['Save'])) {
            /* Save finalized working template to file */
            $sxetemplate->asXML($savefile);
            $bSave = TRUE;
        } elseif (isset($_POST['Preview'])) {
            /* Validate the working template */
            $arRet = validatePAD($sxe, $sxetemplate);
            if (count($arRet) > 0) {
                $bError = TRUE;
                print "<B>ERRORS FOUND</B><br>";
                /* Print out errors returned from validatePAD() */
                foreach ($arRet AS $key=>$value) {
                    print $value[0].": ".$value[1]."<br>";
                }
            } else {
                /* Working template was validated so allow data to be previewed */
                $bPreview = TRUE;
            }
        }
    } else {
```

```
          /* Initial entry point so load the PAD template created from DOM */
          $sxetemplate = simplexml_load_file($padtemplate);
      }
      /* If in working state display the working template for editing or preview */
      if (! $bSave) {
          print '<form method="POST">';
          /* Base64-encoded working template to allow XML to be passed
             in hidden field */
          print '<input type="hidden" name="ptemplate" value="'.
              base64_encode($sxetemplate->asXML()).'">';
          printDisplay($sxe, $sxetemplate, $bPreview);
          print '<br><br>     '.
              '<input type="Submit" name="Preview" value="Preview and Validate PAD">';
          if (!$bError && isset($_POST['Preview'])) {
              /* Working template is valid and in preview mode.
                 Allow additional editing or final Save */
              print '     '.
                  '<input type="Submit" name="Edit" value="Edit PAD">';
              print '     '.
                  '<input type="Submit" name="Save" value="Save PAD">';
          }
          print '</form><br><br>' ;
      } else {
          /* Final PAD file has been saved - Just print message */
          print "PAD File Saved as $savefile";
      }
} else {
    /* Application unable to retrieve the specification file - Error */
    print "Unable to load PAD Specification File";
}
?>
</body>
</html>
```

The important areas to look at within this application are the user variables and the
defined functions. The remainder of the application just pieces it all together. You must set
three user variables. The default values will work just as well, but you can change them with
respect to your current setup. These are the three user variables:

$padspec: Location of PAD specification file. By default it pulls from
http://www.padspec.org, but you can have it reside locally; in that case, modify the value
to point to your local copy.

$padtemplate: Location of the PAD template generated by the DOM extension in Chapter 6.

$savefile: Location to save the final generated PAD file to when done.

The specification file is used in every step of the process, so the first thing the application
does is have SimpleXML load it. Initially, none of the POST variables is set, and SimpleXML is

called on again to load the empty template created by the DOM extension. This is performed only once when the application begins because the template is then passed in $_POST['ptemplate']. Being XML data, it is Base64-encoded within the form and Base64-decoded before being used.

The function printDisplay() takes three parameters. The first is the SimpleXMLElement containing the specification file. The second is the SimpleXMLElement containing the working template. The last parameter is a Boolean used for state. When in a preview state, the system generates display data only; otherwise, it displays editable fields. Being a standardized format, the application loops through the ->Fields->Field elements assuming they always exist. The Field element contains all the information for each node in the template document, including its location in the tree, which is stored in the Path child element. The Path, taking the form of a string such as XML_DIZ_INFO/Company_Info/Company_Name, is split into an array based on the / character, and the first element is removed. You do not need this element because it is the document element, which is already represented by the SimpleXMLElement holding the specification document.

The first element breaks the display output into sections on the screen, skipping all fields that contain the node MASTER_PAD_VERSION_INFO. The information for this node and its children is already provided within the template file. The application then generates the appropriate input tags or displays content based on the state of the application. When input fields are generated, the name of the field corresponds to the location of the element within the document. For example, if you used XML_DIZ_INFO/Company_Info/Company_Name as the Path, the name within the form would be Company_Info[Company_Name]. Values for the fields are pulled from the getStoredValue() function. This is where it gets interesting with SimpleXML usage.

The array containing the elements of the path is iterated. Each time, the variable $sxe, which originally contained the working template, is changed to be the child element of its current element using the $value variable, which is the name of the subnode. Examining a path from the specification file, such as XML_DIZ_INFO/Company_Info/Company_Name, the corresponding array, after removing the first element, would be array('Company_Info', 'Company_Name'). This corresponds to the following XML fragment:

```
<XML_DIZ_INFO>
    <Company_Info>
        <Company_Name />
    </Company_Info>
</XML_DIZ_INFO>
```

Iterating through the array and setting $sxe each time are the equivalent of manually coding this:

```
$sxe = $sxe->Company_Info;
$sxe = $sxe->Company_Name;
```

You can navigate to the correct node using the information from the specification file without needing to know the document structure of the template file. Once iteration of the foreach is finished, the variable $sxe is cast to a string, which is the text content of the node the application is looking for, and is then returned to the application.

When the data is submitted from the UI to the application, the function setValue() is called. As you probably recall, the name of the input fields indicate arrays, such as Company_Info[Company_Name]. No other named fields that are arrays are used in the application, so it assumes all incoming arrays contain locations and values for the PAD template. The `setValue()` function is recursive. As long as the value of the array is another array, the function calls itself with the `$sxe` variable pointing to the field name passed into the function, the new field name, and the new field value. Once the incoming value is no longer an array, it is set as the value of the new field passed to the function of the `$sxe` object passed into the function. The value is also encoded using `htmlentities()` to ensure the data will be properly escaped. For instance, a value containing the & character needs it converted to its entity format, &.

The last use of SimpleXML worth mentioning in this application is within the `validatePAD()` function. PAD contains a `RegEx` field within each `Field` node of the specification. This field defines the regular expression the data needs to conform to in order to be considered valid. The same technique is used to loop through the specification file to find the `RegEx` node and the `Path` node, as you have seen in other functions in this application. The correct element is also navigated to within the template using similar techniques. Once you've gathered all the information, you can test the regular expression against the value of the `$sxe` element from the working template.

This example illustrated how you can use XML and SimpleXML to generate an application including its UI, data storage, and validation rules using a real-world case. If you are a current shareware author, you may already be familiar with the PAD format. Using techniques within this application, you should have no problems writing your own application to generate your PAD files. In any case, this example has shown that even though SimpleXML has a simple API and certain limitations, you can use it for some complex applications, even when you don't know the document structure.

Conclusion

The SimpleXML extension provides easy access to XML documents using a tree-based structure. The ease of use also results in certain limitations. As you have seen, elements cannot be created; only elements, attributes, and their content are accessible, and only limited information about a node is available. This chapter covered the SimpleXML extension by demonstrating its ease of use as well as its limitations. The chapter also discussed methods of dealing with these limitations, such as using the interoperability with the DOM extension and in certain cases with built-in PHP object functions.

The material presented here provides an in-depth explanation of SimpleXML and its functionality; the examples should provide you with enough information to begin using SimpleXML in your everyday coding.

The next chapter will introduce how to parse streamed XML data using the XMLReader extension. Processing XML data using streams is different from what you have dealt with to this point because unlike the tree parsers, DOM and SimpleXML, only portions of the document live in memory at a time.

CHAPTER 8

■ ■ ■

Simple API for XML (SAX)

The extensions covered up until now have dealt with XML in a hierarchical structure residing in memory. They are tree-based parsers that allow you to move throughout the tree as well as modify the XML document. This chapter will introduce you to stream-based parsers and, in particular, the Simple API for XML (SAX). Through examples and a look at the changes in this extension from PHP 4 to PHP 5, you will be well equipped to write or possibly fix code using SAX.

Introducing SAX

In general terms, SAX is a streams-based parser. Chunks of data are streamed through the parser and processed. As the parser needs more data, it releases the current chunk of data and grabs more chunks, which are then also processed. This continues until either there is no more data to process or the process itself is stopped before reaching the end of the data. Unlike tree parsers, stream-based parsers interact with an application during parsing and do not persist the information in the XML document. Once the parsing is done, the XML processing is done. This differs greatly compared to the SimpleXML or DOM extension; in those cases, the parsing builds an in-memory tree; then, once done, interaction with the tree begins, and the application can manipulate the XML.

Background

SAX is just one of the stream-based parsers in PHP 5. What sets it apart from the other stream-based parsers is that it is an event-based, or *push*, parser. Originally developed in 1998 for use under Java, SAX is not based on any formal specification like the DOM extension is, although many DOM parsers are built using SAX. The goal of SAX was to provide a simple way to process XML utilizing the least amount of system resources. Its simplicity of use and its lightweight nature made this parser extremely popular early on and was one of the driving factors of why it is implemented in one form or another in other programming languages.

Event-Based/Push Parser

So, what is an event-based, or push, parser? Well, I'm glad you asked that question. An event-based parser interacts with an application when specific events occur during the parsing of the XML document. Such an event may be the start or the end of an element or may be an encounter with a PI within the document. When an event occurs, the parser notifies the application and provides any pertinent information.

In other words, the parser *pushes* the information to the application. The application is not requesting the data when it needs it, but rather it initially registers functions with the parser for the different events it would like notification for, which are then executed upon notification. Think of it in terms of a mailing list to which you can subscribe. All you need to do is register with the mailing list, and from then on, every time a new message is received from the list, the message is automatically sent to you. You do not need to keep checking the mailing list to see whether it contains any new messages.

SAX in PHP

The xml extension, which is the SAX handler in PHP, has been the primary XML handler since PHP 3. It has been the most stable extension and thus is widely used when dealing with XML. The expat library, `http://expat.sourceforge.net/`, initially served as the underlying parser for this extension. With the advent of PHP 5 and its use of the libxml2 library, a compatibility layer was written and made the default option. This means that by default, libxml2 now serves as the XML parsing library for the xml extension in PHP 5 and later, though the extension can also be built with the depreciated expat library.

Enabled by default, it can be disabled in the PHP build through the `--disable-xml` configuration switch. (But then again, if you wanted to do this, you probably would not be reading this chapter!) You may have reasons for building this with the expat library, such as compatibility problems with your code or application. I will address some of these issues in the section "Migrating from PHP 4 to PHP 5." If this is the case, you can use the `configure` switch `--with-libexpat-dir=DIR` with expat rather than libxml2. This is depreciated and should be used only in such cases where things may be broken and cannot be resolved using the libxml2 library.

One other change for this extension from PHP 4 to PHP 5 is the default encoding. Originally, the default encoding used for output from this extension was ISO-8859-1. With the change to libxml2, the default encoding has changed in PHP 5.0.2 and later to UTF-8. This is true no matter which library you use to build the extension. If any existing code being upgraded to PHP 5 happens to require IISO-8859-1 as the default encoding, this is quickly and easily resolved, as you will see in the next section. Other than the potential migration issues, this chapter exclusively deals with the xml extension built using libxml2.

Using the xml Extension

Working with the xml extension is easy and straightforward. Once you have set up the parser and parsing begins, all your code is automatically executed. You do not need to do anything until the parsing has finished. The steps to use this extension are as follows:

1. Define functions to handle events.

2. Create the parser.

3. Set any parser options.

4. Register the handlers (the functions you defined to handle events) with the parser.

5. Begin parsing.

6. Perform error checking.

7. Free the parser.

Listing 8-1 contains a small example of using this extension, following the previous steps. I have used comments in the application to indicate the different steps.

Listing 8-1. *Sample Application Using the xml Extension*

```php
<?php
/* XML data to be parsed */
$xml = '<root>
<element1 a="b">Hello World</element1>
<element2/>
</root>';

/* start element handler function */
function startElement($parser, $name, $attribs) {
   print "<$name";
   foreach ($attribs AS $attName=>$attValue) {
      print " $attName=".'"'.$attValue.'"';
   }
   print ">";
}

/* end element handler function */
function endElement($parser, $name) {
   print "</$name>";
}

/* cdata handler function */
function chandler($parser, $data) {
  print $data;
}

/* Create parser */
$xml_parser = xml_parser_create();
```

```
/* Set parser options */
xml_parser_set_option ($xml_parser, XML_OPTION_CASE_FOLDING, 0);

/* Register handlers */
xml_set_element_handler($xml_parser, "startElement", "endElement");
xml_set_character_data_handler ($xml_parser, "chandler");

/* Parse XML */
if (!xml_parse($xml_parser, $xml, 1)) {
    /* Gather Error information */
    die(sprintf("XML error: %s at line %d",
    xml_error_string(xml_get_error_code($xml_parser)),
    xml_get_current_line_number($xml_parser)));
}

/* Free parser */
xml_parser_free($xml_parser);
?>
```

To begin examining this extension, you will skip the first step. It is quite difficult to attempt to write event-handling functions without even knowing what the events are and what parameters the functions need. Once the parser has been created and any parse options set, you will return to writing the handler functions. Listing 8-1 may also offer some insight into these functions prior to reaching the "Event Handlers" section.

The Parser

The parser is the focal point of this extension. Every built-in function for xml, other than the ones creating it and two encoding/decoding functions, requires the parser to be passed as a parameter. The parser, when created, takes the form of a resource within PHP 5, just as in PHP 4. The API was left unchanged, unlike the domxml extension, leaving the parser as a resource rather than adding an OOP interface. This not only allows no coding changes when moving from PHP 4 to PHP 5, but the extension already implements a way to use objects with the parser, which is discussed later in this chapter in the "Using Objects and Methods" section.

Creating the Parser

You create the parser using the function xml_parser_create(), which takes an optional parameter specifying the output encoding to use. Input encoding is automatically detected using either the encoding specified by the document or a BOM. When neither is detected, UTF-8 encoded input is assumed. Upon successful creation of the parser, it is returned to the application as a resource; otherwise, this function returns NULL. For example:

```
if ($xml_parser = xml_parser_create()) {
    /* Insert code here */
}
```

Upon successfully executing this code, the variable $xml_parser contains the resource that will be used in the rest of the function calls within this extension.

Setting the Parser Options

After you have created the parser, you can set the parser options. These options differ from those discussed in Chapter 5, which are used by the DOM and SimpleXML extensions. The xml extension defines only four options that can be used while parsing an XML document. Table 8-1 describes the available options, as well as their default values when not specified for the parser.

Table 8-1. *Parser Options*

Option	Description
XML_OPTION_TARGET_ENCODING	Sets the encoding to use when the parser passes the xml information to the function handlers. The available encodings are US-ASCII, ISO-8859-1, and UTF-8, with the default being either the encoding set when the parser was created or UTF-8 when not specified.
XML_OPTION_SKIP_WHITE	Skips values that are entirely ignorable whitespaces. These values will not be passed to your function handlers. The default value is 0, which means pass whitespace to the functions.
XML_OPTION_SKIP_TAGSTART	Skips a certain number of characters from the beginning of a start tag. The default value is 0 to not skip any characters.
XML_OPTION_CASE_FOLDING	Determines whether element tag names are passed as all uppercase or left as is. The default value is 1 to use uppercase for all tag names. The default setting tends to be a bit controversial. XML is case-sensitive, and the default setting is to case fold characters. For example, an element named FOO is not the same as an element named Foo.

You can set and retrieve options using the xml_parser_set_option() and xml_parser_get_option() functions. The prototypes for these functions are as follows:

```
(bool) xml_parser_set_option (resource parser, int option, mixed value)
(mixed)xml_parser_get_option (resource parser, int option)
```

Using these functions, you can check the case folding and change it in the event the value was not changed from the default:

```
if (xml_parser_get_option($xml_parser, XML_OPTION_CASE_FOLDING)) {
   xml_parser_set_option ($xml_parser, XML_OPTION_CASE_FOLDING, 0);
}
```

This code tests the parser ($xml_parser, which was previously created) to see whether the XML_OPTION_CASE_FOLDING option is enabled. If enabled, which in this case it would be since the default parser is being used, the code disables this option by setting its value to 0. You use the other options in the same way even though XML_OPTION_TARGET_ENCODING takes and returns a string (US-ASCII, ISO-8859-1, or UTF-8) for the value.

Caution The parser options XML_OPTION_SKIP_TAGSTART and XML_OPTION_SKIP_WHITE are used only when parsing into a structure. Regular parsing is not affected by these options. The option XML_OPTION_SKIP_WHITE may not always exhibit consistent behavior in PHP 5. Please refer to the section "Migrating from PHP 4 to PHP 5" for more information.

Event Handlers

Event handlers are user-based functions registered with the parser that the XML data is pushed to when an event occurs. If you look at the code in Listing 8-1, you will notice the functions startElement(), endElement(), and chandler(). These functions are the user-defined handlers and are registered with the parser using the xml_set_element_handler() and xml_set_character_data_handler() functions from the xml extension. Many other events are also issued during parsing, so let's take a look at each of these and how to write handlers.

Element Events

Two events occur with elements within a document. The first event occurs when the parser encounters an opening element tag, and the second occurs when the closing element tag is encountered. Handlers for both of these are registered at the same time using the xml_set_element_handler() function. This function takes three parameters: the parser resource, a string identifying the start element handler function, and a string identifying the end element handler function.

Start Element Handler

The function set for the start element handler executes every time an element is encountered in the document. The prototype for this function is as follows:

```
start_element_handler(resource parser, string name, array attribs)
```

When an element is encountered, the element name, along with an array containing all attributes for the element, is passed to the function. When no attributes are defined, the array is empty; otherwise, the array consists of all name/value pairs for the attributes of the element. For example, within a document, the parser reaches the following element:

```
<element att1="value1" att2="value2" />
```

In the following code, a start element handler named startElement has been defined and registered with the parser:

```
function startElement($parser, $element_name, $attribs) {
    print "Element Name: $element_name\n";
    foreach ($attribs AS $att_name=>$att_value) {
        print "   Attribute: $att_name = $att_value\n";
    }
}
```

When the element is reached within the document, the parser issues an event, and the startElement function is executed. The following results are then displayed:

```
Element Name: element
    Attribute: att1 = value1
    Attribute: att2 = value2
```

End Element Handler

The end element handler works in conjunction with the start element handler. Upon the parser reaching the end of an element, the end element handler is executed. This time, however, only the element name is passed to the function. The prototype for this function is as follows:

```
end_element_handler(resource parser, string name)
```

Using the function for the start element handler, an end element handler will be added. This time, since both functions will be defined, the code will also register the handlers:

```
function endElement($parser, $name) {
    print "END Element Name: $name\n";
}

xml_set_element_handler($xml_parser, "startElement", 'endElement');
```

The complete output with the end handler being called looks like this:

```
Element Name: element
    Attribute: att1 = value1
    Attribute: att2 = value2
END Element Name: element
```

Caution The documentation states that setting either of these handlers to an empty string or NULL will cause the specific handler not to be used. At least up to and including PHP 5.1, a warning is issued when the parser reaches such a handler stating that it is unable to call the handler.

Character Data Handler

Character data events are issued when text content, CDATA sections, and in certain cases entities are encountered in the XML stream. Text content is strictly text content within an element in this case. It differs from the conventional text node when the document is viewed as a tree because text nodes can live as children of other nodes, such as comment nodes and PI nodes. You can set a character data handler using the xml_set_character_data_handler() function. Its prototype is as follows:

```
bool xml_set_character_data_handler(resource parser, callback handler)
```

The prototype for the user-defined handler for this function is as follows:

```
handler(resource parser, string data)
```

Caution As you will see in the following sections, character data can be broken up into multiple events, resulting in multiple calls to a character data handler. This is not only dependant upon the content of the data but also upon how lines are terminated because additional character data events may be issued when using \r\n (Windows style) as line feeds compared to just using \n (Unix style).

In the following sections, you will see how this handler deals with different types of data.

Handling Text Content

Text content is character data content for an element. As it is processed, character data events are issued from the parser, and the handler, if set, is executed. In its simplest case, as in the following example, the text content for the element named root is Hello World:

```
<root>Hello World</root>
```

When encountered during processing, this string is passed to the handler for further user processing:

```
function characterData($parser, $data) {
  print "Data: $data END Data\n";
}
```

```
xml_set_character_data_handler($xml_parser, "characterData");
```

When the text is processed, the output from the handler is as follows:

```
Data: Hello World END Data
```

Whitespace also results in the handler being called, as shown in the following code. Remember, the parser option XML_OPTION_SKIP_WHITE is useless unless parsing the XML into a structure, which is explained in the "Parsing a Document" section.

```
$xmldata ="<root>\n<child/></root>";
```

A document containing this string contains an ignorable whitespace, \n, between the opening root tag and the empty-element tag child. When the parser processes the data, this whitespace will be sent to the characterData() function:

```
Data:
 END Data
```

The handler can be called multiple times when processing text content. The content can be chunked and passed to the $data parameter in sequential calls. This occurs from the use of differing terminations of lines. Take the case of using Unix-style line terminations. These consist of just a linefeed (\n), like so:

```
$xmldata ="<root>Hello \nWorld</root>";
```

By using the string contained in $xmldata for the XML data to be processed and running it with the characterData() handler previously defined, you can see that the text content is called only once with the entire content sent to the $data parameter at once:

```
Data: Hello
World END Data
```

In this next instance, Windows-style line feeds (\r\n) are used to terminate lines:

```
$xmldata ="<root>Hello \r\nWorld</root>";
```

This time, the content is broken up into multiple events, and the handler is called twice:

```
Data: Hello  END Data
Data:
World END Data
```

The first event results in just the string "Hello " being passed to the $data parameter. Following the processing, the handler is called again with the string "\nWorld". You might be wondering what happened to \r. The line breaks have been normalized according to the XML specifications.

Note Per the XML specifications, parsers must normalize line breaks. Windows-style line breaks (\r\n) are normalized to a single \n. Also, any carriage return (\r) not followed by a line feed (\n) is translated into a line feed.

The bottom line is that character data can be processed by multiple calls to the handler rather than a single call passing all the data at once. The "Migrating from PHP 4 to PHP 5" section will cover this a bit more, since it is different from the behavior in PHP 4. Line breaks are just one place this occurs. In certain cases, this also occurs when using entities, which will be covered shortly.

Handling CDATA Sections

CDATA sections are handled in a similar fashion to text content but currently exhibit a little different behavior with respect to line endings. This is another area that is covered in the "Migrating from PHP 4 to PHP 5" section of this chapter. Using the same functions defined in the previous section for text content, you can change the XML data to move the text content into a CDATA section block, as follows:

```
$xmldata = "<root><![CDATA[Hello World]]></root>";
```

The resulting output is the same as when the text was used directly as content:

```
Data: Hello World END Data
```

Adding the line feed within the text also produces the same results as demonstrated with the text content:

```
$xmldata = "<root><![CDATA[Hello \nWorld]]></root>";
```

```
Data: Hello
World END Data
```

Using a carriage return, however, exhibits different behavior from what was shown when used within text content:

```
$xmldata = "<root><![CDATA[Hello \r\nWorld]]></root>";
```

```
Data: Hello
World END Data
```

In this case, only a single event was fired. The text was not broken up into multiple sections. The data is also different in this case. If you remember, when the string "Hello \r\nWorld" was used as text content, the data was passed as "Hello " and "\nWorld". The carriage return was never sent to the handler. Inspecting the data sent to the handler when the full string is used within a CDATA section, the whole string, including the carriage return, is passed to the $data parameter. This may be a bug in libxml2 and may change in future releases, but with at least libxml2 2.6.20, the behavior is as I have described.

Handling Entities

In certain cases, entity references will be expanded and sent to the character data handler. In other cases, if defined, entity references will be sent directly to the default handler without being expanded. The first case to look at is the predefined, internal entities.

Per the specifications, the parser implements five predefined entities. They are explained in more detailed in Chapter 2 (and listed in Listing 2-2). When a character data handler is set, these predefined entities automatically are expanded, and their values are sent to the character data handler when encountered. I will use the same functions as defined within the text content section to demonstrate character data handling with entities:

```
$xmldata = "<root>Hello &amp; World</root>";
```

```
Data: Hello  END Data
Data: & END Data
Data:  World END Data
```

The first thing you will probably notice is that three events were triggered for the text content containing the entity &. Encountering an entity reference within a document creates an event. In this case, the parser was processing the character data "Hello ". Upon reaching &, the parser issued the event for "Hello ". The entity reference is then processed alone, which in this case results in another issue of a character data event. Once handled, the parser continues processing the text content.

Note Entity references are handled alone and result in a separate event. When used within text content, this may result in multiple calls to the character data handler.

You probably also notice the resulting text on the second line of output. The entity reference has been expanded, and the actual text for the reference has been sent to the character data handler. In this case, & refers to the character & and the & sent as the $data parameter.

The last cases depend upon whether a default handler has been set. For all other entity references, other than external entity references that have their own handlers, the character data handler is called only when a default handler has not been defined. Just like predefined entities, when passed to the character handler, the entity references are expanded. If a default handler exists, the entity references are not expanded and passed to the handler in their native states. I will cover this in more detail in the "Default Handler" section.

Processing Instruction Handler

PIs within XML data have their own handlers, which are set using the xml_set_processing_instruction_handler() function. When the parser encounters a PI, an event is issued, and if the handler has been set, it will be executed. For example:

```
/* Prototype for setting PI handler */
bool xml_set_processing_instruction_handler(resource parser, callback handler)

/* Prototype for user PI handler function */
handler(resource parser, string target, string data)
```

Data for a processing instruction is sent as a single block. Unlike character data, only a single event is issued per PI:

```
$xmldata = "<root><?php echo 'Hello World'; ?></root>";
```

Using the previous XML data and the following handler, when the instruction is encountered, the function will print the strings from the $target and $data parameters:

```
function PIHandler($parser, $target, $data) {
  print "PI: $target - $data END PI\n";
}
```

```
PI: echo 'Hello World';  END PI
```

External Entity Reference Handler

As you recall from Chapter 3, external entities are defined in a DTD and are used to refer to some XML outside the document. Depending upon the type, they can include a public ID and/or system ID used to locate the resource:

```
/* Examples of External Entities */
<!ENTITY extname SYSTEM "http://www.example.com/extname">
<!ENTITY extname PUBLIC "localname" "http://www.example.com/extname">
```

Within a document, you can reference them using an external entity reference:

```
<root>&extname;</root>
```

Upon encountering the external entity reference, the parser will execute the external entity reference handler, if set, using the xml_set_external_entity_ref_handler() function:

```
/* Prototype for xml_set_external_entity_ref_handler */
bool xml_set_external_entity_ref_handler(resource parser, callback handler)
```

```
/* Prototype for handler */
handler(resource parser, string open_entity_names,
        string base, string system_id, string public_id)
```

Before seeing this functionality in action, you need to be aware of a few issues. The current behavior of these parameters for PHP 5 (at least up to and including PHP 5.1) is that open_entity_names is only the name of the entity reference. Contrary to the documentation, no list of entities exists. Only the name of the entity reference is passed. When using entity references that reference other entities, PHP 5 has an issue, which will be covered in the "Migrating from PHP 4 to PHP 5" section in detail.

Taking these factors into account, the external XML in Listing 8-2, which would live in the file external.xml, will be referenced by the partial document in Listing 8-3. The parser will then process the document in Listing 8-3.

Listing 8-2. *External XML in File* external.xml

```
<?xml version="1.0"?>
<external_element>
   Hello World!
</external_element>
```

Listing 8-3. *XML Document to Be Processed*

```
<?xml version='1.0'?>
<!DOCTYPE root SYSTEM "http://www.example.com/dtd" [
<!ENTITY myEntity SYSTEM "external.xml">
]>
<root>
   <element1>Internal XML Data</element1>
   &myEntity;
</root>
```

The first step you need to take is to write and register the function to handle the external entity:

```
function extEntRefHandler($parser, $openEntityNames, $base, $systemId, $publicId) {
    if ($systemId) {
        if (is_readable($systemId)) {
            print file_get_contents ($systemId);
            return TRUE;
        }
    }
    return false;
}

xml_set_external_entity_ref_handler($xml_parser, "extEntRefHandler");
```

When the parser encounters the external entity reference, &myEntity;, the extEntRefHandler function is executed. Since the entity declaration is defined as SYSTEM, the variable $publicId will be passed as FALSE. The function ensures that the URL defined by $systemId is readable, which in this case is the local file external.xml, and then just prints the contents of the file.

If you have looked at the examples within the PHP documentation, you may notice that the external entity reference handler creates a new parser and parses the data located at the URL from $systemId. According to the XML specifications, the external data must be valid XML, and processing the data with a new parser is perfectly valid and in most cases the desired functionality.

Declaration Handlers

Currently, the extension allows for two specific declaration handlers to be set. You can handle both notation declarations and unparsed entity declarations through their respective handlers. I have grouped them in this section because unparsed entity declarations rely on notation declarations.

Caution For both the user handlers in this section, the public_id and system_id parameters are reversed when using PHP 5 prior to the release of PHP 5.1. This has been fixed for PHP 5.1, so this section is based on the fixed syntax.

The first step in using these handlers is to look at their prototypes:

```
/* Set handler prototypes */
bool xml_set_notation_decl_handler(resource parser, callback note_handler)
bool xml_set_unparsed_entity_decl_handler(resource parser, callback ued_handler)
```

```
/* User function handler prototypes */
note_handler(resource parser, string notation_name, string base, string system_id,
             string public_id)
ued_handler(resource parser, string entity_name, string base, string system_id,
             string public_id, string notation_name)
```

These handlers operate on declaration statements within a DTD. This means these would be processed prior to any processing within the body of the document. This example uses a simplified document; it contains a DTD declaring a notation and an unparsed entity as well as an empty document element:

```
<?xml version='1.0'?>
<!DOCTYPE root SYSTEM "http://www.example.com/dtd" [
<!NOTATION GIF SYSTEM "image/gif">
<!ENTITY myimage SYSTEM "mypicture.gif" NDATA GIF>
]>
<root/>
```

Again, you need to define and register these handlers with the parser:

```
/* Define handlers */
function upehandler($parser, $name, $base, $systemId, $publicId, $notation_name) {
    print "\n---- Unparser Entity Handler ---\n";
    var_dump($name);
    var_dump($base);
    var_dump($systemId);
    var_dump($publicId);
    var_dump($notation_name);
}

function notehandler($parser, $name, $base, $systemId, $publicId) {
    print "\n--- Notation Declaration Handler ---\n";
    var_dump($name);
    var_dump($base);
    var_dump($systemId);
    var_dump($publicId);
}

/* Register Handlers */
xml_set_unparsed_entity_decl_handler($xml_parser, "upehandler");
xml_set_notation_decl_handler($xml_parser, "notehandler");
```

When the notation and unparsed entity declaration are encountered, the respective function is executed and in this case just dumps each of the parameter variables passed to the function. When the document is parsed, the output using these functions is as follows:

```
--- Notation Declaration Handler ---
string(3) "GIF"
bool(false)
string(9) "image/gif"
bool(false)

---- Unparser Entity Handler ---
string(7) "myimage"
bool(false)
string(13) "mypicture.gif"
bool(false)
string(3) "GIF"
```

Default Handler

The intended use of the default handler is to process all other markup that is not handled using any other callback. This handler may not work exactly as expected when running code under PHP 5 that was written for PHP 4. I will cover this in more detail in the section "Migrating from PHP 4 to PHP 5."

■**Caution** Code written for PHP 4 using a default handler may not work as expected under PHP 5. Please refer to the section "Migrating from PHP 4 to PHP 5."

When you use the default handler, you will encounter two issues. The first is dealing with comment tags. When the parser encounters a comment, the entire comment, including the starting and ending tags, is sent to the default handler:

```
function defaultHandler($parser, $data) {
   print "DEFAULT: $data END_DEFAULT\n";
}

xml_set_default_handler($xml_parser, "defaultHandler");
```

Using the following XML data, when the comment tag is processed, the default handler will display the following results:

```
<root><!-- Hello World --></root>
```

```
DEFAULT: <!-- Hello World --> END_DEFAULT
```

Entities, depending upon type, will also use the default handler when registered. Data passed to the default handler is different from that passed when a character data handler is present. If you recall, when a character data handler is registered, all predefined entities will always be sent to that handler with their data expanded. Other entities, except external entity references, will try to use the default handler first and fall back to the character data handler only when a default handler is not present. The data passed to the default handler, however, is not the expanded entity. The entity reference itself is passed. For example:

```
<!DOCTYPE root SYSTEM "http://www.example.com/dtd" [
    <!ENTITY myEntity "Entity Text">
]>
<root><e1>&myEntity;</e1><e2>&amp;</e2></root>
```

To see the difference between using a character data handler and a default handler, the previous XML document will be processed with only a character data handler registered:

```
function characterData($parser, $data) {
    print "DATA: $data END_DATA\n";
}

xml_set_character_data_handler($xml_parser, "characterData");
```

Upon processing, the output is as follows:

```
DATA: Entity Text END_DATA
DATA: & END_DATA
```

Both entities have been expanded, and the strings Entity Text and & have been passed to the $data parameter of the character data handler. Using the same code, you can register a default handler:

```
function defaultHandler($parser, $data) {
    print "DEFAULT: $data END_DEFAULT\n";
}

xml_set_default_handler($xml_parser, "defaultHandler");
```

This time the results are a bit different:

```
DEFAULT: &myEntity; END_DEFAULT
DATA: & END_DATA
```

The default handler is used to process the user-defined entity. It is passed without being expanded, passing the raw &myEntity;, to the default handler. The predefined entity reference, &, on the other hand, is handled by the character data handler, as you can see by the output.

These are currently the only instances when the default handler is used. When using PHP 4 or when building with the expat library, everything not handled by any other handler is processed by the default handler. At this time, it is unknown how the default handler will be used in PHP 5, and it is also possible new functionality may be written to support handling of other data using the xml extension.

Parsing a Document

This chapter has so far explained what the parser is, how you create it, and how to write and register handlers. The code used to this point has shown expected results when a document is processed but has not explained how to process a document. It is important to understand these previous steps prior to processing a document, because they are all required before the processing begins. I will now cover the actual processing, which includes parsing the document, handling error conditions, handling additional functionality within the xml extension, and releasing the parser.

Parsing Data

Unlike the other XML-based extensions, the xml extension parses only string data. Files containing XML must be read and sent to the parser as strings. This doesn't mean, however, that all the data must be sent at once. Remember, SAX works on streaming data. The function used to parse the data is xml_parse(), with its prototype being as follows:

```
int xml_parse(resource parser, string data [, bool is_final])
```

The first parameter, parser, is the resource you have been working with throughout the chapter. The second parameter, data, is the data to be processed. The last optional parameter, is_final, is a flag indicating whether the data being passed also ends the data stream. Let's examine the use of the last two parameters.

Taking the simplest code from the text content section, you can write the complete code, as shown here:

```php
<?php
$xmldata = "<root>Hello World</root>";

function cData($parser, $data) {
  print "Data: $data END Data\n";
}

$xml_parser = xml_parser_create();
xml_set_character_data_handler($xml_parser, "cData");
if (!xml_parse($xml_parser, $xmldata, true)) {
  print "ERROR";
}
?>
```

The variable $xmldata, which is passed to xml_parse(), contains a complete XML document. No other data is needed for the document, so TRUE is passed for the is_final parameter. The xml_parse() function returns an integer indicating success or failure. A value of 1 indicates success, and a value of 0 indicates an error. The "Handling Errors" section shows how to deal with errors.

Chunked Data

The is_final parameter is extremely important to use to have the document parse correctly. The parser works on chunked data, so unless it knows when all available data has been sent, it cannot determine whether a well-formed document is being processed. Consider the following snippet of code where the cData handler from the previous example is being used and has already been registered on the created parser, $xml_parser:

```
$xmldata = "<root>Hello World";
if (!xml_parse($xml_parser, $xmldata, FALSE)) {
    print "ERROR";
}
```

You might expect ERROR to be printed because the XML is not well-formed. Instead, nothing is output when the script is run. In this case, though, the is_final flag is set to FALSE. The parser is sitting in a state expecting more data. Without additional data or the knowledge that the data it has received is the final piece of data, the parser has no way of knowing a problem exists. Changing the is_final parameter to TRUE results in much different output:

```
if (!xml_parse($xml_parser, $xmldata, TRUE)) {
    print "ERROR";
}
```

```
Data: Hello World END Data
ERROR
```

In this case, the parser knows it has all the data it needs to process and not only executes the cData function but also ends in an error state.

Let's now look at trying to process the full document broken up into chunks. You have seen that when is_final is FALSE, the parser waits for more data. Sending the remaining data and setting the is_final flag to TRUE should then allow the parser to continue processing the document:

```
$xmldata = "<root>Hello World";
$xmldata2 = "</root>";

print "Initial Parse\n";
if (!xml_parse($xml_parser, $xmldata, FALSE)) {
    print "ERROR 1";
}

print "Final Parse\n";
if (!xml_parse($xml_parser, $xmldata2, TRUE)) {
    print "ERROR 2";
}
```

```
Initial Parse
Final Parse
Data: Hello World END Data
```

The first call to xml_parse() sends the initial chunk of data, $xmldata, and passes FALSE to is_final. From the results, it is clear that nothing noticeable has happened because nothing has been printed. The last call to xml_parse() sends the remaining chunk of data, $xmldata2, but this time it sets is_final to TRUE. The parser knows that all data has been submitted and is able to call the cData handler with the text content, and it knows that the entire document is well-formed.

File Data

Data coming from a file is typically read in chunks, unless loaded using the file_get_contents() function. In many cases, XML documents are quite large, and loading the entire contents of the file into a string at one time just does not make any sense, especially because of the amount of memory this would require. Using the file external.xml from Listing 8-2, the following PHP file system functions will read chunks of data at a time and process the contents:

```
$handle = fopen("external.xml", "r");
$x= 0;
while ($data = fread($handle, 20)) {
    $x++;
    print "$x\n";
    if (!xml_parse($xml_parser, $data, feof($handle))) {
        print "ERROR";
    }
}
fclose($handle);
```

In this case, the file external.xml is opened and data read in 20 bytes at a time. Each time the bytes are read, they are processed. The variable $x is printed to show the number of times xml_parse() is called. The results of the feof() function, which tests for the end of file, is passed as the is_final flag. The function feof() will return FALSE until the last piece of data is read in the while statement. At this point, the last time xml_parse() is called, the value of the function will be TRUE. When all is said and done, the final results are as follows:

```
1
2
3
4
Data:
   Hello World! END Data
Data:
 END Data
```

You may have an idea of why this code shows an extra call to the cData function. It is a result of a carriage return in the external.xml file. The important thing to notice is that the file was read, and parsing took place for the first 80 bytes of the file prior to any output. This is just because of the location of the text content and because only character data is being handled in this example. In a typical application, it is not usually only the last pieces read from the document that cause the output. If you added an element handler to the code, you would see that the element is handled after 60 bytes have been read.

Parsing into Structures

This extension also includes a function to parse XML data into an array structure of the document. Structures are created using the xml_parse_into_struct() function. Using this function requires no handlers to be implemented or registered, although they could be; in that case, both your handlers would be processed and a final structure would be available when done. The prototype for this function is as follows:

```
int xml_parse_into_struct(resource parser, string data,
                          array &values [, array &index])
```

Note One point to be aware of when using this function is that the data parameter must contain the complete XML data to be processed. Unlike the xml_parse() function that uses the is_final parameter, this function requires all data to be sent at once in a single string.

The new parameters, values and index, return the structures for the XML data. The value parameter must always be passed to this function. It results in an array containing the structure of the document in document order. It contains information such as tag name, level within the tree starting at 1, type of tag, attributes, and in some cases value. For example:

```
$xmldata = "<root><e1 att1='1'>text</e1></root>";
xml_parse_into_struct($xml_parser, $xmldata, $values, $index);
var_dump($values);
```

This piece of code assumes $xml_parser has already been created and case folding has been disabled:

```
array(3) {
  [0]=>
  array(3) {
    ["tag"]=>
    string(4) "root"
    ["type"]=>
    string(4) "open"
    ["level"]=>
    int(1)
  }
  [1]=>
  array(5) {
    ["tag"]=>
    string(2) "e1"
    ["type"]=>
    string(8) "complete"
    ["level"]=>
    int(2)
```

```
    ["attributes"]=>
    array(1) {
      ["att1"]=>
      string(1) "1"
    }
    ["value"]=>
    string(4) "text"
  }
  [2]=>
  array(3) {
    ["tag"]=>
    string(4) "root"
    ["type"]=>
    string(5) "close"
    ["level"]=>
    int(1)
  }
}
```

As you can see, this little document produces a lot of output. Each element is accessed by a numeric key in the topmost array. The key represents the order the specific element was encountered within the document. The elements are then represented by a subarray with associative keys. The elements are as follows:

- tag: Tag name of the element.

- type: Type of tag. The value can be open, indicating an opening tag; complete, indicating that the tag is complete and contains no child elements; or close, indicating the tag is a closing tag.

- level: The level within the document. This value starts at 1 and is incremented by 1 as each subtree is traversed. The level then decrements as the subtree is ascended.

- value: The concatenation of all direct child text content. Only data that would be passed to a character data handler when a default handler is set is present here.

- attributes: An array containing all attributes of the element. The keys of this array consist of the name of the attributes with the values being the corresponding attribute value.

When the option index parameter is passed, the return value is an array pointing to the locations of the element tags within the value array. This means you now have a map you can use to locate specific elements within the other array. Accessing an element by name in the index array returns an array of indexes corresponding to the indexes of the opening and closing tags in the value array. In the case of a complete tag, the array contains only a single index because the opening and closing tag are the same. The result from processing var_dump($index); is as follows:

```
array(2) {
  ["root"]=>
  array(2) {
    [0]=>
    int(0)
    [1]=>
    int(2)
  }
  ["e1"]=>
  array(1) {
    [0]=>
    int(1)
  }
}
```

Reading this array, you can find the root element at indexes 0 and 2 within the values array and the e1 element at index 1. You can access the closing root element using $values[2]. This means the tag name and type should correspond to the closing root element. For example:

```
print $values[2]['tag']."\n";
print $values[2]['type']."\n";
```

```
root
close
```

The xml_parse_into_struct() function is where the options XML_OPTION_SKIP_TAGSTART and XML_OPTION_SKIP_WHITE come into play. These options are used only when building a structure and do not affect data passed to user-defined handler functions. For example:

```
$xmldata = "<root>Content: &amp; &apos; End Content</root>";
xml_parser_set_option ($xml_parser, XML_OPTION_CASE_FOLDING, 0);
xml_parser_set_option ($xml_parser, XML_OPTION_SKIP_WHITE, 1);
xml_parser_set_option ($xml_parser, XML_OPTION_SKIP_TAGSTART , 1);
xml_parse_into_struct($xml_parser, $xmldata, $values, $index);
var_dump($values);
```

```
array(1) {
  [0]=>
  array(4) {
    ["tag"]=>
    string(3) "oot"
    ["type"]=>
    string(8) "complete"
    ["level"]=>
    int(1)
    ["value"]=>
    string(23) "Content: &' End Content"
  }
}
```

The first thing to notice is the value of the tag key, oot. This is referring to the element root from the complete XML document. The option XML_OPTION_SKIP_TAGSTART was set to 1, which, when parsed into a structure, removes the first character of the name of the element tag. The purpose of this option is a bit unknown. My only guess is that prior to supporting the parsing of documents containing namespaces, this option would allow a prefix and the colon to be removed. The only problem with this is that the document must use the same prefixed namespace throughout, or all prefixes must be the same number of characters. The next thing to notice is the value of the value key. XML_OPTION_SKIP_WHITE removes a data parameter that is passed to a character data handler consisting of entirely whitespaces, currently spaces, tabs, and line feeds, in the xml extension. The data is modified only for the value of the structure and not when passed to user-defined character data handlers.

You might wonder why the space between the & and ' characters was removed, because the value is a single string. Remember that character data can be split and sent to the handler in chunks. In this case, when an entity is encountered, the entity is handled as a separate chunk. If the calls to the character data handler were broken down into the substrings sent, it would look like the following. Note the strings are in quotes to show the spaces in the strings.

- "Content: "
- "&"
- " "
- "'"
- " End Content"

The only string containing all whitespace is the space listed between & and '. This string was removed because of the setting for the XML_OPTION_SKIP_WHITE option.

Parsing Information

Byte index, column number, and line number are three pieces of information available while parsing a document. You will also see these again in the "Migrating from PHP 4 to PHP 5" section because these functions have a few quirks. The functions for these pieces of information are xml_get_current_byte_index(), xml_get_current_column_number(), and xml_get_current_line_number(). Each of these functions takes a parser as the parameter and returns either an integer containing the respective data or FALSE if the parser is not valid.

All handler functions are passed the parser as the first parameter. Using this parameter, these functions can be called within user-defined handler functions and not only in the main body of the script where the parse function is called. For example:

```php
<?php
function startElement($parser, $data) {
    print "TAG: $data\n";
    print "Bytes: ".xml_get_current_byte_index($parser)."\n";
    print "Column: ".xml_get_current_column_number($parser)."\n";
    print "Line: ".xml_get_current_line_number($parser)."\n\n";
}
```

```
function endElement($parser, $data) { }

$xmldata = "<root><e1 att1='1'>text</e1></root>";

$xml_parser = xml_parser_create();
xml_parser_set_option ($xml_parser, XML_OPTION_CASE_FOLDING, 0);
xml_set_element_handler($xml_parser, "startElement", "endElement");
xml_parse($xml_parser, $xmldata, true);
?>
```

In this example, every time a starting element tag is encountered, the tag name, the current byte index, the column number of the XML document, and the line number within the document are printed:

```
TAG: root
Bytes: 5
Column: 6
Line: 1

TAG: e1
Bytes: 18
Column: 15
Line: 1
```

The bytes and column information may not be exactly what you were expecting if you first ran this code using PHP 4.x. I will cover this, like much of the other functionality, in the "Migrating from PHP 4 to PHP 5" section. What you can determine, though, is that the number of bytes read is the number of bytes prior to the > marker for the element's opening tag. The column number, on the other hand, is not very accurate. This is an issue with libxml so may change with newer releases of the library.

Handling Errors

Both the XML parse functions return an integer or return FALSE when an invalid parser is passed, indicating any possible error conditions. A return value of 1 indicates successful parsing, and a value of 0 indicates an error has occurred. Upon an error condition, you can obtain the error information through the xml_get_error_code() and xml_error_string() functions:

```
$xmldata = "<root>";
$xml_parser = xml_parser_create();
if (! xml_parse($xml_parser, $xmldata, true)) {
    $code = xml_get_error_code($xml_parser);
    print xml_error_string($code);
}
```

This tests the return value of the xml_parse function. When 0, indicating an error condition, is returned, the if statement evaluates to TRUE and runs the error-handling code.

The first step is getting hold of the actual error code. The parser is passed as the parameter to the xml_get_error_code() function that returns an integer corresponding to the actual error code. With this code, the xml_error_string() function is then executed and returns the error message for the corresponding error code. In this case, the script will print the message Invalid document end.

PHP 5.1 introduced new XML error handling when using libxml2. The new error handling does not even need to be enabled using the libxml_use_internal_errors() function in order to access the last error issued from libxml. The last error is always available from the libxml_get_last_error() function. You can change the previous code to grab any LibXMLError object that may be present upon error, like so:

```
if (! xml_parse($xml_parser, $xmldata, true)) {
    $xmlError = libxml_get_last_error();
    var_dump($xmlError);
}
```

```
object(LibXMLError)#1 (6) {
  ["level"]=>
  int(3)
  ["code"]=>
  int(5)
  ["column"]=>
  int(7)
  ["message"]=>
  string(41) "Extra content at the end of the document"
  ["file"]=>
  string(0) ""
  ["line"]=>
  int(1)
}
```

As you clearly see, the information using this error is much richer than retrieving just code and an error message. The level (indicating the severity of the error), the column, the line, and the filename are also available. The message, although the code is the same as the code returned using xml_get_error_code(), is different within the LibXMLError object. This is because the message from this object is directly from the libxml2 library. The message returned from the xml_error_string() function is defined within the PHP xml extension. You can use either methodology to retrieve information. It all depends upon what information you need and your coding style.

UTF-8 Encoding and Decoding

When dealing with ISO-8859-1 encoded data, this extension provides two functions used to convert to and from UTF-8. They are utf8_encode() and utf8_decode(), as shown in the following code. As you should know by now, libxml stores data in UTF-8 encoding. These functions are here just for convenience since they deal only with converting between ISO-8859-1 and UTF-8. You should typically use other extensions, such as iconv and mbstring, because they support a much broader range of encoding schemes.

```php
<?php
$encodedstring = "contenu d'élément";
print $encodedstring."\n";
$utf8string = utf8_encode($encodedstring);
print $utf8string."\n";
$isostring = utf8_decode($utf8string);
print $isostring."\n";
if ($encodedstring == $isostring) {
   print "Same String";
}
?>
```

The output you will see from this code depends upon the system on which you are running it. The results I receive from running this in my terminal window are as follows:

```
contenu d'.l.ment
contenu d'..l..ment
contenu d'.l.ment
Same String
```

The periods you see in the previous results are because of encoding—because the character cannot be displayed. The results you see when executing this code may differ, but the comparison of the $encodedstring and $isostring variables show they are equal.

Releasing the Parser

The parser is a resource and is automatically freed when the script finishes execution. Sometimes you may want to explicitly free the parser and all its associated memory. You can do this using the xml_parser_free() function. It simply takes a single parameter, and the parser returns TRUE upon successful destruction of the parser or FALSE in the event the variable passed in is not a valid parser. For example:

```
xml_parser_free($xml_parser);
```

Caution Trying to free the parser within a user-defined handler function will cause a crash in versions of PHP 5 prior to PHP 5.1. This has also been fixed in PHP 4.4 for those who may be running multiple versions.

Working with Namespaces

Documents containing namespaces will parse fine using normal parsing methods; however, you may lose important information. Consider the following document and the data passed to the handler functions. Note that case folding is unchanged, which results in using the default of uppercase names.

```
function startElement($parser, $data, $attrs) {
    print "Tag Name: $data\n";
    foreach ($attrs AS $name=>$value) {
        print "      Att Name: $name\n";
        print "      Att Value: $value\n";
    }
}

function endElement($parser, $data) { }

$xmldata = "<a:root xmlns:a='http://www.example.com/a'>
            <a:e1 a:att1='1' /></a:root>";
$xml_parser = xml_parser_create();
xml_set_element_handler($xml_parser, "startElement", "endElement");
xml_parse($xml_parser, $xmldata, true);
```

```
Tag Name: A:ROOT
    Att Name: XMLNS:A
    Att Value: http://www.example.com/a
Tag Name: A:E1
    Att Name: A:ATT1
    Att Value: 1
```

Element and attribute names are passed with the prefixes and local names. The namespace declaration is handled as a normal attribute. This has a few problems. First, you have no way to determine the actual namespace an element or attribute is associated with. Second, the elements and attributes, although they look like they reside in a namespace from the passed data, in reality do not. The namespace declaration is passed as a normal attribute, and the prefixes are just an illusion.

To better show the problem, the following document uses a default namespace:

```
$xmldata = "<root xmlns='http://www.example.com/a'>
            <e1 att1='1' /></root>";
```

```
Tag Name: ROOT
    Att Name: XMLNS
    Att Value: http://www.example.com/a
Tag Name: E1
    Att Name: ATT1
    Att Value: 1
```

Any possible namespace information is completely lost. It may be possible to hack together a script to test attribute names for xmlns and track namespaces as well as associated prefixes, but that is just unrealistic. The good news is that the extension provides a way to deal with namespaced documents.

Note Namespace support requires libxml2 2.6.0 and higher. Although PHP versions 5.1 and higher already meet this requirement, it is possible when running PHP 5.0 that a namespace-aware SAX parser will be unavailable.

The function `xml_parser_create_ns()` creates a namespace-aware parser. It takes two optional parameters. The first is `encoding`, which is the same as the `encoding` parameter for the `xml_parser_create()` function. The second parameter is the `separator`. This is a string, which should be user-identifiable because it is used to separate the namespace from the tag name. I will return to this parameter in a moment. The first step to take is to see the difference that using `xml_parser_create_ns()` makes. Using the code for namespaces and the document using prefixed namespaces, the only change in the following code is in how the parser is created:

```
$xml_parser = xml_parser_create_ns();
```

```
Tag Name: HTTP://WWW.EXAMPLE.COM/A:ROOT
Tag Name: HTTP://WWW.EXAMPLE.COM/A:E1
    Att Name: HTTP://WWW.EXAMPLE.COM/A:ATT1
    Att Value: 1
```

The output is clearly different from the previous output. Rather than a namespace prefix, the elements and attributes are prefixed with the namespace. Within a user handler, the names can be split based on the colon so the actual namespace is accessible. This is much easier than trying to play with prefixes and trying to track namespace declarations. Now, regarding the namespace declaration, it is no longer passed as an attribute. It hasn't just disappeared on you, but before looking at that, let's return to the creation of the parser and the `separator` parameter.

The colon is a valid character to use within the name of a tag, though its use within the name is highly discouraged, as explained in Chapter 2. You might also want to have the namespace easily identifiable from the local name of the tag. The `separator` parameter provides this accessibility. Rather than a colon, the string passed as the `separator` parameter will be used to prefix the namespace with the local name. For example, you could use @ if you like:

```
$xml_parser = xml_parser_create_ns(NULL, "@");
```

```
Tag Name: HTTP://WWW.EXAMPLE.COM/A@ROOT
Tag Name: HTTP://WWW.EXAMPLE.COM/A@E1
    Att Name: HTTP://WWW.EXAMPLE.COM/A@ATT1
    Att Value: 1
```

You could now extract the namespaces and names by splitting the string on the @ character.

Note Any length string can be passed for the `separator` parameter, but only the first character will be used.

Let's return to the namespace declaration. When parsing with a namespace-aware parser, the namespace declaration is not passed as an attribute. Instead, the namespace declaration handler is used and is registered using the xml_set_start_namespace_decl_handler() function. Another migration issue crops up here. The function xml_set_end_namespace_decl_handler() is not used under PHP 5. The functions for dealing with namespace declarations take the following forms:

```
/* Prototypes */
xml_set_end_namespace_decl_handler(resource parser, callback handler)
handler(resource parser, string prefix, string uri)
```

Any time a namespace declaration is encountered during processing, the namespace declaration handler, if defined and registered, is executed. So let's go ahead and add a namespace handler to the code:

```
function nsHandler($parser, $prefix, $uri) {
    print "Prefix: $prefix\n";
    print "URI: $uri\n";
}

xml_set_start_namespace_decl_handler($xml_parser, "nsHandler");
```

```
Prefix: a
URI: http://www.example.com/a
Tag Name: HTTP://WWW.EXAMPLE.COM/A@ROOT
Tag Name: HTTP://WWW.EXAMPLE.COM/A@E1
    Att Name: HTTP://WWW.EXAMPLE.COM/A@ATT1
    Att Value: 1
```

The output shows that the namespace declaration is processed prior to the element tag on which it is defined. Just in case you were interested in tracking the prefixes, they would be available prior to the start element handler being called.

Using Objects and Methods

Handlers are not required to be just functions. You can also use object methods to handle events. Two ways exist to register object methods as handlers, and each requires an already instantiated object. When every handler is a method of the same object, you can use the function xml_set_object(), with the rest of the functionality covered up to now being unchanged. You can also register specific methods from an object directly using handler registration functions. This allows multiple objects to be used for different events.

Using xml_set_object()

Other than defining the class, writing the handlers as methods of the class, and registering an instantiated object of this class with the parser, using this API is no different from what you have seen so far. The xml_set_object() function takes the parser and the instantiated object to be used for handling events as parameters. Handlers are registered in the same way. Only the name of the function, in this case the method, is set with the handler. Parsing then is performed in a normal fashion, except now the object methods will be called. For example:

```php
<?php

class cXML {
      public $eCount = 0;
      public $cCount = 0;

   function startElement($parser, $data, $attrs) {
      print "Tag Name: $data\n";
      $this->eCount++;
   }

   function endElement($parser, $data) { }

   function characterData($parser, $data) {
      print "DATA: $data END_DATA\n";
      $this->cCount++;
   }
}

$xmldata = "<root:a><e1 att1='1'>text</e1></root>";

$xml_parser = xml_parser_create();

/* Create and register Object */
$objXML = new cXML();
xml_set_object($xml_parser, $objXML);

xml_set_element_handler($xml_parser, "startElement", "endElement");
xml_set_character_data_handler($xml_parser, "characterData");
xml_parse($xml_parser, $xmldata, true);

print "\nNumber of Elements: ".$objXML->eCount."\n";
print "Number of Times Character Data Handler Called: ".$objXML->cCount;
?>
```

```
Tag Name: ROOT
Tag Name: E1
DATA: text END_DATA

Number of Elements: 2
Number of Times Character Data Handler Called: 1
```

The code looks only a little different from what you have seen already. The only changes are a class definition and two lines of code that instantiate the object and register it with the parser.

Using Handler Registration

It is not always desirable to have all the handlers belonging to a single object or even to objects from the same class. The handler parameter for the registration functions not only accepts a string identifying the function, or as in the previous section a method call, but also accepts an array containing an object and a method to use as the handler from the object.

The following example will use the same class definition and XML document from the previous example. This time, however, two objects will be instantiated, each handling the processing of different portions of the document.

```
$xml_parser = xml_parser_create();

$objXMLElement = new cXML();
$objXMLChar = new cXML();

xml_set_element_handler($xml_parser, array($objXMLElement, "startElement"),
                                     array($objXMLElement, "endElement"));
xml_set_character_data_handler($xml_parser, array($objXMLChar, "characterData"));
/*******
When uncommenting this block, make sure the previous line of code is commented out

xml_set_character_data_handler($xml_parser, "characterData");
xml_set_object($xml_parser, $objXMLChar);
*******/
xml_parse($xml_parser, $xmldata, true);
print "\n--- objXMLElement ---\n";
print "\nNumber of Elements: ".$objXMLElement->eCount."\n";
print "Number of Times Character Data Handler Called: ".$objXMLElement->cCount."\n";

print "\n--- objXMLChar ---\n";
print "Number of Elements: ".$objXMLChar->eCount."\n";
print "Number of Times Character Data Handler Called: ".$objXMLChar->cCount;
```

If you look closely at this code, two objects, $objXMLElement and $objXMLChar, are instantiated from the xCML class. The element handlers are registered using arrays containing the $objXMLElement object and its startElement() and endElement() methods. The character data handler, on the other hand, is registered with the array containing the $objXMLChar object and its characterData() method. When executed, the results show that the $objXMLElement object had its startElement() method called twice while the $objXMLChar object had its characterData() method called once.

```
Tag Name: ROOT
Tag Name: E1
DATA: text END_DATA

--- objXMLElement ---

Number of Elements: 2
Number of Times Character Data Handler Called: 0
```

```
--- objXMLChar ---
Number of Elements: 0
Number of Times Character Data Handler Called: 1
```

The block of code commented out, at least in this case, results in the same output if it were used rather than the line above it that registered the character data handler. When the xml_set_object() method is used, any method not specifically registered with an associated object will default to the object registered with xml_set_object(). As you might have guessed, you have a lot of possibilities when using objects and the xml extension. For instance, the "Seeing Some Examples in Action" section demonstrates a combination of building a DOM document and using the xml extension and the DOM classes.

Migrating from PHP 4 to PHP 5

As you might have guessed, you might encounter a few issues while migrating code using the xml extension from PHP 4 to PHP 5. The following sections identify what you might be able to expect in terms of problems, possible workarounds, and potential improvements to these issues.

Encoding

As of PHP 5.0.2, the default encoding has changed from ISO-8859-1 to UTF-8. This mainly affects output, which is the target encoding, from the extension, because libxml2 will autodetect the encoding of the document when parsing. This has caused at least a few people some problems, because they were expecting the output to be ISO-8859-1 encoded and in actuality got UTF-8 encoded data.

This is not difficult to resolve, though. You can set the target encoding at the time the parser is created or through the use of the XML_OPTION_TARGET_ENCODING option. When migrating code from PHP 4 or even from any version before PHP 5.0.2, if you have not set the target encoding and have no idea whether you need to, the safest thing to do is add a target encoding of ISO-8859-1 to your script. At least in this case, you will get the same output as you did under PHP 4. You need to use only one of the following methods:

```
/* Setting target encoding during parser creation */
$xml_parser = xml_parser_create('ISO-8859-1');
$xml_parser = xml_parser_create_ns('ISO-8859-1');

/* Setting target encoding using option after parser has been created */
xml_parser_set_option ($xml_parser, XML_OPTION_TARGET_ENCODING, 'ISO-8859-1');
```

Some good news exists in light of all this. The encoding of the source document is automatically detected. It is highly suggested that the document contain an XML declaration with the encoding declaration. When the document is being parsed, the encoding specified in the encoding declaration will be used to read the characters in the document. You might have read that the source encoding must be ISO-8859-1, US-ASCII, or UTF-8, but the encoding can be any encoding supported by libxml2, which includes many more options than just the three listed.

Character Data Handling

Handling character data events is another area that has caused many developers a headache or two. Many developers have coded their applications expecting that character data will behave in a certain manner when being sent to the handler. By this I mean that content can be split and sent to the handler, and many developers have come to think that it is acceptable to assume that data is split the same way every time. Whether or not this always worked in an application under PHP 4 and started causing problems when the code was migrated to PHP 5, the underlying assumption is incorrect; in other words, the application was not coded correctly in the first place. SAX works on streaming data. You cannot assume that character data will not be broken up and sent to the character data handler in chunks; in addition, it is wrong to think that the data will be sent in the same chunks every time.

Line breaks are one area where data is guaranteed to be chunked differently using PHP 5 than when using PHP 4. For example, under PHP 4, you might have code such as the following that expects line feeds within content to cause data to be chunked. In this example, data sent to the characterData handler will be printed surrounded by brackets [ ]:

```
function characterData($parser, $data) {
   print "[$data]";
}

function startElement($parser, $data, $attrs) {
   print "<$data>";
}

function endElement($parser, $data) {
   print "</$data>";
}

$xmldata = "<root>this \n that</root>";
$xml_parser = xml_parser_create();
xml_parser_set_option ($xml_parser, XML_OPTION_CASE_FOLDING, 0);
xml_set_element_handler($xml_parser, "startElement", "endElement");
xml_set_character_data_handler($xml_parser, "characterData");
xml_parse($xml_parser, $xmldata, true);
```

The output when run under PHP 4.*x* looks like this:

```
<root>[this ][
][ that]</root>
```

The line feed caused the data to be sent in three parts to the characterData() function. When run under PHP 5, the output is much different:

```
<root>[this
 that]<root>
```

In this case, the data was not split up but rather sent as a single string to the characterData handler. Any application that begins to have problems after migration because of this issue is coded incorrectly. The only way to resolve this issue is to fix the application code.

Default Handler

The default handler is definitely a problem when migrating from PHP 4 to PHP 5. Unfortunately, this problem has no current workarounds. I will first explain what the default handler is meant to handle. Under PHP 4, the default handler processes anything within a document not handled by any other handler. For example, the default handler processes the XML declaration, element declarations, and attribute declarations. Using PHP 5, the default handler does not currently process any of these. The following code demonstrates how to use the default handler under PHP 4 and under PHP 5:

```php
<?php
function  defaultData($parser, $data) {
   print "$data";
}

function startElement($parser, $data, $attrs) {
   print "<$data>";
}

function endElement($parser, $data) {
   print "</$data>";
}

$xmldata = '<?xml version="1.0"?>
<!DOCTYPE root SYSTEM "http://www.example.com/dtd" [
   <!ENTITY myEntity "Entity Text">
   <!ELEMENT root (e1, e2)>
   <!ELEMENT e1 ANY>
   <!ELEMENT e2 ANY>
]>
<root><e1>&myEntity;</e1><e2/></root>';
$xml_parser = xml_parser_create();
xml_parser_set_option ($xml_parser, XML_OPTION_CASE_FOLDING, 0);
xml_set_element_handler($xml_parser, "startElement", "endElement");
xml_set_default_handler($xml_parser, "defaultData");
xml_parse($xml_parser, $xmldata, true);
?>
```

Running this code under PHP 4, you get the following output:

```
<?xml version="1.0"?>
<!DOCTYPE root SYSTEM "http://www.example.com/dtd" [
   <!ENTITY myEntity "Entity Text">
   <!ELEMENT root (e1, e2)>
   <!ELEMENT e1 ANY>
   <!ELEMENT e2 ANY>
]>
<root><e1>&myEntity;</e1><e2></e2></root>
```

The same code run under PHP 5 produces much different results:

```
<root><e1>&myEntity;</e1><e2></e2></root>
```

The entire prolog of the document is missing.

As I mentioned, this is definitely a problem, and no simple workaround exists. It is possible that in future versions of PHP 5 it may be fixed or new functionality will be added to support capturing this data. Currently, however, PHP 5.1 does not contain any solutions to this issue. If this information is vital to your application, you might want to think about building the xml extension using expat rather than the default libxml2 library.

Parser Information

Byte index and column number are two pieces of information that will not only be different from values obtained running code under PHP 4 but also not be considerably valuable when running under PHP 5. The following example examines the information returned when processing a CDATA section. For brevity, empty data passed to the characterData() function is ignored and not processed:

```php
<?php
function printInfo($parser, $output) {
    printf($output,
        xml_get_current_line_number($parser),
        xml_get_current_column_number($parser),
        xml_get_current_byte_index($parser));
}

function characterData($parser, $data) {
    if (trim($data) == "") return;

    print "Data: $data END Data\n";
    printInfo($parser, "at line %d, col %d (byte %d)\n");
}

$xmldata ='<?xml version="1.0" encoding="iso-8859-1" ?>
<data>
<![CDATA[
multi
line
CDATA
block
]]>
</data>';
$xml_parser = xml_parser_create();
xml_set_character_data_handler($xml_parser, "characterData");
xml_parse($xml_parser, $xmldata, true);
?>
```

The following is the output from PHP 4 or PHP 5 using the expat library:

```
Data: multi END Data
at line 4, col 0 (byte 65)
Data: line  END Data
at line 5, col 0 (byte 72)
Data: CDATA END Data
at line 6, col 0 (byte 79)
Data: block END Data
at line 7, col 0 (byte 86)
```

If you have been using this functionality under PHP 4, the output most likely looks familiar. Columns start at 0 and indicate the starting position of the currently handled data. Line
numbers indicate the current line number of the data being processed. Bytes indicate the
number of bytes processed up until the start of the data being processed. The output from
PHP 5 is much different:

```
Data:
multi
line
CDATA
block
 END Data
at line 3, col 10 (byte 22)
```

Although the data was sent as a single block, the last line is informative, especially when
compared to the last line from the PHP 4 output.

The line numbers here are different because of how the data was chunked. Under PHP 4,
empty data chunks are not processed, and the first character within the CDATA section is a
line feed. This is not displayed in the PHP 4 example but corresponds to line number 3. Compared to the output under PHP 5, the line numbers match correctly. Under PHP 5, the line
number, indicating the starting line of the data being processed, is 3, which corresponds to
the starting line number the initial line feed is on.

The column number is a different story. In each case in the PHP 4 output, the column
number is 0. This is correct because the data being processed begins at column position 0
every time according to the output. Under PHP 5, however, the column number is 10. This
also is correct in this case. Remember, the column number is the starting column for the data
being processed, and with libxml2, the starting column position is 1. The data being
processed begins directly after the opening CDATA tag. Counting the columns for <![CDATA[,
where columns 1 starts before the first <, the line break starts at column 10. I use the term
line break here rather than *line feed* because under Windows your data may contain carriage
returns. Although in this instance the column number is correct, you may run into other
cases where it is not. One such case occurs when processing starting element tags containing
attributes and/or namespace declarations.

The last piece of information, the byte index, is way off under PHP 5. The number of bytes
from PHP 4 is 86, which includes the XML declaration and all data prior to the closing] for the
CDATA section. Line breaks are counted as single line feeds here. The count of 22 under PHP 5
is not even close to this number. The XML declaration alone is 46 bytes. Currently, the byte

count is useless information when running under PHP 5. If your application relies on this to be accurate, it is highly recommended you build this extension with expat rather than libxml2.

Entities

Basic entity processing works just as well under PHP 5 as it did under PHP 4. Issues begin to surface when entities reference other entities. As long as the entities are not being expanded or the expanded entities do not contain additional entity references, migration will not be an issue. In the event an entity being expanded does contain an entity reference, the encapsulated entity reference is included as character data in an unexpanded form. This then also leads to a difference when using the external entity reference handler.

    An entity reference referencing an external entity reference, once expanded, will not handle the contained external entity reference, and the external entity reference handler will not be executed. For example:

```php
<?php
function extEntRefHandler($parser, $openEntityNames, $base, $systemId, $publicId) {
    var_dump($openEntityNames);
    var_dump($systemId);
    return TRUE;
}

$xml_parser = xml_parser_create();
xml_parser_set_option($xml_parser, XML_OPTION_CASE_FOLDING, 0);
xml_set_external_entity_ref_handler($xml_parser, "extEntRefHandler");

$data = '<?xml version="1.0"?>
<!DOCTYPE root SYSTEM "/just/a/test.dtd" [
<!ENTITY systemEntity PUBLIC "aa" "xmltest2.xml">
<!ENTITY testEntity "&systemEntity;">
]>
<root>
    &testEntity;
</root>';

xml_parse($xml_parser, $data, TRUE);
xml_parser_free($xml_parser);
?>
```

The document used in this scenario uses the entity reference &testEntity; within the document. This entity reference contains the entity reference &systemEntity, which in fact is an external entity reference. When the code is executed and the &testEntity; entity reference encountered, one would expect the external entity handler to be executed because of the reference to the external entity reference. In fact, under PHP 4, it does. For example:

```
string(23) "systemEntity?testEntity"
string(12) "xmltest2.xml"
```

The parameters $openEntityNames and $systemId are dumped to the output. As you can clearly see, the $openEntityNames variable contains both of the entities in the stack. The first entity reference encountered was &testEntity;, which contained &systemEntity;. Although the external entity reference handler is executed for the &systmEntity; entity reference, it is initially called by the use of the &testEntity; entity reference in the document.

Running the same code under PHP 5 results in no output. The external entity reference handler is never executed. When the entity reference &testEntity; is encountered in the document, in this case it may be expanded, but no further expansion is performed. Its contents are currently handled as pure character data. This also explains why the parameter $openEntityNames is never a list of entities. Because entity references do not expand entity references they may contain, there is never a stack of entity references to pass. The external entity reference handler will be called only when an external entity reference is used directly within a document.

Seeing Some Examples in Action

I have already provided many small examples throughout this chapter, but it is a good idea for you to see a full example of working with this extension. While thinking about the best way to demonstrate the use of SAX, I remembered that many DOM parsers are built upon SAX. This example will create a DOM parser using this extension yet leverage the DOM API for the tree creation. I realize this may be pointless since DOM already builds a tree from data, but you could also modify the example with custom objects or containers to create a DOM parser without the use of the DOM extension. This example also utilizes much of the functionality within the xml extension, making it an interesting example all around.

Here's the code:

```
class cXML extends DOMDocument {
    private $currentNode = NULL;
    public $separator = ":";


    public function __construct() {
        parent::__construct();
        $this->currentNode = $this;
    }

    function startElement($parser, $data, $attrs) {
        try {
            $nsElement = explode($this->separator, $data);
            if (count($nsElement) > 1) {
                $uri = array_shift($nsElement);
                $name = implode($this->separator, $nsElement);
                $node = $this->createElementNS($uri, $name);
            } else {
                $node = $this->createElement($data);
            }
```

```
        $this->currentNode = $this->currentNode->appendChild($node);
        foreach ($attrs AS $name=>$value) {
            $nsAttribute = explode($this->separator, $name);
            if (count($nsAttribute) > 1) {
                $uri = array_shift($nsAttribute);
                $name = implode($this->separator, $nsAttribute);
                $node = $this->currentNode->setAttributeNS($uri, $name, $value);
            } else {
                $this->currentNode->setAttribute($name, $value);
            }
        }
    } catch (DOMException $e) {
        throw $e;
    }
}

function endElement($parser, $data) {
    $this->currentNode = $this->currentNode->parentNode;
}

function characterData($parser, $data) {
    try {
        $this->currentNode->appendChild(new DOMText($data));
    } catch (DOMException $e) {
        throw $e;
    }
}

function PIHandler($parser, $target, $data) {
    $node = $this->createProcessingInstruction($target, $data);
    $this->currentNode->appendChild($node);
}
}
```

The first step is to define the class that will be used to handle the events. In this case, only the class extends the DOMDocument class. Not only is it kind of neat to be able to use an extended DOM object within the xml parser, but also in this case since the DOM API is being used to create the tree, it offers direct access to the DOMDocument object within the handler events.

Two properties are first defined. The private $currentNode property is used within the methods to keep a handle on the current element in scope. The public $separator property is used for namespaced documents, so the separator used by the xml parser is known and can be used to extract information. The use of these will become clearer as the methods are broken down.

The constructor sets up the initial environment here. When the object is instantiated, the currentNode property needs to be set to point to the instantiated object. At this point, anything that happens as a result of parsing the XML data will be performed within the scope of the DOMDocument. Before looking at the startElement() and endElement() methods, let's jump down to the PIHandler() method.

PIs are valid prior to the document element, so it is a nice and simple method to start with. The xml parser passes the target and data for a PI to the handler. All that is performed in this method is that a new PI node is created and appended to the node specified by the currentNode property. As I said, this is a simple starting point.

The startElement() method is a bit more complex. This example code was created to be able to process and create namespaced documents. This is where the separator property comes into play. The extension prefixes local names with the full namespace separated by a user-definable character. Many namespaces, such as URLs, contain the colon character, so something else will be used. The property just allows the character to be set rather than hard-coded into the class definition, allowing for a bit more flexibility.

The first thing the startElement() method does is explode the tag name being passed in from the xml parser. As long as the separator in use is not contained in any namespaces, the resulting array will either contain a single value, indicating that the element is not in a name-space, or contain two values indicating that the element, whose local name is now in index 1 of the array, is in a namespace, which I identified by index 0 of the array.

If no namespace exists, a new element node is created normally. If a namespace does exist, the namespace is extracted from the array, and the tag name is built by imploding the new array. The implode() function is called in the event the separator character being used also is part of the tag name. The local name for the element would need to be put back together. Once the namespace and local name are pieced back together, a namespaced element node is created. The new node is then appended as a child of the node referenced by the currentNode property, and currentNode is set to this new element. Once a start tag is encountered, the scope moves down a level into the subtree.

Attributes are then handled next. The xml parser passes an array of name/value pairs to the startElement() method holding all the attributes for the element. Namespaces are handled in the same fashion as elements, and the rest of the code should be easy to dissect. The only difference is how attribute nodes are created and appended, which is out of the scope of this chapter; you find can more information about this in Chapter 6.

Just like the start tag moving the scope down a level into the subtree, an ending tag will move the scope up one level. The endElement() method just changes the scope to the parent of the node referenced by the currentNode property. Any processing that occurs after an ending tag occurs on the parent of the node that just ended. Any time the startElement() method is called, a corresponding endElement() method will be called. This is even true for empty-element tags. A tag like <element1 /> will issue both the start element event and the end element event.

The last method for this class is the characterData() method. This method will handle the character data events. Anything being handled by this is created as a text node within the tree. It is currently not possible to determine what type of data it is because this method handles character data, CDATA, and entity references. The text node is just added as a child of the node referenced by the currentNode property.

That defines everything currently within the class. It is not complete and will not work with all documents. For example, prefixes for namespaces are lost, which results in problems because namespaces are being created as default namespaces in every instance. Also, name-spaced attributes will not work correctly either. As mentioned, because of the current state of the character data handler, everything sent there is created as a text node. If you have the desire to do so, expanding upon this example will provide you with some great experience of working with XML and the xml extension. You have the option to continue using the DOM API, which will also give you more exposure to the DOM extension, or create your own custom tree handling routines, which will allow you to work with a DOM-like API without the need for the DOM extension. The latter has been done before, such as with the XML_Tree class; you can find this example in the PEAR repository and referenced later in Chapter 13. For example:

```
$xml_parser = xml_parser_create_ns(NULL, "@");

$objXMLDoc = new cXML();
$objXMLDoc->separator = "@";

xml_set_object($xml_parser, $objXMLDoc);
xml_parser_set_option ($xml_parser, XML_OPTION_CASE_FOLDING, 0);
xml_set_element_handler($xml_parser, "startElement", "endElement");
xml_set_character_data_handler($xml_parser, "characterData");
xml_set_processing_instruction_handler($xml_parser, "PIHandler");

/* The following can be changed to any XML document */
$xmldata = "<root><element1>text</element1><e2>text<e3>more</e3>text</e2></root>";

try {
    if (! xml_parse($xml_parser, $xmldata, true)) {
        $xmlError = libxml_get_last_error();
        var_dump($xmlError);
    }
} catch (DOMException $e) {
    var_dump($e);
}

xml_parser_free($xml_parser);

print $objXMLDoc->saveXML();
```

The remainder of this example is straightforward. A namespace-aware parser is created using the default encoding and using @ for the namespace separator. The object for event handling is created, and its separator property is set to the separator used for the parser. The object is then registered with the parser, and its methods are registered to handle events. The case folding option is disabled, leaving the tag names in their native case rather than forcing them all to uppercase.

This example hard-codes an XML document set in the $xmldata variable. Parsing is then performed all at once. Feel free to try different documents and even stream chunks of the document; the results should be the same. This example uses try/catch blocks because it uses the DOM extension. The parser will throw exceptions in certain cases, so this just ensures they are caught and handled properly.

To recap, this demonstrates how to use the xml extension in a semi-real-world case; I say this because using the DOM API is pointless unless only certain pieces of the document were actually to be built. It may also help with many of the concepts of XML. If you have little to no experience using XML, some of these concepts may be new to you. Being able to see the construction of XML from both a stream parsing view and a tree-based view makes it a bit easier to understand how you put everything together. This example is far from complete and prone to error when using namespaced documents. Fixing the issues and possibly creating a tree structure without using the DOM API is an exercise I will leave up to you.

Conclusion

This chapter has taken a hard look at the xml extension in PHP 5. Through examples and explanations, the API should be fairly clear to you. I have identified many issues you may encounter when migrating from PHP 4 to PHP 5, offering some guidance on how to work around the issues; other examples may leave you with no choice but to recode your application or build the xml extension with expat. It all depends on how XML-extensive the documents you are processing are and what information is critical to the operation of the application.

This chapter introduced you to stream-based parsing and what that means in terms of parsing. It not only offers fast parsing, but it also requires a low amount of system resources. The only issues you may have are the compatibility issues between this extension in PHP 4 and PHP 5.

The next chapter will introduce you to a new stream-based parser, XMLReader. I recommend you read through that chapter carefully; it offers many improvements over parsing with SAX. In fact, many developers who have tried XMLReader prefer it to the xml extension and have rewritten code to take advantage of the new extension. That decision is left up to you, but do not rush to any decision until you have at least read the next chapter.

XMLReader

XMLReader is a new stream-based parser in the PHP 5 lineup. If you skipped the previous chapter on the xml extension and do not know what a stream-based parser is, it may be beneficial to at least review that chapter because it explains in more detail what a stream-based parser is and how it works.

This chapter will introduce you to the XMLReader extension, explain the reasons for the existence of yet another stream-based parser, and show how to use this extension. The chapter will show how to use the API through short examples, with a complete example toward the end of this chapter. You can find additional examples of using this API in other chapters of this book, such as Chapter 14, which covers RDF, and Chapter 17, which covers REST. By the end of this chapter, you should understand what XMLReader is, know what its advantages and disadvantages are, and have a working knowledge of how to use the API in your everyday coding.

■**Caution** Constants have been moved to class constants in PHP 5.1. This differs from PECL version 1.0.1 where constants are regular constants. The examples in this book use class constants to maintain compatibility with the PHP releases.

Introducing XMLReader

The XMLReader extension is an object-oriented API that uses the libxml2 implementation, which in turn is based on the C# implementation of the XmlTextReader API (http://dotgnu.org/pnetlib-doc/System/Xml/XmlTextReader.html). The XMLReader extension is a forward-only, stream-based parser, but unlike SAX, it is a pull rather than a push parser. As you move through a document, the parser's cursor positions itself on the different nodes, allowing you to access information from the current node. It offers many advantages over the xml extension, including additional functionality. As of PHP 5.1, this extension is part of the core PHP code base and can be built using the following configuration option:

```
--with-xmlreader
```

If you are still using PHP 5.0.x, the XMLReader extension is available from the PECL repository at http://pecl.php.net/package/xmlReader. You can install it using the PEAR installer or build it by adding it to your PHP source tree. Refer to the PHP manual for further information about building extensions.

Push vs. Pull Parser

The previous chapter introduced you to stream-based parsing and the xml extension in particular. It explained that a *push* parser, in simple terms, pushes the data to your application while the XML is being parsed. The parser basically controls the flow of your application. A *pull* parser works much differently. It still operates on chunks of data at a time, providing a low memory footprint, but the application is in control of what data it wants and when the data is read from the stream. A pull parser allows you to free yourself from the control a push parser has over your application.

You can think of the difference between the two in terms of watching television. A push parser is like watching television without a digital video recorder. You are sitting there watching a show, and the commercials come on. If you are interested in anything in the commercials, you have to sit there and watch them, deciding which ones you like and which ones you don't. You can't get up and grab a snack, or you might miss something. You are not in control of the commercials. They, speaking in terms of a push parser, are pushed to your television, and you can't skip them, because you might want to watch one and can't pause them.

A pull parser, on the other hand, is like watching television with a digital video recorder (without the rewind feature, of course). By using the play, pause, and fast-forward buttons on the remote, you control the shows and commercials you watch. The current stream of XML data is comparable to the buffer of the digital video recorder. Like in the previous scenario, the commercials come on. Again, you might be interested in one of them. This time, you hit the pause button and grab something to eat. You return and decide you don't want to watch the commercial, so you fast-forward to the next one or even skip the next one. The push parser lets you control the movement of the parser, which is when data is read. When it stops at the point indicated, you can do anything you like in your code. The parser won't start reading more data until you tell it to do so. Your code could even stop reading the XML data and move on to something else. With a push parser, you really have no escape. Your application must read and act on everything in the buffer until all the data in the current stream has been read. It wouldn't be until the next `xml_parse()` call that you could safely stop reading XML data and have your application do something else.

This analogy may be a little over the top, but it should give you the idea. When using a pull parser, you are in control of the processing and of when data should be read. You are not at the mercy of the parser. As you will see in this chapter, this has many advantages over the traditional pull parser model, not to mention is much easier to use.

Advantages Over the xml Extension

If you followed along with the previous section, comparing a push and pull parser to watching television without and with a digital video recorder, you may already have realized one of the advantages of XMLReader over the xml extension. With the XMLReader extension, you control when the data should be accessed. This is just one of the many benefits of this extension. Other advantages include better namespace support, streaming validation support, a simple API, and potentially faster processing.

Namespace Support

From the examples in the previous chapter, you have most likely realized that processing namespaced documents is a real headache. The tag name is sent to the handler in the form of the namespace URI, the separator, and the local name of the element concatenated together. It is up to you, as the developer, to split these based on the separator character just to get access to the name of the element. This doesn't even take into account what it requires to access the prefix, if any, of the element. The same goes for attributes.

Accessing namespace information is much simpler using XMLReader. Once the parser is positioned on an element, you can use the object properties to access both the URI and the prefix for the element. The API also allows access to both the local name and the qualified name of the element. No more jumping through hoops—the information is available in a simple-to-use manner. You can find more details and examples later in the "Dealing with Namespaces" section.

Validation

If you want to perform validation, either by using RELAX NG or by using XML Schemas, you are pretty much out of luck with the xml extension. It will simply parse an XML document without regard to document validity. XMLReader adds the ability to validate a document while parsing. The API supports currently only RELAX NG, but with additions to the libxml2 library released in libxml2-2.6.20, PHP 5.2 should have XML Schema support. You can find further details and examples in the "Performing Validation" section.

Simple API

The xml extension does not have an overly extensive or complicated API. You write handler functions and register them with the parser, and off it goes to do its thing. This sounds simple, right? Well it is, but unless you have used the extension before, XMLReader is much easier to use and understand. In fact, you can implement the majority of the xml extension's API using the XMLReader API with one method and two or three object properties. The XMLReader API is much larger than the xml API (though still very compact), but many of the properties and methods offer information not obtainable from the xml extension. In addition, XMLReader offers advanced functionality that is not available using the xml extension.

Faster Processing

SAX parsing, which is what the xml extension does, should offer the fastest processing of XML data. Using PHP, however, this is typically not true. The numbers are close, but XMLReader can offer faster processing than the xml extension. Because you, as the developer, are in control of the parsing, data will be accessed only when needed. The xml extension, on the other hand, passes data around every time a registered event occurs. If the data from the event is not needed, it still is passed from the libxml2 library through the extension and finally to your handler. This data, to reach and be handled by the handler function, must also be converted into PHP usable data, such as the strings in PHP you already know.

XMLReader, on the other hand, allows you to move through the document, passing the minimal amount of data. When you reach a point of interest, you then request the specific data you want. Consider when the xml extension reaches the start of an element containing attributes. After testing the element tag name, the parser determines it can skip this element. The parser, though, has already processed all the attributes, packaged them, and sent them along as a parameter to the handler. With XMLReader, you request the attributes, so these are not processed until you need or want them. It is small details like these that give XMLReader better performance. Just think of what you would need to do with namespaced documents.

Chapter 11 will return to this issue. Within that chapter, you'll compare all the different parser extensions in PHP 5, with respect to their speeds, using different methods and using different sets of data. You will find hard numbers comparing the processing speeds using the xml extension and using XMLReader, so you will be able to judge for yourself.

Advanced Feature Set

Validation is one feature available using XMLReader and not the xml extension. Advanced namespace support in XMLReader is another. One of the best features of XMLReader, in my opinion, is the ability to be able to determine the type of node. Using the xml extension, in many cases the same handler handles different node types. For example, the character data handler takes care of text content and CDATA sections. You have no way to know what type of character data you are handling at the time. Text content is much different from CDATA, because CDATA can contain characters that are illegal to use as text content. This may affect how you need to handle the data.

Using the XMLReader API, you can easily access the type of node the parser is positioned on through a property from the object. Every type of node is available, so it is simple to process different types of data. A quick summary of some of the other features include the depth with the tree, the number of attributes held by an element, the exporting of nodes to the DOM extension, and the parser control while loading a document. This is just a subset of additional features, but these are some of the more important ones. Throughout this chapter, you will examine these features and see examples of them, so don't worry if you don't fully understand everything presented so far.

Using XMLReader

XMLReader is an object-oriented API. If you couldn't tell by now, I happen to be a bit partial to OOP when dealing with XML APIs. I find it a bit more manageable to deal with documents in this manner. The steps you need to take to process a document are short and simple:

1. Create the XMLReader object.

2. Set any parser options not already set.

3. Parse the document.

Creating the XMLReader Object

You can directly instantiate, or create, the XMLReader object using some methods statically. In this manner, it is similar to creating a DOMDocument object. The techniques aren't very different from each other. Calling the methods statically to create the object saves a line of code. You can directly instantiate the object in the same manner you normally create objects using the new keyword:

```
$objReader = new XMLReader();
```

The constructor takes no arguments and results in an object of type XMLReader.

This doesn't get you too far, though. The object is useless until it has a data stream. Data can be read from a string or directly from a file. This is an advantage over the SAX implementation. Using the xml extension, it is up to you to read the data from a file and then pass it to the parser. Here, the reader can take a URI and pull directly from it. The methods used in these cases are open() and XML():

```
/* method prototypes */
boolean XMLReader::open(string URI)
boolean XMLReader::XML(string source)
```

The open() method is used to read data from a URI, which is specified by the URI parameter. The XML() method reads data from a string containing the document in memory, which is specified by the source parameter. Both methods return a Boolean indicating success or failure:

```
/* Set string data to read */
$data = '<root>my document</root>';
$objReader->XML($data);

/* Set URI pointing to document to parse */
$objReader->open('http://www.example.com/doc.xml');
```

You can also call these methods statically. This eliminates the need to first instantiate the XMLReader object:

```
/* Create object and set string data to read */
$data = '<root>my document</root>';
$objReader = XMLReader::XML($data);

/* Create object and set URI pointing to document to parse */
$objReader = XMLReader:: open('http://www.example.com/doc.xml');
```

Creating the object first and then setting the input or doing it all at once using static methods is clearly up to you. You can save a few additional processing cycles by calling the methods statically, but unless this is critical to you, either way works just as well.

Note Throughout this chapter, the instantiated XMLReader object will simply be referred to as the *reader*.

One thing that is not currently possible using XMLReader but can be done using the xml extension is parsing an in-memory document that is broken up into multiple strings. For example, you can make multiple calls to xml_parse() where each call contains only a portion of the document to process. When using string data under XMLReader, the string must contain the entire document to be processed. This is something that may be expanded on in a future version, but for now when parsing large documents, using a file or stream and using the open() method are your best bets for keeping memory usage low. These do get processed via chunks of data without needing all the data to be residing in memory at one time.

Setting Parser Properties

Once you have created the reader and set the input, you can set parser properties to further control how the document is parsed. You *must* set these properties after setting the input; otherwise, an error will be returned. XMLReader uses different parser options than the DOM and SimpleXML extensions, because of the libxml2 API. It was not possible to combine them into a single set of PHP constants. Table 9-1 describes the parser properties, which are basically a subset of the other libxml parser options from Chapter 5 for XMLReader.

■**Caution** You must set parser properties *after* setting the input data on the XMLReader object. Any attempts to set these properties prior to setting the input will fail and either return FALSE or return an error message.

Table 9-1. *XMLReader Parser Properties*

Property	Value	Description
XMLREADER_DEFAULTATTRS	2	Forces the creation of default attributes within the document as defined in a DTD. With the current state of the XMLReader API in libxml2, default attributes are not available unless directly accessed by name. You can find a further explanation of this in the "Attributes" section later in this chapter.
XMLREADER_LOADDTD	1	Loads the DTD but does not validate the document.
XMLREADER_SUBST_ENTITIES	4	Substitutes entity references with their replaced content. Entity references will not be generated within the document.
XMLREADER_VALIDATE	3	Loads the DTD and validates the document based on the DTD while parsing.

You access parser properties through the getParserProperty() and setParserProperty() methods:

```
/* Method prototypes */
boolean XMLReader::getParserProperty(int property)
boolean XMLReader::setParserProperty(int property, boolean value)
```

The property parameter is one of the properties listed in Table 9-1. The value parameter for the setParserProperty() method is a Boolean indicating whether the specified property is enabled or disabled. The default value for all properties is FALSE. Both methods return a Boolean indicating whether the call succeeded or failed.

■**Note** Some parser properties may not be changed after the initial read of the input data. For instance, a DTD may not be loaded after the reading of the data has already begun.

The following piece of code tests the value of the XMLREADER_SUBST_ENTITIES property. If the current value is FALSE, it then sets it to TRUE. It is a bit redundant and used only to illustrate both methods at once. When setting the value for a parser property, any existing value is over-written, causing the getParserProperty() call in the following code snippet to be unnecessary:

```
if (! $objReader->getParserProperty(XMLREADER_SUBST_ENTITIES)) {
    $objReader->setParserProperty(XMLREADER_SUBST_ENTITIES, TRUE);
}
```

Parsing the Document

Now that the reader is finally prepared, you can begin to parse the document. XMLReader is kind of a hybrid parser. The document is represented as nodes, just like with DOM and SimpleXML, but processed in a manner similar to the xml extension. Parsing the document consists of stopping at nodes along the way where the type of node encountered depends upon the method to position the parser. When performing a normal read with the reader, the parser will stop at all nodes except for attributes. You can access attributes differently than all other node types within a document. For this reason, attributes have their own sec-tion, "Attributes," which deals the functionality available to deal with them. Table 9-2, for PHP 5.1 and higher, and Table 9-3, when using PECL version 1.0.1, describe the constants used for the node types you may encounter when using XMLReader.

Table 9-2. *XMLReader Node Type Constants*

Node Type	Value	Description
XMLREADER::NONE	0	No current node present. This type is encoun-tered prior to the first read and after the entire document has been processed.
XMLREADER::ELEMENT	1	Element node. This type signals the starting tag of an element.
XMLREADER::ATTRIBUTE	2	Attribute node.
XMLREADER::TEXT	3	Text node.
XMLREADER::CDATA	4	CDATA section node.
XMLREADER::ENTITY_REF	5	Entity reference node.
XMLREADER::ENTITY	6	Entity node.
XMLREADER::PI	7	PI node.
XMLREADER::COMMENT	8	Comment node.
XMLREADER::DOC	9	Document node.
XMLREADER::DOC_TYPE	10	Document type node.
XMLREADER::DOC_FRAGMENT	11	Document fragment node.
XMLREADER::NOTATION	12	Notation node.
XMLREADER::WHITESPACE	13	Insignificant whitespace. This type of node is a result of being whitespace and within the scope of a node defining xml:space with the value of default.

Continued

Table 9-2. *Continued*

Node Type	Value	Description
XMLREADER::SIGNIFICANT_WHITESPACE	14	Significant whitespace. This is whitespace that either is being preserved from a node defining xml:space with the value of preserve or not in the scope of xml:space at all.
XMLREADER::END_ELEMENT	15	End element tag.
XMLREADER::END_ENTITY	16	End entity tag.
XMLREADER::XML_DECLARATION	17	XML declaration.

Table 9-3. *XMLReader Node Type Constants for PECL Version 1.0.1*

Node Type	Value	Description
XMLREADER_NONE	0	No current node present. This type is encountered prior to the first read and after the entire document has been processed.
XMLREADER_ELEMENT	1	Element node. This type signals the starting tag of an element.
XMLREADER_ATTRIBUTE	2	Attribute node.
XMLREADER_TEXT	3	Text node.
XMLREADER_CDATA	4	CDATA section node.
XMLREADER_ENTITY_REF	5	Entity reference node.
XMLREADER_ENTITY	6	Entity node.
XMLREADER_PI	7	PI node.
XMLREADER_COMMENT	8	Comment node.
XMLREADER_DOC	9	Document node.
XMLREADER_DOC_TYPE	10	Document type node.
XMLREADER_DOC_FRAGMENT	11	Document fragment node.
XMLREADER_NOTATION	12	Notation node.
XMLREADER_WHITESPACE	13	Insignificant whitespace. This type of node is a result of being whitespace and within the scope of a node defining xml:space with the value of default.
XMLREADER_SIGNIFICANT_WHITESPACE	14	Significant whitespace. This is whitespace that either is being preserved from a node defining xml:space with the value of preserve or is not in the scope of xml:space at all.
XMLREADER_END_ELEMENT	15	End element tag.
XMLREADER_END_ENTITY	16	End entity tag.
XMLREADER_XML_DECLARATION	17	XML declaration.

Not every node type listed in Table 9-2 is currently used. Some may be left over from older libxml2 code, and some may be for future use. For instance, it is doubtful that you will ever run into the node types XMLREADER_ENTITY, XMLREADER_END_ENTITY, and XMLREADER_XML_DECLARATION.

I will not say "never" here, because it is possible they may be used in a future version of libxml2; it is for this reason they are exposed through the XMLReader interface. It would be difficult to deal with node types that get implemented in the libxml2 API but are not exposed through the XMLReader extension, even though the constant has been available in older libxml2 versions.

I will use the document in Listing 9-1 within this chapter unless indicated otherwise. It represents the contents of an XML document within the file named reader.xml.

Listing 9-1. *Contents of File* reader.xml

```
<?xml version='1.0'?>
<!DOCTYPE chapter [
<!ELEMENT chapter (title, para, section)>
<!ELEMENT title (#PCDATA)>
<!ELEMENT para ANY>
<!ATTLIST para name CDATA "default">
<!ELEMENT section ANY>
<!ATTLIST section id ID #REQUIRED>
]>
<chapter>
   <title>XMLReader</title>
   <para>
      First Paragraph
   </para>
   <section id="about">
      <title>About this Document</title>
      <para>
         <!-- this is a comment -->
         <?php echo 'Hi!  This is PHP version ' . phpversion(); ?>
      </para>
   </section>
</chapter>
```

Moving Through the Document

Unless you need access to attributes, moving through the document involves only two methods. These methods are read() and next(). In fact, you can access the entire document using only the read() method. Using the document from Listing 9-1, the reader will move to each node within the document and record the number of nodes accessed:

```
<?php
$objReader = XMLReader::open('reader.xml');
$count = 0;
while ($objReader->read()) {
   $count++;
}
print "Nodes Accessed: $count\n";
?>
```

The result of this example is the text Nodes Accessed: 28. Now I will explain what just happened and what 28 represents.

The read() method instructs the parser to move to the next node in the document, in document order. Once setting the input, think of the parser as being positioned on a document node. This is a concept from the tree parsers, but remember, XMLReader is a hybrid so the same concepts apply. Each time the read() method is called, the parser moves to the next node in the document, returning TRUE or FALSE. A return value of FALSE indicates that movement has failed, normally signaling that the end of the data stream has been reached. When using a well-formed document, this means the parser has reached the end of the document. Because of the construction of this method, you can access every node, except the attribute nodes, using the read() method within a while loop. Once the method returns FALSE, the end of the document has been reached, and execution moves to the next line of code following the end of the while block.

The initial read moves the cursor to the document type node. The XML declaration is skipped in this case. This is one of the cases where a node type is defined, XMLREADER_XML_DECLARATION, but it is not currently in use. No node types are available for the contents of the document type declaration, so the following read skips to the next node after it closes. If you are thinking that the next node encountered is an XMLREADER_ELEMENT node, representing the opening chapter tag, you are incorrect. The next node is actually the line breaks, which are XMLREADER_ SIGNIFICANT_WHITESPACE nodes.

With this in mind, you can count the total number of nodes in the document. The number should total 28 because that is what the code indicated it would be:

- XMLREADER_DOC_TYPE: 1

- XMLREADER_ SIGNIFICANT_WHITESPACE: 11

- XMLREADER_ELEMENT: 6

- XMLREADER_END_ELEMENT: 6

- XMLREADER_TEXT: 2

- XMLREADER_COMMENT: 1

- XMLREADER_PI: 1

And lo and behold, the total number of nodes in the document is 28. You might have come up with 29, but the line breaks within the first para element are actually part of the text content. Not to worry—I had to count a couple of times because my total kept coming out to 29.

The next() method is a little different from read(). It works on elements and moves the cursor much differently than the read() method does. Before trying to understand what it is exactly and how it works, it is necessary to understand the type of information available each time the cursor is positioned on a node. Once you understand how to use and access node information, you will revisit the next() method.

Node Information

You access information for the current node through properties of the reader. All XMLReader properties are read-only. Remember, it's called *XMLReader* for a reason. Table 9-4 describes the properties and descriptions.

Table 9-4. XMLReader *Object Properties*

Property	Return Type	Description
attributeCount	int	The number of attributes when positioned on an element node. All other nodes return a value of 0.
baseURI	string	The base URI for the current node.
depth	int	The number of levels deep within the document tree. The depth begins at zero, so all nodes within the top-level scope of the document, such as the document element start and end tags, return a depth of 0.
hasAttributes	bool	A Boolean indicating the presence of attributes on the current node. This property will return FALSE for all node types other than XMLREADER_ELEMENT.
hasValue	bool	A Boolean indicating whether the current node, based on its type, can have a value. This does not mean that the current node actually has a value.
isDefault	bool	A Boolean indicating whether the attribute was generated from the default value in a DTD. Currently this property is not implemented in libxml2 and always returns FALSE.
isEmptyElement	bool	A Boolean indicating whether the current element is empty or FALSE in all other cases. An empty element is considered to be an empty-element tag only. <a /> will return TRUE, and <a></a> will return FALSE.
localName	string	The local name of the current node.
name	string	The qualified name of the current node.
namespaceURI	string	The namespace URI in which the current node resides.
nodeType	int	An integer representing a node type from Table 9-2 for the current node.
prefix	string	The prefix associated with the namespace for the current node.
value	string	The value for the current node or empty string when no value or node type cannot have a value.
xmlLang	string	The xml:lang in scope for the current node.

Comparing the difference between parsing with the xml extension and XMLReader clearly shows how much easier XMLReader is to use. The following code demonstrates what is involved to parse the reader.xml file and print element tags and character data:

```php
<?php
function startElement($parser, $data, $attrs) {
   print "<".$data.">";
}

function endElement($parser, $data) {
   print $data;
}
```

```php
function characterData($parser, $data) {
    print $data;
}

$xml_parser = xml_parser_create();
xml_parser_set_option ($xml_parser, XML_OPTION_CASE_FOLDING, 0);
xml_set_element_handler($xml_parser, "startElement", "endElement");
xml_set_character_data_handler($xml_parser, "characterData");
$handle = fopen("reader.xml", "r");
while ($data = fread($handle, 4096)) {
    if (!xml_parse($xml_parser, $data, feof($handle))) {
        break;
    }
}
fclose($handle);
?>
```

```xml
<chapter>
    <title>XMLReader</title>
    <para>
        First Paragraph
    </para>
    <section>
        <title>About this Document</title>
        <para>


        </para>
    </section>
</chapter>
```

You can get the same output using XMLReader, which not only is much easier to read but takes fewer lines of coding:

```php
<?php
$objReader = XMLReader::open('reader.xml');
while ($objReader->read()) {
    switch ($objReader->nodeType) {
        case XMLREADER_ELEMENT:
            print "<".$objReader->localName.">";
            break;
        case XMLREADER_END_ELEMENT:
            print "</".$objReader->localName.">";
            break;
```

```
        case XMLREADER_TEXT:
        case XMLREADER_CDATA:
        case XMLREADER_WHITESPACE:
        case XMLREADER_SIGNIFICANT_WHITESPACE:
            print $objReader->value;
    }
}
?>
```

Notice the last four case statements. XMLReader offers greater information for the data encountered in the document. While the reader sends all text and CDATA to the character data handler, each type of node, including whitespace, could be handled differently. In this case, you wanted the same behavior, so all text content is handled the same way. Try removing the whitespace types from the list of cases. The only line breaks in the output would be the line breaks that are part of the First Paragraph text node.

The next() Method

When processing a document, it is not always the case that you need to access every single node. In fact, it is sometimes desirable to bypass an entire subtree and move to the next sibling node. The next() method provides this ability. When called, this method positions the cursor on the next node in the document, bypassing any subtree that may exist for the current node. This means only sibling nodes and nodes following the current node parent's starting tag will be accessed. For example:

```
<?php
$objReader = XMLReader::open('reader.xml');
/* Find the title element */
while ($objReader->read()) {
    if ($objReader->nodeType == XMLREADER_ELEMENT
        && $objReader->localName == "title") {
      break;
    }
}

/* find the section element that is a sibling of title */
while ($objReader->next()) {
    if ($objReader->nodeType == XMLREADER_ELEMENT
        && $objReader->localName == "section") {
      break;
    }
}

/* Descend into subtree of section element */
$objReader->read();
/* First whitespace node is skipped */
```

```
$depth = $objReader->depth;
while ($objReader->next()) {
    /* If depth is less than initial depth, cursor is out of the subtree */
    if ($objReader->depth < $depth) {
        print "\n**** Ascending rest of tree\n";
        print "Current Node: ".$objReader->localName;
        print " Type: ".$objReader->nodeType." Depth: ".$objReader->depth."\n";
        break;
    }
    print "Current Node: ".$objReader->localName;
    print " Type: ".$objReader->nodeType." Depth: ".$objReader->depth."\n";
}
?>
```

The code is a bit longer than it needs to be since the section node could have been initially searched for rather than the first title element node, but this example shows a couple ways of using the next() method.

The purpose of the first while block should be evident. The reader is moving to each node in the document until it encounters the first element start tag with the name title. Instead of using the read() method, the next() method is called, so from the title element node, the cursor moves to each sibling of this node until it encounters the section element node.

If you look at the document in Listing 9-1 again, you should notice the first child node for the section element is a significant whitespace. The cursor is positioned on this node using the read() method, but no processing or testing of the node is performed. Normally, unless you know the exact contents of the document being processed, this is not a good idea. For all you know, the document might not have any whitespaces, and the first child could be an important node type for the application. This is not the case here, so the lone call to the read() method is used to just move the cursor into the subtree of the section element.

The current depth within the document is now stored in the $depth variable, and the processing begins to see what nodes are actually encountered when calling next(). If you think about it, with the cursor positioned on the first text node (which is the significant whitespace), the siblings of this node are the title element, a text node that is whitespace, the para element, and another text node that is whitespace. Executing the code prints the following:

```
Current Node: title Type: 1 Depth: 2
Current Node: #text Type: 14 Depth: 2
Current Node: para Type: 1 Depth: 2
Current Node: #text Type: 14 Depth: 2

**** Ascending rest of tree
Current Node: section Type: 15 Depth: 1
```

The first four lines of output are exactly as expected: the two element nodes interspersed with significant whitespace nodes.

The next part of the output might throw you a bit. While accessing the sibling nodes, no end element nodes were encountered. When working with siblings, there is no need for the cursor to be positioned on the element end tag. The element nodes are encountered during the next() call, and positioning on the end tag would serve no purpose other than be a waste of your time. When the end of a subtree has been reached, on the other hand, positioning back on the parent element node through its end tag can be useful. You may need to perform additional processing with the element based on some information obtained from its subtree. This explains why the last next() performed in the code results in the cursor being positioned on the end tag of the section element. Had processing not been stopped, the end tag for the chapter element would also have been reached.

This method also can take an optional parameter. You can supply the local name for the next node to position. The same rules apply using this parameter as when not using it, but the cursor will skip any nodes with a local name not matching the localname parameter. For instance, you could change the while loop that produced the previous output to stop only at the para element node:

```
while ($objReader->next("para")) {
    /* If depth is less than initial depth, cursor is out of the subtree */
    if ($objReader->depth < $depth) {
        print "\n**** Ascending rest of tree\n";
        print "Current Node: ".$objReader->localName;
        print " Type: ".$objReader->nodeType." Depth: ".$objReader->depth."\n";
        break;
    }
    print "Current Node: ".$objReader->localName;
    print " Type: ".$objReader->nodeType." Depth: ".$objReader->depth."\n";
}
```

```
Current Node: para Type: 1 Depth: 2
```

The localname parameter is not limited to elements. All node types have names, and these can be passed to the next() method as well. Try changing the localname parameter from para to #text in the while loop; your output should look like this:

```
Current Node: #text Type: 14 Depth: 2
Current Node: #text Type: 14 Depth: 2

**** Ascending rest of tree
Current Node: #text Type: 14 Depth: 1
```

Accessing Attributes

You access attributes differently than all other nodes in a document. As you saw earlier in the "Moving Through the Document" section, read() did not stop on any attributes. Attributes are accessible only when positioned on an element node, with either the XMLREADER_ELEMENT node type or the XMLREADER_END_ELEMENT node type. From the list of properties, it is already evident that attributes exist and you can retrieve the number of attributes, but to physically access the attributes themselves involves using additional methods. You have two ways to retrieve information for attributes. You can retrieve attribute values while the cursor is positioned on an element, or you can move the cursor to specific attributes. The following subsections will use a different document to demonstrate the different methods.

```
$data = '<root att1="att1 value" att2="att2 value" att3="att3 value" />';
```

Retrieving Attribute Values

You can retrieve attribute values using the getAttribute(), getAttributeNo(), and getAttributeNS() methods. I will discuss the latter method in the "Dealing with Namespaces" section. The difference between the remaining two methods is that getAttribute() takes a qualified name for its parameter while getAttributeNo() takes a zero-based index, identifying the position of the attribute in relative to the element, for its parameter:

```
$objReader = XMLReader::XML($data);
$objReader->read();
if ($objReader->nodeType == XMLREADER_ELEMENT && $objReader->hasAttributes) {
    print "att1: ".$objReader->getAttribute("att1")."\n";
    print "att2: ".$objReader->getAttribute("att2")."\n";
    print "att3: ".$objReader->getAttribute("att3")."\n";
    for ($x=0;$x < $objReader->attributeCount; $x++) {
        print "Attr Index $x: ".$objReader->getAttributeNo($x)."\n";
    }
}
```

```
att1: att1 value
att2: att2 value
att3: att3 value
Attr Index 0: att1 value
Attr Index 1: att2 value
Attr Index 2: att3 value
```

The results print the attribute value based on name. The last three lines of the results are from the for loop. The for loop executes its body one less time than the number of attributes on the element. The method getAttributeNo() works off a zero-based index, so the first attribute is at index 0. Each iteration through the loop prints the current attribute value based on the index $x and increments $x until it is equal to the number of attributes held on the element.

Moving to Attributes

The problem with using the methods to retrieve attribute values from an element node is that you don't always know the attribute names. Or, the attributes live in namespaces, and you are unsure of the qualified names of the attributes. It is possible to get the values using the attribute index, but that still does not get you any closer to determining the name of the attribute or even whether the attribute lives in a namespace. The XMLReader API has a few methods that move the cursor to attribute nodes, which allows them to be accessed using object properties just like all other node types:

- bool moveToAttribute(string qualifiedName): Moves to an attribute by qualifiedName

- bool moveToAttributeNo(int index): Moves to an attribute by zero-based index

- bool moveToAttributeNs(string localName, string namespaceURI): Moves to an attribute with localName in the specified namespaceURI

- bool moveToFirstAttribute(): Moves to the first attribute in the list on the element

- bool moveToNextAttribute(): Moves to the next attribute in the list on the element

It is pretty obvious what these methods do based on their names. The following block of code will demonstrate how to use these methods, though I will demonstrate the method moveToAttributeNs() in the "Dealing with Namespaces" section.

One other method is handy when positioning the cursor on attributes. When positioned on an attribute, the method moveToElement() will position the cursor back on the element that owns the attribute. This allows the element to be accessed again. Otherwise, when positioned on an attribute, the method read() or next() is called, and the cursor moves as if the method were called while positioned on the element node for the attribute. For example:

```
$objReader = XMLReader::XML($data);
$objReader->read();
if ($objReader->nodeType == XMLREADER_ELEMENT && $objReader->hasAttributes) {
    $objReader->moveToAttribute("att1")."\n";
    print $objReader->localName.": ".$objReader->value."\n";

    $objReader->moveToAttributeNo(2)."\n";
    print $objReader->localName.": ".$objReader->value."\n";
    if ($objReader->moveToFirstAttribute()) {
        do {
            print $objReader->localName.": ".$objReader->value."\n";
        } while ($objReader->moveToNextAttribute());
    }

    $objReader->moveToElement();
    print $objReader->localName."\n";
}
```

```
att1: att1 value
att3: att3 value
att1: att1 value
att2: att2 value
att3: att3 value
root
```

Moving the cursor around attributes is similar to moving through the document, though you have much more freedom with attribute movement than with other types of nodes. Once the cursor is positioned on an attribute, the attribute node is accessible like every other node in the document. This is the only case, however, where the positioning can move in a reverse direction when working with XMLReader.

Exporting to DOM Objects

XMLReader has a big advantage over the xml extension in that because of its internal API and being a hybrid parser, it is possible to export nodes to the DOM extension. You may ask why this is such a big deal. It may or may not be. It depends upon the functionality you need. Consider a few scenarios. You have a 100MB document, and you need to pull only a few nodes from it. You could need to create a new document based on these few nodes, or you could need to process these nodes using the XSL extension.

Of course, you could always load the document into the DOM or SimpleXML extension and access the nodes you need. This, however, will use more than 100MB of memory, because building a tree in memory will require much more memory than the size of the document. A better approach is to scan the document using XMLReader, export the specific nodes, and process them. This will keep memory to a minimum in this case. You can export by using the expand() method. The following example will use a small document to demonstrate this method:

```
$data = '<root><element att1="value">some text</element></root>';
$objReader = XMLReader::XML($data);
while($objReader->localName != "element") {
    $objReader->read();
}
if ($objReader->nodeType == XMLREADER_ELEMENT && $objReader->hasAttributes) {
    $objElement = $objReader->expand();
    var_dump($objElement);

    /* Use DOM API since these are DOM objects */
    $objAttribute = $objElement->attributes->item(0);
    print $objAttribute->nodeValue;
}
```

The cursor first moves to the node named element. Assuming the node is of element type and it has attributes, it is exported to a DOM object. To be precise, it is an element node, so it exports to an object of the DOMElement class, as shown by the var_dump():

```
object(DOMElement)#2 (0) {
}
```

XMLReader is a stream-based parser, meaning that these nodes are not persistent. Exporting a node to DOM creates a copy (which is a real copy equivalent to cloning a node rather than the shared nodes passed between DOM and SimpleXML) of the XMLReader node that is not associated with any document. This is important. Without an associated document, the exported node is pretty much read-only.

Dealing with Namespaces

Handling namespaces with XMLReader is not any harder than handling a document without namespaces. In fact, it works the same way with the same properties and methods you have been using all along. So why is this section dedicated to namespaces? The answer is simple.

It is easier to demonstrate how to work with namespaces after understanding the API rather than trying to understand everything at once.

The only real difference when working with namespaces is that a couple of methods and a few properties are relevant when dealing with namespaces but not otherwise.

Tip The next() method accepts a local name for its optional parameter. When working with prefixed elements, remember to not use the qualified name; just use the local name. The method getAttribute() will retrieve a namespaced attribute based on its local or qualified name, but remember from the XML specification that two attributes in different namespaces with the same local name may exist on the same element. Without using the qualified name and this method, you may not end up with the attribute value you intended to retrieve.

For the purposes of this chapter, I will use the document in Listing 9-2, referring to the file reader2.xml, as the basis for the XML data.

Listing 9-2. *Namespaced Document in File* reader2.xml

```
<?xml version='1.0'?>
<chapter xmlns:a="http://www.example.com/namespace-a"
        xmlns="http://www.example.com/default">
   <a:title>XMLReader</a:title>
   <para>
      First Paragraph
   </para>
   <a:section a:id="about">
      <title>About this Document</title>
      <para>
         <!-- this is a comment -->
         <?php echo 'Hi!  This is PHP version ' . phpversion(); ?>
      </para>
   </a:section>
</chapter>
```

This document is basically the document from Listing 9-1 with the document type declaration removed, a default namespace (http://www.example.com/default) added, and an additional namespace (http://www.example.com/namespace-a) associated with the prefix a. A few of the elements and attributes have also been moved into the http://www.example.com/namespace-a namespace. Just to prove to you that namespaces do not alter the way nodes are accessed, I will run the original node count script again:

```php
<?php
$objReader = XMLReader::open('reader2.xml');
$count = 0;
while ($objReader->read()) {
    $count++;
}
print "Nodes Accessed: $count\n";
?>
```

This time it outputs Nodes Accessed: 27. Now, don't go thinking I am trying to deceive you since the original one counted 28. The document type declaration has been removed, reducing the count by one. Other than that missing node, the cursor has stopped at the same nodes in this document as it did before.

Prefixes and Namespace URIs

Let's take a look at some of the namespace-specific functionality. The first step is to position the cursor on the section element residing within the namespace prefixed by a:

```php
$objReader = XMLReader::open('reader2.xml');
while ($objReader->read()) {
    if ($objReader->nodeType == XMLREADER_ELEMENT
        && $objReader->name == "a:section") {
      break;
    }
}
print $objReader->name;
```

Of course, this prints a:section; otherwise, this would have been futile. You could have also created the test for the node by doing this:

```php
if ($objReader->nodeType == XMLREADER_ELEMENT
    && $objReader->localName == "section" && $objReader->prefix == "a") {
    break;
}
```

It is much easier using the qualified name in this case. Unlike a node not within a namespace or in the default namespace, the properties localName and name do not return the same thing for a node residing in a prefixed namespace. For example, when positioned on the para element, the following comparison is true:

```php
/* This is TRUE for nodes in the default namespace or not residing in a namespace */
If ($objReader->name == $objReader->localName) {
    ...
}
```

Along with the prefix property, the namespaceURI property will return a string containing the namespace URI in which the node resides. Keep in mind the cursor is still positioned on the section element:

```php
print $objReader->namespaceURI;
```

This prints `http://www.example.com/namespace-a`. As far as object properties go, `prefix` and `namespaceURI` are the only two that have meaning when dealing with namespaces and return empty strings in all other cases. The remaining properties, which you have already encountered, work the same way.

Attributes

Attributes work pretty much in the same manner as explained previously. A few additional methods are specific to namespace usage as well as to the namespace declarations themselves. The first things to look at are the attribute methods. Two previously mentioned methods are `getAttributeNs()` and `moveToAttributeNs()`.

Both of these methods take two parameters. The first is the local name of the attribute, and the second is the `namespaceURI` in which the attribute is located. The `section` element, where the cursor is still positioned, has a single attribute with the local name `id` in the namespace `http://www.example.com/namespace-a`. You can retrieve the value of the attribute with any of the following calls:

```
print $objReader->getAttribute('id');
print $objReader->getAttribute('a:id');
print $objReader->getAttributeNs('id', 'http://www.example.com/namespace-a');
```

All three of these will print the value of the attribute named `id`. The first method is not recommended when working with namespaces. If an additional `id` attribute existed not within the same namespace, you have no guarantee which attribute value is being retrieved. Consider what might be printed if the start tag for the section element looked like `<a:section a:id="about" id="2">`. The value for the first attribute would be retrieved even though it was the second one you wanted.

Caution Do not use `getAttribute()` without qualified names unless trying to access a non-namespaced attribute. As of libxml2 2.6.21, this method will not retrieve values for namespaced attributes.

The `moveTo` methods work just like the `getAttribute` methods with regard to the qualified name. The `moveToAttribute()` method, however, does not have the bug the `getAttribute()` method has. When passing in a local name for the attribute, only non-namespaced attributes are retrieved:

```
$objReader->moveToAttribute('id');
print $objReader->value."\n";
$objReader->moveToAttribute('a:id');
print $objReader->value."\n";
$objReader->moveToAttributeNs('id', 'http://www.example.com/namespace-a');
print $objReader->value."\n";
```

Although you would expect the same results as using the `getAttribute` methods, it is slightly different:

```
/* first line is a blank line */
about
about
```

The output is actually correct. The moveToAttribute() method does not contain the bug in the getAttribute() method. In actuality, the previous results should have looked like these.

Namespace Declarations

Namespace declarations are handled as regular attributes within XMLReader. They have their own section because the implementation is not complete in the libxml2 library so can be accessed only from certain attribute methods. These methods are currently the moveTo methods, except the moveToAttributeNs() method. This method currently does not move the cursor to namespace declarations. For this example, the parser needs to be reset so the chapter element can be used:

```php
<?php
$objReader = XMLReader::open('reader2.xml');
while ($objReader->read()) {
    if ($objReader->nodeType == XMLREADER_ELEMENT
        && $objReader->name == "chapter") {
        break;
    }
}

$objReader->moveToAttributeNo(0);
print $objReader->value."\n";
$objReader->moveToAttributeNo(1);
print $objReader->value."\n";

$objReader->moveToAttribute("xmlns:a");
print $objReader->value."\n";
$objReader->moveToAttribute("xmlns");
print $objReader->value."\n";

$objReader->moveToFirstAttribute();
print $objReader->value."\n";
$objReader->moveToNextAttribute();
print $objReader->value."\n";
?>
```

```
http://www.example.com/namespace-a
http://www.example.com/default
http://www.example.com/namespace-a
http://www.example.com/default
http://www.example.com/namespace-a
http://www.example.com/default
```

It is possible in the near future that additional attribute methods will support namespace declarations, but currently only the ones used previously in this chapter have been implemented as of libxml2-2.6.20.

Performing Validation

One of the advantages over the xml extension is XMLReader's ability to perform validation while processing a document. Currently, only DTD and RELAX NG validation is supported, but by the time you read this, XML Schema support may have been added. Depending upon the type of validation being performed, you may need to prepare validation support before calling the initial read() method but after setting the input data stream. While processing the document, you can check the validity using the isValid() method. This method returns a Boolean indicating the state of document validity.

Note When not performing validation on a document, the isValid() method will always return FALSE.

Validating with DTD

You specify validation using a DTD with the XMLREADER_VALIDATE parser property. When this property must be set depends upon a few conditions. When you need to load an external subset, you must set this property prior to the initial call to read() unless the XMLREADER_LOADDTD property has been set prior to the initial call to read(). By default an external subset is not loaded, so in order to ensure it is used, it must be loaded in order to validate the document. When the document does not contain an external subset, such as the document in Listing 9-1, you can set this property at any time during script execution. Until the XMLREADER_VALIDATE property has been set, however, any calls to isValid() will return FALSE, even though the document may be valid. Once the property has been set, isValid will begin to return the actual validity status of the document. For example:

```php
<?php
$objReader = XMLReader::open('reader.xml');
$objReader->setParserProperty(XMLREADER_VALIDATE, TRUE);
while ($objReader->read()) {
    if (! $objReader->isValid()) {
        print "NOT VALID\n";
        break;
    }
}
?>
```

This piece of code results in no output. The only possible output would occur if the document were not valid at any time during processing.

Validating with RELAX NG

RELAX NG validation works differently than DTD validation. The isValid() method is still used to check validity, but you instruct the reader to perform validation through the setRelaxNGSchema() method or the setRelaxNGSchemaSource() method. It is mandatory to call either method after setting the input data and prior to the first call to the read() method. Once the document has begun processing, the reader cannot be instructed to perform RELAX NG validation. For example:

```php
<?php
$schema = '<?xml version="1.0" encoding="utf-8" ?>
<element name="chapter" xmlns="http://relaxng.org/ns/structure/1.0">
   <element name="title">
      <text/>
   </element>
   <element name="para">
      <text/>
   </element>
   <element name="section">
      <attribute name="id" />
      <text/>
   </element>
</element>';

$objReader = XMLReader::open('reader.xml');
$objReader->setRELAX NGSchemaSource($schema);

libxml_use_internal_errors(TRUE);
while ($objReader->read()) {
   if (! $objReader->isValid()) {
      $xmlError = libxml_get_last_error();
      var_dump($xmlError);
      exit;
   }
}
?>
```

The schema defined by the $schema variable is used to validate the document from Listing 9-1 and is designed to fail. The reader is first instantiated, and the input data is set. With the reader prepared for parsing, the RELAX NG schema to validate against is set using the setRelaxNGSchemaSource() method, taking a string containing the entire schema as its parameter. For this example, the new error handling for XML, added in PHP 5.1, is used. This will allow the application to query for an XML error rather than having warnings displayed during script execution. Using the read() method, the reader moves throughout all the nodes in document order, checking the document validity at each stop, with $objReader->isValid(). Once the document fails validation, the script pulls the last error generated from the libxml library and dumps the structure to the output.

The section element from the schema is defined to allow only text content, but in the XML document itself, it actually contains child elements. Upon the reader encountering the child title element of the section element, the document fails the validity check, and the script prints the dump of the LibXMLError object obtained from the libxml_get_last_error() call:

```
object(LibXMLError)#2 (6) {
  ["level"]=>
  int(2)
  ["code"]=>
  int(38)
  ["column"]=>
  int(0)
  ["message"]=>
  string(35) "Did not expect element title there"
  ["file"]=>
  string(0) ""
  ["line"]=>
  int(0)
}
```

You can work with a RELAX NG schema from a file in the same manner. The only change would be to reference the schema as a file using setRelaxNGSchema(), passing the filename or URI as the parameter, rather than using a schema loaded into a string variable.

Seeing Some Examples in Action

Throughout this chapter you have seen how XMLReader processes documents, but most examples have been small code snippets or code focusing on a particular functionality of the XMLReader API. It is time to look at a larger application that uses a good portion of the API and see how the code breaks down. For this example, just as in the previous chapter, I will process a document and build an in-memory tree. Although you could easily do this by exporting nodes using the expand() method, this example will not use that method; the node information will be processed using reader properties. The DOM extension will still be used to create the internal tree, but without relying on the expand() functionality, it is possible for you to easily implement your own tree creation storage by replacing the DOM functionality.

Note The complete example in this chapter presents the full API for the XMLReader extension in a single application. You can find real-world examples of using XMLReader in later chapters such as Chapter 14 and Chapter 17.

Here's the code:

```php
<?php
class cReader extends XMLReader {
    private $document = NULL;
    private $currentNode = NULL;
    const xmlns = "http://www.w3.org/2000/xmlns/";

    public function __construct() {
        /* Create the base document for the tree */
        $this->document = new DOMDocument();
        $this->currentNode = $this->document;
    }

    function attributes() {
        /* DOM throws exceptions so try/catch used */
        try {
            if ($this->moveToFirstAttribute()) {
                do {
                    /* Attributes are always prefixed when in a namespace */
                    if ($this->prefix) {
                        if ($this->prefix != "xmlns") {
                            $this->currentNode->setAttributeNS($this->namespaceURI,
                                                    $this->name, $this->value);
                        } else {
                            /* This is a namespace declaration.
                               Ensure it is created as it may not be used on element */
                            $this->currentNode->setAttributeNS(self::xmlns,
                                                    $this->name, $this->value);
                        }
                    } else {
                        /* No need to handle default namespace declarations.
                           DOM already creates them with the element */
                        if ($this->name != "xmlns") {
                            $this->currentNode->setAttribute($this->name, $this->value);
                        }
                    }
                } while ($this->moveToNextAttribute());
            }
        } catch (DOMException $e) {
            throw $e;
        }
    }
```

```php
    function startElement() {
        try {
            if ($this->namespaceURI) {
                $node = $this->document->createElementNS($this->namespaceURI,
                                                          $this->name);
            } else {
                $node = $this->document->createElement($this->name);
            }
            $this->currentNode = $this->currentNode->appendChild($node);
            if ($this->hasAttributes) {
                $this->attributes();
            }
        } catch (DOMException $e) {
            throw $e;
        }
    }

    function endElement() {
        $this->currentNode = $this->currentNode->parentNode;
    }

    function characterData() {
        try {
            $this->currentNode->appendChild(new DOMText($this->value));
        } catch (DOMException $e) {
            throw $e;
        }
    }

    function PIHandler() {
        $node = $this->document->createProcessingInstruction($this->name,
                                                             $this->value);
        $this->currentNode->appendChild($node);
    }

    function saveXML() {
        return $this->document->saveXML();
    }
}

$xmldata = "<root><element1>text</element1><e2>text<e3>more</e3>text</e2></root>";

$objReader = new cReader();
$objReader->XML($xmldata);
```

```
try {
    while ($objReader->read()) {
        switch ($objReader->nodeType) {
            case XMLREADER_ELEMENT:
                $objReader->startElement();
                break;
            case XMLREADER_END_ELEMENT:
                $objReader->endElement();
                break;
            case XMLREADER_TEXT:
            case XMLREADER_CDATA:
            case XMLREADER_WHITESPACE:
            case XMLREADER_SIGNIFICANT_WHITESPACE:
                $objReader->characterData();
                break;
            case XMLREADER_PI:
                $objReader->PIHandler();
                break;
        }
    }
} catch (DOMException $e) {
    var_dump($e);
}

print $objReader->saveXML();
?>
```

```
<?xml version="1.0"?>
<root><element1>text</element1><e2>text<e3>more</e3>text</e2></root>
```

This example performs the same functionality as shown in the example for the xml extension in Chapter 8. It is a bit longer because namespace support has been added. As you may infer from that, handling namespaces is much easier to deal with in XMLReader than in the xml extension. Let's take a look at the actual functionality contained in this example.

The cReader class is a class extending the XMLReader class. The only advantage of having written the functionality as object methods is that it is encapsulated and possibly a bit easier to follow. Before examining the class structure, let's jump right down to the actual body of the script itself where the cReader object is instantiated (again to be referred to as the *reader*) and then returned to the class itself.

The reader sets the input to the XML to process and is processed using the read() method. This ensures that the parser stops at each node within the document. The nodeType test mimics the behavior of the event handlers used in the previous chapter. This is the reason all the content type nodes—XMLREADER_TEXT, XMLREADER_CDATA, XMLREADER_WHITESPACE, and XMLREADER_SIGNIFICANT_WHITESPACE—are grouped into the same functionality. The behavior needs to be the same for all of these, although XMLReader-specific processing can be performed for each individual type. As each of the types listed in the switch statement are processed, the application calls the specified method from the object. This is similar to an event being called, but in this case the application controls the call; using the xml extension, it is called automatically.

The first type of node the document encounters is typically an element node. This is not always the case if you recall the possible legal structure of an XML document, but for this exercise, the document element will be the first node. When encountered, the startElement() method is called. The method first tests for a namespaceURI on the current node. When empty, a regular element is created; otherwise, the element resides in a namespace and is created as such. Notice that the element is created using the name property. This returns the qualified name of the node rather than using localName, which would return the name of the node without the appropriate prefix. The method then checks whether the element has attributes using the hasAttributes property. Remember that attributes are not a node type that the parser stops on. They must be requested when positioned on an element.

Assuming the element has attributes, the attributes() method is then called. This method may look a bit confusing. Support for namespace declarations has been added here because XMLReader handles namespace declarations just like any other attribute. The reader positions itself on the first attribute and begins the attribute processing. Attributes do not inherit the default namespace, so it is safe to assume that if an attribute has a prefix, the attribute is a namespaced attribute. Without the prefix, the attribute is handled as a normal attribute.

The case for a normal attribute also tests to make sure the attribute is not a default namespace declaration. In the case of this example, a default namespace would already have been created when the element was created. If you are unsure of the reason for this, refer to Chapter 6. Namespaced elements also need to test their prefixes for the string "xmlns". These are also namespace declarations but define a prefix for the namespace as well. The DOM extension normally handles creating these when the element is created, but namespace declarations can also be defined on elements even though the element is not within the namespace. In a case like this, the namespace declaration simply needs to be created on the current element. Once the reader finishes with the current attribute, it moves to the next attribute using the moveToNextAttribute() method. This method is used as the truth expression for the do/while loop. This guarantees that the loop will be executed at least once, which is needed for the initial attribute, and will continue to be executed as long as the reader can move to the next attribute. The TRUE/FALSE return values from XMLReader methods make this extension extremely easy to use in control structures.

The remaining methods within the cReader class are fairly straightforward. The name and value properties retrieve the needed XML information. If you compare these methods to the equivalent ones from the previous chapter, you will find little difference other than how the XML information is passed and obtained. It also demonstrates how simple it can be to convert an existing application using the xml extension rather than using the XMLReader extension.

Again, you can customize this example if you like to use custom XML tree storage rather than the DOM extension. The DOM extension was used only for brevity, because it natively handles building an XML tree.

Conclusion

This chapter introduced the XMLReader extension as well as many of the advantages it has over the xml extension. As of PHP 5.1, XMLReader has been included as part of the core PHP distribution but is also available from PECL for those running PHP 5.0.*x*. The explanations, code snippets, and examples in this chapter should provide you with enough information to immediately begin using this API. You can find additional real-world uses in Chapters 14 and 17. These may also help you understand some of the benefits of using XMLReader for XML processing.

XMLReader is the last of the native XML parsers in PHP. The next chapter will introduce you to XSLT and the XSL extension. You will begin to look at how you can transform XML data from one structure to another. If you have ever wondered how to use XML as a data source to produce many different types of output, such as HTML, XHTML, WAP, and so on, then the XSL extension is most likely what you have been seeking. Not only will you examine the extension, but you will learn how to write XSL templates as well.

■ ■ ■

CHAPTER 10

Extensible Stylesheet Language Transformations (XSLT)

The parsers you have read about allow applications to process XML data. Two of them, DOM and SimpleXML, are directly relevant when working with the XSL extension. DOM is the primary and required extension when working with the XSL extension, but as you will see in this chapter, you can also pass documents from SimpleXML to the XSL extension. Before proceeding with this chapter, you should make sure you have at least a basic understanding of what DOM and SimpleXML are and how they work.

This chapter will introduce Extensible Stylesheet Language (XSL) and Extensible Stylesheet Language Transformations (XSLT) and show how to create style sheets for transforming data. I will show how to use some of the common features in the language to create these style sheets. With a working knowledge of the XSLT basics, you will then look at the XSL extension and how you can use it with style sheets to transform XML data.

■**Note** The first part of this chapter deals with general information about XSL and XSLT, including how to build style sheets. If you already understand XSL style sheets, you may want to skip to the "Introducing the XSL Extension" section where I will discuss the PHP XSL extension specifically.

Introducing XSL and XSLT

You have already been exposed to an XSL language in Chapter 4, XPath. You can find out more about XSL, a W3C specification, at `http://www.w3.org/TR/xsl/`. While XML defines languages that describe data, XSL defines languages that can transform data, navigate documents, use XPath, and format XML documents. The term *XSL* is often misused, because many people think it is the same as XSLT, which is what this chapter is about, but in fact, XSLT is a subset of XSL.

You can find more information about XSLT, also a W3C specification, at `http://www.w3.org/TR/xslt`. It is a language written in XML that can transform an XML document into another XML document. For example, you can use XSLT to take some XML data and, using a style sheet, transform it into other output, such as XHTML or WAP, using an XSL processor. The processor in this case is the PHP XSL extension. Listing 10-1 shows an example of a style sheet written using XSLT.

Listing 10-1. *Sample XSLT Style Sheet*

```
<?xml version="1.0" encoding="UTF-8" ?>
<xsl:stylesheet xmlns:xsl="http://www.w3.org/1999/XSL/Transform" version="1.0">
  <xsl:output method="html"/>
  <xsl:template match="/">
    <html>
      <body>
        <xsl:apply-templates select="/sites/site"/>
      </body>
    </html>
  </xsl:template>
  <xsl:template match="/sites/site">
    <p><xsl:value-of select="./name"/> : <xsl:value-of select="./url"/></p>
  </xsl:template>
</xsl:stylesheet>
```

This style sheet may look familiar. You first saw it in Chapter 5. Looking at it more closely, you may notice XPath syntax. XSLT utilizes XPath for navigational functionality, processing functionality, and text-generation functionality. At this point, you should understand the XPath language. (You can find detailed coverage of XPath in Chapter 4.) With a general idea of what XSLT is and what it's used for, you can examine the style sheet to figure out what it is doing and how to write one.

Introducing Style Sheets

Style sheets define template rules that can identity and transform data from a source XML document. You create a style sheet using elements that are defined by the XSLT specification and are bound to the `http://www.w3.org/1999/XSL/Transform` namespace URI. Throughout this chapter, I will use the prefix `xsl` to refer to the XSLT namespace. Creating a style sheet begins with the root element, which must be either the `xsl:stylesheet` element or the `xsl:transform` element:

```
<xsl:stylesheet xmlns:xsl="http://www.w3.org/1999/XSL/Transform" version="1.0" />
<xsl:transform xmlns:xsl="http://www.w3.org/1999/XSL/Transform" version="1.0" />
```

The choice of element to use is completely up to you when creating a style sheet, but the most commonly one used is the `xsl:stylesheet` element. No matter which element you choose to use, they both must define the XSLT namespace, which in these examples is associated with the `xsl` prefix but may be associated with any prefix you choose.

The `version` attribute is also required and typically set to `1.0`. Any value other than this enables forward-compatible processing. I will explain this in more detail in the "Using Output" section, but for now it just means that when the `version` attribute has any value other than `1.0`, an XSLT processor based on the XSLT version 1.0 specification will bend some of the rules and ignore certain instances that would cause an error according to the XSLT 1.0 specification.

■**Note** The style sheets explained in this chapter are full style sheets and not simplified inline XSLT. You can use simplified inline versions only for style sheets containing a single template for the root node. The XSLT namespace and version are defined on the root node, and XSLT elements are then embedded directly into the output, rather than output tags being embedded within templates. The majority of style sheets you will encounter in the real world will be complete style sheets. With an understanding of them, you will have no problem understanding a simplified style sheet if you ever run into one.

Introducing Templates

Templates define rules that are processed when a matching node is encountered. You specify them using an xsl:template element:

```
<xsl:template match="pattern" name="qname" priority="number" mode="qname" />
```

An xsl:template element doesn't do much by itself because the rules are defined with the scope of the element, but its attributes do define how data is to be processed by the rules.

The match Attribute

The match attribute specifies the node from the XML data document for which the rule set applies. The value of the attribute is a *pattern*. (This is a term you should be familiar with because it refers to an XPath pattern from Chapter 4.) XSLT locates nodes in a document using XPath patterns. Notice the two xsl:template elements in the style sheet in Listing 10-1:

```
<xsl:template match="/">
<xsl:template match="/sites/site">
```

The first element matches on /, which refers to the root node of the XML data document. The second element uses the pattern /sites/site. Based on what you read in Chapter 4, this will match all site elements that are children of the document element, which is sites. This attribute is not always required and depends upon whether the name attribute is being used and how the template is being called.

The name Attribute

The name attribute defines a name for the current template. As you will see shortly in the "Using Templates" section, you can call templates by name rather than by matching nodes. When calling a template in this manner, the match attribute is not required since it's not going to be used. When both match and name attributes are defined, you can call the template either by node matching or by name. This means a match attribute, a name attribute, or both attributes can exist on this element, but at least one is required.

The priority Attribute

You can use priority attributes to help resolve conflicts between matching templates. Templates having a higher priority take precedence over other matching templates. For example, given two templates where one matches the node() pattern and the other matches the element's `site` pattern, a `site` element node would match both templates. Assigning priorities to these templates allows the correct one to be selected:

```
<xsl:template match="node()" priority="0" />
<xsl:template match="site" priority="1" />
```

When matching on a `site` element node, the second template is chosen, even though it matches both templates, because the `priority` value 1 is higher than the `priority` value 0 in the first template. This can become quite complicated when defining many templates because it is up to you to keep track of all the `priority` values. The value for this attribute is a numeric.

When the `priority` attribute is not specified, XSLT computes a default value based on a set of criteria:

- A pattern with a QName or PI literal preceded by a child or attribute axis specifier has a priority of 0.

- A pattern with a name preceded by a child or attribute axis specifier has a priority of -0.25.

- A pattern testing for node type preceded by a child or attribute axis specifier has a priority of -0.5.

- All other patterns have a priority of 0.5.

So, based on these rules, the `xsl:template` element matching on * has a priority of -0.5, and the one that matches on `sites/site` has a priority of 0.5, unless a `priority` attribute is explicitly used.

The mode Attribute

The `mode` attribute is another mechanism to handle conflicting template matches. You can use this attribute only when a `match` attribute is specified on the `xsl:template` element. As you will see later in the "Applying Templates" section, this attribute is similar to using a `name` attribute, except it works with the `match` attribute. This probably gives you an idea of what might be coming up when you get into applying templates. If you have no idea why this may be useful, then the next section will be helpful.

Using Templates

When processing style sheets, the template matching the root node, `match="/"`, is automatically processed because of some built-in default templates (which are explained later in the "Using Built-in Templates" section). For example, the following is a modified version of the style sheet from Listing 10-1:

```
<?xml version="1.0" encoding="iso-8859-1"?>
<xsl:stylesheet xmlns:xsl="http://www.w3.org/1999/XSL/Transform" version="1.0">
  <xsl:output method="html"/>
  <xsl:template match="/">
```

```
    <html>
      <body>
          Some text
      </body>
    </html>
  </xsl:template>
  <xsl:template match="/sites/site">
    <p><xsl:value-of select="./name"/> : <xsl:value-of select="./url"/></p>
  </xsl:template>
</xsl:stylesheet>
```

Two templates are still defined, but the content of the body element has been changed to not use the XSLT language. The following XML data will be used for the transformation against this new style sheet:

```
<?xml version="1.0" encoding="iso-8859-1"?>
<sites>
   <site>
      <name>PHP</name>
      <url>http://www.php.net/</url>
   </site>
   <site>
      <name>XML C Parser</name>
      <url>http://www.xmlsoft.org/</url>
   </site>
</sites>
```

When the transformation occurs, the resulting data is as follows:

```
<html><body>
                Some text
      </body></html>
```

Ignore the formatting because this is based on the spacing used within the style sheet. The output, though, shows that the template matching the root node, /, was called, but the one matching /sites/site was not. The output consists of the content of the matched xsl:template element that is not from the http://www.w3.org/1999/XSL/Transform name-space. The output is not usually a snapshot of the xsl:template content, as it is here. The XSLT language is usually intermixed with other content to allow for more advanced transformations, as you will see later in the "Using Templates and XSLT" section.

Applying Templates

If you look closely at this new style sheet and the one from Listing 10-1, you will notice that the xsl:apply-templates element was removed. This element is what is used to access other templates within the style sheet:

```
<xsl:apply-templates select="node-set-expression" mode="qname" />
```

The xsl:apply-templates element has two attributes, neither of which is required.

The `select` attribute specifies a node set to be processed based on the value of the attribute, which is an XPath expression. Taking the `xsl:apply-templates` element from the style sheet in Listing 10-1, `<xsl:apply-templates select="/sites/site"/>`, the `select` attribute results in the node set containing all `site` elements that are children on the document element, which is `sites`. When the main template is processed and this element is encountered, the node set from the XML data document, based on the XPath expression, is processed. This results in the second template, `<xsl:template match="/sites/site">`, being called because the node set from the `xsl:apply-templates` `select` attribute matches the `match` attribute on the second `xsl:template`. So, this time, running the `sites` XML data document against the original template in Listing 10-1, the results include the output from the second template, as follows:

```
<html><body>
<p>PHP : http://www.php.net/</p>
<p>XML C Parser : http://www.xmlsoft.org/</p>
</body></html>
```

Absolute paths are not required for the `match` attribute or the `select` attribute. Each operates using the current node as the context. Based on this, Listing 10-2 shows an equivalent style sheet to the one in Listing 10-1.

Listing 10-2. *Alternative Expressions in Style Sheet*

```xml
<?xml version="1.0" encoding="iso-8859-1"?>
<xsl:stylesheet xmlns:xsl="http://www.w3.org/1999/XSL/Transform" version="1.0">
  <xsl:output method="html"/>
  <xsl:template match="/">
    <html>
      <body>
        <xsl:apply-templates select="sites/site" />
      </body>
    </html>
  </xsl:template>
  <xsl:template match="site">
    <p><xsl:value-of select="./name"/> : <xsl:value-of select="./url"/></p>
  </xsl:template>
</xsl:stylesheet>
```

The `xsl:apply-templates` element selects all `site` elements that are children of the `sites` elements, which in turn are children of the context node, which in this case is the document node. It works just like XPath in this respect. The `xsl:template` element matches on all `site` element nodes. Running the data against this style sheet produces the same output.

Omitting the `select` attribute results in all the child nodes of the current context node to be used for the node set. You could change the `xsl:apply-templates` and `xsl:template` elements to reflect this:

```
<xsl:apply-templates />
```

```
<xsl:template match="sites/site">
```

Using the current style sheet, the output will be the same, even though the node set from `xsl:apply-templates` is a bit different. Originally, the node set was being explicitly set. In this case, the children of the document node, which could possibly include text nodes, comments, and PIs, are being used for the node set. You must be careful when omitting the `select` attribute in the event that some data you might not have been expecting in the XML data suddenly appears.

The `mode` attribute specifies the mode to use when matching a template. When this attribute is present, it will match only against templates that have the same mode specified. When this attribute is omitted, it will match only against templates that also have omitted the `mode` attribute. This attribute can be useful when transforming data into different results based on some condition. For example, XML data that might be used for a publication will go through stages. Before reaching the released version, it may be in an editing stage where reviewers are commenting on the content. When processed in the editing stage, you would want these comments to be included with the output. You would also want to perform this using a single style sheet. In this case, you could define two templates that match the same expression but with different modes. When the document is to be processed, you could select the mode conditionally, such as by using parameters, which will be discussed in the "Using Variables and Parameters" section. The style sheet would end up having multiple elements for this:

```
<xsl:template match="chapter" mode="editing" />
<xsl:template match="chapter" mode="publish" />
```

You would then specify the template to use by setting the `mode` attribute on the `xsl:apply-templates` element:

```
<xsl:apply-templates select="chapter" mode="editing" />
```

Using Built-in Templates

When no matching template is found for a node set, XSLT uses some built-in templates in an attempt to process the data. The first template is used for the element and the root node. When no matching template is found when either of these nodes is being processed, the default template is as follows:

```
<xsl:template match="*|/">
   <xsl:apply-templates/>
</xsl:template>
```

This template just calls `xsl:apply-templates` without a `select` attribute to process all the child nodes of the current node. To see what this actually means, compare the following style sheet with those you have seen so far in this chapter:

```
<?xml version="1.0" encoding="iso-8859-1"?>
<xsl:stylesheet xmlns:xsl="http://www.w3.org/1999/XSL/Transform" version="1.0">
   <xsl:output method="html"/>
   <xsl:template match="site">
      <p><xsl:value-of select="./name"/> : <xsl:value-of select="./url"/></p>
   </xsl:template>
</xsl:stylesheet>
```

This has a single template matching `site` elements. The XSL processor first tries to match the root node. In this example, that template was removed. It ends up falling back on the built-in template, which in turn tries to apply templates on the child nodes, since no `select` attribute exists on the `xsl:apply-templates` element of the root node. At this point, the `sites` element is in the node set. Again, no matching template exists for this node, so the built-in template also processes it. This time the `site` elements are in the node set and do match a template defined in your style sheet. At this point, these nodes are processed, and no further recursion takes place on them. This doesn't mean that processing stops, because all the previous node sets will still be completely processed.

The second built-in template is almost the same as the first, except it also passes the `mode` attribute along. This applies only if a mode has been defined somewhere in the style sheet and, while in the context of the mode, a built-in template was called for a node in the node set. For example:

```
<xsl:template match="*|/" mode="m">
    <xsl:apply-templates mode="m"/>
</xsl:template>
```

The last built-in template that affects the results works with text and attribute nodes. If you have been playing around with changing some of the XPath used in this section, you might have noticed that spacing is sometimes different in the results. This is because of running into a text node being processed by a built-in template:

```
<xsl:template match="text()|@*">
    <xsl:value-of select="."/>
</xsl:template>
```

This template results in the output of the value of a text node or attribute. If you take the style sheet from Listing 10-2 and remove the `select` attribute (rather than using the expression `sites/site`) from the `xsl:apply-templates` element, you will notice that the document is spaced differently. Without the `select` attribute, all child nodes are selected for the node set, including text nodes. The style sheet does not define a template to handle text nodes, and whitespace text is not disabled (which is an option covered later in the "Using Output" section). In addition, the XSL processor uses the value of these text nodes, currently spaces and line feeds in the XML data, in the results.

Calling Templates

Previously, I mentioned that you can give templates names using the `name` attribute on the `xsl:template` element. You can call a template by name using the `xsl:call-template` element:

```
<xsl:call-template name="qname" />
```

Unlike the `xsl:apply-templates` element, this element does not allow a node set to be specified. Instead, it calls a template that has a matching value for the `name` attribute as that specified by the value of the `name` attribute on this element. The node set used is also the current node set being processed, rather than the children:

```
<xsl:template name="siteurl">
 : <xsl:value-of select="./url"/>
</xsl:template>

<xsl:template match="site">
   <p>
      <xsl:value-of select="./name" />
      <xsl:call-template name="siteurl" />
   </p>
</xsl:template>
```

When the last template, matching on site, is being processed, the site node is also processed by the named template siteurl to return the value of the url child element. Other than some additional line feeds and spaces this has introduced (which was done for easier readability), the results should be the same as the previously used style sheets working on the data set.

Using Templates and XSLT

So far you have seen basic templates and how to call them. The only results so far have used literal result elements (such as the HTML markup used within the templates) to show a few examples of the xsl:value-of element. This element is part of XSLT and will help you write rich style sheets. The following sections will explore some of the more commonly used elements and demonstrate how to use them.

Creating Nodes

You can create nodes in the transformed tree literally, as you have seen in the examples. The HTML tags used within the templates demonstrate this. When transformed, these nodes are automatically created within the result tree. Using the XSLT language, it is also possible to create nodes dynamically. This means node names and values do not need to be hard-coded within a template but can be created based on some criteria. I will now explain how to create different nodes and show examples of using the XSL elements for performing these operations.

Attribute Value Templates

Within many of the XSL elements that follow, some of the attribute values of the defining element are interpreted as attribute value templates, which allow the use of expressions. Curly braces surround expressions that are to be evaluated within the attribute value and look like {expression}. For example, to generate the local name of the current node in context along with the value of an attribute named num from the current node, the attribute value template would look like this:

{local-name(.)}{@num}

The attribute templates are not restricted to expressions only. You can also use literal values within these templates. Note that in order to use a literal curly brace, you must use double braces. The double braces will be replaced by a single brace. For instance, {{ evaluates to a literal {, and }} evaluates to a literal }. So, when writing these templates using this:

```
{local-name(.)}unevaluated{@num}
```

it evaluates to the following when the element `<site num="1" />` is in context:

```
siteunevaluated1
```

Creating Elements

Sometimes you need to create elements in the result trees and literal elements just won't do. For instance, you cannot add elements that are named based on values from the context node using literals. This is where you can use the `xsl:element` element:

```
<xsl:element name={qname} namespace={uri-reference} use-attribute-sets=qnames />
```

All attribute values of this element within the curly braces ({}) are interpreted as attribute value templates for the values. The final result of the template, though, must be the type specified. The content of this element is a template to define attributes and children of the element being created.

The name Attribute   The `name` attribute specifies the name of the element to be created. You can use it to mimic literal elements within the style sheet as well as to create dynamically named elements:

```
<!-- Using literal p elements -->
<p>
    <xsl:value-of select="./name" />
    <xsl:call-template name="siteurl" />
</p>
```

You can also use `xsl:element` to produce the same `<p></p>` tags in the result tree:

```
<xsl:element name="p">
    <xsl:value-of select="./name" />
    <xsl:call-template name="siteurl" />
</xsl:element>
```

The element name could also be dynamically created rather than using a hard-coded name. When sharing templates that match multiple nodes of the same name, you might want the name of the current node in the result tree. It doesn't make sense to write a bunch of conditional code, which I haven't explained yet, and hard-code names based on the conditions. Attribute templates come in handy in this case:

```
<xsl:element name="{local-name(.)}">
    <xsl:value-of select="./name"/> : <xsl:value-of select="./url"/>
</xsl:element>
```

Assuming this is within a matching template and an element named `site` is currently being processed, the portion of the resulting tree looks like the following (depending upon the values of the subnodes, of course):

```
<site>PHP : http://www.php.net/</site>
```

The only condition when using attribute value templates is that the final result must be a valid QName as defined in the XML specification.

The namespace Attribute The namespace attribute defines the namespace for the element when created. The value of this attribute is also interpreted as an attribute value template. The result of the attribute value template should be a URI reference, though it is not an error if it is not legal. When the QName has a prefix, it will be associated with the namespace; otherwise, the namespace is considered to be a default namespace. When it results in an empty string, the created element will be considered to have a NULL namespace. Using the same site element from the previous example as the context, the following code creates the resulting tree with namespaced elements:

```
<xsl:element name="ns:{local-name(.)}" namespace="http://www.example.com/ns">
   <xsl:element name="ns:{local-name(.)}" namespace="http://www.example.com/ns" />
   <xsl:element name="{local-name(.)}" namespace="http://www.example.com/ns" />
</xsl:element>
```

Here the first xsl:element will create an element with the QName ns:site with the ns prefix associated with the namespace http://www.example.com/ns. An empty child ns:site element is also created and bound to the same namespace. An additional site element is created, but this time without a prefix so the namespace will become the default namespace for the element in the results. Processing this snippet from the style sheet would result in the following piece of output:

```
<ns:site xmlns:ns="http://www.example.com/ns">
   <ns:site></ns:site>
   <site xmlns="http://www.example.com/ns"></site>
</ns:site>
```

The use-attribute-sets Attribute The use-attribute-sets attribute allows the use of a predefined set of attributes that will be created with the element. The value of this attribute is a whitespace-separated list of attribute set names. Before you try to understand what attribute sets are, you first need to understand how attributes are created.

Creating Attributes

You can create attributes in the same manner as elements. The xsl:attribute element defines a new attribute:

```
<xsl:attribute name={qname} namespace={uri-reference} />
```

You define the attributes of this element in the same way as the respective attributes from the xsl:element element. The content of this attribute defines the value for the created attribute:

```
<xsl:element name="site">
   <xsl:attribute name="{local-name(.)}att">
      <xsl:value-of select="@num"/>
   </xsl:attribute>
</xsl:element>
```

Based on this code, an element named `site` will be created with an attribute named by appending `att` to the local name of the context node. Its value will be set by the value of the `num` attribute of the current context node. Using an element node defined by `<site num="1" />` as the context would result in the following:

```
<site siteatt="1"></site>
```

Named Attribute Sets

You can group sets of attributes within a named attribute set so that you do not need to add each individual attribute every time you need it:

```
<xsl:attribute-set name=qname use-attribute-sets=qnames />
```

The `name` attribute specifies the name of the named attribute set being defined. The value is a literal QName and *not* an attribute value template like you saw with previous elements. The value specified by the name is what is used to reference the attribute set from other elements such as the value specified by the `use-attribute-sets` attribute from the `xsl:element` element. The `use-attribute-sets` attribute on the `xsl:attribute` set element can specify additional named attribute sets that this `name` attribute set includes. The value consists of a list of `name` attribute sets separated by whitespace. Attributes that are being defined within the attribute set, and not coming from other attribute sets from the `use-attribute-sets` attribute, are defined within the content of the `xsl:attribute-set` element. For example:

```
<xsl:attribute-set name="attset1">
   <xsl:attribute name="att1">1</xsl:attribute>
</xsl:attribute-set>

<xsl:attribute-set name="attset2" use-attribute-sets="attset1">
   <xsl:attribute name="att2">2</xsl:attribute>
</xsl:attribute-set>

<xsl:template match="site">
   <xsl:element name="site" use-attribute-sets="attset2">
      <xsl:attribute name="att3">3</xsl:attribute>
   </xsl:element>
</xsl:template>
```

This code defines two attribute sets. The set `attset1` defines a single attribute named `att1` having the value 1. The set `attset2` uses the named attribute set `attset1` as well as defines an attribute named `att2` having the value 2. When `attset2` is referenced from another element, such as the `xsl:element` element in the previous code, it would have the same effect as defining the `att1` and `att2` `xsl:attribute` elements within the content of the `xsl:element` element. Assuming the previous `xsl:element` is within a matched template, the result from the processing would be as follows:

```
<site att1="1" att2="2" att3="3"></site>
```

It is important to note that the same rules for the xsl:attribute element, such as using expressions, pertain when used within attribute sets. Any expression would be evaluated just as if the xsl:attribute elements had been defined within the content of the xsl:element element.

Caution It is an error for an attribute to directly or indirectly reference itself.

Creating Text

You can easily create text using literal text as well as some other XSLT elements not yet introduced. Even so, you can also use the xsl:text element to explicitly create text in the results because it offers a bit of control over how the text is handled:

```
<xsl:text disable-output-escaping = "yes" | "no" />
```

The content of this element is what is to be used as the content of the resulting text node. It may be controlled to a degree using the disable-output-escaping attribute. This attribute may have the value yes or no and determines whether the text within the contents of the xsl:text element will be escaped in the resulting XML document. By default, the XSL processor will escape characters, so the default attribute value is no. For example:

```
<xsl:text disable-output-escaping="yes">
   This &amp; That
<xsl:text>
```

```
<xsl:text disable-output-escaping="no">
   This &amp; That
</xsl:text>
```

The difference between these two is significant. Processing the first will result in This & That as the content in the final resulting XML document, which in reality is malformed XML. The second block instructs the XSLT processor to escape the text content using the disable-output-escaping attribute with the value no, which results in the text This & That, which is legal and well-formed XML. The attribute, in this case, didn't need to be specified since it uses no, which is the default value anyway. This is something to keep in mind, especially when processing CDATA sections that have not been converted to text nodes because the disable-output-escaping attribute will not work with CDATA sections. (This is covered in more detail in the "Using Output" section.)

Creating Processing Instructions

You can create PIs just like all the other node types you have seen so far. You do this using the xsl:processing-instruction element:

```
<xsl:processing-instruction name={ncname} />
```

The name attribute, whose value is interpreted as an attribute value template, specifies the target of the PI being created. The content of the element defines the data for the PI:

```
<xsl:processing-instruction name="php">
  print "Hello World";
</xsl:processing-instruction>
```

When this block is encountered within a template, it creates the following PI:

```
<?php print "Hello World"; ?>
```

■**Caution** When the output method is html, processing instructions are terminated by > and not by ?>. This means you need to manually add ? as part of the content of the xsl:processing-instruction element.

Creating Comments

Comments are another type of node you can create dynamically; you do this by using the xsl:comment element:

```
<xsl:comment />
```

As you may notice, this element has no attributes, and its content defines the text for the comment:

```
<xsl:comment>
  Node named <xsl:value-of select="local-name()" /> was processed
</xsl:comment>
```

Using the site element from the XML data source as an example, a comment is dynamically generated when this element is processed within a template. Although the xsl:value-of element has not yet been introduced, you might already have an idea of what it does. The comment will include the literal text as well as the local name of the node in context when processed:

```
<!-- Node named site was processed -->
```

Copying Nodes

You can copy nodes directly to the result tree using the xsl:copy element or the xsl:copy-of element. The differences between these two are the depth of the actual copy and the node to be copied.

xsl:copy This is the syntax for xsl:copy:

```
<xsl:copy use-attribute-sets=qnames />
```

The copy is only a shallow copy, so attributes and child nodes are not part of the copied node. Namespace nodes, however, are copied along with the node. When the node being copied is an element type node, you can use the `use-attribute-sets` attribute to indicate the named attribute set to be created with the copied element. For example:

```
<xsl:template match="site">
    <xsl:copy use-attribute-sets="attset2" />
    <xsl:copy />
    <xsl:copy>Some Text</xsl:copy>
</xsl:template>
```

When a `site` element is matched against this template, three copies of the element are created in the resulting tree. The first `xsl:copy` creates attributes based on the `name` attribute set, `attset2`. The second `xsl:copy` copies only the element, which ends up being the open element tag with a closing element tag because no attributes or children are copied and no named attribute set has been specified. The third `xsl:copy` element creates a copy of the element and adds text content. It would also be valid for the content of the `xsl:copy` element to create attributes and apply other templates. Applying this template to one of the `site` elements produces the following:

```
<site att2="2" att1="1"/>
<site/>
<site>Some Text</site>
```

xsl:copy-of The `xsl:copy-of` element performs a deep copy of the node. Namespaces, attributes, and children are all copied along with the node. Here's the syntax:

```
<xsl:copy-of
    select = expression />
```

The value of the `select` attribute specifies the expression used to define the node set or result tree fragment to be copied into the result tree. An expression evaluating to any other type causes the results to be converted to a string and inserted into the result tree. This case would be similar to having called `xsl:value-of` with the expression. Later in the "Using Variables and Parameters" section, you will be introduced to the concepts of variables and parameters in XSLT. These add a data type called a *result tree fragment*, which is similar to the `DOMDocumentFragment` object. The `xsl:copy-of` element is efficient in handling these, as well as node sets, when they are to added to the final result tree. Rather than converting the nodes to strings, the nodes can be copied directly to the resulting tree. For example:

```
<xsl:template match="site">
    <xsl:copy-of select="." />
</xsl:template>
```

The following is an example of a portion of the resulting tree using this template:

```
<site num="2">
    <name>XML C Parser</name>
    <url>http://www.xmlsoft.org/libxslt/index.php</url>
</site>
```

Text Generation

The xsl:value-of element is an element you have seen many times within the examples but has yet to be fully explained. You can use it to generate text nodes in the resulting tree:

```
<xsl:value-of select=string-expression disable-output-escaping = "yes" | "no" />
```

The difference between this element and the xsl:text element is because of the select attribute on the xsl:value-of element. This element takes no child elements like many of the other ones and uses the results from the select attribute to generate the text. The results from the select attribute are automatically converted to a string if not so already, just as if the string function were called. In the event the expression results in an empty string, no text node is created. The disable-output-escaping attribute works the same way as the attribute on the xsl:text element works. For example:

```
<xsl:template match="site">
   <p><xsl:value-of select="./name"/> : <xsl:value-of select="./url"/></p>
</xsl:template>
```

A site element matching this template would have text nodes created from the xsl:value-of elements based on the resulting string from the child name and url elements:

```
<p>PHP : http://www.php.net/</p>
```

Example Generating an HTML Document

Before continuing, I will demonstrate many of the concepts presented so far using a small example that transforms some XML data into an HTML page. The page will end up containing two links with a description of each link. I will use the following XML document for the input data:

```
<?xml version="1.0" encoding="iso-8859-1"?>
<sites>
   <site>
      <name>PHP</name>
      <url>http://www.php.net/</url>
      <description>PHP: Hypertext Preprocessor</description>
   </site>
   <site>
      <name>XML C Parser</name>
      <url>http://www.xmlsoft.org/</url>
      <description>The XML C parser and toolkit of Gnome</description>
   </site>
</sites>
```

This document is almost a duplicate of the previous one in this chapter. I have added a child element to each site element, providing a short description of the site. I will use the following style sheet to transform this data:

```
<?xml version="1.0" encoding="iso-8859-1"?>
<xsl:stylesheet xmlns:xsl="http://www.w3.org/1999/XSL/Transform" version="1.0">
  <xsl:output method="html"/>
```

```
<xsl:template match="/">
   <html>
      <body>
         <!-- Process the site elements -->
         <xsl:apply-templates select="/sites/site" />

      </body>
   </html>
</xsl:template>

<xsl:template match="site">
   <!-- Build the anchor tag -->
   <xsl:comment>Link for <xsl:value-of select="name" /></xsl:comment>
   <a>
      <xsl:attribute name="href">
         <xsl:value-of select="url" />
      </xsl:attribute>
      <xsl:value-of select="name"/>
   </a>

   <!-- display description in a paragraph -->
   <p><xsl:value-of select="description"/></p>

</xsl:template>
</xsl:stylesheet>
```

Upon transformation, the main template matches the root node. Not only does this provide the skeleton HTML, but it also instructs the processor to apply templates to the site elements.

For each of the site elements in the XML document, a comment is created that includes the addition of the value of the name element within the comment. An anchor tag is then created, in which an href attribute must be built. The value of this attribute is pulled from the url element from the current site element being processed. The content of the anchor tag, which is the clickable text displayed when rendered, is then taken from the name element. Last, the value of the description element is added within p tags. This occurs once for each site element within the XML document and in this case would be twice. Figure 10-1 shows the output in a browser when finally rendered.

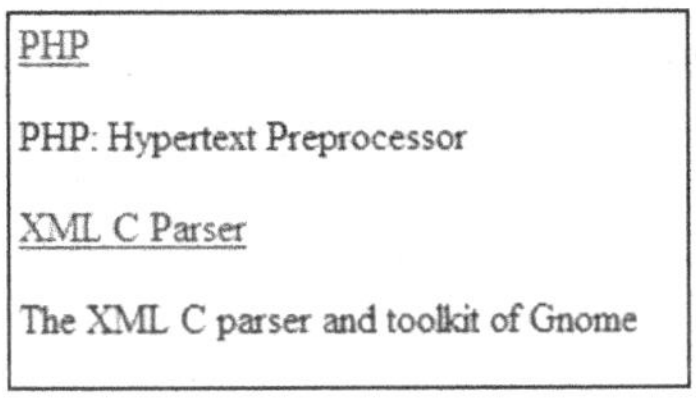

```
PHP

PHP: Hypertext Preprocessor

XML C Parser

The XML C parser and toolkit of Gnome
```

Figure 10-1. *HTML output of transformation view in browser*

Performing Repetitive Processing

It is not required that nodes always be processed using the xsl:apply-templates element or the xsl:call-template element. You can choose a node set and directly instantiate a template using the xsl:for-each element. This element will iterate through the selected node set, and its contents will be used as the template for each node in the set:

```
<xsl:for-each select=node-set-expression>
   <!-- Content: (xsl:sort*, template) -->
</xsl:for-each>
```

The select attribute defines the expression used to select the nodes to be iterated, just as it has worked on many of the other elements in XSLT. The content of this element is the template for the selected node set. You might notice the xsl:sort element in the definition as well. I will discuss this element in the "Sorting" section, but basically you can use it to define the sort order of the node set being iterated:

```
<xsl:for-each select="/sites/site">
   <p><xsl:value-of select="./name"/> : <xsl:value-of select="./url"/></p>
</xsl:for-each>
```

This syntax often depends upon coding style. If you think about what this is actually doing, you might wonder what the difference is between using this and using xsl:apply-templates. Either of these will take the set of site nodes and result in the same set of nodes in the resulting tree. My recommendation, however, is to lean toward using xsl:apply-templates and to fall back on xsl:for-each only if necessary. For instance, you could rewrite the previous block using the following:

```
<xsl:template match="site">
   <p><xsl:value-of select="./name"/> : <xsl:value-of select="./url"/></p>
</xsl:template>

<!-- assume following called in scope of sites element with site children -->
<xsl:apply-templates />
```

This also adds a bit more reusability to the style sheet because the site elements are handled by a common template rather than handled directly inline where the xsl:for-each element is used.

Performing Conditional Processing

The xsl:if and xsl:choose elements provide support for conditional processing within templates. Using conditionals is another instance, like xsl:for-each, that in many cases could be handled by calling another template. Again, it comes down to coding style and how style sheets are managed.

xsl:if

The xsl:if element works as a simple if/then statement:

```
<xsl:if test=boolean-expression>
   <!-- Content: template -->
</xsl:if>
```

The test attribute specifies the expression to test. It is evaluated as a Boolean, and when it evaluates to TRUE, the contents of the xsl:if element are processed. There is no else case for this element, so an evaluation of FALSE would skip over any processing defined in the content:

```
<xsl:template match="site">
   <xsl:if test="@num = 2">
      <p><xsl:value-of select="./url"/></p>
   </xsl:if>
</xsl:template>
```

Using the sites document you have been using in this chapter, the num attribute is tested for the value 2 when the site elements match this template. Only the site element passing this condition is processed by the contents of the xsl:if element, which would result in the following:

```
<p>XML C Parser : http://www.xmlsoft.org/</p>
```

As previously mentioned, you could also do this using xsl:apply-templates:

```
<xsl:template match="/sites/site">
   <p><xsl:value-of select="./url"/></p>
</xsl:template>

<!-- Called within the template matching document node -->
<xsl:apply-templates select="sites/site[@num=2]"/>
```

The test is not always this simple, and in some cases it might just be too difficult or might create some unreadability issues when trying to force the use of the apply-templates element. Again, it comes down to coding style, extensibility, and manageability when deciding which type to use.

xsl:choose

The xsl:choose element, along with the xsl:when and xsl:otherwise elements, is used to test for multiple conditions, each with different results. It has a similar effect as using if/elseif/else statements in PHP:

```
<xsl:choose>
   <!-- Content: (xsl:when+, xsl:otherwise?) -->
</xsl:choose>

<xsl:when test=boolean-expression>
   <!-- Content: template -->
</xsl:when>

<xsl:otherwise>
   <!-- Content: template -->
</xsl:otherwise>
```

The xsl:choose element is the container for the conditional. It consists of one or more xsl:when elements followed by an optional xsl:otherwise element. The xsl:when element defines the expression to test using the test attribute. This is the same as the test attribute on the xsl:if element. When it evaluates to TRUE, the content of the element is instantiated; otherwise, the next xsl:when element is tested. If all the tests from the xsl:when elements fail, the content from the xsl:otherwise element, if present, is instantiated. For example:

```
<xsl:template match="/sites/site">
    <xsl:choose>
        <xsl:when test="@num=1">
            <xsl:value-of select="./url"/>
        </xsl:when>
        <xsl:when test="@num=3">
            Site Number 3
        </xsl:when>
        <xsl:otherwise>
            No matching Sites
        </xsl:otherwise>
    </xsl:choose>
</xsl:template>
```

This template tests the num attribute of the current site element in context. When using the following XML data with a style sheet containing the template:

```
<?xml version="1.0" encoding="iso-8859-1"?>
<sites>
    <site num="1">
        <name>PHP</name>
        <url>http://www.php.net/</url>
    </site>
    <site num="2">
        <name>XML C Parser</name>
        <url>http://www.xmlsoft.org/</url>
    </site>
</sites>
```

the resulting tree from the template would be as follows:

```
http://www.php.net/
No matching Sites
```

Sorting

You can sort node sets within an xsl:apply-templates or xsl:for-each element using an xsl:sort element. When used within an xsl:for-each element, it must be the first child element but may come after an xsl:param element within the contents of an xsl:apply-templates element:

```
<xsl:sort select = string-expression

        lang = { nmtoken }                                                    ‘
        data-type = { "text" | "number" | qname-but-not-ncname }
        order = { "ascending" | "descending" }
        case-order = { "upper-first" | "lower-first" } />
```

This element specifies the sort key for the node set from the parent element. You can use multiple xsl:sort elements to create sort keys, which are then processed in order.

The sort key is created based on the resulting string from the expression defined in the select attribute. When not present, the select attribute defaults to ., causing the text value of the current node to be used as the sort key. For example:

```
<xsl:for-each select="/people/person">
   <xsl:sort select="./last-name" />
   <xsl:sort select="./first-name" />
   <p>
      <xsl:value-of select="./last-name"/>. <xsl:value-of select="./first-name"/>
   </p>
   <xsl:text>
   </xsl:text>
</xsl:for-each>
```

This for-each selects all person elements that are children of the people element, sorts them by last-name, and then sorts them by the first-name elements that are children of the person elements. This may sound a bit confusing and is much easier to see in an example. The xsl:text element has been inserted to allow line feeds to be inserted. The following XML data is used for the input:

```
<people>
    <person>     .
        <first-name>John</first-name>
        <last-name>Smith</last-name>
    </person>
    <person>
        <first-name>Tom</first-name>
        <last-name>Jones</last-name>
    </person>
    <person>
        <first-name>Joe</first-name>
        <last-name>Smith</last-name>
    </person>
</people>
```

The resulting output is as follows:

```
<p>Jones, Tom</p>
<p>Smith, Joe</p>
<p>Smith, John</p>
```

The remaining optional attributes on this element control how the list of sort keys is sorted. The values for these attributes are all attribute template values so may be dynamically created.

The lang Attribute

The lang attribute specifies the language of the sort keys. The acceptable values for this attribute follow the same rules as those for an xml:lang attribute (http://www.w3.org/TR/REC-xml/#sec-lang-tag). When not specified, the language is determined from the system environment. For example, to specify German as the language used for the sort keys, you would write the element as <xsl:sort lang="de" />.

The data-type Attribute

The data-type attribute specifies how the value of the resulting select expression should be interpreted for sorting purposes. The possible value for this attribute is text (which is the default value), number, or a QName. Any other value other than text or number should not be used. Using a QName for this attribute, which would be any valid QName other than the string text or number, is dependant upon a specific processor that understands what the value of the QName represents. The value text causes the data to be sorted lexicographically according to the language specified by the lang attribute.

The order Attribute

The order attribute accepts either ascending or descending for its value and determines whether the data should be ordered by the respective value. The default value for this attribute is ascending.

The case-order Attribute

The case-order attribute is valid only when the data-type is text, which of course is the default type for the data-type attribute. It can have the value lower-first or upper-first, and the default value is dependant upon the language (the value of the lang attribute) used for the keys.

Note ·With the current version of libxslt, 1.1.14 (which is the XSLT library used for PHP 5), the case-order and lang attributes have not yet been implemented and will have no bearing on sort orders.

Numbering

The xsl:number element inserts formatted numbers into the results tree:

```
<xsl:number
    level = "single" | "multiple" | "any"
    count = pattern
    from = pattern
    value = number-expression
```

```
format = { string }
lang = { nmtoken }
letter-value = { "alphabetic" | "traditional" }
grouping-separator = { char }
grouping-size = { number } />
```

The value attribute contains an expression that is converted to a number as if the number function had been executed on the result of the expression. The number is then rounded to an integer and converted to a string based on the values of the format, lang, letter-value, grouping-separator, and grouping-size attributes. The actual process for the number-to-string conversion is beyond the scope of this chapter. You can find information about how to use these attributes to control the conversion in the XSLT specification at http://www.w3.org/TR/xslt#convert.

The grouping-separator and grouping-size attributes are both optional, but unless they both are specified on the element, either one is ignored by itself. These attributes define how and what separators are used for a number. For example, a comma is typically used to separate thousands within a number. Think of it in terms of the number_format() function in PHP, except it has no decimals or decimal places. The grouping-separator attribute specifies the character used to separate the digits, just like the thousands_sep parameter. Unlike the PHP function, the separator is not forced to separate thousands. Although it typically separates every three digits, it can separate at any number of digits. For example, the following:

```
<xsl:number grouping-separator="," grouping-size="3" value="1000000" />
```

results in this:

```
1,000,000
```

Changing the separator character to the pound sign (#) and grouping on every two digits, like so:

```
<xsl:number grouping-separator="#," grouping-size="2" value="1000000" />
```

results in the following:

```
1#00#00#00
```

When the value attribute is not specified, a number based on the position of the current node in the source XML document is inserted. The attributes level, count, and from can control how this number is derived. The following descriptions come from the XSLT specifications:

- The level attribute specifies what levels of the source tree should be considered; it has the value single, multiple, or any. The default is single.

- The count attribute is a pattern that specifies what nodes should be counted at those levels. If the count attribute is not specified, then it defaults to the pattern that matches any node with the same node type as the current node and, if the current node has an expanded name, with the same expanded name as the current node.

- The from attribute is a pattern that specifies where counting starts.

The number constructed using the level, count, and from attributes is driven by the value of the level attribute. It determines which nodes will be used to match against the expressions defined in the count and from attributes. The following document demonstrates how to use these attributes:

```
<book>
    <chapter>
        <section>
            <p>c1 s1 p1</p>
        </section>
    </chapter>
    <chapter>
        <section>
            <p>c2 s1 p1</p>
        </section>
        <section>
            <p>c2 s2 p1</p>
            <p node="context">c2 s2 p2</p>
            <p>c2 s2 p3</p>
        </section>
        <section>
            <p>c2 s3 p1</p>
        </section>
    </chapter>
</book>
```

The node that will be used as the context node is the p element having the attribute node with the value context. In XPath terms, the node can be identified by the expression /book/chapter[2]/section[2]/p[@node='context'].

When level="single", it searches for the first node in the ancestor-or-self axis that matches the count pattern. Once a node has been found, it counts the number of preceding siblings of this node that also match the count pattern and adds 1 to the count. The reason for the count being incremented by 1 is to take into account the first matching node. If the from attribute is specified, then the search is limited to ancestors of the node that are also descendants of the nearest ancestor matching the from pattern:

```
<xsl:number level='single' count='p' />
```

When used within a style sheet against the context node, this would return 2. The first matching node ends up being the context node. The number of preceding sibling nodes that are named p, based on the pattern specified by the value of the count attribute, are then counted. In this case, you have only a single preceding sibling, and it matches, so the count is 1. You then add 1 to this number, which causes the final result to be 2.

When level="multiple", the search works in a similar manner to single, except in this case, once a match is found, the search continues moving up one level in the hierarchy, allowing multiple nodes to be located. Counting is then performed for each of the located nodes using the pattern defined by the count attribute to match against previous siblings. The value returned is a list of numbers based on the results of each count. They are ordered based on the location of the node, found from the search, in document order. The `from` attribute works in the same manner as described for using `single`:

```
<xsl:number level='multiple' count='chapter|section|p' />
```

Here the `count` pattern will match elements named `chapter`, `section`, and p. This causes the search to locate the context node itself (matching on p), the parent element of p (matching on `section`), and the second `chapter` element in the document because it is the `chapter` node in the hierarchy of the context node. Based on document order, counting starts with the `chapter` element. The number of preceding siblings that match the `count` pattern is 1, which would be the first `chapter` element in the document. Then, 1 is then added to this to take into account the `chapter` node you are starting from, which results in 2. Counting is then performed using the next node in document order, which is the `section` element. There is only one preceding sibling that matches the pattern and adding 1 to this, the count also returns 2. Finally, the matching preceding siblings from the context node are counted. Again, only a single node matches, to which 1 is added, giving the final result of 2. The final value ultimately returned by this is `2.2.2`.

■**Note** You can control the value returned using the `format` attribute. In this case, the attribute was not specified, and each count was separated by a decimal. If you used the attribute `format="I.A.1"`, the result would have been `II.B.2` because the first numeric in the result would be formatted using Roman numerals, indicated by `I`; the second numeric would be an alpha based on its numeric position from `A`, where A is position 1; and the last numeric is returned as a numeric based on the use of `1` for the third position in the `format` value. The `xsl:number` element is quite useful, especially in a case like this where you could use it as a label indicating the current chapter, section, and paragraph.

When `level="any"`, simply every node that matches the `count` pattern and that either is the context node or precedes the context node in document order is counted. This means the count includes preceding sibling nodes and ancestor nodes of the context, which match the `count` pattern, as well as nodes matching the pattern within the subtrees of those nodes. If the `from` attribute is specified, then only nodes matching the `count` pattern that fall within the scope of the node matching the `from` pattern and its subtree (excluding any node that comes after the context node in document order) and the context node are counted. For example:

```
<xsl:number level='any' count='p' />
```

This returns the value 6. Only six p elements in the document consist of the context node and all the nodes that come before the context node in document order. The `from` attribute could limit this further to count only the p elements that fall within the context node and its ancestor `chapter` element:

```
<xsl:number level='any' count='p' from="chapter" />
```

This would return the value 4 because the p elements within the first `chapter` element are not within the scope being matched even though they do precede the context node in document order.

Using these attributes may be intimidating to those new to XPath and XSLT. It is a good idea to review the XPath material in Chapter 4, because it explains in more detail the organization of the tree, its axes, and its node sets.

Using Variables and Parameters

Variables and parameters allow values to be bound to a name using the elements xsl:variable and xsl:param. The actual names are a bit misleading because the difference between the two is that, once bound, the value for a variable cannot be changed; but when a value is bound to a parameter, the value acts only as the default value. Parameters can be passed to a template or style sheet that is used in place of the default values. For example: •

```
<xsl:variable
    name = qname
    select = expression>
    <!-- Content: template -->
</xsl:variable>

<xsl:param
    name = qname
    select = expression>
    <!-- Content: template -->
</xsl:param>
```

The name attribute is a required attribute for each of these elements. The value is a QName that specifies the name of the variable or parameter and is used to reference it within the style sheet. The select attribute is an optional attribute and can be used for an expression that, when evaluated, defines the value:

```
<xsl:param name="phpText" select="PHP" />
```

This creates a parameter named phpText with a default value consisting of the string PHP. Because the value of the select attribute is an expression, the value can be any resulting type of an expression valid under XPath. This means variables and parameters could even be node sets.

Using the select attribute is only one way to define a value. Each of these elements can also instantiate templates that become the value of the variable or parameter. Templates result in result trees, which consist of nodes. When defining the value within the content of the xsl:variable or xsl:param element, the element is bound to a resulting tree fragment. This means the resulting node set is wrapped within a root node, which is automatically created. If you are familiar with the DOM tree, it is equivalent to creating the resulting node set within a DOMDocumentFragment:

```
<xsl:param name="phpText">PHP</xsl:param>
```

Although this looks similar to the previous parameter of the same name, it is actually quite different. Using the select attribute select="PHP" results in the parameter phpText being bound to the string PHP. When the text PHP is used within the content of the xsl:param element, a text node with the value PHP is actually bound to the phpText parameter. Although this might not seem like a big difference, it actually could be, depending upon how the variable or parameter is used because it's not always the case that the node set operates in the same manner as a native string or numeric type would.

When the select attribute is not present and the element contains no content, the value is defined as an empty string:

```
<xsl:param name="emptyVar />
```

This is equivalent to writing the following:

```
<xsl:param name="emptyVar" select="'''" />
```

When referencing a variable or parameter, the name is prefixed with the dollar sign ($). Taking the previous binding for the emptyVar parameter, it would be used within an expression in the form of $emptyVar:

```
<xsl:value-of select="$emptyVar" />
```

Setting Global Variables and Style Sheet Parameters

Variables and parameters are used as top-level elements, meaning they are direct children of the xsl:stylesheet element, are declared globally, and are visible everywhere in the style sheet. As a result of parameters being able to be passed to style sheets and templates, top-level xsl:param elements declare parameter elements for the style sheet, which can be passed to the style sheet by an XSLT processor. The context of either of these types of elements, when residing as top-level elements, is the root node of the source document. This is something to keep in mind when writing any expressions for the values of these elements. It is also worthy to note that the values must be computed prior to the variable or parameter being referenced. For example:

```
<xsl:stylesheet xmlns:xsl="http://www.w3.org/1999/XSL/Transform" version="1.0">
    <xsl:param name="x" select="1"/>
    <xsl:template match="/">
        <value>
            <xsl:value-of select="$x" />
        </value>
    </xsl:template>
</xsl:stylesheet>
```

When a document is processed with this style sheet, the default results are as follows:

```
<value>1</value>
```

The XSLT processor may pass a different value for the parameter named x, such as the value 5. This time, processing the document results in the following:

```
<value>5</value>
```

Setting Variables and Parameters in Templates

Variables and parameters used within templates are local to those templates. In other words, they are visible to all sibling nodes and their descendants. All xsl:param elements must be declared as the first child elements of an xsl:template element. The xsl:variable elements, on the other hand, can be declared anywhere within the list of children of an `xsl:template` element. The parameter or variable, however, cannot be referenced by any elements that precede its declaration. For example:

```
<!-- ERROR: variable used before being declared -->
<xsl:template name="mytemplate">
    <xsl:value-of select="$x" />
    <xsl:variable name="x" select="1" />
</xsl:template>
```

Think of the `xsl:variable` and `xsl:param` elements in terms of variable scope in PHP. Global variables can be accessed from anywhere, including from within functions. Variables declared within functions are visible only within the function. It is also perfectly valid for a local variable to have the same name as a global variable. Within XSLT, this is called *shadowing*. For example:

```
<!-- The Following is invalid -->
<xsl:template match="/">
    <xsl:param name="x" select="1"/>
    <xsl:variable name="x" select="1"/>
</xsl:template>
```

This template is invalid because an `xsl:variable` element with the same name as an `xsl:param` element is within the same scope. To be able to reuse an `xsl:variable` or `xsl:param` name, they must be of different scope, or shadowed. For instance, the following style sheet binds a parameter within the global scope yet shadows the binding within a template:

```
<xsl:stylesheet xmlns:xsl="http://www.w3.org/1999/XSL/Transform" version="1.0">
    <xsl:param name="x" select="1"/>
    <xsl:template match="/">
        <xsl:param name="x" select="3"/>
        <value>
            <xsl:value-of select="$x" />
        </value>
    </xsl:template>
</xsl:stylesheet>
```

This template is perfectly legal. The parameter, x, defined within the template shadows the global parameter binding. Within the template, unless a parameter of the same name is passed to it, the default value of 3 is used for the x parameter. Once the processor is finished with the template, the local parameter loses scope, causing the global parameter to once again take effect. The same rules apply to variables, although there is no possibility of a variable being passed to a template. A variable is considered bound and usable based on it being in scope.

Passing Parameters to Templates

Just like the XSLT processor can pass parameters to style sheets overriding the default parameter values, you can call templates with parameters to override default values bound within the template. You can use the `xsl:with-param` element for this purpose:

```
<xsl:with-param
   name = qname
   select = expression>
   <!-- Content: template -->
</xsl:with-param>
```

This element is applicable within the content of an xsl:call-template or xsl:apply-templates element. The required name attribute is the name of the parameter, and you can use the optional select attribute to define the value. They work in the same fashion as an xsl:param element and use any child elements to specify content. The context for an expression used within the select attribute or template created within the content is the same as that used for the xsl:call-template or xsl:apply-templates element in which it resides. For example:

```
<?xml version="1.0" encoding="iso-8859-1"?>
<xsl:stylesheet xmlns:xsl="http://www.w3.org/1999/XSL/Transform" version="1.0">
   <xsl:param name="x" select="2"/>

   <xsl:template match="/">
      <xsl:apply-templates select="sites/site">
         <xsl:with-param name="x" select="count(.)" />
      </xsl:apply-templates>
   </xsl:template>

<xsl:template match="site">
   <xsl:param name="x" select="10"/>
   <xsl:value-of select="$x" />
   <xsl:text>
</xsl:text>
   </xsl:template>
</xsl:stylesheet>
```

This is a bit more complex. The parameter x is bound globally with the default value of 2. The entry template, matching /, applies any templates of the site elements that are children of the sites element and passes a parameter x with the value being the count of the current node set. Based on this expression, the value will always be 1. The matching template also defines the parameter x with the value 10. This is a shadow binding since it is declared locally yet the style sheet has the global parameter x as well. The value 10 for the local parameter is just the default value. As you can see from the results, the value passed from the xsl:with-param element is what is used for the actual value of the parameter within the template:

```
1
1
1
1
```

The template processed four site elements, which caused 1 to be output for each element. The xsl:text element was used only to add line feeds to the results.

Using Functions

XPath is the foundation for much of XSLT, so all the functionality and functions from XPath are available within the XSLT language. XSLT, though, extends the functionality of the core XPath library with some of its own functions not available under XPath. The following sections will introduce you to these functions and show how to use them within a style sheet.

Multiple Source Documents

Documents outside the source document are accessible using the document() function:

```
node-set document(object, node-set?)
```

The simplest case when using this function is with a single parameter. When the object parameter is not a node set, the object is simply converted into a string and treated as a URI reference:

```
<xsl:value-of select="document('http://www.example.com/file.xml')" />
```

The result of the document() function is a node set, so it is also perfectly legal to use it as part of a path for an expression:

```
<xsl:value-of
    select="document('http://www.example.com/file.xml')/html/head/style" />
```

The URI may also be a fragment, so only certain nodes from the document will be returned by the function.

When a node set is passed as a single parameter, the result is the union, for each node in the set, of having called the document() function with the string value of the current node from the set. For example, assume a list of elements containing URLs:

```
<sites>
    <site>http://www.example.com/file1.xml</site>
    <site>http://www.example.com/file2.xml</file>
</sites>
```

Both of these documents could be returned in a node set and their values determined:

```
<xsl:value-of select="document(/sites/site)" />
```

The last possibility is using two parameters, with a node set being passed in as the first parameter. In this case, for each of the nodes in the node set, the function would be called using the string value of the node and passing the second argument passed to the original function call as the second argument for the current document() call. The final resulting node set would be a union of all the accumulated results.

Keys

Keys in XSLT are similar to IDs in XML documents, except they do not have the same limitations as using IDs. They are used in combination of the xsl:key element and the key() function:

```
<xsl:key
   name = qname
   match = pattern
   use = expression />
```

```
node-set key(string, object)
```

You declare keys using the xsl:key element. The name attribute specifies the name for the key. The match attribute is a pattern that causes nodes matching the pattern to be used as keys. The use attribute is an expression specifying what information for the nodes to use as the key value. Keys work like indexes and are optimized to find what you are seeking.

Think about book data stored in XML format. Each book has a unique ISBN to clearly identify it. The following is a short example of such a document:

```
<books>
   <book isbn="159059xxxx">
      <title>Book 1</title>
      <author>Author 1</author>
   </book>
   <book isbn="159059yyyy">
      <title>Book 2</title>
      <author>Author 2</author>
   </book>
   <book isbn="159059zzzz">
      <title>Book 3</title>
      <author>Author 3</author>
   </book>
</books>
```

This document has no IDs defined, but the document can still be indexed for fast retrieval within XSLT:

```
<xsl:stylesheet version="1.0" xmlns:xsl="http://www.w3.org/1999/XSL/Transform">
   <xsl:key name="ISBN" match="book" use="@isbn"/>

   <xsl:template match="/">
      <xsl:value-of select="key('ISBN', '159059yyyy')/title" />
   </xsl:template>

</xsl:stylesheet>
```

Processing this style sheet with the book data, the resulting output is Book 2.

The xsl:key element is a top-level element, so it must live as a direct child of the xsl:stylesheet element. The element used here defines the key named ISBN that matches on book elements and uses the isbn attribute of the book elements as the key value. The key() function is used as the expression within the select element. The first parameter is the name of the key to use. This value must match a predefined key, which in this case is ISBN. The second value is the value of the key to match. Looking at the source document, the second book element contains the value 159059yyyy for its isbn attribute. The resulting node set is then used as part of the path within the expression, which ultimately returns the value Book 2.

Number Formatting

The format-number() function creates formatted numbers. It is similar to using the number_format() function from PHP, but it offers much more capability. It works in conjunction with the xsl:decimal-format element, which controls the interpretation of a format pattern used by the function. For example:

```
string format-number(number, string, string?)
```

```
<xsl:decimal-format
    name = qname
    decimal-separator = char
    grouping-separator = char
    infinity = string
    minus-sign = char
    NaN = string
    percent = char
    per-mille = char
    zero-digit = char
    digit = char
    pattern-separator = char />
```

The format-number() function takes two required parameters plus an optional third parameter. The first parameter is the number to be formatted. If it is not of the type number, it is converted according to the rules defined in the XPath specifications. The second argument defines the format pattern used to format the number. The last parameter is optional. When passed, it uses the named xsl:decimal-format element to provide different behavior than the default decimal-format to interpret the format pattern. This explanation is a bit useless unless you know how the xsl:decimal-format element interprets the pattern based on its defined attributes as well as the defaults.

The name attribute is not required for the xsl:decimal-format attribute. It is used to create a named decimal format, which could then be called directly by the format-number() function. When a name is not specified by this element, the interpretation defined by the rest of the attributes becomes the default decimal format, which overrides the built-in default decimal format. The remaining attributes control interpretation of the format pattern and are explained nicely in the XSLT specification. The following list comes from the specification at http://www.w3.org/TR/xslt#format-number.

The following attributes both control the interpretation of characters in the format pattern and specify characters that may appear in the result of formatting the number:

- decimal-separator specifies the character used for the decimal sign; the default value is a period (.).

- grouping-separator specifies the character used as a grouping (for example, the thousands separator); the default value is a comma (,).

- percent specifies the character used as a percent sign; the default value is a percent character (%).

- per-mille specifies the character used as a per-mille sign; the default value is the Unicode per-mille character (#x2030) .

- zero-digit specifies the character used as the digit zero; the default value is a digit zero (0).

The following attributes control the interpretation of characters in the format pattern:

- digit specifies the character used for a digit in the format pattern; the default value is a number sign (#).

- pattern-separator specifies the character used to separate positive and negative subpatterns in a pattern; the default value is a semicolon (;).

The following attributes specify characters or strings that may appear in the result of formatting the number:

- infinity specifies the string used to represent infinity; the default value is the string Infinity.

- NaN specifies the string used to represent the NaN value; the default value is the string NaN.

- minus-sign specifies the character used as the default minus sign; the default value is a hyphen (-, #x2D).

Based on all these rules, the following demonstrates how different formats work with different values:

```
<xsl:decimal-format name="euros" decimal-separator="," grouping-separator="."/>

<xsl:value-of select="format-number('A', '.00')" />
<xsl:value-of select="format-number('1.99', '.00')" />
<xsl:value-of select="format-number('1.99', '.###')" />
<xsl:value-of select="format-number('9999.99', '#.###,##', 'euros')" />
```

```
NaN
1.99
1.99
9.999,99
```

Miscellaneous Functions

XSLT defines four functions that are not as significant as the other functions yet can sometimes be useful.

current() The current() function returns a node set that contains only the current node as its members:

```
node-set current()
```

This function may not immediately seem to have a purpose because you could easily access the current node using . or self::. When used within a predicate, though, it can provide much different results:

```
<code>
   <functions>
      <function name="foreach">
         <!-- function information -->
      </function>
      <function name="do">
         <!-- function information -->
      </function>
   </functions>
   <control name="do" params="0">
      <!-- more info -->
   </control>
</code>
```

```
<xsl:template match="control">
   <xsl:apply-templates select="/code/function[@name=current()/@name]" />
</xsl:template>
```

Using the current control element matched in the template, the xsl:apply-templates element applies any matching template to the function element whose name attribute has the same value as the name attribute for the current node being processed. This is greatly different from writing this:

```
/code/function[@name=./@name]
```

This is equivalent to writing this:

```
/code/function[@name=@name]
```

The node sets are completely different, because the latter expression would select every function element rather than a single function element.

unparsed-entity-uri() The unparsed-entity-uri() function returns the URI of the unparsed entity with the specified name that resides in the same document as the context node. When the entity does not exist, an empty string is returned:

```
string unparsed-entity-uri(string)
```

Assume the XML source document contains a DTD with the following entity declaration:

```
<!ENTITY systemEntity SYSTEM "http://www.example.com/file.xml">
```

You could then use the unparsed-entity function to look up the URI for this entity during processing:

```
<xsl:value-of select="unparsed-entity-uri('systemEntity')" />
```

This would result in the string http://www.example.com/file.xml.

generate-id() The generate-id() function will return a string that uniquely identifies the argument node set that is first in document order:

```
string generate-id(node-set?)
```

An empty node set passed in as the node-set parameter will result in an empty string. When no parameter is passed in, the context node is used. This function will always return the same string for the same node, yet no two nodes in a document will generate the same ID.

■Caution The identifier returned by this function cannot be used to identify node sets between transformations. An identifier is guaranteed to be the same only within a single transformation. Performing another transformation on a subsequent call to a PHP page or even within the same PHP page, even when the same document and style sheet are used, may result in a different identifier being used during the transformation.

For example:

```
<xsl:template match="site">
    <xsl:value-of select="generate-id()" />
</xsl:template>
```

When matched, the unique identifier for the current site element being processed is returned:

```
id337632
```

system-property() This property returns the value of the system property passed in as the argument:

```
object system-property(string)
```

The string argument is a QName, which is expanded using the namespace declarations in scope for the expression. For instance, three system properties are required by the XSLT specifications because they reside in the XSLT namespace:

```
<xsl:template match="/">
    <xsl:value-of select="system-property('xsl:vendor')" />
    <xsl:value-of select="system-property('xsl:vendor-url')" />
    <xsl:value-of select="system-property('xsl:version')" />
</xsl:template>
```

```
libxslt
http://xmlsoft.org/XSLT/
1.0
```

Using Messages

Debugging XSLT is not always the easiest of tasks. You can use the xsl:message element to produce XML fragments that do not become part of the result tree, but you can capture them using other methods depending upon the XSLT processor. Within PHP 5, any output from an xsl:message is captured as an error. More particularly, an E_WARNING is generated with the output from the xsl:message as the error message. Using PHP 5.1, you can capture them using the new XML error handling by means of calling libxml_use_internal_errors(TRUE);. This way, the messages will be contained within the message property of LibXMLError objects:

```
<xsl:message terminate = "yes" | "no">
   <!-- Content: template -->
</xsl:message>
```

The terminate attribute instructs the XSLT processor whether it should terminate upon encountering and after processing the xsl:message element. The default value is no, so processing will continue, no E_WARNINGS will be issued, and no LibXMLError objects (explained in Chapter 5) will be captured. The content of this element is the template used to create the XML fragment that becomes the message for the warning:

```
<xsl:template match="site">
   <xsl:message>
      Debug: <xsl:value-of select="./name" />
   </xsl:message>
   <p><xsl:value-of select="./name" /></p>
</xsl:template>
```

The resulting tree can contain the following:

```
<p>PHP</p>
<p>XML C Parser</p>
```

The PHP warnings or message properties of LibXMLError objects would contain the following:

```
Debug: PHP
Debug: XML C Parser
```

Using Extensions

Extensions, naturally, are a way of extending the regular capability of the XSLT processor. They allow you to add your own custom functions, which are then callable from the XSLT style sheets. Several extensions are often built into the processor, such as those provided by EXSLT (http://www.exslt.org/), which is a community initiative to provide extensions to XSLT. To utilize extension functionality, you need to define namespaces and associate them with prefixes on the xsl:stylesheet element for specific extensions. Table 10-1 presents some of the common prefixes and associated namespaces used for some of the EXSLT modules.

Table 10-1. *EXSLT Modules and Associated Namespaces*

Module	Prefix	Namespace URI
Date	date	http://exslt.org/dates-and-times
Dyn	dyn	http://exslt.org/dynamic
Common	exsl	http://exslt.org/common
Functions	func	http://exslt.org/functions
Math	math	http://exslt.org/math
Random	random	http://exslt.org/random
RegEx	regexp	http://exslt.org/regular-expressions
Sets	set	http://exslt.org/sets
Strings	str	http://exslt.org/strings

So, to use the functionality of the Math module from EXSLT, the first thing is to add the namespace to the xsl:stylesheet element:

```
<xsl:stylesheet xmlns:xsl="http://www.w3.org/1999/XSL/Transform" version="1.0"
                xmlns:math="http://exslt.org/math">
```

Calling Functions

You can now use functions from this module by prefixing the function name with the math prefix, which instructs the processor to use the extension from the appropriate module. For example, the Math module includes the lowest() function. It takes a node set as its parameter and returns the lowest value. Using the sites document that has numeric values for the num attribute of the site elements, you can determine the lowest value with this function:

```
<xsl:stylesheet xmlns:xsl="http://www.w3.org/1999/XSL/Transform" version="1.0"
                xmlns:math="http://exslt.org/math">
  <xsl:template match="/">
    <xsl:value-of select="math:lowest(/sites/site/@num)" />
  </xsl:template>
</xsl:stylesheet>
```

If you look at the expression for the xsl:value-of element, you will notice the lowest() function has been prefixed by math. When the processor evaluates the expression, functions that are prefixed are treated as extension functions and are evaluated according to their namespace association. The result of processing the data is the value 1, which is the lowest value for the num attributes on site elements.

Extension Elements

Some extensions also define extension elements. To use the functionality of these elements within a style sheet, you must specify an additional attribute, extension-element-prefixes, on the xsl:stylesheet element. This attribute takes a whitespace-separated list of registered namespace prefixes associated with any of the extensions from which the use of its elements is needed. One such module is the EXSLT Common module. It includes an exsl:document element, which can be used to actually save a result tree to a URI during transformation:

```
<xsl:stylesheet xmlns:xsl="http://www.w3.org/1999/XSL/Transform" version="1.0"
                xmlns:exsl="http://exslt.org/common"
                extension-element-prefixes="exsl">

    <xsl:template match="/">
        <exsl:document href="exsl.xml">
            <mydoc>New document saved to a URI</mydoc>
        </exsl:document>
    </xsl:template>

</xsl:stylesheet>
```

For this example to work, extension-element-prefixes must include the exsl prefix in its value list. Omitting this attribute or the exsl value results in the exsl:document element being treated as a regular element in the template. With the prefix within the attribute, the result tree does not contain the exsl:document element or its content. Instead, the content within the element is output to the URI defined by the href attribute rather than to the result tree.

User-Defined Functions

You can implement user-defined functions in one of two forms. The first is a generic method that works with XSLT processors implementing the EXSLT Functions module. The second method is specific to the XSL extension in PHP 5, which allows user-defined PHP functions to be called from within an XSLT style sheet. I will discuss this method later in the "Calling PHP Functions from XSL" section after the XSL extension has been introduced.

The generic way is using the func:function and func:result elements from the EXSLT Functions module. The function is written using syntax available when writing XSLT style sheets, so a custom function may contain functionality from additional extensions and modules:

```
<func:function name = QName>
    <-- Content: (xsl:param* | template) -->
</func:function>
```

```
<func:result select = expression>
    <-- Content: template -->
</func:result>
```

The func:function element defines the function to be used within the style sheet. This element is a top-level element, so it lives as a direct child of the xsl:stylesheet element. The name attribute defines the name of the function. Its value is a QName and must include a prefix associated with a namespace. Because these are user-defined functions, the prefix and namespace should be something unique to the style sheet author.

Based on this, you should already be aware that you need to add two namespaces to the `xsl:stylesheet`: one for the `func` prefix and one for the unique prefix and namespace. You will also need to add the `extension-element-prefixes` attribute with the value `func`; as explained in the previous section, you need this in order to use elements prefixed with `func`. The opening `xsl:stylesheet` element should look something similar to the following, where the prefix `rob` is associated with the `http://www.ctindustries.net/xslfunctions` namespace, which will be used for the user-defined function:

```
<xsl:stylesheet xmlns:xsl="http://www.w3.org/1999/XSL/Transform" version="1.0"
                xmlns:func="http://exslt.org/functions"
                xmlns:rob="http://www.ctindustries.net/xslfunctions"
                extension-element-prefixes="func">
```

With this in place, you can now build the function. It will be a simple function that accepts up to three parameters. The first two will be numbers and, depending upon the value of the third parameter, will either be added or be subtracted with the result returned to the callee:

```
<func:function name="rob:myFunc">
    <xsl:param name="val1" select="0" />
    <xsl:param name="val2" select="0" />
    <xsl:param name="subtractit" select="0" />
    <xsl:choose>
        <xsl:when test="$subtractit = 0">
            <func:result select="$val1 + $val2" />
        </xsl:when>
        <xsl:otherwise>
            <func:result select="$val1 - $val2" />
        </xsl:otherwise>
    </xsl:choose>
</func:function>

<xsl:template match="/">
    <xsl:value-of select="rob:myFunc(4)" />
    <xsl:value-of select="rob:myFunc(1, 2)" />
    <xsl:value-of select="rob:myFunc(15, 3, 1)" />
</xsl:template>
```

You define function parameters using the `xsl:param` element. Within the `rob:myFunc` function, three parameters (`val1`, `val2`, and `subtractit`) are defined with default values of 0. The first two parameters, `val1` and `val2`, are the numbers to either be added or be subtracted. The last parameter, `subtractit`, is a flag signaling the operation to perform. Any value other than 0, which is the default value, causes the function to return the difference between `val1` and `val2`.

Only a single `func:result` element can be instantiated within the `func:function` element. This is why the `xsl:choose` element is used. If `xsl:if` had been used, one `func:result` element would need to live within `xsl:if` and the other outside of it. This would cause an error; any time `test` evaluated to TRUE for an `xsl:if`, the first `func:result` would be instantiated, and then after exiting the `xsl:if` block, the last one would try to be instantiated.

Moving down to the `xsl:template` element, you can see how the function is called within the `xsl:value-of` elements. Because parameters have default values, the function can take zero to three parameters. So, instantiating the template results in the following output:

```
4
3
12
```

Trying to call the function with more than three arguments will result in an error while the data is being transformed.

Tip User-defined functions not only allow more compact style sheets, such as when a function needs to be referenced from multiple spots within a style sheet, but they also make it easier to port specific functionality to another style sheet as well as provide a single location when changes or bug fixes need to be made to the functionality.

Using Fallback

When writing XSLT, it's not always possible to know whether certain functionality has been implemented by an XSLT processor or whether some type of extended functionality is available to the processor. You can use the `xsl:fallback` element to define some fallback capabilities in the event one of these conditions is encountered during processing:

```
<xsl:fallback>
    <!-- Content: template -->
</xsl:fallback>
```

The content of this element is instantiated when a fallback condition arises:

```
<xsl:template match="site">
    <xsl:function value="robtest">
        Function EXECUTED
        <xsl:fallback>
            FALLBACK Condition Encountered
        </xsl:fallback>
    </xsl:function>
</xsl:template>
```

Within this template, an `xsl:function` element has been used. This is an *invalid* element within the XSLT namespace. An `xsl:fallback` element has also been implemented within this invalid `xsl:function` element. When a `site` element matches this template, the `xsl:function` element is processed. If it were a valid element, the text `Function EXECUTED` would be added to the result tree. However, this element is invalid, and the fallback condition is instantiated. The resulting text for this template is as follows:

```
FALLBACK Condition Encountered
```

Using Output

The xsl:output element is a top-level element, meaning it is a direct child of the xsl:stylesheet element. It is not a required element but is often used to provide some instruction on how the resulting tree should be output:

```
<xsl:output
    method = "xml" | "html" | "text" | qname-but-not-ncname
    version = nmtoken
    encoding = string
    omit-xml-declaration = "yes" | "no"
    standalone = "yes" | "no"
    doctype-public = string
    doctype-system = string
    cdata-section-elements = qnames
    indent = "yes" | "no"
    media-type = string />
```

The XSLT processor can create three types of output. They are xml, html, and text, which are also the possible values for the method attribute. By definition, the method attribute can also take a QName that must contain a prefix, but this is processor dependant and often not supported.

Note The XSL extension in PHP 5 supports only the values xml, html, and text for the method attribute.

When this attribute is not specified or the xsl:output element is omitted from the style sheet, the default output method is chosen based on the contents of the result tree. A result tree meeting the following conditions defaults to the html output method:

- The root node of the result tree has an element child.

- The expanded name of the first element child of the root node (that is, the document element) of the result tree has the local name HTML (in any combination of uppercase and lowercase) and a NULL namespace URI.

- Any text nodes preceding the first element child of the root node of the result tree contain only whitespace characters.

If any of these conditions is not met, the default output method is xml.

The remaining attributes are used as parameters for the output method. The following descriptions come from the W3C XSLT specification at http://www.w3.org/TR/xslt#output. (These are just general descriptions because some are further explained or used in examples in the following sections.)

- version specifies the version of the output method.

- indent specifies whether the XSLT processor can add whitespace when outputting the result tree; the value must be yes or no.

- encoding specifies the preferred character encoding that the XSLT processor should use to encode sequences of characters as sequences of bytes. The value of the attribute is case-insensitive, and the value must contain characters only in the range from #x21 to #x7E (that is, the printable ASCII characters). The value should either be a character set registered with the Internet Assigned Numbers Authority (IANA) from RFC-2278 or start with X-.

- media-type specifies the media type (MIME content type) of the data that results from outputting the result tree. The charset parameter should not be specified explicitly; instead, when the top-level media type is text, a charset parameter should be added according to the character encoding actually used by the output method.

- doctype-system specifies the system identifier to be used in the document type declaration.

- doctype-public specifies the public identifier to be used in the document type declaration.

- omit-xml-declaration specifies whether the XSLT processor should output an XML declaration; the value must be yes or no.

- standalone specifies whether the XSLT processor should output a stand-alone document declaration; the value must be yes or no.

- cdata-section-elements specifies a list of the names of elements whose text node children should be output using CDATA sections.

XML Output Method

When the result tree is output as XML, the processor creates a well-formed tree or issues errors when this is not possible. It is important that any literal tags you may use within templates are written as well-formed XML as well. For instance, creating the start tag for an element, yet never closing, it would cause an error:

```
<!-- This is an error because it does not produce well-formed XML -->
<?xml version="1.0" encoding="iso-8859-1"?>
<xsl:stylesheet xmlns:xsl="http://www.w3.org/1999/XSL/Transform" version="1.0">
  <xsl:output method="xml"/>
   <xsl:template match="/">
      <unbalanced>
      <xsl:value-of select="2"/>
   </xsl:template>
</xsl:stylesheet>
```

XML Declaration Attributes Roughly half the attributes affect any XML declaration that would be included with the output. The primary attribute in this case is omit-xml-declaration. When set to yes, no XML declaration is included with the output, which basically renders most of the other attributes that affect it useless. Setting the value to no or omitting this attribute results in an XML declaration being included in the output.

The version attribute specifies the version of XML used in the output, with the default being 1.0. You could use other version numbers, such as 1.1 or 2.0; 2.0 is not even a valid version number for XML and would be indicated in the resulting declaration, but the processor will actually use whatever version it supports if not supporting the version specified to create the document. When the standalone attribute is specified, it is included in the declaration with the value set by this attribute. The last attribute affecting the declaration is the encoding attribute.

The encoding attribute does two things. First, when specified, it adds an encoding attribute to the declaration of the resulting document. The value is the same as the value set in the xsl:output element. Second, it sets the encoding for the processor to use while creating the resulting document. You can find detailed information about encoding, especially with respect to the support under PHP 5, in Chapter 5.

```
<xsl:output method="xml" version="1.0" standalone="yes" encoding="UTF-8" />
```

Used within a style sheet, this would cause the processor to produce an XML document with the following XML declaration:

```
<?xml version="1.0" encoding="UTF-8" standalone="yes"?>
```

Other Attributes The remaining attributes offer control over certain aspects of the tree structure as well as the MIME type for the resulting data. I will first address the MIME type because it currently does not do anything when using the XSL extension in PHP. This is because of the media-type attribute not being implemented in the current version of libxslt, which at this time is 1.1.14. Documents output in XML format typically are of the text/xml MIME type, which is also the default value for this attribute when XML is output. MIME types are used so when a client is requesting a document, the MIME type can be sent in the headers and the client is able to use it to determine how to handle the content. Even though it is not implemented, it has little bearing on the PHP XSL extension. Typical usage is through a Web server, and the encompassing PHP application is able to modify the content headers in any event.

The indent attribute works in a similar fashion to the formatOutput property in DOM. When it is set to yes, the resulting XML is "beautified" by indenting and by adding line feeds at the different levels of the tree. The default value is no for this attribute—for good reason. Whitespaces are significant and could possibly alter a document in such a way that the serialized version does not match what the resulting document was. When working with documents that have elements containing mixed content, the safest bet is to not use indenting.

You can also add system and public identifiers to the resulting document using the doctype-system and doctype-public attributes. When using these attributes, a document declaration is included in the resulting document with the document element automatically added. To specify a system identifier, add the doctype-system attribute to the xsl:output element with the value of the system identifier. Using the sites document for the XML data (where the sites element is the document element), the following would add a system identifier to the resulting document:

```
<xsl:output method="xml" doctype-system ="http://www.example.com"/>
```

This would cause the following to be added to the final results:

```
<?xml version="1.0"?>
<!DOCTYPE sites SYSTEM "http://www.example.com">
```

A public identifier is defined using both the `doctype-system` and `doctype-public` attributes. When both attributes are specified, the system identifier portion of the public identifier is taken from the value of the `doctype-system` attribute. When a `doctype-public` attribute is used alone, then the system identifier portion is empty. For example:

```
<xsl:output method="xml" doctype-public="publicid" omit-xml-declaration="yes" />

<!-- Resulting Document Declaration -->
<!DOCTYPE sites PUBLIC "publicid" "">


<xsl:output method="xml" doctype-public="publicid"
            doctype-system ="http://www.example.com/" omit-xml-declaration="yes" />

<!-- Resulting Document Declaration -->
<!DOCTYPE sites PUBLIC "publicid" "http://www.example.com/">
```

The last attribute on this element is `cdata-section-elements`. This attributes takes a whitespace-separated list of element names whose direct child text nodes should be output as CDATA sections rather than text nodes. Any text nodes to be converted to CDATA sections that contain the sequence of characters]]> are converted to two sequential CDATA sections. The first CDATA section is closed after the]] characters. An additional CDATA section is created, with the first character containing the > character and including the rest of the text:

```
<xsl:stylesheet xmlns:xsl="http://www.w3.org/1999/XSL/Transform" version="1.0">
  <xsl:output method="xml" cdata-section-elements="node2 node4 node6" indent="yes"/>
    <xsl:template match="/">
      <newdoc>
        <node1>some text</node1>
        <node2>some text</node2>
        <node3><![CDATA[native CDATA section]]></node3>
        <node4><![CDATA[native CDATA section]]></node4>
        <node5>CDATA chars ]]&gt;</node5>
        <node6>CDATA chars ]]&gt;</node6>
      </newdoc>
    </xsl:template>
</xsl:stylesheet>
```

This style sheet shows the effects of creating some text as CDATA sections. Text is first output as a text node and followed by the corresponding text as CDATA. Because of the `cdata-section-elements` attribute (`node2`), `node4` and `node6` will generate CDATA sections for their child text nodes; the rest of the elements will output straight text nodes:

```
<?xml version="1.0"?>
<newdoc>
  <node1>some text</node1>
  <node2><![CDATA[some text]]></node2>
  <node3>native CDATA section</node3>
  <node4><![CDATA[native CDATA section]]></node4>
  <node5>CDATA chars ]]&gt;</node5>
  <node6><![CDATA[CDATA chars ]]]]><![CDATA[>]]></node6>
</newdoc>
```

HTML Output Method

Even if this is your first time dealing with XSL, you are probably familiar with HTML. HTML is not the same as XHTML, and using the html output method will generate HTML rather than XML-conformant XHTML.

■**Note** To output XHTML, which is not a valid output method in XSLT 1.0, use the xml output method.

This being said, some of the syntax within your document may be altered a bit when it is output. For instance, under HTML, many empty tags are written as a start element with no corresponding closing tag. If within the style sheet, which must be XML conformant, you use `<br />` or `<br></br>`, you would see only `<br>` when the document is output.

Another alteration that occurs is the addition of a META element. If the HTML document contains a HEAD element, a META tag is added as the first child of the HEAD element that specifies character encoding. If your result tree looked similar to the following:

```
<html>
  <head></head>
  <body>content</body>
</html>
```

it would be changed upon output to the following:

```
<html>
  <head>
    <meta http-equiv="Content-Type" content="text/html; charset=UTF-8">
  </head>
  <body>content</body>
</html>
```

■**Caution** Some of the material presented in this section is specific to the libxslt library, which is used by the XSL extension in PHP 5.

The version attribute for HTML output corresponds to the HTML version for the resulting document, such as 4.01 to specify that the document conforms to the HTML 4.01 specification. Specifying this attribute automatically sets the document declaration using the appropriate identifiers for the specified HTML version:

```
<xsl:output method="html" version="4.01"/>
```

Assuming you used the HTTML element and it is the document element of the tree, the resulting output would automatically include the document type declaration:

```
<!DOCTYPE html PUBLIC "-//W3C//DTD HTML 4.01 Transitional//EN"
                      "http://www.w3.org/TR/1999/REC-html401-19991224/loose.dtd">
```

Setting either the doctype-system attribute or the doctype-public attribute disables the automatic creation of a document declaration based on the version attribute. Using either of these attributes works the same as when the output method is xml. For example:

```
<xsl:output method="html" version="4.01" doctype-public="publicid"/>
```

The only change to this element has been the addition of the doctype-public attribute, but it alters the resulting output greatly:

```
<!DOCTYPE html PUBLIC "publicid">
```

The media-type attribute, again, is applicable to this output method but does not currently serve a usable purpose under PHP using the XSL extension. The default value, in any case, is text/html.

Putting all this together using the sites document again and the following style sheet, an HTML page can be output containing an ordered list of all site names:

```
<?xml version="1.0" encoding="iso-8859-1"?>
<xsl:stylesheet xmlns:xsl="http://www.w3.org/1999/XSL/Transform" version="1.0">
  <xsl:output method="html" version="4.01" />

  <xsl:template match="/">
    <html>
      <head>
      </head>
      <body>
        <ol>
           <xsl:apply-templates select="/sites/site/name" />
        </ol>
      </body>
    </html>
  </xsl:template>

  <xsl:template match="name">
    <li><xsl:value-of select="." /></li>
  </xsl:template>

</xsl:stylesheet>
```

```
<!DOCTYPE html PUBLIC "-//W3C//DTD HTML 4.01 Transitional//EN"
                      "http://www.w3.org/TR/1999/REC-html401-19991224/loose.dtd">
<html>
<head><meta http-equiv="Content-Type" content="text/html; charset=UTF-8"></head>

<body><ol>
<li>XML C Parser</li>
<li>PHP</li>
<li>PHP</li>
<li>XML C Parser</li>
</ol></body>
</html>
```

Text Output Method

Text output is simple. You output the result tree by outputting the string value for each text node in the document without performing any escaping. The only two applicable attributes for this method are media-type, which does not affect anything using the XSL processor in PHP, and the encoding attribute, which instructs the processor to encode the output using the specified encoding. Using the style sheet from the CDATA example and modifying the xsl:output to output as text, you'll see that the results are radically different now:

```
<?xml version="1.0" encoding="iso-8859-1"?>
<xsl:stylesheet xmlns:xsl="http://www.w3.org/1999/XSL/Transform" version="1.0">
  <xsl:output method="text" />
   <xsl:template match="/">
      <newdoc>
         <node1>some text</node1>
         <node2>some text</node2>
         <node3><![CDATA[native CDATA section]]></node3>
         <node4><![CDATA[native CDATA section]]></node4>
         <node5>CDATA chars ]]&gt;</node5>
         <node6>CDATA chars ]]&gt;</node6>
      </newdoc>
   </xsl:template>
</xsl:stylesheet>
```

```
some textsome textnative CDATA sectionnative CDATA sectionCDATA chars ]]>CDATA chars
]]>
```

Introducing the XSL Extension

The XSL extension is the new XSL processor for PHP 5. Prior to its creation, XSLT was available through the domxml extension (when built with XSLT support) and the XSLT extension, which was based on the Sablotron library. During the reimplementation of domxml, XML and XSLT were split into new extensions. This is how the DOM and XSL extensions came about in PHP 5. Both domxml and the XSLT extension have been moved to PECL (http://pecl.php.net/), although neither has packages built for it, and both must be accessed via the CVS repository. Enough talk of those ancient extensions! The focus here is the XSL extension.

Note The term *XSL* used within the rest of this chapter refers to the XSL extension in PHP 5.

XSL is based on the libxslt library (http://xmlsoft.org/XSLT/), which in turn is based on the familiar libxml2 library. It makes a fine fit with the rest of the XML-based extensions in PHP 5, because they all use the same common library, thus fitting into the interoperability scheme. XSL requires that the DOM extension, enabled by default, also be available. This ensures a tree-based parser is available to perform transformations to an in-memory tree.

Enabling XSL

By default, XSL is not built into PHP, though it's included with the core. It must be specified when configure is executed:

```
--with-xsl
```

Before adding this to your configure routine, make sure you have libxslt installed along with the header files. The minimum version that can be used with XSL is 1.0.18. XSL also supports some EXSLT functionality, which requires that libexslt, a sister library to libxslt, also be installed along with its headers. It is not required to build XSL with EXSLT support, but without it, the extended functionality it offers will be unavailable.

Note Unless building from source, Windows users can ignore this and use the DLL included with the package from the PHP download site. Just make sure it is also enabled in the php.ini file.

Using XSL Constants

Table 10-2 describes XSL's short list of constants.

Table 10-2. *Constants from XSL*

Constant Name	Value	Description
XSL_CLONE_AUTO	0	Autodetect whether document needs to be cloned.
XSL_CLONE_NEVER	-1	Never clone the document.
XSL_CLONE_ALWAYS	1	Always clone the document.

All the constants deal with how the style sheet document is handled when imported by the processor. I will explain how to use these constants later in the "The cloneDocument Property" section.

Using the XSLTProcessor Class

XSL is an object-oriented API and works using a single class. The XSLTProcessor handles all the functionality to transform XML data into another form. The API is simple, consisting of one property and nine methods, yet provides some powerful functionality.

The cloneDocument Property

Earlier versions of libxslt (those prior to 1.1.5) caused problems with the XML data document when using keys in a style sheet. The problems resulted in a corrupt XML data document, making it useless for any further processing and possibly causing a crash. Originally, prior to this being changed with libxslt 1.1.5, the data document would be copied and the copy was used by XSL. Though this did prevent any problems, it also resulted in an increase in system resources because two document trees were in memory at the same time for the same document.

Because this issue was specific to using keys, it made no sense to always force a document copy. The cloneDocument property allows a developer to explicitly specify whether the document should be cloned or left as is or specify that XSL should determine whether the document needed to be cloned. The value of this property is one of the constants described in Table 10-2.

The default value for this property is XSL_CLONE_AUTO, so the processor will attempt to autodetect the use of keys in a style sheet. If keys are detected, a copy of the XML data document is used for the transformation. When using libxslt 1.1.5 or newer, there really is no need for the document to ever be cloned, because using keys in a style sheet does not cause any issues with the interoperability of extensions like earlier versions did. Depending upon your style sheet and library versions, you may want to explicitly set the handling of document cloning. When using this property, you can use the following guidelines to determine the proper setting depending upon the version of libxslt you're using. The variable $proc refers to an already instantiated XSLTProcessor object.

- When using libxslt 1.1.5 or newer, the data document never needs to be cloned. You can disable cloning by calling $proc->cloneDocument = XSL_CLONE_NEVER;.

- When using libxslt 1.1.4 or earlier and the style sheet makes no use of keys, then you can disable cloning: $proc->cloneDocument = XSL_CLONE_NEVER;.

- When using libxslt 1.1.4 or earlier and the style sheet *does* use keys, then you should perform cloning: $proc->cloneDocument = XSL_CLONE_ALWAYS;.

Even if your system is running libxslt 1.1.4 or earlier, the XSL_CLONE_AUTO option works well determining whether cloning needs to take place. The only disadvantage to this is that because it is out of your control, you will never know whether a document is being cloned. Programmatically it does not matter, but if your systems administrator were to ask about any sudden spikes in server memory usage, this would be a good place to start if using XSL.

The XSLTProcessor Methods

Table 10-3 lists the methods implemented by the XSLTProcessor class.

Table 10-3. XSLTProcessor *Methods*

Method	Description
getParameter()	Gets the value of a parameter
hasExsltSupport()	Determines whether PHP has EXSLT support
importStylesheet()	Imports style sheet
registerPHPFunctions()	Enables the ability to use PHP functions as XSLT functions
removeParameter()	Removes parameter
setParameter()	Sets value for a parameter
transformToDoc()	Transforms to DOMDocument
transformToURI()	Transforms to URI
transformToXML()	Transforms to string

The descriptions for these methods are generic. You'll see explanations and examples of these methods in the next section.

Using the XSL Extension

The API for this extension is easy to use, and you can perform simple transformations with just a few lines of code. Before transforming any documents, you first need to create the XSLTProcessor using the new keyword:

```
$proc = new XSLTProcessor();
```

With the XSLTProcessor now instantiated as $proc, you need to decide whether the default document cloning setting needs to be overridden.

Importing the Style Sheet

The next step in the process is to import the style sheet into the processor by using the importStylesheet() method. By importing the style sheet, the processor not only loads the style sheet document but also compiles it so that it is ready to transform data:

```
void importStylesheet(DOMDocument stylesheet)
```

The method takes one parameter, which, according to the documentation, is a DOMDocument object containing the style sheet:

```
$xsl = new DOMDocument();
$xsl->load('my_stylesheet.xsl');
$proc->importStylesheet($xsl);
```

Although a DOMDocument object is an acceptable and preferred object for the method, it is also possible to pass SimpleXMLElement objects and other DOM node types to this method.

You might wonder how any other type of node than a document node could be used to contain a style sheet. The answer to this is that it can't. The reasoning behind allowing other node types is because of the inner workings of SimpleXML. SimpleXML has no concept of a document node. The first SimpleXMLElement object is created from one of the simplexml_load_xxx() functions, and the resulting object refers to the document element. To allow SimpleXML to interact with XSL, any SimpleXMLElement type object passed to this method automatically imports the document node associated with the SimpleXMLElement node. This then opens the door for different types of DOM objects, as long as they inherit from the DOMNode class, to be passed as well as to exhibit the same behavior. For example:

```
/* Load style sheet from SimpleXMLElement object */
$xsl = simplexml_load_file('my_stylesheet.xsl');
$proc->importStylesheet($xsl);


/* Load from a DOMElement object */
$xsl = new DOMDocument();
$xsl->load('my_stylsheet.xsl');
$child = $xsl->documentElement;
$proc->importStylesheet($child);
```

Transforming Data

An XSLT processor loaded with a style sheet is ready to transform some data. You have three methods to transform data. The difference between them lies with where the resulting data is output. Do not confuse this with the xsl:output method that determines how the result tree is output. Data can be returned as a string using the transformToXML() method, sent to a URI using the transformToURI() method, or even returned as a DOMDocument object using the transformToDoc() method.

As you will see, each method takes a doc parameter. The doc parameter, being an object of the DOMDocument type, is the XML document containing the data to be transformed using the already imported style sheet. This parameter, just like the one from the importStylesheet() method, may also be a SimpleXMLElement object or DOMNode object and follows the same rules for determining the document node.

Caution Many developers make the mistake of thinking that because this method accepts nodes other than document nodes, only a fragment of the XML document will be processed. This is incorrect. No matter what node is passed in as the parameter, the full document, starting with the document node, is transformed.

Returning Results As a String

When transforming XML using XSLT within a Web server environment, it is often the case that the result tree is an HTML document that is to be returned to the requesting browser. It is also possible that the result tree contains an RSS document that is to be sent to a requesting client. Either way, each of these would use the transformToXML() method. The name of this method is a bit misleading at first. The ToXML part might make you think that only XML will be returned, which is not the case when working with HTML. All this method does is return the resulting tree as a string. The ToXML is used to be consistent with the other XML methods (such as saveXML() in DOM and asXML() in SimpleXML) where the methods are just returning their tree, which happen to be XML data, as a string:

```
string transformToXML(DOMDocument doc)
```

The doc parameter, which has already been explained, contains the XML data to be transformed. This method returns the output as a string, which could then possibly be sent through a Web server back to the requesting client. The example in Listing 10-3 illustrates a transformation where the results are just printed.

Listing 10-3. *Transforming to a String*

```
$xsl = new DOMDocument();
$xsl->load('my_stylesheet.xsl');

$proc->importStylesheet($xsl);

$dom = new DOMDocument();
$dom->load('my_xmldata.xml');

print $proc->transformToXML($dom);
```

Sending Results to a URI

Output can also be sent to a URI, such as a file or remote system. Just like the previous XML-based extensions in this book, PHP streams handle the data transfer. This opens up many different avenues for dealing with URIs:

```
int transformToURI(DOMDocument doc, string uri)
```

I will skip over the doc parameter because you have seen this parameter a few times now and should understand what it is. The uri parameter is a string containing the URI for where the resulting data is to be sent. This method returns an integer that specifies the number of bytes written to the URI. Using the code from Listing 10-3 and just changing the transformation call, you could send the results to multiple places:

```
/* Save results to a local file.*/
$proc->transformToURI($dom, 'transform_results.xml');

/* Send results to remote Web server */
$proc->transformToURI($dom, 'http://www.example.com/process.php');
```

Returning Results As a DOMDocument Object

The last method for transformation returns the result tree as a DOMDocument object:

```
DOMDocument transformToDoc(DOMNode doc)
```

Even though the doc parameter is a DOMNode type object in the documentation, it is the same as the doc parameter used for the previous transformation methods and follows the same rules. The return value in this case is truly a DOMDocument object. There is no gray area with respect to the returned object type. Again, using the code from Listing 10-3 and changing the transformation call, XSL can return a DOMDocument object that can be used for further processing:

```
$transDoc = $proc->transformToDoc($dom);
```

You might wonder how this could be useful. It is unlikely you would need to edit the resulting document, especially since it could have been performed using the style sheet. In most cases, the new document would either be processed within an application or be quite possibly used as the XML data for a different transformation. The possibilities are numerous.

Using Parameters in XSL

XSL provides functionality to pass parameters to a style sheet. The parameters and values themselves are not passed to a style sheet until a document is being transformed. In the meantime, XSL provides three methods—setParameter(), getParameter(), and removeParameter()— to manage the parameters that will be passed for use during the transformation. These methods can be called at any time after the XSLTProcessor object has been instantiated and before a transformation call.

■**Note** Parameters passed by the XSLT processor affect only top-level parameters. These are xsl:param elements that are immediate child elements of the xsl:stylesheet element.

Setting Parameters

Naturally, the setParameter() method sets parameters for the style sheet:

```
bool setParameter(string namespace, string name, string value)
bool setParameter(string namespace, array options)
```

As you can see, you have two ways to call this method. In each case, the namespace parameter is currently not used, so any value can be passed there because it will be ignored anyway. It is a good idea, though, to pass NULL or an empty string just to reduce any possible confusion. The style sheet used for these examples looks like the following:

```
<xsl:stylesheet xmlns:xsl="http://www.w3.org/1999/XSL/Transform" version="1.0">
    <xsl:param name="param1" select="0" />
    <xsl:param name="param2" select="0" />
    <xsl:param name="param3" select="0" />
```

```
<xsl:template match="/">
   <xsl:value-of select="$param1" />
   <xsl:value-of select="$param2" />
   <xsl:value-of select="$param3" />
</xsl:template>
</xsl:stylesheet>
```

The first prototype accepts a name and value, where name is the name of the parameter in the style sheet and value is the value for which the parameter should be set:

```
$proc->setParameter(NULL, 'param1', 'newval');
```

This sets the value for param1 to the string newval. When the transformation occurs, the resulting output looks like the following:

```
Newval
0
0
```

The second prototype takes an array containing name/value pairs. This allows you to set multiple parameters at the same time:

```
$proc->setParameter(NULL, array('param1'=>2, 'param2'=>3));
```

This operation sets the value of param1 to 2 and the value of param2 to 3. The resulting output in this case is as follows:

```
2
3
0
```

Retrieving Parameter Values

The getParameter() method retrieves values for parameters set using the setParameter() method. Parameters defined in the style sheet have no bearing on this method call. For example:

```
string getParameter(string namespaceURI, string localName)
```

Again, the namespaceURI currently has no bearing and should be set to NULL or the empty string until it is implemented. The localName parameter is the name of the parameter to retrieve:

```
/* Parameter not set on processor but exists in style sheet */
var_dump($proc->getParameter(NULL, 'param3'));

/* Parameter set on processor and exists in style sheet */
$proc->setParameter(NULL, 'param1', 'newval');
var_dump($proc->getParameter(NULL, 'param1'));
```

```
/* Parameter set on processor but not existing in style sheet */
$proc->setParameter(NULL, 'param4', 4);
var_dump($proc->getParameter(NULL, 'param4'));
```

A parameter that has not been set using setParameter() results in a return value of FALSE. The following is the output from the preceding example. The last result demonstrates that a parameter does not need to be specified in the style sheet to set and retrieve values for it on the processor. When passed to the style sheet, it is simply ignored.

```
bool(false)
string(6) "newval"
string(1) "4"
```

Removing Parameters

You can remove parameters set by setParameter() by using the removeParameter() method:

```
bool removeParameter(string namespaceURI, string localName)
```

The parameters are the same as those for the getParameter() method. The namespaceURI is not used, and the localName is the name of the parameter. Using the results from the getParameter() example, it is clear that param4 has the value 4. For this example, param4 will be removed, and then its nonexistent value can be retrieved:

```
var_dump($proc->getParameter(NULL, 'param4'));

$proc->removeParamater(NULL, 'param4');

var_dump($proc->getParameter(NULL, 'param4'));
```

```
string(1) "4"
bool(false)
```

Calling PHP Functions from XSL

EXSLT is a collection of additional modules providing extended functionality to XSLT. As long as libexslt is included when building XSL (which, as long as you have it and the header files installed, should build in automatically), the functions are available to be used within a style sheet. Calling the hasExsltSupport() method will indicate whether your XSLT processor supports EXSLT, based on the value of the returned Boolean:

```
if ($proc->hasExsltSupport()) {
    /* EXSLT support available */
}
```

Using the function module from EXSLT, you can create and use user-defined functions within style sheets. The functions, however, are limited to XSLT syntax and the functionality supported by the XSLT processor. XSL extends XSLT even further by adding its own module to support calling PHP functionality from within a style sheet. Because the functionality is implemented by the parser and not by the libxslt/libexslt libraries, it is available whether or not EXSLT support is enabled.

Setting Up the Processor

The registerPHPFunctions() method sets up the processor to allow PHP function calls to be made from within the style sheet:

```
void registerPHPFunctions([mixed names])
```

Under PHP 5.0.*x*, the registerPHPFunctions() method takes no arguments. Calling it simply enables PHP function support in the style sheet. With the release of PHP 5.1, some steps to secure the use of this method were added. The names parameter was added, allowing a developer to restrict the PHP functions available to be used in a style sheet. The value can be a single string identifying a function to allow or an array containing multiple functions to allow. When setting acceptable functions to be called using a string, the registerPHPFunctions() method can be called multiple times, adding each function to the list of acceptable functions. It is much easier, however, to just use an array containing all the function names in this case because the method then needs to be called only once:

```
/* Setting up parser to support PHP functions - all PHP 5 versions */
$proc->registerPHPFunctions();

/* Restricting callable functions by single function at a time - PHP 5.1 + only */
$proc->registerPHPFunctions('date');
$proc->registerPHPFunctions('time');

/* Restricting callable functions using array - PHP 5.1 + only */
$proc->registerPHPFunctions(array('date', 'time'));
```

Functions are not limited to built-in functions either. User-defined functions are perfectly valid:

```
function myFunction() {
    return "myFunction called";
}

$proc->regsiterPHPFunctions('myFunction');
```

■**Caution** Calling the registerPHPFunctions() method without any arguments allows all functions available within a PHP script, including user-defined functions, to be called from an XSLT style sheet. Specifying function names as the parameter will restrict callable functions to only those registered with the processor. This will help prevent untrusted style sheets from calling PHP functions that they are not allowed to call or should not call.

Setting Up the Style Sheet

Using PHP functions is just like using EXSLT modules. You must add the proper namespace to the xsl:stylesheet element. The PHP namespace for its own module is http://php.net/xsl. Typically, the php prefix is used with this namespace, but you are free to specify any prefix you like:

```
<xsl:stylesheet xmlns:xsl="http://www.w3.org/1999/XSL/Transform" version="1.0"
                xmlns:php="http://php.net/xsl">
```

This style sheet will use the prefix php to access PHP functionality.

Calling the Functions

With the processor set up to allow PHP functions and the namespace properly added to the xsl:stylesheet element, the only thing left is to explain how functions are called within the style sheet. The PHP XSL module provides two callable functions from a style sheet that are used to access the PHP functions. Assuming the php prefix is associated with the PHP namespace, they are php:function and php:functionString. The difference between these two is how arguments to be passed to the PHP functions are handled. When using php:functionString, arguments that are node sets from XSLT are converted to strings and then passed to the PHP function. When using php:function, arguments that are node sets are converted into corresponding DOM objects based on the type of node and passed to the PHP function as an array of DOM objects.

Using Function Parameters

Each of these functions takes a variable number of parameters. The first parameter is required and specifies the name of the PHP function or static method to call. A method call cannot be made against an instantiated object because the object is not directly accessible from the style sheet, but it could be called indirectly by calling a function that in turn calls the object. All additional parameters are the parameters to be passed to the PHP function when called. The additional parameters are specified in the order they are passed to the PHP functions:

```
php:function('testFunction', 'a', .);
```

When called from the style sheet, this would call the PHP function named testFunction and pass the string 'a' for the first parameter and an array containing the context node, as a DOMNode type, for the second parameter:

```
php:functionString('testFunction', 'a', .);
```

This function performs the same actions as the previous one, except in this case, the string value of the context node is passed as the second argument.

Making the Call

The following function is defined within a PHP script that is performing some XSLT processing:

```
function MYFUNC($var = NULL) {
    return var_export($var, true)."\n\n";
}

$proc->registerPHPFunctions('MYFUNC');
```

It accepts a single parameter, defaulting to NULL, and returns the results of calling var_export(), which, by passing TRUE as the second argument to it, returns a parsable string representation of a variable. To call this function, you need to use the php:function() function or the php:functionString() function in the style sheet:

```
<xsl:stylesheet xmlns:xsl="http://www.w3.org/1999/XSL/Transform" version="1.0"
                xmlns:php="http://php.net/xsl">

    <xsl:template match="/">
        <xsl:value-of select="php:function('MYFUNC', 1)" />
        <xsl:value-of select="php:function('MYFUNC', .)" />
        <xsl:value-of select="php:functionString('MYFUNC', .)" />
    </xsl:template>
</xsl:stylesheet>
```

The XML data that will be used for this transformation looks like this:

```
<sites>
    <site><name>XML C Parser</name></site>
    <site><name>PHP</name></site>
</sites>
```

The result from the transformation is as follows:

```
<?xml version="1.0"?>
1

array (
  0 =&gt;
  class DOMDocument {
  },
)


        XML C Parser
        PHP

```

Note The only type of object that can be returned from the PHP function is one that is based on the DOMNode class, which includes the majority of the classes from the DOM extension. All other types of objects result in PHP issuing a warning and an empty string being used as the result. You'll see an example of this in the "Processing a Style Sheet Built Using the DOM Extension" section.

Looking at the template within the style sheets, you will see three calls made to the PHP functions. The first call uses `php:function` to call the `MYFUNC` function, passing a number 1 as its parameter. From the output you can see that the variable was truly passed as the integer 1. The second call uses `php:function` to call the `MYFUNC` function, passing in the context node as the parameter. Based on the rules of conversion for node sets, it is converted to a DOM object with the type based on the node type and sent to the function as an array. From the output, you can see that the array contains a `DOMDocument` object. The last call uses the `php:functionString` function to call `MYFUNC`, again passing in the context node. This time, the node is converted to a string using the rules defined by XPath and then passed to the `MYFUNC` function. The output shows that the argument passed was a string containing all the text nodes from the XML data document.

Seeing Some Examples in Action

XSL is not a complex extension to use. The majority of difficulty comes from creating the style sheets used in the transformations. Examples of using the different functionality of the `XSLTProcessor` are abundant. I'll demonstrate two examples in the following sections. The first is a continuation of the example in Chapter 6 where a style sheet was manually created using the DOM methods. The second example is a bit larger. It aggregates some RSS feeds (which are thoroughly covered in Chapter 14) using the XSL extension and a variety of XSLT functionality for displaying in a web page.

Processing a Style Sheet Built Using the DOM Extension

One of the biggest problems developers have using the DOM extension is creating documents with namespaces. The last example in Chapter 6 manually created an XSLT style sheet using the DOM API. As you are now well aware, XSLT requires extensive use of namespaces, and they must be used properly. This example will show the processing of that manually created document.

From the DOM example, the code for building an XSLT style sheet ended with the `$stylesheet` variable, which is a `DOMDocument` object, containing a style sheet created manually. Using this already created variable, the XML data from Chapter 6 (which will be re-created here), will be transformed.

Here's the code:

```
$xml = <<<EOF
<sites>
    <site>
        <name>Libxml</name>
        <url>http://www.xmlsoft.org</url>
    </site>
    <site>
        <name>W3C DOM Level 3 Specification</name>
        <url>www.w3.org/TR/DOM-Level-3-Core/</url>
    </site>
</sites>
EOF;
```

```
$dom = new DOMDocument();
$dom->loadXML($xml);

$proc = new xsltprocessor();

$proc->importStylesheet($stylesheet);

print $proc->transformToXML($dom);
```

The code is straightforward and simple to understand. The code demonstrates that manually created style sheets, as long as they are namespaced properly, work fine with XSL. Running the code with the code from Chapter 6, the output you will see should look similar to this:

```
<html><body>
<p>Libxml : http://www.xmlsoft.org</p>
<p>W3C DOM Level 3 Specification : www.w3.org/TR/DOM-Level-3-Core/</p>
</body></html>
```

Aggregating RSS Feeds Using XSL

This example demonstrates how to use the XSL extensions and some of the XSLT functionality using RSS for the source data, since it is a data source everyone should be able to access. I will not explain the structure and workings of RSS (covered in detail in Chapter 14) in this example because the focus is on using the extension and XSLT functionality.

This example will show how to combine a couple of the PHP news feeds into a single XML data source and store them locally. The feed to be accessed or identified in a configuration file is named siteconfig.xml and contains the following document:

```
<?xml version="1.0"?>
<sites>
   <site>
      <name>PHP General</name>
      <url>http://news.php.net/group.php?group=php.general&amp;format=rss</url>
   </site>
   <site>
      <name>PHP Pear Dev</name>
      <url>http://news.php.net/group.php?group=php.pear.dev&amp;format=rss</url>
   </site>
</sites>
```

Two sites have been configured. The first one is the feed for the PHP General newsgroup, and the second is the feed for the PHP PEAR Dev group. The url element for these groups points to the locations of the respective RSS feeds from which you will pull the XML data.

This data is used by a style sheet, identified by the file rsscache.xsl, to transform the data from each feed into a single document, which is then stored locally in the file named rsscache.xml. This local file works as a cache; here it must be updated manually, but it is possible to have this file automatically update on some specified schedule.

The style sheet that performs the transformation is as follows:

```
<?xml version="1.0"?>
<xsl:stylesheet xmlns:xsl="http://www.w3.org/1999/XSL/Transform"
                xmlns:php="http://php.net/xsl" version="1.0">
  <xsl:output method="xml" indent="yes" />

  <xsl:template match="/">
     <xsl:element name="channels">
        <xsl:apply-templates select="/sites/site"/>
     </xsl:element>
  </xsl:template>

  <xsl:template match="site">
     <xsl:variable name="siteurl" select="url" />
     <xsl:apply-templates select="php:functionString('retrieveRSS',
                                              $siteurl)/channel">
        <xsl:with-param name="sitename" select="name" />
     </xsl:apply-templates>
  </xsl:template>

  <xsl:template match="channel">
     <xsl:element name="channel">
        <xsl:element name="title">
           <xsl:copy-of select="$sitename" />
        </xsl:element>
        <xsl:copy-of select="link" />
        <xsl:apply-templates select="item"/>
     </xsl:element>
  </xsl:template>

  <xsl:template match="item">
     <xsl:element name="item">
        <xsl:copy-of select="title" />
        <xsl:copy-of select="link" />
        <xsl:copy-of select="pubDate" />
        <xsl:element name="timestamp">
           <xsl:value-of select="php:functionString('strtotime', pubDate)" />
        </xsl:element>
     </xsl:element>
  </xsl:template>

</xsl:stylesheet>
```

Looking at this file, you will notice that the http://php.net/xsl namespace has been added. This will allow PHP functions to be called, assuming the processor calling the style sheet has enabled the use of PHP function calls. The output method has been set to xml, because the output is to be a locally cached XML document, and indenting has been enabled, which will allow easier readability if you happen to open the resulting rsscache.xml file in an editor.

Upon processing the configuration data, each of the site elements is selected for further processing, matching on site. The template handling these nodes retrieves the remote RSS data. Rather than using the XSLT document() function, this calls a PHP function. This PHP function has been defined within the encompassing script and is written as follows:

```
function retrieveRSS($url) {
    $doc = new DOMDocument();
    if ($doc->load($url)) {
        return $doc->documentElement;
    }
    return 0;
}
```

It accepts a single argument, $url, that is then retrieved using a DOMDocument object. Looking at the template making this call, a variable has been used and is set to the content of the url element. This value is then passed to the retrieveRSS() function from which the document element of the resulting XML document is returned or 0 is returned upon failure.

Note The variable is not needed in this instance because using url rather than $siteurl would also work, but a variable was used for demonstration instead.

Assuming the document element was returned from the function, the template then calls xsl:apply-templates, selecting the channel element from the returned node set. By "node set," I am simply referring to the document element. This would occur once for each of the site elements from the configuration file, but note that each time the retrieveRSS() function is called, any returned node set is processed by the templates before the next call to the function. When applying the templates to the channel element, a parameter is also being passed. The content of the name element for the specific site being processed is passed using the sitename parameter. The reason for this will be shown in the template matching on the channel element.

Upon matching a channel element, a new channel element is created to encapsulate the data you want pulled into the new XML document. The reason xsl:element is used instead of literal <channel> and </channel> tags is because of the data being worked upon. The document came from the external PHP function residing in the php namespace. Using a literal element tag causes the php namespace declaration to be added to the elements. The resulting document does not need any namespace information for this example, so by using xsl:element, the channel element is specifically created with no namespace information. This is where the parameter passed from the previous template comes into play. Rather than use the title for the channel from the RSS feed, you would like to have the name you defined in the config file for the channel used instead for the new document. You do not need to do anything special with the link, so it is simply copied, using xsl:copy-of, into the new document. The template then applies templates to the item elements from the channel.

The template matching on item just pulls a few elements from the RSS feed for each item. They are still contained within an item element, but the nodes being copied are only title, link, and pubDate. When the data from this resulting document is finally to be transformed into HTML, it would be nice to be able to do some sorting using the XSLT sorting functionality.

You have no way to perform date sorting natively, so add a timestamp element. The value here simply takes the date specified by pubDate and calls the PHP strtotime() function to convert the date into a Unix time stamp. You can then use this value, being purely numeric, to perform date sorting.

The local rsscache.xml file is created using the previous XML data and style sheet from the following script. This is a single script, so the function you are interested in is buildCache(). This function uses a generic function to load the DOMDocument objects, create the XSLT processor, transform the data, and save the result document to a file.

The entire script for this example, referenced by the filename rssrender.php, appears as follows:

```php
<?php
/* The configuration file storing the sites to pull RSS data from.
   It must be readable by the Web server */
$site_config = 'siteconfig.xml';
/* Template used to render the cached RSS */
$render_xsl = 'itemrender.xsl';
/* This file stores the summarize RSS information.
   It must be read/writable by the Web server */
$rsscache = 'rsscache.xml';
/* Template used to build the RSS cache */
$rsscache_xsl = 'rsscache.xsl';

/* function called from the $rsscache_xsl template */
function retrieveRSS($url) {
    $doc = new DOMDocument();
    if ($doc->load($url)) {
        return $doc->documentElement;
    }
    return 0;
}

/* Generic function to transform XML data using XSL extension */
function genericProcess($xmlfile, $xslfile, $params=NULL, $outputfile=NULL) {
    $doc = new DOMDocument();
    $doc->load($xmlfile);

    $xsl = new DOMDocument();
    $xsl->load($xslfile);

    $proc = new xsltprocessor();
    $proc->registerPHPFunctions();
    $proc->importStylesheet($xsl);

    if (is_array($params)) {
        foreach ($params AS $key=>$value) {
            $proc->setParameter(NULL, $key, $value);
        }
    }
```

```php
    if ($outputfile == NULL) {
        if ($outdoc = $proc->transformToDoc($doc)) {
            $outdoc->formatOutput = TRUE;
            return $outdoc->saveXML();
        }
    } else {
        return $proc->transformToURI($doc, $outputfile);
    }
}

/* Build the RSS Cache file */
function buildCache() {
    genericProcess($GLOBALS['site_config'], $GLOBALS['rsscache_xsl'], NULL,
                   $GLOBALS['rsscache']);
}

$xslparams = NULL;
$cacheBuilt = FALSE;
$sorted = NULL;

/* Perform actions based on HTML form submissions */
if (isset($_POST['buildcache']) && ! empty($_POST['buildcache'])) {
    buildCache();
} elseif (isset($_POST['sortit']) && ! empty($_POST['sortit']) &&
          isset($_POST['sort']) && ! empty($_POST['sort'])) {
    $sorted = $_POST['sort'];
    $xslparams = array('sortparam'=>$_POST['sort']);
}

if (file_exists($rsscache)) {
    $cacheBuilt = TRUE;
}

?>
<html>
    <body>
        <b>RSS Items:</b><br>
        <form method="post">
        <table>
            <tr>
                <td><input type="submit" name="buildcache" value="Update Cache">
                        </td>
<?php if ($cacheBuilt) { ?>
```

```
        <td>
            <select name="sort">
                <option value="">Published Date</option>
                <option value="channel" <?php if ($sorted == "channel")
                                    print "selected"; ?>>Channel</option>
                <option value="title" <?php if ($sorted == "title")
                                    print "selected"; ?>>Item Title</option>
            </select>  
            <input type="submit" name="sortit" value="Sort">
        </td>
<?php } ?>
        </tr>
    </table>
    </form><br><br>
    <?php
    if ($cacheBuilt) {
        print genericProcess($rsscache, $render_xsl, $xslparams);
    } else {
        print "Cache not built. Please update Cache.";
    } ?>
    </body>
</html>


<?xml version="1.0"?>
<xsl:stylesheet xmlns:xsl="http://www.w3.org/1999/XSL/Transform" version="1.0">
    <xsl:param name="sortparam" select="datetime" />
    <xsl:output method="html"/>

    <xsl:template match="/">
        <table>
            <xsl:apply-templates select="//channel/item">
                <xsl:sort select="../title[$sortparam='channel']" order="ascending" />
                <xsl:sort select="./title[$sortparam='title']" order="ascending"
                        case-order="lower-first" />
                <xsl:sort select="./timestamp" order="descending" />
            </xsl:apply-templates>
        </table>
    </xsl:template>

    <xsl:template match="channel">
        <xsl:element name="channel">
            <xsl:copy-of select="title" />
            <xsl:copy-of select="link" />
                <xsl:apply-templates select="item"/>
        </xsl:element>
    </xsl:template>
```

```
<xsl:template match="item">
    <tr>
        <td colspan="3">
            <a>
                <xsl:attribute name="href">
                    <xsl:value-of select="link" />
                </xsl:attribute>
                <xsl:value-of select="title"/>
            </a>
        </td>
    </tr><tr>
        <!-- Insert some non breaking spaces.
            Rather than add DTD for nbsp numeric codes are used instead. -->
        <td>     </td>
        <td>Channel:
            <a>
                <xsl:attribute name="href">
                    <xsl:value-of select="../link" />
                </xsl:attribute>
                <xsl:value-of select="../title"/>
            </a>
        </td>
        <td>Published: <xsl:copy-of select="pubDate" /></td>
    </tr>
</xsl:template>

</xsl:stylesheet>
```

The only part of this template that probably needs explaining is the sortparam parameter and how sorting takes place. The sortparameter is passed into the style sheet from the XSLT processor based upon the form submission. This allows you to choose how the sorting should be performed in the resulting HTML output. The problem you run into is that the xsl:sort element can be used only within the context of the xsl:apply-templates and xsl:for-each elements. The possible solutions would be to create multiple templates to process item elements and call them based on the type of sorting that needs to be performed, use xsl:choose and select the xsl:apply-templates call based on the value of the sortparam, or find a way to work around the issue, as in this example.

You can request three types of sorting. The default is a simple datetime sort. The items are ordered by their pubDate in descending order. This was the reason the additional timestamp element was added. The sorting is actually performed on that element. The second sorting method is by channel title, using the name that came from the site's config file, in ascending order followed by pubDate in descending order. Lastly, the items can be sorted by the title of the item in ascending order followed by pubDate in descending order. Now the question you most likely have is, how can this work when all the xsl:sort elements are called within the scope of the same xsl:apply-templates call?

The first xsl:sort element defined performs a sort based on the title element from the parent of the current item. The qualifier for the select, however, tests the equality of the sortparam. Unless the value channel was passed from the XSLT processor, the qualifier fails, resulting in nothing being selected for this sort. The same trick is used in the second `xsl:sort` element, but this time it checks for the value `title`. If the value matches, then sorting is performed on the `title` element of the item. The last `xsl:sort` has no such qualifier. If you remember the sort ordering, the last sort key for every sorting is the `datetime`. This key will always be used and thus is never invalidated by a qualifier.

■**Note** Although this sorting trick does work, it will result in a slower transformation compared to using `xsl:choose` or defining multiple templates. It does, however, create a more compact style sheet. The performance issue really depends upon the amount of data being processed.

When running this example within a Web server, the cache can be created and/or updated by clicking the Update Cache button. Sorting is simply changed by selecting the desired sort option and clicking the Sort button. Figure 10-2 shows a rendered page that has been sorted by the item name.

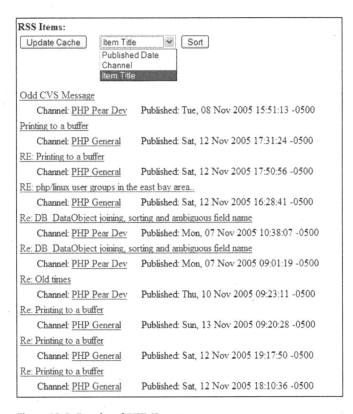

Figure 10-2. *Rendered HTML page*

Conclusion

XSLT is a powerful technology for transforming XML data into different results. This chapter introduced and explained the XSLT language. As you can see, the bulk of the work is creating the style sheet using the XSLT language. Style sheets can become quite complex. But the more experience you get using the language, the easier it becomes to write more complex rules.

This chapter also explored XSLT functionality. Using EXSLT modules, an abundance of more complex functions are available to be used within style sheets. The XSL extension takes this a step further by allowing you to create your own functions using PHP that can be called from a style sheet. This opens up endless possibilities for what can be performed during a transformation.

This extension is the last of the internal PHP XML parsers and processors to be examined. The next chapter covers how to develop with XML. It compares the different extensions and technologies, including everything from the pros and cons to optimizations and interoperability. After you have finished the next chapter, you should be prepared for your next XML-based project using PHP 5.

■ ■ ■

CHAPTER 11

Effective and Efficient Processing

With so many different ways to process a document, it is often difficult to decide which is the best method. This chapter will cover the strengths and weaknesses of the different parsing methodologies to help you make an educated decision about which will work best for you. In some cases, a single technology may not be enough, so this chapter will also cover how to effectively combine technologies. By the end of this chapter, you should be able to determine which technologies fit your needs and understand how to use them together to effectively and efficiently process XML.

■**Note** I performed all the tests in this chapter using debug builds of PHP and libxml2. This adds overhead in both memory usage and processing time. The results of the tests will vary between systems as well as between different release builds of PHP and libxml2. You should not take the results presented in this chapter as absolutes but as the basis to compare performance and memory utilizations among the different extensions. When dealing with performance and optimizations, you should also consider ease of development and debugging. It is possible you may overoptimize your code, leaving it difficult to maintain. How code is organized is something left up to you to decide.

Looking at the Pros and Cons of Parsers

Each of the XML-based parsers in PHP 5 provides its own unique way to interact with XML data. The most noticeable difference is the classification of tree-based parsers versus streaming parsers. You can break this classification down even further, because the extensions in each category differ significantly from each other. No single extension can handle every task because each has its own pros and cons. The following sections will summarize and compare the parsers available, which will eventually help you choose a specific parser.

Comparing Tree-Based and Streaming Parsers

As you recall, *tree-based parsers* build an in-memory representation of an XML document while parsing it. Once loaded, the tree can be navigated, modified, and finally saved. Parsers that fall under this category potentially use a high level of system resources. Consider loading a 10MB document using a tree-based parser. The entire document is loaded into memory in a tree structure, which ends up consuming much more than the original 10MB of memory. On the other hand, because the document resides in memory, navigating the tree is fast—once the internal tree has been built, of course. The PHP 5 extensions falling into this category are DOM and SimpleXML. Although they are fundamentally similar, their usage and their functionality are significantly different from each other.

Streaming parsers are lightweight parsers. An XML document is simultaneously parsed and processed. Data is read in chunks, and once specific data is processed, it is typically discarded. Once parsing has been completed, no further processing can be performed. These parsers differ greatly from tree-based parsers. Navigation is forward only. You cannot dynamically access specific locations in an XML document, and the parser cannot access previously processed data. The XML document is not memory resident, so modifications cannot be made natively and then be saved to the original document. On the other hand, without the need for a memory-resident structure, streaming parsers use memory effectively, keeping its usage to a minimum. The two extensions falling into this category, though very distinct from each other, are the xml extension and XMLReader.

Comparing Individual Parsers

With all the different functionality and nuances between the parsers, it's not easy to figure out how they are operationally different. Table 11-1 presents a matrix of the extensions and some of the more significant differences. Following this table, I'll discuss each of the differences in more detail and how these features pertain to the specific extensions.

■**Note** Within the following sections when referring to the parsers, the term *xml* refers to the SAX-based xml extension.

Table 11-1. *Comparative Breakdown of Extensions*

	Tree-Based Parsers		Streaming Parsers	
Feature	**DOM**	**SimpleXML**	**xml**	**XMLReader**
System resources	Variable	Variable	Minimal	Minimal
Document navigation	Excellent	Good	Forward-Only	Forward-Only
Document editing	Excellent	Good	None	None
Ease of use	Difficult	Simple	Simple	Easy
Namespace support	Excellent	Decent	Minimal	Excellent
Parsing/processing speed	Variable	Variable	Fast	Fast

System Resources

Overall, the streaming parsers win in this area. Unlike the tree-based parsers, xml and XML-Reader do not need to build in-memory tree structures. Processing begins immediately as the data streams through the parser. Once the data has been processed, the parser is free to release the data. Memory usage remains low while parsing large documents. By "large documents," I mean ones that are megabytes in size.

The tree-based parsers, DOM and SimpleXML, are memory hogs. The amount of system resources used depends upon the size and structure of the XML document being processed. The larger the document, the more resources that are required. Processing with one of these extensions takes place on the in-memory tree. The parser, however, must first build the entire tree from the data before any processing can take place, and the tree, containing all the information for the document, ends up using much more memory than a serialized version of the tree itself.

Table 11-2 shows the internal memory used by libxml2 from each of the extensions parsing a 12.5MB document called `bigxml.xml`. These figures do not represent the memory used by PHP but, rather, the actual memory required to parse the document, which would be on top of the memory used by PHP. The document consists of 200,000 child nodes; a snippet looks like this:

```
<books>
    <book id="1"><title>1</title><pages>1</pages></book>
    <book id="2"><title>2</title><pages>2</pages></book>
    <!-- Remaining book elements -->
</books>
```

Table 11-2. *Internal Memory Usage by Extension*

DOM	SimpleXML	xml	XMLReader
85.6MB	85.6MB	26KB	177KB

I performed all tests using PHP 5.1 with libxml2-2.6.20 built in debug mode on a Pentium 4 2.6GHz system with 1GB of physical memory running under Windows XP SP 2. Similar tests run on older hardware (a Pentium III 350MHz system with 512MB memory and various versions of Linux) resulted in similar results. All results in Table 11-2 have been rounded to the nearest kilobyte or to the first tenth in the case of megabytes.

Note I performed all tests under Windows using a debug build of PHP CLI and a debug build of libxml2. Performance will differ based on platform, so although tests performed on your platform may not compare to the results in this chapter, the numbers should be comparable when running the same tests with different extensions.

DOM

Loading a document 12.5MB in size and requiring 85.6MB of memory probably makes you think the DOM extension must be doing a lot of editing on this document. You may be surprised to find out this is the amount of memory just to create the DOMDocument object:

```php
<?php
$dom = DOMDocument::load('bigxml.xml');
?>
```

Working with large documents definitely requires some finesse or some decent hardware when using the DOM extension. Imagine the memory it would require to work with a document on the scale of 100MB. Unfortunately, I am unable to supply any information on that; after consuming about 700MB of system memory (not to mention the memory already being used by the operating system and other applications), my test machine started to fail and had to be rebooted.

SimpleXML

SimpleXML results in similar memory consumption as the DOM extension. Before rounding off the figures, SimpleXML actually resulted in about 114 bytes less memory consumption, but looking at the figures, the difference really doesn't matter. Just like the DOM example, SimpleXML did nothing other than load the document. No processing was actually performed. The following is the actual script used for the result in Table 11-2:

```php
<?php
$sxe = simplexml_load_file('bigxml.xml');
?>
```

As far as system resources go, both tree-based parsers are pretty much equal. The larger the document, the more memory required to parse it.

xml

After looking at the figures for the previous two extensions, the number for xml is probably shocking. The xml extension required only 26KB of memory to parse the 12.5MB file. Again, this number does not reflect the amount of memory used by PHP, just the libxml2 library. Even considering the memory used by PHP and the rest of your code, the number pales in comparison to a number such as 85.6MB.

The stream-based parsers do not create in-memory structures, so the memory requirements depend entirely upon your code. The result for xml was based on reading 4,096 bytes of the document at a time and feeding them to the parser. No handlers were implemented, so the data just simply parsed the following:

```php
<?php
$handle = fopen("bigxml.xml", "r");
while ($data = fread($handle, 4096)) {
    if (!xml_parse($parser, $data, feof($handle))) {
        print "error";
        break;
    }
}
?>
```

■**Note** Memory usage remained consistent using xml and XMLReader even when the document doubled in size from 12.5MB to 26MB. The same cannot be said for DOM and SimpleXML, which caused memory usage to peak at about 172MB.

XMLReader

Although not as low as xml, XMLReader is attractive with its 177KB memory usage. XMLReader is a pull parser, so you must instruct it to keep parsing the document because the cursor stops along the way. For example:

```php
<?php
$reader = XMLReader::open('bigxml.xml');
while ($reader->read()) {
    // do nothing
}
?>
```

Summary

Streaming parsers, xml, and XMLReader are the most memory-efficient parsers in terms of the libxml2 memory usage. This comes with the cost of less functionality, however. The tree-based parsers, DOM and SimpleXML, use quite a lot of memory because the actual usage depends upon the size and structure of the document. Typically, creating the in-memory tree requires four to seven times more memory than the actual size of the serialized document. This varies not only based on the size of the document but also based on the composition of the document.

Document Navigation

Document navigation is the ability to move around and/or dynamically access locations within a document. Streaming parsers offer virtually no navigation because they move only forward through the document. The minor exception to this is XMLReader, with its ability to move between attributes and elements. Neither xml nor XMLReader, though, allows movement to previously processed data. Neither extension allows the document to be dynamically accessed either, such as through XPath queries. Document navigation is one of the biggest strengths of tree-based parsers, because they allow free movement to any point in the tree. Trees can be descended, ascended, and even queried.

xml and XMLReader

As previously stated, these extensions make a single pass through a document. Without an in-memory tree, navigation is not possible. XMLReader is a minor exception to this. Even though the cursor moves only forward through a document, movement between an element and its attributes is possible. Attributes are a special case within XMLReader, and unless instructed to do so, the cursor never stops on an attribute. You can also use the next() method for navigational purposes. The cursor still will move only forward but can skip subtrees. Other than these two cases, it could be argued that the read() function is considered to be navigational functionality; however, in my opinion, this method is integral to the "pull" philosophy and relates more to its parsing method than to actual document navigation. The cursor will move only to the next node, rather than to a node specified by the developer.

DOM

Support for working with a document is rich in the DOM extension. You can descend the tree as well as ascend it. You can access the document node, document element node, child nodes, and parent for the current node for node types through the object's properties. DOM provides navigational functionality to siblings and many other node types through simple method calls. You can also use XPath to retrieve collections of nodes queried by an expression.

Because DOM supports access to an entire document, it is not always simple to access a specific node without using XPath. For example, take the following document, where $element is a DOMElement object referring to the body node:

```
<body>
    <child1/>
    <child2/>
    <child3/>
</body>
```

Navigating to the child3 element without using XPath is not as simple as asking the DOMElement object to get a specific node. In this instance, getElementsByTagName() could work; except in a larger document, every node named child3 would be retrieved, but only the single child element of the body element should be retrieved. You could do this in a few ways, but they all look something like the following:

```
$node = $element->firstChild;
while ($node && $node->nodeName != 'child3') {
    $node = $node->nextSibling;
}
```

The tree needs to be walked, in some manner, with each node being tested for the specified criteria.

SimpleXML

SimpleXML does not have as rich of navigational functionality as DOM, but it is so much easier to access elements. First I will cover some of the navigational limitations. SimpleXML does not ascend a tree. For instance, while working with a bunch of SimpleXMLElement objects and the object for the document element goes out of scope, you have no way to return to the top of the tree. Another aspect of SimpleXML is that only elements and attributes within a document are accessible. All other types of nodes—excluding text nodes, which make up the content of these nodes—are inaccessible.

These deficiencies, in many cases, are outweighed by the ease of use SimpleXML offers when descending a tree. For instance, in the example document for DOM, with the variable $sxe referencing the body element, what took a few lines of code including a loop to walk the tree using the DOM API takes only a single line of code using SimpleXML:

```
$node = $sxe->child3;
```

SimpleXML allows you to work with the tree as an object, removing the need to manually locate elements within the document.

Summary

Neither xml nor XMLReader offers any real document navigational functionality, because they are both streaming parsers. DOM and SimpleXML, being tree parsers, allow movement through the in-memory tree. The difference between DOM and SimpleXML is mainly because of the API. SimpleXML, having a much smaller API, is restrictive in the allowable navigation. For example, with a `SimpleXMLElement` object, you have no way to directly access the document element or even the parent element without using XPath or keeping the object for the node in scope and accessible. DOM allows direct access to the navigational functionality so a tree can be descended and ascended. SimpleXML, on the other hand, allows intuitive movement through the document using element names as object properties, making the API easier for many developers to use.

Document Editing

Document editing involves editing an existing document as well as creating documents from scratch. DOM and SimpleXML excel in this area, though DOM is the real winner. xml and XMLReader are read-only parsers, so forget about either one of them if you require document editing. SimpleXML does not provide the full capabilities of DOM, which offers complete access to a document, but SimpleXML is convenient to use when working with uncomplicated documents or when requiring simple text modification. Advanced editing is typically performed with the DOM extension.

xml and XMLReader

Both of these extensions offer read-only access to the XML document. Any modifications that a script may make are not performed on the actual XML document. For example, exporting a node from XMLReader returns a copy of the node and not the actual node within the document. The xml extension, on the other hand, works only with the string values of the document contents and not the physical document.

DOM

DOM offers complete document-editing capabilities. The document is loaded into memory, and its structure and contents can be altered and saved. With a rich API, probably with more functionality than the majority of developers would ever use, virtually every aspect of a document can be edited, including creating documents from scratch.

SimpleXML

SimpleXML provides limited editing capabilities. Although, like DOM, the document is loaded into memory and ultimately saved, editing functionality is limited to existing elements and attributes. You can remove elements and attributes from documents to a point, but you cannot add them. This prevents you from creating documents from scratch as well as limits the changes you can make to a document's structure.

Summary

Looking at the extensions, the only viable options for document editing are DOM and SimpleXML. Although you can use SimpleXML for simple editing functions such as changing the content of an element or attribute, you cannot make more advanced structural modifications. For complete editing capabilities, you need to use the DOM extension.

Ease of Use

Ease of use refers to the difficulty factor when using a particular extension. XMLReader is the easiest extension to use. SimpleXML is also easy to work with, but people tend to have some initial difficulty working with namespaces. The xml extension has a small API, but it is difficult to distinguish certain data. Also, it provides challenges when working with namespaces. The size of the DOM API alone causes this extension to rank last in this area.

xml

The xml extension is not overly difficult to use but does have its own quirks. At first glance you might think you just need to define a few handlers and that you can start parsing. Although generally speaking this is correct, you need to consider a few other issues. For starters, xml does not directly parse a document from a file. The file must be loaded into strings that are sent to the parser. You must determine ahead of time whether the document is to be parsed with namespace support. Two functions exist to create the parser, and only one supports namespaces. When dealing with namespaces, you must manually separate namespace URIs from node names within the callbacks. Although a few areas may make this extension a bit confusing, it still is not overly difficult to use. In any event, read on to see how XMLReader overcomes many of these deficiencies.

XMLReader

Of all the extensions, XMLReader is the easiest of the XML-based parsers to use. You can control the parsing using a single method, and you can query information using a small list of object properties. XMLReader is able to parse strings directly from files, and namespaced documents require no special setup. When you need namespace information, you can request it directly from the reader.

DOM

Most people either love or hate DOM. This extension has a large API based on the W3C specifications and is often intimidating for those who have never used it before. It provides a lot of functionality but tends to require a decent knowledge of the basic XML specifications. In many cases, it takes a good amount of coding to get the information you are seeking. This area relates to document navigation. Even though DOM has a more complex API, being based on the specifications, developers who have used DOM parsers in other languages will have few problems utilizing this one in PHP. The learning curve definitely depends upon your background.

SimpleXML

The purpose of SimpleXML was to make parsing XML as simplistic as possible. I still consider XMLReader easier to use when dealing with namespaced documents; SimpleXML comes in second when reading or performing minor editing on documents. The problem areas often encountered with SimpleXML tend to occur when working with namespaced documents or documents with complex structures. For documents dealing with mainly elements, attributes, and text, SimpleXML really shines. For example, consider using SimpleXML with the following document:

```
<root>
  <child1 att1="a">text</child1>
</root>
```

Assuming this document has been loaded into the SimpleXMLElement object $sxe, how much easier can it be to work with a tree than the following? Not much!

```
/* Print element contents */
print $sxe->child1;

/* Print value of att1 attribute */
print $sxe->child1["att1"];
```

Summary

Although I find XMLReader the easiest API to work with, it is a toss-up between that and SimpleXML. As you will learn after reading this chapter, every extension has some drawback. How easy an extension is to use is just one factor you must consider when trying to determine which one to use. A balance must exist—you must be comfortable with the extension but also be able to get the job done in an efficient manner.

Namespace Support

Working with namespaced documents is not always so simple because they can get quite complex. This is not only true when trying to write code for these documents but also when reading them in serialized form. The following sections will compare how each extension does when dealing with a namespaced document.

xml

The xml extension deals with namespaces when the parser is created with the xml_parser_create_ns() function. In PHP 5, namespace declarations are handled only by the xml_set_start_namespace_decl_handler() function. The end handler is never called. Data available from the handler is the prefix and namespace URI. The element handlers prefix the local name of the element with the namespace URI, separated by a user-definable character. Looking back at the start namespace handler in Chapter 8, the handler is a little bit useless. All that the handler would provide is the ability to map prefixes with namespace URIs for possible use within other handlers. The problem is that it is up to the developer to do this, which means scoping issues need to be dealt with and need to be tracked for the prefix/namespace URI combination within the element handlers. This is a complete waste of time because the prefix has little meaning to an XML document. The namespace URI is what really matters.

The namespace declaration handlers are not the only issue you may run into problems with. You must consider namespaces within the element handlers as well. Assume a document using namespaces is being parsed and the xml parser has been created to handle namespaced documents. No special options have been used, other than the defaults and a disabling of case folding. The parser encounters the element name `mynode` residing in the `http://www.example.com/mydoc` namespace. What gets passed to the element handler is `http://www.example.com/mydoc:mynode`.

This must now be split apart into the namespace URI and the element local name, and it is up to the developer to do this. If the namespace URI used in the document for this particular element is known ahead of time, then it is not too difficult to handle. But this often is not the case. Looking at the data passed for the element name, you might think about splitting it into an array based on the : or searching for a substring after the last :. This is fine, but consider what would happen in the rare case that the local name for the element contained the : character. Now you need to think a bit more and possibly change the namespace separator character to something not used in a namespace URI. You also need to consider that some elements may not reside in any namespace, so these would also need to be handled in the callbacks. Everything pertaining to elements also pertains to attributes.

As you can see, while xml supports handling namespaces, it is not as simple as you might like. You need to consider many issues and code for them ahead of time. So all in all, although you can work with namespaces, I do not consider this extension as having minimal namespace support. It's there, but it's not particularly easy to use.

XMLReader

XMLReader is one of the best and easiest extensions when dealing with namespaces in documents. You don't need to perform any special parsing or processing. The reader will stop at every element in the document, just like the xml extension will handle each element. It doesn't matter whether namespaces are in use. Namespace information is easily obtainable if so desired using the `namespaceURI`, `prefix`, `name`, and `localName` properties of the reader. When positioning the cursor on attributes, the same properties are used in the same manner. As an alternative with attributes, the `getAttributeNs()` method can also retrieve attribute values directly based on the `namespaceURI` parameter passed to the method.

One of the differences between xml and XMLReader is how namespace declarations are handled. Within xml, you must use a special handler. Within XMLReader, you can handle namespace declarations as normal attributes. What distinguishes these from regular attributes is the namespace URI. Per the XML Namespace specification, the namespace `http://www.w3.org/2000/xmlns/` is always bound to the `xmlns` prefix. When this value is returned from checking the `namespaceURI` property of an attribute, the attribute is a namespace declaration and not a regular element attribute.

DOM

DOM provides full support for namespaces when reading and editing XML documents. When reading a document, similar properties to XMLReader retrieve namespace information for the current node. Namespace declarations are handled differently in DOM than in XMLReader, however. Within DOM, they are of type `DOMNameSpaceNode` and not usually handled as regular attributes.

DOM, being a tree-based parser, goes well beyond the capabilities of XMLReader. You can create elements and attributes within namespaces, as well as create namespace declarations. Although reading documents within namespaces is not too difficult, many developers new to

DOM get confused when editing namespaced documents. Editing namespaced documents often requires a good knowledge of what namespaces are and how they work within XML.

SimpleXML

SimpleXML is not one of my favorite extensions when working with namespaced documents. It supports them, but unless you already know the document structure and which elements and attributes are in which namespace, you can forget about trying to read the document with this extension. For instance, say you are pulling in some XML data from a remote location, `http://www.example.com/remote.xml`. You know nothing of the structure, so you write some code like the following:

```php
<?php
$sxe = simplexml_load_file("http://www.example.com/remote.xml");
$children = $sxe->children();
foreach($children AS $node) {
   print $node;
}
?>
```

Much to your surprise, you get no output. Physically opening the document, you find out everything is in a prefixed namespace:

```
<ns:root xmlns:ns="http://www.example.com/ns">
   <ns:element1>some content</ns:element1>
   <ns:element2>more content</ns:element2>
</ns:root>
```

Without specifying the namespace URI, you cannot access any of the child elements. The children need to be accessed by `$children = $sxe->children("http://www.example.com/ns");`.

You will run into the same problem with namespaced attributes as you did with elements. To top it all off, the namespace declarations are inaccessible using SimpleXML, so you have no way to even find out what namespaces have been declared within a document.

Summary

You have probably guessed that the degree of namespace support implemented by each extension varies greatly, and each one has problems. XMLReader is probably the easiest extension to use while providing excellent namespace support. It requires no special setup and works the same regardless of working with or without a namespaced document. DOM follows XMLReader in the namespace area. It can be as easy as XMLReader but begins to add some complexity when editing namespaced documents. SimpleXML places third in my list. It provides decent namespace support but requires the developer to know the document structure and namespaces ahead of time. The xml extension is my least favorite extension when working with namespaces. It requires too much additional coding on the developer's side to use namespace information effectively. This is one of the major reasons I prefer XMLReader over xml.

Parsing/Processing Speed

Determining the speed that each extension takes to parse and process a document depends upon what type of processing needs to take place and the code written by the developer. This section covers the time it takes for each extension to find an element within a document. Only the basic functions of the extensions will be used. (You will take a look at optimizations later in the "Optimizing Parsing and Processing" section.) The document used for this test is the same one used when looking at the system resources. It is 12.5MB in size and contains 200,000 book elements. The document resides in the file bigxml.xml; a small snippet of the document looks like the following:

```
<books>
    <book id="1"><title>1</title><pages>1</pages></book>
    <book id="2"><title>2</title><pages>2</pages></book>
    <!-- Remaining book elements -->
</books>
```

Each extension will use basic, unoptimized functionality to search for the book element with the id attribute containing the value 5000. You'll see more optimized code later in this chapter (in the "Optimizing Parsing and Processing" section), and for now the functions and methods used are ones that are familiar even to developers new to these extensions. Table 11-3 shows the results for each extension. The table shows the average time from ten executions for each extension.

Table 11-3. *Average Time in Seconds for Unoptimized Search for an Element*

xml	XMLReader	DOM	SimpleXML
0.930624079704	0.699739193916	7.1625934124	7.1127900362

The times differ dramatically for the stream-based parsers compared to the tree-based parsers. The time is calculated from when the parser begins parsing to when the element is found. The stream-based parsers do not have to load the entire document and therefore result in much faster times. For the code within each of the following sections, two common functions have been defined:

```
function starting_time() {
    $mtime = microtime();
    $mtime = explode(" ",$mtime);
    return $mtime[1] + $mtime[0];
}

function ending_time() {
    $mtime = microtime();
    $mtime = explode(" ",$mtime);
    return $mtime[1] + $mtime[0];
}
```

These calculate the starting time and the ending time to come up with an approximate execution time.

xml

Although not the fastest, the average time for the xml extension to locate the element is quite impressive. The code used for this test is as follows:

```
function startElement($parser, $data, $atts) {
    if ($data == "book" && $atts["id"] == 5000) {
        $endtime = ending_time();
        print $endtime - $GLOBALS['starttime'];
        exit;
    }
}

function endElement($parser, $data) { }

$parser = xml_parser_create();
xml_parser_set_option ($parser, XML_OPTION_CASE_FOLDING, 0);
xml_set_element_handler($parser, "startElement", "endElement");
$handle = fopen("bigxml.xml", "r");
$starttime = starting_time();
while ($data = fread($handle, 4096)) {
    if (!xml_parse($parser, $data, feof($handle))) {
        print "error";
        break;
    }
}
```

The starting time begins after the parser has been set up and the file is opened for reading. The time calculation includes only the time it took for the extension to parse the data up to the point the book element with the id attribute having the value 5000 is encountered. At this point, the total time is calculated, and parsing stops.

XMLReader

XMLReader clearly outperforms all the extensions when locating an element. It performed 25 percent faster than xml, which came in with the second fastest time. You'll be surprised to know that this is without any optimizations, which will be demonstrated later in the "Optimizing Performance" section, so it can actually run even faster. The code used in this test also measures the time after the parser has been set up until the element has been found, at which point total execution time is calculated and parsing stops:

```
$reader = new XMLReader();
$reader->open('bigxml.xml');
$starttime = starting_time();
while ($reader->read()) {
    if ($reader->nodeType == XMLREADER::ELEMENT &&
        $reader->name == "book" && ($reader->getAttribute("id") == 5000))
    {
        $endtime = ending_time();
        print $endtime - $starttime;
        exit;
    }
}
```

Looking at the code, you should see that no special tricks have been used. The standard read() method is called each time, and the nodeType, name and id attribute values are tested.

DOM

DOM tends to be the slowest extension in the pack, though its testing time is quite close to that of SimpleXML. Remember that this is unoptimized code, and the document is an unknown structure. The entire tree must be walked until the first element named book with the attribute id containing the value 5000 is encountered. The majority of the time is due to the initial parsing. Before any processing can begin, the entire document is loaded into memory:

```
function checkChild($node) {
    if ($node->nodeType != XML_ELEMENT_NODE) {
        return;
    }
    if ($node->nodeName == "book" && ($node->getAttribute("id") == 5000)) {
        $endtime = ending_time();
        print $endtime - $GLOBALS['starttime'];
        exit;
    }
    foreach ($node->childNodes AS $child) {
        checkChild($child);
    }
}

$dom = new DOMDocument();
$starttime = starting_time();
$dom->load('bigxml.xml');
checkChild($dom->documentElement);
```

The code needs to walk to tree, so it recursively calls the checkChild() function. Any node that is not an element is immediately ignored, and control returns to the parent calling function. Elements are the only node types that can contain child elements, so if the name of the current element is not book and its attribute is of the wrong value, the code iterates through the children of the node, passing each one to the checkChild() function. Again, this is not optimized code, so it can run faster.

SimpleXML

SimpleXML displays decent results for a parser that needs to load the entire tree in memory before processing. Like the code for DOM, the code used for the SimpleXML test is also unoptimized, and the document structure is unknown:

```
function checkChild($sxe) {
    foreach ($sxe->book as $book) {
        if ($book["id"] == 5000) {
            $endtime = ending_time();
            print $endtime - $GLOBALS['starttime'];
            exit;
        }
```

```
      checkChild($book);
   }
   $children = $sxe->children();
   foreach ($children AS $node) {
      checkChild($node);
   }
}

$starttime = starting_time();
$sxe = simplexml_load_file('bigxml.xml');
checkChild($sxe);
```

SimpleXML works on elements. If you look at the first `foreach` loop in the `checkChild()` function, it iterates over `book` elements, skipping all other node types. For each `book` node that does not have the attribute `id` does not exist or the attribute does not equal 5000, it is then processed by a call to `checkChild()`. When no matching `book` elements occur, a general processing of all children takes place. This presents an issue that skews this test, though. It is possible that a `book` element may occur as a subchild that wouldn't get processed until after the `book` elements but appears before the `book` element in document order. The name of nodes is not available using this extension, making working with unknown document structures difficult.

Summary

The tests performed here are not perfect indicators of overall performance, but they should give you a good idea. The stream-based parsers crushed the tree-based parsers in terms of locating the element, but the further the element is in the document, the longer it takes the streamers to find it. In addition, more of the document has to be parsed and processed. The tree parsers have no choice but to parse the entire tree because processing can't begin until that happens. Within the "Optimizing Parsing and Processing" section in this chapter, you will see more numbers based on different techniques and different processing tasks. One thing is for sure—you will be surprised to see the results of an optimized XMLReader example performing the same processing that was done in this chapter. If you haven't been able to tell by now, I am a little biased toward XMLReader when needing to process a document in a single pass.

Choosing a Parser

Many times developers choose a particular parser because they are comfortable with the API. This is not always the best choice, because the developer may need to do additional coding and also because of many of the factors discussed in the previous sections. Sometimes it makes sense to use a different technology, which may require learning a new API. The following sections will explore some of the factors to think about when choosing a parser and will offer some guidance on which one may be the right choice for you.

Tree-Based or Stream-Based Parser?

The first decision is determining whether a tree-based or stream-based parser is the right choice. From the tests in the previous sections, a stream-based parser is highly efficient both in memory usage and in speed. The drawbacks, on the other hand, limit the processing that can be performed. You should first ask yourself the following questions about the problem you are trying to solve:

- Do I need to edit the content of the XML document?

- Do I need to perform multiple searches in the document in no particular order?

- Do I need to be able to navigate through the document in all directions?

- Do I need to use the document with the XSL extension?

- Do I need to traverse the trees within the document more than once?

If you can answer "yes" to any of these questions, then you will most likely need to use a tree-based parser, which would be either DOM or SimpleXML. A few fringe cases are the exceptions to some of these questions, but generally DOM or SimpleXML is a safe bet to use. Now that you have determined the type of parser, you need to think about the specific parser to choose.

xml or XMLReader?

Unless you have an application using xml under PHP 4 and encounter none of the issues that exist with the extension when moving it to PHP 5, I highly recommend using XMLReader for stream-based parsing. As you have read in this chapter and possibly in Chapter 9, it is faster, has an intuitive and simple API, offers better namespace support, and offers advanced features such as validation and exporting nodes to DOM. The amount of resources required is comparable to that of the xml extension, so when it comes down to a choice, I recommend XMLReader over xml. I have yet to find a case where XMLReader cannot perform the same functionality or a case where the performance difference between the two is significant enough to justify using the xml extension instead.

DOM or SimpleXML?

The choice between DOM and SimpleXML is not as clear-cut as that of xml versus XMLReader. Everything that can be accomplished in SimpleXML can also be accomplished in DOM, but the same cannot be said the other way around. This, however, comes at a price. SimpleXML is extremely straightforward and has an intuitive and simple API. DOM has a large learning curve and an extremely large and complex API. Deciding between these two extensions requires you to answer another set of questions about what you are trying to accomplish:

- Do I need to work with node types other than just elements, attributes, and text?

- Do I need to edit anything more than existing text content?

- Do I need the ability to ascend trees without resorting to XPath or having to worry about variable scope?

- Am I working with an unknown document structure?

- Do I need advanced XPath querying to retrieve more than just elements, attributes, and text nodes?

If you answered "yes" to any of these questions, you should probably consider using DOM. Although much more complex to use, it overcomes many of the areas SimpleXML was not meant to handle. These questions are handled with respect to SimpleXML, because DOM already offers this functionality and is presented in Chapter 6.

SimpleXML works only with elements, attributes, and text content within a document:

```
$sxe->elementName
$sxe->elementName["attributeName"]
```

Other node types are not supported. SimpleXML was not designed to be a full-fledged XML editing tool like the DOM extension but rather a lightweight, easy-to-use extension for developers to access XML. For this reason, the majority of developers have no need to access any other node types.

SimpleXML was also not designed to create XML documents. Again, most developers are working with preexisting documents, such as RSS feeds, and just need to process them. SimpleXML provides the ability to edit existing content, such as changing text content and attribute values, removing attributes and elements, and adding new attributes, but anything beyond this is beyond the editing capabilities of SimpleXML.

Navigation is primarily based on named element access using the object properties. Although you can perform unnamed access using the children() and attribute() methods, you have no way to access ancestor nodes directly from a SimpleXMLElement object. You have to use XPath, or the object for a node further up in the tree must be accessible. Take the following code, for instance:

```
function loadxml() {
    $xml = "<root><node1/><node1/><node2/></root>";
    $sxe = simplexml_load_string($xml);
    return $sxe->node1;
}
$xml = loadxml();
```

The variable $xml is a SimpleXMLElement object that iterates the node1 nodes. The problem is that you have no way to get back to the root of the document without resorting to XPath:

```
$arXMLPath = $xml->xpath('/*');
$root = $arXMLPath[0];
```

Remember to keep scope in mind when working with SimpleXML or be prepared to use XPath.

Unknown document structures present a real problem for SimpleXML when namespaces end up being used. Normally the methods children() and attributes() are used when the structure is not known, but unless a namespace URI is passed, they return only the elements and attributes that are either not in a namespace or in the default namespace. All other cases require you to know the namespace ahead of time.

XPath won't save you in this case like it did with navigation. XPath in SimpleXML returns only elements, attributes, and text nodes. Queries searching for any other type of information result in an empty array.

Summary

Probably the easiest decisions to make when choosing a parser are deciding between a stream-based and tree-based parser and deciding between xml and XMLReader. It gets a little more challenging when deciding between DOM and SimpleXML. You might lean toward the ease of use of SimpleXML but are worried about needing some of the functionality of DOM down the road. I have good news for you in this respect. As you will see in the section "Combining Technologies," it is easy to use the two extensions together, so when you run into areas where something is too difficult or impossible to implement using SimpleXML, you can use the functionality from DOM. Before jumping right into this interoperability, you will first examine how to optimize parsing and processing.

Optimizing Parsing and Processing

I have thrown many aspects of parsing and processing at you in this chapter. Some of these aspects are beneficial, and others are problematic. It's not always possible to choose the most efficient parser because the functionality is just not sufficient to accomplish the task. Take, for instance, document editing. Of course, xml and XMLReader are fast and use minimal amounts of memory, but you just cannot do document editing with them. You need to use either DOM or SimpleXML. This means the amount of memory required will be much greater than that used by either xml or XMLReader. The following sections will address some of these issues and offer ideas and techniques to efficiently and effectively parse and process XML to employ in your everyday usage of the extensions.

Using Memory Efficiently

Memory is one issue to be aware of when working with XML documents. This is not particularly an issue using xml or XMLReader but is pertinent when using DOM and SimpleXML. The following sections will cover a few of the common issues encountered when working with these extensions that relate to memory usage.

Working with Large Documents: Part I

Large document is really an arbitrary term. The amount of memory used depends upon the size of the document, which then must be evaluated with the resources available on the hardware running the software. If you refer to Table 11-2, you will see that using either DOM or SimpleXML with a 12.5MB file consumes 85.6MB of memory internally. This should give you an idea of how to judge whether a document is considered large.

You cannot specifically do anything using DOM or SimpleXML to avoid the memory issue. This is something you need to handle within the document. Breaking a document up into logical sections and storing each section within its own file will allow you to work with smaller pieces of it at a time, thus reducing the memory usage. You can do this using entity references or XInclude. It is likely that the entire document will rarely need to be processed at once. You can perform editing within the individual sections and pull them together only when needed. At these times, editing usually is not being performed, so you can perform the final processing using one of the stream-based parsers such as XMLReader. Take, for example, the following document, which is a reader's digest version of a large document:

```
<document>
   <section1><!-- All the content for section1 --></section1>
   <section2><!-- All the content for section2 --></section2>
   <section3><!-- All the content for section3 --></section3>
</document>
```

Logically, this document might be broken up into three sections where each section is stored in its own file. You could then rewrite the base document, in this case using XInclude, so that the different sections are just pointed to within the base document:

```
<document xmlns:xi="http://www.w3.org/2001/XInclude">
   <xi:include href="section1.xml"/>
   <xi:include href="section2.xml"/>
   <xi:include href="section3.xml"/>
</document>
```

Editing the sections would involve editing one of the three files listed in this new document. This immediately will reduce your memory usage by about a third of what it used to be. Currently, only DOM is able to perform XIncludes, $dom->XInclude(), but the technique is similar using external entities:

```
<!DOCTYPE document [
   <!ENTITY section1 SYSTEM "section1.xml">
   <!ENTITY section2 SYSTEM "section2.xml">
   <!ENTITY section3 SYSTEM "section3.xml">
]>
<document>
   &section1;
   &section2;
   &section3;
</document>
```

Using entity references, any of the extensions could process the final document. This way, if final document processing is performed by DOM or SimpleXML, the memory hit you will end up taking will be a one-time thing and not every time a section of the document is edited.

General Memory Considerations

Large documents are only one of the potential areas that cause a high usage of memory. Multiple documents in memory at a time can cause problems just as a single large document. I can recall an instance when a developer sent me an email about using domxml under PHP 4. He was trying to process more than 1,000 XML documents within a single script, and his machine was crashing. The extensions in PHP 5 handle documents and memory much differently than domxml did back in the day. A document is kept in memory as long as an object is referencing it or any portion of the document. Consider the effects of executing the following piece of code:

```php
<?php
$dom = new DOMDocument();
$dom->load('bigxml.xml');
$root = $dom->documentElement;
$dom->load('bigxml.xml');
?>
```

At first glance, you might think this script isn't so bad. Although it's using the 12.5MB XML file, it's loaded into the same variable, so the document from the first load() call should go away and the memory used should be destroyed, right? Wrong. You may have forgotten about the $root variable. With the second call to load(), the $dom variable is associated with the second document and no longer associated with the first, but $root still remains. Until $root is destroyed, the first document continues to reside in memory. Prior to loading the document a second time, $root should be destroyed by calling unset($root);. When load() is called the second time, the initial document will first be removed from memory before loading the new document. This also is true when using SimpleXML, but be careful when calling unset(). Make sure it is called on the object and not on an object accessing a property, or you will end up removing an element from the document rather than dereferencing the object:

```php
/* Dereferencing a SimpleXMLElement */
unset($sxe);

/* Deletes an Element from the XML document*/
unset($sxe->elementName);
```

When trying to work with multiple documents in succession, you may want to write the code within a function:

```php
<?php
function processDoc($file) {
   $dom = new DOMDocument();
   $dom->load($file);
   $root = $dom->documentElement;
   /* Additional Code Here */
}

$arFiles = array('bigxml.xml', 'section1.xml', 'section2.xml');

foreach ($arFiles AS $filename) {
   processDoc($filename);
}
?>
```

What's so special about doing this? Using a function for the DOM functionality keeps all the variables within the scope of the function processDoc(). The function allows you to not have to worry about tracking all variables referencing the document. Once the function finishes, all the variables automatically go out of scope; thus, all the objects are destroyed and the document is released from memory. Using the code shown here, only a single document is in memory at a time, and when the foreach loop has finished processing, there is no cleanup needed. This is not always a good idea. It is very dependent upon the application you are writing.

■**Caution** Segregating XML functionality into user-defined functions so that variable scope is automatically managed is not always a good idea. Refer to the section "Working with Large Documents: Part II" for additional information.

Optimizing Performance

Performance is another area where some code tweaks and use of some certain functions can make all the difference between a script that is slow and one that provides a decent level of performance. Many issues can affect performance when dealing with XML that are not within your control. It has happened to all of us before that a remote file is being read in, and the network unexpectedly goes down. In a case like this, you cannot do anything other than use cached copies of the files when available. The following sections will cover issues that are within your control in order to make optimal use of the extensions.

Working with Large Documents: Part II

When working with DOM or SimpleXML, execution time relates to the size of the document. The larger the document, the more time it takes to load. Breaking the document into sections and working with smaller portions of it at a time not only reduces the amount of memory required but also reduces the amount of time the document takes to load.

Load time is not the only factor to consider. Unloading the document also requires a good amount of time. Using the 12.5MB file `bigxml.xml` again and comparing the amount of time it takes to load the document to that of unloading it, you will see that unloading the document actually takes a little longer. Table 11-4 presents the time it takes the DOM and SimpleXML extensions to load and unload `bigxml.xml`.

Table 11-4. *Time in Seconds to Load and Unload* `bigxml.xml`, *Which Is 12.5MB*

DOM: Loading	DOM: Unloading	SimpleXML: Loading	SimpleXML: Unloading
6.42168030739	6.75953874588	6.40448312759	6.7824942112

Unloading the document seems to take about almost 10 percent longer than it takes to load the document. The difference between the times of the two extensions is negligible because the test is not 10 percent accurate; however, it is close because they are performing virtually the same action.

This relates to managing memory by encapsulating XML functionality within functions. Although doing this helps to manage the lifetime of documents and keep memory down, script execution time increases. In a typical Web request, getting the data to the user is the primary objective, and the amount of time it takes the script to shut down is not a primary concern as long as the data has been sent to the user. Here you need to achieve a balance. You need to balance how much memory you can use (without sacrificing too much system resources) with trying to process as fast as possible. The fewer number of documents that need to be freed during script execution will result in fast processing to get the data to the user and require a longer shutdown time, but it will also increase memory usage.

Working with Known Document Structures

Earlier in this chapter, in Table 11-3, I showed the results of testing the speed of the parsers when searching for a single element in a document. The tests performed were all unoptimized searches. I'll now show the result of rewriting the tests for each extension using the assumption that the document structure is known ahead of time. I will use the same document, bigxml.xml, weighing in at 12.5MB. Table 11-5 shows the results of the optimized tests by extension. I applied the same criteria for measuring time in these tests. The time does not include the initial time to set up the parser. This includes only the actual time the extension spent parsing, which includes loading the document, until the point the element found is measured.

Table 11-5. *Average Time in Seconds for Optimized Search for an Element*

xml	XMLReader	DOM	SimpleXML
0.930624079704*	0.237751293182	6.6229793787	6.5837672472

* No optimizations could be made to the xml code, so there is no difference in time.

When I initially stated that the document structure was known, the extensions are using only the assumption that book elements are children of the books document element. Other types of elements could be mixed in, but this one part of the structure is a given, and the extensions are coded for the possibility of the existence of other elements within the children of the books element. For this reason, as shown in Table 11-5, I could not make any additional optimizations to the code for the xml extension. To ensure the environment was still the same for the tests, I ran xml ten times, which resulted in little difference from the original results in Table 11-3, so I used the original result in Table 11-5.

XMLReader

The optimized version of the XMLReader script runs 66 percent faster than the original. This is a dramatic increase in processing speed without any side effects. It does not require any additional memory usage or system resources. Before I explain the optimizations, you should look at the code used:

```php
<?php
$reader = new XMLReader();
$reader->open('bigxml.xml');
$starttime = starting_time();

while ($reader->nodeType != XMLREADER::ELEMENT || $reader->name != "book") {
    $reader->read();
}
```

```
do {
   if ($reader->getAttribute("id") == 5000) {
      $endtime = ending_time();
      print $endtime - $starttime;
      exit;
   }
} while ($reader->next("book"));
?>
```

The first optimization, which was also used in the original test since it's not specific to the extension, is testing for the node type. The nodeType property is an integer and is much faster to test for than a string, such as name. The document contains many text nodes, and rather than having to test the name against the value book, they are quickly ignored by failing the nodeType test, causing the reader to move the cursor using the read() method. The initial while loop locates the first book element, at which point the real optimization can take place.

The document structure is known, so it is safe to assume that all book elements contain the attribute id and that book elements are siblings of each other. The value of the id attribute for the first book element is tested against the search criteria, which is the value of 5000 in this case. Upon failing, the while() portion of the do/while loop is executed, and $reader->next("book") is called.

The next() method skips subtrees and positions the cursor on the next sibling of the current node. In this case, the value book is supplied, instructing the reader to move to the next book sibling rather than stopping at the real next sibling of the node. In actuality, the next sibling would have been a significant whitespace, but since these are useless to the search, they are skipped, which allows the script to run even faster. If you recall, the document contains 200,000 book elements, so it ends up containing 200,001 significant whitespace siblings in total.

Although the actual execution time will vary depending upon the location of the element in the document, it is quite impressive that 5,000 book elements can be processed, which also includes the time to read the data from disk, in less than 0.3 seconds. The further within the document the element resides, the longer the execution time; but considering that the time should be no longer than a tree-based parser and should not introduce any memory penalties, the results certainly demonstrate the efficiency of XMLReader.

DOM

An optimization of the DOM test resulted only in a 7 percent decrease in total time. In the following code, you can see that it is not as complicated as the previous test:

```
<?php
$dom = new DOMDocument();
$starttime = starting_time();
$dom->load('bigxml.xml');
$root = $dom->documentElement;
$child = $root->firstChild;
while ($child->nodeType != XML_ELEMENT_NODE || $child->localName != "book" ||
      ($child->getAttribute("id") != 5000)) {
   $child = $child->nextSibling;
}
$endtime = ending_time();
print $endtime - $starttime;
?>
```

Only the children of the document element need to be tested. Just like XMLReader, the nodeType is the first test in the while() statement. It executes the fastest and is used to rule out the text nodes. As long as any of the criteria do not match, the current node's sibling is retrieved. This process continues until the specified book element is found.

You might think that a 7 percent reduction in time is not all too significant, but in actuality it is. The total time includes the time to load and build the in-memory tree. The actual time to walk the tree and locate the specified book element is only 0.17 seconds. Consider this important piece of information. It took less than two-tenths of a second to process 5,000 elements. The further the element is located in the document, the longer it will take to find it; but the time is much smaller than that of XMLReader because XMLReader parses and processes at the same time, while DOM just has to process the already loaded document.

SimpleXML

The figures for SimpleXML are comparable to those of DOM. An optimized version on the SimpleXML test code also resulted in a 7 percent decrease in the execution time. The code for this test is also much simpler than that of the original test case:

```php
<?php
$starttime = starting_time();
$sxe = simplexml_load_file('bigxml.xml');

foreach($sxe->book AS $book) {
    if ($book["id"] == 5000) {
        $endtime = ending_time();
        print $endtime - $starttime;
    }
}
?>
```

SimpleXML processes the document in a similar fashion to DOM. The foreach iterates each of the book elements and tests the value of the id attribute. The amount of time, taking out the factor of loading the document into memory, is also comparable to that of DOM. SimpleXML also took roughly 0.17 seconds to iterate and locate the specified book element. Generally speaking, DOM and SimpleXML are relatively close in performance figures based on the tests performed in this chapter.

XPath

I tested searching for the element using XPath with both DOM and SimpleXML. The results are not indicated in Table 11-5, as they couldn't even come close to anything presented there. The average time starting right before the document is loaded to the time it took to set up XPath and perform the query was approximately 25 seconds. It took about 18 seconds to perform the query alone. This cannot be considered an optimization; removing the time to load the document from the results of the DOM and SimpleXML tests, they each took approximately 0.16 seconds to walk the tree and locate the specified element. Just in case you think this number is a typo, it is not; it takes less than two-tenths of a second to walk the tree using optimized code and locate the element. Even taking into account the time to load the document into memory, the total time DOM and SimpleXML take is less than the XPath query alone.

The problem here is because of how XPath works. The query used to test XPath was the following:

```
/books/book[@id=5000]
```

XPath had to check every single book element, totaling 200,000, and compare the id attribute to the value 5000. You cannot just tell it to stop checking after it finds the first one. Even if you tried to use the position() function, it still would check them all. The position() function works on node sets, and the node set it would operate on would be the node set containing every book node having an attribute named id with the value 5000. The only way it could determine this would be to again check every single book element.

■**Note** Performing the XPath tests on an inferior machine running Linux resulted in drastically different numbers. The query took only 7 seconds on the Linux machine compared to that of 18 seconds on the Windows machine. Other tests were also performed, but none differed in such great amount as using XPath. Debug builds of both the PHP CLI and libxml2 libraries were used in both environments when performing the tests.

Summary

The optimizations shown in the previous sections have dealt with working within a single extension and making effective usage of memory and execution time. From the results, it is clear that whenever possible, you should use XMLReader. Not only is memory efficiently handled because of the streaming nature of the data but also it has proven to be the fastest parser of all the extensions. It is inevitable that at one time or another you will need a tree parser. When using DOM or SimpleXML, it is important to maintain a balance between the memory usage and script execution speed. A script that uses too much memory can take down a server or result in a slowdown on the entire system. A script that runs too slow, on the other hand, may result in an unusable application. You need to think about this when using DOM or SimpleXML because it's not always the case that you are in control of the XML document.

One extension I have not mentioned up to this point is XSL. It works in combination with other extensions, so you need to do any optimization either using the partner extension, which would be either DOM or SimpleXML, or using the XSLT language. In the next section, I will cover not only working with the XSL extension in an optimized manner but also combining the different extensions to achieve the desired results and providing efficient and effective usage.

Combining Technologies

One of the original philosophies for XML in PHP 5 was interoperability among the various extensions. This is true for all the new extensions, but the xml extension still stands alone. Unlike the other extensions, the xml extension does not have any hooks to work natively with the other extensions. The major benefit to the interoperability is that selecting a primary parser to use in your application won't always lock you into only the functionality provided by the extension. DOM and SimpleXML are able to completely work together, but because of the differences in parsing technology, some, yet limited, functionality allows XMLReader to work with DOM, which in turn means it can work with SimpleXML. In the following sections, I will cover some techniques that allow the extensions to work together efficiently. You will also take a look at the XSL extension and ways to optimize performance using the interoperability amongst the extensions.

Using DOM and SimpleXML Together

DOM and SimpleXML are able to work together on the same document at the same time. Nodes can be imported from one extension to the other, which means the node can be shared between the extensions without being a copy. Actions performed on the node from one extension are reflected within the object from the other extension. DOM imports nodes from SimpleXML using the dom_import_simplexml() function, and SimpleXML imports nodes from DOM using the simplexml_import_dom() function.

The majority of times DOM needs to export a node to SimpleXML is when a document is being created from scratch and then passed off to SimpleXML or when the node is coming from another extension such as XMLReader or XSL, which support only the creation of DOM objects, and is being sent to SimpleXML for processing.

The reason for this is that a developer who prefers to process documents using SimpleXML will use SimpleXML as the primary parser and export a node to DOM only so that functionality not supported by SimpleXML can be performed. A developer who works with DOM as the primary parser has all the functionality needed already available and would have loaded the document using SimpleXML had its API been the preferable one to read the document with.

■ **Note** Importing nodes using either function does not copy the underlying libxml2 structure. This structure simply becomes accessible from either DOM or SimpleXML. This is significant because there is no performance loss importing nodes from one extension to the other.

Importing Nodes into SimpleXML

First let's look at how SimpleXML imports a node from DOM. If SimpleXML is your parser of choice, then this functionality is handy to be able to work with XMLReader and XSL. The simplexml_import_dom() method takes one required parameter, node, and one optional parameter, class_name. The node parameter is a DOM object containing the document node to be imported, which inherits from the DOMNode class. The optional class_name parameter allows the class name to create the returned SimpleXMLElement object. Any class name passed as the optional argument must extend the SimpleXMLElement class.

The following code will demonstrate a document being loaded into a DOMDocument object, exported to SimpleXML, modified by SimpleXML, and then serialized by DOM:

```php
<?php
$dom = new DOMDocument();
$dom->loadXML('<books><book/></books>');
```

```
/* Import document into SimpleXML */
$sxe = simplexml_import_dom($dom);

/* Edit the book element */
$sxe->book = "Edited Book Title";

/* Print the serialized document using DOM */
print $dom->saveXML();
?>
```

A document containing an empty book element is loaded into a DOMDocument object. This object is then imported into SimpleXML and results in the SimpleXMLElement object, $sxe. The value of the book element is modified using $sxe, and the document is serialized using the original DOMDocument object. When the script is run, the output you will see is the modified document:

```
<?xml version="1.0"?>
<books><book>Edited Book Title</book></books>
```

Importing Nodes into DOM

Developers preferring the SimpleXML API for handling XML will find the dom_import_simplexml() function extremely handy. You can achieve the best of both worlds by using a combination of these two extensions. The biggest complaints I have seen from developers all revolve around SimpleXML having a small API and lacking functionality. This was pretty much the purpose of SimpleXML in the first place. It was meant to be easy to use, and any functionality that it doesn't implement can be handled using DOM. The top two complaints are that the name of the current node is unobtainable and elements cannot be created. Both of these are easily solvable with interoperability.

In Chapter 7, you read about extending the SimpleXMLElement class and looked at the simple example using the dom_import_simplexml() function. That example can be extended even further. It all depends upon how much functionality you require. For example:

```php
<?php
class mySXE extends SimpleXMLElement {
    function nodeName() {
        $node = dom_import_simplexml($this);
        return $node->nodeName;
    }

    function addChildElement($name, $value=NULL) {
        $node = dom_import_simplexml($this);
        $child = $node->appendChild(new DOMElement($name, $value));
        return simplexml_import_dom($child, "mySXE");
    }
}
```

```
$books= new mySXE("<books/>");
/* Print the name of the document element */
print $books->nodeName()."\n";

/* Add book nodes to document */
$book = $books->addChildElement("book");
$book->addChildElement("title", "Title1");
$book->addChildElement("pages", 10);

$book = $books->addChildElement("book");
$book->addChildElement("title", "Title2");
$book->addChildElement("pages", 20);

/* Iterate through the books, and print titles */
foreach ($books->book AS $book) {
    print "Title: ".$book->title."\n";
}
?>
```

This code is not overly optimized and just demonstrates how you can add DOM functionality to SimpleXML. Each time one of the extended functions is called, the node is imported into DOM, and the desired functionality is performed. In this case, a function to retrieve the current node name and a function to append a child element have been added to the class. The final output results in the following:

```
books
Title: Title1
Title: Title2
```

Using XMLReader and DOM Together

Even using XMLReader, which is a streaming parser, it is possible to interface with DOM, which in turn opens the window to interoperate with other extensions. XMLReader has an expand() method that "expands" the current node the reader is positioned on and returns a DOM object that is a copy of the node. This means you won't be working on the original document itself, just a copy of one of its subtrees.

The benefits of this method are found more often when working with large documents. You can use XMLReader to locate nodes and then copy them out to DOM objects. Think about the original problem in this chapter when working with large documents. One idea was to break them up into logical areas and use XInclude. The problem is, this large document already exists, so how are you going to go about breaking it up? The following document, which was previously used in the example, resides in the file bigxml2.xml:

```
<document>
    <section1><!-- All the content for section1 --></section1>
    <section2><!-- All the content for section2 --></section2>
    <section3><!-- All the content for section3 --></section3>
</document>
```

You can use XMLReader to move through the document and locate each of the section elements. When the cursor is positioned on the element, it will be expanded to a DOMElement object, appended to a new empty document, and saved to disk using the element name as the filename. At the same time, a new main document is created, defining each section as an XInclude link. The generated file should look similar to the one presented within the "Working with Large Documents: Part I" section:

```php
<?php
define('XINCLUDEURI', "http://www.w3.org/2001/XInclude");

/* Adds new xi:include elements to the new document */
function addXISection($xidoc, $filename) {
    $root = $xidoc->documentElement;
    $newXI = $xidoc->createElementNS(XINCLUDEURI, "xi:include");
    $root->appendChild($newXI);
    $newXI->setAttribute("href", $filename);
}

/* Create the main document that will hold the XInclude links */
$domXI = new DOMDocument();
$root = $domXI->appendChild(new DOMElement("document"));
$root->setAttributeNS("http://www.w3.org/2000/xmlns/", "xmlns:xi", XINCLUDEURI);

/* Create the reader, and begin to parse document */
$reader = new XMLReader();
$reader->open('bigxml2.xml');

/* Following two lines, position cursor on the document element node */
$reader->read();
$reader->read();

/* Move cursor to first child node of document element */
if ($reader->read()) {
    /* Perform tests, and use next() method to traverse sibling nodes */
    do {
        if ($reader->nodeType == XMLREADER::ELEMENT) {
            /* XInclude filenames will be based on element names */
            $filename = $reader->localName.".xml";
            $node = $reader->expand();

            /* Add expanded node to a DOMDocument, and serialize it to file */
            $subdom = new DOMDocument();
            $subdom->appendChild($node);
            $subdom->save($filename);

            /* Free document from memory */
            unset($subdom);
```

```
            addXISection($domXI, $filename);
        }
    } while($reader->next());
}
$domXI->formatOutput = TRUE;
$domXI->save("segmented.xml");
?>
```

The resulting file is named segmented.xml and would be the file used when you need to perform the final processing on the entire document. You can now perform editing using the smaller files created for the elements expanded by XMLReader. This is only one instance that the expand() method is useful and should give you ideas for other ways you might employ this functionality in your code.

■**Note** Unlike the SimpleXML and DOM import functions, the expand() method performs a full copy of the XML node. This means that the larger the subtree of the node, the more memory will be consumed and the more time it will take to perform the node copy.

Using XSL with XMLReader

In the previous chapter, you read about XSL; it requires the use of the DOM extension. In the current chapter, you have seen how XMLReader can interface with the DOM extension. If you haven't gotten the idea where I am going with this yet, let me make it a bit clearer. Using a combination of XMLReader, DOM, and XSL, it is possible to transform very large documents, which ordinarily wouldn't be possible without running some real heavyweight hardware. For example:

```
<?php
/* Set up the XSLT processor */
$xslDoc = new DOMDocument();
$xslDoc->load("bigxml2.xsl");
$xsltProc = new XsltProcessor();
$xsltProc->importStylesheet($xslDoc);

$reader = new XMLReader();
$reader->open('bigxml2.xml');
/* Following two lines, position cursor on the document element node */
$reader->read();
$reader->read();
/* Move cursor to first child node of document element */
```

```
if ($reader->read()) {
    /* Perform tests, and use next() method to traverse sibling nodes */
    do {
        if ($reader->nodeType == XMLREADER::ELEMENT) {
            /* XSL output filenames will be based on element names */
            $filename = $reader->localName.".xml";

            $node = $reader->expand();
            /* Add expanded node to a DOMDocument, and transform it */
            $dom = new DOMDocument();
            $dom->appendChild($node);
            $xsltProc->transformToUri($dom, $filename);
            unset($dom);
        }
    } while($reader->next());
}?>
```

This example is similar to the previous XMLReader and DOM example except that rather than creating an XInclude document, subtrees are being transformed using XSL. The file bigxml2.xsl could consist of any XSL templates you like. That is not provided in this example and is left up to you to implement if you choose to do so.

Conclusion

No single parser will solve every problem. Each has its own strengths and weaknesses, and it's not always easy to determine which one to choose. This chapter covered the XML extensions available in PHP 5 and provided some insight into how to go about determining which one may be best suited for a particular problem at hand. It is not always easy to determine ahead of time the right balance between memory usage and execution speed. Many aspects affect these issues so the best you can do is plan as far enough ahead as possible, perhaps even making some assumptions and writing code based on those assumptions. You can try to write as efficient code as possible without being detrimental to the effectiveness of the application. After reading this chapter and examining the results of the different tests, you should realize that, when possible, you should use XMLReader. It not only uses minimal resources but also provides excellent execution speed. Alternatively, it may be beneficial to see whether using a combination of the technologies would help you.

This chapter concludes the coverage of specific XML-based extensions included with PHP 5. This does not mean this is all that you can do with XML in PHP. The remaining chapters in this book will cover some of the other XML technologies and how you can use the extensions to leverage them. The next chapter will introduce you to XML security, including XML signatures and XML encryption. Currently, no extension provides this support directly, but you can use the extensions to write some supporting functionality for XML security.

CHAPTER 12

■■■

XML Security

PHP 5 provides many mechanisms to deal with XML documents. Applications can take advantage of the tree-based parsers (DOM and SimpleXML) and the stream-based parsers (xml and XMLReader), as well as document transformations using XSL. Processing, although one of the primary tasks for an application, is just one aspect that you need to consider when writing XML-based applications. Security and authentication of the data are often important as well. This chapter will cover some standards and methods you can use to provide support for XML encryption and digital signatures in documents.

■**Note** No built-in extension or package in PHP natively provides encryption and digital signatures. Currently, it is possible to write code to perform limited XML security functions for simple documents using an encryption extension, such as OpenSSL, mcrypt, or the sha1() function, and using a tree-based parser, such as DOM. The examples within this chapter require that the DOM extension is available on the development machine. This chapter will focus more on how you can implement digital signatures and encryption using PHP rather than cover the complete specification. For this reason, I will use SHA1 and HMAC-SHA1 within the examples for digital signatures, because it is possible to use these algorithms without requiring additional extensions, and I will use mcrypt for the examples of XML encryption because of its flexibility.

Introducing XML Security

Security is a topic that is always making headline news. In fact, reading news stories about sensitive data being stolen is almost becoming commonplace. When you speak to people about security measures they have taken, many times you hear that they use Secure Sockets Layer (SSL) and a logon to protect their application and data. They just don't realize that this is only one layer—if someone breached that layer of security, it would be all over.

Therefore, you should handle security in layers. The application must be protected, the network must be protected, and the data must be protected. The methods used for each of these layers vary depending upon your needs and the purpose an application serves. Using XML security is one such method that can protect data.

With XML being used more and more to transmit data between remote locations, it is vital in many cases that this information is protected. How the data is protected depends upon what the data contains. In some instances, it may be fine that the data is transmitted in plain text. The real concern is that the data has not been altered and that you can verify the source of the data. An acquaintance of mine works in a company that deals with the remote automation of machinery. Commands are sent in XML format and processed to control different machinery. The XML structure and data are not sensitive data, but ensuring that the center issuing the commands is. Imagine what would happen if somehow an attacker gained access to the application and began sending their own XML instruction sets. This would be a worst-case scenario. To provide additional authentication of the commands, the XML structures are digitally signed using XML signatures. By adding a layer of complexity to the application (because the XML must be signed on the sending side and verified for both integrity and sender authenticity), you in turn add an extra layer of security to the system.

Determining how to implement security when working with XML, whether you need signatures or encryption, is often a daunting task. You must consider how secure your data needs to be. If you work within a small office and you have XML data containing employee reviews, you might want that data secured from the employees in the office. The security needs for this data is much less than that of, say, credit card information contained within XML being sent to a remote system across the Internet.

Another area to think about is interoperability. If the data is being passed to other systems, possibly running different software and/or operating systems, you cannot expect those systems to handle data in the same manner as your system. You might think this is not an issue because XML is vendor neutral. But this, although true to a point, cannot be expected to hold true when working with XML security. You cannot be positive that a remote system handles whitespace or even orders attributes, which have no real order in XML, when the data is loaded. You can find in-depth coverage of this particular issue in the section "Introducing Canonical XML."

This chapter is broken down into two types of security implementations. The section "Introducing Basic Security" covers some simple methods you can use to provide data integrity and encryption when working with XML. Although easy to implement, much stronger methods to protect data could be deployed. The section "Introducing Enterprise Security," as well as most of the material in the rest of the chapter, deals with W3C specifications designed for XML security. The methods employed can provide greater security and interoperability, but they come with a price. The methods are not even remotely close to being simple. In PHP, it is possible to implement enterprise security to a point, but you may be begging for mercy by the time you are done.

Introducing Basic Security

What I call *basic security* does not mean data is insecure. Rather, it refers to implementing security in a manner that you do not need complex systems, you control the environments or rules for all systems involved, and you are not concerned with interoperability. Basically, you have the leeway to implement security in any manner you like, and all parties involved will respect and follow your decision. This all falls within the umbrella term *basic security*, and under these guidelines I will explain how you can work with XML securely.

Message Integrity

Message integrity means that data has not been altered from its original state. If you create an XML document and either store it on the file system or send it to another party, you want to make sure it remains unchanged; otherwise, a possibility exists that an unknown party has altered the document in some malicious way. Using a digital signature, you can verify the integrity of your data.

A simple example of this is hashing XML without getting a parser involved. Once you bring an XML parser into the picture, things can drastically change. Assume you have an XML document stored in some arbitrary place. It could be within a database or, as in this example, stored on the file system in the file xmlsec.xml, which appears as the following:

```
<?xml version="1.0"?>
<root>
    <data>My Data</data>
</root>
```

Once a document is in serialized form, you can create a digital signature of it. For example, the following code loads the document from the file system and creates both an SHA1 hash, which stands for the Secure Hash Algorithm, and an MD5 hash, which stands for Message Digest 5. Only one of these hashes is needed, but both are shown here in case you have a personal preference:

```
/* Generate SHA1 hash */
$sha1hash = sha1_file('xmlsec.xml');

/* Generate MD5 hash */
$md5hash = md5_file('xmlsec.xml');

/* Print resulting hashes */
print $sha1hash."\n";
print $md5hash."\n";
```

This technique is nothing new and might be something you are already doing with regular files. The resulting hash, whichever one you decide to use, must be stored in a secure yet accessible location. The next time you open the document, you can verify its signature to ensure the data has not changed. For example:

```
if (sha1_file('xmlsec.xml') == $sha1hash) {
    /* Open and modify the XML document */
    $dom = new DOMDocument();
    $dom->load('xmlsec.xml');
    $root = $dom->documentElement;
    $root->appendChild($dom->createElement('data', 'More data'));
    $dom->save('xmlsec.xml');

    /* Create and store a new hash for the next time document is accessed */
    $sha1hash = sha1_file('xmlsec.xml');
    print 'New Hash: '.$sha1hash."\n";
} else {
    print 'File has been altered!';
}
```

This approach has some drawbacks, such as what happens when the document needs to be sent to another party. The outside party would need both the hash and the document. They cannot be sent together because a third party could intercept the communication, generate an altered XML document, and replace the provided hash. When the intended recipient receives this malicious message, they have no idea this happened. The new hash matches against this new document.

This is where HMAC comes in. HMAC calculates a hash with a secret key. Not only can you verify the message integrity, but you can also verify the authenticity of the message. For HMAC, you use the mhash extension. (If this extension is unavailable, you can use a generic HMAC function, which is shown later in this chapter in Listing 12-4.) There is little change to the workflow using HMAC. The biggest difference is that you can provide your secret key to the recipient of the XML documents at any time. You also can send the document and the hash at the same time because without the secret key, the hash is nearly impossible to reproduce.

For example, if the value of the secret key were secret, the data hmac would be created using either of the two following calls:

```
$secret_key = 'secret';

/* Generate HMAC-SHA1 hash */
$hmac_sha1hash = bin2hex(mhash(MHASH_SHA1, file_get_contents('xmlsec.xml'),
                               $secret_key));

/* Generate MD5 hash */
$hmac_md5hash = bin2hex(mhash(MHASH_MD5, file_get_contents('xmlsec.xml'),
                              $secret_key));
```

Assuming the receiver already has your secret key, the XML document and the hmac could be sent to the receiver, such as by being passed as parameters in a URL or through HTTP POST.

■**Note** When sending an XML document and an HMAC, the XML document should be Base64 encoded, and the data must be verified prior to being loaded by a parser. It is also required that both parties use the same algorithms when performing message verification and authentication.

The following code is a simple example of receiving a document and hmac using HTTP POST. It assumes that the XML document is Base64 encoded and passed as the value of the xmldoc parameter and the hmac is passed as the value of the hmac parameter. HMAC-SHA1 is the mechanism being used by the sender and receiver in this example.

```
<?php
$secret_key = 'secret';

if (isset($_POST['xmldoc']) && isset($_POST['hmac'])) {
    $xmldata = base64_decode($_POST['xmldoc']);

    /* Generate the expected HMAC */
    $hmac_sha1hash = bin2hex(mhash(MHASH_SHA1, $xmldata, $secret_key));
```

```
    /* Verify message integrity and authenticity */
    if ($hmac_sha1hash == $_POST['hmac']) {
        $dom = new DOMDocument();
        $dom->loadXML($xmldata);
        print $dom->saveXML();
    } else {
        print 'DATA HAS BEEN ALTERED!!!';
    }
} else {
    print 'Missing Arguments';
}
?>
```

Data Encryption

Message integrity and authentication are good measures to use to ensure that the data came from the real originating party and was not altered, but they do not help when you need to keep data secret. For example, if you run an e-commerce site that is remotely hosted and from which credit card information is submitted and then sent to your company's internal systems for processing, you need to protect that data at all costs. Consider sending the following XML document across the Internet:

```xml
<?xml version="1.0"?>
<order>
    <items>
        <item>
            <id>123</id>
            <quantity>2</quantity>
            <unit_price>9.99</unit_price>
        </item>
    </items>
    <customer>
        <name>John Smith</name>
        <address>123 Doe Lane</address>
        <city>Portland</city>
        <state>Maine</state>
        <zip>04101</zip>
    </customer>
    <creditcard>
        <number>1234 1234 123 1234</number>
        <ccv>123</ccv>
        <exp>0107</exp>
    </creditcard>
</order>
```

Doing so in plain text is just asking for trouble, not to mention against the regulations of credit card companies. It wouldn't even matter if the data were not altered in any way; the simple fact that it was intercepted is cause for alarm. A situation like this is a prime candidate for using encryption in XML.

The following example demonstrates how you can encrypt the credit card information in the XML, allowing it to be safely transmitted across the Internet. This example uses the mcrypt library, but you can use any cryptographic tools you have available. The variable $orderxml used in the example is assumed to contain the previous order.

```
$secret_key = 'secret';

$dom = new DOMDocument();
$dom->loadXML($orderxml);
$order = $dom->documentElement;
foreach ($order->childNodes AS $node) {
    if ($node->nodeName == 'creditcard') {
        /* Get serialized creditcard node */
        $data = $dom->saveXML($node);

        /* Encrypt the serialized node */
        $td = mcrypt_module_open(MCRYPT_3DES, '',  MCRYPT_MODE_CBC, '');
        $iv = mcrypt_create_iv(mcrypt_enc_get_iv_size($td),  MCRYPT_RAND);
        mcrypt_generic_init($td, $secret_key, $iv);
        $encrypted_data = rtrim(mcrypt_generic($td, $data));
        mcrypt_generic_deinit($td);
        mcrypt_module_close($td);

        /* Create a new replacement node containing encrypted data */
        $encNode = $dom->createElement('encrypted', base64_encode($encrypted_data));
        $order->replaceChild($encNode, $node);

        /* Add the Initialization Vector as an attribute */
        $encNode->setAttribute('iv', base64_encode($iv));
        break;
    }
}

$enc_document = $dom->saveXML();
```

Note that within the example, the encrypted data, as well as the initialization vector (IV) used on the decryption side, are both Base64 encoded. This ensures that the data is valid XML syntax. The resulting document would look like the following:

```
<?xml version="1.0"?>
<order>
    <items>
        <item>
            <id>123</id>
            <quantity>2</quantity>
            <unit_price>9.99</unit_price>
        </item>
    </items>
```

```
<customer>
    <name>John Smith</name>
    <address>123 Doe Lane</address>
    <city>Portland</city>
    <state>Maine</state>
    <zip>04101</zip>
</customer>
<encrypted iv="5Fl6lc4xjwA=">Jhm3UYs9OvxaOkD6OWfKsaO/zm3GOaCNft/9/57qzmODhz51
WC3fL8dxuPzexlE9aNworn1dn7YFT2bP+WjHUP/qzvOpIQh9vVQ48TlOl8Z/Qeh4ffyfVThCVpt4esau
yhalLSOeqJaE2/GW5sOnEEgqM7p9iHj4</encrypted>
</order>
```

On the receiving end, you simply do the reverse of what was done during the encryption process. The variable $enc_document will be used for the input XML document, as shown in the following code. The value for this variable depends upon how the XML is being passed to the receiver of the encrypted data, so it may have come from an HTTP POST variable.

```
$dom = new DOMDocument();
$dom->loadXML($enc_document);
$order = $dom->documentElement;
foreach ($order->childNodes AS $node) {
    if ($node->nodeName == 'encrypted') {
        /* Get Initialization Vector */
        $iv = base64_decode($node->getAttribute('iv'));

        /* Get data, and decode it */
        $data = base64_decode($node->nodeValue);

        /* Decrypt the data */
        $td = mcrypt_module_open(MCRYPT_3DES, '',  MCRYPT_MODE_CBC, '');
        mcrypt_generic_init($td, $secret_key, $iv);
        $decrypted_data = rtrim(mdecrypt_generic($td, $data));
        mcrypt_generic_deinit($td);
        mcrypt_module_close($td);

        $frag = $dom->createDocumentFragment();
        /* Functionality available in PHP 5.1 */
        $frag->appendXML($decrypted_data);

        /* Replacement node */
        $order->replaceChild($frag, $node);
        break;
    }
}

print $dom->saveXML();
```

As you can see, the `encrypted` node is located, and the content and `iv` attribute are retrieved and decoded. The content is then decrypted and loaded into a `DOMDocumentFragment` using the `asXML()` method (which is available in PHP 5.1), and the old encrypted node is replaced with the new fragment. This ultimately results in the original `creditcard` element and its contents being put back into the tree. If you execute these scripts, you will see that the resulting data is the same as the original.

The material you have seen so far about message verification and data encryption is only the beginning. In many cases, these techniques might be all you ever need. However, you might find yourself in the position some day that you no longer can control both end points of the system, or your company might deal with numerous vendors on any number of platforms. It is not feasible to be implementing custom security schemes and structures every time. It might be time to start looking at a common methodology for performing XML security. This is where I make the distinction between the terms *basic security* and *enterprise security*.

Introducing Enterprise Security

For those of you who need something more than basic security and do not want to deal with proprietary formats, the W3C has developed some specifications for encrypting and digitally signing XML. The XML-Signature Syntax and Processing specification (`http://www.w3.org/TR/xmldsig-core/`) defines processing rules and syntax to provide integrity, message authentication, and signer authentication services. The XML Encryption Syntax and Processing specification (`http://www.w3.org/TR/xmlenc-core/`) defines a process for encrypting data and representing the result in XML.

The only catch to all of this is that although PHP offers the tools to perform this in a limited fashion, it is up to the developer to write the code to hook it all together. The idea of writing an extension to provide this capability in an easy-to-use manner has been tossed around but has yet to come to fruition. In the meantime, I will cover what these technologies are and how you can implement them using the current tool set provided by PHP. I will use DOM as the parser in the examples, since it offers the greatest flexibility; I will use SHA1, via the built-in `sha1()` function, for the digital signatures portion, because it is available as part of the core PHP install from the Strings extension and offers enough functionality to demonstrate and utilize the technologies covered in this chapter. You could implement certain examples using one of the other XML parsers and OpenSSL, but in order to cover the most areas of XML security, I will show examples using DOM, SHA1 (used for digital signatures), and 3DES-CBC (used for XML encryption utilizing mcrypt) for consistency. Using different algorithms depends not only upon what your system supports but also upon whether the algorithm is applicable for the specific task. For instance, a one-way hash is pretty much useless for data encryption, because you still need a way to decrypt the data, but it is perfect for verifying the integrity of data. Table 12-1 lists some of the algorithms and their identifiers that you can use when working with XML security. (I'll cover algorithms and their identifiers throughout this chapter.)

Table 12-1. *Algorithms and Their Identifiers*

Algorithm	Type	Identifier
Triple DES	Block	`http://www.w3.org/2001/04/xmlenc#tripledes-cbc`
AES-128	Block	`http://www.w3.org/2001/04/xmlenc#aes128-cbc`
AES-256	Block	`http://www.w3.org/2001/04/xmlenc#aes256-cbc`
AES-192	Block	`http://www.w3.org/2001/04/xmlenc#aes192-cbc`
RSA-v1.5	Key transport	`http://www.w3.org/2001/04/xmlenc#rsa-1_5`
RSA-OAEP	Key transport	`http://www.w3.org/2001/04/xmlenc#rsa-oaep-mgf1p`
Diffie-Hellman	Key agreement	`http://www.w3.org/2001/04/xmlenc#dh`
Triple DES	Symmetric key wrap	`http://www.w3.org/2001/04/xmlenc#kw-tripledes`
AES-128	Symmetric key wrap	`http://www.w3.org/2001/04/xmlenc#kw-aes128`
AES-256	Symmetric key wrap	`http://www.w3.org/2001/04/xmlenc#kw-aes256`
AES-192	Symmetric key wrap	`http://www.w3.org/2001/04/xmlenc#kw-aes192`
SHA1	Message digest	`http://www.w3.org/2000/09/xmldsig#sha1`
SHA256	Message digest	`http://www.w3.org/2000/09/xmldsig#sha256`
SHA512	Message digest	`http://www.w3.org/2000/09/xmldsig#sha512`
RIPEMD-160	Message digest	`http://www.w3.org/2001/04/xmlenc#ripemd160`
Base64	Encoding	`http://www.w3.org/2000/09/xmldsig#base64`

One of the most difficult tasks when working with XML security is that documents that can be logically equivalent can be physically represented differently. Consider a document that has been created in one application and is sent to another. The receiving application may have a slightly altered document. It is possible the original application decided to format the output to make it more readable. These two documents are logically equivalent, but is the original document considered altered? With respect to document verification, it would be because the original document added these whitespaces after the fact only when serializing. To overcome this problem, the W3C developed the XML canonicalization specifications.

Introducing Canonical XML

The Canonical XML specification (`http://www.w3.org/TR/xml-c14n`) establishes a method for determining whether two documents are identical. The underlying problem is that documents can be created that mean the same thing and that have the same content yet have different physical representations. This makes it difficult to determine whether the two documents are actually identical. With Canonical XML, two documents having the same canonical form are considered identical even if their physical representations are not identical.

Before going further, you should understand what *canonical form* is. The specification defines canonical form of a document to be the physical representation of the document as created using the following methods:

- The document is encoded in UTF-8.

- Line breaks normalize to #xA on input, before parsing.

- Attribute values are normalized, as if by a validating processor.

- Character and parsed entity references are replaced.

- CDATA sections are replaced with their character content.

- The XML declaration and DTD are removed.

- Empty elements are converted to start-end tag pairs.

- Whitespace outside the document element and within start and end tags is normalized.

- All whitespace in character content is retained (excluding characters removed during line feed normalization).

- Attribute value delimiters are set to quotation marks (double quotes).

- Special characters in attribute values and character content are replaced by character references.

- Superfluous namespace declarations are removed from each element.

- Default attributes are added to each element.

- Lexicographic order is imposed on the namespace declarations and attributes of each element.

If you look through this list, you will see a few items that make things difficult when using PHP to create canonical XML. You can resolve many of these issues using parser options when loading a document. Using LIBXML_NOENT, LIBXML_DTDLOAD, LIBXML_DTDATTR, and LIBXML_NOCDATA in combination will substitute entity references with their content, load the DTD to ensure IDs are handled, default all attributes so they are physically created in the tree, and convert all CDATA to text content. This does leave a few items that are not performed automatically.

You could handle the DTD in a couple of ways. Create a new document, and then do a deep copy or import the document element into the new document. Then, output the document using the document element as the context, or employ XSL. You can also handle the XML declaration in two ways. Using DOM, you can output the document using the document element as the context. Or, using XSL, assuming you used the already mentioned parser options, you can perform a transformation on the document where the style sheet just returns document element to the result tree and omits the XML declaration if being serialized. For example:

```
<xsl:stylesheet xmlns:xsl="http://www.w3.org/1999/XSL/Transform" version="1.0">
    <xsl:output omit-xml-declaration="yes"/>

    <xsl:template match="/">
        <xsl:copy-of select="." />
    </xsl:template>
</xsl:stylesheet>
```

If this is used to return a DOMDocument object, the DTD and XML declaration will have been removed when serializing by using the document element as the context when serializing:

```
$root = $doc->documentElement;
print $doc->saveXML($root);
```

■**Note** Serializing a document using the DOM API in order to remove the DTD and XML declaration can be done only when serializing to a string. Serializing to a file does not support a content node.

Data Model

If you decide to read the XML canonicalization specifications, you will notice that everything is defined in terms of XPath node sets, where the node set contains the nodes to be converted into canonical form. PHP has no native canonicalization support for XML, so using XPath depends upon how you decide to implement some form of canonicalization. Based upon the XPath data model, the types of nodes that are significant to create canonical form are root, element, comment, PI, text, attribute, and namespace nodes.

This doesn't mean you need to handle other types of nodes. As you have already seen, attributes need to be defaulted, CDATA sections need to be converted to text nodes, and character and parsed entity references need to be resolved. You can handle them, however, while the document is being loaded:

```
$dom = new DOMDocument();
$dom->loadXML($xmlstring, LIBXML_NOENT | LIBXML_DTDLOAD | LIBXML_DTDATTR |
                          LIBXML_NOCDATA);
```

The resulting document may still contain irrelevant nodes, such as a document type declaration, but you will be able to discard them when creating the canonical form.

Node ordering is also important when creating the canonical form. Luckily, if using XPath, node sets should already be in document order, but to produce correct canonical form, you need to handle a few more issues:

- Namespace nodes come before attribute nodes.

- Namespace nodes are sorted lexicographically based on their local names, where a default namespace would always come first in the list.

- Attribute nodes are also sorted lexicographically but are sorted based on their namespace URIs and then based on their local names. Attributes not within a namespace have an empty URI and would come before any namespaced attributes.

This prevents another challenge that you need to handle through coding. If XSL is being used to create the output, then some creative use of templates could help you achieve this. You could also perform this using the DOM API. Although attributes are unordered, when serialized, namespaces are always serialized prior to attributes. In addition, both are serialized in the order they are defined on an element. For instance, the first attribute added to the element is the first attribute serialized. The same goes for the namespaces. The following element:

```
<node a:attr="a-attr" b:attr="b-attr" attr2="attr2" attr="attr"
   xmlns:b="http://www.example.com/b"
   xmlns:a="http://www.example.com/a"
   xmlns="http://www.example.com" />
```

would automatically serialize to the following:

```
<node xmlns:b="http://www.example.com/b" xmlns:a="http://www.example.com/a"
      xmlns="http://www.example.com" a:attr="a-attr" b:attr="b-attr"
      attr2="attr2" attr="attr"/>
```

This still is not what you actually need. The namespace declarations are not sorted, and the attributes are not sorted. Using the DOM API means re-creating the tree using only the appropriate nodes and applying all the appropriate rules. In this case, when the new element is being created, namespaces and attributes need to be created in the proper order. The code in Listing 12-1 is just an example of how to accomplish this. It is unoptimized and broken down into multiple steps to illustrate what needs to happen. The variable $node used within the code refers to a DOMElement object referencing the earlier node element.

Listing 12-1. *Sorting Namespaces and Attributes*

```
/* Generic Attribute Sorting And Appending Function */
function sortAndAddAttrs($element, $arAtts) {
   $newAtts = array();
   foreach ($arAtts AS $attnode) {
      $newAtts[$attnode->nodeName] = $attnode;
   }
   ksort($newAtts);
   foreach ($newAtts as $attnode) {
      $element->setAttribute($attnode->nodeName, $attnode->nodeValue);
   }
}

$dom2 = new DOMDocument();
$element = $dom2->createElementNS("http://www.example.com", "node");
$dom2->appendChild($root);

/* Create DOMXPath based on original document $dom */
$xPath = new DOMXPath($dom);

$nsnode = $xPath->query('namespace::*', $node);

/* Add namespace nodes */
foreach ($arNS AS $nsnode) {
   /* Skip default namespace because it was already added with element node
      Skip xml namespace because it is automatic for document */
   if ($nsnode->prefix != "" && $nsnode->prefix != "xml") {
      $element->setAttributeNS("http://www.w3.org/2000/xmlns/",
                               "xmlns:".$nsnode->prefix, $nsnode->namespaceURI);
   }
}
```

```
/* Get attributes not in a namespace, and then sort and add them */
$arAtts = $xPath->query('attribute::*[namespace-uri(.) = ""]', $node);
sortAndAddAttrs($element, $arAtts);

/* Get namespaced attributes */
$arAtts = $xPath->query('attribute::*[namespace-uri(.) != ""]', $node);

/* Create an array with namespace URIs as keys, and sort them */
$arNS = array();
foreach ($arAtts AS $attnode) {
   $arNS[$attnode->namespaceURI] = 1;
}
ksort($arNS);

/* Loop through the URIs, and then sort and add attributes within that namespace */
foreach ($arNS as $nsURI=>$val) {
   $arAtts = $xPath->query('attribute::*[namespace-uri(.) = "'.$nsURI.'"]', $node);
   sortAndAddAttrs($element, $arAtts);
}
```

Upon serializing this, where the element was just created as the document element of $dom2, the output shows the namespaces and attributes correctly ordered:

```
<node xmlns="http://www.example.com" xmlns:a="http://www.example.com/a"
         xmlns:b="http://www.example.com/b" attr="attr" attr2="attr2"
         a:attr="a-attr" b:attr="b-attr"/>
```

Node Processing

Only nodes that are in the node set are processed when creating the canonical form. Once completely processed, the node is removed from the set. If you are reading the specification, you might be a little confused about how this occurs. I will attempt to explain this in simple terms. When a node in the node set is processed, any attribute nodes, namespace nodes, and child nodes are also processed *only* for those nodes that are also in the node set. Based on this, the following sections explain how each node type is processed.

■**Note** The term *process* as used within the following sections is meant as the act of processing the node into canonical form.

Root Node

The root node is the document and encompasses all nodes within a document. It has no physical representation and upon being processed will not generate an XML declaration or process the document type declaration. So, the only children nodes that would possibly be processed are the document element and comments or PIs that are direct children of this node.

Element Node

An element node is processed through the creation of a start tag using the QName of the element, the processing of any namespace and attributes nodes, and the processing of any child nodes and an end tag for the element. I will not explain the semantics of this generation because the PHP extensions actually handle the actual generation of the serialized form.

■**Tip** In canonical form, element nodes must always have a starting and ending tag. Empty tags are not allowed. You must write `<element />` as `<element></element>`.

One point I would like to mention, though, concerns using empty namespace declarations. Within a document, you can use them to indicate that an element is not in any namespace. Typically, however, this is used only when within a default namespace and indicates that nodes within the current scope are not within a default namespace. For example:

```
<element1 xmlns="http://www.example.com>
   <element2>
      <element3 xmlns=""></element3>
   </element2>
</element1>
```

The element node `element1` sets the default namespace to `http://www.example.com`. This namespace is automatically inherited by `element2`. The `element3` node removes the default namespace by setting `xmlns=""` so that any element falling within the children of `element3` would not be in any namespace unless otherwise set by one of those node. With respect to canonical form, only elements that would otherwise be in a default namespace can set an empty namespace. So, based on this rule, the following is invalid:

```
<!-- The following is invalid -->
<element1 xmlns="">
   <element2></element2>
</element1>
```

The node `element1` is not within a default namespace so cannot define an empty default namespace in canonical form. In canonical form, it looks like this:

```
<element1>
   <element2></element2>
</element1>
```

Namespace Node

Namespace nodes are processed only if they are not in scope based on the same prefix and namespaceURI of an ancestor element also within the node set. Consider the following document:

```
<element1 xmlns:a="http://www.example.com/a" xmlns:b="http://www.example.com/b">
   <element2 xmlns:a="http://www.example.com/a" xmlns:b="http://www.example.com/Z">
      <element3></element3>
   </element2>
</element1>
```

The canonical form of this document looks like this:

```
<element1 xmlns:a="http://www.example.com/a" xmlns:b="http://www.example.com/b">
   <element2 xmlns:b="http://www.example.com/Z">
      <element3></element3>
   </element2>
</element1>
```

You can see that the namespace with the prefix a was removed from element2. The namespaceURI and prefix are both in scope from its parent so are not serialized. The namespace with prefix b on element2 was included because the namespaceURI for that prefix changed and is no longer the same namespace.

Attribute Node

The PHP extensions already handle the processing of attribute nodes when being serialized. The only possible issue may deal with the values of attributes. The serialized value of the node is modified by replacing the characters &, <, and " with their entity references and the whitespace characters #x9 (tab), #xA (line feed), and #xD (carriage return) with their character references. Notice that the > character is not modified. Basically, you will modify the attribute values when serialized if using any special characters. If this is the case, then XSL may be helpful because you can use a template to match attributes, which in turn calls a PHP function to process the attribute value and return a modified string. For the sake of this chapter and because of having to build all this manually, I will use simplified attribute values that need no special handling.

Text Node

Text nodes are processed by converting the characters &, <, and > to their entity references. The whitespace character #xD is also replaced by .

Processing Instruction Node

PI nodes will already have been taken care for you during serialization, unless the value is empty. They consist of the <? characters followed by the target, a space, the value, and the closing ?> characters. An empty value would not place a space after the target. Do not confuse an empty value with a value consisting of whitespaces. Consider the following:

```
<?php?>
<?php ?>
<?php     ?>
```

The canonical forms of these are as follows:

```
<?php?>
<?php?>
<?php?>
```

Each of these has no value, so no additional space was added.

■**Caution** PIs that have empty values will need to be handled like attributes when creating the canonical form. The suggested method is to use XSL to create the values properly. This, of course, is needed only if the document can have PI nodes with empty values. In all other cases, serialization using the PHP extensions will work correctly.

Comment Node

Comment nodes are a little special. Canonical form can be generated without comment nodes. If this is the case, comment nodes have no bearing during serialization. In this case, you need to remove all comments in the document. Again, you could do this using XSL or using the DOM API. This is an example of doing this with DOM in combination with XPath:

```
$xPath = new DOMXPath($dom);
$cnodes = $xPath->query('//comment()');
foreach ($cnodes AS $cnode) {
    $cnode->parentNode->removeChild($cnode);
}
```

Introducing Exclusive XML Canonicalization

An issue faced earlier in the chapter when working with canonical XML dealt with extracting a document subset and inserting it into a different context. This caused many problems because canonical XML includes the document subset's ancestor namespace declarations and attributes within the XML namespace. For instance, a wrapper node encapsulates a subset and might be used for something like transport. If you are familiar with SOAP, you know this would be equivalent to its envelope. The following document is in canonical form:

```
<subdoc>
    <element>content</element>
</subdoc>
```

The document subset is then encapsulated within an envelope:

```
<envelope xmlns="http://www.example.com" xml:lang="en">
    <subdoc>
        <element>content</element>
    <subdoc>
</envelope>
```

When canonical XML is applied to the subset in this case, the serialized version is much different:

```
<subdoc xmlns="http://www.example.com" xml:lang="en">
  <element>content</element>
</subdoc>
```

Dealing with something like digital signatures becomes a nightmare. The original document no longer has the same canonical form as the latter one even though it is the same document/subset. Trying to extract the subset and place it within a different context, such as within another document, becomes impossible. This is why you might also hear canonical XML referred to as *inclusive canonical XML*. It includes the context of a subset's ancestors.

To deal with this issue, *exclusive XML canonicalization* was devised. It excludes, rather than includes, the context of a subset's ancestors. This means namespace declarations and attributes in the XML namespace from a subset's ancestors are not part of the canonicalization process when performing exclusive XML canonicalization. Taking the enveloped subdoc and using exclusive XML canonicalization, the results are probably more of what you had originally expected:

```
<subdoc>
  <element>content</element>
<subdoc>
```

The document subset remains in the same form as it originally was. This area is where canonical XML and exclusive XML canonicalization differ.

Data Model

The data model for exclusive XML canonicalization is the same as that for canonical XML with a few exceptions. These exceptions, as previously noted, fall into the area of namespace declaration handling. You have already seen that a search of ancestor nodes not within the node set for namespace declarations and attributes from the XML namespace is not performed under exclusive XML canonicalization. Serialization of namespace declarations themselves also differs and depends upon a few factors.

You can use an `InclusiveNamespaces PrefixList` parameter with exclusive XML canonicalization. It is a list containing prefixes and/or a token that indicates a default namespace. This parameter plays a role in how namespaced nodes are rendered in canonical form.

■**Note** For the sections dealing with prefixes not in the `InclusiveNamespace PrefixList`, assume the list is `NULL`, meaning it does not contain any prefixes or tokens. This will help you understand the process.

Prefixed Namespace Nodes

Namespaced nodes with a prefix not in the `InclusiveNamespaces PrefixList`, if used, are rendered if they meet the following criteria:

- The parent element is in the node set.

- The namespace is visibly utilized by the element, which includes its attributes.

- The prefix has not already been rendered by an ancestor within the output, or the prefix has been rendered by an ancestor yet refers to a different namespace.

The term *visibly utilize* means that either the element or one of its attributes uses the prefix of the namespace within its qualified name. The following document will be serialized using exclusive XML canonicalization. It is assumed that all nodes are within the node set.

```
<n1:element1 xmlns:n1="http://www.example.com/ns1"
            xmlns:n2="http://www.example.com/ns2">
   <n2:element2 n1:att1="value" xmlns:n3="http://www.example.com/ns3">
      some content
   </n2:element2>
</n1:element1>
```

Based on the rules for namespace serialization, the canonical form ends up like the following:

```
<n1:element1 xmlns:n1="http://www.example.com/ns1">
   <n2:element2 n1:att1="value" xmlns:n2="http://www.example.com/ns2">
      some content
   </n2:element2>
</n1:element1>
```

As you can see, the n2 namespace was not serialized on the n1:element1 element. It is not visibly utilized there. Moving to the n2:element2 element, the n2 namespace declaration is added because it meets all the criteria. Its parent element, n2:element2, is in the node set, it is visibly utilized by the element (notice the n2 prefix for the element name), and the prefix has not yet been rendered. The n3 namespace was not rendered because it is not visibly utilized. The n2:element2 element is not in the n3 namespace and does not contain any attributes within the n3 namespace.

Default Namespace Nodes

The rules for processing tokens that represent default namespace nodes not in the InclusiveNamespaces PrefixList are different from those for canonical XML for empty namespaces, xmlns="". The empty namespace is output only if the element visibly utilizes the default namespace, the element does not define a default namespace that is in the node set, and the nearest ancestor that is output and that visibly utilizes the default namespace has a default namespace in the node set. This may sound a little confusing, so take a look at the following document:

```
<element1 xmlns="">
   <element2 xmlns="http://www.example.com/default">
      <element3 xmlns="">
         <element4 xmlns="">
            Some Content
```

```
        </element4>
      </element3>
    </element2>
</element1>
```

The canonical form using exclusive XML canonicalization is as follows:

```
<element1>
  <element2 xmlns="http://www.example.com/default">
    <element3 xmlns="">
      <element4>
        Some Content
      </element4>
    </element3>
  </element2>
</element1>
```

The only element that declares an empty default namespace is element3.

InclusiveNamespaces PrefixList

The InclusiveNamespaces PrefixList throws a little curve to the rules already defined for handling namespace nodes. A namespace node matching a prefix or token in the list is rendered according to the rules of canonical XML rather than those of exclusive XML canonicalization. Namespace nodes in the node set that match a prefix or token in the list, unlike those not in the list, do not need to have parent elements in the node set. This can make your output look a little strange because it can result in non-well-formed XML, which is perfectly acceptable when generating a canonical form for a document subset. For the sake of sanity (because this leads to much greater complexity than you are already dealing with), the discussion of namespace nodes without an element in the node set is out of the scope of this chapter. Documents and document subsets used within this chapter will conform to those described in the next section.

Constrained Implementation (Non-Normative)

Section 3.1 of the Exclusive XML Canonicalization specification deals with a non-normative way to implement exclusive XML canonicalization. It assumes that subsets are well-formed and that when an element is in a node set, so is its namespace axis. When an element is not in a node set, neither is its namespace axis. These are the types of documents and document subsets that will be used within this chapter when working with the XML extensions in PHP. The following steps come directly from the specifications for section 3.1:

1. Recursively process the entire tree (from which the XPath node set was selected) in document order starting with the root. (The operation of copying ancestor xml: namespace attributes into output apex element nodes is not done.)

2. If the node is not in the XPath subset, continue to process its children element nodes recursively.

3. If the element node is in the XPath subset, then output the node in accordance with canonical XML except for namespace nodes, which are rendered as follows:

   a. ns_rendered is a copy of a dictionary, off the top of the state stack, of prefixes and their values that have already been rendered by an output ancestor of the namespace node's parent element.

   b. Render each namespace node if and only if it is visibly utilized by the immediate parent element or one of its attributes or if it is present in InclusiveNamespaces PrefixList *and* if its prefix and value do not appear in ns_rendered.

   c. Render xmlns="" if and only if the default namespace is visibly utilized by the immediate parent element node or the default prefix token is present in InclusiveNamespaces PrefixList *and* the element does not have a namespace node in the node set declaring a value for the default namespace *and* the default namespace prefix is present in the dictionary ns_rendered.

4. Insert all the rendered namespace nodes (including xmlns="") into the ns_rendered dictionary, replacing any existing entries. Push ns_rendered onto the state stack, and recurse.

5. After the recursion returns, pop the state stack.

This list contains generalized instructions on how exclusive XML canonicalization could be implemented. As you get into the "Introducing XML Signatures" and "Introducing XML Encryption" sections, you will see examples using PHP that demonstrate this generalization.

▪Note The canonical forms used with digital signatures and encryption are generated using exclusive XML canonicalization.

Introducing XML Signatures

XML signatures can verify the integrity and source of data and that the data has not been altered from its original state. It does this by using keys. One of the most commonly used methods involves public and private keys. An author of a document would use a private key to sign the data. This would create a digital signature, which is then added to an XML document. The receiver, who must have a copy of the author's public key, would then use that key to verify the signed data. Upon a successful verification, the receiver knows three things:

- The author is the genuine originator of the document, which is known as *signer authentication*.

- The data has not been altered from its original form, which is called *integrity*.

- Neither the data nor the checksum has been tampered with, which may occur if someone is trying to alter data while keeping the integrity of the data in order to deceive the receiver of the data. This is commonly known as *message authentication*.

The XML-Signature Syntax and Processing specification (http://www.w3.org/TR/xmldsig-core/) specifies the syntax and processing rules for creating and representing digital signatures. It is named such because it uses XML syntax for the signature. You can apply XML signatures to virtually any type of digital data including data within an XML document as well as remote resources accessible from a URI.

Understanding the Types of Signatures

Three types of XML signatures exist: enveloped signatures, enveloping signatures, and detached signatures.

Enveloped Signatures

Enveloped signatures are signatures that are contained within the XML content that is being signed. In simple terms, an enveloped signature is an XML signature structure that is a child of a signed document. For example:

```
<mydocument>
    <mydata1>some data</mydata1>
    <mydata2>more data</mydata2>
    <Signature>
       <!-- Signature Data -->
    </Signature>
</mydocument>
```

The XML signature, denoted by the Signature element and its contents, is placed within the document being signed. In this case, the data would include the data from the mydocument element and all of its content but exclude the actual XML signature structure, which begins with the Signature element.

Enveloping Signatures

XML signatures can also be *enveloping*. This means the data being signed lives within the XML signature structure:

```
<mydocument>
    <mydata2>more data</mydata2>
    <Signature>
       <!-- Signature Data including the reference to the Object element -->
       <Object Id="mydata">
          <mydata1>some data</mydata1>
       </Object>
    </Signature>
</mydocument>
```

Although the XML signature structure does not need to be embedded within an XML document since its structure is in XML format, I have shown it this way because you have not been introduced to the structure and because it illustrates how an enveloping signature can be encapsulated within another document, for which the encapsulating document has no bearing on the signature. In this case, the signature would include a reference to the Object element. The data within the `Object` element is the data being signed. I will explain how to reference data later in the "Introducing the XML Signature Structure" section.

Detached Signatures

Enveloped signatures means the signature is encapsulated within a document being signed. It is not necessary that the entire document be signed, and it is quite possible you have only a single element in the document that is signed. In fact, it is also quite possible that the data being signed does not even live within the document and resides remotely and is accessible through a URI. *Detached signatures* are used just for these purposes:

```
<mydocument>
    <mydata2>more data</mydata2>
    <Signature>
        <!-- Signature Data including the reference to the Object element -->
    </Signature>
    <Object Id="mydata">
        <mydata1>some data</mydata1>
    </Object>
</mydocument>
```

With this example, the data within the `Object` element is again being signed. This time, however, the element lives outside the signature, and the signature is being applied only to that particular element and not the entire document:

```
<Signature>
    <!-- Signature Data including the reference to remote data -->
</Signature>
```

This example refers to data being signed that lives outside the document entirely. Rather than referencing the `Object` element from the previous examples, the XML signature, in this instance, references remote data using a URI. Again, I will explain this in detail in the "Introducing the XML Signature Structure" section when I break down the structure. Just as in the previous example, it would also be valid to encapsulate the XML signature within a document, and the document has no bearing on the signature or the referenced data.

Introducing the XML Signature Structure

The structure of XML signatures can get quite complex. An entire book could be written on this subject alone. For this reason, I will keep things simple and cover only the core syntax. This chapter will introduce how to create and verify basic XML signatures using PHP. After you understand this, you should be able to implement more advanced signatures based on the specifications.

The document in Listing 12-2 illustrates a valid enveloping signature.

■**Note** The XML signature in Listing 12-2, as well as all other examples in this chapter, uses the string "secret" for the HMAC key. Attributes named Id are ID attributes. No DTDs are being used in this section, although you could use a DTD to automatically define these as IDs within the document. Refer to the specifications for the schemas for each element and attribute list.

Listing 12-2. *Example of Enveloping Signature*

```
<Signature xmlns="http://www.w3.org/2000/09/xmldsig#">
  <SignedInfo>
    <CanonicalizationMethod
        Algorithm="http://www.w3.org/TR/2001/REC-xml-c14n-20010315" />
    <SignatureMethod Algorithm="http://www.w3.org/2000/09/xmldsig#hmac-sha1" />
    <Reference URI="#object">
      <DigestMethod Algorithm="http://www.w3.org/2000/09/xmldsig#sha1" />
      <DigestValue>nTZuluErIxkl4DgMsBO/E5TiLRA=</DigestValue>
    </Reference>
  </SignedInfo>
  <SignatureValue>OUubDO2l6XUIODuLSjKAtjYlaTk=</SignatureValue>
  <Object Id="object">Hello World!</Object>
</Signature>
```

The data being signed in this case is the Object element. It lives within the Signature element, thus creating an enveloping signature. Using this example, you'll now see how the XML signature is composed and structured.

Signature Element

The Signature element is the root of an XML signature and is bound to the http://www.w3.org/2000/09/xmldsig# namespace. This element contains all the information needed to verify an XML signature.

SignatureValue Element

The SignatureValue element contains the Base64-encoded value of the actual digital signature, which in Listing 12-2 is the value OUubDO2l6XUIODuLSjKAtjYlaTk=. I'll explain how to compute this value later in the "Generating a Signature" section as well as when you get into actually generating an XML signature.

SignedInfo Element

The SignedInfo element is a container element that provides information regarding how a signature is processed, the location of the data that is signed, and the value for data integrity. This element also accepts an optional Id attribute. Using this attribute allows the element to be referenced by other signatures or objects.

CanonicalizationMethod Element

The CanonicalizationMethod element defines the type of canonicalization that must be applied to the SignedInfo element when processing a digital signature. Implementations must at least support canonical XML without comments, as noted by the value http://www.w3.org/TR/2001/REC-xml-c14n-20010315. Other possible values include, but are not limited to, http://www.w3.org/TR/2001/REC-xml-c14n-20010315#WithComments, which is canonical XML with comments, and http://www.w3.org/TR/xml-exc-c14n/, which is exclusive canonical XML. As shown in Listing 12-2, the value for this element is http://www.w3.org/TR/2001/REC-xml-c14n-20010315, so canonical XML will process the SignedInfo element.

SignatureMethod Element

The SignatureMethod element specified the algorithm used to create and verify the digital signature. Depending upon the algorithm used, this element can have child elements, such as HMACOutputLength, to provide additional information for the algorithm. You specify the actual algorithm to be used in the Algorithm attribute. The algorithms are specified by URI and define the role. You can find a few of the possible values at http://www.w3.org/TR/xmldsig-core/#sec-AlgID within the specification. The value used in Listing 12-2 is http://www.w3.org/2000/09/xmldsig#hmac-sha1, which corresponds to HMAC-SHA1. So, it is now safe to assume that HMAC-SHA1 is the algorithm used in this chapter for digital signatures.

Reference Element

Reference elements specify what data is signed. You can use more than one Reference element. For the sake of this chapter, however, the digital signatures used here will contain only a single Reference element. This element can take any of three optional attributes. You can use an Id attribute so that the element can be easily referenced from other places. The Type attribute is a URI that specifies the type of data. For instance, the attribute can be Type="http://www.w3.org/2000/09/xmldsig#Object" or Type="http://www.w3.org/2000/09/xmldsig#Manifest". The value has no bearing on how the signature is generated. It can, however, be used by an application for its own purpose. The last optional attribute is URI. This has much more bearing on data than the other attributes.

The URI attribute identifies the location of the data object, using a URI as its value. The attribute is considered optional, because it is possible that an application already knows where the data resides. For instance, if the same XML structure is always used, it may be agreed upon by both the author and the receiver of the document that a certain element within the document will always be signed. Typically, though, it is safest to always include a URI. The example in Listing 12-2 is using data that is located within the document. The URI attribute has the value #object. This identifies the node set containing the element with an ID, defined by the Id attribute, of object.

Note The Transforms element, which is an optional child of a Reference element, will be omitted from this chapter. Its use is out of scope because it is a bit advanced at this point to attempt to use the current XML functionality in PHP.

DigestMethod Element

The DigestMethod element defines the algorithm that is applied to the data being signed. You specify the actual algorithm using a URI for the value of the Algorithm attribute. This attribute works in the same manner as the one located on the SignatureMethod element. The example in Listing 12-2 used the value http://www.w3.org/2000/09/xmldsig#sha1. The digest will be computed using an SHA1 hash.

DigestValue Element

The DigestValue element contains the Base64-encoded value of the digest. Using the signature from Listing 12-2, the digest is simply the SHA1 hash of the canonical form of the data being signed. Do not worry if you do not fully understand this at this point. This will be made extremely clear when I cover how to create and verify the signatures in the "Creating a Signature" and "Verifying a Signature" sections.

KeyInfo Element

The KeyInfo element is an optional element that can allow the recipients to obtain the needed keys, certificates, or public key management information. The XML signature in this chapter uses the string "secret", which is private and known only to the author and recipient because of the algorithm specified in the SignatureMethod element. Other algorithms use public/private key pairs, making it perfectly viable to include public keys, certificates, or information about accessing a public key within the XML signature.

This element serves as a container to provide the needed information, which may be contained in any number of possible child elements. The content of a KeyName element is a string containing a key identifier for the recipient. It indicates to the recipient information what key to use for the document. A KeyValue element defines a single public key, such as DSA or RSA public keys, which can verify and validate the signature. You can use a Retrieval element to reference KeyInfo information stored in another location. It has a URI and Type attribute and works in the same manner as a Reference element. The remaining possible elements, X509Data, PGPData, SPKIData, and MgmtData, are used depending upon the type of algorithm being used. For example, you can use X509 certificates, and an X509Data element could contain certificate chains, revocation lists, or a SubjectKeyIdentifier. Again, these elements are out of the scope of this chapter but are covered in more detail within the specification at http://www.w3.org/TR/xmldsig-core/#sec-KeyInfo.

Object Element

An Object element is a container to hold any type of data. It has three optional attributes. The Id attribute is an ID used to reference the element. The XML signature in Listing 12-2 uses the name object for the Id attribute, which is then referenced by the Reference element through its URI attribute. A MimeType attribute specifies the MIME type of the data. The value must be a valid MIME type as defined in RFC 2045 (http://www.ietf.org/rfc/rfc2045.txt). The last attribute is Encoding. The value defines the encoding used within the object. The MimeType and Encoding attributes are purely informational. It is completely up to the application whether they need to be used.

Creating a Signature

Creating a signature involves generating the Reference and SignatureValue elements. The rest of the information within a Signature element defines how the values are generated or, when using an enveloping signature, could be data that is being signed. The first steps are determining the type of encryption algorithm that will be used and are determining what rules are to be used when the signature is created; they also determine the rules an application must follow to verify the signature.

In this case, the XML signature being created is the one in Listing 12-2. The following is a list of rules that will be used to create the signature:

- The signature will be enveloping. The Reference element will refer to an Object element with the Id object within the document. Specifically, the Object element will be a child of the Signature element.

- XML canonicalization will be used. This determines the value for the Algorithm attribute on the CanonicalizationMethod element.

- HMAC SHA1, using the string "secret" for the key, will be used for the signature. This determines the value of the Algorithm attribute on the SignatureMethod element.

- SHA1 will be used for message integrity. This determines the value of the Algorithm attribute on the DigestMethod element.

Based on this list, you can create a skeleton Signature, as shown in Listing 12-3.

Listing 12-3. *Skeleton Enveloping Signature Document*

```
<Signature xmlns="http://www.w3.org/2000/09/xmldsig#">
  <SignedInfo>
    <CanonicalizationMethod
        Algorithm="http://www.w3.org/TR/2001/REC-xml-c14n-20010315" />
    <SignatureMethod Algorithm="http://www.w3.org/2000/09/xmldsig#hmac-sha1" />
    <Reference URI="#object">
      <DigestMethod Algorithm="http://www.w3.org/2000/09/xmldsig#sha1" />
    </Reference>
  </SignedInfo>
  <Object Id="object">Hello World!</Object>
</Signature>
```

■**Note** A Reference element is created for each data object being signed. This example has only a single data object, so the Reference element was created with the overall skeleton rather than generating them because the DigestValue elements are calculated for each data object.

The only piece of information within the skeleton not mentioned in the list is the text Hello World!; that text, as well as the encompassing Object element, is the message to be signed. The last steps here are to generate the DigestValue and generate the actual signature.

Generating the Reference

According to the specification, DigestValues are created while Reference elements are created. The reason for this is that multiple objects can be used within a single XML signature. In this case, the data is simple, and the Reference element pointing to the data has already been created.

No transforms are being used, so you can move directly to the DigestValue calculation. This is calculated by performing the following steps:

1. Obtain the raw data specified by the Reference element. In this case, it is the Object element.

2. Apply any Transforms. This example does not use any.

3. If the transforms (or the raw data in the event there are no Transforms defined) result in a node set, then use canonical XML to serialize the node set. In this example, there are no transforms, and the raw data is the Object element. Canonicalization performed in this step is true canonical XML, meaning inclusive. The value from the CanonicalizationMethod element has no bearing on this step because that element pertains to Signature generation and not Reference generation.

4. Using the algorithm specified by the DigestMethod element, calculate the DigestValue using the resulting data from step 3.

5. Add the DigestValue to the tree. Again, the specifications build the Reference element during these steps, so if you decide to follow that method or have a complex signature requiring the steps to be performed in that manner, then create the Reference element and its children at this point and append it as a child to the SignedInfo element.

From step 1, the raw data is the Object element. For this example, I will use the variable $doc, which represents the skeleton signature from Listing 12-3. This can either be loaded from a file or be built manually using the DOM methods from Chapter 6.

■**Caution** When creating the signature document manually using the DOM API, the Signature element defines the default namespace http://www.w3.org/2000/09/xmldsig#. Elements within its scope must be created using namespace-aware methods, such as createElementNS, in order for this to work properly.

For example:

```
$xPath = new DOMXpath($doc);
/* Following line split into two lines because of length */
$query = '//*[local-name()="Reference" and '.
         'namespace-uri()="http://www.w3.org/2000/09/xmldsig#"]';
$nodeset = $xPath->query($query);
$refElement = $nodeset->item(0);
$dataURI = $refElement->getAttribute("URI");
```

This returns the value #object. Because a DTD was not specified, you are unable to retrieve the Object element using the getElementByID method from DOM. You must do it manually. You can use the following code to perform this operation. Note that it assumes the URI value contains an ID and not a URL to external data:

```
$ID = substr ($dataURI, 1);
$query = '//*[@Id="'.$ID.'"]';
$nodeset = $xPath->query($query);
$Object = $nodeset->item(0);
```

The resulting $Object variable should be a DOMElement object referencing the Object element in the document. Serialization using $doc->saveXML($Object) should produce the following:

```
<Object Id="object">Hello World!</Object>
```

There are no Transforms, and the result of the first step is a node set containing the Object element. This node set (read: element) must be serialized in canonical form:

```
<Object xmlns="http://www.w3.org/2000/09/xmldsig#" Id="object">some text</Object>
```

Canonical XML is used here, which is inclusive. This means the default namespace defined by the Signature element, which is an ancestor of the Object element, is serialized with the Object node. A quick and simple way to canonicalize this element is copying it to another document and serializing the new document. The copy must be a deep copy so that all attributes and children are copied. During the copy, because this node becomes the top-level node, the inherited default namespace is re-created on the copy. Because of the structure of the XML signature and data you are working with, this is the only thing you need to do prior to serialization to result in the correct canonical form. For more complex structures, you would need to use the techniques described in the "Introducing Canonical XML" section:

```
$dom = new DOMDocument();
$copyObject = $dom->importNode($Object, TRUE);
$dom->appendChild($copyObject);
```

■**Caution** This works only because the content of the Object element is simple text and not an XML subtree. If the contents were a subtree, you would need to apply the rules and techniques described in the "Introducing Canonical XML" section so that namespaces and attributes in particular are generated correctly.

Using the algorithm from the DigestMethod element, the canonical form of the data generates the digest. This value is then encoded using Base64 encoding and set as the content of the DigestValue element:

```
$query = '//*[local-name()="DigestMethod" and '.
    'namespace-uri()="http://www.w3.org/2000/09/xmldsig#"]';
$nodeset = $xPath->query($query);
$digMethod = $nodeset->item(0);
$algorithm = $digMethod->getAttribute("Algorithm");
if ($algorithm == "http://www.w3.org/2000/09/xmldsig#sha1") {
    $canonical = $dom->saveXML($copyObject);
```

```php
/* Create SHA1 hash of the canonical form of the Object element */
$hash = sha1($canonical);
$bhash = pack("H*", $hash);
$digValue = base64_encode($bhash);

/* Following is done in example only to add proper whitespacing */
$addPrev = NULL;
$addPost = NULL;
if ($digMethod->previousSibling->nodeType == XML_TEXT_NODE) {
   $addPrev = clone $digMethod->previousSibling;
}
if ($digMethod->nextSibling->nodeType == XML_TEXT_NODE) {
   $addPost = clone $digMethod->nextSibling;
}
/* End custom whitespaces */

/* Create DigestValue element, and append to parent of DigestMethod */
$digestValue = $doc->createElementNS("http://www.w3.org/2000/09/xmldsig#",
                                    "DigestValue", $digValue);
$digMethod->parentNode->appendChild($digestValue);

/* Following is done in example only to add proper whitespacing */
if ($addPrev) {
   $digMethod->parentNode->insertBefore($addPrev, $digestValue);
   $digMethod->parentNode->removeChild($digMethod->nextSibling);
}
if ($addPost) {
   $digMethod->parentNode->appendChild($addPost);
}
/* End addition of whitespaces */
} else {
   print "Unhandled Encoding";
   exit;
}
```

This piece of code finds the algorithm for the digest, and if it can be handled, then it continues processing. In this case, you are handling only SHA1. The SHA1 hash of the canonical form previously obtained is converted to binary form. The sha1() function is being used, because it is available by default in PHP. To avoid having to convert the value into binary form, you can use mhash, $bhash = mhash(MHASH_SHA1, $canonical);, because it returns the hash as a binary rather than as a hexadecimal. In any event, the binary value is then Base64 encoded. A DigestValue element is then created using the createElementNS method and passing in the encoded value.

The additional code for handling whitespace is *not* needed when generating a signature. The reason it has been added in this example is because whitespace is significant in canonical form. To present a document in an easily presentable form, such as the one shown in Listing 12-2, I added whitespaces. These whitespaces are included within a signature in order to present you with a readable form as well as correct values for the DigestValue and SignatureValue elements.

Generating a Signature

Signature generation involves using the key, which in this case is the string "secret", to apply the algorithm specified by the Algorithm on the SignatureMethod element to the SignedInfo element in canonical form. This time the canonical form is generated using the method specified by the CanonicalizationMethod element. Rather than explain every single step in the process, because you should be experienced enough at this point to find nodes and values, I will demonstrate only the steps specific to generating the signature. This being said, the following variables and values will be assumed:

- $canonMethod: "http://www.w3.org/TR/2001/REC-xml-c14n-20010315";

- $signedInfo: DOMElement for SignedInfo element

- $Object: DOMElement for Object element

- $key: "secret";

Listing 12-4 defines a generic HMAC function. To use the sha1() function without additional dependencies, I will use the function in Listing 12-4 within the example.

Listing 12-4. *Generic HMAC Function*

```
function hmac ($key, $data)
{
    $b = 64; // byte length
    if (strlen($key) > $b) {
        $key = pack("H*",sha1($key));
    }
    $key  = str_pad($key, $b, chr(0x00));
    $ipad = str_pad('', $b, chr(0x36));
    $opad = str_pad('', $b, chr(0x5c));
    $k_ipad = $key ^ $ipad ;
    $k_opad = $key ^ $opad;

    return sha1($k_opad  . pack("H*",sha1($k_ipad . $data)));
}
```

The process for generating the signature is similar to generating the digest. A different node set is used, and HMAC SHA1 is being performed; however, in this example, the element SignedInfo is being converted into its canonical form, and the signing algorithm is applied. The resulting value is then set as the content for the SignatureValue element and appended as a child to the Signature element. For example:

```
$dom = new DOMDocument();
$copyInfo = $dom->importNode($signedInfo, TRUE);
$dom->appendChild($copyInfo);
/*
  Following works only with PHP 5.1 and above. LIBXML_NOEMPTYTAG used to
  create start and end tags for empty elements. Document element $copyInfo passed
  to dump the node, which does not generate an XML declaration output
```

```
*/
$canonical = $dom->saveXML($copyInfo, LIBXML_NOEMPTYTAG);

/* Calculate HMAC SHA1 */
$hmac = hmac($key,$canonical);
print $hmac."\n";
$bhmac = base64_encode(pack("H*", $hmac));

/* Handle whitespaces for presentation layout */
$addPrev = NULL;
$addPost = NULL;
if ($Object->previousSibling->nodeType == XML_TEXT_NODE) {
  $addPrev = clone $Object->previousSibling;
}
if ($Object->nextSibling->nodeType == XML_TEXT_NODE) {
  $addPost = clone $Object->nextSibling;
}
/* END Handle whitespaces for presentation layout */

/*
   Create and append the SignatureValue element as child of Signature element
   insertBefore used with whitespacing to generate output in Listing 12-2.
*/
$sigValue = $doc->createElementNS("http://www.w3.org/2000/09/xmldsig#",
                                  "SignatureValue", $bhmac);
if ($addPrev) {
  $Object->parentNode->insertBefore($sigValue, $Object->previousSibling);
} else {
  $Object->parentNode->insertBefore($sigValue, $Object);
}

/* Following is done in example only to add proper whitespacing */
if ($addPost) {
  $Object->parentNode->insertBefore($addPrev, $sigValue);
}

print $doc->saveXML();
```

The resulting document should look exactly like the document in Listing 12-2, down to the same whitespaces used.

Verifying a Signature

Verifying a signature is similar to creating a signature but is a bit simpler. A tree is not being created, so you do not need to deal with insert nodes or add any whitespace to make it look nice. Verification requires validating the reference to ensure the integrity of the message and validating the signature to ensure the message and signer authenticity. The XML signature in

Listing 12-2 should be the same as the signature you just saw created. You can use either in the following sections because it will be used as the XML signature being verified.

Validating the Reference

The steps for validating the reference are almost identical to creating the value for the DigestValue content when creating a signature. The only difference is that the elements and content already exists, so no modifications to the document are made. Normally, the following steps would be performed for each Reference element in the XML signature, but in this case, there is only a single Reference element.

Steps 1 to 4 of generating a reference from the "Creating a Signature" section are performed on the XML signature. The resulting digest value is then compared to the value within the DigestValue element in the XML signature. Remember that the value within the signature is Base64 encoded. Although in many cases a Base64-to-Base64 comparison should work, the specification recommends a binary-to-binary comparison in the event that additional whitespaces ended up in the document. This is a simple comparison because the content of the DigestValue is just the Base64-encoded binary value. A simple call to base64_decode() will convert the value to binary form. The following code uses the resulting XML signature, referenced by the $doc variable, as the document being verified:

```
/* Retrieve Reference node and location of data */
$xPath = new DOMXpath($doc);
$query = '//*[local-name()="Reference" and
 namespace-uri()="http://www.w3.org/2000/09/xmldsig#"]';
$refElement = $xPath->query($query)->item(0);
$dataURI = $refElement->getAttribute("URI");

/* Retrieve Digest Value for current Reference */
$query = 'string(./*[local-name()="DigestValue" .
   'and namespace-uri()="http://www.w3.org/2000/09/xmldsig#"])';
$signedDigest = $xPath->evaluate($query, $refElement);

$ID = substr ($dataURI, 1);
$query = '//*[@Id="'.$ID.'"]';
$Object = $xPath->query($query)->item(0);

/* Create canonical form for Object element */
$dom = new DOMDocument();
$copyObject = $dom->importNode($Object, TRUE);
$dom->appendChild($copyObject);
$canonical = $dom->saveXML($copyObject);

/* Assume digest algorithm retrieved and SHA1 was found */
/* Create SHA1 hash of the canonical form of the Object element */
$hash = sha1($canonical);
$bhash = pack("H*", $hash);
$digValue = base64_encode($bhash);
```

```
if ($signedDigest != $digValue) {
   print "Digest Authentication Failed";
   exit;
} else {
   print "Digest Authentication Success!";
}
```

Validating a Signature

The steps for validating the signature are also similar to creating the signature, though the tree is not modified. Again, the algorithm specified by the SignatureMethod element is applied to the canonical form of the SignedInfo element. The canonical form is generated using the method specified by the CanonicalizationMethod element. The same rules apply for verifying the value as those from verifying a reference. In the following example, the binary values, rather than the Base64-encoded values, are compared to determine the authenticity of the message and signer:

```
/* Retrieve Value for SignatureValue element */
$query = 'string(//*[local-name()="SignatureValue" '.
   'and namespace-uri()="http://www.w3.org/2000/09/xmldsig#"])';
$signature = base64_decode($xPath->evaluate($query));

/* Generate canonical form of SignedInfo element*/
$signedInfo = $xPath->query("//*[local-name() = 'SignedInfo']")->item(0);
$dom = new DOMDocument();
$copyInfo = $dom->importNode($signedInfo, TRUE);
$dom->appendChild($copyInfo);
/*
  Following works only with PHP 5.1 and above
  LIBXML_NOEMPTYTAG used to create start and end tags for empty elements
  document element $copyInfo passed dump the node which does not generate
  an XML declaration output
*/
$canonical = $dom->saveXML($copyInfo, LIBXML_NOEMPTYTAG);
$key = "secret";
$hmac = hmac($key,$canonical);
$calc_signature = pack("H*", $hmac);

if ($signature != $calc_signature) {
   print "Signature Authentication Failed";
} else {
   print "Signature Authentication Success!";
}
```

▓Caution The steps to generate and verify signatures as well as the type of signatures used in this chapter are only a small subset of what can be performed using XML signatures. The steps are meant as an introduction to get you started using digital signatures. Signatures can become quite complex working with multiple sets of data, data residing in different locations, different types of data, and different algorithms. The material presented here is intended only as a starting point, and you should refer to the specifications to work with more advanced and complex XML signatures.

Introducing XML Encryption

In many instances, an XML document can contain sensitive data. For example, an e-commerce system can collect customer and payment information and send that to a secure server for processing rather than storing the information on a public server. This type of scenario pertains more toward smaller businesses because they typically lack the resources to implement a large, secure environment and tend to host their e-commerce systems with a hosting provider.

In this day and age, it is extremely unlikely for sensitive data to be left on these public servers. In some cases, online credit card processors are used, leaving the small business with the freedom of not having to deal with storing and managing this information. Some companies, however, still process credit card information internally. It is possible they also have a brick and mortar store and handle sales processing together. It is important to these companies to transmit the sensitive information from their public site to their more secure internal network. SSL is one possible method of handling this. The data is encrypted during transit. Though once received, the data is back to clear text. This may not be a desirable situation. This is a case where XML encryption may come in handy.

Introducing XML Encryption

XML signatures only get you so far. They provide the mechanisms to verify the integrity and authenticity of the data, but the data is still, in most cases, in plain text. The W3C has defined some specifications in order for systems to implement a common format to perform XML encryption. The XML Encryption Syntax and Processing specification (http://www.w3.org/TR/xmlenc-core/) specifies a process for encrypting data and representing the result in XML. The XML Encryption Requirements specification (http://www.w3.org/TR/xml-encryption-req/) specifies the requirements for implementing XML encryption.

Encryption Granularity

You can use XML encryption to sign virtually any type of data. This includes both XML and non-XML-based data. Just like XML signatures, the data can even be located outside the XML encryption document. This section will explain the granularity available using XML encryption. This means examining the different pieces and types of data that could be encrypted and their relation to the XML encryption document. Consider the example of an order from an e-commerce site explained earlier. If using XML format to describe the order, it may appear in the following form, which is a stripped-down version of some payment information:

```
<payment>
    <order_number>1001</order_number>
    <customer>Joe Smith</customer>
    <creditcard>
        <number>4111 1111 1111 1111</number>
        <expiration_month>01</expiration_month>
        <expiration_year>2007</expiration_year>
        <ccv2>123</ccv2>
    </creditcard>
</payment>
```

This is not the type of information you would want to store or pass around in plain text. Rather, it will be encrypted, and the information to be encrypted within the structure is completely up to your needs and/or security concerns.

Element Encryption

Element encryption involves encrypting an element within the document. It includes the opening and closing tags as well as all of its content. For example, you may want to encrypt the entire creditcard element within the payment document. This will protect the payment information by not only encrypting the credit card number but also the type of payment:

```
<payment>
    <order_number>1001</order_number>
    <customer>Joe Smith</customer>
        <EncryptedData Type='http://www.w3.org/2001/04/xmlenc#Element'
                    xmlns='http://www.w3.org/2001/04/xmlenc#'>
        <CipherData><!-- Encryption Information Here --></CipherData>
    </EncryptedData>
</payment>
```

If someone were to intercept this document, the only information they would be able to see is the order number and the customer's name. The rest of the data is encrypted, so for all they know the customer may have opted to pay by cash on delivery (COD).

Mixed Content Encryption

If hiding the type of payment made by a customer is not necessary, then the content of the creditcard element could be encrypted rather than the entire element. This would then allow some, internal to the company, to be able to examine the XML document and know the type of payment being made without needing access to any of the encrypted information. For example:

```
<payment>
    <order_number>1001</order_number>
    <customer>Joe Smith</customer>
    <creditcard>
        <EncryptedData xmlns='http://www.w3.org/2001/04/xmlenc#'
                    Type='http://www.w3.org/2001/04/xmlenc#Content'>
```

```
      <CipherData><!-- Encryption Information Here --></CipherData>
    </EncryptedData>
  </creditcard>
</payment>
```

Character Data Encryption

Those even less concerned with the security of all but the actual credit card number may opt to encrypt only the value of the number element. This would effectively encrypt the text content of the number element. For example:

```
<payment>
    <order_number>1001</order_number>
    <customer>Joe Smith</customer>
    <creditcard>
      <number>
        <EncryptedData xmlns='http://www.w3.org/2001/04/xmlenc#'
                       Type='http://www.w3.org/2001/04/xmlenc#Content'>
          <CipherData><!-- Encryption Information Here --></CipherData>
        </EncryptedData>
      </number>
      <expiration_month>01</expiration_month>
      <expiration_year>2007</expiration_year>
      <ccv2>123</ccv2>
    </creditcard>
</payment>
```

Arbitrary Data and XML Document Encryption

As I said before, you can encrypt any type of data. Someone may want the entire payment document encrypted so if it were intercepted, the interceptor would have no idea what information was contained within the XML encryption document. For example:

```
<EncryptedData xmlns='http://www.w3.org/2001/04/xmlenc#'
               MimeType='text/xml'>
    <CipherData><!-- Encryption Information Here --></CipherData>
</EncryptedData>
```

Based on the resulting structure, for all one knows, the data that was encrypted was a JPEG image rather than an XML payment document (though the size of the resulting structure may give it away). The data being encrypted does need to be an XML document or have anything to do with XML. XML encryption is just a process and standard structure for encrypting some data, packing it up as a standard structure, and possibly providing some information about the type of encryption and data used.

Super Encryption

Data that is encrypted more than once is called *super encryption*. It's possible you are a security zealot and are trying to prevent an attacker from ever gaining access to your data. Or it's also possible you have an XML document that already contains some encrypted data, and you have added some information to the XML document and would like to encrypt this new, modified document. In this case, you want the original encrypted data to be included in your set of data to be encrypted rather than adding an EncryptedData element to the document, which would then contain two sets of encrypted data. Based on the syntax of XML encryption, which I will be coming to shortly, it is invalid for an EncryptedData element to have an EncryptedData as an ancestor. It is perfectly valid, however, to encrypt an EncryptedData element to create a new EncryptedData element:

```
<!-- First Encrypted Data -->
<EncryptedData Id="encrypt1" xmlns='http://www.w3.org/2001/04/xmlenc#'
               MimeType='text/xml'>
   <CipherData><!-- Encryption Information Here --></CipherData>
</EncryptedData>

<!-- Super Encrypted Data Containing EncryptedData element with Id encrypt1 -->
<EncryptedData Id="encrypt2" xmlns='http://www.w3.org/2001/04/xmlenc#'
               MimeType='text/xml'>
   <CipherData><!-- Encryption Information Here --></CipherData>
</EncryptedData>
```

Formats of XML Encryption

XML encryption can either be enveloping or be detached. The examples you have seen so far have all been enveloping structures. The physical location of the encrypted data does not need to live within the XML encryption structure. The information provided within the CipherData element, which is broken out when the structure is explained, could point to the location of the encrypted data rather than include it within its content:

```
<!-- Example of Enveloping structure -->
<EncryptedData xmlns='http://www.w3.org/2001/04/xmlenc#'
               MimeType='text/xml'>
   <CipherData>
      <CiperValue><!-- Encrypted Data --></CipherValue>
   </CipherData>
</EncryptedData>

<!-- Example of Detached structure -->
<EncryptedData xmlns='http://www.w3.org/2001/04/xmlenc#'
               MimeType='text/xml'>
   <CipherData>
      <CipherReference URI="http://www.example.com/encrypted_data.enc" />
   </CipherData>
</EncryptedData>
```

Introducing the XML Encryption Structure

Depending upon the algorithm used and any optional information provided to the recipient to aid in key retrieval and additional decryption information, the structure can become a bit complex. This chapter will be using the Triple DES algorithm for encryption, and the structure explained in the following sections will provide enough information to support the use of this algorithm.

■**Note** Using different encryption algorithms may require the use of elements and attributes not covered in this chapter. The goal of this chapter is to provide enough information and examples so that you can understand at least the basic concepts of XML encryption and can begin implementing it using PHP and Triple DES encryption after reading the material. This topic is quite lengthy, and complete coverage is beyond the scope of this book. You can find additional information regarding algorithms, structure, and processing in the specifications identified at the beginning of this chapter.

EncryptedData Element

The EncryptedData element is the root of the XML encryption structure. It is the container for the structure and holds information regarding the encryption used, key retrieval, and the encrypted data. This element replaces the data being encrypted within an XML document or becomes the root of an XML document if the data being encrypted is an entire XML document or is not an XML document and does not reside within a document.

The element lives within the http://www.w3.org/2001/04/xmlenc# namespace, as do most of its children. The possible children of this element are a CipherData element, which is required, and EncryptionMethod, KeyInfo, and EncryptionProperties elements, which are all optional. Four optional attributes exist. Other than the Id attribute, the attributes help the recipient restore the encrypted data to its original form during decryption:

- The Id attribute specifies an ID for the element.

- The type attributes identifies the type of data prior to encryption. For example, the value http://www.w3.org/2001/04/xmlenc#Element specifies the original data is XML containing either an empty-element tag or a single element and its contents. The value http://www.w3.org/2001/04/xmlenc#Content indicates that the original data is XML containing the contents of an element, which could consist of mixed content. You can use other values to help in restoring the data to its original state during decryption.

- The MimeType attribute can describe the media type of the data that has been encrypted.

- The optional Encoding attribute can indicate the encoding of the original data.

Based on this, an element that has been encrypted would be replaced with the following EncryptedData element:

```
<EncryptedData xmlns="http://www.w3.org/2001/04/xmlenc#"
               Type="http://www.w3.org/2001/04/xmlenc#Element">
   <!-- Contents of EncryptedData element -->
</EncryptedData>
```

EncryptionMethod Element

The EncryptionMethod element is an optional element. It describes the algorithm that was used to encrypt the data. Without this element, the recipient must already know the algorithm used in order to decrypt the data. The child elements on EncryptionMethod depend upon the type of algorithm used, which is specified by the value of the Algorithm attribute. In this case, the algorithm is Triple DES:

```
<EncryptionMethod Algorithm="http://www.w3.org/2001/04/xmlenc#tripledes-cbc"/>
```

No child elements are required for this algorithm. For additional information about possible child elements when using other algorithms, refer to the specifications for this element at http://www.w3.org/TR/xmlenc-core/#sec-EncryptionMethod.

KeyInfo Element

The KeyInfo element provides information about obtaining the key needed to decrypt the data. It is not required, but when not provided, the recipient must already know the correct key to use in order to decrypt data. This element is from the XML-Signature Syntax and Processing specification and used according to that specification. Please refer to the section "Introducing XML Signatures" or the specification for more information.

■**Tip** Remember that this element lives in the http://www.w3.org/2000/09/xmldsig# namespace and, when used within XML encryption, must be namespaced properly.

The examples of XML encryption within this chapter do not offer any hints about the key used. The key for the examples is just the string "secret", and the only additional key information that will be provided is the name of the key, which will be mcryptiv, and the value used for the initialization vector for the mcrypt functions. This value is created when the IV is created during encryption and then sent within the KeyValue element so that the data can be properly decrypted:

```
<KeyInfo xmlns="http://www.w3.org/2000/09/xmldsig#">
  <KeyName>mcryptiv</KeyName>
  <KeyValue><!-- Value generated while encrypting --></KeyValue>
</KeyInfo>
```

CipherData Element

The CipherData element is a required element that provides the encrypted data through inclusion or by providing a reference to the location of it. It is a container for either a CipherValue element or a CipherReference element. Only one of these elements can be present as the content for this element.

CipherValue Element

The `CipherValue` element includes encrypted data within the XML encryption structure. The content of this element is the Base64-encoded value of the encrypted data:

```
<CipherValue>NMIYVAUsrK/P4+W1N2P811DL2Hpkg9SeCplIp9kxJpGfhXYFM2n29A==</CipherValue>
```

CipherReference Element

The `CipherReference` element works in a similar manner to `Reference` elements used in XML signatures. It can contain `Transforms` elements, which are not covered in detail in this chapter, but must have a URI attribute used to locate the encrypted data. After processing the URI, which includes processing any `Transforms` that may be used, the resulting data must contain the encrypted value. This means that if the data were Base64 encoded, like it is when using a `CipherValue` element, it must be decoded prior to finishing processing:

```
<CipherReference URI="http://www.example.com/remotedata.enc" />
```

This example would use the data located at `http://www.example.com/remotedata.enc`.

Encrypting Data

The process for encrypting data is not overly complicated. In this case, it is actually quite simple because many of the elements and attributes from the specification are not even used. It is one thing if you are trying to create a generic XML encryption encrypt/decrypt processor, but that is out of the scope of this chapter. Most developers just need to understand how to perform these operations to implement some type of XML encryption scheme using PHP within their applications, which is the focus of this chapter. For example:

```
<payment>
    <order_number>1001</order_number>
    <customer>Joe Smith</customer>
    <creditcard>
        <number>4111 1111 1111 1111</number>
        <expiration_month>01</expiration_month>
        <expiration_year>2007</expiration_year>
        <ccv2>123</ccv2>
    </creditcard>
</payment>
```

The formal specifications define the steps used for encrypting data. They are performed for each data item to be encrypted. These steps are generic and do not have to be performed in the exact order presented. As you will see through this demonstration, some steps are performed out of order. For instance, the content of the `KeyValue` element depends upon the IV used by the mcrypt functions. For this reason, the encryption is performed before the `KeyInfo` element is created, although all but the IV is known prior to the data encryption. The following steps are taken from the XML Encryption Syntax and Processing specification (`http://www.w3.org/TR/xmlenc-core/`) for those needing to perform more advanced encryption than that shown in this chapter:

1. Select the algorithm (and parameters) to be used in encrypting this data.

2. Obtain and (optionally) represent the key.

   a. If the key is to be identified (via naming, via a URI, or included in a child element), construct the ds:KeyInfo as appropriate (for example, ds:KeyName, ds:KeyValue, ds:RetrievalMethod, and so on).

   b. If the key itself is to be encrypted, construct an EncryptedKey element by recursively applying this encryption process. The result may then be a child of ds:KeyInfo, or it may exist elsewhere and may be identified in the preceding step.

3. Encrypt the data.

   a. If the data is an element or is element content, obtain the octets by serializing the data in UTF-8 as specified in the XML 1.0 specification. The encryptor can do the serialization. If the encryptor does not serialize, then the application must perform the serialization.

   b. If the data is of any other type that is not already octets, the application must serialize it as octets.

   c. Encrypt the octets using the algorithm and key from steps 1 and 2.

   d. Unless the decryptor will implicitly know the type of the encrypted data, the encryptor should provide the type for representation.

4. Build the EncryptedType (EncryptedData or EncryptedKey) structure.

   a. If the encrypted octet sequence obtained in step 3 is to be stored in the CipherData element within the EncryptedType, then the encrypted octet sequence is Base64 encoded and inserted as the content of a CipherValue element.

   b. If the encrypted octet sequence is to be stored externally to the EncryptedType structure, then store or return the encrypted octet sequence, and represent the URI and transforms (if any) required for the decryptor to retrieve the encrypted octet sequence within a CipherReference element.

5. Process EncryptedData.

   a. If the Type of the encrypted data is an element or is element content, then the encryptor must be able to return the EncryptedData element to the application. The application can use this as the top-level element in a new XML document or insert it into another XML document, which may require a re-encoding.

   b. If the Type of the encrypted data is not element or element content, then the encryptor must always return the EncryptedData element to the application. The application can use this as the top-level element in a new XML document or insert it into another XML document, which may require a re-encoding.

Prior to beginning any coding, the first things you need to decide are the algorithms to be used and the data to be encrypted. In this case, the payment document will be used as the original document, which needs the creditcard element to be encrypted. The variable $doc will represent this data loaded into a DOMDocument object. The encryption algorithm will be Triple DES in Cipher Block Chaining (CBC) mode and use "secret":

```
$key = "secret";
```

Obtain the data to be encrypted, which in this case is the creditcard element:

```
$xpath = new DOMXPath($doc);
$creditcard = $xpath->query("//creditcard")->item(0);
$plaintext = $doc->saveXML($creditcard);
```

When encrypting XML, you should use canonical form. This is to ensure that namespaces are properly carried along with encrypted data. This example does not use any namespaces, so this is not a concern. As you have seen, converting data to canonical form can be quite complex. The good news is that it is only because of namespaces that using canonical form is recommended. The order of attributes and the handling of whitespaces are not issues when performing XML encryption like they are when adding XML signatures. So, rather than trying to deal with writing a routine to create the canonical form, a really fast and easy shortcut is to create a new document and import the node to be encrypted, as demonstrated in Listing 12-5.

Listing 12-5. *Serializing a Namespace Element and Preserving Namespace Information*

```
/* Preserving Namespace information */
$tempdoc = new DOMDocument();
$newnode = $tempdoc->importNode($node_to_encrypt);
$plaintext = $tempdoc->saveXML($newnode);
```

No matter which method you need, you now have a serialized version of the data being encrypted, $plaintext. The next step is to perform the actual encrypting of the data:

```
$td = mcrypt_module_open(MCRYPT_3DES, '', MCRYPT_MODE_CBC, '');
$iv = mcrypt_create_iv(mcrypt_enc_get_iv_size($td), MCRYPT_RAND);
mcrypt_generic_init($td, $key, $iv);
$encrypted_data = rtrim(mcrypt_generic($td, $plaintext));
mcrypt_generic_deinit($td);
mcrypt_module_close($td);
```

Now that you have the information needed for the KeyInfo, you need to create it. To ensure that the initialization vector value, $iv, remains intact, it must be Base64 encoded and then set as the content of the KeyValue element:

```
$keyInfo = $doc->createElementNS("http://www.w3.org/2000/09/xmldsig#", "KeyInfo");

$keyTmp = $doc->createElementNS("http://www.w3.org/2000/09/xmldsig#",
                                "KeyName", "mcryptiv");
$keyInfo->appendChild($keyTmp);

/* Base64 encode the IV value, and set to KeyValue content */
$keyTmp = $doc->createElementNS("http://www.w3.org/2000/09/xmldsig#",
                                "KeyValue", base64_encode($iv));
$keyInfo->appendChild($keyTmp);
```

The last step is to put all the pieces together within an EncryptedData element. The type of encrypted data is an XML element, so the Type attribute will be set accordingly. At this point, you can swap out the creditcard element with the new EncryptedData element:

```
$encData = $doc->createElementNS("http://www.w3.org/2001/04/xmlenc#",
                              "EncryptedData");
$encData->setAttribute("Type", "http://www.w3.org/2001/04/xmlenc#Element");
$creditcard->parentNode->replaceChild($encData, $creditcard);
```

Add the EncryptionMethod element so the recipient knows the algorithm being used. This is completely optional. If both parties have already agreed on an algorithm, then it is not necessary that this be added:

```
$encMethod = $doc->createElementNS("http://www.w3.org/2001/04/xmlenc#",
                              "EncryptionMethod");
$encMethod->setAttribute("Algorithm",
                      "http://www.w3.org/2001/04/xmlenc#tripledes-cbc");
$encData->appendChild($encMethod);
```

Add the KeyInfo element created earlier:

```
$encData->appendChild($keyInfo);
```

Create the CipherData element, which in this example would require a CipherValue element. It is important to remember that when using a CipherValue element, the content *must* be Base64 encoded.

■**Caution** You must use the octet form of the data for encryption. When encrypting XML data, it must be serialized using UTF-8 encoding. Serializing a node using saveXML($node) will automatically have the proper encoding, but when serializing an entire document using saveXML(), the encoding of the original document is used. If using an encoding that does not fit into octet form, convert the encoding to UTF-8 prior to encoding. Calling $doc->encoding = "UTF-8" prior to serialization will change the encoding to output the correct data to be encrypted.

For example:

```
$cipherData = $doc->createElementNS("http://www.w3.org/2001/04/xmlenc#",
                              "CipherData");
$encData->appendChild($cipherData);

/* Base64 encode the value to be used as the element content */
$encoded = base64_encode($encrypted_data);
$cipherValue = $doc->createElementNS("http://www.w3.org/2001/04/xmlenc#",
                              "CipherValue", $encoded);
$cipherData->appendChild($cipherValue);
```

The serialized value of this document will look like the following. (Note that the output has been cleaned up and formatted for presentational purposes.)

```
<payment>
    <order_number>1001</order_number>
    <customer>Joe Smith</customer>
    <EncryptedData xmlns="http://www.w3.org/2001/04/xmlenc#"
                   Type="http://www.w3.org/2001/04/xmlenc#Element">
        <EncryptionMethod Algorithm="http://www.w3.org/2001/04/xmlenc#tripledes-cbc"/>
        <KeyInfo xmlns="http://www.w3.org/2000/09/xmldsig#">
            <KeyName>mcryptiv</KeyName>
            <KeyValue>5Fl6lc4xjwA=</KeyValue>
        </KeyInfo>
        <CipherData>
            <!-- CipherValue has been formatted for display -->
            <CipherValue>
                Jhm3UYs9OvxaOkD6OWfKsaO/zm3GOaCNhS//zoBMUysNZllY/cn8lbHX+d
                6vPu/TZEytA+S1W1lehMFgxL2pWvW3UrCdypAocMln+FneJbfDUjVMRSYe
                kYjgghdwWPcOaKlC9UAEm/ZTyTyo2xix4DHPBbIE1xf4SL8xhfOpcTPX+A
                OeRYxU7r+wVRRq5wno2OQHHILMgMkaywQlS3qAk7YdXmfYZu1K4PCOHGEq
                stOW5OvW+oNZa37i6yqdVcOX
            </CipherValue>
        </CipherData>
    </EncryptedData>
</payment>
```

Decrypting Data

Decrypting the data is even easier than encrypting the value. This time the tree does not need to be modified, unless you want to re-create the entire original document rather than just use the resulting creditcard element. Using the resulting data from the "Encrypting Data" section, the variable $encdom will be used as the DOMDocument object with the loaded data.

■**Note** Decryption processing for other algorithms or complex structures is more involved than what is presented in this chapter. The steps presented here are enough to handle most cases using basic structures, such as the one from the previous section, and allow you to begin working with XML encryption once you have finished reading the chapter. To use other algorithms or handle more complex structures, refer to the XML Encryption Syntax and Processing specification.

The steps to decrypt the data depend heavily upon how data needs to be decrypted. The example shown here is within a controlled environment. You know what has been encrypted and how it has been encrypted, so you do not need to create a generic processor to handle all types of algorithms and XML encryption structures. Because of this, you can skip many steps and even perform them in a different order than defined in the specification. For those who may need to handle different types of encryption algorithms and structures, the following are the steps detailed in the specifications. They are performed for each EncryptedData or EncryptedKey element within the document.

1. Process the element to determine the algorithm, parameters, and ds:KeyInfo element to be used. If some information is omitted, the application must supply it.

2. Locate the data encryption key according to the ds:KeyInfo element, which may contain one or more children elements. These children have no implied processing order. If the data encryption key is encrypted, locate the corresponding key to decrypt it. (This may be a recursive step because the key-encryption key may itself be encrypted.) Or, one might retrieve the data encryption key from a local store using the provided attributes or implicit binding.

3. Decrypt the data contained in the CipherData element.

   a. If a CipherValue child element is present, then the associated text value is retrieved and Base64 decoded so as to obtain the encrypted octet sequence.

   b. If a CipherReference child element is present, the URI and transforms (if any) are used to retrieve the encrypted octet sequence.

   c. The encrypted octet sequence is decrypted using the algorithm/parameters and key value already determined from steps 1 and 2.

4. Process decrypted data of a Type element or element content.

   a. The clear-text octet sequence obtained in step 3 is interpreted as UTF-8 encoded character data.

   b. The decryptor must be able to return the value of Type and the UTF-8 encoded XML character data. The decryptor is not required to perform validation on the serialized XML.

   c. The decryptor should support the ability to replace the EncryptedData element with the decrypted element or element content represented by the UTF-8 encoded characters. The decryptor is not required to perform validation on the result of this replacement operation. The application supplies the XML document context and identifies the EncryptedData element being replaced. If the document into which the replacement is occurring is not UTF-8, the decryptor must transcode the UTF-8 encoded characters into the target encoding.

5. Process decrypted data if Type is unspecified or is not an element or element content.

   a. The clear-text octet sequence obtained in step 3 must be returned to the application for further processing along with the Type, MimeType, and Encoding attribute values when specified. MimeType and Encoding are advisory. The Type value is normative because it may contain information necessary for the processing or interpretation of the data by the application.

   b. Note this step includes processing data decrypted from an EncryptedKey. The clear-text octet sequence represents a key value and is used by the application in decrypting other EncryptedType element(s).

Based on these steps, the first step you need to do is locate the information supplied regarding how the data was encrypted and possibly what type of data was encrypted. Using the loaded document, the first step is to locate the EncryptedData element and determine the algorithm, KeyInfo element, and parameters to use:

```
$xpath = new DOMXPath($encdom);
$query = "//*[local-name()='EncryptedData' and ".
         "namespace-uri()='http://www.w3.org/2001/04/xmlenc#']";
$nodeset = $xpath->query($query);
if ($nodeset->length == 0) {
   exit;
}
encData = $nodeset->item(0);

/* Get information on type of data encrypted */
$encType = $encData->getAttribute("Type");
```

The algorithm is not difficult to obtain. It is found on the EncryptionMethod element. The following example first defines a default algorithm. In the event the element does not exist, it assumes the Triple DES is being used.

```
/* default algorithm */
$algorithm = "http://www.w3.org/2001/04/xmlenc#tripledes-cbc";

/* Find the algorithm used for encryption */
$query = "//*[local-name()='EncryptionMethod' and ".
         "namespace-uri()='http://www.w3.org/2001/04/xmlenc#']";
$nodeset = $xpath->query($query);
if ($nodeset->length == 1) {
   $attrAlgorithm = $nodeset->item(0)->getAttribute("Algorithm");
   if ($attrAlgorithm) {
      $algorithm = $attrAlgorithm;
   }
}
```

Once the algorithm is located, the code then determines how and if this algorithm can be used. Again, the current application can handle only Triple DES in CBC mode and will produce an error for any other algorithm. The mcrypt extension is being used for encryption, so based on the algorithm, some initial values are prepared for when mcrypt is used in the decryption process:

```
switch ($algorithm) {
   case "http://www.w3.org/2001/04/xmlenc#tripledes-cbc":
      $mcryptalg = MCRYPT_3DES;
      $mcryptblock = MCRYPT_MODE_CBC;
      break;
   default:
      print "Unhandled Algorithm";
      exit;
}
```

You must now obtain the KeyInfo information. This is a controlled environment, and you know that it contains a KeyName and KeyValue element. The value you are mainly concerned with is the KeyValue because this is where the value for the initialization vector resides for the mcrypt functions. The following code uses the DOMXPath evaluate() method. The queries convert the proper elements to strings, which, according to the XPath specification, return the contents of the elements.

```
/* Find Key Information */
$query = "string(//*[local-name()='KeyName' and ".
        "namespace-uri()='http://www.w3.org/2000/09/xmldsig#'])";
$keyName = $xpath->evaluate($query);
$query = "string(//*[local-name()='KeyValue' and ".
        "namespace-uri()='http://www.w3.org/2000/09/xmldsig#'])";

/* KeyValue is Base64 encoded and must be decoded */
$keyValue = base64_decode($xpath->evaluate($query));
```

Now that you have the algorithm and the rest of the processing rules, you must locate the encrypted data. The CipherData element needs to be located and then its children examined for either a CipherValue element or a CipherReference element. The CipherData element can have only one of these elements as its child; based on which one it has, it determines the location of the encrypted data:

```
/* Find the Cipher Information */
$node = NULL;
$query = "//*[local-name()='CipherData' and ".
        "namespace-uri()='http://www.w3.org/2001/04/xmlenc#']";
$nodeset = $xpath->query($query);
if ($nodeset->length == 1) {
   $CipherData = $nodeset->item(0);
   /* Find the child element as this element may have only one */
   foreach ($CipherData->childNodes AS $node) {
      if ($node->nodeType == XML_ELEMENT_NODE) {
         break;
      }
   }
}

/* Error out if no child elements found */
if (! $node) {
   print "Unable to find Encrypted Data";
   exit;
}
```

```
/* Based on the element name, find the data and obtain encrypted octet sequence */
if ($node->nodeName == "CipherReference") {
   /* Handle CipherReference here
       $encryptedData = ..... 
   */
} elseif ($node->nodeName == "CipherValue") {
   /* Base64 decode the value to obtain encrypted octet sequence */
   $encryptedData = base64_decode($node->nodeValue);
}
```

Using the information obtained earlier for the algorithm used, decrypt the data:

```
$td = mcrypt_module_open($mcryptalg, '',  $mcryptblock, '');

/* IV was passed with KeyValue and must be used to properly decrypt */
mcrypt_generic_init($td, $key, $keyValue);
$decrypted_data = rtrim(mdecrypt_generic($td, $encryptedData));
mcrypt_generic_deinit($td);
mcrypt_module_close($td);
```

The variable $decrypted_data should now contain the decrypted creditcard element. Any type of data may actually be decrypted, so the following block demonstrates how to generically handle the decrypted data. It is based on the information supplied by the content of the EncryptedType element, which has been stored in $encType:

```
$newdoc = NULL;
switch ($encType) {
   case "http://www.w3.org/2001/04/xmlenc#Element":
      /* load element into a new document */
      $newdoc = new DOMDocument();
      $newdoc->loadXML($decrypted_data);
      break;
   case "http://www.w3.org/2001/04/xmlenc#Content":
      /* This may be a fragment so create a doc with a root node,
         load the data into a fragment - PHP 5.1 only - and append
         the fragment to the document element. */
      $newdoc = new DOMDocument();
      $newdoc->loadXML('<root />');
      $frag = $newdoc->createDocumentFragment();
      $frag->appendXML($decrypted_data);
      $newdoc->documentElement->appendChild($frag);
      break;
   default:
      /* Data is generic type and possibly not XML */
}

if ($newdoc) {
   print $newdoc->saveXML();
}
```

If you followed this demonstration starting with the "Encrypting Data" section, the output you should see is as follows:

```
<?xml version="1.0"?>
<creditcard>
    <number>4111 1111 1111 1111</number>
    <expiration_month>01</expiration_month>
    <expiration_year>2007</expiration_year>
    <ccv2>123</ccv2>
  </creditcard>
```

Conclusion

Security is always a concern for a developer and becomes more of an issue the more publicly available an application is. It is no different when working with XML. In many cases, it becomes more of an issue because XML documents are sent to and received from remote sources. It becomes important that the data can be trusted before being processed. Many developers I have spoken to rely on SSL and some type of application authentication to provide security for their data. The XML is then sent through an SSL tunnel. This may be fine when working with Web servers, but it becomes quite a task for many when this is not the case.

The payment example shown in the chapter is just a small example of how you can protect sensitive data. It is inexcusable for anyone to send credit card information in plain text across the Internet. With the number of security-related issues in the news, sometimes even occurring within a company, it is not even safe to have this data in plain text on a secured network. XML encryption adds a layer of security by keeping the data secret and accessible only to those with the keys to access the data. Therefore, you have no reason to have this data in plain text, and using XML encryption allows for easy storage as well as provides an easy packaging for transport.

An advantage of XML security is that it is just a format and process for securing data. The data does not have to be in XML format, and it does not have to reside within the structure. Using this common format, any type of data, processed correctly, can be safeguarded and (assuming the correct keys and algorithms used) processed in a standardized way. The technology does not define the algorithms or keys available for use; this means you can use whatever encryption tools you have available, or you can change to some other algorithm and key system.

This chapter introduced XML security by demonstrating how to use both XML signatures and XML encryption using PHP. I touched on only the tip of these technologies because an entire book could be written on them alone. The information presented, though, should provide a decent foundation to not only begin using these technologies but also to understand how you can handle other algorithms, key systems, and more complex structures using the specifications as a reference.

The next chapter is a break in the examination of XML technologies and provides an introduction to PEAR and some of the XML packages it offers. The packages provide functionality written in PHP that can be used rather than having to write your own custom code for many of the common XML needs and technologies.

CHAPTER 13

■■■

PEAR and XML

With the introduction of PHP 5 came a bunch of new tools to work with XML. From XML parsers to an XSLT processor and a SOAP service, the available extensions provide enough functionality to serve the majority of your needs. Problems some developers face, however, include that the extensions are not included on the server they are working with (and therefore not under their control) and that the extensions do not natively support some specific functionality. You can at least work around the latter problem. You would just be required to code the specific functionality by hand using the available tools.

The former issue is a bit more difficult to handle. In a similar fashion, you could choose to write the functionality by hand but would need to start at the ground level and would be forced to re-create functionality that otherwise would have been available through any of the extensions not currently available. In cases like these, many developers will search the Internet for preexisting code to leverage rather than starting from scratch. The PHP Extension and Application Repository (PEAR) solves some of these problems.

This chapter will introduce PEAR and many of the packages you can use to work with XML data.

What Is PEAR?

PEAR (http://pear.php.net/) is a centralized location for open source libraries, known as *packages*, that developers can leverage within their applications. What sets PEAR apart from many of the repositories on the Internet is that the packages available through PEAR must conform to a set of defined guidelines. This helps to ensure that the packages are high quality and will be maintained. Therefore, you know that reported bugs will be fixed, or at least dealt with; new features may be added, as long as they won't break existing functionality; and updated packages will be made available. This should provide you with at least some feeling of ease; in other words, once you start using a package, you will not be completely on your own in the event of a problem. The following list summarizes the purpose of PEAR:

- PEAR provides a centralized location for libraries, called *packages*, written by the PHP community.

- PEAR provides a distribution and management mechanism for these packages.

- Packages within PEAR follow set coding standards.

- PEAR consists of a large community with support available through its Web site and mailing lists.

- PEAR is governed by the PEAR group, which enforces that packages conform to guidelines and maintainers continue to follow the set guidelines.

PEAR is not an ad hoc repository. Packages must first be submitted and approved by the community before being added to the repository. This ensures that the package conforms to PEAR's guidelines and standards, and it also makes sure the package provides some needed functionality. Of course, not all developers like using code they have not written and may not be interested in what PEAR has to offer. For those who do, however, PEAR is a perfect place to search for quality code without having to worry about being left stranded in the event a problem arises.

Using PEAR

The easiest way to work with PEAR is to use the PEAR Package Manager. Unless specifically built without PEAR support or running under Windows, the PEAR Package Manager, as well as a few core packages, is installed with the core PHP installation.

Note Currently, it appears that PEAR will not be included with a default installation of PHP 6. You must manually install the PEAR core and installer.

In the event your system does not include the core PEAR installation, you can install it with some simple commands. In a Linux/Unix environment, depending upon the name of your command-line browsers, one of the following should install and set up the PEAR core:

```
lynx -source http://go-pear.org/ | php
links -source http://go-pear.org/ | php
```

Installing in a Windows environment is just a bit different. The core PHP installation includes a BAT file named go-pear.bat. Execute this file, and follow the instructions it provides.

In the event you are on a shared host or cannot install a systemwide PEAR installation, additional options are available, such as installing a local copy of PEAR. To install packages as described in this chapter, you should have the PEAR Package Manager installed and an available Internet connection. You can find instructions for performing manual installations of PEAR packages within the PEAR manual at http://pear.php.net/manual/index.php.

You can access the PEAR Package Manager from the command line using the pear command:

```
pear <command>
```

Although several commands are available, Table 13-1 presents the most commonly used ones.

Table 13-1. *PEAR Package Manager Commands*

Command	Argument	Description
info	\<package name\>	Displays information about the supplied package
install	\<package name\>	Installs the specified package
list		Lists all the installed PEAR packages
list-all		Lists all the packages and shows versions for both the available and installed packages
list-upgrades		Lists all the packages with upgrades available
remote-info	\<package name\>	Displays information about the specified package
remote-list		Lists the packages and versions from the remote repository
upgrade	\<package name\>	Upgrades the specified package
upgrade-all		Upgrades all the packages with upgrades available

Using the commands listed in Table 13-1, the following sequence of commands will list all currently installed PEAR packages, upgrade any installed packages with available upgrades, display information about the XML_Parser package, and install the package (assuming it is not already installed):

```
pear list
pear upgrade-all
pear remote-info XML_Parser
pear install XML_Parser
```

Using PEAR and XML Together

The majority of XML packages in PEAR require at least the xml extension. This is not a serious stumbling block because this extension has been part of the core PHP installation since the pre–PHP 4 days. The xml extension is the oldest XML-based extension. With a lot of applications and other extensions based on the xml extension, it's difficult to find an installation of PHP that does not include this extension.

PEAR provides many different branches in its tree. Each branch provides a grouping of a certain type of functionality. The packages I will present in this chapter deal specifically with XML functionality. Chapter 20 will cover packages relating to Web service functionality. PEAR has an active community, and packages are proposed and added often. At the time of this writing, PEAR contains 28 XML-based packages, but I will present only a few in this chapter.

If you use any of the XML packages, your script needs to include the library. Each of these packages lives in the XML branch and is included using the normal PEAR syntax `require_once 'XML/<package_name>';`. You can find the require statement for each of the packages in the following sections of this chapter.

XML_Parser Package

The XML_Parser package provides an object-oriented interface to the xml extension. If you read Chapter 8, you are probably wondering what advantage this offers, because the extension can already use class methods natively. XML_Parser expands upon the built-in OOP functionality offered by the extension; it provides some additional common functionality that normally has to be written by a developer, such as handling different types of input for XML documents, and it provides new methods of parsing. This package consists of two classes, each providing a different method to parse XML. They are the XML_Parser and XML_Parser_Simple classes. Before going into details, I have to say that I am not a fan of the XML_Parser_Simple class. I will elaborate on this in the "XML_Parser_Simple Class" section.

XML_Parser Class

The XML_Parser class is the base class within the package. It provides common methods for loading XML data, a simple way to register callbacks, standard error handling through standard PEAR errors, and two different modes affecting how the callbacks operate. To use this package, assuming the location for the PEAR packages has been set up in the php.ini file, your script must include the package:

```
require_once 'XML/Parser.php';
```

You can instantiate the class in two ways. Using a single object, you can extend the class with the custom class implementing the methods for the callbacks to be used. Callbacks are automatically registered based on the names of the methods defined in the class. The following is a list of methods that can be defined in a class, which would be called by the parser while it parses a document:

- startHandler(resource parser, string name, array attribs): This method is called when a starting element tag is encountered.

- endHandler(resource parser, string name): This method is called when an ending element tag is encountered.

- cdataHandler(resource parser, string data): This method is called when character data is encountered.

- defaultHandler(resource parser, string data): This method is called for default handling.

- piHandler(resource parser, string target, string data): This method is called when a PI is encountered.

- unparsedHandler(resource parser, string entity_name, string base, string system_id, string public_id, string notation_name): This method is called when an unparsed entity is encountered.

- notationHandler(resource parser, string notation_name, string base, string system_id, string public_id): This method is called when a notation is encountered.

- entityrefHandler(resource parser, string open_entity_names, string base, string system_id, string public_id): This method is called when an external entity reference is encountered.

Using these standard methods makes working with the parser quite convenient, because you no longer need to register them manually. For example:

```
class myClass extends XML_Parser
{
    function startHandler($parser, $name, $attribs)
    {
        print "<$name>\n";
    }

    function endHandler($parser, $name)
    {
        print "</$name>\n";
    }
}
```

Once this class is instantiated and the input set, parsing can begin immediately. The callbacks are automatically registered.

Input Settings

The xml extension works on string data. Anytime you want to use a file or stream, it is up to you to write the supporting code to read the data into strings that could then be passed to the parser. XML_Parser simplifies this through the implementation of three methods. They are setInputString(), setInputFile(), and setInput().

setInputString() The setInputString() method takes a single argument, which is the string to parse. The method operates in the same fashion as working with the native xml extension and passing the is_final parameter set to TRUE to the xml_parse() function. When working with large documents, this is not very efficient because the entire document is loaded into the string and parsed as a whole rather than being chunked into smaller pieces of data.

setInputFile() The setInputFile() method is convenient to use when working with a document from a file or a stream. It accepts a filename or URI, and it handles the opening of the resource and the reading of the data for you. No longer do you need to write any code to handle the file I/O because it will automatically be handled for you.

setInput() The setInput() method accepts a resource, such as that returned from the fopen() function, as its parameter. Input would be read starting at the current position of the file position indicator. This could be useful in cases where you are creating an XML document by writing to a file and would like to then parse the file. You do not need to close the file. You would just need to position the pointer back to the beginning of the file, and then you would need to pass the resources to this method.

Parser Modes

XML_Parser operates in one of two modes. In event mode, it operates in the normal fashion as the xml extension. The start and end element handlers, startHandler() and endHandler(), are called for each element encountered in the document. This is the default mode and what you are most likely used to dealing with if you have worked with the xml extension. In func mode, the methods called for an element are based upon the name of the element. Methods are written in the form xmltag_[element name]() for the start of the element and in the form xmltag_[element name]_() for the closing element tag. These methods, respectively, take the same arguments as the startHandler() and endHandler() methods. For example, given the following XML document:

```
<root>
    <title>My Title</title>
    <description>My Description</description>
</root>
```

you can create a class with the following methods:

```
function xmltag_title($parser, $name, $attribs) { … }
function xmltag_title_($parser, $name) { … }
```

Unless additional element handlers are created, the only two events that will occur are the start of the title element and the closing title element tag. The remaining handlers, which all deal with other node types in the document, operate as normal in this mode. It is only the element handlers that differ between modes.

You can set the mode in one of two ways. The first method is setting it via the object constructor:

```
__construct($srcenc, $mode, $tgtenc)
```

The first parameter, $srcenc, is the source encoding for the document. The second parameter, $mode, is the parser mode. It can be set to event, which is the default value, or func. The last parameter, $tgtenc, is the target encoding.

The second way to set the mode is through the setMode() method. Once you have instantiated the object, you can change the mode by passing the value func or event as a parameter to this method:

```
$myParser->setMode("func");
```

Object Handler

You have one additional way to work with the XML_Parser class. Rather than extending the class and creating the handler methods within an extended class, you can create a handler class, which allows you to work directly with an instantiated XML_Parser class. The handler class defines the methods for the callbacks and, when instantiated, is set as the object handler for an instantiated XML_Parser object. For example:

```
require_once 'XML/Parser.php';

class MyHandler {
    function startHandler($parser, $name, $attribs)
    {
        print "<$name>\n";
    }
}
```

```
    function endHandler($parser, $name)
    {
        print "</$name>\n";
    }
}

$parser = new XML_Parser();
$objHandler = new MyHandler();
$result = $parser->setHandlerObj($objHandler);
...
```

XML_Parser_Simple Class

As I mentioned, the XML_Parser_Simple class is not one I particularly favor. It is a class extending the XML_Parser class and operates by issuing an event for an element only upon encountering the closing element tag. At this point, the element name, its attributes, and all character data that resides as a direct child of the element are sent to the handler. No events are issued for the start of the element, and character data as character data isn't sent to the element handler where appropriate. You must include the package in your script using this:

```
require_once 'XML/Parser/Simple.php';
```

The method that handles the element and character data is the handleElement() method:

```
handleElement($name, $attribs, $data)
```

The remaining handlers work as they normally do by using the XML_Parser class. Consider the following document, contained in the string $xml:

```
<root>
    <element1>
        <child1>some text</child1>
        <child2>more text</child2>
    </element1>
    <element2>element2 text</element2>
</root>
```

The following code then parses the document:

```
class simpleClass extends XML_Parser_Simple {
    function handleElement($name, $attribs, $data)
    {
        print "$name : $data\n";
    }
}

$o = new simpleClass();
$o->setInputString($xml);
$o->parse();
```

When looking at the following results, you have to keep in mind that the handler for the element is called when the closing tag is encountered in the document. (I have modified the following results to remove some additional line feeds to save space.)

```
CHILD1 : some text
CHILD2 : more text
ELEMENT1 :
ELEMENT2 : element2 text
ROOT :
```

For a simple document containing a document element and child elements consisting of text-only content, then this type of parsing might be useful. In terms of parsing real XML, which covers all types of document structures, this type of parsing makes absolutely no sense; in fact, it is contrary to how XML works. Nodes are no longer in document order because the lowest descendant of a tree is processed first; however, text content that is a child of an element is processed with the element closing tag. This also means attributes used on an element are not available to be handled until the element close tag occurs.

Note Although the XML_Parser_Simple class may look appealing for simple tasks, I recommend handling XML parsing in a proper manner and using the standard XML_Parser class. This will help you understand XML and will keep you away from developing some potential bad habits that are counterproductive in the long run.

XML_Tree Package

The XML_Tree package allows you to use DOM functionality without needing the DOM extension. It relies on the XML_Parser package, so you need the core xml extension to utilize this package. Version 2 of this package (which has been in beta for more than a year), or newer, is required to use it with PHP 5.x and newer. You can install or upgrade to the beta version (unless it has been marked as stable by the time you are reading this) using one of the following pear commands:

```
/* Upgrade an existing XML_Tree package */
pear upgrade XML_Tree-beta

/* Install XML_Tree package */
pear install XML_Tree-beta
```

Note that you can add -beta to the package name so the installer will select the latest version rather than the latest stable version.

Caution At this time, the extension is marked as a beta version and must be installed using one the methods mentioned here. This extension still has some issues under PHP 5, but the examples demonstrated here will work. Possible deviations from the code presented here may result in fatal errors.

The package consists of two classes. The primary class, XML_Tree, is equivalent to a document node, and XML_Tree_Node is equivalent to element nodes. Attributes are handled via name/value arrays. Method names are similar to those used in DOM, but some differences exist; therefore, you cannot use this package as a one-to-one replacement for the DOM extension (not to mention that only a small subset of node types are supported). The API for this package is of decent size, so I will use an example to demonstrate this package rather than show the entire API.

XML_Tree enables you to build, navigate, and modify an XML document. Again, you have some limits on what you can perform, but for the majority of cases that typically are element- and attribute-based documents, you should not have any issues. The first aspect I will demonstrate is document creation. I will show how to build the following XML document using the XML_Tree package:

```xml
<?xml version="1.0"?>
<book lang="en>
   <bookinfo>
      <title>Sample Book</title>
      <author>
         <firstname>Rob</firstname>
         <surname>Richards</surname>
      </author>
   </bookinfo>
   <chapter id="navigation">
      <title>Navigating The Tree</title>
      <para>This chapter explains how to navigate a tree</para>
   </chapter>
</book>
```

The following document is similar to one from Chapter 6 used to illustrate some of the DOM functionality:

```php
<?php
require_once 'XML/Tree.php';

$tree = new XML_Tree();

/* Create document element, and add lang attribute */
$book = $tree->addRoot('book');
$book->setAttribute("lang", "en");

/* create and add bookinfo element */
$binfo = $book->addChild('bookinfo');

/* create title element, and add to tree */
$title = new XML_Tree_Node("title", "Sample Book");
$binfo->addChild($title);
```

```
/* Create author element and its children */
$author = $binfo->addChild("author");
$fname = $author->addChild("firstname");
$fname->setContent("Rob");
$author->addChild("surname", "Richards");

/* Create chapter element and id attribute, and add to tree */
$catts = array("id"=>"navigation");
$chapter = new XML_Tree_node("chapter", NULL, $catts);
$book->addChild($chapter);

/* Create and add title and para elements */
$chapter->addChild("title", "Navigating The Tree");
$strContent = "This chapter explains how to navigate a tree";
$chapter->addChild("para", $strContent);

/* Print the resulting XML document */
print $tree->dump();
?>
```

You may notice that this document uses the same methods in multiple manners. For example, the addChild() method may accept an element name, an XML_Tree_Node object, or an XML_Tree object. When using an element name and any additional information pertinent to the element, you can both create and append the method. Using an object of either XML_Tree type will just append the passed object to the tree.

Navigation is also a bit different from using DOM. It is possible to access child elements using the children property, which returns an array of child elements, but the syntax for other methods may seem a little odd. Based on the previous example, you can use the following code to dump the title element:

```
$title = $book->getElement(array(1,0));
print $title->dump();
```

From the book element, this piece of code accesses the title element and prints it:

```
<title>Navigating The Tree</title>
```

Many of the methods accept a path as an argument. The path is an array indicating the position of the child element to be accessed. Using array(1,0) with the getElement() method from the book element results in accessing the second child of the book element, which is the chapter element, and then results in accessing the first child of that element. (Remember, arrays have zero-based indexes.)

You can modify trees just like using DOM. Again, the parameters may look a little strange. Some methods accept either a path or a position to locate an element. Positions can be either positive, which locates the child element in document order, or negative, which locates the element starting from the last child element and moving to the previous siblings. For example:

```
/* remove last child element from the bookinfo element */
$binfo->removeChild(-1);

/* Remove all children, and set text content */
$chapter->children = array();
$chapter->setContent("In progress");

print $tree->dump();
```

The result tree looks like the following document:

```
<?xml version="1.0"?>
<book lang="en">
  <bookinfo>
    <title>Sample Book</title>
  </bookinfo>
  <chapter id="navigation">In progress</chapter>
</book>
```

All in all, when tree-based parsers are just not an option, XML_Tree can provide the needed functionality when the XML documents are not overly complex.

XML_Util Package

XML_Util contains a variety of functionality that can be used when creating XML documents. It has no dependencies on any XML extension or package, but it requires the use of the pcre extension. It allows you to create XML without needing any XML-based libraries. You don't even need to instantiate the XML_Util class because you can call the methods statically.

This package is similar in functionality to the XMLWriter extension available from the PECL repository. Intuitive methods create a document in a simple-to-understand fashion. XML_Util returns the newly created piece of the XML document as a string, so they must all be concatenated together or appended to a file because the document is created to result in a complete XML document. This means, however, that it is not necessary to create complete documents. It is possible to create just small pieces of a document even if it results in malformed XML. The API for this class is not complex and is documented on the PEAR site. As an example to demonstrate the functionality, I will show how to construct the following document using XML_Util:

```
<?xml version="1.0" encoding="UTF-8"?>
<element name="courses" xmlns="http://relaxng.org/ns/structure/1.0">
    <zeroOrMore>
        <element name="course">
            <element name="title">
                <text/>
            </element>
        </element>
    </zeroOrMore>
</element>
```

This document is a RELAX NG schema, which was used with DOM in Chapter 6. You can construct it with XML_Util in fewer than 20 lines of code:

```php
<?php
require_once "XML/Util.php";


$doc = XML_Util::getXMLDeclaration("1.0", "UTF-8");


$atts = array("name"=>"courses");
$doc .= XML_Util::createStartElement("element", $atts,
                                     "http://relaxng.org/ns/structure/1.0");
$doc .= XML_Util::createStartElement("zeroOrMore");
$doc .= XML_Util::createStartElement("element", array("name"=>"course"));
$doc .= XML_Util::createStartElement("element", array("name"=>"title"));
$doc .= XML_Util::createTag("text");
$doc .= XML_Util::createEndElement("element");
$doc .= XML_Util::createEndElement("element");
$doc .= XML_Util::createEndElement("zeroOrMore");
$doc .= XML_Util::createEndElement("element");


print $doc;
?>
```

The resulting document does not contain the indentation and line breaks found in the original document. Although indentation and line breaks are not required to use this schema, you can easily format it using the XML_Beautifier package rather than having to do it by hand to produce an XML document for presentation.

XML_Beautifier Package

The XML_Beautifier package can format an XML document for presentational purposes. It is similar to using the formatOutput property in DOM but also allows for some additional formatting for comments and multiline starting element tags. The XML_Beautifier package depends upon the XML_Parser and XML_Util packages, and the current stable release, which is version 1.1, works with PHP 5 and newer. The package currently consists of four classes, but the class you will most likely be concerned with is the XML_Beautifier class. You can control much of the formatting by using options with the XML_Beautifier class, as shown in Table 13-2.

Table 13-2. *XML_Beautifier Options*

Option	Default	Description
caseFolding	FALSE	Boolean indicating whether to enable or disable case folding.
caseFoldingTo	uppercase	When caseFolding is enabled, this option sets the folding to either uppercase or lowercase.
indent	Four spaces	A string that is used for indenting.
linebreak	\n	A string that is used for line breaks. For instance, under Windows you may want to set this to \r\n.

Option	Default	Description
maxCommentLine	-1	Maximum length of comment line before being wrapped. The value -1 means to not limit the length.
multilineTags	FALSE	Boolean indicating whether a line break should be inserted after each attribute in a starting element tag and also be indented.
normalizeComments	FALSE	Boolean indicating whether whitespaces within comments are to be normalized and line breaks removed.
removeLineBreaks	TRUE	Boolean indicating whether line breaks are to be removed from CDATA sections.

You can manipulate the options in a variety of ways. The easiest method is to pass them as the parameter value to the constructor of the class. Using this method, the options are passed as an array containing name/value pairs:

```
$options = array("indent"=>"   ", removeLineBreaks=>FALSE);
$xmlformat = new XML_Beautifier($options);
```

This creates an XML_Beautifier object that will use three spaces for indentation and will not remove line breaks from CDATA sections. You can also set options using the setOption() method or the setOptions() method. The difference between these two is that setOption() will set a single option at a time using the option name passed as the first parameter and the value passed as the second parameter. The setOptions() method will set any number of options at a time because it takes a single parameter that consists of an array of options, just like the constructor does:

```
$xmlformat->setOption("multilineTags", TRUE);
$xmlformat->setOptions(array("casFolding"=>FALSE, "normalizeComments"=>FALSE));
```

You can also quickly revert options to the original defaults with the resetOptions() method that takes no parameters:

```
$xmlformat->resetOptions();
```

Once you have set all the appropriate options, you can easily format the XML using the formatFile() method or the formatString() method. The method to use depends upon the location of the XML document to be formatted:

```
string formatString(string $string [, string $renderer = "Plain"])
mixed formatFile(string $file [, string $newFile=NULL [, string $renderer=Plain"]])
```

The formatString() method takes a string containing the document to be formatted and returns the formatted document as its return value. You can safely omit the $renderer parameter. You use this parameter to select the renderer to use; currently, only a Plain renderer has been implemented and is the default value for the parameter. The formatFile() method accepts the filename, passed by the $file parameter, of the XML document to be formatted. The optional $newFile parameter can be a filename for the formatted document to be saved to; the value XML_BEAUTIFIER_OVERWRITE, which causes the resulting document to overwrite the original file with the new document; or NULL, which is the default value and results in the formatted document to be returned as the return value. The last parameter is the same as the one for the formatString() method; you can safely ignore it at this time.

The following example demonstrates how to format an XML document that is loaded into a string, $xml, and printed to the output:

```
<?php
$xml = '<doc><element1 att1="attvalue" att2="att2value"/>
<element2>content</element2><!-- This
is a
comment --></doc>';

require_once 'XML/Beautifier.php';
$fmt = new XML_Beautifier(array("multilineTags"=>TRUE, "normalizeComments"=>
TRUE));
$result = $fmt->formatString($xml);
print $result;
?>
```

The document contained in the variable $xml contains line breaks with the most noticeable ones being used within the comment node. The options multilineTags and normalizeComments have been enabled. The resulting output based on this code looks like the following:

```
<doc>
    <element1 att1="attvalue"
             att2="att2value" />
    <element2>content</element2>
    <!-- This is a comment -->
</doc>
```

The element1 start tag has been split into several lines with only a single attribute per line. This is caused by the multilineTags option. The comment has also been altered by using the normalizeComments option. All line breaks have been removed and whitespaces have been normalized, which, if you recall from Chapter 2, means that multiple whitespaces used in succession are normalized into a single whitespace.

XML_HTMLSax Package

Normally, XML parsers cannot handle HTML documents because they are not well formed. I say *normally* because it is possible to load an HTML document using DOM, but no other parser handles it, unless, of course, it is XHTML. The XML_HTMLSax package was designed to allow HTML to be parsed just like XML documents using either the xml extension or the XML_Parser package. XML_HTMLSax offers its own set of options rather than the ones defined by the xml extension, as shown in Table 13-3.

Table 13-3. *XML_HTMLSax Options*

Option	Description
XML_OPTION_CASE_FOLDING	Element opening and closing tags are converted to uppercase.
XML_OPTION_ENTIES_PARSED	Entities are passed to the data handler parsed using the html_entity_decode() function.
XML_OPTION_ENTIES_UNPARSED	Entities are passed to the data handler unparsed.
XML_OPTION_LINEFEED_BREAK	Line feeds generate calls to the data handler.
XML_OPTION_TAB_BREAK	Tabs generate calls to the data handler.
XML_OPTION_TRIM_DATA_NODES	Trims leading and trailing whitespace from data passed to the data handler.

You register handlers in a similar fashion as the XML_Parser package. You must create a user-defined class that defines the handler functions. You then register this class and its associated handlers with an instantiated XML_HTMLSax object. Parsing takes place on string data, so unlike XML_Parser, you must manually read data from a file. You can supply data from a file in a single chunk returned from a function such as file_get_contents() or can split it into chunks and parse it within a while loop. The following example reads the data from the page http://www.php.net/support.php using file_get_contents() and parses it based on the handlers defined in the myHTMLParser class that has been registered with an instantiated XML_HTMLSax class, $parser:

```php
<?php
require_once('XML/XML_HTMLSax.php');

class myHTMLParser {
    function openHandler($parser, $name, $attrs) {
        print "<$name";
        foreach ($attrs AS $attname=>$attvalue) {
           print ' '.$attname.'="'.$attvalue.'"';
        }
        print ">\n";
    }

    function closeHandler($parser, $name) {
       print "</$name>";
    }

    function dataHandler($parser, $data) {
       print $data;
    }

    function piHandler($parser, $target, $data) {
       print "<?$target $data?>";
    }
}
```

```
/* Create parser and handler object */
$parser = new XML_HTMLSax();
$myHandler = new myHTMLParser();

/* Set the handler object */
$parser->set_object($myHandler);

/* Set options */
$parser->set_option('XML_OPTION_TRIM_DATA_NODES');

/* Set the handlers */
$parser->set_element_handler('openHandler','closeHandler');
$parser->set_data_handler('dataHandler');
$parser->set_pi_handler('piHandler');

/* Parse document by string */
$doc = file_get_contents("http://www.php.net/support.php");
$parser->parse($doc);
?>
```

XML_Serializer Package

XML_Serializer provides the ability to quickly and easily transform arrays and objects into XML documents, as well as the other way around. It depends upon the XML_Parser and XML_Util packages, so make sure these are installed before trying to use this package. The package consists of two classes, XML_Serializer, which performs the serialization of a data structure, and XML_Unserializer, which takes an XML document and returns an array or objects based on the contents.

■**Note** This package is currently at beta status and must be installed or upgraded using either pear install XML_Serializer-beta or pear upgrade XML_Serializer-beta.

XML_Serializer Class

The XML_Serializer class transforms your data into XML documents. It can operate in one of two modes. The difference between modes is how *indexed arrays* are handled. Indexed arrays are arrays that use numeric keys. Two possible modes exist, as shown in Table 13-4.

Table 13-4. *XML_Serializer Modes*

Name	Constant	Description
default	XML_SERIALIZER_MODE_DEFAULT	When serializing indexed arrays, the default tag is used as the tag name.
simplexml	XML_SERIALIZER_MODE_SIMPLEXML	When serializing indexed arrays, the key of the parent value is used as a tag name.

To illustrate the difference between these two modes, look at the following results serializing an array consisting of the values a, b, and c and using each mode and no other options:

```
$vals = array('a', 'b', 'c');

/* Result using default serialization */
<array>
<XML_Serializer_Tag>a</XML_Serializer_Tag>
<XML_Serializer_Tag>b</XML_Serializer_Tag>
<XML_Serializer_Tag>c</XML_Serializer_Tag>
</array>

/* Result using SimpleXML serialization */
<array>a</array>
<array>b</array>
<array>c</array>
```

As you can clearly see, simplexml mode uses the parent tag, which is array for each of the tag names. In this case, it also does not generate well-formed XML. This mode is generally used when an array is a property of an object or an XML fragment is desired. You set the mode through the XML_Serializer options. Table 13-5 lists all the options you can use when serializing data.

Table 13-5. *XML_Serializer Options*

Name	Constant	Default Value	Description
indent	XML_SERIALIZER_OPTION_INDENT	' '	String used for indentation.
linebreak	XML_SERIALIZER_OPTION_LINEBREAKS	\n	String used for newlines.
typeHints	XML_SERIALIZER_OPTION_TYPEHINTS	FALSE	Automatically adds type hint attributes.
addDecl	XML_SERIALIZER_OPTION_XML_DECL_ ENABLED	FALSE	Adds XML declaration.
encoding	XML_SERIALIZER_OPTION_XML_ENCODING	NULL	Encoding specified in the XML declaration.
defaultTagName	XML_SERIALIZER_OPTION_DEFAULT_TAG	XML_Serializer_ Tag	Tag used for indexed arrays or invalid names.
classAsTagName	XML_SERIALIZER_OPTION_CLASSNAME_ AS_TAGNAME	FALSE	Uses class name for objects in indexed arrays.
keyAttribute	XML_SERIALIZER_OPTION_ATTRIBUTE_KEY	_originalKey	Attribute where original key is stored.
typeAttribute	XML_SERIALIZER_OPTION_ATTRIBUTE_TYPE	_type	Attribute for type (only if typeHints are enabled).
classAttribute	XML_SERIALIZER_OPTION_ATTRIBUTE_ CLASS	class _	Attribute for class of objects (only if typeHints enabled).
scalarAsAttributes	XML_SERIALIZER_OPTION_SCALAR_AS_ ATTRIBUTES	FALSE	Scalar values (strings, ints, and so on) will be serialized as attributes.
prependAttributes	XML_SERIALIZER_OPTION_PREPEND_ ATTRIBUTES	' '	Prepends string for attributes.

Continued

Table 13-5. *Continued*

Name	Constant	Default Value	Description
indentAttributes	XML_SERIALIZER_OPTION_INDENT_ATTRIBUTES	FALSE	Indents the attributes; if set to _auto, it will indent attributes so they all start at the same column.
mode	XML_SERIALIZER_OPTION_MODE	XML_SERIALIZER_MODE_DEFAULT	Sets the mode for XML_Serializer. Must be one of the modes listed in Table 13-4.
addDoctype	XML_SERIALIZER_OPTION_DOCTYPE_ENABLED	FALSE	Adds a doctype declaration.
doctype	XML_SERIALIZER_OPTION_DOCTYPE	NULL	Supplies a string or an array with ID and URI.
rootName	XML_SERIALIZER_OPTION_ROOT_NAME	NULL	Name of the root tag.
rootAttributes	XML_SERIALIZER_OPTION_ROOT_ATTRIBS	array()	Attributes of the root tag.
attributesArray	XML_SERIALIZER_OPTION_ATTRIBUTES_KEY	NULL	All values in this key will be treated as attributes.
contentName	XML_SERIALIZER_OPTION_CONTENT_KEY	NULL	This value will be used directly as content; instead of creating a new tag, this can be used only in conjunction with attributesArray.
commentName	XML_SERIALIZER_OPTION_COMMENT_KEY	NULL	This value will be used directly as a comment; instead of creating a new tag, this can be used only in conjunction with attributesArray.
tagMap	XML_SERIALIZER_OPTION_TAGMAP	array()	Tag names that will be changed.
encodeFunction	XML_SERIALIZER_OPTION_ENCODE_FUNC	NULL	Function that will be applied before serializing.
namespace	XML_SERIALIZER_OPTION_NAMESPACE	NULL	Namespace to use.
replaceEntities	XML_SERIALIZER_OPTION_ENTITIES	XML_SERIALIZER_ENTITIES_XML	Type of entities to replace.
returnResult	XML_SERIALIZER_OPTION_RETURN_RESULT	FALSE	The serialize() method returns the result of the serialization instead of TRUE.
ignoreNull	XML_SERIALIZER_OPTION_IGNORE_NULL	FALSE	Ignores properties that are set to NULL.

One way you can set options is through the XML_Serializer constructor. You pass the constructor as an array with the name of the option as the key and with the value as the value of the item in the array. For instance, you can create an object that will add the XML declaration with the encoding set to UTF-8, with the document element named mydoc, with the default tag named myelement, and with tabs for indenting like this:

```
$options = array(
    'addDecl' => TRUE,
    'encoding' => 'UTF-8',
    'indent' => "\t",
    'defaultTagName' => 'myelement',
    'rootName' => 'mydoc'
);
$objSerializer = new XML_Serializer($options);
```

You can specify options by using their actual names or by using the appropriate constants listed in Table 13-5. In this case, I used the actual name of the option, but this is not required. Similarly to some of the other XML packages in this chapter, you can also set options using the setOption() or setOptions() method. The first, setOption(), accepts a name and a value parameter. You can use this to set a single option at a time. The method setOptions() accepts an array of options; these options are merged with any currently set options for the object. You can reset options to their default values with a simple call to resetOptions().

You can also set options when the serialize() method is called. This method performs all the work required to transform the data, which is passed as the first parameter into an XML document. You can pass a special option, named overrideOptions (which is not listed in Table 13-5 since it is pertinent to this method only), with the value TRUE and with the array of options to instruct the object to use only the options passed to the method rather than any that have been previously set. Putting together everything up to this point, the full code to serialize the initial array is as follows:

```php
<?php
require_once 'XML/Serializer.php';

$vals = array('a', 'b', 'c');

$options = array(
    'addDecl' => TRUE,
    'encoding' => 'UTF-8', .
    'indent' => "\t",
    'defaultTagName' => 'myelement',
    'rootName' => 'mydoc'
);

$Serializer = new XML_Serializer($options);
$result = $Serializer->serialize($vals, array('returnResult' => TRUE));

print $result."\n";
$result = $Serializer->getSerializedData();
?>
```

You should note a couple of things about this script. The first is the use of options passed to the serialize() method. Unlike setting other options, any options passed to this method are set only temporarily. Once the method has returned, the options will revert to their previous states. This occurs even when the overrideOptions option is passed. The second thing you should note is the actual option being passed to this method. By default, the serialize() method returns TRUE. Using the returnResult option causes this method to return the serialized XML document. This means the last line calling the getSerializedData() method, which just returns the current serialized document contained by the XML_Serializer object, is redundant. In both lines of code, $result will contain the same XML document. The output you should see upon script execution is as follows:

```
<?xml version="1.0" encoding="UTF-8"?>
<mydoc>
        <myelement>a</myelement>
        <myelement>b</myelement>
        <myelement>c</myelement>
</mydoc>
```

XML_Unserializer Class

You can use the XML_Unserializer class for the reverse transform of the XML_Serializer class. It takes XML documents and transforms them into the appropriate arrays or objects. The options available are specific to this class, as shown in Table 13-6. Unlike those available to the XML_Serializer class, no preexisting constants have been defined for these options.

Table 13-6. *XML_Unserializer Options*

Name	Default Value	Description
complexType	array	Complex types will be converted to arrays, if no type hint is given.
keyAttribute	_originalKey	Get array key/property name from this attribute.
typeAttribute	_type	Get type from this attribute.
classAttribute	_class	Get class from this attribute (if not given, use tag name).
tagAsClass	true	Use the tag name as the class name.
defaultClass	stdClass	Name of the class that is used to create objects.
parseAttributes	FALSE	Parses the attributes of the tag into an array.
attributesArray	FALSE	Parses them into separate array (specify name of array here).
prependAttributes	' '	Prepends attribute names with this string.
contentName	_content	Puts CDATA found in a tag that has been converted to a complex type in this key.
tagMap	array()	Uses this to map tag names.
forceEnum	array()	These tags will always be an indexed array.
encoding	NULL	Specifies the encoding character of the document to parse.
targetEncoding	NULL	Specifies the target encoding.
decodeFunction	NULL	Function used to decode data.
returnResult	FALSE	The unserialize() method returns the result of the unserialization instead of TRUE.

The XML_Unserializer class has similar methods as the XML_Serializer class. You can set options through the constructor, the setOption() and setOptions() methods, and the resetOptions() method. The only difference to remember is that the option used must be an option listed in Table 13-6. Using the serialized XML document from the previous example, which is stored in the variable $result, you can transform it back into an array using the following code:

```
require_once 'XML/Unserializer.php';

$XMLUnserializer = new XML_Unserializer();

$result2 = $XMLUnserializer->unserialize($result, FALSE,
                                         array('returnResult' => TRUE));

if (PEAR::isError($result2)) {
   die($result2->getMessage());
}

var_dump($XMLUnserializer->getUnserializedData());

print "\n".$XMLUnserializer->getRootName()."\n";
```

The unserialize() method takes three arguments in this case. The first, which is required, is the XML document to unserialize. The second optional argument is a Boolean indicating whether the value of the first parameter is the name of a file or just a string containing the XML document. In this example, FALSE is passed, which indicates that the variable $result is a string containing the XML document. The last optional parameter is an array of options to be used for unserializing the document. Again, this uses the returnResult option so rather than returning a TRUE/FALSE value, the method will return the unserialized data. It is not required to return the value at this point because it can also be retrieved using the getUnserializedData() method. The last line outputs the tag name of the root element. This must be called only after the data has been unserialized. The output of this code is as follows:

```
array(1) {
  ["myelement"]=>
  array(3) {
    [0]=>
    string(1) "a"
    [1]=>
    string(1) "b"
    [2]=>
    string(1) "c"
  }
}

mydoc
```

This may look a bit odd. The original data was array('a', 'b', 'c'). The array does exist in the output, but it is actually the value of the myelement key of an array. The problem is that the original data being serialized was a numeric indexed array. When it was unserialized, XML_Unserializer had to make some guesses about the data. You can avoid using the typeHints option when serializing the data. Had it been used in the XML_Serializer example, the resulting XML document would have looked like the following: .

```
<?xml version="1.0" encoding="UTF-8"?>
<mydoc _type="array">
        <myelement _originalKey="0" _type="string">a</myelement>
        <myelement _originalKey="1" _type="string">b</myelement>
        <myelement _originalKey="2" _type="string">c</myelement>
</mydoc>
```

Attributes have been added to each of the myelement elements to identify the key for each item in the array. When this is unserialized, the XML_Unserializer uses the attributes to determine how the data is to be reconstructed. Had this been used originally, the var_dump() of the resulting data would have been as follows:

```
array(3) {
  [0]=>
  string(1) "a"
  [1]=>
  string(1) "b"
  [2]=>
  string(1) "c"
}
```

This is the original array properly reconstructed.

Summary

I have demonstrated only a small portion of the XML_Serializer package; it actually provides some powerful features. Dubbed "the Swiss Army knife for reading and writing XML files," it can easily serialize complex structures into XML documents, and vice versa. The possibilities are pretty much endless of what can be performed using this package. Imagine how easy it would be to convert data retrieved from a MySQL database into XML. You could convert rows of returned records into XML and append them together to form a complete recordset. Add type hinting to this, and you now have the basic data structure that could be sent to some remote application. If you think about it, it starts leading you down the path of Web services.

XML_RSS Package

RSS, covered in detail in Chapter 14, is an XML format for content syndication. The XML_RSS package consists of the XML_RSS class, which simplifies the process of reading and extracting information from RSS feeds. The only dependency of this package is the XML_Parser package. To parse remote feeds, which are typically required when working with RSS, PHP must be allowed to access remote URLs through the allow_url_fopen INI setting. XML_RSS uses the XML_Parser package, which in turn uses the xml extension, so the same rules that apply to the xml extension for processing PHP streams apply to the XML_RSS package. The API is compact and demonstrated further in the next chapter when I explain RDF and RSS.

XML_DTD Package

XML_DTD offers the capabilities to parse DTDs as well as validate documents against these DTDs without needing a validating parser such as DOM. In fact, the only dependency this package has is the XML_Tree package and its dependencies. The package consists of three classes. XML_DTD_Parser performs the actually parsing of a DTD, which results in an object of the XML_DTD_Tree class. You can use this to extract information from the parsed DTD. The last class, XML_DTD_XmlValidator, validates an XML document against a DTD. This package is still in an alpha release but will work to some degree under PHP 5.

Caution Whitespaces are not properly ignored when validating a document. Elements that can consist only of child elements will fail to validate if ignorable whitespaces exist between the child elements. When setting the list of acceptable elements, #PCDATA must also be allowable content, or the whitespaces must be removed from the document prior to it being validated. This issue exists with the alpha release 0.4.2 so it may be fixed by the time you read this.

Depending upon the class being used, the DTD can reside within a file or be contained in a string. In either case, the DTD is handled as an external subset, so it does not consist of a document type declaration. Listing 13-1 contains an example of a DTD that could be used by this package. The subset defined in this listing could be referred to by the file xmldtd.dtd.

Listing 13-1. *External Subset in* xmldtd.dtd

```
<!ELEMENT courses (course+)>
<!ELEMENT course (title, description)>
<!ELEMENT title (#PCDATA)>
<!ELEMENT description (#PCDATA)>
```

The document in Listing 13-2 comes from Chapter 3, which explained document validation. The document, located in the file courses.xml, is considered valid when validated using the DOM extension.

Listing 13-2. *Courses Document Residing in the File* courses.xml

```
<courses>
   <course>
      <title>French I</title>
      <description>Introductory French</description>
   </course>
   <course>
      <title>French II</title>
     <description>Intermediate French</description>
   </course>
</courses>
```

The XML_DTD_Parser class creates a tree that you can use to inspect the DTD. It has a single method, parse(), that parses the DTD and returns an XML_DTD_Tree object. This method takes one required parameter, which is the DTD to be parsed, and an optional parameter, which indicates whether the first parameter is a file location or a string containing the DTD. The default value of the second parameter is TRUE, indicating that the first parameter refers to a file location. The following code demonstrates how to parse a DTD and outputs a dump of the returned XML_DTD_Tree object:

```php
<?php
require_once 'XML/DTD.php';
$dtdfile = "xmldtd.dtd";

$dtdParser = new XML_DTD_Parser;
$tree = $dtdParser->parse($dtdfile);
var_dump($tree);
?>
```

Using the XML_DTD_Parser class requires that the appropriate class definition file be loaded. In this case, it is located at XML/DTD.php. The php_ini file has been configured to include PEAR packages automatically, so complete pathing is not required and actually should be configured in this manner for PEAR to operate properly. The following is the output returned after executing the code. (It contains more than what appears but has been edited to save space.)

```
object(XML_DTD_Tree)#2 (1) {
  ["dtd"]=>
  array(1) {
    ["elements"]=>
    array(4) {
      ["courses"]=>
      array(4) {
        ["child_validation_dtd_regex"]=>
        string(25) "(#PCDATA,course,#PCDATA)+"
        ["child_validation_pcre_regex"]=>
        string(39) "((,?#PCDATA),?(,?course),?(,?#PCDATA))+"
/* Additional output omitted */
    }
  }
}
```

As you can see from the output, you could access XML_DTD_Tree directly using the arrays contained within the object. For convenience, some methods have also been defined, which are listed in Table 13-7, for the class to access specific information from the tree as well.

Table 13-7. XML_DTD_Tree *Methods*

Method	Prototype	Description
elementIsDeclared	bool elementIsDeclared(string $elem)	Indicates whether the element specified by the $elem parameter has been defined in the DTD
getAttributes	array getAttributes(string $elem)	Returns all the defined attributes for the specified element
getChildren	array getChildren(string $elem)	Returns all the defined child elements for the specified element

Method	Prototype	Description
getContent	string getContent(string $elem)	Returns any content defined for the element
getDTDRegex	string getDTDRegex(string $elem)	Returns the DTD element definition for the specified element
getPcreRegex	string getPcreRegex(string $elem)	Returns the Perl regular expression used for validating the children of the specified element

The primary use of this package is for validating XML documents, which you can do by using the XML_DTD_XmlValidator class. The class is easy to use because its constructor has no arguments and has only two public methods. The isValid() method does the bulk of the work from this class. It takes two parameters. The first is the filename for the DTD, and the second is the filename of the XML document. The method returns a Boolean indicating whether the file was successfully validated. Upon a failure, you can use the getMessage() method to retrieve the specific errors that occurred during validation. The following code uses the DTD from Listing 13-1 to validate the XML document from Listing 13-2:

```php
<?php
require_once 'XML/DTD/XmlValidator.php';

$DTDValidator = new XML_DTD_XmlValidator;
if (! $DTDValidator->isValid('xmldtd.dtd', 'courses.xml')) {
   echo $DTDValidator ->getMessage();
}
?>
```

The output is probably not what you are expecting:

```
line 2: <#PCDATA> not allowed under <courses>
line 6: <#PCDATA> not allowed under <courses>
line 3: <#PCDATA> not allowed under <course>
line 4: <#PCDATA> not allowed under <course>
line 7: <#PCDATA> not allowed under <course>
line 8: <#PCDATA> not allowed under <course>
```

The problem here is because of line breaks in the XML. These are currently not handled correctly when this package is used under PHP 5.

■**Note** The issues with whitespaces causing XML documents to not validate may have been resolved by the time you read this.

A workaround for this issue is to write DTDs that take the whitespaces into account. The downside to this is that a DTD can no longer be written to strict measures. The following is the DTD from Listing 13-1 modified to correctly validate the XML document from Listing 13-2:

```
<!ELEMENT courses (#PCDATA | course)*>
<!ELEMENT course (#PCDATA | title | description)*>
<!ELEMENT title (#PCDATA)>
<!ELEMENT description (#PCDATA)>
```

Although this package currently has issues, it still provides the mechanism to validate XML documents without needing any built-in XML-based extensions.

XML_FastCreate Package

XML_FastCreate provides the ability to easily create XML and XHTML documents. It differs from other packages that provide similar functionality in the way these documents are created. It also can leverage other packages such as XML_DTD, XML_Beautifier, and XML_Tree to provide document validation, format output, and return data in a form other than a simple string. As long as the specific package has been installed, XML_FastCreate automatically takes care of loading the appropriate class and performing the specific functionality using the XML_FastCreate API.

■**Note** The additional packages are not required to use XML_FastCreate. Without XML_DTD, you cannot perform document validation. Without XML_Beautifier, you cannot indent documents for presentation. Without XML_Tree, you can use only the Text driver.

Although only a few methods are defined in the API, it is quite dynamic. The following piece of code, although not complete, demonstrates how to create documents:

```
$oFastCreate->html(
    $oFastCreate->head(
        $oFastCreate->title("XML_FastCreate Sample")
    ),
    $oFastCreate->body(
        $oFastCreate->p("Hello World!"),
        $oFastCreate->br(),
        $oFastCreate->p("End of Sample")
    )
);
```

You can create tags by using dynamic methods. The name of the tag you want to create becomes the name of the method to be called. The resulting document would look like this:

```
<?xml version="1.0" encoding="UTF-8" standalone="no" ?>
<html>
<head>
<title>XML_FastCreate Sample</title></head>
<body>
<p>Hello World!</p>
<br />
<p>End of Sample</p></body></html>
```

An XML_FastCreate object is not directly instantiated. A factory method is called statically from the class, which determines the driver that will be used when creating a document, as well as any options listed in Table 13-8 to use with the driver:

```
object XML_FastCreate::factory(string $driver, [array $options = array()])
```

Currently, two different drivers extend the XML_FastCreate class. You can use the Text driver when a string is the desired output. This driver is built in and requires no other supporting packages. When the XML_Tree package has been installed, you can also use the XML_Tree driver. This driver returns the results as an XML_Tree object rather than a plain string.

Table 13-8. *XML_FastCreate Options*

Name	Default Value	Description
dtd	' '	Sets the DTD file to perform validity checking. Using this option requires the XML_DTD package to be installed.
indent	FALSE	Boolean to enable or disable output indentation. Using this option requires the XML_Beautifier package to be installed.
version	1.0	Sets the XML version.
encoding	UTF-8	Sets the encoding character set.
standalone	no	Sets the standalone attribute. Value can be yes or no.
doctype	Not Set	String containing the document type declaration or one of the constants defined by this package: XML_FASTCREATE_DOCTYPE_XHTML_1_1, XML_FASTCREATE_DOCTYPE_XHTML_1_0_STRICT, XML_FASTCREATE_DOCTYPE_XHTML_1_0_FRAMESET, XML_FASTCREATE_DOCTYPE_XHTML_1_0_TRANSITIONAL, XML_FASTCREATE_DOCTYPE_HTML_4_01_STRICT, XML_FASTCREATE_DOCTYPE_HTML_4_01_Frameset, or XML_FASTCREATE_DOCTYPE_HTML_4_01_Transitional.
quote	TRUE	Boolean indicating whether to autoquote attributes and contents.
translate	NULL	Hash table of tags to translate to another: 'translate' => array('title' => array('<h1 class="title"><span>', '</span></h1>'), and 'date' => array('<span class="date">', '</span>').
exec	' '	Sets external tool to valid the document.
file	' '	Writes the validation output to a file.
expand	FALSE	Boolean indicating whether empty tags should have opening and closing tag (TRUE) or just an empty-element tag.
apos	TRUE	Changes apostrophe to '. The setting depends upon whether you are creating XML or HTML.
singleAttribute	FALSE	Boolean indicating whether attributes may be written with just a name (TRUE), such as <input type="checkbox" checked />, which is valid for HTML, or must conform to XML standards and require a value (FALSE) even when empty.

So, to create a new XML_FastCreate object using the Text driver along with a few options, you do this:

```
require_once 'XML/FastCreate.php';

$options = array(
   'doctype' => XML_FASTCREATE_DOCTYPE_XHTML_1_0_TRANSITIONAL,
   'singleAttribute' => TRUE);

$oFastCreate = XML_FastCreate::factory('Text', $options);
```

It is with this $oFastCreate object that you can create the document. In a similar fashion to the SimpleXML extension, CDATA sections and comments cannot be created using the dynamic method access. For this reason, XML_FastCreate incorporates the methods cdata() and comment(). Both of these methods accept a single parameter, which is the content for these nodes in the XML document. A simple example of creating the courses document from Listing 13-2 and adding a couple of comments within the document is as follows:

```
<?php
require_once 'XML/FastCreate.php';

$oFastCreate = XML_FastCreate::factory('Text');

$oFastCreate->courses(
   $oFastCreate->comment('Intro to French Course'),
   $oFastCreate->course(
      $oFastCreate->title('French I'),
      $oFastCreate->description('Introductory French')
   ),
   $oFastCreate->comment('Intermediate French Course'),
   $oFastCreate->course(
      $oFastCreate->title('French II'),
      $oFastCreate->description('Intermediate French')
   )
);

$xml = $oFastCreate->getXML();
print $oFastCreate->indentXML($xml);
?>
```

The example is similar to the snippet of code presented earlier. The output is performed in two steps. To get the XML document in a presentational state, the method indentXML() is used. This method takes a string containing the XML to make presentable and also requires that the XML_Beautifier package be installed. It is not required that the XML_FastCreate object hold any XML document to perform the transformation because the string passed to the method is what is used to be "beautified." This is the reason the getXML() method is used. This method retrieves the XML document created by the object as a string. This string is then passed to the indentXML() method with the final result printed to the output.

This package provides more functionality than demonstrated here. As previously mentioned, documents can also be validated. The isValid() method, which requires the XML_DTD package to be installed, works in the same manner as the XML_DTD package, except that it validates the XML document currently existing within the XML_FastCreate object based on the DTD, which is passed as a filename to the method. XML_FastCreate is also able to perform validation, indentation, and output all through a single method call. Based on the options set when the object was created, the toXML() method will perform any necessary validation, indent if necessary, and send the final document directly to output. The method does not return the final document; rather, it returns TRUE or a PEAR error object. You can find additional information about class methods and arguments in the PEAR manual for this package.

Conclusion

The PEAR repository is a place where you can find preexisting code covering many different topics. The XML section alone contains 28 packages ranging from simple parsers to an object-oriented API for creating SVG documents. This chapter introduced PEAR, its installer, and a few of the XML-related packages. Many of these packages can come in handy, especially in cases where DOM or SimpleXML are just not available. The only requirement of many of these packages is for the xml extension to be installed, which it is in almost every installation. Although they might not be able to provide all the functionality that could be performed using DOM or SimpleXML, the PEAR packages can do a lot with XML. Some packages are also written to perform specific functionality. One such package is XML_RSS. The next chapter introduces RDF and RSS, where you will also find an example of processing an RSS feed using the XML_RSS package.

■■■

CHAPTER 14

Content Syndication: RSS and Atom

Content syndication is not something new—it has been around for many years but has never been as widely used as it is today. The term *content syndication* refers to publishing information on the Internet that can then be used by other sites as well as by stand-alone reader applications. The explosion of Web logs (commonly referred to as *blogs*) breathed new life into content syndication. Before, the syndicated content, known as *feeds*, was typically found on news sites only. Once blogs began proliferating on the Internet, content started being shared left and right, and users began using readers and aggregators to track their favorite blogs. Many people, mostly nontechnical ones, probably have never heard of the acronym RSS or probably do not understand the concept of content syndication yet unknowingly utilize it as they download MP3 files to their music players. In addition, those who subscribe to podcasts are actually using technology built on RSS. Whether providing a feed for a blog, providing a feed of changes for some software you may be writing, or doing your own podcast, the applications for content syndication are almost endless, and its usage is growing at a phenomenal rate every day.

This chapter will cover the formats used for these feeds, including a brief history of them. Once you understand their basic structures, I will show how to use XML technologies in PHP to create your own publishers and readers for these feeds.

■**Tip** Trying to figure out whether a feed is valid is not always simple to do. No matter how closely you follow the specifications, you can create hours of work for yourself by having to track down the smallest typographical error. The site Feed Validator (http://feedvalidator.org/) is a great resource for validating all the types of feeds mentioned in this chapter.

Understanding the Evolution of RSS and Atom

The acronym RSS is pretty ambiguous. The evolution of feeds is quite interesting and explains the reason why the acronym RSS can stand for RDF Site Summary, Rich Site Summary, or Really Simple Syndication. The history of content syndication actually goes back further than RSS, but it didn't start to get interesting until about 1999 when Netscape released RSS 0.9.

For its portal site, Netscape released RDF Site Summary (RSS) 0.9, which was based upon RDF. RDF, formally known as the Resource Description Framework, is a W3C specification for describing metadata (http://www.w3.org/RDF/). With it, you can describe almost everything with a URI. But RDF is not a simple technology. Although RSS 0.9 wasn't really RDF, it was still more complicated than RSS needed to be.

Dave Winer, the founder of UserLand Software, was one of the most vocal critics of Netscape's implementation of RSS. He, as well as many others, thought it was still too complex and that it lacked necessary features. Netscape quickly released RSS 0.91, which was no longer based on RDF; Netscape dropped namespace support from the document, added a DTD, and added a few new features from UserLand's scriptingNews format. No longer supporting RDF, the technology was now called Rich Site Summary. Although this step toward simplification appeased those looking for an easier-to-use technology, it, at the same time, upset those who favored the RDF approach and who thought the original RSS 0.9 had not gone far enough. Not shortly after this, Netscape, no longer interested in the portal business, stopped developing RSS completely. This is where RSS's history begins to get interesting.

The developer community, rather than a single company, continued to work on RSS, but developers could not agree on what the next version of RSS should entail. The RDF backers began working on RSS 1.0, using RSS 0.9 as its basis and causing quite a battle in the developer community. Everything that was deemed wrong with the original format and simplified by RSS 0.91 was brought back to life. In December 2000, RSS 1.0 (named RDF Site Summary) was officially released. Winer quickly countered this with his release of RSS 0.92, which was a continuation of RSS 0.91.

Thus, RSS had forked, which began the confusion most people have today when looking at the different RSS versions.

Although RSS 1.0 was considered finalized, Winer continued developing the 0.9x branch by releasing 0.93 and 0.94. Trying to bridge the gap between the two paths, Winer proposed RSS 2.0, which was basically RSS 0.92 with some optional elements and namespace support. It still did not include RDF, angering many of those in the RSS 1.0 group. Fighting even occurred about whether discussions should take place on a mailing list (favored by the RSS 1.0 group) or blogs (favored by Winer). In the end, Winer released a final version of RSS 2.0, not taking into account many of the concerns from those in the RSS 1.0 group. This caused those developers to return to working on their own RSS branch.

The ongoing feud had no end in sight. About a year later, in mid-2003, Sam Ruby led a new group with the goal of creating a blog format using the following guidelines:

- 100 percent vendor neutral

- Implemented by everybody

- Freely extensible by anyone

- Cleanly and thoroughly specified

RSS 0.9 was a Netscape initiative and a driving force behind its portal business. Netscape was not worried about trying to create a vendor-neutral format, though. After all, when the two RSS groups could not agree on anything, how could they all implement the same format and allow extensibility by everyone? Therefore, rather than trying to guess the future and develop new features, Sam Ruby created Atom based on what was known to work when dealing with content syndication. In addition, he kept it simple with a minimal feature set.

Introducing RSS 1.0: RDF Site Summary

RSS 1.0, released in December 2000, is the successor to RSS 0.9 in terms of an RDF-based feed. This section will explain the structure of an RSS 1.0 document; Listing 14-1 shows a sample RSS 1.0 document. I will cover as much detail as possible for RSS 1.0 in this chapter, and you can find additional information in the full specification at `http://web.resource.org/rss/1.0/spec`. Many people don't need all the features of RSS 1.0 and prefer to use RSS 0.91, RSS 2.0, or Atom, but RSS 1.0 is probably the most complex structure to deal with, so I will cover it in more detail than the others. Once you understand an RSS 1.0 document, the other syndication formats will be much easier to use.

Listing 14-1. *Sample RSS 1.0 Document*

```
<?xml version="1.0"?>
<rdf:RDF
   xmlns:rdf="http://www.w3.org/1999/02/22-rdf-syntax-ns#"
   xmlns="http://purl.org/rss/1.0/" >

   <channel rdf:about="http://www.exmaple.com/news.rss">
      <title>Example RSS News</title>
      <link>http://www.example.com/</link>
      <description>
         This is an example RSS feed from www.example.com.
      </description>

      <image rdf:resource="http://www.example.com/images/rss_channel.gif" />

       <items>
          <rdf:Seq>
             <rdf:li resource="http://www.example.com/pub/article1.html" />
             <rdf:li resource="http://www.example.com/pub/article2.html" />
          </rdf:Seq>
       </items>
   </channel>

   <image rdf:about="http://www.example.com/images/rss_channel.gif">
      <title>Example RSS News Feed</title>
      <link>http://www.example.com</link>
      <url>http://www.example.com/images/rss_channel.gif</url>
   </image>

   <item rdf:about="http://www.example.com/pub/article1.html">
      <title>Article 1</title>
      <link>http://www.example.com/pub/article1.html</link>
      <description>
         This is the description for article 1.
      </description>
   </item>
```

```
<item rdf:about="http://www.example.com/pub/article2.html">
    <title>Article 2</title>
    <link>http://www.example.com/pub/article2.html</link>
    <description>
        This is the description for article 2.
    </description>
</item>
</rdf:RDF>
```

Introducing the RSS 1.0 Structure

An RSS 1.0 document should always include an XML declaration. Although optional for an XML document, its use is normally recommended and is needed if trying to maintain backward compatibility with RSS 0.9. The document root of all RSS 1.0 documents is a namespaced RDF element in the RSS syntax schema namespace that also defines the RSS 1.0 schema as the default namespace for the document. Although you can use any prefix to bind to the RSS syntax schema, rdf is normally used; in fact, you must use rdf when maintaining backward compatibility with RSS 0.9. For example:

```
<?xml version="1.0"?>
<rdf:RDF
    xmlns:rdf="http://www.w3.org/1999/02/22-rdf-syntax-ns#"
    xmlns="http://purl.org/rss/1.0/">
```

Besides the required namespace declarations, the RDF element must contain the following structure:

- One and only one channel element

- An optional image element

- One or more item elements

- Zero or more textinput elements

You can also declare additional namespaces on this element, which allow for the extensibility of the document, by using modules (explained later in the "Introducing Modules" section).

channel Element

The channel element is the container that holds the information describing the channel. In my opinion, the structure of the channel element is more difficult to work with than the other RSS branch and than Atom because the channel is not self-contained. RSS 1.0 allows only a single channel in a feed and is not self-contained. The individual item elements are not contents of the element but, rather, are contents of the RDF element.

An rdf:about attribute is required for a channel element. The value is a URI that identifies a channel and must be unique in regard to all rdf:about attributes in the document. In this respect, it is similar to an XML ID type attribute. Typically, the URI is the URL of the home page for the site or the URL for the RSS feed, but it could be any URI you like as long as it is unique from all other rdf:about values. For example:

```
<channel rdf:about="http://www.example.com/news.rss">
```

A `channel` element needs to contain one `title` element, one `link` item, one `description` item, and one `items` element. Depending upon whether the channel has an associated `image` and/or `textinput` element as a child of the `rdf:RDF` element, an associated `image` and/or `textinput` element is required within the `channel` element. It is invalid for an `image` or `textinput` element to exist as a child of an `rdf:RDF` element and not have the corresponding child element within the `channel` element. The same goes for the reverse of this statement.

title

The `title` element defines the title of the channel. It is a required element that contains #PCDATA with a suggested maximum length of 40 characters. The length can exceed 40 characters, but doing so breaks backward compatibility with RSS 0.9. For example:

```
<title>Example RSS News</title>
```

link

The `link` element, which is required, defines the URL for an HTML page to which the `title` element links. Normally this is the site's home page or a news page on the site. The only valid protocols for the URL are HTTP, HTTPS, and FTP (specified by `http`, `https`, and `ftp`, respectively). For example:

```
<link>http://www.example.com/</link>
```

description

The `description` element describes the channel. It is a required element containing #PCDATA with a suggested maximum length of 500 characters. Again, although only a suggestion, lengths of more than 500 characters break compatibility with RSS 0.9 parsers. For example:

```
<description>This is an example RSS feed from www.example.com.</description>
```

items

The `items` element, also required, acts as a table of contents for the child `item` elements of the `rdf:RDF` element. It defines the sequencing for the how the `item` elements should be ordered when parsed. For example:

```
<items>
   <rdf:Seq>
      <rdf:li resource="http://www.example.com/pub/article1.html" />
      <rdf:li resource="http://www.example.com/pub/article2.html" />
   </rdf:Seq>
</items>
```

The child `rdf:Seq` element denotes that its child elements, the `rdf:li` elements, are to be sequenced in the order its child `rdf:li` elements appear. Because RSS 1.0 requires a minimum of at least one `item` element, this element is required, and at least one `rdf:li` element is required.

The `rdf:li` elements are associations to the document's `item` elements. The `resource` attribute corresponds to the `item` element's `rdf:about` attribute and must contain the same value as the corresponding `rdf:about` attribute. If you consider the `rdf:about` attributes to be

XML ID type attributes, then the resource attribute would be an IDREF type attribute. It points to and locates the item element in the document.

image

The image element is optional and used to associate an image element with the channel. It is required only if an image element exists as a child of the rdf:RDF element. Similar to how rdf:li elements work, the image element contains an rdf:resource attribute. For some reason, the rdf:li resource attribute was not namespaced in the RSS 1.0 specification but must be with the image element. The value must be identical to the image element's rdf:about value so that the image can be located within the document. For example:

```
<image rdf:resource="http://www.example.com/images/rss_channel.gif" />
```

This element must always be an empty element.

textinput

The textinput element associates an optional child textinput element of the rdf:RDF element with the channel. It is required only when such a child element exists in the document. Being an associative element, it is an empty element with only an rdf:resource attribute. Again, the value of the rdf:resource attribute must be identical to the value of the rdf:about attribute of the master textinput element. For example:

```
<textinput rdf:resource="http://www.example.com" />
```

This element was not used in Listing 14-1 but is written as demonstrated here.

image Element

An image element, which is a child of the rdf:RDF element, associates an image with an HTML rendering of the channel. It is not required that you use an image with a feed, but when supplied, the associated image element within the channel element must also exist. This element requires an rdf:about attribute whose value is a URL locating the physical image. Like all URLs in the RSS 1.0 specification, the protocol must be HTTP, HTTPS, or FTP (specified by http, https, or ftp, respectively).

The format of the physical image has no restrictions (though it should be a common format for the greatest Web browser support). The height and width depend upon the RSS version compatibility you are trying to obtain. The RSS 0.91 specification allows an image height from 1 to 144 and a width from 1 to 400. RSS 0.9, however, dictates an image of exactly 88 × 31. For example:

```
<image rdf:about="http://www.example.com/images/rss_channel.gif">
    <title>Example RSS News Feed</title>
    <link>http://www.example.com</link>
    <url>http://www.example.com/images/rss_channel.gif</url>
</image>
```

The image element, when used, cannot be an empty element. It must contain a title element, a url element, and a link element.

title

The `title` element supplies the alternate text for the image when the channel is rendered as HTML. Its content becomes the value for the image's `alt` attribute in the rendered HTML. Following the same format as the other `title` elements within the document, its content contains `#PCDATA` and has a suggested maximum length of 40 characters. Again, the suggested length is required only when maintaining backward compatibility with RSS 0.9. For example:

```
<title>Example RSS News Feed</title>
```

url

The `url` element specifies the URL to the physical location of the image. When the channel is rendered as HTML, the contents of this element become the value for the image's `src` attribute in the rendered HTML. It is important to remember that only HTTP, HTTPS, and FTP (specified by `http`, `https`, and `ftp`, respectively) are valid protocols for the URL. When maintaining compatibility with RSS 0.9, the length of the content can be no greater than 500 characters. For example:

```
<url>http://www.example.com/images/rss_channel.gif</url>
```

link

The `link` element specifies the URL to which the image should link when the channel is rendered as HTML. The contents could become the value for the `href` attribute of an anchor tag surrounding the rendered image tag when displayed as HTML. The value is typically the site's home page or a news page and, to maintain compatibility with RSS 0.9, must have a length no greater than 500 characters. The URL must also use only HTTP, HTTPS, or FTP (specified by `http`, `https`, or `ftp`, respectively). For example:

```
<link>http://www.example.com</link>
```

item Element

The master `item` elements, which are those that are children of the `rdf:RDF` element, contain the specific information for a block of content. This content could be anything identifiable by a URI, such as news information, a job listing, or a blog entry. A minimum of one `item` element is required and, when maintaining compatibility with RSS 0.9 or 0.91, must be limited to a maximum of 15 `item` elements.

Each `item` element must contain a unique `rdf:about` attribute. The attribute must be unique within the entire document and not just among the different `item` elements. The value for this attribute is a URL to the specific content. For example, if the particular `item` element were based on a blog entry, the attribute would contain the URL to the specific entry within the blog. This value must also be identical to the content of the child `link` element, as well as to the value of the `resource` attribute from the `rdf:li` element used within the `channel` element. For example:

```
<item rdf:about="http://www.example.com/pub/article1.html">
    <title>Article 1</title>
    <link>http://www.example.com/pub/article1.html</link>
    <description>
        This is the description for article 1.
    </description>
</item>
```

All item elements must contain a title element and a link element. The description element is optional, but it is common to see one within an item element.

title

The title element contains the title of the item. Using a blog entry as an example, the content for this item would be the same as the title used for the entry within the blog. Its format is #PCDATA with a suggested maximum length, for RSS 0.9 compatibility, of 100 characters. For example:

```
<title>Article 1</title>
```

link

The link element contains the URL to a specific item. In the case of a blog entry, the content of this element is the direct URL to the specific blog entry to which the item refers. The rules for this element are the same as all other link and url elements from the RSS 1.0 specification. The URL protocol must be HTTP, HTTPS, or FTP (specified by http, https, or ftp, respectively), and the suggested maximum length is 500 characters. For example:

```
<link>http://www.example.com/pub/article1.html</link>
```

description

The description element provides a brief description or abstract of the content to which the item is referring. It consists of #PCDATA with a suggested maximum length of 500 characters. This element is optional, but it's almost always used. For example:

```
<description>This is the description for article 1.</description>
```

Although not mentioned in the specification, it is generally acceptable to use HTML in a description. Early in RSS's history, plain text was considered the only valid content. However, the original UserLand RSS reader never filtered out HTML, and developers began using it within content. This pretty much became the norm and is where RSS 1.0 stands today; all readers are generally expected to be able to handle HTML. You need to consider, though, that RSS, being in XML format, must properly encode entities. It is also common to see developers using CDATA sections to contain the content.

textinput Element

The textinput element generates a form, such as a search box or subscription form, that would use the GET method when the feed is rendered into HTML. This is an optional element, and I have yet to come across it in any RSS feeds. It most likely exists to maintain compatibility with RSS 0.9. Being a child of the rdf:RDF element, it contains an rdf:about attribute that has a unique value corresponding to the location where the form should be submitted. This value must not only be identical to the content of the child link element but also be identical to the value of the rdf:resource attribute for the textinput element contained within the channel element. For example:

```
<textinput rdf:about="http://www.example.com/search.php">
    <title>Channel Search</title>
    <name>str_search</name>
    <description>Search all information within channel</description>
    <link>http://www.example.com/search.php</link>
</textinput>
```

When this element is used, it needs to contain title, description, name, and link elements.

title

The title element provides a descriptive title for the textinput field. Its content is #PCDATA with a suggested maximum length of 40 characters. For example:

```
<title>Channel Search</title>
```

description

The description element briefly describes the purpose of the form. Its content is #PCDATA with a suggested maximum length of 100 characters. For example:

```
<description>Search all information within channel</description>
```

name

The name element defines the name attribute of the textinput field when rendered as HTML. This means that when the form is submitted, the value of the name element will be the name of the parameter passed to the site when the form is submitted. The content of this element is #PCDATA with a maximum length of 500 characters. For example:

```
<name>str_search</name>
```

link

The link element defines the URL to which the form will be submitted using the GET method. Its content is #PCDATA with a suggested maximum length of 500 characters. Following the URL standards in the RSS 1.0 specification, the protocol can be HTTP, HTTPS, or FTP (specified by http, https, or ftp, respectively). For example:

```
<link>http://www.example.com/search.php</link>
```

Introducing Modules

Modules provide the means to compartmentally extend RSS. They reside within their own namespaces and are designed to provide specific, narrowly focused functionality. The RSS 1.0 specification includes three built-in modules that you can use to extend its basic functionality:

- Dublin Core

- Syndication

- Content

Dublin Core

The Dublin Core module provides some standard metadata elements that can provide additional descriptions of the data contained within the RSS feed. The module is defined by the http://purl.org/dc/elements/1.1/ namespace, typically bound to the dc prefix and declared on the rdf:RDF element:

```
<rdf:RDF
    xmlns:rdf="http://www.w3.org/1999/02/22-rdf-syntax-ns#"
    xmlns="http://purl.org/rss/1.0/"
    xmlns:dc="http://purl.org/dc/elements/1.1/" >
```

You can use the elements defined by this module, listed in Table 14-1, within all child elements of the rdf:RDF element. This means the elements can be children of the channel, item, image, and textinput elements. It is important to remember the difference between the RSS elements because many share the same name though provide different functionality. The easiest way to remember which elements can use these module elements is to use the module elements only within elements that have an rdf:about attribute. It also doesn't hurt to remember that the image and textinput elements within the channel element must be empty so cannot contain child elements—or any content.

Table 14-1. *Dublin Core Module Elements*

Element	Description
dc:title	A name given to the resource.
dc:creator	An entity primarily responsible for making the content.
dc:subject	A topic of the content.
dc:description	A description of the content.
dc:publisher	An entity responsible for making the resource available.
dc:contributor	An entity responsible for making contributions to the content.
dc:date	The date of an event, such as the creation date.
dc:type	The type or nature of the content.
dc:format	The physical or digital manifestation of the resource, such as the media type.
dc:identifier	A unique reference to the resource, such as the URI or ISBN.
dc:source	A reference to a resource from which the current resource is derived.
dc:language	The language of the content, such as en or en-GB.
dc:relation	A reference to a related resource.
dc:coverage	The scope of the resource.
dc:rights	Information about the rights held in and over the resource. When this element is absent, no assumption can be made about any rights concerning the resource.

Using the module, you can extend the channel element to include the publisher, creator, and date. Each of these elements provides additional information about the channel. Taking the channel element from Listing 14-1, an extended channel element using the Dublin Core module would look like the following:

```
<channel rdf:about="http://www.exmaple.com/news.rss">
    <title>Example RSS News</title>
    <link>http://www.example.com/</link>
    <description>This is an example RSS feed from www.example.com.</description>

    <image rdf:resource="http://www.example.com/images/rss_channel.gif" />

    <items>
        <rdf:Seq>
            <rdf:li resource="http://www.example.com/pub/article1.html" />
            <rdf:li resource="http://www.example.com/pub/article2.html" />
        </rdf:Seq>
    </items>
    <dc:publisher>Apress</dc:publisher>
    <dc:creator>Rob Richards (mailto:rrichards@php.net)</dc:creator>
    <dc:date>2005-10-01T12:00+00:00</dc:date>
</channel>
```

Syndication

The Syndication module provides additional information to aggregators and others accessing the RSS feed regarding how often the feed is updated. Using this information, you can reduce the amount of times you have to access the feed in order to keep up-to-date, which can also help reduce your bandwidth usage. This module resides within the http://purl.org/rss/1.0/ modules/syndication/ namespace bound to the prefix sy:

```
<rdf:RDF
    xmlns:rdf="http://www.w3.org/1999/02/22-rdf-syntax-ns#"
    xmlns="http://purl.org/rss/1.0/"
    xmlns:sy="http://purl.org/rss/1.0/modules/syndication/" >
```

The Syndication module is extremely simple to use because it provides only three elements, shown in Table 14-2.

Table 14-2. *Syndication Module Elements*

Element	Description
sy:updatePeriod	The period over which the channel format is updated. The content of this element can be hourly, daily, weekly, monthly, or yearly. When this element is omitted, the default value daily is used.
sy:updateFrequency	The frequency of updates in relation to the updatePeriod. The value must be a positive integer and defaults to 1 when omitted.
sy:updateBase	Defines a base date and time that are used with the updatePeriod and updateFrequency to establish a publishing schedule. The content of this element must take the format YYYY-MM-DDTHH:MM.

You can use these elements only to describe a channel, and therefore you can use them only as child elements of the `channel` element. For instance, you can extend the `channel` element from Listing 14-1 to include a publishing schedule, as follows:

```
<channel rdf:about="http://www.exmaple.com/news.rss">
    <title>Example RSS News</title>
    <link>http://www.example.com/</link>
    <description>This is an example RSS feed from www.example.com.</description>

    <image rdf:resource="http://www.example.com/images/rss_channel.gif" />

    <items>
        <rdf:Seq>
            <rdf:li resource="http://www.example.com/pub/article1.html" />
            <rdf:li resource="http://www.example.com/pub/article2.html" />
        </rdf:Seq>
    </items>

    <sy:updatePeriod>daily</sy:updatePeriod>
    <sy:updateFrequency>4</sy:updateFrequency>
    <sy:updateBase>2005-01-01T12:00+00:00</sy:updateBase>
</channel>
```

Based on the last three elements within the `channel` element, the content is updated every six hours (four times per day) starting at noon Greenwich mean time (GMT).

Content

The Content module provides support for the actual content of Web sites and the information about how it is to be interpreted. This module lives within the `http://purl.org/rss/1.0/modules/content/` namespace bound to the `content` prefix:

```
<rdf:RDF
    xmlns:rdf="http://www.w3.org/1999/02/22-rdf-syntax-ns#"
    xmlns="http://purl.org/rss/1.0/"
    xmlns:content="http://purl.org/rss/1.0/modules/content/" >
```

This module currently contains five approved elements: `content:items`, `content:item`, `content:format`, `rdf:value`, and `content:encoding`.

content:items

The `content:items` element is a container for `content:item` elements. It can be a child of an RSS `item` or `channel` element, and it takes the following form:

```
<content:items>
    <rdf:Bag>
        <rdf:li>
            <!-- content:item elements located here -->
        </rdf:li>
    </rdf:Bag>
</content:items>
```

The additional `rdf` namespaced elements are necessary when using this element and are from the RDF specification.

content:item

The `content:item` element describes a single version of the content for its parent item. This attribute can contain an `rdf:about` attribute whose value is the URI of the content. When this attribute is not used with this element, you need to use a child `rdf:value` element. For example:

```
<!-- Without rdf:about attribute -->
<content:item>
  <!-- information about the item goes here -->
  <!-- content:item children -->
</content:item>

<!-- Using rdf:about attribute -->
<content:item rdf:about="http://www.example.com/image.jpg">
  <!-- content:item children -->
</content:item>
```

The content of this element can consist of a required `content:format` element, an `rdf:value` element that depends upon the existence of an `rdf:about` attribute, and an optional `content:encoding` element.

content:format

The `content:format` element is a required, empty element with an `rdf:about` attribute. The value of this attribute is a URI that represents the content of the item. Normally the value is one of the URIs specified by the Resource Directory Description Language (RDDL) natures at `http://www.rddl.org/natures/`. For example, an item that consisted of strict XHTML content would have a `content:format` element like the following:

```
<content:format rdf:resource="http://www.w3.org/TR/xhtml1/DTD/xhtml1-strict" />
```

rdf:value

The `rdf:value` element contains the content of the `content:item` element. `rdf:value` is required only when the `content:item` element does not contain an `rdf:about` attribute that points to the content. When `rdf:value` is used, its content is encoded as specified by a `content:encoding` element. The following two examples of the `rdf:value` element have no encoding defined and thus are considered to contain character data:

```
<rdf:value>This is &lt;b&gt;Bold Text&lt;/b&gt;.</rdf:value>
<rdf:value><![CDATA[This is <b>Bold Text</b>.]]></rdf:value>
```

When content is included as unencoded XML, you should use the attribute `rdf:parseType="Literal"` so as to not confuse RDF parsers.

content:encoding

The `content:encoding` element is an empty element with an `rdf:resource` attribute. The value of this attribute is a URI representing the encoding of the `content:item` element. For example, when the content of the `rdf:value` element is well-formed XML, you should use the URI `http://www.w3.org/TR/REC-xml/#dt-wellformed`. For example:

```
<content:item>
   <content:format rdf:resource="http://www.w3.org/1999/xhtml" />
   <content:encoding rdf:resource="http://www.w3.org/TR/REC-xml#dt-wellformed" />
   <rdf:value rdf:parseType="Literal" xmlns="http://www.w3.org/1999/xhtml">
      <p>This is <b>Bold Text</b>.</p>
   </rdf:value>
</content:item>
```

Example Item Element

Putting all this together, the following code shows how to create a new item for the document in Listing 14-1 and includes information about the content using the Content module. Some simple XHTML markup, `<p>This is <b>Bold Text</b>.</p>`, is included within the content, and the content module informs the parser and aggregator how to handle this data.

```
<item rdf:about="http://www.example.com/pub/article3.html">
   <title>Article 3</title>
   <link>http://www.example.com/pub/article3.html</link>
   <content:items>
      <rdf:Bag>
         <rdf:li>
            <content:item>
               <content:format rdf:resource="http://www.w3.org/1999/xhtml" />
               <content:encoding
                       rdf:resource="http://www.w3.org/TR/REC-xml#dt-wellformed" />
               <rdf:value rdf:parseType="Literal"
                    xmlns="http://www.w3.org/1999/xhtml">
                  <p>This is <b>Bold Text</b>.</p>
               </rdf:value>
            </content:item>
         </rdf:li>
      </rdf:Bag>
   </content:items>
</item>
```

Introducing RSS 2.0: Really Simple Syndication

The RSS 2.0 specification (`http://blogs.law.harvard.edu/tech/rss`) was released in July 2003. Although it does supercede the previous 0.9x versions, many people continue to use RSS 0.91 because of its simplicity. RSS 2.0 is not much more complex than RSS 0.91, but it does allow extensibility through the use of namespaces. You can use elements not defined in the specification within an RSS 2.0 document as long as they are namespaced. This section will break down the structure of an RSS 2.0 document; Listing 14-2 shows the same feed as the RSS 1.0 document from Listing 14-1 but written using RSS 2.0.

Listing 14-2. *Sample RSS 2.0 Document*

```
<?xml version="1.0"?>
<rss version="2.0">
   <channel>
      <title>Example RSS News</title>
      <link>http://www.example.com/</link>
      <description>
         This is an example RSS feed from www.example.com.
      </description>

      <image>
         <title>Example RSS News Feed</title>
         <link>http://www.example.com</link>
         <url>http://www.example.com/images/rss_channel.gif</url>
      </image>

      <item>
         <title>Article 1</title>
         <link>http://www.example.com/pub/article1.html</link>
         <description>This is the description for article 1.</description>
         <pubDate>Sun, 02 Oct 2005 11:05:27 GMT</pubDate>
      </item>
      <item>
         <title>Article 2</title>
         <link>http://www.example.com/pub/article2.html</link>
         <description>This is the description for article 2.</description>
         <pubDate> Sun, 02 Oct 2005 11:35:47 GMT </pubDate>
      </item>

   </channel>
</rss>
```

One of the biggest differences between these documents, excluding the mandatory use of namespaces in an RSS 1.0 document, is the channel encapsulation. All information pertaining to the channel (including the items) is contained within the channel element. This eliminates the need to reference items, image, and textinput elements from within a channel element, like you need to do in RSS 1.0.

Introducing the RSS 2.0 Structure

All RSS 2.0 documents start with a root rss element. The XML declaration is optional, but as always, it is general practice to include it in the document. The rss element encapsulates the information for the feed and uses a required version attribute to denote the RSS version being used. This element contains a single channel element that defines the channel and includes the feed content.

It may seem odd that the document contains a `channel` element even though the document can contain only a single channel, rather than just having its contents live directly as children of the `rss` element, but I assume this is because of the structure RSS had in versions 0.9 and 0.91. To keep compatibility, these elements were kept within the structure. This is only a guess, but otherwise it would be just as intuitive that all children of an `rss` element would pertain to the channel, since it can contain only a single channel.

The `channel` element contains all the information for the feed, other than the version of RSS being used. Its structure requires that the elements in Table 14-3 are implemented and allows for additional information using the optional elements listed in Table 14-4.

Table 14-3. *Required* `channel` *Elements*

Element	Description	Example
title	The name of the channel. If the feed contains information from your Web site, the title should be the same as that of the Web site or specific page name from the Web site.	"Example RSS News"
link	The URL to the Web site or specific page to which the feed refers.	"http://www.example.com"
description	The description of the channel.	"This is an example RSS feed from www.example.com."

Table 14-4. *Optional* `channel` *Elements*

Element	Description	Example
language	The language in which the channel is written. The value should be a language code as specified by Netscape (http://blogs.law.harvard.edu/tech/stories/storyReader$15) or defined by the W3C in RFC 1766 (http://www.ietf.org/rfc/rfc1766.txt).	en-us
copyright	Copyright notice for content in the channel.	Copyright 2005, Example Holder
managingEditor	Email address for the party responsible for editing the content.	editor@example.com (Managing Editor)
webMaster	Email address for party responsible for handling technical issues.	webmaster@example.com (Webmaster)
pubDate	The publication date for the content in the channel.	Mon, 03 Oct 2005 13:00:01 GMT
lastBuildDate	The last date and time the content changed.	Mon, 03 Oct 2005 13:15:26 GMT
category	The category (or categories) to which this channel belongs. This element follows the same rules as the category element for an item.	`<category>PHP</category>`

Element	Description	Example
generator	A string indicating the program used to generate the channel.	My PHP RSS Generator v1.0
docs	A URL to the documentation for the RSS format used. Unless you have written your own documentation for RSS 2.0, you should use `http://blogs.law.harvard.edu/tech/rss`.	`http://blogs.law.harvard.edu/tech/rss`
cloud	Specifies a Web service implemented in HTTP-POST, XML-RPC, or SOAP 1.1, which supports the `rssCloud` interface, allowing a process to register with and be notified of updates.	`<cloud domain="soap.example.com" port="80" path="/rsscloud.php" registerProcedure="rssNotify" protocol="soap"/>`
ttl	The number of minutes a channel can be cached before refreshing from the source (time to live).	`<ttl>60</ttl>`
image	Specifies a GIF, JPEG, or PNG image to display with the channel. This element contains child elements that define the image.	See the "image Element" section for an example.
rating	The Platform for Internet Content Selection (PICS) rating for the channel. PICS is a W3C specification found at `http://www.w3.org/PICS/` to rate content so users can control the type of material they are allowed to access.	`<rating>(PICS-1.1 "http://www.classify.org/safesurf/" l r (SS~~000 1))</rating>`
textInput	Used to create a text input box to display with the channel.	See the "textInput Element" section for an example.
skipHours	Contains up to 24 `<hour />` child elements with values from 0 to 23, indicating when the channel should not be read. This element is rarely used within a feed but is still valid. From various statistics I could find, fewer than 2 percent of feeds utilize this element.	`<skipHours><hour>0</hour> <hour>12</hour><skipHours>` This would ask an aggregator to not access the channel from noon to 1 p.m. GMT or from midnight to 1 a.m. GMT.
skipDays	Contains up to seven `<day />` child elements with values of `Monday`, `Tuesday`, `Wednesday`, `Thursday`, `Friday`, `Saturday`, or `Sunday`, indicating days the channel should not be read. This element seems to be used even less than `skipHours`. The best usage statistics I could find for this element came in at less than 0.2 percent.	`<skipDays><day>Thursday</day> </skipDays>` Do not read channel on Thursdays.

A few of the optional elements require some additional explanation because they are more than simple text content containers. These elements are image, cloud, and textInput. I'll explain the category element in more detail in the context of an item in the "item Element" section. The rules for using this element as a child of channel are the same as when used as a child of an item element.

image Element

The image element defines the image associated with the channel and allows the image to be rendered when the feed is rendered. You can use only GIF, JPEG, or PNG images for a channel. When using an image element, you also need three child elements:

title: The title of the image. The value of this element is used as the value for the alt attribute on the img tag when rendered as HTML. The value is normally the same as the value of the channel's title element.

url: The URL of the image. The value of this element is used as the value for the src attribute of the img tag when rendered as HTML.

link: The URL of the site or Web page to which the image should link. You would use this value to create an anchor tag with the value of the href attribute being the value of the link element. In practice, this value is typically the same as the channel's child link element.

An image element can also define three additional optional elements to provide more information for the image:

height: The height of the image in pixels. The value can be an integer from 1 to 400. When omitted, the default value of 31 is used for the image's height.

width: The width of the image in pixels. The value can be an integer from 1 to 144. When omitted, the default value of 88 is used for the image width.

description: A description of the content to which the link element points. The value of this element is used as the value for the title attribute of the link that surrounds the rendered image.

The following structure uses the image element from the RSS document in Listing 14-2 and adds the optional elements to define a GIF with the dimension 100×35 that will link to http://www.example.com/ when selected in the rendered HTML:

```
<image>
    <title>Example RSS News Feed</title>
    <link>http://www.example.com</link>
    <url>http://www.example.com/images/rss_channel.gif</url>
    <width>100</width>
    <heigth>35</heigth>
    <description>Example RSS News Feed</description>
</image>
```

textinput Element

The textInput element works in the same manner as that from the RSS 1.0 specification (though note the difference in case for the element name). The textInput element generates a form, such as a search box or subscription form, that would use the GET method when the feed is rendered into HTML. When using it, you must also use the four required child elements:

`title`: The label of the Submit button in the text input area.

`description`: Explanation of the text input area.

`name`: The name of the text object in the text input area. The value of this element is used as the parameter name passed to the processing script.

`link`: The URL of the script that processes the request upon submission.

For example:

```
<textInput>
    <title>Channel Search</title>
    <name>str_search</name>
    <description>Search all information within channel</description>
    <link>http://www.example.com/search.php</link>
</textInput>
```

item Element

The `item` elements contain the actual content for the feed. Unlike RSS 1.0, it is legal to have a feed without any items, though the feed would not serve much purpose in that case. Also, unlike RSS 1.0, these elements are children of the `channel` element rather than just pointers to items. Although the basic structure is similar to that used in RSS 1.0, additional optional elements, defined by the RSS 2.0 specification, can further describe the item rather than having to extend the structure like what you must do in RSS 1.0.

title

The `title` element, which is required, contains the title of the item. Using a blog entry as an example, the content for this item would be the same as the title used for the entry within the blog. Other than containing character data, this element has no further restrictions. For example:

```
<title>Article 1</title>
```

link

The `link` element, which is required, contains the URL to a specific item. In the case of a blog entry, the content of this element would be the direct URL to the specific blog entry to which the item refers. This element has no further restrictions for the content. Protocols are not restricted under RSS 2.0 like they are when using RSS 1.0. For example:

```
<link>http://www.example.com/pub/article1.html</link>
```

description

The `description` element provides a brief description or abstract of the content to which the item is referring. Unlike RSS 1.0, this element is required within an `item` element. For example:

```
<description>This is the description for article 1.</description>
```

author

The author element is optional and is used to identify the author of the current item. The content contains the email address of the author. This element is useful when the feed contains items from many different authors rather than from a single source. For example:

```
<author>rrichards@php.net (Rob Richards)</author>
```

category

The category element is an optional child element for both an item element and a channel element. It associates one or more categories with either an item or a channel, depending upon the context. It has one optional attribute, domain, whose value identifies a categorization taxonomy. The value of the element is a slash-separated string that identifies a hierarchic location in the indicated taxonomy. For example:

```
<category>PHP</category>
```

Here's another example (which has been split into three lines for readability):

```
<category domain="http://www.dmoz.org">
    Computers/Programming/Languages/PHP/
</category>
```

comments

The comments element includes the URL to a comments page for the particular item. For example, most blog entries contain a section for user comments. The contents of the comments element for this item would be the URL pointing to the user comment page or section. For example:

```
<comments>http://www.exmaple.com/2005/10/01/article1.html#comments</comments>
```

enclosure

An enclosure element is optionally used to locate and describe some type of content associated with the current item. For example, an item for a news entry could refer to a multimedia clip in MPEG format that shows the actual footage of the event. You could use an enclosure element so that the video could be retrieved along with the feed. This way, if feed retrieval were automated, you could retrieve the video clip with the feed, allowing it to stored and viewed on a local machine rather than streaming it across the Internet.

This element was pretty much added to the RSS 2.0 specification specifically to allow for the syndication of audio files, eventually termed *podcasts*. Its structure consists of an empty element with three required attributes:

url: An HTTP URL locating the enclosure

length: The size of the enclosure in bytes

type: The MIME type of the enclosure

For example:

```
<enclosure url="http://www.example.com/news/article1.mpg"
           length="9312164" type="video/mpeg" />
```

guid

The content of the optional guid element is a globally unique identifier for the item. It is a string that an aggregator can use to determine whether the item is new. You can use an optional isPermaLink with either the value true, which is the default value, or the value false. When the value is true, an aggregator assumes that the value of the element is a URL pointing to the item that could be opened in a Web browser. For example:

```
<!-- GUID is not a URL -->
<guid isPermaLink="false">1234567890</guid>

<!-- GUID is a URL that can be opened -->
<guid isPermaLink="true">http://www.example.com/pub/article1.html</guid>
<!-- GUID is a URL that can be opened using default value for isPermaLink -->
<guid>http://www.example.com/pub/article1.html</guid>
```

pubDate

The optional pubDate element contains the date the current item was published. The value of this element is a date in the format defined in RFC 822 (http://asg.web.cmu.edu/rfc/rfc822.html#sec-5). When a future date is used, an aggregator can choose to not display the current item until the specified date and time is reached. For example:

```
<pubDate>Sun, 02 Oct 2005 18:10:01 GMT</pubDate>
```

source

An optional source element supplies the name of the RSS channel from which the item came. It has one required attribute, url, which links to the XML from the source. For example:

```
<source url="http://www.example.net/foreign.xml">Third Party Feed</source>
```

The url attribute, in this case, points to the www.example.net domain, which is the originator of the item. This allows the proper credits to be given to the originator when a feed incorporates items from other feeds.

Extending RSS 2.0

You can extend RSS 2.0 in the same way you can extend RSS 1.0 documents. Elements outside the RSS 2.0 specification must reside in a unique namespace when used within the feed. It uses modules, but unlike RSS 1.0, no default modules are built into the specification. This does mean, on the other hand, that you can use the modules explained earlier with an RSS 2.0 feed. For more information about extending RSS 2.0, please refer to the earlier "Introducing Modules" section.

Introducing Atom 1.0

As you read earlier, Atom was created because of all the problems and disagreements in the RSS community a few years back. It is a new format, built from the ground up and not relying on any of the existing RSS formats as its foundation. Atom not only defines a format for a feed but also defines an API for creating, retrieving, and editing documents. This section will focus on the format of an Atom 1.0 document. You can find additional information, including the API, at http://www.atomenabled.org/. The document in Listing 14-3 is an example of the same feed that has been shown in RSS 1.0 and RSS 2.0 formats but this time is converted to Atom 1.0 format.

Listing 14-3. *Example Atom 1.0 Document*

```
<?xml version="1.0"?>
<feed xmlns="http://www.w3.org/2005/Atom">

  <title>Example RSS News</title>
  <link href="http://www.example.com/"/>

  <updated>2005-10-02T11:35:27Z</updated>
  <author>
    <name>Rob Richards</name>
    <email>rrichards@php.net</email>
  </author>
  <id>http://www.example.com/</id>

  <entry>
    <title>Article 1</title>
    <link href="http://www.example.com/pub/article1.html"/>
    <id>http://www.example.com/pub/article1.html</id>
    <updated>2005-10-02T11:35:27Z</updated>
    <summary>This is the description for article 1.</summary>
  </entry>
  <entry>
    <title>Article 2</title>
    <link href="http://www.example.com/pub/article2.html"/>
    <id>http://www.example.com/pub/article2.html</id>
    <updated>2005-10-02T11:25:47Z</updated>
    <summary>This is the description for article 2.</summary>
  </entry>
</feed>
```

The syntax is a little different from either RSS format. It uses a default namespace like RSS 1.0 does.

Introducing the Atom 1.0 Structure

Atom defines two different types of documents: Atom feed documents and Atom entry documents. An *Atom feed document* is similar to an RSS feed. It provides all the information for the feed as well as the content, which are called *entries* rather than *items*. An *Atom entry document* represents a single entry that lives outside the context of a feed. The type of document being created determines the document element that must be used. Atom feed documents, which are most common, begin with a feed element, and Atom entry documents begin with an entry element. In both cases, the elements reside within the http://www.w3.org/2005/Atom namespace, which is set as the default namespace on the element. For example:

```
<?xml version="1.0" encoding="UTF-8"?>
<feed xmlns="http://www.w3.org/2005/Atom">
   <!-- Atom Feed elements -->
</feed>

<?xml version="1.0" encoding="UTF-8"?>
<entry xmlns="http://www.w3.org/2005/Atom">
   <!-- Atom Entry elements -->
</entry>
```

Atom uses internationalized resource identifiers (IRIs), as defined in RFC 3987, located at http://www.ietf.org/rfc/rfc3987.txt. IRIs extend the URI syntax to support a greater number of characters. This means that a URI is an IRI, but not all IRIs are URIs. Section 3.1 from RFC 3987 explains how an IRI can be mapped to a URI. I will not go into detail about this; if you decide to use IRIs with Atom, it is important you understand how mappings are created because you must take two facts into consideration with Atom. First, when you use an IRI that is not also a URI for dereferencing, you must map it to a URI. This means when a resource needs to be retrieved, the IRI must have a mapping to a URI so that the resource can be located and retrieved. You can also use an IRI for resource identification, such as when used as the value of Atom id elements. In this case, the IRI alone is used for uniqueness, and the mapped URIs are not used.

Second, all Atom elements can contain xml:base and xml:lang attributes. As you saw in earlier chapters, xml:base sets the base URI or IRI for resolving any relative paths found in the scope of a particular element. You can identify the natural language for an element and its descendants using the xml:lang attribute. This attribute is significant only for elements and attributes defined as being "language-sensitive" from the Atom specification.

In terms of the structure of an Atom document, these attributes are part of a common definition, atomCommonAttributes, that can be applied to any element. This definition consists of zero or one xml:base attribute, zero or one xml:lang attribute, and any number of unspecified attributes. The unspecified attributes would constitute namespaced attributes, outside the Atom namespace, used to extend the Atom specification.

Common Constructs

Many of the elements defined in the Atom specification share the same structure. The following sections will present these common structures and their definitions. When an Atom element is identified as being one of these types, it must adhere to the requirements for the particular construct.

■**Caution** Whitespace must not be used in a Date construct or any IRI. Doing so results in the creation of invalid Atom documents.

Text

A Text construct, `atomTextConstruct`, contains human-readable text. This construct can either be an `atomPlainTextConstruct` or an `atomXHTMLTextConstruct`. The difference is the type of content allowed within the element, which is explained in more detail within the context of the `type` attribute in the "type Attribute" section. Other than the difference in content, a Text construct consists of `atomCommonAttributes`, an optional `type` attribute, and its contents.

type Attribute

The `type` attribute specifies the type of content contained within the element. It can take the value `text`, `html`, or `xhtml`. When this attribute is omitted from a Text construct, the value `text` is used by default. The following is a breakdown of how content is treated based on the value of the `type` attribute.

text

The value `text` indicates that the content is plain text with no entity-escaped HTML. This doesn't mean that entities do not have to be escaped. The content still must be valid XML. For example:

```
<title type="text">Using PHP &amp; XML</title>
```

Because this is plain text, an Atom processor can remove whitespace and format the text for display, such as justifying text or using changing fonts.

html

The value `html` indicates that the content is suitable to be displayed as HTML. All markup must be properly escaped, and the content should be able to be displayed within an HTML DIV tag. For example:

```
<title type="html">Using &lt;B&gt;PHP&lt;B&gt; &amp; &lt;B&gt;XML&lt;B&gt;</title>
```

xhtml

The value `xhtml` indicates that the content is valid XHTML. When using this type, the content is contained within a `div` tag, which is not considered part of the content. This tag, as well as the appropriate content, must reside within http://www.w3.org/1999/xhtml, just like when writing an XHTML document. You can define the namespace anywhere within the Atom document as long as it is in scope when using the construct. For example:

```
<!-- Using default namespace on div tag -->
<title type="xhtml">
   <div xmlns=" http://www.w3.org/1999/xhtml ">
      <b>PHP</b> &amp; <b>XML</b>
   </div>
</title>
```

```
<!-- Using a prefixed namespace -->
<title type="xhtml" xmlns:xhtml="http://www.w3.org/1999/xhtml">
    <xhtml:div>
        <xhtml:b>PHP</xhtml:b> &amp; <xhtml:b>XML</xhtml:b>
    </xhtml:div>
</title>
```

As you can clearly see, the easiest manner to handle the namespacing is to set it as a default namespace on the div element. Defining it anywhere above this element requires using a prefix to keep it separate from the Atom namespaced elements and attributes, which then must be used for every piece of XHTML written.

Person

A Person construct describes a person or other entity. It is constructed with atomCommonAttributes, a single name element, an optional uri element, an optional email element, and any number of extension elements. Extension elements are elements outside the Atom namespace that can provide additional information about the particular element. Table 14-5 describes the Atom-specific elements for this construct.

Table 14-5. Person *Construct Child Elements*

Element	Description
name	A required element containing a human-readable name for the person or entity. The content is language-sensitive.
uri	An optional element containing an IRI associated with the person or entity.
email	An optional element containing the email address associated with the person or entity.

Date

A Date construct defines an element containing a date and time conforming to those specified in RFC 3339. It is constructed with atomCommonAttributes and has a date and time as the content. The date and time are separated by the uppercase letter *T* and, when a numeric time zone offset is not used, must contain the uppercase letter *Z* for the time zone. For example:

```
<!-- No time zone offset specified -->
<updated>2005-10-02T11:30:00Z</updated>
```

```
<!-- Time zone offset used -->
<updated>2005-10-02T11:30:00-4:00</updated>
```

link

A link element defines a reference from a feed or entry to a Web resource. It consists of atomCommonAttributes, a required href attribute, and five optional attributes:

href: A URL or IRI that can be dereferenced to a resource.

rel: This attribute describes the meaning of the link. It can be a full URI or one of the predefined values:

- alternate: An alternate representation of the entry of a feed, such as a link to the page to which a feed refers.

- enclosure: A related resource that may require additional handling, such as a video. When this attribute is used, it is also recommended that the length attribute be provided.

- related: A resource related to the feed or entry.

- self: The feed or entry itself.

- via: The source of the information provided in the entry or feed.

type: The media type of the resource.

hreflang: The language of the resource.

title: The title for the link.

length: The size of the resource in bytes.

For example:

```
<link href="http://www.example.com/news/article1.mpg" rel="enclosure"
    length="9312164" type="video/mpeg" />
```

Category

A category element associates a category with either a feed or an entry. It consists of atomCommonAttributes, a required term attribute, an optional scheme attribute, and an optional label attribute:

term: A string identifying the category

scheme: An IRI identifying the categorization scheme

label: A language-sensitive, human-readable label that can be displayed in user applications

For example:

```
<category term="PHP" />
```

or:

```
<category term="PHP"
        scheme="http://www.dmoz.org/Computers/Programming/Languages/PHP/"/>
```

content

A content element either links or contains the content of an entry element. Its structure depends upon the type and location of the actual content. All content elements contain a type attribute and, depending upon its value, may require an src attribute. The content of this element depends upon the value of the type attribute as well as the use of the src attribute.

In most cases, the value of the type attribute will be text, html, or xhtml. In these instances, the content element does not have an src attribute and uses the rules defined by a Text construct based on its type value. In the rest of the cases, the type attribute must contain a valid MIME type, which excludes composite types.

When the src attribute is used, it contains the URI locating the content. The type attribute in this case indicates the MIME type of the remote content. When the src attribute is not used, and the type attribute does not contain one of the already mentioned values, then the content is determined as follows:

- If the type attribute ends in +xml or /xml, the src attribute is not used, and the content of the element is an inline XML document.

- If the type attribute starts with text, then the src attribute is not used, and the content of the element is an inline, escaped document.

- In all other cases, the content of the element is a Base64-encoded document of the media type defined by the type attribute.

For example:

```
<content type="xhtml" xml:lang="en">
    <div xmlns="http://www.w3.org/1999/xhtml">
        <b>PHP</b> &amp; <b>XML</b>
    </div>
</content>
```

feed Element

The feed element is the document element for an Atom feed document containing the metadata and data for the feed. Its children consist of atomCommonAttributes, a number of metadata elements (listed in Table 14-6), a number of extension elements, and zero or more entry elements (which are described in the following section).

Table 14-6. feed *Metadata Elements*

Element	Use	Description
title	Required	A Text construct containing the title or name of the feed.
id	Required	A permanent and universally unique IRI. If this is not a URI, it is *not* dereferenced and is compared on a character-to-character basis, just like a URI.
updated	Required	A Date construct indicating the date and time of the last significant modification.

Continued

Table 14-6. *Continued*

Element	Use	Description
author	Recommended	A Person construct providing information about the author of a feed. A feed element must contain one or more author elements unless every entry element contains at least one author element.
link	Recommended	A link, as defined in the "Common Constructs" section, to a related Web page.
category	Optional	Associates a category, as defined in the "Common Constructs" section, with the feed. A feed can have zero or more category elements.
contributor	Optional	A Person construct providing information for a contributor to the feed. You can use zero or more contributor elements.
generator	Optional	Identifies the agent used to create the feed.
icon	Optional	Identifies a small image, by means of a URL, for the feed.
logo	Optional	Identifies a larger image, by means of a URL, for the feed.
rights	Optional	A Text construct containing any rights, such as copyrights, for the feed.
subtitle	Optional	A Text construct containing a description or subtitle for the feed.

A document using the metadata elements from Table 14-6 could look something like the one in Listing 14-4.

Listing 14-4. *Sample Atom Feed Document Using Optional Elements*

```xml
<?xml version="1.0" encoding="UTF-8"?>
<feed xmlns="http://www.w3.org/2005/Atom">
   <title>Example Feed</title>
   <id>http://www.example.com/</id>
   <updated>2005-10-02T15:15:00Z</updated>
   <author>
      <name>John Smith</name>
   </author>
   <author>
      <name>Jane Doe</name>
   </author>
   <link rel="self" href="/atom/" />
   <category term="technology"/>
   <category term="PHP"/>
   <contributor>
      <name>John Doe</name>
   </contributor>
   <generator uri="/phpatomgen.php" version="1.0">
      Example PHP Atom Generator
   </generator>
```

```
<icon>http://www.example.com/feedicon.jpg</icon>
<logo>http://www.example.com/feedlogo.jpg</logo>
<rights> &copy; 2005 John Smith </rights>
<subtitle>Description of Example Atom Feed</subtitle>

<!-- Zero or more entry elements -->
</feed>
```

entry Element

Atom does not require a feed to contain any entry elements, which is similar to RSS 2.0, because it does not require items. Using the Atom format, however, an entry element can be part of a feed and also can be its own document. This section will cover the structure of an entry element because it is the same whether used a child element of a feed element or used stand-alone as the document element of an Atom entry document. The only difference is that because Atom elements must live within the Atom namespace, an entry element used as an Atom entry document must declare the namespace, http://www.w3.org/2005/Atom, while a child entry element within a feed would normally already be within the scope of this namespace. Many of the possible child elements, shown in Table 14-7, of an entry element are used in a similar fashion as those used by the feed element.

Table 14-7. *Entry Child Elements*

Element	Use	Description
title	Required	A Text construct containing the title or name of the entry.
id	Required	A permanent and universally unique IRI. If this is not a URI, it is *not* dereferenced and is compared on a character-to-character basis like a URI.
updated	Required	A Date construct indicating the date and time of the last significant modification.
author	Recommended	A Person construct providing information about the author of a feed. An entry element must contain at least one author element unless one is contained by the feed or is provided within a source element for the current entry.
content	Recommended	Contains or links to the complete content, as defined in the "Common Constructs" section, of the entry. This element must be provided if the entry does not contain an alternate link and should be provided if there is no summary.
link	Recommended	A link, as defined in the "Common Constructs" section, to a related Web page. An alternate link must be used if the entry does not contain a content element.
summary	Recommended	A Text construct that provides a short summary or description of the entry. It is recommended that a summary element be used when no content element is used, the content is remote and uses an src attribute, or the content is Base64-encoded.
category	Optional	Associates categories, as defined in the "Common Constructs" section, with the entry. A feed can have zero or more category elements. There can be zero or more category elements.

Continued

Table 14-7. *Continued*

Element	Use	Description
contributor	Optional	A Person construct providing information for a contributor to the entry. You can use zero or more contributor elements.
published	Optional	A Date construct containing the initial creation date and time of the entry.
source	Optional	A source element is used when an entry is copied from another feed. I will explain this element in further detail following this table.
rights	Optional	A Text construct containing any rights, such as copyrights, for the entry.

I have explained each of the elements in Table 14-7 elsewhere in the chapter. The only element that needs more clarification is the source element. You use a source element when an entry is copied from another feed. Its children can be any of those used by the entry's original parent feed element except for entry elements, especially when the element is not already contained by the entry. For example, if you used an entry from Listing 14-3 to create an Atom entry document, it could look like the following:

```
<?xml version="1.0" encoding="UTF-8"?>
<entry xmlns="http://www.w3.org/2005/Atom">
    <title>Article 1</title>
    <link href="http://www.example.com/pub/article1.html"/>
    <id>http://www.example.com/pub/article1.html</id>
    <updated>2005-10-02T11:35:27Z</updated>
    <summary>This is the description for article 1.</summary>
    <source>
        <link href="http://www.example.com/"/>
        <author>
            <name>Rob Richards</name>
            <email>rrichards@php.net</email>
        </author>
    </source>
</entry>
```

If you look at the source element, you will see that it used the link and author elements from the original feed. This pertains to Atom entry documents and also when an entry from one feed is incorporated into another feed. The original feed information for the entry is maintained with the entry, keeping it completely separate from the current feed yet allowing the entry to reference its original feed. The author, contributor, rights, and category elements are some elements to preserve from the original feed because they provide the most important information pertaining to the origins and rights for the entry.

Choosing a Format

With three competing technologies, how do you choose one to use? If you are going to be subscribing to a feed, the answer is simple. You use what is offered and what your reader supports.

The hard part comes when you are the one creating the feed. Personally, when faced with a decision like this, I often will check around to see what the big corporations are doing. It is normally a safe bet that if several of them are using the same technology, it means good support exists for it. Of course, big companies also have a decent amount of resources behind them, so even if the support is not there, it usually arrives quickly.

In my opinion, RSS 2.0 looks like a safe bet, although I am not ruling out the others. With a quick look at some RSS 2.0 implementers, you will see names such as Yahoo, the *Wall Street Journal*, MSNBC, and IBM. This does not even include those providing podcasts. This, however, doesn't mean you have to use RSS 2.0 or even select just a single format.

If you look at the open source community, it is not surprising to find sites providing feeds in all three formats. Unlike a company that normally mandates how its information is accessed, open source sites tend to lean more toward freedom of choice. No matter what aggregator or reader you are using, as long as it's compatible with at least one of the technologies, you will be able to access the information.

Comparing the three formats, my first choice is RSS 2.0. It is simple to use and has a high usage rate. Second on my list is Atom. I consider Atom to be a wildcard format. It has a great structure and offers more flexibility than RSS 2.0, but it does not yet have the user base RSS 2.0 does. Remember, Atom was created as a competing format because of all the problems between the two RSS camps. So, unlike the RSS branches that already had user bases (though divided), Atom started from the bottom. I consider it a wildcard because it still has the possibility of gaining more widespread usage. RSS 1.0 is my least favorite. I think the structure is a bit awkward, and the use of namespaces a bit extensive for my liking. You should also take into account that RSS 1.0 is built on RDF technology, which in my opinion just overcomplicates things.

In the end, the choice is up to you. Everything here has been my opinion, not the voice of the Great Oz. Only you understand who your audience is and your users' needs. You know the type of content your feed will be supplying. Finally, you will be the one who has to support it. The advice offered should help you decide which format (or even formats) best suits your needs.

Seeing Some Examples in Action

Content syndication varies depending upon the technologies you are comparing. For this reason, the examples in the following sections are not overly complex examples that attempt to demonstrate the complete functionality of each of the formats. I will demonstrate a simple API for creating minimal RSS 1.0, RSS 2.0, and Atom feeds using DOM; a simple RSS 2.0 parser using SimpleXML; and a simple Atom parser using XMLReader. You could extend each of these examples to create much more feature-rich applications.

Creating Simple Feeds Using DOM

Depending upon the type of feed and the different support being added to it, building a feed manually using DOM can become complex, especially when trying to support multiple formats. This example will demonstrate how to use DOM to create feeds in multiple formats and support the minimal requirements for each format. The code is split into four classes. The Syndicator class is the base class, which is not instantiated directly, that provides the bulk of functionality for building a feed. The remaining classes, which extend the Syndicator class, are the ones that are instantiated to create a feed in a specific format. The RSS1 class supports an RSS 1.0 feed, the RSS2 class supports RSS 2.0 feeds, and the Atom class supports Atom 1.0 feed documents.

Syndicator Class

The Syndicator class is the base class and provides the majority of functionality for creating a feed. Because of the differing feed formats, much has been generalized in this class with specifics provided by the extending classes. This class is not meant to be directly instantiated. In actuality, this class should be made abstract, but in the event you are not fluent with OOP or some of the newer aspects of PHP 5, I have written it as a regular class:

```
class Syndicator {
    protected $rssDoc = NULL;
    protected $docElement = NULL;
    protected $root = NULL;
    protected $items = NULL;
    protected $hasChannel = TRUE;
    protected $tagMap = array('item'=>'item', 'feeddesc'=>'description',
                              'itemdesc'=>'description');


    const ITEM = 0;
    const FEED = 1;
```

All class properties are protected because they are not meant to be accessed outside an instantiated object. The first three properties are required because of the differing structures. The rssDoc property holds the DOMDocument object you are using to create the feed. The docElement property holds the DOMElement object to which item or entry elements are added. This normally is the document element except in the case of RSS 2.0. The item elements are added to the channel element in that format, which is actually a child of the document element. The docElement property acts as a pseudo-document element, so you can add item and entry elements using common functionality. The root property holds the DOMElement to which you add the metadata for the feed. Again, this varies depending upon the format you are using. For an Atom feed, the value of this property is the feed element, which is the document element. For an RSS 1.0/RSS 2.0 feed, the value of this property is the channel element. I will show how to use the remaining properties later in the example. The defaults for these, however, are for the RSS 1.0 and 2.0 feeds.

```
/* Common element creation function that handles namespace creation properly */
protected function createSyndElement($namespace, $name, $value=NULL)
{
    if (is_null($namespace)) {
        return $this->rssDoc->createElement($name, $value);
    } else {
        return $this->rssDoc->createElementNS($namespace, $name, $value);
    }
}
/* Default link element creation function as Atom has a different format */
protected function createLink($parent, $url)
{
    $link = $this->createSyndElement($this->NS, 'link', $url);
    $parent->appendChild($link);
}
```

The following function, createRSSNode(), adds a title, link, and description to the element passed as the first parameter. In the case of an Atom feed, it also creates the updated and id elements. Links in Atom feeds are created differently than in RSS 1.0 and RSS 2.0 feeds; thus, the example uses a createLink() function. As you will see in the Atom class, it is overridden so the element is created in the proper format. A $type variable is passed into this method to indicate the type of element for which these child elements are being created. The reason for this is to determine the element for the description. RSS 1.0 and RSS 2.0 use the element description for both the channel and item elements. Atom, on the other hand, uses subtitle for the feed element and content for the entry element. Based on the type, the proper name is taken from the tagMap array, which is also overridden in the Atom class.

```
/* Generic method to create appropriate title, link, and
   description for an element */
protected function createRSSNode($type, $parent, $title, $url,
                                 $description, $pubDate = NULL, $id=NULL)
{
   $this->createLink($parent, $url);
   $title = $this->createSyndElement($this->NS, 'title', $title);
   $parent->appendChild($title);
   if ($type == Syndicator::ITEM) {
      $titletag = $this->tagMap['itemdesc'];
   } else {
      $titletag = $this->tagMap['feeddesc'];
   }
   $description = $this->createSyndElement($this->NS, $titletag, $description);
   $parent->appendChild($description);
```

The remaining functionality of the createRSSNode() method is specific to Atom. These methods could be supported with additional coding for both RSS 1.0 and 2.0 but are currently out of the scope of this example. To do so would require supporting extending modules, the Dublin Core in particular, for RSS 1.0. These are required for a valid Atom feed so currently work properly only for that format.

```
   /* id elements and updated elements are specific to Atom
      - corresponding elements from other formats not currently supported */
   if (! is_null($id)) {
      $idnode = $this->createSyndElement($this->NS, 'id', $id);
      $parent->appendChild($idnode);
   }
   if (! is_null($pubDate)) {
      $datenode = $this->createSyndElement($this->NS, 'updated', $pubDate);
      $parent->appendChild($datenode);
   }
}
```

The constructor performs all the initial setup for the feed. Each class defines a SHELL property, which is just a template for the document. It is used to easily create a document with the initial namespaces declared properly. The hasChannel property is set to FALSE for the Atom class because it is the only format not using a channel element. Once the object is instantiated, the constructor will have properly set up the properties mentioned earlier and set the initial metadata for either the feed element or the channel element based on the values passed to the constructor.

```php
function __construct($title, $url, $description, $pubDate = NULL, $id=NULL)
{
    try {
        $this->rssDoc = new DOMDocument();
        $this->rssDoc->loadXML($this->SHELL);
        $this->docElement = $this->rssDoc->documentElement;
        if ($this->hasChannel) {
            $root = $this->createSyndElement($this->NS, 'channel');
            $this->root = $this->docElement->appendChild($root);
        } else {
            $this->root = $this->docElement;
        }
        $this->createRSSNode(Syndicator::FEED, $this->root, $title,
                            $url, $description, $pubDate, $id);
        return;
    } catch (DOMException $e) {
        throw new Exception($e->getMessage());
    }
    throw new Exception("Unable to Create Object");
}
```

The addItem() method is pretty simple. It creates an element using the name pulled from the tagMap, which is entry for Atom and item for RSS 1.0 and 2.0. The new element is then appended to the node held by the docElement property. The createRSSNode() method is then called, passing the type Syndicator::ITEM constant, which will result in the title, link, description, possible ID, and updated elements to be created on this new element.

```php
public function addItem($title, $link, $description=NULL,
                        $pubDate = NULL, $id=NULL)
{
    $item = $this->createSyndElement($this->NS, $this->tagMap['item']);
    if ($this->docElement->appendChild($item)) {
        $this->createRSSNode(Syndicator::ITEM, $item, $title, $link,
                            $description, $pubDate, $id);
        return TRUE;
    }
    return FALSE;
}

/* Method used as a holder and is overridden in the Atom class */
public function addAuthor($name)
{
    trigger_error("Function not yet implemented");
    return FALSE;
}
```

```php
/* Simple method to return the formatted XML document as a string */
function dump()
{
    if ($this->rssDoc) {
        $this->rssDoc->formatOutput = TRUE;
        return $this->rssDoc->saveXML();
    }
    return "";
}
}
```

RSS1 Class

The RSS1 class is the class to be instantiated when creating an RSS 1.0 feed. It has a format much different than RSS 2.0 and Atom do and therefore must override some methods to support its structure properly. The first area to look at is the properties and the constant it defines. The RDFNS constant is used only within this class. It defines the rdf namespace because it is quite long and because the constant makes it easier to use. This namespace is needed for a few elements, and attributes are specific to RSS 1.0. The NS property sets the common namespace used within the Syndicator class. Using the property allows the Syndicator class to use generalized code shared amongst the classes when creating elements.

```php
class RSS1 extends Syndicator {
    const RDFNS = 'http://www.w3.org/1999/02/22-rdf-syntax-ns#';
    protected $NS = 'http://purl.org/rss/1.0/';

    /* Following is formatted for readability */
    protected $SHELL =
        '<rdf:RDF xmlns:rdf="http://www.w3.org/1999/02/22-rdf-syntax-ns#"
                xmlns="http://purl.org/rss/1.0/" />';
```

The addToItems() method is unique to this class. RSS 1.0 requires items to be referenced within the channel element. The items property, which you saw defined in the Syndicator class, holds the DOMElement to which the rdf:li elements are added. Upon the addition of the first item, the structure is set up, which includes the items element and the rdf:Seq element, which is the parent for the rdf:li items. This method is never called publicly, and hence you have the private accessor. Instead, it is called by the overridden addItem() method in this class.

```php
private function addToItems($url)
{
    if (is_null($this->items)) {
        $container = $this->createSyndElement($this->NS, 'items');
        $this->root->appendChild($container);
        $this->items = $this->rssDoc->createElementNS(self::RDFNS, 'Seq');
        $container->appendChild($this->items);
    }
```

```
$item = $this->rssDoc->createElementNS(self::RDFNS, 'li');
$this->items->appendChild($item);
$item->setAttribute("resource", $url);
}
```

The only reason that the addItem() method has been overridden is to support the cre-ation of the rdf:li elements. This method first calls the parent addItem() method and then makes a call to the internal addToItems() method.

```
public function addItem($title, $link, $description=NULL,
                        $pubDate = NULL, $id=NULL)
{
    if (parent::addItem($title, $link, $description, $pubDate, $id)) {
        $this->addToItems($link);
        return TRUE;
    }
    return FALSE;
}
```

As you probably recall from the RSS 1.0 section, the channel and item elements must con-tain an rdf:about attribute. The createRSSNode() method is overridden to create this attribute prior to the createRSSNode() method from the Syndicator class being called.

```
protected function createRSSNode($type, $parent, $title, $url,
                                 $description, $pubDate = NULL)
{
    $parent->setAttributeNS(self::RDFNS, 'rdf:about', $url);
    parent::createRSSNode($type, $parent, $title, $url, $description, $pubDate);
}
}
```

RSS2 Class

The RSS2 class instantiates an object to create an RSS 2.0 document. This class is extremely simple. RSS 2.0 does not use a namespace, so the NS property is set to NULL, and the tem-plate is simply the rss element with a version. The structure of an RSS 2.0 feed differs from that of RSS 1.0; as in RSS 2.0, all elements reside within the channel element. The construc-tor has been overridden so that once the constructor from the Syndicator class has been called, the docElement property can be set to point to the proper node. In this case, both the root and docElement properties point to the channel element.

```
class RSS2 extends Syndicator {
    protected $NS = NULL;
    protected $SHELL = '<rss version="2.0" />';
```

```
function __construct($title, $url, $description, $pubDate = NULL, $id=NULL)
{
    try {
        parent::__construct($title, $url, $description, $pubDate, $id);
        $this->docElement = $this->root;
    } catch (Exception $e) {
        throw new Exception($e->getMessage());
    }
}
}
```

Atom Class

The Atom class, used to instantiate an object to create an Atom 1.0 feed, is not much more difficult than using the RSS2 class. Its NS property is set to the Atom namespace, and the SHELL property is set to the initial feed element. The hasChannel variable is set to FALSE in this case. When the constructor is called, a channel element will not be created, and the docElement property will be set accordingly. The class also defines a custom tagMap. Atom tags vary slightly from the RSS 1.0 and 2.0 tags, which is the reason for the use of this array mapping.

```
class Atom extends Syndicator {
    protected $NS = 'http://www.w3.org/2005/Atom';
    protected $SHELL = '<feed xmlns="http://www.w3.org/2005/Atom" />';
    protected $hasChannel = FALSE;
    protected $tagMap = array('item'=>'entry', 'feeddesc'=>'subtitle',
                              'itemdesc'=>'content');
```

Atom has a different syntax for a link element. This method overrides the default method so that the link is created in the proper format:

```
protected function createLink($parent, $url) {
    $link = $this->rssDoc->createElementNS($this->NS, 'link');
    $parent->appendChild($link);
    $link->setAttribute('href', $url);
}
```

Atom also requires that the feed and entry elements contain an updated id element. In the event no value has been passed to these parameters for the constructor and addItem() methods, the values are automatically populated. The id is set to the URL, and the pubDate is set to the current date and time.

■Note If you are not familiar with the value c passed to the date function, it is a new format character as of PHP 5 that formats dates in ISO 8601 format. This format is compatible with the Atom Date construct.

For example:

```
function __construct($title, $url, $description, $pubDate = NULL, $id=NULL)
{
    try {
        if (empty($id))
            $id = $url;
        if (empty($pubDate))
            $pubDate = date('c');
        parent::__construct($title, $url, $description, $pubDate, $id);
    } catch (Exception $e) {
        throw new Exception($e->getMessage());
    }
}
```

The addAuthor() method is specific to Atom. An author element is required either within the feed or within every entry element. Rather than supporting some version of this for the RSS formats, the method defined in the Syndicator class will issue a user notice when called and not overridden by the current instantiated class. This method, when called, adds a simple author and child name element to the feed. This is the minimal amount of data required to create a valid Atom document.

```
public function addAuthor($name)
{
    $author = $this->rssDoc->createElementNS($this->NS, 'author');
    if ($this->docElement->appendChild($author)) {
        $namenode = $this->rssDoc->createElementNS($this->NS, 'name', $name);
        if ($author->appendChild($namenode)) {
            return TRUE;
        }
    }
    return FALSE;
}

public function addItem($title, $link, $description=NULL,
                        $pubDate = NULL, $id=NULL)
{
    if (empty($id))
        $id = $link;
    if (empty($pubDate))
        $pubDate = date('c');
    return parent::addItem($title, $link, $description, $pubDate, $id);
}
}
```

You can use the following code with the classes defined previously to create simple feeds in each format. Currently, the RSS2 class is the default type of feed to be created. Executing the code will create an RSS 2.0 document containing two articles and will print the resulting document to the output. Depending upon how the script is being accessed (CLI versus Web page), you need to use the correct input variable. It is currently set up to use CLI, but commenting the line requesting the $_SERVER['argv'] and uncommenting the $_GET['format'] line will allow the script to run within a Web page. In CLI mode, passing the value rss1 will create an RSS 1.0 feed, atom will create an Atom feed, and anything else will result in an RSS 2.0 feed. When executed within a Web page, the same values are used, although they need to be named with the parameter format.

```php
$type = "";

/* Uncomment the following when using within a Web server environment
if (isset($_GET ['format'])) {
    $type = (string)$_GET['format'];
}
*/

/* Comment out the following to disable CLI mode */
if (isset($_SERVER['argc']) && $_SERVER['argc'] > 1) {
    $type = (string) $_SERVER['argv'][1];
}

swtich ($type) {
    case 'rss1':
        $test = new RSS1("RSS1 Title", "http://www.example.com/rss1.xml",
                        "My RSS1 Feed");
        break;

    case 'atom':
        $test = new Atom("Atom Title", "http://www.example.com/atom.xml",
                        "My Atom Feed");
        /* Author is only applicable to an Atom feed */
        $test->addAuthor('Rob Richards');
        break;
    default:
        $test = new RSS2("RSS2 Title", "http://www.example.com/rss2.xml",
                        "My RSS2 Feed");
}




$test->addItem('Article 1', 'http://www.example.com/pub/article1.html',
                'This is the description for article 1.');
$test->addItem('Article 2', 'http://www.example.com/pub/article2.html',
                'This is the description for article 2.');
print $test->dump();
```

```xml
<?xml version="1.0"?>
<rss version="2.0">
    <channel>
        <link>http://www.example.com/rss2.xml</link>
        <title>RSS2 Title</title>
        <description>My RSS2 Feed</description>
        <item>
            <link>http://www.example.com/pub/article1.html</link>
            <title>Article 1</title>
            <description>This is the description for article 1.</description>
        </item>
        <item>
            <link>http://www.example.com/pub/article2.html</link>
            <title>Article 2</title>
            <description>This is the description for article 2.</description>
        </item>
    </channel>
</rss>
```

Creating a Simple RSS 2.0 Parser Using SimpleXML

SimpleXML provides a simple way to parse feeds. As long as no default namespaces have been used in the feeds, you have little to deal with other than understanding the structure. As you are already aware from Chapter 7, you access elements as properties by name, and you access attributes like an array with string indexes.

```php
<?php
/* Define some RSS 2.0 and other compatible feeds */
$rssfeed = array();
/* The PHP RSS feeds are RSS version 0.93 */
$rssfeed['PHPGEN'] = 'http://news.php.net/group.php?group=php.general&format=rss';
/* The YAHOO RSS feeds are RSS version 2.0 */
$rssfeed['YAHOOTOPNEWS'] = 'http://rss.news.yahoo.com/rss/topstories';
/* The Planet PHP RSS feed is RSS version 0.91 */
$rssfeed['PLNTPHP'] = 'http://www.planet-php.org/rss/';
/* Apress new book list feed - RSS 2.0 */
$rssfeed['APRESSBOOKS'] = 'http://www.apress.com/rss/whatsnew.xml';


/* Loop through and process each defined feed */
foreach($rssfeed AS $name=>$url) {
    $rssParser = simplexml_load_file($url);

    /* Output the channel information */
    print $rssParser->channel->title."\n";
    print "   URL: ".$rssParser->channel->link."\n";
    print "   ".$rssParser->channel->description."\n\n";
```

```
    /* Iterate through the items, and output each one */
    foreach ($rssParser->channel->item AS $item) {
        print $item->title."\n";
        print $item->link."\n";
        print $item->pubDate."\n";
        print $item->description."\n\n";
    }
}
?>
```

As you can see, in only a few lines of code the basic information from RSS feeds ranging from version 0.91 to 2.0, excluding RSS 1.0, is easily parsed using SimpleXML.

Creating a Simple Atom Parser Using XMLReader

This example uses XMLReader to parse an Atom feed from Planet PHP (http://www.planet-php.org). Although the feed uses Atom 0.3, the code written here based on Atom 1.0 is compatible with the older version feed. It is basic because it outputs only the feed title, URL, and a subtitle, if one is defined. It then outputs the title, link, and content for each entry element in the feed. The amount of code to perform this simple task is much greater than that of SimpleXML. XMLReader is a streaming parser, so the entire tree is not loaded into memory. Although it is extremely fast and uses a low amount of memory, the code is much more difficult to write because positioning must be tracked to retrieve the correct information from the feed.

Note Within the following example, you may notice $$curnode being used. This is not a typo but rather the use of a *variable variable*. A variable variable allows access to variables using dynamic names. For example, $a = 'myvariable'; $$a = 1; print $myvariable; results in the output of 1. You can find detailed information concerning variable variables in the PHP manual.

Here's the code:

```php
<?php
$rssURL = 'http://www.planet-php.org/atom/';

function outputChannelInfo($channelTitle, $channelLink, $channelDesc)
{
    print "Title: $channelTitle\n";
    print "URL: $channelLink\n";
    print "Description: $channelDesc\n";
    print "------------------------\n\n";
    $GLOBALS['printTitle'] = TRUE;
}
```

```php
/* This function processes an entry element and its contents */
function processItem($rssParser)
{
    $content = "";
    $link = "";
    $title = "";
    $curnode = NULL;

    /* Keep processing the entry until the closing entry tag is encountered */
    while ($rssParser->read() && $rssParser->localName != "entry") {
        switch ($rssParser->nodeType) {
            case XMLREADER::ELEMENT:
                $curnode = NULL;
                switch ($rssParser->localName) {
                    case "title":
                    case "content":
                        $curnode = $rssParser->localName;
                        break;
                    case "link":
                        $link = $rssParser->getAttribute('href');
                }
                break;
            case XMLREADER::TEXT:
            case XMLREADER::CDATA:
                if (! is_null($curnode)) {
                    $$curnode = $rssParser->value;
                }
        }
    }
    print "  Title: $title\n";
    print "  URL: $link\n";
    print "  Description: $content\n\n";
}

/* Create a new XMLReader, and begin reading from the remote location */
$rssParser = new XMLReader();
$rssParser->open($rssURL);
$printTitle = FALSE;
$subtitle = "";
$link = "";
$description = "";
$curnode = NULL;
```

```
while ($rssParser->read()) {
    switch ($rssParser->nodeType) {
        case XMLREADER::ELEMENT:
            $curnode = NULL;
            switch ($rssParser->localName) {
                case "entry":
                    if (! $printTitle) {
                        /* output the feed information before the first entry element */
                        outputChannelInfo($title, $link, $description);
                    }
                    /* If the entry is not empty, then process the contents */
                    if (! $rssParser->isEmptyElement) {
                        processItem($rssParser);
                    }
                    break;
                case "title":
                case "subtitle":
                    $curnode = $rssParser->localName;
                    break;
                case "link":
                    $link = $rssParser->getAttribute('href');
            }
            break;
        case XMLREADER::TEXT:
        case XMLREADER::CDATA:
            if (! is_null($curnode)) {
                $$curnode = $rssParser->value;
            }
    }
}
/* In the event the feed contained no entry elements, output the feed information */
if (! $printTitle) {
    outputChannelInfo($title, $link, $subtitle);
}
?>
```

XMLReader has an easy API to understand. The code should be more than enough to understand how it is being parsed.

Using PEAR XML_RSS

The PEAR XML_RSS class, mentioned in Chapter 13, provides an easy way to read RSS feeds without having to even know XML. Although it cannot be used to read Atom-based feeds, it should work with most RSS version 1.0 and 2.0 feeds. The only requirements to use this class, other than having to install it on the machine, are that the XML_Parser package is installed and that remote file access is enabled (unless all feeds being accessed are local files, which is highly unlikely).

You create the RSS parser by instantiating an XML_RSS object and by passing a URI or file handle for the RSS data to be parsed to the constructor:

```
$rss_parser = new XML_RSS('http://www.example.com/feed.rss');
```

In this instance, the RSS feed, located at http://www.example.com/feed.rss, is set as the data to be parsed for the instantiated XML_RSS object, $rss_parser. Once created, the parse() method must be called to read and parse the data, which will then, barring any errors, be available to access by means of the API:

```
$rss_parser->parse();
```

The API is quite simple, having only five methods. Each method returns an array of data, which corresponds to a specific group of information from the RSS document. The first piece of information that is typically requested concerns the channel. The getChannelInfo() method returns an associative array containing information about the channel itself. You can use the following keys to access specific channel information from the array:

title: Title of the channel

link: URI of the channel

description: Description of the channel

image: An image associated with the channel

The availability of these keys depends upon the actual data contained in the RSS feed, so it is usually prudent to check that a certain key exists in the array prior to trying to retrieve a value.

The next area of the RSS feed typically accessed is the items contained in the feed. The getItems() method returns a two-dimensional array containing each RSS item, which is then accessed in a similar fashion as the channel information. Unlike a channel, no image is associated with an item, but XML_RSS does provide access to the publication date for an item, if available, through the pubDate key.

You can quickly access all images from the RSS document by using the getImages() method. It returns a two-dimensional array containing information about each image. The available keys for an image are as follows:

title: Name of the channel

link: URL to the site

url: URL to the image

Text inputs are not all that common in feeds but can be accessed through the getTextinputs() method. This method returns an array accessed through the following keys:

title: The label of the Submit button

description: The description of the input field

link: The URL of the script that processes text input requests

name: The name of the text object in the text input area

The last method, getStructure(), provides a quick way to retrieve the entire RSS document as a structure. The return value for this method is an array, but its composition depends upon the RSS document itself so has no defined set form.

Listing 14-5 shows the RSS document that is parsed by Listing 14-6, which also displays some of its basic information on the console.

Listing 14-5. *RSS File Located at* http://www.example.com/feed.rss

```
<?xml version="1.0" encoding="UTF-8"?>
<rss version="0.91">
   <channel>
      <title>My RSS Feed</title>
      <link>http://www.example.com/feed.rss</link>
      <description>My Example Rss Feed</description>
      <language>en</language>
      <item>
         <title>CDATA Section contained within description</title>
         <link>http://www.example.xom/cdata.html</link>
         <description><![CDATA[<p>CDATA sections contain the content for
            the description element so may contain any type
            of characters</p>]]></description>
      </item>
      <item>
         <title>RSS 0.91 does not have any namespaces</title>
         <link>http://www.example.com/namespaces.html</link>
         <description><![CDATA[<p>No need to deal with namespaces when
            using RSS 0.91.]]></description>
      </item>
   </channel>
</rss>
```

This document uses an older format of RSS, version 0.91, to demonstrate the flexibility of the XML_RSS class. The code in Listing 14-6 could easily use a different feed without you having to change anything other than the URL passed to the XML_RSS constructor:

Listing 14-6. *RSS Parser Example*

```
<?php
/* Require XML_RSS package */
require "XML/RSS.php";

/* Create RSS Parser */
$rss_parser = new XML_RSS("http://www.example.com/feed.rss");

/* Parse RSS Feed */
$rss_parser->parse();
```

```php
/* Get and Display Channel Information */
$channel = $rss_parser->getChannelInfo();
echo 'Channel: '.$channel['title']."\n";
echo '   Link: '.$channel['link']."\n";
echo '   Description: '.$channel['description']."\n";
echo "---------------------------------------\n\n";

/* Get and Display Items */
foreach ($rss_parser->getItems() as $value) {
    echo 'Item: '.$value['title']."\n";
    echo '   Link: '.$value['link']."\n\n";
}
?>
```

```
Channel: My RSS Feed
   Link: http://www.example.com/feed.rss
   Description: My Example Rss Feed
-----------------------------------------

Item: CDATA Section contained within description
   Link: http://www.example.xom/cdata.html

Item: RSS 0.91 does not have any namespaces
   Link: http://www.example.com/namespaces.html
```

Conclusion

Content syndication has become popular mainly because of the numerous blogs available on the Web. The most popular formats for this are RSS 1.0, RSS 2.0, and Atom. These formats had rough evolutions. With all the discontent between the RSS 1.0 and RSS 2.0 camps, a bunch of developers decided to start things from scratch, which resulted in Atom. In this chapter, you saw how documents in all of these formats are structured and learned how to create and parse them using tools available in PHP. Through the recent chapters, you have gotten closer to working with XML and the Internet, with content syndication being primarily an XML-based Web technology.

In the next chapter, you will begin to enter the world of Web Services, starting with Web Distributed Data Exchange (WDDX).

■■■

Web Distributed Data Exchange (WDDX)

With the exception of content syndication, the material presented to this point has been about general XML technologies and tools. Moving forward, the remaining chapters focus more on Web services and data exchange through the use of XML. This chapter will cover WDDX, which is a common XML format for exchanging data structures; specifically, the chapter will explain what WDDX is, how to use it, and how to use the wddx extension in PHP. Although WDDX itself is not a Web service, it can be used to create Web services.

Introducing WDDX

WDDX is an XML technology that allows data and data structures to be exchanged between systems in a system-neutral format while keeping the data types intact. It defines an XML structure that is used to pass the data but does not define the mechanism the data is passed between; therefore, WDDX itself cannot be considered a Web service but can be used to build a Web service, in the general sense, using any form of transport you like, including (but not limited to) HTTP, File Transfer Protocol (FTP), Simple Mail Transfer Protocol (SMTP), and Post Office Protocol (POP). Basically, you can use any protocol that supports transferring textual data.

Background

Allaire created WDDX in 1998 to provide distributed computing support to its ColdFusion platform. With WDDX, variables (which include a name, data type, and value) can be serialized into an XML document from one application and sent to another. The receiving application can then unserialize the XML document and re-create these variables in their native data types and values. Data types are not limited just to the simple number and string types but also include more complex structures such as arrays, structures, and recordsets.

WDDX is platform and language agnostic. This allows other languages on a variety of platforms to take advantage of this technology, thus letting an application on one platform written in one language send data to another application on another platform using a different language. The receiving application is then able to unserialize the data into its own native data types.

WDDX is not a formal standard but is built upon open standards, specifically XML 1.0, and is freely available for both use and redistribution. WDDX development and future evolution has moved to an open project, OpenWDDX.org (http://www.openwddx.org). Although you can find some information and software development kits (SDKs) at this site, you won't find much activity from the past few years. This does not mean the WDDX technology is dead. It is still actively used on a number of platforms and programming languages, especially PHP.

WDDX Data Types

Thinking of the data in terms of variables and their data types in PHP, the question becomes, how can you send the data to another system, using XML, for processing? For example, you might have the following variables, whose values need to be sent to another system:

```
$myinteger = 1;
```

Using XML, you might serialize the values, which simply means converting them to a textual representation, and then send them in an XML document:

```
<data>1</data>
```

Depending upon the type of processing you need to perform, this might be sufficient. The drawback to this is that you lose the native data types. Of course, the systems might already have some predetermined structure and therefore map the structure accordingly, or some sort of type hinting might be included in the document, like so:

```
<data type='integer'>1</data>
```

This does provide more flexibility, but any systems that are exchanging data have to understand the structure and know how it should be processed. A different solution might involve using XML Schemas to indicate data types, but, again, the system needs to know how to process the document.

WDDX provides a solution to this problem. Through its common format, the value would serialize to the following:

```
<wddxPacket version="1.0">
    <header/>
    <data>
        <number>1</number>
    </data>
</wddxPacket>
```

When passing a single value, this format might be acceptable, but XML is a descriptive language. All you know from this structure is that it contains 1. You could never pass multiple values in this format because nothing descriptive sets them apart. The majority of cases will be serializing the actual variable rather than just the value, allowing for some descriptive information to be passed. For instance, serializing the following variables, rather than single values, produces something much more useful:

```
$mystring = 'Text Data';
$myinteger = 1;
```

```
<wddxPacket version="1.0">
    <header/>
    <data>
        <struct>
            <var name="mystring">
                <string>Text Data</string>
            </var>
            <var name="myinteger">
                <number>1</number>
            </var>
        </struct>
    </data>
</wddxPacket>
```

This structure clearly shows that it contains a variable named mystring, which is a string containing the value Text Data, and a variable named myinteger, which is a number containing the value 1. WDDX is not limited to just these simple data types; WDDX provides support for several abstract types that are represented in a number of languages, as shown in Table 15-1.

Table 15-1. *WDDX Data Types and Language Mappings*

WDDX	PHP	Java	ECMAScript	COM Type
null	NULL	null	null	VT_NULL
boolean	boolean	java.lang.Boolean	boolean	VT_BOOL
number	integer, float, double	java.lang.Double	number	VT_R8
dateTime		java.lang.Date	Date	VT_DATE
string	string	java.lang.String	String	VT_BSTR
array	array	java.lang.Vector	Array	VT_ARRAY | VT_VARIANT
struct	array, object	java.lang.Hashtable	Object	IWDDXStruct
recordset		com.allaire.util. RecordSet	WddxRecordset	IWDDXRecordset
binary		com.allaire.util.Binary	WddxBinary	V_ARRAY | UI1

Understanding the Structure of WDDX

The structure of WDDX documents has remained consistent since 1999 with the release of WDDX 1.0. Although the structure looks simple based on the DTD (http://www.openwddx.org/downloads/download.cfm), the actual complexity of the document depends upon the data being serialized. The more complex the structure of a variable (for instance, containing multi-dimensional arrays or classes), the more complex the composition of the WDDX document will be. The following sections will cover the structure of WDDX documents; you can build them manually using an extension such as DOM or XMLWriter (covered in Chapter 2), or you can build them using the wddx extension in PHP, which requires little to no knowledge of XML structures.

WDDX Packets

Data exchange using WDDX takes place through *packets*. Packets are simply XML documents passing data in WDDX format; they begin with the wddxPacket element. This document element contains a single header element and a single data element, providing a container for notes or comments and a container for the actual data being exchanged, respectively. It also contains a version attribute with the version of WDDX being used. Because currently only a single version exists, the value will always be 1.0. When adding notes and comments to the packet, you use a comment element, which is an optional child of the header element; otherwise, the header element is just an empty element. For example:

```
<!-- Packet without notes or comments -->
<wddxPacket version='1.0'>
    <header/>
    <data>
        <!-- WDDX data goes here -->
</wddxPacket>

<!-- Packet with a comment -->
<wddxPacket version='1.0'>
    <header>
        <comment>
            This packet contains a comment
        </comment>
    </header>
    <data>
        <!-- WDDX data goes here -->
</wddxPacket>
```

The data element contains the meat of the packet, which is the data you are exchanging. It contains only a single element, which depends upon the data being added to the packet. The following is a list of valid child elements, which are explained in the next sections, for the data element:

- null
- boolean
- number
- dateTime
- string
- array
- struct
- recordset
- binary

Simple Data Type Elements

Simple data types are simple structures that cannot contain additional data types within their contents. These elements include null, boolean, number, dateTime, and string. These data types simply contain a value of the specified type as its contents or are empty in the case that the data type does not or cannot have a value, such as NULL.

null

The null element represents a NULL value or empty string, depending upon whether the language supports a NULL type. In the case of PHP, NULL is supported, but just keep in mind that if exchanging data with another system using another language, it *may* be interpreted as an empty string rather than NULL when unserialized. This is the element's syntax:

```
<null/>
```

boolean

The boolean element represents a Boolean value. The value of this element can be true or false. Case sensitivity is important here. These values must be lowercase in order to be considered valid values according to the WDDX DTD. Even though mixed case may work in certain cases, using all lowercase is highly recommended. This is the element's syntax:

```
<boolean>false</boolean>
```

number

The number element is used for floating-point numbers. In PHP this covers both the integer types and the float types. The range of numbers for the value of this element is restricted to +/-1.7E+/-308 with the precision restricted to a maximum of 15 digits after the decimal point. This is comparable to an 8-byte floating-point representation, which is the common maximum value for floats within PHP.

The following elements contain the serialized values for the numbers 12345, -12345, 12.345, -12.345, and 123456789012345:

```
<number>12345</number>
<number>-12345</number>
<number>12.345</number>
<number>-12.345</number>
<number>1.2345678901235E+014</number>
```

dateTime

The dateTime element carries date and time information in ISO 8601 format. PHP does not have a native datetime type. This does not mean you cannot use this element, though. For instance, you can set values using the date() function with either the c format parameter added in PHP 5 (that is, date('c')) or the DATE_ISO8601 constant added in PHP 5.1 (that is, date(DATE_ISO8601)) to create ISO 8601–formatted dates. This is the element's syntax:

```
<dateTime>2005-10-08T17:28:04-04:00</dateTime>
```

string

The string element contains arbitrary-length strings that must not contain embedded NULLs. You can handle control characters, falling into the UTF-8 range 00–1F, using child char elements. The char element is an empty element with a code attribute. The value of this attribute is a single character using the hexadecimal code. You do not need to handle tab (09) and newline (0A) characters by using a char element. These characters are valid within XML text content. Therefore, when setting a string value containing any of the special control characters, the value of the string element will contain mixed content. For example, XML removes carriage returns from XML data. Line endings in a Windows environment consist of a carriage return and a newline. You can preserve these using the char element. The following examples illustrate how to use the string element as well as the char element:

```
<string>This is a string value without any control characters</string>
<string>Line 1<char code="0D"/><char code="0A"/>Line2</string>
```

Complex Data Type Elements

Complex data type elements include the array, struct, recordset, and binary elements. These elements are used for more complex data structures, such as PHP arrays and classes. Only two of these elements, array and struct, have direct mappings to native PHP types, but the remainder can be converted into data usable by an application.

array

The array element holds data for an integer-based array. In PHP, arrays can have numeric or string indexes. Only numeric-indexed arrays map to the array element. String-based indexed arrays are handled with the struct element.

■**Note** Numeric index arrays in PHP are zero-based arrays. Creating arrays that are not zero-based, even though they are numerically indexed, may not result in using the array element. For instance, the arrays array(2=>'a', 4=>'b', 6=>'c') and array(0=>'a', 2=>'b') serialized using the wddx extension would result in a struct with named variables rather than array elements.

The children of an array element consist of the values held at each index. These values can be both simple and complex data types. This means an array element can have one or more data type child elements, which are the same child elements valid for use within the data element. The array element also contains a length attribute. The value of this attribute is the number of values held within the array. In PHP terms, the value of the length attribute is the value from calling the count() function on the array being serialized.

For instance, the following PHP arrays, which are both numerically indexed, are serialized into the same WDDX array structure:

```
array('a', 1, false);
array(0=>'a', 1=>1, 2=>false);
```

```
<array length='3'>
   <string>a</string>
   <number>1</number>
   <boolean value='false'/>
</array>
```

struct

Structures are string-indexed collections of data. The struct element identifies the contents as being such a structure. In PHP, structures pertain to string-indexed arrays and objects. It is also important to note that any non-zero-based numerically indexed array or zero-based index array not having sequentially indexed items can result in the use of a struct element rather than an array element.

The struct element is a container for zero or more var elements. These elements represent variables or class properties identified by the required name attribute. Each var element contains a single child data type element, consisting of any element that is valid as a child of the data or array element. Thus, if you took a few variables from PHP:

```
$myint = 12345;
$mystring = "This is a string";
$mykeys = array('key1'=>1, 'key2'=>2);
```

their serialized representations of the var element, which would live within a struct element, would be as follows:

```
<var name='myint'>
   <number>12345</number>
</var>

<var name='mystring'>
   <string>This is a string</string>
</var>

<var name='mykeys'>
   <struct>
      <var name='key1'>
         <number>1</number>
      </var>
      <var name='key2'>
         <number>2</number>
      </var>
   </struct>
</var>
```

As you can see from the serialization of the $mykeys variable, it is a complex data structure. The variable contains an associative array; thus, the var element itself not only is a child of a struct element but also contains a struct element. This struct element then contains additional var elements that identify each item in the array. If you remember that the definition of a WDDX structure is not complicated but the resulting serialized document can become quite complex, you should now have an idea of what this means. The complexity of the structure being serialized is directly related to the complexity of the resulting WDDX packet. This will become even clearer within the "Using WDDX" section where you will see an object being serialized into a WDDX structure.

PHP is a case-sensitive language, so the statement $myVar = array('key'=>1, 'KEY'=>2); results in an associative array with two distinct keys: key and KEY. WDDX, being used by many languages (some not case sensitive), does not differentiate variable names or key names of different case. A WDDX structure containing two variables with the same name, even if they differ in case, will use the value of the last variable when the structure is deserialized. If you serialized $myVar, your resulting structure might look like this:

```
<struct>
    <var name='myVar'>
        <struct>
            <var name='key'><number>1</number></var>
            <var name='KEY'><number>2</number></var>
        </struct>
    </var>
</struct>
```

While using PHP, you might end up with the same $myVar after unserializing the packet as the original $myVar variable, but if this structure were passed to some other system using a language that is not case sensitive, the resulting data would be an associative array, or language-equivalent structure, containing only a single index, the string key, and the corresponding value of a numeric 2. The first value overwrites the second value because the names, even though differing in case, are not unique. For interoperability, it is important to uniquely identify names without any regard to case sensitivity.

recordset

The recordset element is used for tabular data, which is two-dimensional data such as data in comma-separated value (CSV) format or records from a database. The data is in a format that can be represented in a row and column format. Data serialized into this format can be composed only of simple data types. It is not required that you use the recordset element for two-dimensional data, and in many cases, developers use a struct instead. This tends to be the case when data contains complex types, which cannot be used with a recordset element, and because many languages do not have many direct mappings to a recordset type. In addition, as you will see by its composition, some developers just do not like its structure.

A recordset element contains any number of field elements as its children. It does require two attributes: rowCount defines the number of rows, and fieldNames defines the names of the fields being used within its contents. The value of the rowCount attribute is simply the number of rows of data encapsulated by the recordset element. The value of the fieldNames attribute is a comma-separated list of the names of the fields used for the data. For example:

```
<recordset rowCount="2" fieldNames="ID,FIRST_NAME,LAST_NAME">
    <!-- field elements -->
</recordset>
```

Based on this structure, you know that the recordset contains two records, each having three fields identified by the names listed in the `fieldNames` attribute. This means the `recordset` element will contain three `field` elements.

A `field` element contains the data for every row in the recordset for a specific field. It contains a `name` attribute that identifies the name of the field, which must be one of the names from the `fieldNames` attribute on the parent `recordset` element. Its child elements are composed of any number of simple data type elements, which means `null`, `boolean`, `dateTime`, `number`, `string`, or `binary`. Each one represents the data from a specific row for a field within the tabular data. Because a single data type usually defines the data from a field, only one of the data types will be used for every child element within a `field` element.

The structure of the `recordset` element, because of the layout of the `field` elements, often looks odd to developers, and this is why they often use a struct instead. Rather than the XML being broken down by rows of data, it is broken down by fields, which are then broken down by rows. Consider the data from a database, as shown in Table 15-2, which is broken down by the fields for each row.

Table 15-2. *Database Data*

ID	FIRST_NAME	LAST_NAME
1	John	Smith
2	Jane	Doe

When using XML for this data, it is common to use a structure similar to the following:

```
<row>
    <ID>1</ID>
    <FIRST_NAME>John</FIRST_NAME>
    <LAST_NAME>Smith</LAST_NAME>
</row>
<!-- Additional row elements -->
```

You can also use a general `field` element name with a `name` attribute set to the name of the field. In any case, the data per row is usually grouped together. In a WDDX packet, however, the data is serialized into the following format when using a `recordset` element:

```
<recordset rowCount="2" fieldNames="ID,FIRST_NAME,LAST_NAME">
    <field name="ID">
        <number>1</number>
        <number>2</number>
    </field>
    <field name="FIRST_NAME">
        <string>John</string>
        <string>Jane</string>
    </field>
```

```
    <field name="LAST_NAME">
        <string>Smith</string>
        <string>Doe</string>
    </field>
</recordset>
```

As you can see, the data is grouped by field, so when reading this document logically, you are processing the data for every row for a specific field rather than processing the data per row for each field. Because of this reason alone, you may prefer using a struct element, where the data can be serialized by row, rather than a recordset element. Unfortunately, when receiving data, this might be out of your control.

binary

The binary element represents binary large objects (BLOBs), which are strings of binary data. You may recall from previous chapters that passing binary data in its native form within XML is not safe. Not all characters produce proper XML. WDDX 1.0 mandates that the binary element contain the Base64-encoded data, although previous versions may have allowed other encodings. In any event, you set the type of encoding used on the encoding attribute, which under WDDX 1.0 is a fixed attribute containing the value base64. This element also allows the length of the binary data and MIME type of the binary data to be included using the length and type attributes. There is not a native binary type in PHP, so you will typically handle this data using PHP strings. For example:

```
<binary encoding="base64" length="9312164" type="video/mpeg">
    <!-- Base64-encoded data here -->
</binary>
```

Using WDDX

Although you could work with WDDX using the XML parsers in PHP, the wddx extension provides quick and simple functionality for performing the majority of serialization and unserialization routines required to convert data and WDDX packets in PHP. Although not every WDDX data type element can be created during serialization using this extension, they are all supported during unserialization into some sort of native PHP data type.

Note All output produced by the wddx extension shown in this chapter has been formatted for presentation. Because WDDX serialization does not add additional whitespace such as indentation and newlines, I have altered the output for readability.

On the Windows platform, the wddx extension is enabled by default. It is built into PHP, so you don't need to modify the php.ini file to use the extension. On other platforms, you must build PHP with wddx support. You can accomplish this using a configure flag:

```
--enable-wddx
```

The wddx extension is built upon the xml extension, which also must be present. You can find additional information about the xml extension, including how to build it with PHP, in Chapter 8.

Serializing Data

You can serialize data into WDDX packets in two ways. The first method is using a single function call that builds a complete packet based upon the parameters passed. The second method is slightly more involved, but not much, and allows variables to be added to the structure in multiple calls. The method used really depends upon the data an application is processing and when it is available. For instance, you could serialize a few predetermined variables easily in a single function call, but when trying to serialize data from database results, it is usually easier to serialize rows as you iterate through the result set.

Simple Serialization

Depending upon the desired content of a WDDX packet, you can call either the wddx_serialize_value() function or the wddx_serialize_vars() function. Each of these functions creates a complete WDDX packet using a single line of code. The simplest of these functions is wddx_serialize_value(). It takes a single parameter (a variable whose value is to be serialized) and an optional string to add a comment to the header element, returning the resulting WDDX packet. This function is useful only when you want to exchange a single unnamed data type with another system. For example:

```
$myArray = array(1,2,3);

print wddx_serialize_value($myArray, 'This is an un-named array');
```

```
<wddxPacket version='1.0'>
   <header>
      <comment>This is an un-named array</comment>
   </header>
   <data>
      <array length='3'>
         <number>1</number>
         <number>2</number>
         <number>3</number>
      </array>
   </data>
</wddxPacket>
```

The more commonly used wddx_serialize_vars() function, demonstrated in Listing 15-1, allows for an arbitrary number of variables to be serialized by name all at once. A struct element is automatically created, and each variable passed to the function is created as a var element mapping the name of the variable to the name attribute on the var element. The only task you cannot perform using this function is adding a comment to the header. This, in my opinion, is minor compared to how easily you can create a packet. In any case, you could use the second method of creating a packet, covered in the next section, if a comment is absolutely necessary.

Listing 15-1. *Serializing Variables in WDDX*

```php
<?php
class myClass
{
    public $prop1;
    public $prop2 = 'default';
    public $prop3 = 0;
    /* Additional functionality here */
}

$objMyClass = new myClass();
$objChildClass = new myClass();

/* Set prop1 to the $objChildClass */
$objMyClass->prop1 = $objChildClass;

$myInteger = 2;

/* Serialize the variables
The variable names are passed not the actual variables */
$output = wddx_serialize_vars('myInteger', 'objMyClass');

print $output
?>
```

The script in Listing 15-1 demonstrates the serialization of a variable containing an integer, $myInteger, and an object, $objMyClass, that has its prop1 property set to another object of the same class. All the variables to be serialized are passed at once, passing their names, not the actual variables, to the wddx_serialize_vars() function. The function returns the resulting WDDX packet, which is shown here:

```
<wddxPacket version="1.0">
    <header/>
    <data>
        <struct>
            <var name="myInteger">
                <number>2</number>
            </var>
            <var name="objMyClass">
                <struct>
                    <var name="php_class_name">
                        <string>myClass</string>
                    </var>
```

```
            <var name="prop1">
               <struct>
                  <var name="php_class_name">
                     <string>myClass</string>
                  </var>
                  <var name="prop1">
                     <null/>
                  </var>
                  <var name="prop2">
                     <string>default</string>
                  </var>
                  <var name="prop3">
                     <number>0</number>
                  </var>
               </struct>
            </var>
            <var name="prop2">
               <string>default</string>
            </var>
            <var name="prop3">
               <number>0</number>
            </var>
         </struct>
      </var>
   </struct>
   </data>
</wddxPacket>
```

From the output you can see both the myInteger variable and the objMyClass variable set as the var elements beneath the topmost struct element. What is of interest is the structure created for objMyClass. This is an object serialized into a struct element.

You are most likely wondering where the var elements with the name attribute set to php_class_name originated. Anytime an object is serialized using the wddx extension, a var element with the name attribute set to php_class_name is added as the first child element of the object's struct element. The value of the element is a string element containing the name of the class from which the object was instantiated. This way when the packet is unserialized, the object can be instantiated in the values returned. I will demonstrate how to do this in the "Unserializing Data" section.

Complex Serialization

Don't be fooled by the heading "Complex Serialization." This does not mean it is complex to serialize data. Quite the contrary—it is still quite simple to serialize data. This section will just detail how to handle complex data, which would be data that could not be serialized (or would be difficult to do so) all at a single time. You can handle serialization in this fashion through three functions: wddx_packet_start(), wddx_add_vars(), and wddx_packet_end().

These functions work using a packet_id resource that is created by the wddx_packet_start() function. This function not only creates the packet_id, but an optional comment can be passed as a parameter, which will create a comment element within the header element for the final packet. For example:

```
$wddxid = wddx_packet_start('Building a packet in pieces');
```

You then add variables using the wddx_add_vars() function. This function, besides the fact that it takes the packet_id resource as its first argument, serializes variables in the same manner as the wddx_serialize_vars() function. The noticeable difference is that using wddx_add_vars() just adds the var element and its contents to the WDDX packet rather than creating a stand-alone packet. This means that after you have a packet_id, you can make multiple calls to wddx_add_vars() until all data has been added, at which time wddx_packet_end() is called to close and return the resulting packet. For example:

```
/* The following two variables represent the number of rows from the database
   and the number of fields per row. These have been hard-coded for presentation */
$rowCount = 10;
$fieldCount = 2;

wddx_add_vars($wddxid, 'rowCount', 'fieldCount');

/* This section assumes SQL was run against some type of database and assumes the
   resulting records are contained in $db. The dummy function fetch_db_data()
   represents a function that returns the records one row at a time as associative
   arrays */
$row = 0;
while ($line = fetch_db_data($db)) {
   $row++;
   /* var names must be unique so you create a variable name called
      row with the row number appended to the end. */
   $varname = 'row'.$row;

   /* Use variable variable to set the array to the new named variable */
   $$varname = $line;

   /* You need to pass the variable name.
      This is now stored in the variable $varname */
   wddx_add_vars($wddxid, $varname);
}

$output = wddx_packet_end($wddxid);
print $output;
```

This code is not actually working code. It assumes a SQL query has been run that returns some records. The number of rows returned would be stored in $rowCount, and the number of fields per row would be stored in $fieldCount. These variables are then added to the WDDX packet.

The function fetch_db_data() is a dummy function. It represents some function that returns the current row as an associative array from the returned records. The code loops through these records and, using a variable variable (because var elements must have unique name attributes), adds the arrays to the packet one at a time. Once done, the call to wddx_packet_end() closes the packet. The resulting packet should look similar to the following document. The structure, of course, depends upon the fields and number of records being returned from the SQL query.

```
<wddxPacket version="1.0">
    <header>
        <comment>Building a packet in pieces</comment>
    </header>
    <data>
        <struct>
            <var name='rowCount'><number>10</number></var>
            <var name='fieldCount'><number>2</number></var>
            <var name="row1">
                <struct>
                    <var name="catid"><string>1</string></var>
                    <var name="name"><string>John Smith</string></var>
                </struct>
            </var>
            <var name="row2">
                <struct>
                    <var name="catid"><string>2</string></var>
                    <var name="name"><string>Jane Doe</string></var>
                </struct>
            </var>
            <!-- Additional rows --->
        </struct>
    </data>
</wddxPacket>
```

Unserializing Data

You can unserialize data by using a single function call, wddx_deserialize(). This function takes a string containing a WDDX packet and returns the corresponding native PHP data type.

■**Note** As of PHP 5.1, the function wddx_deserialize() is an alias of the wddx_unserialize() method. Although this chapter refers to wddx_deserialize(), you should use wddx_unserialize() when running under PHP 5.1 or newer.

In the majority of cases, a struct element is a child of the data element, so an array containing the data is returned. In all other cases, the data is simply returned. In both instances, the returned data is of the type specified in the packet. The following example, using the packet created in Listing 15-1, demonstrates how the packet is unserialized. Rather than re-creating the serialized packet, the code uses the resulting $output variable from the listing. For example:

```
class myClass
{
    public $prop1;
    public $prop2 = 'default';
    public $prop3 = 0;
    /* Additional functionality here */
}

$unserialized = wddx_deserialize($output);
var_dump($unserialized);
```

The WDDX packet contains a serialized object, which is instantiated when the packet is unserialized. Without using any additional features, such as autoloading, you must define the class within the script so you can instantiate it. A var_dump() of the resulting $unserialized variable shows the following:

```
array(2) {
  ["myInteger"]=>
  int(2)
  ["objMyClass"]=>
  object(myClass)#3 (3) {
    ["prop1"]=>
    object(myClass)#4 (3) {
      ["prop1"]=>
      NULL
      ["prop2"]=>
      string(7) "default"
      ["prop3"]=>
      int(0)
    }
    ["prop2"]=>
    string(7) "default"
    ["prop3"]=>
    int(0)
  }
}
```

This is an array containing two items. Because the packet contained var elements, the resulting array is an associative array containing the names of the original serialized variables as the keys. This makes it extremely simple to re-create the original variables if so desired. For example:

```
foreach ($unserialized AS $key=>$value) {
   /* variable variable used to re-create the original serialized variable */
   $$key = $value;
}

print $objMyClass->prop2;
```

This results in the output of the string default.

It is not always possible to perform an operation such as this. The wddx_serialize_value() function does not maintain any information for the variable. Only the value is serialized. Although an array may be the resulting data structure after unserializing a packet, it is also quite possible that just a string, integer, float, or object is returned. Again, this is not all that common, because passing a single value, whether it is a simple or complex type, without any descriptive information is quite useless, unless written for some specific task that both applications understand.

Seeing Some Examples in Action

The wddx extension is not difficult to use, but alone it is not very useful. After all, it is called Web Distributed Data *Exchange* for a reason—data is meant to be exchanged with other systems. In the following sections, I will present two examples. The first is another example of serializing and unserializing data. This will re-enforce what you have read in this chapter. The second example will take working with wddx a step further. It will show how you can create a Web service, both the client and server portions, using WDDX.

Seeing Simple Serialization/Unserialization in Action

You have seen how to use the different data types in PHP when creating a WDDX packet. The following example brings them all together and demonstrates how a packet is created using a number of variables with different data types. Listing 15-2 shows the resulting WDDX packet from this code.

```
<?php
/* Some variables to pass */
$myinteger = 1;
$mystring = "My String";
$mysecondstring = "Second\nString";
$myarray = array('a', 'b', 'c');
$mystruct = array('key1'=>'a', 'key2'=>'b', 'key3'=>'c');

/* Multiple variables being serialized at once */
$serialized_out = wddx_serialize_vars('myinteger', 'mystring', 'mysecondstring',
                      'myarray', 'mystruct');
echo $serialized_out;
?>
```

Listing 15-2. *Resulting WDDX Packet*

```
<wddxPacket version='1.0'>
    <header/>
    <data>
        <struct>
            <var name='myinteger'>
                <number>1</number>
            </var>
            <var name='mystring'>
                <string>My String</string>
            </var>
            <var name='mysecondstring'>
                <string>Second<char code='0A'/>String</string>
            </var>
            <var name='myarray'>
                <array length='3'>
                    <string>a</string>
                    <string>b</string>
                    <string>c</string>
                </array>
            </var>
            <var name='mystruct'>
                <struct>
                    <var name='key1'>
                        <string>a</string>
                    </var>
                    <var name='key2'>
                        <string>b</string>
                    </var>
                    <var name='key3'>
                        <string>c</string>
                    </var>
                </struct>
            </var>
        </struct>
    </data>
</wddxPacket>
```

The unserialization of this data, using the resulting $serialized_out from the serialization example represented by the packet in Listing 15-2, is performed with a single call:

```
$arOut = wddx_deserialize($serialized_out);
var_dump($arOut);
```

The output, shown in Listing 15-3, is an array containing the values of each serialized variable that is associated with the original variable by the index of the array.

Listing 15-3. *Unserialized WDDX Packet*

```
array(5) {
  ["myinteger"]=>
  int(1)
  ["mystring"]=>
  string(9) "My String"
  ["mysecondstring"]=>
  string(13) "Second
String"
  ["myarray"]=>
  array(3) {
    [0]=>
    string(1) "a"
    [1]=>
    string(1) "b"
    [2]=>
    string(1) "c"
  }
  ["mystruct"]=>
  array(3) {
    ["key1"]=>
    string(1) "a"
    ["key2"]=>
    string(1) "b"
    ["key3"]=>
    string(1) "c"
  }
}
```

Because you know the original structure, the following code quickly re-creates the original variables with their native types in PHP:

```
foreach($arOut AS $key=>$value) {
    $$key = $value;
}

var_dump($myinteger);
```

As you can see from the output, the $myinter variable, which was set in the original script, is re-created with its original value:

```
int(1)
```

Of course, for more complex structures, this little piece of code simply wouldn't do, but it should give you a starting point if you want to expand it to support the different data types in WDDX.

Creating a Simple Web Service Using WDDX

I have broken this example into two parts. I will show how to create a server component that is designed to run beneath a Web server and how to create a client component. The client piece is generic and written for the command line, but you can expand and embed it in a local Web page. The service allows the client to request a record based on an ID from a database. The request is packaged in a WDDX packet. The server receives the packet unserialized, and the requested record returned is packaged in a WDDX packet to the client.

■**Caution** These scripts do not implement any form of security, and data is sent in plain text. When creating a Web service, authentication and secure transmissions are often important to implement. You could do this using combinations of secure sockets, authentication mechanisms, and encryption. For instance, one possible combination is SSL, XML signatures, and XML encryption.

WDDX Web Service Server

The database used in this example is SQLite, because by default it is included in almost every PHP 5+ build. It may be necessary to repath or modify permissions for the database, wddxdb, to be created. The server accepts only those POST requests sending a WDDX packet containing a structure with a var element having a name attribute set to recid. This element contains the ID of the record to be retrieved from the database.

The server then retrieves the id and name fields from the database based on the recid and serializes the results into a WDDX packet, which is then sent to the client. This example uses the sqllite_fetch_all() function so you can expand the example and request a range of record IDs. The function returns a multidimensional array, which is easily serialized using the wddx_serialize_value() function.

■**Note** To try this example, the server code should reside in a directory accessible by the Web server and be named wddxserver.php. Using a different name for this script will require the name to be changed in the client portion as well.

Here's the code:

```php
<?php
/* If the database does not exist, then create it and populate it with some data */
if (! file_exists('wddxdb')) {
    if ($dbhandle = sqlite_open('wddxdb', 0666)) {
        sqlite_query($dbhandle, 'CREATE TABLE wddx (id int, name varchar(15))');
        for ($x=1; $x< 11; $x++) {
            sqlite_query($dbhandle,
                    "INSERT INTO wddx VALUES (".$x.", 'Data Num: ".$x."')");
        }
```

```
        sqlite_close($dbhandle);
    }
}

/* Function to retrieve data from database and return the results in a
   serialized WDDX packet. Upon failure return a NULL value in the packet */
function getDBData($recid) {
    if (is_numeric($recid) && $dbhandle = sqlite_open('wddxdb')) {

        $query = sqlite_query($dbhandle,
                                'SELECT id, name FROM wddx where id='.$recid);
        $result = sqlite_fetch_all($query, SQLITE_ASSOC);
        return wddx_serialize_value($result);
    } else {
        return wddx_serialize_value(NULL);
    }
}

/* Requests are only accepted from a POST with the data set in the
   packet variable. */
if (isset($_POST['packet'])) {
    $wddx_packet = $_POST['packet'];
    /* retrieve data based on the requested recid, and return resulting packet */
    if ($wddx_packet && $arData = wddx_deserialize($wddx_packet)) {
        if (is_array($arData) && array_key_exists('recid', $arData)) {
            print getDBData((int)$arData['recid']);
            exit;
        }
    }
}

/* On bad requests send a NULL value in the packet */
print wddx_serialize_value(NULL);
?>
```

WDDX Web Service Client

The client portion is simple. The majority of the code is handling the sockets to the server for posting and retrieving data, as well as the displayed output of the results. The sample code was designed to be run at a command though can be embedded within HTML to operate under a Web server. The first three variables must be set correctly to point to the server hosting the wddxserver.php file, which is the server piece of this example, and to the port for the Web server accepting HTTP requests. The connection will be made using TCP, set by the $remote_protocol variable.

Here's the code:

```php
<?php
/* Address of remote server - Set these to the server and port where the
   remote server script is located. */
$remote_protocol = 'tcp';
$remote_server = 'localhost';
$remote_server_port = 80;

/* The serialized packet. In this case, being an example, it is hard-coded
   to request the record having an id of 5. */
$packet = wddx_serialize_value(array('recid'=>5));

/* Make POST request using sockets */
$remote_connect = $remote_protocol.'://'.$remote_server;
$sock = fsockopen($remote_connect, $remote_server_port, $errno, $errstr, 30);
if (!$sock) die("$errstr ($errno)\n");

/* Use var name packet for the POST */
$data = 'packet='.urlencode($packet);

fwrite($sock, "POST /wddxserver.php HTTP/1.0\r\n");
fwrite($sock, "Host: $remote_server\r\n");
fwrite($sock, "Content-type: application/x-www-form-urlencoded\r\n");
fwrite($sock, "Content-length: " . strlen($data) . "\r\n");
fwrite($sock, "Accept: */*\r\n");
fwrite($sock, "\r\n");
fwrite($sock, "$data\r\n");
fwrite($sock, "\r\n");

$headers = "";
while ($str = trim(fgets($sock, 4096)))
  $headers .= "$str\n";

$packet = "";
while (!feof($sock))
  $packet .= fgets($sock, 4096);
fclose($sock);
/* END POST Request */

/* Unserialize packet data, and output resulting data */
$arData = wddx_deserialize($packet);
if (is_array($arData)) {
   if (count($arData) > 0) {
      foreach ($arData AS $rownum=>$arRow) {
         foreach ($arRow AS $fieldname=>$fieldvalue) {
            print $fieldname.": ".$fieldvalue."\n";
         }
```

```
        print "\n";
      }
   } else {
      print "No Records Returned";
   }
} else {
   /* Some type of error happened */
   var_dump($arData);
}
?>
```

Because this is merely an example, the record to be retrieved has been hard-coded to 5. This effectively is requesting the record from the database with an ID of 5. It is fairly trivial to modify this example to make the record number dynamic as well as to allow ranges of records to be requested at once. Rather than serializing a variable named recid, it is just as easy to serialize an associative array mapping recid to the record number being requested.

Once the packet has been created, the client opens a socket connection to the server and posts the data, using the variable packet to identify the WDDX packet being sent. Once the server has processed the request within the packet, it returns the results in another WDDX packet. If it unserializes into an array, it is safe to assume, based on the server script, that the data was queried and returned. This does not mean that any rows were returned, just that no errors were encountered. An unserialized value of NULL indicates that some problem occurred. I did not break errors out in the example, so this could include a problem accessing the database and an improper request to the Web server.

The data returned, if an array, is a multidimensional array. This is the format returned by the sqlite_fetch_all() function. Only simple output processing takes place here, printing each field name and value on a single line. Each row, if the script were expanded to allow multiple record requests, would be separated by two lines. Modifying this example to perform more complex operations and different output is an exercise I will leave to you.

Using PEAR XML_WDDX

When the wddx extension is unavailable or for some reason you just don't want to use it, you can use the PEAR XML_WDDX package to serialize and unserialize WDDX packets. It is compatible with PHP 5 and newer, so it will work correctly when migrating code from PHP 4 that might have used this package. Although XML_WDDX will use the wddx_deserialize() function if the wddx extension is available, this package is not an exact replacement for the extension, as you will see in this section.

You can install the package by using the PEAR installer. (You can find additional information about PEAR and its installer in Chapter 13.)

```
pear install XML_WDDX
```

At the time of this writing, the current stable release is 1.0.1, and the only dependency is the xml extension. When the wddx extension is present on the system, it is leveraged by XML_Wddx to unserialize packets. Once you have installed the package, you can use the XML_Wddx class within your script by adding the appropriate require statement:

```
require 'XML/Wddx.php';
```

The class is then instantiated using the new keyword. You don't have to pass any parameters to the constructor, so the call is simply as follows:

```
$objWddx = new XML_Wddx();
```

XML_Wddx provides only two public methods: serialize() and deserialize(). The serialize() method works just like the wddx_serialize_value() function from the wddx extension. It accepts only a single parameter that contains the data to be serialized. It does not provide any mechanism for creating a comment but does create and return the entire packet from the method call.

Note Control characters within strings are not handled using char elements. Any string that contains a control character, explained in the earlier "string" section, is encapsulated within a CDATA section. To clarify this, the entire string, and not just the control characters, is encapsulated.

You can unserialize a packet using the deserialize() method. This method takes one parameter containing the packet and returns the unserialized data as a native PHP data type. How the packet is unserialized depends upon whether the wddx extension was installed with PHP. When present, the wddx_deserialize() method is used when the XML_Wddx deserialize() method is called; otherwise, the native XML_Wddx code is used. This impacts unserialization because the wddx extension provides support for more data types and XML_Wddx. The following is a list of some of the differences between the two:

- XML_Wddx does not handle a recordset element.

- XML_Wddx does not handle a dateTime element.

- The wddx extension Base64 decodes the contents of binary elements and returns the actual binary data. XML_Wddx does not, and the data is returned as a Base64-encoded string that the user must decode.

For example:

```php
<?php
/* Require the XML_Wddx package */
require 'XML/Wddx.php';

/* Some variables to pass */
$myinteger = 1;
$mystring = 'My String';
$mysecondstring = "Second\nString";
$myarray = array('a', 'b', 'c');
$mystruct = array('key1'=>'a', 'key2'=>'b', 'key3'=>'c');

/* Multiple variables must be passed within an array */
$myvalues = array($myinteger, $mystring, $mysecondstring, $myarray, $mystruct);
```

```
$objWddx = new XML_Wddx();

echo $objWddx->serialize($myvalues);
?>
```

The output of this script should look a bit familiar to you. The same variables were serialized in Listing 15-2 using the wddx extension. The output has a few noticeable differences, however.

```
<wddxPacket version='1.0'><header/><data>
  <array length='5'>
    <number>1</number>
    <string>My String</string>

      <string><![CDATA[Second
String]]></string>


      <array length='3'>
        <string>a</string>
        <string>b</string>
        <string>c</string>
      </array>


      <struct>
        <var name='key1'><string>a</string></var>
        <var name='key2'><string>b</string></var>
        <var name='key3'><string>c</string></var>
      </struct>

  </array>
</data></wddxPacket>
```

The first thing you will notice is that this code uses an array element rather than a struct element as the child for the data element. XML_Wddx does not accept multiple variables for serialization; thus, you must place them in an array that is then serialized. Because they are passed by array and no key is specified, var elements are not created. The other noticeable difference is the use of the CDATA section within the second string element. The wddx extension does not use CDATA sections but rather escapes the characters <, &, and >, and it converts control characters to char elements.

XML_Wddx, however, does understand char elements during deserialization. The output from the deserialization() method depends upon whether the wddx extension has been installed with PHP. When it exists, the XML_Wddx deserialization() method natively uses it; otherwise, the built-in deserialization routine is used. The following example uses the data from $serialized_out in Listing 15-2:

```
require 'XML/Wddx.php';

$objWddx = new XML_Wddx();

/* $serialized_out is the resulting serialized data from Listing 15-2. */
$arRet = $objWddx->deserialize($serialized_out);
var_dump($arRet);
```

The following is the resulting data structure from the var_dump() call. Remember, this output is based on that the wddx extension was not installed with PHP and the internal deserialization routine from the XML_Wddx class is being used. If you are trying this code on a machine that has the wddx extension installed, your output will be the same as the output in Listing 15-3.

```
array(5) {
  ["myinteger"]=>
  string(1) "1"
  ["mystring"]=>
  string(9) "My String"
  ["mysecondstring"]=>
  string(13) "Second
String"
  ["myarray"]=>
  array(3) {
    [0]=>
    string(1) "a"
    [1]=>
    string(1) "b"
    [2]=>
    string(1) "c"
  }
  ["mystruct"]=>
  array(3) {
    ["key1"]=>
    string(1) "a"
    ["key2"]=>
    string(1) "b"
    ["key3"]=>
    string(1) "c"
  }
}
```

Conclusion

WDDX is an XML format that allows data and its corresponding data types to be exchanged between two independent systems. It is platform agnostic and supported through a number of languages. Although not a Web service on its own, it can be used to create Web services, and its format is much simpler than a SOAP document. It never became as much of a buzzword as SOAP, but it provides a quick and easily created format that can be leveraged when needing to connect systems.

This chapter dissected the WDDX structure and covered how both the wddx extension and the XML_Wddx class can create WDDX documents. Within the examples, you learned how to create a simple Web service using WDDX as the data envelope.

The next chapter progresses further into the area of Web services with a discussion of XML-RPC. Unlike WDDX, XML-RPC is a complete service that includes how the data is transported between systems.

CHAPTER 16

■■■

XML-RPC

XML-RPC may have spawned the term *Web service*. Although XML was probably being passed between systems to perform similar functionality, XML-RPC was the first platform-neutral technology with a defined standard that did not require developers to learn proprietary formats or transports. By the end of this chapter, you should understand what XML-RPC is, its format, and how you can leverage it in PHP through the xmlrpc extension or the XML_RPC package in PEAR. This chapter will not cover the history of XML-RPC and its association to SOAP. You can find that material in Chapter 1.

■**Caution** This chapter will not detail any type of security that you may need or want to implement. Publicly implemented Web services can be dangerous when not properly protected because you are possibly allowing anonymous users to execute code on your server. You must take the same care when building a Web application as when implementing an XML-RPC server. This includes, at a minimum, checking data inputs and possibly performing data encryption.

Introducing XML-RPC

XML-RPC stands for XML-based Remote Procedure Call. A *procedure call*, if you are not familiar with the term, is simply a function call in terms of PHP. It is some code that you can call, passing in parameters that the block of code can use, and from which you can possibly receive a return value. A *remote procedure call* is effectively the same except the code being called exists in and is executed by a different application and possibly by a different machine.

For a remote procedure call to take place, the call to the function, as well as any parameters needed by the remote function and any results, must be exchanged between the two systems. This of course cannot occur in the usual manner. Instead, everything must be *marshaled*. Marshaling involves taking some data and converting it to a common format, which then can be sent somewhere (including over a network), received by a remote system, and then converted into data understandable by the receiver. If you read the previous chapter, this should sound familiar. WDDX takes native PHP data, converts it to a common XML structure that could be passed to some other system, and converts it into the other system's native data types.

XML-RPC performs similar marshaling to what WDDX does; it converts the native data types into an XML structure, but XML-RPC goes further than WDDX and is why it's considered to be a true Web service. It not only specifies the format for the XML message, but it also defines how the message is transported. An HTTP POST request is the mechanism used as the transport in XML-RPC. Being a complete specification (http://www.xmlrpc.com/spec), as well as defining ways to call remote procedures, XML-RPC is a much more well-known and more commonly used technology than WDDX. Now, don't get me wrong—I still think WDDX can be useful, especially since it does not define a specific transport, leaving the possibilities endless.

Exploring the XML-RPC Structure

Structure within XML-RPC depends upon the direction of the data. Though the two share many aspects, a request takes a different form than a response. Not only does each have its own XML structure, but also each requires specific information in the HTTP headers. The following sections will cover each of these aspects and provide examples of the structure used. Before getting into any specific area, it is first important to know and understand some of the common XML elements shared between the request and the response.

Common Elements

Parameters passed to a function and return values are all pieces of data that have specific data types. Not only is it important that the value for these is passed, but the value's corresponding data type must be kept intact. PHP is a loosely typed language, so, for instance, you can add a string to a numeric, which would result in a numeric:

```
$float_as_string = "1.1";
var_dump($float_as_string);
$newval = 1 + $float_as_string;
var_dump($newval);
```

The output confirms that $float_as_string is actually a string and the resulting $newval is a float with the value 2.1:

```
string(3) "1.1"
float(2.1)
```

It does not always work this way with other languages. Try doing something similar in C, for example. The resulting value would not be anything close to what you would expect in PHP.

When passing values between systems, XML-RPC wraps each value within a value element. The content of this element is a single element identifying the data type and containing the data to be passed. For example, the following represents 1.1 in its serialized format:

```
<value>
    <double>1.100000</double>
</value>
```

Most languages share many of the common data types, but this is not always the case. Marshaling the data creates a common format that allows a different system to interpret data into its own native types. The following sections will break down the common XML-RPC types and how they relate to the data types in PHP.

int

The int or i4 element passes a 4-byte signed integer. In terms of PHP data types, this is simply an integer type. XML-RPC defines two elements for this data type, although they both mean the same thing. I will use the int element within this chapter when referring to integers. This is the syntax:

```
/* PHP Data Type */
(int) 5

/* XML-RPC format */
<value>
    <int>5</int>
</value>
```

double

The double element is used for floating-point numbers. These are of the types float, double, and real in PHP. To give you an idea of what to expect for output, I used the PHP xmlrpc extension to generate the serialized values in the following code. You will notice that doubles add a trailing zero to create at least six decimal places. Numbers containing more than six decimal places are truncated to seven decimal places, so the number -12.12345678 is truncated to -12.1234567 and not rounded up.

```
/* PHP Data Type */
(float) -12.345

(float) -12.12345678

/* XML-RPC format */
<value>
    <double>-12.345000</double>
</value>

<value>
    <double>-12.123457</double>
</value>
```

boolean

A boolean element is used in XML-RPC for Boolean data types. The physical value of the element is either 1 for TRUE or 0 for FALSE. This is the syntax:

```
/* PHP Data Type */
(bool) FALSE

/* XML-RPC format */
<value>
    <boolean>0</boolean>
</value>
```

string

A string element is used for the string data type. In PHP, many things are strings. No date or binary types exist, because these are handled using strings. As you will see with the next two types, you do not always have a direct one-to-one mapping of a native PHP data type to an XML-RPC type. In terms of usage within PHP, you can use the string element when the data is to be interpreted textually rather than what is held within the string, such as a date/time value. This is the syntax:

```
/* PHP Data Type */
(string) "Some text string"

/* XML-RPC format */
<value>
    <string>Some text string</string>
</value>

/* Alternative XML-RPC String Format */
<value>Some text string</value>
```

■**Note** When a data type is not specified, such as in the example for the alternative XML-RPC string format, the type is automatically assumed to be that of string by default. It is best practice, however, to always explicitly type data.

---

dateTime

The dateTime.iso8601 element represents a date and time in ISO 8601 format (http://www.iso.org/iso/en/prods-services/popstds/datesandtime.html). The format allowed is actually only a subset of the allowed dates from ISO 8601. In XML-RPC, the date is in the basic format of CCYYMMDDTHH:MM:SS.

■**Note** The date does not include time zone information. The time zone used depends upon the application. Normally, the server portion of the application dictates what time zone is being used for any dates passed back and forth. To create a correct date within PHP, you must use a call similar to date('Ymd\TH:i:s'), because date('c') or date(DATE_ISO8601) includes hyphens within the date portion and includes the time zone in the time information, which must not be passed.

Some languages have a native datetime type, while others, like PHP, do not. In PHP, date and times are held in strings. For example, calling $mydate = date('c'); returns the current data and time in ISO 8601 format, but the type of $mydate is still a string. The type needs to be converted to the proper XML-RPC format, as will be demonstrated in the "Encoding and Decoding Data" section. This is the syntax:

```
/* PHP Data Type Example */
(string) date('Ymd\TH:i:s')

/* XML-RPC format */
<value>
   <dateTime.iso8601>20051014T16:16:11</dateTime.iso8601>
</value>
```

base64

The base64 element is similar to the dateTime.iso8601 element with respect to PHP. It denotes binary data that has been Base64 encoded. Again, PHP does not have a binary data type or a Base64 type. The data is simply a string. The type, as well as the data, needs to be converted to a proper XML-RPC format. I will demonstrate how to do this in the "Handling Non-Native PHP Data Types" section. This is the syntax:

```
/* PHP Data Type Example */
(string) file_get_contents('binaryfile.bin')

/* XML-RPC format */
<value>
   <base64><!-- content omitted because of length  --></base64>
</value>
```

array

PHP arrays are multipurpose. The indexes can be numeric, which really specifies order or location, or can be strings that operate like a hash table or dictionary. I will refer to the latter array types as *associative arrays*. An XML-RPC array is simply a vector or list. In PHP, this corresponds to a numerically indexed array.

An array is a complex type. This means its structure is not simply a value element containing a type element containing a value. An array is a container for multiple values and thus can contain any number of value elements. The value elements (for some reason that I do not know) are contained within a data element. This data element is a child element of the array element. This may sound a bit confusing and is probably much easier to see within the XML structure:

```
<value>
   <array>
     <data>
        <!-- Any number of value elements -->
     </data>
   </array>
</value>
```

The comment within this structure indicates that several value elements can exist as children of the data element. The value element, again, is a wrapper element for any of the XML-RPC data types discussed in this chapter. If you think about some complex data structures, such as multidimensional arrays, the XML structure can become quite complex, because it entails arrays within arrays. For example:

```
/* PHP Data Type */
(array) array('a', 'b', 'c')

/* XML-RPC format - value elements compacted on single line to save space */
<value>
   <array>
      <data>
         <value><string>a</string></value>
         <value><string>b</string></value>
         <value><string>c</string></value>
      </data>
   </array>
</value>
```

Structures

Associative arrays, which are arrays with string indexes, and objects in PHP are serialized into struct elements. These are complex structures containing a member element for each item in an array or property of an object. Each member element consists of a name element, indicating the index name or object property, and a value element. The value, again, is simply the wrapper for any of the XML-RPC data types mentioned within this chapter. This is the syntax:

```
/* PHP Data Type - both the following serialize into same XML-RPC format */
(array) array('a'=>1, 'b'=>2, 'c'=>3)
(object) class myclass { public $a=1; public $b=2; public $c=3; }

/* XML-RPC format - value elements compacted on single line to save space */
<value>
   <struct>
      <member>
         <name>a</name>
         <value><int>1</int></value>
      </member>
      <member>
         <name>b</name>
         <value><int>2</int></value>
      </member>
      <member>
         <name>c</name>
         <value><int>3</int></value>
      </member>
   </struct>
</value>
```

The structure shown here is not an overly complex structure. The values within the struct element are all scalars, which basically means they are single values rather than complex values like arrays or objects. It is quite possible to have extremely complex structures, such as when dealing with multidimensional arrays or objects whose properties contain arrays or additional objects.

Request Header

XML-RPC uses an HTTP POST as its transport. You might wonder why you need to worry about the format for this. Whether you are creating your own XML manually or using the xmlrpc extension, it is up to you to provide the functionality to transport the data. An example of a request header, defined by the XML-RPC specification, is as follows:

```
POST /rpcserver.php HTTP/1.0
User-Agent: PHPRPC/1.0
Host: rpc.example.com
Content-Type: text/xml
Content-length: 181
```

These are the minimum headers required to properly transport the data. The URI in the first POST line is the location of the XML-RPC server to which the data is being sent. The User-Agent, which is some identifiable name for the client sending the data, and the Host, which is the address of the remote server, are both required headers. The Content-Type must be set to text/xml, and the Content-length must be correctly set to the length of the data being sent. Both of these headers are also required.

It is up to you what method or functionality you use to send the data, as long as it conforms to the rules specified here. For instance, you could use the Client URL Request Library (CURL) or sockets to open a connection, send the request, and read the response.

Listing 16-1 contains two functions, either of which can be used to make the XML-RPC calls. One, call_using_sockets(), works using network sockets. (This is the one I will use within the examples in this chapter.) The other, call_using_curl(), uses the curl extension to interact with the XML-RPC server. If you decide to try the examples in this chapter, you can use either function. Note that when using the call_using_curl() function, you need an additional parameter to identify the protocol, such as http. This is not required when using network sockets because tcp is assumed.

Listing 16-1. *Functions to Transport XML-RPC*

```
/* Function using network sockets */
function call_using_sockets($remote_server, $remote_server_port,
                            $remote_path, $request) {
  $sock = fsockopen($remote_server, $remote_server_port, $errno, $errstr, 30);
  if (!$sock) die("$errstr ($errno)\n");

  fwrite($sock, "POST $remote_path HTTP/1.0\r\n");
  fwrite($sock, "User-Agent: PHPRPC/1.0\r\n");
  fwrite($sock, "Host: $remote_server\r\n");
  fwrite($sock, "Content-type: text/xml\r\n");
  fwrite($sock, "Content-length: " . strlen($request) . "\r\n");
  fwrite($sock, "Accept: */*\r\n");
  fwrite($sock, "\r\n");
  fwrite($sock, "$request\r\n");
  fwrite($sock, "\r\n");
```

```
    $headers = "";
    while ($str = trim(fgets($sock, 4096))) {
        $headers .= "$str\n";
    }

    $data = "";
    while (!feof($sock)) {
        $data .= fgets($sock, 4096);
    }
    fclose($sock);
    return $data;
}

/* Function using curl */
function call_using_curl($protocol, $remote_server, $remote_server_port,
                         $remote_path, $request) {

    $url = "$protocol://$remote_server:$remote_server_port/";

    $header = "POST $remote_path HTTP/1.0\r\n";
    $header .= "User-Agent: PHPRPC/1.0\r\n";
    $header .= "Host: $remote_server\r\n";
    $header .= "Content-type: text/xml\r\n";
    $header .= "Content-length: " . strlen($request)."\r\n";
    $header .= "Accept: */* \r\n\r\n";
    $header .= "$request\r\n\r\n";

    $ch = curl_init();
    curl_setopt($ch, CURLOPT_URL, $url);
    curl_setopt($ch, CURLOPT_RETURNTRANSFER, 1);
    curl_setopt($ch, CURLOPT_TIMEOUT, 1);
    curl_setopt($ch, CURLOPT_USERAGENT, 'PHPRPC/1.0');
    curl_setopt($ch, CURLOPT_CUSTOMREQUEST, $header);
    curl_setopt($ch, CURLOPT_POSTFIELDS, $request);

    $data = curl_exec($ch);
    if (curl_errno($ch)) {
        print curl_error($ch);
    } else {
        curl_close($ch);
        return $data;
    }
}
```

Tip Performing a POST using HTTPS is also an acceptable transport when the data needs to be encrypted between the client and the server.

Request Format

The purpose of XML-RPC is to make remote function calls, performing one call per request. The root of every request document is a methodCall element. This element contains a single methodName element and possibly a params element. The methodName element contains the name of the procedure to be called in the remote application. The procedure name can contain only uppercase and lowercase alphanumeric characters, underscores, periods, colons, and slashes. All other characters are invalid for the contents of this element. For example:

```
/* Valid methodName contents */
<methodName>addNumbers</methodName>
<methodName>myApp.addNumbers</methodName>
<methodName>myApp::addNumbers</methodName>
<methodName>myApp/addNumbers</methodName>
<methodName>add_2_numbers</methodName>

/* Invalid methodName contents */
<methodName>addNumbers!</methodName>
<methodName>myApp?addNumbers</methodName>
<methodName>myApp#addNumbers</methodName>
<methodName>add_*2*_numbers</methodName>
<methodName>+_2_numbers</methodName>
```

The use of the params element depends upon whether the procedure being called takes any parameters. When the procedure does not take any parameters, this element is not required as part of the XML request; otherwise, it is required and takes a single param element for each of the parameters being passed. Each of the param elements has a child value element that corresponds to any of the data types in the "Common Elements" section for the respective parameter. For example, consider the following PHP function:

```php
function getUserInfo($userid)
{
    /* Logic to retrieve user information */
}
```

The getUserInfo() function takes a single integer as its parameter. This parameter identifies the user record to retrieve. When making an XML-RPC request to a server exposing this function, the request would appear in the format shown in Listing 16-2.

Listing 16-2. *Example XML-RPC Request Document*

```xml
<?xml version="1.0" encoding="UTF-8"?>
<methodCall>
    <methodName>getUserInfo</methodName>
    <params>
        <param>
            <value>
                <int>5</int>
            </value>
        </param>
    </params>
</methodCall>
```

The remote function getUserInfo takes only one integer as a parameter, so the request contains only a single param element whose value is the integer 5. This value instructs the function to retrieve the user information for the user with a user ID of 5.

Likewise, a function not requiring any parameters, such as function getCurrentDateTime() { /* Logic Here */ }, does not contain any param elements; thus, the params element is not required, as shown here:

```
<?xml version="1.0" encoding="UTF-8"?>
<methodCall>
    <methodName>getCurrentDateTime</methodName>
</methodCall>
```

The order of the param elements is important when passing multiple parameters. Because they are not named parameters, they must be ordered in the exact order as defined by the remote function. For example, the following function defines three parameters:

```
function myfunc($parm1, $parm2, $parm3) { ... }
```

The parameters are broken down like this: $param1 takes an integer, $param2 takes a string, and $param3 takes a float. To illustrate this point, examine the requests in Listing 16-3 and Listing 16-4. Only the request in Listing 16-3 is technically valid to call the remote function. I say *technically* here because some languages are strictly typed, while others are loosely typed (like PHP) or even typeless. Languages that are not strictly typed can convert types, allowing the parameters to be used.

Listing 16-3. *Valid Request for* myfunc

```
<?xml version="1.0" encoding="UTF-8"?>
<methodCall>
    <methodName>myfunc</methodName>
    <params>
        <param>
            <value><int>5</int></value>
        </param>
        <param>
            <value><string>Parameter String</string></value>
        </param>
        <param>
            <value><double>12.345</double></value>
        </param>
    </params>
</methodCall>
```

Listing 16-4. *Invalid Request for* my func

```
<?xml version="1.0" encoding="UTF-8"?>
<methodCall>
    <methodName>myfunc</methodName>
    <params>
        <param>
            <value><string>Parameter String</string></value>
        </param>
        <param>
            <value><int>5</int></value>
        </param>
        <param>
            <value><double>12.345</double></value>
        </param>
    </params>
</methodCall>
```

In Listing 16-4, the string type parameter is the first, in document order, of the param elements. This means it maps to the first parameter of myfunc(). The first parameter for the function, however, requires an integer.

Response Header

For the greatest interoperability with XML-RPC clients, it is best practice to follow the guidelines set forth in the specification regarding the response headers. The following is an example of the headers that should be sent when data is returned:

```
HTTP/1.1 200 OK
Connection: close
Content-Length: 158
Content-Type: text/xml
Date: Fri, 14 Oct 2005 23:57:08 GMT
Server: PHPRPC/1.0
```

In a more controlled environment, it is not always required that the specified headers be followed exactly. For instance, when creating a server running within a Web server where you know what the clients are expecting for return data, it is not always necessary to modify the headers and allow the Web server to handle the headers directly. In most cases, the Content-Type would not be correct, because the type would generally be returned as text/html, and possibly the Server would not be correctly identified. However, unless clients need to detect these, they can often use the default Web server headers. You should already understand how to modify headers in PHP, so the examples you see in this chapter will rely strictly on the default behavior of a Web server. I will leave any modifications you may need to make in your own environment up to you.

Response Format

The methodResponse element serves as the root of a response document. The content of this element is either a single params element or a single fault element. Unless the server is returning an error condition, a params element will be used even when not returning a value. This allows the client to know, at the least, that the procedure was executed without errors, such as the response in Listing 16-5.

Listing 16-5. *XML-RPC Response Without a Return Value*

```
<?xml version="1.0"?>
<methodResponse>
    <params/>
</methodResponse>
```

Returning Values

Just like return values from functions, only a single return value can be returned from the XML-RPC server. XML-RPC has no concept of passing parameters by reference, so you should not be expecting to be able to retrieve modified parameters. The return value from the server is returned in the same format as that in Listing 16-5. The difference here is that the params element is not empty. It contains a single param element containing a single value element. Its format would look similar to the params subtree of an XML-RPC request document that passes a single parameter:

```
<?xml version="1.0"?>
<methodResponse>
    <params>
        <param>
            <value><!-- data type element and resulting return value --></value>
        </param>
    </params>
</methodResponse>
```

Look at the request from Listing 16-2 making a call to a getUserInfo() function. Without getting into any specifics of the logic within the function, the ultimate return value is an array containing the name, address, and ZIP code for the specified user. So, if the function were to return array("name"=>'John Doe', 'address'=>'123 Example Drive', 'zipcode'=>'12345'), the resulting XML-RPC response document would be as follows:

```
<?xml version="1.0" encoding="UTF-8"?>
<methodResponse>
    <params>
        <param>
            <value>
                <struct>
                    <member>
                        <name>name</name>
                        <value><string>John Doe</string></value>
                    </member>
```

```
        <member>
            <name>address</name>
            <value><string>123 Example Drive</string></value>
        </member>
        <member>
            <name>zipcode</name>
            <value><string>12345</string></value>
        </member>
      </struct>
    </value>
  </param>
  </params>
</methodResponse>
```

Returning an Error

Errors are returned to the client using the fault structure. Rather than using the params element within the response, the fault element is used instead. This element contains a single value element containing a struct element. This structure has two named members: a faultCode with a corresponding integer value and a faultString with a corresponding error message contained in a string. For example:

```
<?xml version="1.0"?>
<methodResponse>
  <fault>
    <value>
      <struct>
        <member>
          <name>faultCode</name>
          <value><int>-1</int></value>
        </member>
        <member>
          <name>faultString</name>
          <value><string>Invalid Procedure Requested</string></value>
        </member>
      </struct>
    </value>
  </fault>
</methodResponse>
```

A fault takes this exact form. The only modifications you need to make are to the integer value for the faultCode and to the string value for the faultString. You cannot make any other modifications or additions to this structure.

■ **Note** XML-RPC does not define any standard faultCodes or faultStrings. These depend on the server and can take any values as long as the faultCode is an integer and the faultString is a string.

Special Remote Calls

Many XML-RPC implementations offer support for some server introspection. In simple terms, a client can request the server to provide some additional support information, such as a list of available functions. Although not an inclusive list, Table 16-1 describes a few of these calls.

Table 16-1. *Server Introspection Methods*

Method Name	Return Type	Arguments	Description
system.listMethods	array		Returns an array containing the methods that a client can call
system.methodHelp	string	string methodName	Returns a string containing any documentation for the method specified by the methodName parameter
system.methodSignature	array	string methodName	Returns an array containing the methodSignature of the method specified by the methodName parameter

A client can call any of these methods in the same manner as all other remote methods are requested. It is not guaranteed that a server has implemented any or all of these methods, and it is also possible that the server may implement some additional ones.

Using xmlrpc in PHP

The xmlrpc extension has existed in PHP since 4.1.0. It is based upon the xmlrpc-epi library (http://xmlrpc-epi.sourceforge.net/), provides support for encoding and decoding XML-RPC requests and responses, and provides some additional functionality specific to a server. Although the extension is still marked as experimental, it has been available in PHP for more than four years now, and it is highly unlikely that its API will change.

With the release of PHP 5, this extension now leverages libxml2 rather than expat by default; however, just like the xml extension, the flag --with-libexpat-dir causes xmlrpc to be built with expat. You can enable this extension through the configure script:

```
--with-xmlrpc[=DIR]
```

When DIR is not specified, the bundled xmlrpc-epi library is used; otherwise, DIR specifies the path to search for the xmlrpc-epi include files. Under Windows, you can enable the extension through the php.ini file, which places the php_xmlrpc.dll file in the directory containing your PHP extensions:

```
extension=php_xmlrpc.dll
```

The following sections will cover how to use the xmlrpc extension in PHP. First, I will cover some generic functionality. These functions, while part of the extension, are not completely

specific to XML-RPC. They allow the encoding and decoding of native PHP data into a serialized XML format that would either allow you to manually build request and response structures
or allow you to transport the structures using protocols not defined by the XML-RPC specification. Next, I will cover how to create an XML-RPC client, making calls to some fictional server.
Finally, I will show how to create a fictitious server so that it and the client can communicate
with one another.

Looking at the Generic Functionality

The xmlrpc extension contains a few functions that I consider general functionality. You can use
them when creating either a client or a server as well as when creating a service not conforming
to the XML-RPC specification. Many of these functions are useful when working manually with
data, as you will see in the "Creating an XML-RPC Client" and "Creating an XML-RPC Server"
sections; in fact, you can use some quick and easy methods to implement XML-RPC.

Encoding and Decoding Data

You can encode and decode data similarly to how you do so using WDDX, as described in
Chapter 15. The functions xmlrpc_encode() and xmlrpc_decode() can perform these operations, but they do not generate a full XML-RPC request or response. They strictly handle the
data and its types.

The xmlrpc_encode() function creates a params structure. This in itself is not enough to
make a request because the root methodCall element is missing and because the corresponding methodName is missing. For example:

```
$encoded = xmlrpc_encode(array(1, 2));
echo $encoded;
```

Calling this code creates a params structure containing an array holding the values 1 and 2:

```
<params>
   <param>
      <value>
         <array>
            <data>
               <value><int>1</int></value>
               <value><int>2</int></value>
            </data>
         </array>
      </value>
   </param>
</params>
```

Although not a complete request, the data can be converted to native PHP data types
using the corresponding xmlrpc_decode() function:

```
$phpdata = xmlrpc_decode($encoded);
var_dump($phpdata);
```

```
array(2) {
  [0]=>
  int(1)
  [1]=>
  int(2)
}
```

The question now becomes, why would you ever use these functions?

When making a request, you do not have any functions like when using wddx to build the XML document incrementally. It is an all-or-nothing deal. Although you could use DOM on the resulting params structure and manually build a request document, you could use these functions to create a Web service that does not conform to the XML-RPC specification. You could pass the params structure back and forth, between the client and the server, just like you pass a WDDX structure. No method name would be defined in the structure, but you could use a technology such as REST, covered in Chapter 17, for this purpose.

The xmlrpc_decode() function is a little more flexible. It decodes both full XML-RPC request documents, which are those containing the methodCall and methodName elements, and those created by the xmlrpc_encode() function. The results from calling the function are the same regardless of the type of document being decoded. Any method information is discarded, and only the information contained within the params element is decoded.

Handling Non-Native PHP Data Types

The xmlrpc extension defines both a base64 data type and a dateTime.iso8601 data type, neither of which is a native type in PHP. You can use the xmlrpc_set_type() and xmlrpc_get_type() functions to convert PHP data into these respective XML-RPC types and determine the type so they are compatible with the extension and can be used directly. You can use these functions when implementing either a client or a server so that the data is exchanged properly.

Consider the following piece of code that attempts to encode a date without setting its type:

```
$isodate = date('c');
echo xmlrpc_encode($isodate);
```

This simply results in a string element for the value:

```
<string>2005-10-19T12:24:42-04:00</string>
```

To the application reading this data, the data is simply a string and not identified as a date. Setting the type of the $isodate variable to datetime, on the other hand, allows it to be encoded properly into a dateTime.iso8601 type. For example:

```
$isodate = date('c');
xmlrpc_set_type($isodate, "datetime");
$encoded_iso = xmlrpc_encode($isodate);
echo $encoded_iso;
```

This time, the resulting content of the value element is as follows:

```
<dateTime.iso8601>20051019T12:38:16</dateTime.iso8601>
```

The base64 data type is handled in the same manner. The variable being set by the xmlrpc_set_type() function will contain the raw binary data and the type base64 passed as the type to the function. Upon encoding, not only will the base64 element be used to hold the contents, but also the raw binary data is automatically Base64 encoded within the resulting structure.

Caution Using the xmlrpc_set_type() function to create datetime and base64 data types will convert the data type of any variable passed to the function into an object usable by the xmlrpc extension. This means trying to perform a function such as echo on the resulting variable will not work as expected.

When decoding an XML structure, unless absolutely positive that it does not contain a dateTime.iso8601 or base64 type, you should check the type of variable. Any data of these types would be returned as objects. The values for these data types must be read through the object properties as follows:

xmlrpc_type: The data type set using xmlrpc_set_type().

scalar: The value for the data returned as a PHP string.

timestamp: This property is valid only for date/time data and is the value of the scalar in time-stamp format.

For example:

```
$phpdata = xmlrpc_decode($encoded_iso);

echo xmlrpc_get_type($phpdata)."\n\n";
var_dump($phpdata);
```

Using the $encoded_iso variable from the previous example, the data is decoded, the type is output, and the resulting PHP data is output using the var_dump() function:

```
datetime

object(stdClass)#2 (3) {
  ["scalar"]=>
  string(17) "20051019T13:21:40"
  ["xmlrpc_type"]=>
  string(8) "datetime"
  ["timestamp"]=>
  int(1129742500)
}
```

Creating an XML-RPC Client

You can create a compliant XML-RPC client using a combination of the functions introduced earlier. This would require building a complete request and would require some additional work. The extension, however, provides a quick and simple function, allowing you to create a client—at least building the request structure—in as little as a single line of code. As previously mentioned, the extension does not provide a mechanism for the data transport, so you will use the `call_using_sockets()` function from Listing 16-1 instead.

Using the xmlrpc_encode_request() Function

Calling the `xmlrpc_encode_request()` function with the appropriate arguments will create and return a complete XML-RPC request document that includes the `methodCall` and `methodName` information:

```
string xmlrpc_encode_request(string method, mixed params [, array output_options])
```

The `method` parameter is simply the name of the method to be called on the remote server. The value passed to this parameter becomes the content of the `methodName` element in the request. The `params` parameter contains the PHP data that will be passed as the parameters to the server. If you have ever played around with this extension, you might have become a bit confused by the data passed to this argument.

Passing any scalar type, such as an integer or string or even an object, to this parameter creates a single `param` element for the data. Passing a numerically indexed array, on the other hand, creates a `param` element for each item in the array. So, to create a request that consists of a single parameter containing an array, the array needs to be passed as an item of an array:

```
echo xmlrpc_encode_request('remoteMethod', array(1, 2));
```

At first glance, you might think that a request containing a single parameter, which is an array, would be created. The resulting request structure, however, proves this to be wrong:

```
<?xml version="1.0" encoding="iso-8859-1"?>
<methodCall>
    <methodName>mymethod</methodName>
        <params>
            <param>
                <value><int>1</int></value>
            </param>
            <param>
                <value><int>2</int></value>
            </param>
        </params>
</methodCall>
```

In fact, to pass the array as a single parameter, you need to send it as the only item within an encapsulating array:

```
echo xmlrpc_encode_request('remoteMethod', array(array(1, 2)));
```

Here you can see that to send array(1, 2) as a single parameter, you need to pass it within an array as array(array(1, 2):.

```
<?xml version="1.0" encoding="iso-8859-1"?>
<methodCall>
    <methodName>remoteMethod</methodName>
    <params>
        <param>
            <value>
                <array>
                    <data>
                        <value><int>1</int></value>
                        <value><int>2</int></value>
                    </data>
                </array>
            </value>
        </param>
    </params>
</methodCall>
```

The last optional parameter, output_options, is an associative array containing any options that you may want to pass. The following are the possible options:

verbosity: Determines how the resulting XML is formatted. Available values are no_white_space, newlines_only, and pretty, which is the default.

escaping: Determines how and if certain characters are escaped. The value for this option can be one or many values. When setting multiple values, you pass them as an array. The possible values for this option are cdata, non-ascii, non-print, and markup. The default for this option is the combination of non-ascii, non-print, and markup.

version: Specifies the format of the XML document. Possible values are xmlrpc, soap 1.1, and simple. The keyword auto is also recognized and will create a response in the same format a request came in. The default for this option is auto (when applicable) and xmlrpc. (This chapter does not use this option, and all data is in xmlrpc format.)

encoding: The encoding for the XML document. The default encoding is iso-8859-1.

Decoding the Response

A client decodes responses it receives from the server using the xmlrpc_decode() function described in the earlier "Encoding and Decoding Data" section. The response can either contain any return values or contain a fault structure. As you will see in the next section, the fault structure allows the client to perform error handling when the server encounters an error trying to fulfill the request. For example:

```
$phpdata = xmlrpc_decode($retval);
```

Handling Errors

Whether or not the server produces an error when a request is made, a response is returned in XML format. After decoding the response, a client is able to determine whether the response is an error using the xmlrpc_is_fault() function. This function takes the return value from the xmlrpc_decode() function and returns TRUE if an error condition is detected and FALSE if no errors occurred from the request. For example:

```
$phpdata = xmlrpc_decode($retval);
/* check for errors */
if (xmlrpc_is_fault($phpdata)) {
    print "Error Code: ".$phpdata['faultCode']."\n";
    print "Error Message: ".$phpdata['faultString']."\n";
} else {
    /* Process return value */
}
```

When a fault is detected, the resulting data is an array containing faultCode and faultString members. The actual structure of the XML document for a fault will be shown in the "Creating an XML-RPC Server" section. For now it is enough to understand that the faultCode is an int data type and that the faultString is a string data type. These are the only two members allowed within a fault structure. The faultCode is application dependant. The XML-RPC specification does not have any predefined codes, so if you are handling errors based on the code, it is necessary that the creator of the XML-RPC server being accessed provides the list of codes that can be returned.

Seeing an XML-RPC Client in Action

I will show a real example of an XML-RPC client later in this chapter in the "Seeing Some Examples in Action" section. However, that section shows only a client, so here, in order to explain both sides of the equation, I will show how to create a client that makes stock trades that are executed on a remote server. I explain and demonstrate the server in the "Creating an XML-RPC Server" section.

I wrote the following example to be executed from the command line using PHP CLI. With a little HTML and a few <BR> tags, it is quite easy to adapt it to run under a Web server. I wrote the server, created in the next section, to be executed from within a Web server. If you decide to try this code, make sure you add the call_using_sockets() function from Listing 16-1, or the equivalent function, to the script. In addition, make sure to set the remote server, sent as the first parameter, accordingly. Currently, the script assumes localhost running on port 80 and assumes the script being called is named stocktrader.php and lives in the document root of the Web site. Here's the code:

```
<?php
/* An array to hold data returned from server */
$arMessage = array();

/* The userid is obtained through some other mechanism */
$userid = 1;
```

```
/* Common function to make XML-RPC requests */
function make_request($request_xml, &$arMessage, $stockSymbol,
                      $stockQuantity, $transtype) {
   $retval = call_using_sockets('localhost', 80, '/stocktrader.php', $request_xml);

   $data = xmlrpc_decode($retval);

   if (is_array($data) && xmlrpc_is_fault($data))
   {
      $arMessage[] = "Unable to $transtype $stockQuantity shares of $stockSymbol";
      $arMessage[] = "Error Code: ".$data['faultCode'];
      $arMessage[] = "Error Message: ".$data['faultString'];
   } else {
      $arMessage[] = $data;
   }
}

/* Stock symbol, quantity, and type of transaction (buy/sell) are obtained
   through some mechanism such as an HTML form */

/* Purchase 100 shares of Yahoo */
$stockSymbol = "YHOO";
$stockQuantity = 100;

$request_xml = xmlrpc_encode_request('stockPurchase', array($userid, $stockSymbol,
                                                  $stockQuantity));
make_request($request_xml, $arMessage, $stockSymbol, $stockQuantity, 'Purchase');

/* Add an blank to the message array to add extra line feed during output */
$arMessage[] = "";

/* Sell 50 shares of Google */
$stockSymbol = "GOOG";
$stockQuantity = 50;
$request_xml = xmlrpc_encode_request('stockSale', array($userid, $stockSymbol,
                                                  $stockQuantity));

make_request($request_xml, $arMessage, $stockSymbol, $stockQuantity, 'Sell');

/* Add an blank to the message array to add extra line feed during output */
$arMessage[] = "";

/* Buy 10 shares of Microsoft */
$stockSymbol = "MSFT";
$stockQuantity = 50;
$request_xml = xmlrpc_encode_request('stockPurchase', array($userid, $stockSymbol,
                                                  $stockQuantity));
```

```
make_request($request_xml, $arMessage, $stockSymbol, $stockQuantity, 'Purchase');

/* Output the messages received from the server */
foreach ($arMessage AS $message) {
   print $message."\n";
}
?>
```

This sample code begins with some initialization. First, the $arMessage and $userid variables are set up. The $arMessage variable is an array that will hold any return data or error information from the remote server. This will be used at the end of the script to output all the messages. The $userid variable is given the value 1. This variable represents the user ID for the person or entity making the stock transaction and is hard-coded for this example.

Second, the make_request() function is a common function that will send an encoded request to the server using the call_using_sockets() function from Listing 16-1. It takes five parameters. The first is the encoded XML-RPC request to be sent. The second is the $arMessage array passed by reference so that messages can be added and eventually used elsewhere in the script. The remaining three parameters strictly add some information in the event the server returns an error. As you can see within the error handling within the function, their text values are simply inserted into the error messages being created.

Once the request has been made, the returned data is then decoded and tested for an error. A fault structure is decoded into an array, and because a server can return any data type, the type must first be tested for an array prior to checking whether it is a fault. In the event the server returned an error, the error is dissected, and the error information is placed into the $arMessage array. In all other cases, the actual decoded data is placed directly in the array.

For the actual client calls, you can see in the code that three stock transactions are to be made. The first transaction attempts to purchase 100 shares of Yahoo stock. The second transaction attempts to sell 50 shares of Google, and the last attempts to purchase 50 shares of Microsoft. They are all hard-coded for this example, but you could create a simple Web interface to allow for dynamic input.

The xmlrpc_encode_request() function creates the request document. As you can probably guess from looking at the function calls, the two methods being called on the remote server are stockPurchase and stockSale. Each takes three parameters: the user ID, stock symbol, and stock quantity. The corresponding variables are simply passed as items within an array.

Once all requests have been made and the return values and/or errors are processed, the script simply loops through the $arMessage array and outputs the messages. Although the server for this client has yet to be written, the following is the final output you would get once everything is assembled and the script ran:

```
Bought 100 shares of Yahoo!

Sold 50 shares of Google

Unable to Purchase 50 shares of MSFT
Error Code: -1
Error Message: Stock Symbol MSFT cannot be traded
```

The first two messages are the values returned directly from the remote server. They show that the first two stock transactions were successfully executed. The last demonstrates a fault returned when trying to purchases 50 shares of Microsoft. To see how and why the return values were created, you need to take a look at the server being used.

Creating an XML-RPC Server

You have two ways to handle the request data received from the client using the xmlrpc functions. The first is a more manual method where it is up to the developer to decode the data, handle the method call, and create the resulting response document. The second method involves creating an XML-RPC server, registering methods, and allowing the server to process the raw request and create the resulting document. In both cases, the result document must be returned to the client.

The example server uses the second method to service the client. Before I get to that, I will provide an overview of the functions that can process a request using the first method, as well as show how you can access the request in the first place. Understanding these functions will at least provide you with the flexibility of being able to create a server in either scenario depending upon your needs.

Retrieving the Request Data

The request is sent using an HTTP POST to the server. It is not passed as a parameter, so trying to retrieve it using the $_POST superglobal is out of the question. It is strictly raw data. In some cases, it can be retrieved using $HTTP_RAW_POST_DATA. This, however, depends upon INI settings and is not always available. A much more universal and less memory-intensive way to get the data exists. Using streams, the URI php://input grants you access to this raw data. Within your XML-RPC server script, you would read the data just as you would a normal file:

```
$raw_post_data = file_get_contents("php://input");
```

No matter which method you choose to handle a request, you still need to retrieve the raw POST data. This chapter, ensuring that the data is available for any PHP server setup, will use only the streams functionality to retrieve this data.

Manually Handling a Request

Now that you have the raw request, you need to do something with it. The first step is to decode the request structure. You require the method that needs to be executed here, so the xmlrpc_decode() function is out of the question, since it will return only the parameters for the method. The xmlrpc_decode_request() function is basically an extended version of the function, because the return values are still the parameters of the request; however, this function also takes an additional parameter as input, which is passed by reference, and contains the name of the requested method once the xmlrpc_decode_request() function has successfully returned:

```
$method_name = "";
$decoded = xmlrpc_decode_request($raw_post_data, $method_name);
```

Using the raw POST data from the previous section, calling this function will return the parameters to be passed, which are then set to the $decoded variable. After calling this function, the variable $method_name will now contain the name of the method being requested. This is the value set within the methodName element of the request.

Assuming that the requested function (the one named in the $method_name variable) exists and is publicly available for remote requests, you now need to call the function. It is up to you how you would like to handle the function call. Some possible methods are using the call_user_func() or call_user_func_array() function, which could also be tested prior to the actual call using the is_callable() function to ensure that the function can be called in the first place. In any event, the response document you need to create depends upon whether the function call was successful or an error condition was encountered.

The same function used to create the request, xmlrpc_encode_request(), is used to create the response. This may seem a little odd because previously you saw that this function created the entire request document, but the response document has a different structure. The difference in its usage lies with the first parameter. Passing in NULL as the method parameter causes this function to generate the methodResponse structure. For example:

```
$response = xmlrpc_encode_request(NULL, $retVals);
```

Unlike when creating a request, you can pass any of the XML-RPC data types as $retVals. A response contains only a single param element, so wrapping $retVals in an array will cause only the param to be an array that contains each of the $retVals as items, rather than creating multiple param elements.

But how are errors returned from the server? This is actually quite simple. You can create a fault structure by creating an associative array containing a faultCode key and a faultString key, with their values being the value that should be set as the content of the element when serialized into XML format. For example, suppose the request method does not exist, and you have defined code 500 to designate this error:

```
$arFault = array('faultCode'=>500, 'faultString'=>'Unknown Method Requested');
```

The $arFault array is then passed as the data to be passed back to the client:

```
$response = xmlrpc_encode_request(NULL, $arFault);
```

If you were to look at the resulting $response string, the document would look like the following:

```
<methodResponse>
   <fault>
     <value>
        <struct>
           <member>
             <name>faultCode</name>
             <value><int>500</int></value>
           </member>
           <member>
             <name>faultString</name>
             <value><string>Unknown Method Requested</string></value>
           </member>
```

```
      </struct>
    </value>
  </fault>
</methodResponse>
```

The only thing left to do, whether the response contains a return value or a fault, is to return the data to the client. The easiest way to do this is when running the server within a Web server. The response just needs to be echoed. Remember, though, that the data needs to be identified as XML, so you must properly set the Content-Type header:

```
header('Content-Type: text/xml');
echo $response;
```

Using a Server to Handle a Request

You can write an XML-RPC server much more easily using the extension's server rather than having to do everything manually. The server in this case is a PHP resource that allows the registration of functions that are automatically called when a request document is passed to the server. The server then also automatically creates the entire response document based on the return value of the called function. From this description alone, you probably already have the feeling that this is going to be much easier than having to manually perform all of the operations yourself.

The following creates a server using the xmlrpc_server_create() function and subsequently destroys it using the xmlrpc_server_destroy() function:

```
/* Create XML-RPC server */
$rpcserver = xmlrpc_server_create();

/* Destroy XML-RPC server */
xmlrpc_server_destroy($rpcserver);
```

Being a resource, it is not required that the server be destroyed; although it is automatically cleaned up once PHP has finished serving the request, it is often good practice to do so anyway.

Once you have a hold of a server, you need to register the functions to be served using the xmlrpc_server_register_method() function. The function takes three parameters: the server resource itself, the public name of the function called by the clients, and the internal name of the function, which is the function definition. For instance, using the server just created, $rpcserver, the following code maps the internal function buy_stock() to a publicly identifiable method named stockPurchase and registers it with the server:

```
xmlrpc_server_register_method($rpcserver, "stockPurchase", "buy_stock");
```

This function returns a Boolean indicating whether the function was registered successfully. Functions that are registered must conform to the standard prototype used for callbacks. For example:

```
mixed function_name(string method_name, array args, mixed user_data)
```

So, based on this prototype, you would define the buy_stock() function as follows:

```
function buy_stock($method_name, $args, $user_data) { . . . }
```

You would then reference this function from an XML-RPC request using the method name stockPurchase.

Once you have defined and registered all functions with the server, all that is left to do—once a request is made, of course—is access the raw post data, have the server process this data, and finally return the results from the processing. As mentioned earlier in this chapter, the best way to access the raw post data is by using PHP streams:

```
$request_data = file_get_contents('php://input');
```

This data is then passed to the server for processing by means of the xmlrpc_server_call_method() function. This function takes the raw post data, parses the request, calls the proper function, and returns the resulting response document:

```
mixed xmlrpc_server_call_method(resource server, string xml,
                              mixed user_data [, array output_options])
```

The parameters are pretty much straightforward. The server is the XML-RPC server that has been created. The request data is passed to the xml parameter. The user_data parameter allows data to be passed to the function being called. Whatever is passed to this parameter is passed directly to the called function as its user_data parameter. The last parameter is the same as the output_options parameter defined earlier in this chapter. It gives you control over how the resulting response document is created.

You may be curious as to why this function can return mixed results. In most cases, the return value will be a string containing the XML-RPC response. One output_option option, output_type, was not covered earlier in this chapter. The default value for this option is the value xml. It is also possible to specify the value php, which causes the results to be returned as native PHP data types and ignores types not native to PHP. (I intentionally omitted this option because the XML-RPC discussed in this chapter is written based upon the formal specifications for the greatest interoperability. Everything contained in this chapter deals strictly with the xml output_type.)

The response document is created based on the return value of the function it calls to service the request. One special case exists when the returned data alters the response structure, and that is when a fault is created. Simply returning an associative array containing the keys faultCode and faultString causes the XML-RPC server to create a fault structure using the values for these items as the contents of the fault elements. For example, a function called by xmlrpc_server_call_method() and returning the array array('faultCode'=>100, 'faultString'=>'Function Error Message') results in the following fault:

```
<?xml version="1.0" encoding="utf-8"?>
<fault>
   <value>
      <struct>
         <member>
            <name>faultCode</name>
            <value><int>100</int></value>
         </member>
```

```
        <member>
            <name>faultString</name>
            <value><string>Function Error Message</string></value>
        </member>
    </struct>
    </value>
</fault>
```

▐Tip Remember to set the Content-Type header to text/xml prior to returning the resulting response document.

Putting this all together, you can create a server to service the request from the client created in the previous section. It defines two functions, buy_stock() and sell_stock(), that are registered with an XML-RPC server. The only two stocks, defined in the $arStocks array, that can be used within these functions are Yahoo (YHOO) and Google (GOOG). The following is the complete code for the server, referenced as the file stocktrader.php by the client. I wrote it to run within a Web server because it leverages the header creation performed by the Web server.

```php
<?php
/* Stocks available to be traded */
$arStocks = array('YHOO'=>'Yahoo!', 'GOOG'=>'Google');

/* Function that performs the actual stock purchase */
function buy_stock($method_name, $args, $app_data) {
    if (! is_array($args) || count($args) <> 3) {
        return array('faultCode'=>-2,
                     'faultString'=>'Invalid Number of Parameters');
    }
    $userid = $args[0];
    $symbol = $args[1];
    $quantity = $args[2];
    if (array_key_exists($symbol, $GLOBALS['arStocks'])) {
        return "Bought $quantity shares of ".$GLOBALS['arStocks'][$symbol];
    } else {
        return array('faultCode'=>-1,
                     'faultString'=>"Stock Symbol $symbol cannot be traded");
    }
}
```

```php
/* Function that performs stock sale */
function sell_stock($method_name, $args, $app_data) {
    if (! is_array($args) || count($args) <> 3) {
        return array('faultCode'=>-2,
                        'faultString'=>'Invalid Number of Parameters');
    }
    $userid = $args[0];
    $symbol = $args[1];
    $quantity = $args[2];
    if (array_key_exists($symbol, $GLOBALS['arStocks'])) {
        return "Sold $quantity shares of ".$GLOBALS['arStocks'][$symbol];
    } else {
        return array('faultCode'=>-1,
                        'faultString'=>"Stock Symbol $symbol cannot be traded");
    }
}


$request_xml = file_get_contents("php://input");

/* Create XML-RPC server, and register the functions */
$xmlrpc_server = xmlrpc_server_create();
xmlrpc_server_register_method($xmlrpc_server, "stockPurchase", "buy_stock");
xmlrpc_server_register_method($xmlrpc_server, "stockSale", "sell_stock");

/* Set content type to text/xml */
header('Content-Type: text/xml');

/* Process the XML-RPC request */
print xmlrpc_server_call_method($xmlrpc_server, $request_xml, array());
?>
```

The only portions of this example I expect you to have questions about are the functions written to provide the requested functionality. Because arguments are passed as an array to your functions, a simple check ensures it is an array, and the correct number of parameters is passed. If the client does not send exactly three, the functions issue an error stating this. This error is then returned to the calling client. The other error condition arises if the requested stock is not one of your supported stocks. If you look at the earlier client example, you will see the request to purchase 50 shares of Microsoft stock (MSFT). This symbol is invalid and causes the fault with a faultCode of -1 to be returned to the client.

Using XML_RPC in PEAR

The XML_RPC package from PEAR provides an object-oriented API for creating XML-RPC clients and servers. Unlike the xmlrpc extension, it also provides the mechanisms for transporting data between the client and server. The only requirement for using this package is that the xml extension in PHP be installed. You can install the package, just like other PEAR packages you have encountered so far, using the PEAR installer:

```
pear install XML_RPC
```

In many PHP installations, this package is already installed.

Note If you are manually searching for this package on the PEAR site, it is grouped within the Web service packages rather than within the XML packages.

Like all PEAR packages, the first thing you need to do when using the package is to include it in the script being written:

```
require_once 'XML/RPC.php';
```

This now makes available the XML_RPC_Value, XML_RPC_Client, XML_RPC_Server, XML_RPC_Message, and XML_RPC_Response classes. This package provides much more functionality than that provided natively by the xmlrpc extension, but unless you absolutely need to utilize it all, I find the xmlrpc extension a bit easier to use.

This introduction to XML_RPC is not an in-depth coverage of the package functionality. I will touch on only a few methods from the XML_RPC_Value, XML_RPC_Client, XML_RPC_Message, XML_RPC_Response, and XML_RPC_Server classes and demonstrate a brief example of creating a client. You can find more complete coverage of the API at the PEAR site for this package.

XML_RPC_Value

This package does not use native PHP variables and their data types. Rather, values are wrapped within an XML_RPC_Value object. To create an object of this type, a PHP variable and a string containing the data type defined in the XML-RPC specification are passed as parameters to the constructor. Both parameters are strictly optional, because an empty XML_RPC_Value object can be set after the fact using its methods, and the data type has a default type of string when the type is not specified. For example:

```
/* Creating XML_RPC_Value objects */
$intValue = new XML_RPC_Value(1, 'int');
$stringValue = new XML_RPC_Value('string1', 'string');
$string2Value = new XML_RPC_Value('string2');
$arrayValue = new XML_RPC_Value(array(1, 2), 'array');
```

Because all values are objects, you need to access the underlying data using the object methods rather than accessing the data directly. Although many different methods exist depending upon what needs to be done, the only method you will be concerned with for the sake of this object is scalarval(). This method returns the underlying PHP data using its native data type. For example, using the $arrayValue object created previously, you can retrieve the internal array using this method:

```
$val2 = $ arrayValue->scalarval();
var_dump($val2);
```

```
array(2) {
  [0]=>
  int(1)
  [1]=>
  int(2)
}
```

XML_RPC_Message

An XML_RPC_Message object contains the actual request sent to the server. It defines both the method to be called and the parameters to be passed to the remote function:

```
XML_RPC_Message(string methodName, array parameterArray)
```

The first parameter, methodName, is the name of the remote function to be invoked. The parameterArray parameter is an array containing XML_RPC_Value objects for each of the function's parameters. Take, for example, a remote function named calcNumbers() with the following prototype:

```
function calcNumbers($num1, $operator, $num2) { . . . }
```

Caution This prototype illustrates what the native function looks like. This is not the format used when called by an XML_RPC_Server object. Refer to the "XML_RPC_Server" section for additional information about defining internal functions.

It accepts three parameters. The $num1 parameter represents the first number for the calculation. The $operator parameter is the operation to perform, such as +, -, /, or *. The last parameter, $num2, is the second number for the calculation. Creating the request message for this function to add the numbers 1 and 2 looks like this:

```
$objMessage = new XML_RPC_Message('calcNumbers', array(new XML_RPC_Value(1, 'int'),
                                         new XML_RPC_Value('+'),
                                         new XML_RPC_Value(2, int)));
```

XML_RPC_Message objects are also passed to the function being called on the server side. The important methods here are getNumParams() and getParam(). Just like when working with the xmlrpc extension, parameters from an XML-RPC request are passed to functions as a single argument. In this case, it is an XML_RPC_Message object from which the parameters must be extracted. You can retrieve the number of parameters contained in the XML_RPC_Message by calling the getNumParams() method. It takes no parameters and returns an integer. Each parameter is then accessed by calling the getParam() method, passing the offset of the parameter to return as the argument. The parameter returned is also contained within an XML_RPC_Value object, just like all other values in this package. For example:

```
$paramcount = $objMessage->getNumParams();
for ($x=0; $x < $paramcount; $x++) {
    $objRPCValue = $objMessage->getParam($x);
    /* Do something with parameter */
}
```

XML_RPC_Client

Using the client is extremely easy in this package. Virtually all you need to do is create an XML_RPC_Client object and send an XML_RPC_Message. For example:

```
XML_RPC_Client(string path, string server [, integer port [, string proxy [, integer
               proxy_port [, string proxy_user [, string proxy_pass]]]]])
```

As you can see from the parameters for the construction, the client performs the necessary transport based on the parameter values. You do not need to use any of the previously defined functions, such as the one from Listing 16-1. The following list describes each of the parameters and what they are used for:

path: The path on the server that services the request.

server: The URL of the remote server.

port: The port number to which to connect. The default value is 80 for HTTP and 443 for HTTPS and SSL.

proxy: The URL of the proxy server if needed.

proxy_port: The port number of the proxy server. This defaults to 80 for HTTP and 443 for HTTPS and SSL.

proxy_user: The username to be used to authenticate with the proxy server.

proxy_pass: The password to be used to authenticate with the proxy server.

For example:

```
$objRPCClient = new XML_RPC_Client('/rpcscript.php', 'example.com');
```

Using the newly created XML_RPC_Client object, the request is simply made by creating the message, using the XML_RPC_Message object, and calling the send() method:

```
mixed XML_RPC_Client::send(XML_RPC_Message xmlrpc_message [, int timeout])
```

The method takes only an XML_RPC_Message object, using $objMessage from the previous section, and an optional timeout value. Unless a communications error occurs or some other error besides a returned fault structure occurs, which would cause the return value of the method to be 0, an XML_RPC_Response object is returned:

```
$objResponse = $objRPCClient->send($objMessage);
```

XML_RPC_Response

Both a server and a client use the XML_RPC_Response class. As already demonstrated, it is returned by an XML_RPC_Client object when calling the send() method. On the server side, it is created and used as the response returned to the client. When needing to create a response while creating an XML-RPC server, the parameters for the construction depend upon what type of response is being sent. Returning a response with a return value simply happens by passing an XML_RPC_Value object as the only parameter. For example:

```
$objResponse = new XML_RPC_Response(new XML_RPC_Value(1, 'int'));
```

Creating a fault structure for the response takes three parameters, with the first parameter always being 0. The remaining parameters are, respectively, the fault code and the fault message. For example:

```
$objFault = new XML_RPC_Response(0, -100, 'Invalid Method Requested');
```

Again, the object must be accessed using its methods to retrieve the response information. The following is a list of available methods and their descriptions that can be called from an XML_RPC_Response object. None of them take any parameters.

faultCode(): The numeric fault code or 0 if there is no error.

faultString(): The error message from the fault or empty if no error.

value(): Returns the XML_RPC_Value object containing with the response. This method should not be called when the value returned by faultCode() is not 0.

serialize(): Returns the XML document of the response.

XML_RPC_Server

An XML_RPC_Server object works in a similar fashion as an XML-RPC server from the PHP extension. Rather than having to call multiple functions, however, the majority of the work happens by passing the information as arguments to the object's constructor. For example:

```
XML_RPC_Server(array dispMap, int serviceNow = 1, int debug = 0)
```

Before getting to the first parameter, I will describe the remaining two, because they are not used in this chapter. The serviceNow parameter indicates to the server whether it should service the request immediately, which is during construction, or wait until instructed. When told to wait by passing in the value 0 as the serviceNow argument, the server will not process anything until its service() method is called. The debug parameter turns on debug mode when the value 1 is passed as the argument.

The dispMap parameter is an associative array using the publicly known method name as the key associated with another associated array that defines the internal function to be used. The array held by each item is broken down into the following keys:

function: The value is the name of the internal function to be called. This key is mandatory within the array.

signature: The signature for the function. This is explained in more detail in a few moments. Using this key is optional.

docstring: A string containing any documentation for the function. Using this key is optional.

Before demonstrating how to create an XML_RPC_Server object, I will explain the signature key. The signature key is an array containing additional arrays where each of these arrays defines the data type for the return value and the data types for each of the accepted parameters. Its usage is purely optional but can formally declare the procedure, number of arguments, and type of arguments. For example:

```
function myfunct($arg1, $arg2="") {
    return TRUE;
}
```

This is how a normal function is written when not working with xmlrpc. Its name is myfunct, and it accepts two parameters. In this case, I will say $arg1 is an integer, and $arg2 is a string. The return value is clearly a Boolean. Because $arg2 is optional, you actually have two different signatures. One signature exists for when $arg2 is not passed, and the other is for when $arg2 is passed to the function. Rewriting this function to be used with XML_RPC, it looks like the following:

```
function myfunct($args) {
    /* $args is an XML_RPC_Message object */
    return TRUE;
}
```

Returning to the signatures, the first item of a signature array item is the return type of the function. The remaining items are the data types for each parameter. Because the function has two signatures, the signature is written as follows:

```
array(
        /* Signature when both parameters are passed */
        array('boolean', 'int', 'string'),
        /* Signature when only the required first parameter is passed */
        array('boolean', 'int')
)
```

Again, PHP is a loosely typed language. When a variable is passed to a function, it does not care about the type of the variable. The value of the variable is converted as needed to an appropriate type based on its usage. Values in XML-RPC do have a specific type. Using signatures, you can restrict the types of variables that will be passed to the PHP functions. For example, when myfunc() is used without a signature, anything can be passed as arguments. On the other hand, using signatures, such as the previous one, myfunct() is limited to accepting a value that has an int data type and optionally a string for the second parameter. This also illustrates how optional parameters are handled with signatures.

Now when creating the XML_RPC_Server object, registering only the single myfunct() function, you could do it in a few ways:

```
$objServer = new XML_RPC_Server(array("example.MyFunct" =>
                                    array("function" => "myfunct")));
```

You can also create it with a signature like this:

```
$objServer = new XML_RPC_Server(array("example.MyFunct" =>
                                array("function" => "myfunct",
                                      "signature" =>
                                        array(
                                            array('boolean', 'int', 'string'),
                                            array('boolean', 'int')
                                        )))));
```

Because the serviceNow parameter is not used, creating $objServer automatically processes the request that was sent and returns the appropriate response. You can find additional documentation and examples on the PEAR site for this package.

XML_RPC_Client Example

The following example illustrates how to write an XML-RPC client using the XML_RPC package from PEAR. The following client interacts with the stock server created using the xmlrpc extension in PHP. It performs only a single transaction, but it works in the same manner as the previous stock client does.

```php
<?php
require_once 'XML/RPC.php';

$userid = 1;
$stockSymbol = "YHOO";
$stockQuantity = 100;

$params = array(new XML_RPC_Value($userid, 'int'),
                new XML_RPC_Value($stockSymbol, 'string'),
                new XML_RPC_Value($stockQuantity, 'int'));
$msg = new XML_RPC_Message('stockPurchase', $params);

$objStock = new XML_RPC_Client('/stocktrader.php', 'localhost');

$retVal = $objStock->send($msg);

if (!$retVal) {
    echo 'Error: ' . $objStock->errstr;
} else {
    if (!$retVal->faultCode()) {
        $xmlrpcValue = $retVal->value();
        echo $xmlrpcValue->scalarval()."\n";
    } else {
        echo "Unable to Purchase $stockQuantity shares of $stockSymbol";
        echo "Error Code: ".$retVal->faultCode()."\n";
        echo "Error Message: ".$retVal->faultString()."\n";
    }
}
?>
```

Bought 100 shares of Yahoo!

Seeing Some Examples in Action

Throughout this chapter, you have seen a few examples of interaction using XML-PRC. For a final example, I will use a real-world scenario. You may not be aware of this, but interacting with the PEAR repository using its tools occurs over XML-RPC.

■**Note** As of PEAR 1.4.0, REST, covered in the next chapter, is now the service of choice for interacting with PEAR and its channels. XML-RPC is still available for supporting earlier versions of PEAR.

Leveraging this fact, you can create a custom interface to interact with PEAR directly. This example will demonstrate how to retrieve information for a specific package from the PEAR database. You can retrieve the full list of publicly accessible functions, which you could use to expand upon this example, by calling the remote system.listMethods function. I will use the xmlrpc extension in PHP to create the client.

This example has two files. The file pearxmlrpclib.php, shown in Listing 16-6, is the code that performs all the work.

■**Note** I have omitted the code for the call_using_sockets() function from the example because you can find it in Listing 16-1. If sockets are unavailable on your system, you can exchange it with the call_using_curl() function as long as you change the appropriate call within the library as well.

Listing 16-6. *Search Library Referenced As* pearxmlrpclib.php

```php
<?php

function call_using_sockets($remote_server, $remote_server_port,
                            $remote_path, $request) {
/* Code for this function found in Listing 16-1. */
}

/* Initialize variables */
$results = NULL;
$cur_package = '';
$pear_server = 'pear.php.net';
$pear_server_port = 80;
$pear_rpc_page = '/xmlrpc.php';

/* If form posted, then request the package information from PEAR
   Invalid submissions are not being checked in this example */
if (! empty($_POST['submit'])) {
    $cur_package = (string)$_POST['pkg_name'];
    $request_xml = xmlrpc_encode_request('package.info', array($cur_package));
```

```
    /* call_using_curl may be substituted here */
    $retval = call_using_sockets($pear_server, $pear_server_port,
                                 $pear_rpc_page, $request_xml);
    $results = xmlrpc_decode($retval);
}
?>
```

You need to place the code for the Web page, shown in Listing 16-7, somewhere within a Web site where it can be called from a browser. If the library file from Listing 16-6 is not placed in the same directory, make sure to correctly change the reference so the Web page can include it.

Listing 16-7. *Web Page for Search Referenced As* pearxmlrpc.php

```php
<?php include('pearxmlrpclib.php'); ?>
<!DOCTYPE HTML PUBLIC "-//W3C//DTD HTML 4.01 Transitional//EN"
                      "http://www.w3.org/TR/html4/loose.dtd">
<html>
<body>
<p><b>PEAR Package Information</b></p>

<form name="pear_search" method="post">
   Package Name: <input type="text" name="pkg_name"
                        value="<?php echo $cur_package; ?>">
      
   <input type="submit" name="submit" value="Search">
</form>

<?php
/* If we have results and it is an array, then output the key/value pairs */
if ($results && is_array($results)) {
?>
<table border="0">
   <tr>
      <th colspan="2">Package Information for <?php echo $cur_package; ?></th>
   </tr>
<?php
   foreach($results AS $key=>$value) {
      /* Skip output of empty and complex values */
      if (empty($value) || is_array($value))
         continue;
?>
   <tr>
      <td align="right"><?php echo $key; ?>:</td>
      <td align="left"><?php echo $value; ?></td>
   </tr>
```

```php
<?php } /* End foreach */
} /* End if */
?>
</table>
</body>
</html>
```

Entering XML_RPC as the package on which to search results in the page shown in Figure 16-1.

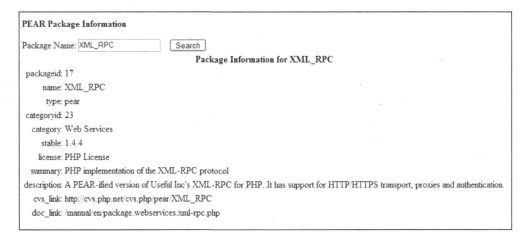

Figure 16-1. *Example output information for the XML_RPC package*

Conclusion

Calling remote procedures is not something new. Many technologies, such as DCOM and CORBA, allow for RPC to take place. However, many of these are difficult to implement and are even tied to specific platforms. XML-RPC was developed as a platform- and language-neutral mechanism of exchanging data and allowing remote functions to be called, marshaling the data in XML format. It also defined a universal transport agent, HTTP POST, allowing virtually every computer to be able to interact with each other.

XML-RPC was pretty much the first official Web service. I say *official*, as you will see in the next chapter, because XML has been exchanged between systems since it was conceived, although no official nomenclature was ever given to the method until recently. With SOAP and REST becoming more popular, XML-RPC usage has been on a decline, with many services switching over to these other technologies. This does not mean XML-RPC is no longer used. When compared to the other technologies, XML-RPC does have its place. For instance, compared to using REST, XML-RPC provides a defined format for marshaling data, while REST does not. SOAP, on the other hand, provides all the features of XML-RPC and then some, but many feel overwhelmed by the complexity of it; XML-RPC is much easier to use.

The next chapter will begin the coverage of the common methods for using and implementing Web services. The first of these is REST.

CHAPTER 17

Representational State Transfer (REST)

Representational State Transfer (REST) is not a specific standard like many of the other technologies covered in this book. Instead, it is an architectural style utilizing commonly found technologies and protocols that in this case will be used to implement and utilize REST-based Web services. This chapter will provide some background and information regarding REST, but it focuses more on utilizing REST for Web services and uses the services available from Yahoo and Amazon as examples.

Introducing REST

In 2000, Roy Fielding wrote his doctoral dissertation (http://www.ics.uci.edu/~fielding/pubs/dissertation/abstract.htm) about architectural styles and designs of network-based software architectures. Within it, he speaks of Web architectures where any information or concept that can be named, referred to as a *resource*, is identified by a *resource identifier*, such as a URI. In common terms, you can think of the PHP home page as a resource with a resource identifier of http://www.php.net/.

Components in this architecture perform actions on the resource using its representation. For instance, using a browser to request the resource, a server transfers the current state of a Web page to the browser. The browser is then able to perform the action of rendering the representation. Simply put, the server sends the data for the requested page in its current state, and the data is rendered. Navigating to any of the links within the rendered page causes a state transition because the next page, which could be considered another state of an application, is transferred to the browser for rendering.

This style of architecture was dubbed REST. It has become quite popular because it uses components and technologies most developers already know. Using PHP, you can request a remote resource as follows:

```
$representation = file_get_contents('http://www.php.net/');
```

PHP file functions and streams make accessing Web services simple in the REST world.

Introducing REST Web Services

Although there is much more to REST than just the material presented in the previous section, this chapter will focus on using it specifically for Web services. You should now have at least a general idea what REST represents. It is fine if that is just a conceptual idea right now. This section will cover how REST is used for Web services. I will explain both the client side and the server side and will demonstrate them by showing how to create a custom Web service. Later sections will show how to interact with some real-world Web services, such as those from Yahoo and Amazon.

Using the REST methodology for a Web service involves the use of the following components:

XML: XML is the format for the representation of the resource.

HTTP: The methods GET, HEAD, POST, PUT, and DELETE indicate the action to be taken.

URI: The URI, typically a URL, is the resource identifier that locates the Web service (resource).

MIME type: Because the data being passed to the client is in XML format, `text/xml` is the MIME type used.

Of all these components, the only topics you have not seen used in this book are the HEAD, PUT, and DELETE methods when using HTTP. Everything else in this list should be familiar to you. This does not mean you can use these components hazardously, though, as you will see throughout the next sections.

■**Note** The MIME type should already be evident at this point. When a server is returning data, the MIME type must be `text/xml` so it is correctly interpreted.

XML Representation

When making a call to a Web service, the data is returned in XML format. REST is different from most technologies because it's not a standard but an architectural style. REST has no standard structure for the XML. By contrast, when working with XML-RPC or WDDX, the same format is used no matter what system you access, as long as the system's data conforms to either of these technologies. A REST Web service returns XML as a structure defined by the implementer of the service.

For example, assume you are accessing two independent Web services, Service A and Service B, and each returns a set of customer data. The XML in Listings 17-1 and 17-2 return the same set of data yet are structurally completely different.

Listing 17-1. *Customer Data from Service A*

```xml
<?xml version="1.0" encoding="UTF-8"?>
<customers>
    <customer>
        <custid>1</custid>
        <fname>John</fname>
        <lname>Smith</lname>
    </customer>
    <customer>
        <custid>2</custid>
        <fname>Jane</fname>
        <lname>Doe</lname>
    </customer>
</customers>
```

Listing 17-2. *Customer Data from Service B*

```xml
<?xml version="1.0" encoding="UTF-8"?>
<!DOCTYPE customer_list [
    <!ELEMENT customer_list (customer+)>
        <!ELEMENT customer (first_name, last_name)>
        <!ATTLIST customer custid ID #REQUIRED>
        <!ELEMENT first_name (#PCDATA)>
        <!ELEMENT last_name (#PCDATA)>
]>
<customer_list>
    <customer custid="1">
        <first_name>John</first_name>
        <last_name>Smith</last_name>
    </customer>
    <customer custid="2">
        <first_name>Jane</first_name>
        <last_name>Doe</last_name>
    </customer>
</customer_list>
```

Each of these documents returns the same customer data, John Smith and Jane Doe, but structurally, they are completely different. They have no standard structure, so the caller must already know what to expect. Typically, a public Web service offers a published API for this purpose, but it is possible to use WSDL or Web Resource Description Language (WRDL). Although this book does not cover WRDL, I will explain WSDL in Chapter 18 in relation to SOAP.

From the REST-based Web services I have seen, these technologies are rarely used. WRDL is a descriptive language specifically for REST-based architectures, but it really never became popular. The more commonly known WSDL, in my opinion, is like a black art because of its complexity. Those who prefer REST to SOAP often do so because REST is easier to implement and understand. From a client perspective, REST leverages technologies most developers are already comfortable using. SOAP, on the other hand, although not difficult to use with WSDL, requires a developer to learn a new API and potentially use something they do not understand. When implementing a service, REST has the same advantages as from the client perspective. The developer already is comfortable writing code based on the existing technologies. Implementing a SOAP service leads to learning a new API, writing a WSDL document, and adding levels of complexity that many do not want to handle.

HTTP Methods

HTTP is the protocol used in a REST architecture. If you have researched REST at all, you have probably come across the methods GET, HEAD, POST, PUT, and DELETE. In a purist view of REST, each of these methods provides certain types of functionality often explained using the database acronym CRUD. CRUD refers to Create, Retrieve, Update, and Delete. As you will see in some of the real-world applications demonstrated in this chapter, this concept is really a gray area.

Unless these methods are used in the manner shown in Table 17-1, a REST purist would say that the service is not RESTful. Personally, I believe technology in general is a completely gray area. It is all about getting the job done as simply as possible, without sacrificing security and stability and without adding unnecessary layers of complexity. So, as long as the methods are used in a similar fashion as listed in Table 17-1, it's close enough to say the service is RESTful. Aren't there enough acronyms out there already?

Table 17-1. *HTTP Methods for REST*

Method	CRUD Operation	Description
GET	Retrieve	Retrieves the representation of a resource.
HEAD		Retrieves metadata for the representation and resource.
POST	Create	In the strict sense, POST creates a resource. In the real world, however, POST is typically used to create, update, and even delete a resource. It is normal to use REST services that support only GET and POST.
PUT	Update	Updates a resource. More often than not, you will not see this method used in the real world but instead will see POST used to perform the actions.
DELETE	Delete	Deletes a resource. Just like PUT, in the real world this is rarely used, and instead POST is used in its place.

Although it might be worthwhile to understand the differences between how the different methods are used in the purist world, this chapter will be limited to the GET and POST methods because these are more often than not what you will encounter in real-world usage.

HTTP GET

You should use the GET method only to retrieve a representation of a resource. You might be tempted to create a service that uses only GET to perform all operations, which may work fine for you, but you should perform any resource modifications, additions, and deletions using POST. This will allow the separation of functionality and will also reduce the possibility of inadvertent mistakes. This doesn't mean a service is never implemented using only HTTP GET.

Take RSS, for example, which fits in perfectly within the REST definition of a Web service. From a user perspective, the only action that can be taken is to retrieve the resource, so an HTTP GET call is made, the XML is returned, and the result can be parsed and processed as a user sees fit.

When trying to use GET for all actions, though, the only differentiation between the retrieval and the deletion of a resource is a combination of the URL and parameters. For example, assume a service is running at the location `http://www.example.org/myservice.php`. The difference between retrieving a record and deleting a record is the following:

```
/* Retrieve representation of resource 1 */
$representation = file_get_contents('http://www.example.org/myservice.php?resid=1');

/* Delete resource 1 */
file_get_contents('http://www.example.org/myservice.php?resid=1&del=1');
```

The service itself is able to know only that an operation is being performed on the resource based on parameters:

```
/* Service Determination of Operation */
if (isset($_GET['del'])) {
   /* Delete resource identified by $_GET['resid'] */
} else {
   /* Retrieve resource identified by $_GET['resid'] */
}
```

This has too much room for mistakes. If the del parameter was accidentally passed, the resource could be deleted even though the intended operation was a simple retrieval. It is also possible that different URLs could be used, such as `http://www.example.org/myservice_retrieve.php` to retrieve the representation and `http://www.example.org/myservice_delete.php` to delete the resource. This, however, goes against the REST architecture. The URL identifies the resource, and in this case, you end up with two URLs for the same resource where the difference is the operation to perform. To summarize this, it is best practice to use GET for retrievals and POST for other operations on the resource.

HTTP POST

The POST method performs some type of action, other than a simple retrieval, on a resource. Anytime a new resource is being created, modified, or deleted, it should be done using POST. As you just read in the previous section, there are reasons for this. Not following this methodology (even though I still believe in gray areas) goes completely against the REST approach. Although there is still room for potential errors since parameters are still used to determine the type of modification to make, with a POST request you can at least know that something should change, and from there you can implement checks to ensure that an inappropriate action is not being requested.

This is one reason purists believe in using PUT and DELETE. The action is removed from the parameter list and is determined by the HTTP method. Again, this is seldom used in the real world and just adds complexity that really does not need to be there. Of course, I will probably take some heat for suggesting the use of POST rather than the other distinct methods, but technology seems to be overly complicated. I don't know about you, but if I can find a simple way to do something and achieve the same results, then I prefer the simpler method.

URI

Although you are already familiar with URIs and URLs, it is important to understand their significance within a REST Web service. You might be curious why most of the URLs you see used within Web services do not contain the actual Web page. They just point to some location. For example, the Yahoo Web Search service, which I will demonstrate later in the "Introducing the Yahoo Web Services" section, uses `http://api.search.yahoo.com/WebSearchService/V1/webSearch`. URIs point to resources, and they should not change over time. If you decide to use the URL `http://www.example.org/myservice.php` for your service and then after time decide to implement it in another language, you will need to change the page name. Clients will no longer be able to locate the service because they will be referencing an old location.

Note The URL structures discussed in this section refer to more general usage of REST. When dealing with Web services, as you will see in the examples throughout this chapter, URLs are not always provided in the XML response. Sometimes you may receive identifiers for resources that can be used with a different service to locate the actual resource or more additional information pertaining to the resource.

When choosing a URL for resources, you need to make sure it is descriptive but not overly descriptive. It should be obvious based on the URI what the resource is or provides. Making it overly descriptive in nature limits future extensibility. For instance, suppose you are creating a service to provide information about automobiles. In particular, you are currently providing information about Fords. This is one possible URL:

`http://www.example.org/FordAutos`

You can differentiate different makes of Fords by using further pathing in the URL:

`http://www.example.org/FordAutos/escort`
`http://www.example.org/FordAutos/explorer`

Down the line, say you decide to add some manufacturers; now you have a problem. Of course, you can create similar structures like this:

`http://www.example.org/ChevyAutos`
`http://www.example.org/NissanAutos`

However, structurally this is not too intuitive. A much better structure is to use a structure such as this:

`http://www.example.org/auto/Ford`
`http://www.example.org/auto/Chevy`
`http://www.example.org/auto/Nissan`

The entry point is of course `http://www.example.org/auto`. Although not critical when creating a service, it is a good idea to put some thought into its structure prior to making it publicly accessible.

When using a fixed URI, you need to think about how to handle API versioning. It's inevitable that eventually changes will be made and you will require a new version, so this is something to plan for in advance. You can handle this in a few ways based on personal preference. One way is to pass the version number as a parameter in the query string. There is no specification on how you have to do this, so the parameter name and value are completely up to you. For example:

```
http://www.example.org/auto/Ford?apiver=1.0
http://www.example.org/auto/Ford?apiver=2.0
```

It can also be part of the URL:

```
http://www.example.org/V1/auto/Ford
http://www.example.org/V2/auto/Ford
```

In certain cases where HTTP POST is used to call a service, you can also identify the version by some required element in an XML document:

```
<request>
   <version>1.0</version>
</request>

<request>
   <version>2.0</version>
</request>
```

No matter which method you choose to employ, handling API versioning is always something to think about ahead of time so you encounter fewer problems in the future.

Creating a REST Web Service

The easiest Web services to create are those where clients simply make requests. Because no data modifications are taking place, you need to handle only the GET method. For example, suppose you want to write a service that simply adds two integers passed by the client. This is not a very useful service, but it demonstrates the functionality nonetheless. Say you can access this fictitious service at http://www.example.com/addit. It requires two parameters, num1 and num2. If either of these parameters is absent, an error is returned in the form of an <error /> structure containing message elements citing the specific errors; otherwise, it returns a value element containing the results of the addition.

Here's the code:

```php
<?php

function generate_error($messages) {
    $error = '<error>';
    /* A message does not contain any characters invalid for element content */
    foreach ($messages AS $message) {
        $error .= '<message>'.$message.'</message>';
    }
    $error .= '</error>';
    return $error;
}
```

```php
function addit($num1, $num2) {
   $retval = '<value>';
   $retval .= $num1 + $num2;
   $retval .= '</value>';
   return $retval;
}

/* Set content type for XML */
header('Content-type: text/xml');
print '<?xml version="1.0"?>';

$errors = array();
if (isset($_GET['num1'])) {
   if (isset($_GET['num2'])) {
      print addit((int)$_GET['num1'], (int)$_GET['num2']);
   } else {
      $errors[] = 'Missing num2 parameter';
   }
} else {
   $errors[] = 'Missing num1 parameter';
   if (! isset($_GET['num2'])) {
      $errors[] = 'Missing num2 parameter';
   }
}

print generate_error($errors);
?>
```

Calling this service using the URL http://www.example.com/addit?num1=1&num2=2 results in the following data:

```
<?xml version="1.0"?>
<value>3</value>
```

Clearly this example is an overly simplified version of a Web service because services can offer a great amount of functionality. It does, however, provide a good starting point to examine a bit more complex service.

The examples from Yahoo and Amazon use the GET method for accessing their Web services. Although Yahoo's Flickr service employs POST when modifying or creating photos, I will not demonstrate how to use it in this chapter. Furthermore, Amazon uses GET exclusively for its services shown in this chapter even when creating and modifying data. To demonstrate how to effectively use GET and POST with a REST Web service, I will show how to create a service that allows the retrieval and modification of an XML file. (In reality, the data can be stored in any format as long as it is converted to and from XML format for transport.) This file simply contains content, such as paragraphs that can render an HTML page. Once you've built the service, I will demonstrate a simple client that accesses this service using GET and POST methods depending upon the desired action.

■**Caution** I haven't implemented any security in this example and have implemented only limited data checking. If following along with the example, ensure that you execute it within a controlled environment. An alternative is to expand upon this example by adding security features and additional data checking to prevent adverse effects from possible unauthorized usage.

The server portion consists of two files. The file restserver.php is used for the service and contains the publicly accessible methods doc.view, doc.add, doc.update, and doc.delete. The file myresource.xml is the XML document containing the data to be accessed and modified. These are meant to reside within an accessible directory within a Web site, and the Web server must have read/write access to the myresource.xml file. The following code shows the initial contents of the XML file. It defines an internal subset so that an ID can be defined, and it provides a root element that will contain the modifiable data.

```xml
<?xml version="1.0" encoding="UTF-8"?>
<!DOCTYPE root [
    <!ELEMENT courses (course)*>
    <!ELEMENT p (#PCDATA)>
    <!ATTLIST p ID ID #REQUIRED>
]>
<root/>
```

■**Caution** The following example is written to be executed using PHP 5.1 or newer. The DOM load() method is passing the options parameter to default DTD attributes and to create IDs. To use this code under PHP 5.0, you must set either the resolveExternals property or the validateOnParse property to TRUE for $doc in the getResource() function prior to loading the XML document.

The code for the server is a bit longer than the XML file:

```php
<?php
/* Filename for the XML data - must be read/writable by Web server */
$resource_filename = 'myresource.xml';

/* Generic error returned when problem encountered */
function get_error() {
    /* includes prologue as the value returned is sent directly to the client */
    return '<?xml version="1.0"?><error code="-1">Invalid Request</error>';
}
```

```php
/* Load the XML document from file system, and make sure IDs are properly handled */
function getResource() {
    $doc = new DOMDocument();
    /* The following call uses the optional options parameter available
       only in PHP 5.1 and higher */
    if ($doc->load($GLOBALS['resource_filename'], LIBXML_DTDATTR)) {
        return $doc;
    }
    return NULL;
}


/* Add a new p element using ID $id with the contents $value.
   If $id already exists in document do not add new content */
function addResource($id, $value) {
    if ($doc = getResource()) {
        if (($element = $doc->getElementById($id)) == NULL) {
            $element = $doc->documentElement->appendChild($doc->createElement('p',
                                                                       $value));
            $element->setAttribute('ID', $id);
            if ($doc->save($GLOBALS['resource_filename'])) {
                return $doc->saveXML();
            }
        }
    }
    return get_error();
}


/* Update or delete an existing p element based on $id.
   If $id does not exist in document return generic error */
function updateResource($id, $value, $isdel = FALSE) {
    if ($doc = getResource()) {
        if ($element = $doc->getElementById($id)) {
            if ($isdel) {
                $element->parentNode->removeChild($element);
            } else {
                while($element->firstChild) {
                    $element->removeChild($element->firstChild);
                }
                $element->appendChild($doc->createTextNode($value));
            }
            if ($doc->save($GLOBALS['resource_filename'])) {
                return $doc->saveXML();
            }
        }
    }
    return get_error();
}
```

```
$action = '';

/* Set content type for XML */
header('Content-type: text/xml');

/* Determine action based on POST or GET */
if (isset($_POST) && isset($_POST['action']) && $_POST['action'] != 'doc.view') {
    $action = $_POST['action'];
} else if (isset($_GET) && isset($_GET['action']) &&
    $_GET['action'] == 'doc.view') {
    $action = 'doc.view';
}

/* Perform specified action as long as needed parameters have been passed */
if ($action == 'doc.add' && isset($_POST['id']) && isset($_POST['value'])) {
    echo addResource((int)$_POST['id'], $_POST['value']);
} else if ($action == 'doc.delete' && isset($_POST['id'])) {
    echo updateResource((int)$_POST['id'], NULL, TRUE);
} else if ($action == 'doc.update' && isset($_POST['id']) &&
    isset($_POST['value'])) {
    echo updateResource((int)$_POST['id'], $_POST['value']);
} else if ($action == 'doc.view') {
    /* The raw XML document could just be returned,
       but here we ensure it is proper XML before sending.
       If it is not proper, it will not load into the DOMDocument */
    if ($doc = getResource()) {
        echo $doc->saveXML();
    } else {
        echo get_error();
    }
} else {
    echo get_error();
}
?>
```

Four generic functions are defined: get_error(), which generates a basic nondescriptive error; getResource(), which loads the XML data from the file system into a DOMDocument object; addResource(), which adds a new element, as long as the ID is unique, to the XML data; and updateResource(), which updates and deletes an element based on the ID. Based on the value of the action parameter and the HTTP method used to call the service, the service will then either perform the request operation and return the new XML data structure or return the generic error message, indicating a failure.

The client piece for this is extremely simple, as shown next. I have written it to be executed using PHP CLI, and it requests each of the accessible actions in sequence. It wouldn't require much additional effort to integrate it with some type of UI.

```php
<?php
/* Define remote server and path to script on remote server */
$server = 'http://localhost';
$path = '/restserver.php';

/* Function to make POST requests using PHP streams */
function make_post_request($url, $data) {
    $opts = array(
        'http'=>array('method'=>"POST", 'content'=>$data,
        'header'=>"Content-Type: application/x-www-form-urlencoded\r\n")
    );

    $context = stream_context_create($opts);
    return file_get_contents($url, FALSE, $context);
}

/* Example Get Resource */
$url = $server.$path.'?action=doc.view';

$dom = new DOMDocument();
$dom->load($url);
print $dom->saveXML()."\n";

/* Example Add Resource */
/* Select a new ID and request a new p tag be added */
$id = 5;
$value = 'Some Text';
$data = 'action=doc.add&id='.$id.'&value='.rawurlencode($value);
$url = $server.$path;
echo "Results After adding New Item:\n";
print make_post_request($url, $data)."\n";

/* Example Update Resource */
$value = 'New Modified Text';
$data = 'action=doc.update&id='.$id.'&value='.rawurlencode($value);
$url = $server.$path;
echo "Results After Editing Existing Item:\n";
print make_post_request($url, $data)."\n";

/* Example Delete Resource */
$data = 'action=doc.delete&id='.$id;
$url = $server.$path;
echo "Results After Deleting Item:\n";
print make_post_request($url, $data)."\n";
?>
```

The client makes POST requests using PHP streams and the file_get_contents() function. As you progress through the client code, the appropriate URL is created and called. Using the REST methodology, retrieving the data takes place with a simple GET call passing the appropriate parameters. The additional three calls that modify the data take place using the HTTP POST method.

Note The text being added and modified is simple text in this example, and the `rawurlencode()` function is used. In real-world applications, you must ensure that the data is handled correctly, either when passed from the client or when being handled by the server, because entities must be properly escaped before they can be added to the remote XML data document.

If you are trying this code on your own, as long as the server paths, filenames, and remote permissions have been properly set, you should see the following output:

```
<?xml version="1.0" encoding="UTF-8"?>
<!DOCTYPE root [
<!ELEMENT courses (course)*>
<!ELEMENT p (#PCDATA)>
<!ATTLIST p ID ID #REQUIRED>
]>
<root/>

Results After adding New Item:
<?xml version="1.0" encoding="UTF-8"?>
<!DOCTYPE root [
<!ELEMENT courses (course)*>
<!ELEMENT p (#PCDATA)>
<!ATTLIST p ID ID #REQUIRED>
]>
<root><p ID="5">Some Text</p></root>

Results After Editing Existing Item:
<?xml version="1.0" encoding="UTF-8"?>
<!DOCTYPE root [
<!ELEMENT courses (course)*>
<!ELEMENT p (#PCDATA)>
<!ATTLIST p ID ID #REQUIRED>
]>
<root><p ID="5">New Modified Text</p></root>

Results After Deleting Item:
<?xml version="1.0" encoding="UTF-8"?>
<!DOCTYPE root [
<!ELEMENT courses (course)*>
<!ELEMENT p (#PCDATA)>
<!ATTLIST p ID ID #REQUIRED>
]>
<root/>
```

The document has gone through three different iterations to end up in the same state it was prior to calling the client code.

The following sections will cover some REST-based Web services found in the real world. Yahoo and Amazon are just two of many companies and organizations providing publicly accessible Web services. The examples in the next sections will show only a small subset of functionality found in a few of the services. Using the ideas and techniques presented, you should have no problems expanding the examples or even trying some of the other services these companies offer.

Introducing the Yahoo Web Services

Yahoo provides a variety of Web services at http://developer.yahoo.net/, from searching the Web to interfacing with Flickr (Yahoo's photo-sharing community). Using REST, you can easily add integration for them within a Web page or larger application. Although several services are available, this chapter will demonstrate how to perform a Web search (http://developer. yahoo.net/search/web/) and how to perform a product search (http://developer.yahoo.net/ shopping/V1/productSearch.html). Using the ideas and techniques presented in the examples, it is quite easy to apply them to access other offered services. It is important to read the documentation for a particular service to understand the different parameters and results used for a particular service.

■**Note** To utilize the Web services offered by Yahoo, you must be a registered user and obtain an application ID (from http://api.search.yahoo.com/webservices/register_application) that uniquely identifies the application accessing the service.

An application ID is required to access the services provided by Yahoo. This allows application usage to be tracked but is not used to limit access. Access is controlled based on IP address. The Flickr service, which is not covered in this chapter, requires its own API key. Although a lot of functionality does not require authentication, to upload photos you must also register for an API secret key (at http://www.flickr.com/services/api/registered_keys.gne) once you have your API key.

Results

As previously mentioned, Flickr returns its own result structures, so the structure presented here does not pertain to that service. The majority of the remaining services use a ResultSet structure. Although the default namespace and schemas may vary between services, they all return a document with a ResultSet element as the document element. This element also contains three common attributes, though you can use additional attributes for different services. For example:

```
<ResultSet totalResultsAvailable="1285" totalResultsReturned="5"
        firstResultPosition="1">
  <-- Zero or more Result Elements -->
  <Result>
     <!-- Result Content -->
  </Result>
</ResultSet>
```

The ResultSet element will always contain the attributes totalResultsAvailable, totalResultsReturned, and firstResultPosition. As their names indicate, they provide the total number of results available from the query as well as the total number of results returned in the XML document. The firstResultPosition attribute indicates the position of the first Result element in relation to the total number of available results. Based on the previous structure, the query resulted in a total of 1,285 hits where 5 have been returned in the resulting XML document and where the first Result element represents the first result from the 1,285 results. This means the ResultSet element contains 5 Result child elements where the 5th element relates to the 5th result from 1,285. The structure of the Result element depends upon the service being called and is documented in each of the APIs from Yahoo.

Web Search

Yahoo provides a variety of search services, including audio, video, and Web searches. This example will focus on performing a Web search, but you can find additional information about performing other types of searches at http://developer.yahoo.net/search/index.html. Although the URL to access the different searches is different, the methods and techniques that will be demonstrated here are the same. The APIs, made up of the different parameters and result structures, are the only things to be aware of when using any of these other services. The developer site provides documentation for the APIs for all the available services.

The Yahoo Web Search service allows you to integrate an application with the Yahoo search engine. Just like performing a search using your browser, programmatically you can make remote calls to the Yahoo Web service, process the resulting XML document, and use the results directly in your application. For instance, you could make a custom user interface that allows a search and displays the results in your own format. You can find additional information for this service at http://developer.yahoo.net/search/web/V1/webSearch.html.

All interaction with the Web search is performed using HTTP GET calls, which are made against the following URL:

http://api.search.yahoo.com/WebSearchService/V1/webSearch

To make a request, parameters indicate the criteria and options used to perform the search. At a minimum, you need the application ID, specified by the appid parameter, and the search terms, specified by the query parameter, to avoid generating an error. Table 17-2 describes the acceptable parameters.

Table 17-2. *Web Search Request Parameters*

Parameter	Type/Value	Description
appid	string	Your registered Yahoo application ID. This is a request parameter.
query	string	Terms on which to search. This is a required parameter.
type	all/any/phrase	This value indicates the type of search. The default value returns results containing all query terms. The value any returns results containing one or more query terms. The value phrase returns results matching the query terms as a phrase.
results	integer	The number of results to return. The default value is 10, and 100 is the maximum.
start	integer	The starting position of the results to be returned. The finishing position (start + results - 1) cannot exceed 1,000. The default value is 1.
format	any/html/msword/ pdf/ppt/rss/txt/ xls	Specifies the kind of file for which to search. The default value, any, indicating any file type, is used when nothing is specified.
adult_ok	No value or 1	When the value 1 is passed, results containing adult content can be returned.
similar_ok	No value or 1	When the value 1 is passed, multiple results with similar content can be returned.
language	string	The language, as defined in the Yahoo documentation, in which the results are written. The default value is en.
country	string	The country code, as defined in the Yahoo documentation, for the country in which the Web site is located.
site	string	A domain to which to restrict your searches. Up to a maximum of 30 values, each specified by its own parameter, can be used. When omitted, searches are not restricted to any domain.
subscription	string	Any subscriptions to premium content that should also be searched. You can submit multiple values, and you can find supported subscription codes in the Yahoo documentation.
license	any/cc_any/ cc_commercial/ cc_modifiable	The Creative Commons license under which the contents are licensed. The default value any is used when nothing is supplied. You can specify multiple values using multiple parameters.

Because the service is called by a simple GET request, it is easy to see what the structure of a resulting search request looks like. Using the file_get_contents() function, you can query the service for the term *php web services*, returning only a single result record and only those in English. The code in Listing 17-3 demonstrates how to make this query and print the resulting XML to the output.

Listing 17-3. *Example Querying Web Search Service*

```php
<?php
/* This is the application ID you registered with Yahoo */
$appid = "<your Yahoo! application id>";

/* URL to Web Search service */
$url = 'http://api.search.yahoo.com/WebSearchService/V1/webSearch';

/* The query is separate here because the terms must be encoded. */
$url .= '?query='.rawurlencode('php web services');

/* Complete the URL adding the App ID, limit to 1 result and only English results */
$url .= "&appid=$appid&results=1&language=en";

print file_get_contents($url);
?>
```

Assuming you have correctly set the application ID, $appid, and did not encounter any unexpected errors, you should receive the following output. Note that the output has been formatted for display purposes. Specifically, I have added the line feeds and indentations for readability.

```xml
<?xml version="1.0" encoding="UTF-8"?>
<ResultSet xmlns:xsi="http://www.w3.org/2001/XMLSchema-instance"
          xmlns="urn:yahoo:srch"
          xsi:schemaLocation="urn:yahoo:srch
http://api.search.yahoo.com/WebSearchService/V1/WebSearchResponse.xsd"
          totalResultsAvailable="4376512" totalResultsReturned="1"
          firstResultPosition="1">
   <Result>
      <Title>ASPN : Web Services : Simple Web Services API</Title>
      <Summary>... Perl Web Services. PHP Web Services. Python Web Services ... Go
ogle Search Modules. Reference. PHP Web Services Quickstart ...</Summary>
      <Url>http://aspn.activestate.com/ASPN/WebServices/SWSAPI/phptut</Url>
      <ClickUrl>http://rds.yahoo.com/SIG=12qmiikdg/EXP=1130551351/**http%3A%2F%2Fa
spn.activestate.com%2FASPN%2FWebServices%2FSWSAPI%2Fphptut</ClickUrl>
      <ModificationDate>1127977200</ModificationDate>
      <MimeType>text/html</MimeType>
      <Cache>
         <Url>http://rds.yahoo.com/SIG=19gaac6ij/EXP=1130551351/**http%3A%2F%2F216.
109.125.130%2Fsearch%2Fcache%3Fei%3DUTF-8%26eo%3DUTF-8%26ac%3D0%26n%3D1%26b%3D1%
26va%3Dphp%2Bweb%2Bservices%26vm%3Dr%26fl%3D1%26vl%3Dlang_en%26u%3Daspn.activest
ate.com%2FASPN%2FWebServices%2FSWSAPI%2Fphptut%26w%3Dphp%2Bservices%26d%3DEQG5K2
FULnbk%26icp%3D1%26.intl%3Dus</Url>
         <Size>18495</Size>
      </Cache>
   </Result>
</ResultSet>
<!-- ws01.search.re2.yahoo.com uncompressed Thu Oct 27 19:02:31 PDT 2005 -->
```

The results from the Web search are fairly straightforward. The element names are descriptive so it's easy to deduce what each of the elements is used for. To aid in your understanding of the results, Table 17-3 describes the elements found within a Result element.

Table 17-3. *Web Search* Result *Elements*

Element	Description
Title	The title of the Web page
Summary	Summary text associated with the Web page
Url	The URL for the Web page that can be used for display purposes
ClickUrl	The URL for linking to the page
MimeType	The MIME type of the page
ModificationDate	The date the page was last modified, in Unix time-stamp format
Cache	An element containing a URL element indicating the URL of the cached result and a Size element specifying its size in bytes

Now that you have an idea of how the service is called and what will be returned, it is quite easy to integrate this using any of the XML extensions in PHP. For example, once you have built the query, you can query the service and load the resulting XML into an object using a single SimpleXML call. Once you have done this, the SimpleXML interface provides easy access to the underlying results, as shown in Listing 17-4.

Listing 17-4. *Using SimpleXML to Query the Web Search Service*

```php
<?php
/* This is the application ID you registered with Yahoo */
$appid = "<your Yahoo! application id>";

/* URL to Web Search service */
$url = 'http://api.search.yahoo.com/WebSearchService/V1/webSearch';

/* The query is separate here because the terms must be encoded. */
$url .= '?query='.rawurlencode('php5 xml');

/* Complete the URL adding App ID, limit to 5 results and only English results */
$url .= "&appid=$appid&results=5&language=en";

$sxe = simplexml_load_file($url);

/* Check for number of results returned */
if ((int)$sxe['totalResultsReturned'] > 0) {
   /* Loop through each result and output title, url and modification date */
   foreach ($sxe->Result AS $result) {
      print 'Title: '.$result->Title."\n";
      print 'Url: '.$result->Url."\n";
      print 'Mod Date: '.date ('M d Y', (int)$result->ModificationDate)."\n\n";
   }
}
?>
```

The code to query the Web service in Listing 17-4 is similar to that of the code in Listing 17-3. The only real differences are that the query has been changed to search for the terms *php5* and *xml*, asking for five results, and that SimpleXML is being used to process the results. This time something actually happens with the resulting XML document. SimpleXML loops through each of the Result elements and outputs the contents of the Title, Url, and ModificationDate elements. The resulting output should look similar to the following:

```
Title: Zend Technologies - PHP 5 In Depth - XML in PHP 5 - What's New?
Url: http://www.zend.com/php5/articles/php5-xmlphp.php
Mod Date: Oct 29 2005

Title: Workshop: XML in PHP5
Url: http://php5.bitflux.org/phpconf2004
Mod Date: Mar 05 2005

Title: XML with PHP5 - encoding
Url: http://www.topxml.com/forum/fb.asp?m=1470
Mod Date: Oct 26 2005

Title: XML with PHP5 - encoding
Url: http://www.topxml.com/forum/m_1470/printable.htm
Mod Date: Oct 18 2005

Title: XML in PHP5: An in-depth look into advanced XML features
Url: http://slides.bitflux.ch/phpconf2003
Mod Date: Oct 10 2005
```

As clearly demonstrated, using REST to interface with the Yahoo Web Search service is not much different from working with XML from files. The difference is just that the file in this case is a remote service where parameters are being passed. Once the results are returned, you can handle them in the same manner you handle any other XML results using the extension of your choice.

The next example will demonstrate how to access the Yahoo Product Search service. Though accessing the service is not much more difficult than accessing the Yahoo Web Search service, the ResultSet can be a bit more complicated.

Shopping

Performing a shopping search on Yahoo allows you to search matching products, see specific offers from merchants, view user ratings, and compare products. Through the various shopping Web services that Yahoo provides, it is also possible to perform these actions programmatically. The example in this section will demonstrate how to perform product searches using the Yahoo Product Search service. You can find additional information and documentation for this service at http://developer.yahoo.net/shopping/V1/productSearch.html. The service itself, which is the URL you will be making your requests against, is at the following location:

```
http://api.shopping.yahoo.com/ShoppingService/V1/productSearch
```

The simplest case for a product search is a basic search using only query terms. Just like Yahoo's Web interface, the service also allows products to be searched by price range, department, and merchant. Table 17-4 describes the available parameters for use with the service.

Table 17-4. *Product Search Request Parameters*

Parameter	Type/Value	Description
appid	string	Your registered Yahoo application ID. This is a request parameter.
query	string	Terms on which to search. This is a required parameter.
results	integer	The number of results to return. The default value is 10, and 50 is the maximum.
start	integer	The starting position of the results to be returned. The finishing position (start + results - 1) cannot exceed 1,000. The default value is 1.
merchantid	integer	If specified, returns only products from a specified merchant.
highestprice	float	Sets the maximum price (in USD) for products to be returned.
lowestprice	float	Sets the minimum price (in USD) for products to be returned.
sort	relevance/price	Determines the sorting of the results. The default value relevance sorts by relevance; price sorts by price from lowest to highest.
department	integer	Sets the department to search for products in as defined in the list at http://developer.yahoo.net/shopping/departments.html.

If you look closely at this table, you will most likely notice that in order to search within a particular merchant, you need the merchant ID, passed with the merchantid parameter. This is not something you normally will have the first time you perform a query. This value is normally obtained from within the result of querying this service or one of the other applicable shopping services.

The structure of the resulting document depends upon how specific the query searched upon was. It still contains the ResultSet and individual Result elements, but the content of the Result elements can be either a Catalog element, whose structure is broken out in Table 17-5, or an Offer element, as shown in Table 17-6.

Table 17-5. Catalog *Response Elements*

Element	Description
Url	The URL for the corresponding catalog page on Yahoo Shopping
ProductName	The name of the product
PriceFrom	The lowest price (in U.S. dollars) for the product in this catalog
PriceTo	The highest price (in U.S. dollars) for the product in this catalog
Thumbnail	The URL of a product thumbnail image and its height and width in pixels
Summary	A short description of the product
Description	A longer description of the product
UserRating	An enclosing tag for user rating information for this product

Element	Description
MaxRating	A value from 1 (worst) to 5 (best) representing the maximum rating given to this product by a user
NumRatings	The number of users who have rated this product
AverageRating	A value from 1 (worst) to 5 (best) representing the average rating given to this product by a user
RatingUrl	The URL to the ratings page for this product on Yahoo Shopping
CreateRatingUrl	The URL to the page for posting reviews of this product on Yahoo Shopping
SpecificationList	Contains product specifications in key/value pairs
Specification	Contains an individual key/value specification pair
SpecificationLabel	Contains the label for the specification
SpecificationValue	Contains the value for the specification

For example, if you performed a product search with the term *linksys* and only the second result was returned using the following code:

```php
<?php
/* This is the application ID you registered with Yahoo */
$appid = "<your Yahoo! application id>";

/* URL to Product Search service */
$url = 'http://api.shopping.yahoo.com/ShoppingService/V1/productSearch';

/* The query is separate here because the terms must be encoded. */
$url .= '?query='.rawurlencode(' linksys ');

/* Complete the URL with App ID, limit to 1 result and start at second record */
$url .= "&appid=$appid&results=1&start=2";

print file_get_contents($url);
?>
```

the resulting output would be the following XML document (note that it has been formatted for easier readability):

```xml
<?xml version="1.0" encoding="ISO-8859-1"?>
<ResultSet xmlns:xsi="http://www.w3.org/2001/XMLSchema-instance"
           xmlns="urn:yahoo:prods"
           xsi:schemaLocation="urn:yahoo:prods
 http://api.shopping.yahoo.com/shoppingservice/v1/productsearch.xsd"
           totalResultsAvailable="13640" firstResultPosition="2"
           totalResultsReturned="1">
   <Result>
     <Catalog ID="1990338714">
       <Url><![CDATA[http://shopping.yahoo.com/p:Linksys%20Instant%20Broadband%20
```

```
EtherFast%20Cable%2FDSL%20Router:1990338714]]></Url>
        <ProductName><![CDATA[Linksys Instant Broadband EtherFast Cable/DSL Router
]]></ProductName>
        <PriceFrom>39.99</PriceFrom>
        <PriceTo>61.61</PriceTo>
        <Thumbnail>
            <Url><![CDATA[http://us.f3.yahoofs.com/shopping/3029653/simg_t_ti18804jp
g70?rm____DM3g.XsS6]]></Url>
            <Height>53</Height>
            <Width>70</Width>
        </Thumbnail>
        <Description><![CDATA[Linksys, a provider of networking hardware for the s
mall/medium business (SMB), small office/home office (SOHO), and enterprise mark
ets and broadband networking hardware for the home, has announced the new EtherF
ast Cable/DSL Router. The first in the new Instant Broadband series, this Linksy
s broadband router will enable home or office users to connect their computers t
o a cable or DSL modem and securely share Internet access and perform networking
 tasks such as file and printer sharing. The built-in hardware firewall gives us
ers the security of sharing files without fear of intruders hacking into the net
work. ]]></Description>
        <Summary><![CDATA[Ethernet, Fast Ethernet ...]]></Summary>
        <UserRating>
            <MaxRating>5</MaxRating>
            <NumRatings>10</NumRatings>
            <AverageRating>4.0</AverageRating>
            <RatingUrl><![CDATA[http://shopping.yahoo.com/p:Linksys%20Instant%20Broa
dband%20EtherFast%20Cable%2FDSL%20Router:1990338714:page=user-reviews]]></Rating
Url>
            <CreateRatingUrl><![CDATA[http://shopping.yahoo.com/p:Linksys%20Instant%
20Broadband%20EtherFast%20Cable%2FDSL%20Router:1990338714:page=post-reviews]]></
CreateRatingUrl>
        </UserRating>
        <SpecificationList>
            <Specification>
                <SpecificationLabel>
                    <![CDATA[Networking Standards]]>
                </SpecificationLabel>
                <SpecificationValue>
                    <![CDATA[Ethernet, Fast Ethernet]]>
                </SpecificationValue>
            </Specification>
        </SpecificationList>
        </Catalog>
    </Result>
</ResultSet>
```

The catalog result is a more generalized result. Along with product information, it shows the lowest and highest prices found for the product, as well as the user rating information. An offer is a bit more specific, as described in Table 17-6.

Table 17-6. Offer *Response Elements*

Element	Description
Field	Contains the description.
Offer	Contains the data for an individual merchant offering of a product.
Url	Contains the URL for the corresponding catalog page on Yahoo Shopping.
ProductName	Contains the name of the product.
Price	Contains the price of the product in USD.
Thumbnail	Contains the URL of a product thumbnail image and its height and width in pixels.
Summary	Contains a short description of the product.
Merchant	Contains a Name element with the name of the merchant making this offer. The Merchant element also has an ID attribute specifying the merchant ID.

If you used a more specific query, such as *Linksys Wireless-G Broadband Router WRT54G Router*, and the second result from the resulting records is returned, the Result element would contain an Offer element, broken out in Table 17-6, instead. For example:

```php
<?php
/* This is the application ID you registered with Yahoo */
$appid = "<your Yahoo! application id>";

/* URL to Product Search service */
$url = 'http://api.shopping.yahoo.com/ShoppingService/V1/productSearch';

/* The query is separate here because the terms must be encoded. */
$url .= '?query='.
        rawurlencode('Linksys Wireless-G Broadband Router WRT54G Router');

/* Complete the URL with App ID, limit to 1 result and start at second record */
$url .= "&appid=$appid&results=1&start=2";

print file_get_contents($url);
?>
```

The output this time is much different. In this case, the result is an offer, which is specific to a merchant.

```xml
<?xml version="1.0" encoding="ISO-8859-1"?>
<ResultSet xmlns:xsi="http://www.w3.org/2001/XMLSchema-instance"
        xmlns="urn:yahoo:prods"
        xsi:schemaLocation="urn:yahoo:prods
```

```
http://api.shopping.yahoo.com/shoppingservice/v1/productsearch.xsd"
            totalResultsAvailable="155" firstResultPosition="2"
            totalResultsReturned="1">
  <Result>
     <Offer>
        <Url><![CDATA[http://store.yahoo.com/i-software/109246.html]]></Url>
        <ProductName><![CDATA[Wireless-G Broadband Router [ Linksys WRT54G Wireles
s ]]]></ProductName>
        <Price>65.40</Price>
        <Thumbnail>
           <Url><![CDATA[http://us.f3.yahoofs.com/shopping/mcid17_37651/simg_t_tiso
ftware_1869_19594097.th?rm____Ddq1xgH7W]]></Url>
           <Height>64</Height>
           <Width>70</Width>
        </Thumbnail>
        <Summary><![CDATA[Wireless-G is the upcoming 54Mbps wireless networking st
andard that's almost the new screaming fast Wireless-G standard as your needs gro
w. The Linksys Wireless-G Broadband Router is really three devices in one box. F
irst, there's the Wireless...]]></Summary>
        <Merchant ID="1009413">
           <Name><![CDATA[BITS.com]]></Name>
        </Merchant>
     </Offer>
  </Result>
</ResultSet>
```

As you can see, only some brief product information is included, and the price within this data is specific for the merchant identified in the Merchant element. If you recall the input parameters from Table 17-4, the merchantid parameter takes an integer identifying the merchant to the queried. Using the ID attribute from the Merchant element is one way to retrieve such an identifier. You could also use this identifier to search for additional information about the merchant using the Yahoo Merchant Search service, which is also a part of the Yahoo Shopping service.

There is a reason the second result was queried. A mix of Catalog and Offer elements will often return the results. After running a few queries, it appears that the catalog results are returned before the offer results, but this is not something I can say for sure. The more generic the query, the more number of catalog results. Likewise, the more specific the query, the fewer number of catalog results. Take the prior example, for instance; when the query *Linksys Wireless-G Broadband Router WRT54G Router* was used, the first result was actually a Catalog result, and the remaining Offer results were specific to individual merchants. The second result was chosen in order to skip over the initial Catalog result because only one was contained in that result set and to demonstrate the output of an Offer.

To demonstrate how to work with mixed results, I will show an example using the XSL extension. This example, shown in Listing 17-5, is quite different from those you have previously seen using the XSL extension. In this case, the XML document being passed to the XSLTProcessor contains a single element whose content is the request (URL) to the Yahoo Product Search service. XSL uses this URL to make the request, receive the resulting document, and transform the results into HTML output. For the best results, the code should run under a Web server and be called from a browser. The code expects the style sheet yahooprod.xsl to reside in the same directory.

This example also uses hard-coded values for the query terms, but you can easily extend it to be passed from a form or as parameters. If you make modifications along these lines, make sure you properly encode the terms and query. Notice that the parameter separators have been coded as & rather than &. You must also be careful with the terms themselves. The example here performs a simple rawurlencode. This is not enough if additional special characters, such as &, appear in the search terms.

Listing 17-5. *Using XSL to Transform Product Search*

```php
<?php
/* This is the application ID you registered with Yahoo */
$appid = "<your Yahoo! application id>";

/* URL to Product Search service */
$url = 'http://api.shopping.yahoo.com/ShoppingService/V1/productSearch';

/* The query is separate here because the terms must be encoded. */
$url .= '?query='.
        rawurlencode('Linksys Wireless-G Broadband Router WRT54G Router');

/* Complete the URL with App ID, limit to 5 results*/
$url .= "&amp;appid=$appid&amp;results=5";

/* Create document, and set url to url document element */
$dom = new DomDocument();
$dom->appendChild(new DOMElement('url', $url));

/* Load the style sheet yahooprod.xsl from Listing 17-6. */
$xsl = new DOMDocument();
$xsl->load('yahooprod.xsl');

/* Have the style sheet make the request and transform the results */
$proc = new xsltprocessor();
$proc->importStylesheet($xsl);
print $proc->transformToXML($dom);
?>
```

Listing 17-6 shows the style sheet. First, the results from the Yahoo services contain default namespaces. If you recall from dealing with namespace in XPath and XSL, you need to register namespaces in some manner. In this case, the namespace is declared in the xsl:stylesheet element. The prefix prod has been added and refers to the urn:yahoo:prod namespace, which comes from the data being returned by the service. All elements referenced from the result document must be prefixed with the prod prefix in order to be accessed.

Listing 17-6. *XSL Template for Product Search:* yahooprod.xsl

```
<xsl:stylesheet xmlns:xsl="http://www.w3.org/1999/XSL/Transform"
                xmlns:prod="urn:yahoo:prods" version="1.0">
<!-- urn:yahoo:prods namespace added with prefix prod matching the default namespace
     of result document from the Yahoo Product Search Service -->
  <xsl:output method="html"/>

  <xsl:template match="prod:Thumbnail">
    <br />
    <img>
      <xsl:attribute name="src">
        <xsl:value-of select="prod:Url"/>
      </xsl:attribute>
      <xsl:attribute name="height">
        <xsl:value-of select="prod:Height"/>
      </xsl:attribute>
      <xsl:attribute name="width">
        <xsl:value-of select="prod:Width"/>
      </xsl:attribute></img>
  </xsl:template>

  <xsl:template match="prod:Catalog">
    <p><b>Catalog</b><br />
    <xsl:apply-templates select="prod:Thumbnail"/><br />
    Product: <a>
      <xsl:attribute name="href">
        <xsl:value-of select="prod:Url"/>
      </xsl:attribute>
      <xsl:value-of select="prod:ProductName"/>
    </a><br />
    Price Range: <xsl:value-of select="prod:PriceFrom"/> -
                 <xsl:value-of select="prod:PriceTo"/>
    </p>
  </xsl:template>

  <xsl:template match="prod:Offer">
    <p><b>Offer</b><br />
    Product: <a>
      <xsl:attribute name="href">
        <xsl:value-of select="prod:Url"/>
      </xsl:attribute>
      <xsl:value-of select="prod:ProductName"/>
    </a><br />
    Merchant: <xsl:value-of select="prod:Merchant/prod:Name"/><br />
    Price: <xsl:value-of select="prod:Price"/>
    </p>
  </xsl:template>
```

```
<!-- Entry point -->
<xsl:template match="/">
    <html>
        <body>
            <!-- Apply templates on document pulled from url defined
                 in passed in DOMDocument.
            We are only interested in selecting the Result elements -->
            <xsl:apply-templates
                select="document(./url)/prod:ResultSet/prod:Result"/>
        </body>
    </html>
</xsl:template>
</xsl:stylesheet>
```

The other interesting aspect of this example is how the request is made. The main entry match point calls xsl:apply-templates, passing the document() function. Using the content of the url element from the DOMDocument object created in code, the style sheet makes the request and then, with the resulting document, applies the templates to the Result elements. Calling this from a browser results in output similar to that shown in Figure 17-1.

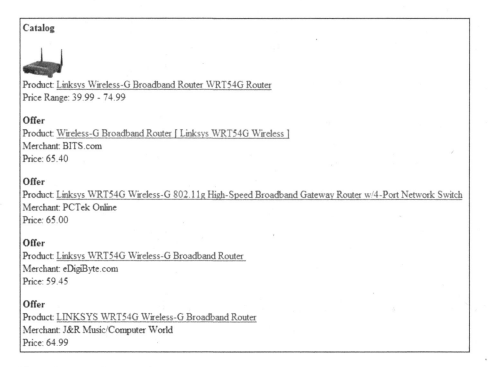

Figure 17-1. *Product search output*

Standard Errors

One topic I haven't covered yet is what happens when an error is encountered. Things don't always work exactly as planned, and eventually a request will result in an error for one reason or another. The majority of the Yahoo Web services use a standard error format. (However, Flickr has its own response format that includes errors so does not use this standard error format.) Depending upon the error, you will either receive an HTTP error code, which will be one of the codes listed in Table 17-7, or receive an XML error document, illustrated in Listing 17-7. Depending upon how the request is made, such as making the request directly with an XML extension or the file_get_contents() function, an HTTP error will result in a PHP warning.

Table 17-7. *Error Codes*

Error Code	Description
400	Bad request. The parameters passed to the service did not match as expected. The Message element should tell you what was missing or incorrect.
403	Forbidden. You do not have permission to access this resource or are over your rate limit.
500	Service unavailable. An internal problem prevented Yahoo from returning data to you.

The XML document in Listing 17-7 is a generic structure. When an error is returned, the Message element contains the actual text for the encountered error.

Listing 17-7. *Error Message Structure*

```
<Error xmlns="urn:yahoo:api">
    The following errors were detected:
  <Message>error message</Message>
</Error>
```

■**Note** In cases where a 400 code is returned, an XML error document will not be accessible because the PHP streams will automatically generate a warning and not return an error document.

Introducing the Amazon Web Services

Amazon also provides a number of accessible Web services. You can find more information within the Amazon site (http://www.amazon.com/):

- The Alexa Web Information Service allows the data collected by the Alexa Web crawler and its usage analysis to be remotely and programmatically accessed.

- The Amazon Simple Queue Service offers hosted queues that can be used to buffer messages between distributed applications.

- The Amazon Historical Pricing service provides access to more than three years of sales data.

- The Amazon E-Commerce Service, which I will demonstrate in this section, provides much of the functionality found within the Amazon Web site. You can search products, you can retrieve personal lists such as wish lists or wedding registries, you can access seller information, and you can control remote shopping carts.

Before accessing the Amazon services, you must register with the Amazon Web Services Program to receive an access key ID. This key is passed with every request made to the services through the AWSAccessKeyId parameter and not only controls access to the service but also allows usage to be tracked. You can obtain a key by registering at the following URL:

```
http://www.amazon.com/gp/aws/registration/registration-form.html
```

Registering for a key will allow you to try the examples provided in this section, which consist of an item search (similar to a product search using the Yahoo service) and some remote shopping cart functionality. The URL you need to use to access the Web service depends upon your locale and is broken down by country code, as shown in Table 17-8.

Table 17-8. *Amazon E-commerce Service URL by Locale*

Locale	URL
Amazon.com (US)	http://webservices.amazon.com/onca/xml?Service=AWSECommerceService
Amazon.co.uk (UK)	http://webservices.amazon.co.uk/onca/xml?Service=AWSECommerceService
Amazon.de (DE)	http://webservices.amazon.de/onca/xml?Service=AWSECommerceService
Amazon.co.jp (JP)	http://webservices.amazon.co.jp/onca/xml?Service=AWSECommerceService
Amazon.fr (FR)	http://webservices.amazon.fr/onca/xml?Service=AWSECommerceService
Amazon.ca (CA)	http://webservices.amazon.ca/onca/xml?Service=AWSECommerceService

The examples in the following sections will use the URL for the United States, http://webservices.amazon.com/onca/xml?Service=AWSECommerceService. Feel free to change this to a URL from Table 17-8 that matches your locale.

Introducing the Error Format

When errors are encountered, the response contains an Errors structure. Depending upon the type of error or errors, this structure can be the document element or can be contained further within the resulting XML document. In both cases, however, the actual Error structure is the same:

```
<Errors>
   <Error>
      <Code><!-- Error Code defined in Amazon Web Services documentation --></Code>
      <Message><!-- Error Message defined in Amazon documentation --></Message>
   </Error>
   <!-- Any number of Error elements: One per error -->
</Errors>
```

For instance, when making an invalid request to the service, such as omitting the Service parameter used to identify which service is being accessed, the error is returned as a top-level error. This means that the returned XML document is an Errors structure. The request http://webservices.amazon.com/onca/xml? results in the following response:

```
<?xml version="1.0" encoding="UTF-8"?>
<Errors>
   <Error>
      <Code>AWS.MissingServiceParameter</Code>
      <Message>Your request is missing the Service parameter.
      Please add the Service parameter to your request and retry.</Message>
   </Error>
</Errors>
```

When the error is related to some issue concerning more specified functionality, such as the omission of a parameter required for an operation, the Errors structure appears deeper within the resulting XML document. For example, when performing an ItemSearch and omitting your access key ID, such as when requesting http://webservices.amazon.com/onca/xml?Service=AWSECommerceService&Operation=ItemSearch, the resulting document is as follows:

```
<?xml version="1.0" encoding="UTF-8"?>
<ItemSearchResponse
             xmlns="http://webservices.amazon.com/AWSECommerceService/2005-10-05">
   <OperationRequest>
      <HTTPHeaders>
         <Header Name="UserAgent"/>
      </HTTPHeaders>
      <RequestId>1H7BW92GT4GAKMBG38DV</RequestId>
      <Arguments>
         <Argument Name="Service" Value="AWSECommerceService"/>
         <Argument Name="Operation" Value="ItemSearch"/>
      </Arguments>
      <Errors>
         <Error>
            <Code>AWS.MinimumParameterRequirement</Code>
            <Message>Your request should have atleast 1 of the following parameters:
                  AWSAccessKeyId, SubscriptionId.</Message>
         </Error>
      </Errors>
   </OperationRequest>
</ItemSearchResponse>
```

If you look toward the end of this response, you can see the Errors structure with the message indicating the access key ID is missing. Because of the differing placements of the error, it is not always so simple to determine whether the response is in error. According to the Amazon documentation, you should use XPath to query for an error. Using SimpleXML or DOM, you can do this easily:

```php
<?php
$query = 'http://webservices.amazon.com/onca/xml?Service=AWSECommerceService'.
         '&Operation=ItemSearch';

/* Example Error checking using DOM */
$dom = new DOMDocument();
$dom->formatOutput = TRUE;
$dom->load($query);
$xpath = new DOMXPath($dom);
$errors = $xpath->query('//*[local-name()="Error"]');
if ($errors && $errors->length > 0) {
   /* Dump first error */
   echo $dom->saveXML($errors->item(0));
} else {
   /* Result is valid so process */
}

/* Example Error checking using SimpleXML */
$sxe = simplexml_load_file($query);
$xpath = $sxe->xpath('//*[local-name()="Error"]');
if (is_array($xpath) && count($xpath) > 0) {
   /* Dump first error */
   echo $xpath[0]->asXML();
} else {
   /* Result is valid so process */
}
?>
```

Usually you wouldn't need such detailed examples of error detection and extraction, but in this case there is a bit of a difference depending upon where the error is positioned. When returned as a top-level error, the document does not use any namespaces. When returned within a result document, however, default namespaces come into play. Unless you are coding for a specific query, such as in this case where an ItemSearchResponse document is being returned, the default namespace varies. It depends upon the resulting document. To create a generic error-handling routine using XPath, you cannot register a namespace, so Error elements are searched by matching on their local names using the local-name() function. You run into even more problems when trying to use the xml or XMLReader extension. XPath is not an option. The only way around this is to parse the result document, expecting it to be valid and erroring out when you encounter an Errors element.

Performing an Item Search

Performing item searches with the Amazon Web service is similar to that of using Yahoo's, except that Amazon allows for quite a number of parameters. Table 17-9 lists only a subset of the parameters that are valid for this type of search.

Table 17-9. *Subset of* ItemSearch *Parameters*

Parameter	Description
Operation	The operation to perform. This parameter is required and must be set to ItemSearch to search items.
SearchIndex	The Amazon store for which to search. This parameter is required, and valid values vary by locale and are found within the API documentation.
Keywords	The keywords for which to search. When SearchIndex is set to MusicTracks, the keyword searches song titles.
Artist	Artist's name for which to search.
Author	Author's name for which to search.
Actor	Actor's name for which to search.
Director	Director's name for which to search.
Manufacturer	Manufacturer for which to search.
Publisher	Publisher for which to search.
ItemPage	Results are returned ten at a time. This value indicates which page from the result set to return. When not specified, the first ten, or all items if there are fewer than ten, are returned. Values can be from 1 to 3200.
Sort	Identifies how the results are ordered. You can find acceptable values in the API documentation, and they are based on the value of SearchIndex and your locale.
MinimumPrice	The minimum price for results to be returned. The value is specified in pennies or equivalent local currency.
MaximumPrice	The maximum price for resulting products. The value is specified in pennies or equivalent currency.
ResponseGroup	This parameter controls the resulting XML structure. The default value Small returns only limited item information. By using one of the other acceptable values specified in the API documentation, such as Medium or Large, you can return additional information such as price and image data in the resulting structure. You can specify multiple groups by supplying them as a single comma-separated value.

This also doesn't even account for the parameters that control the format and presentation. Yes, you can supply a URL to a style sheet and return the resulting output rather than XML. This is not something that I will demonstrate because by now you should be able to take the resulting XML and do that yourself.

Except for the difference in handling the errors and the different resulting XML structure, the procedure for making calls to this service is the same as when using the Yahoo services. For this reason, I will not show a complete example. Instead, I will show a simple call using DOM and the resulting document output. For example:

```php
<?php
$access_key = '&AWSAccessKeyId=<your access key id>';

$query = 'http://webservices.amazon.com/onca/xml?Service=AWSECommerceService';
$query .= $access_key;
$query .= '&Operation=ItemSearch&Keywords='.rawurlencode('linksys');
$query .= '&SearchIndex=Electronics';
```

```
$dom = new DOMDocument();
$dom->formatOutput = TRUE;
$dom->load($query);
print $dom->saveXML();
?>
```

The query that has been constructed contains the minimal amount of parameters to perform an item search of any relevance. The Service parameter has been set to AWSECommerceService. Because Amazon uses a single access point for its Web services, it is mandatory to properly indicate the particular service against which the operations should be performed. The Operation parameter, having the value ItemSearch, instructs the service that the values being passed are to be used to search for an item. The Keywords parameter contains the keywords to be used in the search. In this case, the same linksys value that was used for one of the Yahoo product searches is being used here. This allows you to compare the results from the two services using the same search criteria. Although the particular value does not need to be encoded, the rawurlencode() function is a reminder to encode any values you may be passing here. The last parameter of interest is SearchIndex. The value for this comes from a list of acceptable values as defined in the Amazon documentation. It indicates the department to be searched and is mandatory to make a request without an error. When the code is actually executed, the returned document should look similar to the one in Listing 17-8.

Note I have modified Listing 17-8 for readability. I have added formatting, and I have removed eight of the ten resulting Item elements for brevity. Your results may vary based on current search results from Amazon as well as any differences in locale.

Listing 17-8. ItemSearch *Result Document*

```
<?xml version="1.0" encoding="UTF-8"?>
<ItemSearchResponse
          xmlns="http://webservices.amazon.com/AWSECommerceService/2005-10-05">
  <OperationRequest>
    <HTTPHeaders>
      <Header Name="UserAgent"/>
    </HTTPHeaders>
    <RequestId>1YJRG7ORVP7HRZWPY57X</RequestId>
    <Arguments>
      <Argument Name="Service" Value="AWSECommerceService"/>
      <Argument Name="AWSAccessKeyId" Value="XXXXXXXXXXXXXXXXX"/>
      <Argument Name="SearchIndex" Value="Electronics"/>
      <Argument Name="Keywords" Value="linksys"/>
      <Argument Name="Operation" Value="ItemSearch"/>
    </Arguments>
    <RequestProcessingTime>0.0499119758605957</RequestProcessingTime>
  </OperationRequest>
```

```
<Items>
  <Request>
    <IsValid>True</IsValid>
    <ItemSearchRequest>
      <Keywords>linksys</Keywords>
      <SearchIndex>Electronics</SearchIndex>
    </ItemSearchRequest>
  </Request>
  <TotalResults>484</TotalResults>
  <TotalPages>49</TotalPages>
  <Item>
    <ASIN>B00007KDVI</ASIN>
    <DetailPageURL>http://www.amazon.com/exec/obidos/redirect?tag=ws%26link_co
de=xm2%26camp=2025%26creative=165953%26path=http://www.amazon.com/gp/redirect.ht
ml%253fASIN=B00007KDVI%2526tag=ws%2526lcode=xm2%2526cID=2025%2526ccmID=165953%25
26location=/o/ASIN/B00007KDVI%25253FSubscriptionId=XXXXXXXXXXX</DetailP
ageURL>
    <ItemAttributes>
      <Manufacturer>Linksys</Manufacturer>
      <ProductGroup>CE</ProductGroup>
      <Title>Linksys WRT54G Wireless-G Router</Title>
    </ItemAttributes>
  </Item>
  <Item>
    <ASIN>B0007MGG2M</ASIN>
    <DetailPageURL>http://www.amazon.com/exec/obidos/redirect?tag=ws%26link_co
de=xm2%26camp=2025%26creative=165953%26path=http://www.amazon.com/gp/redirect.ht
ml%253fASIN=B0007MGG2M%2526tag=ws%2526lcode=xm2%2526cID=2025%2526ccmID=165953%25
26location=/o/ASIN/B0007MGG2M%25253FSubscriptionId=XXXXXXXXXXX</DetailP
ageURL>
    <ItemAttributes>
      <Manufacturer>Linksys</Manufacturer>
      <ProductGroup>CE</ProductGroup>
      <Title>Linksys Compact Wireless-G Broadband Router WRT54GC</Title>
    </ItemAttributes>
  </Item>
  <!-- 8 additional Item elements omitted -->
</Items>
</ItemSearchResponse>
```

Using the Remote Shopping Cart

The operations for a remote shopping cart are actually pretty interesting. Using this functionality, it is possible to remotely create a shopping cart and add, remove, and update items
within the cart. You can also retrieve all carts within 90 days of the last access date. Using
a combination of operations available within the Amazon E-Commerce Service, such as the
item search, it is possible to create a custom Amazon shop where visitors can add items to

their carts, and when they are ready to purchase, you hand them off to Amazon for order processing. Although this might not sound worthwhile, if you happen to be an Amazon associate, you can collect referral fees for the items purchased.

The steps for working with the remote shopping cart are fairly simple:

1. Create a new cart or retrieve existing cart.

2. Add/remove/update/clear the cart.

3. Hand off to Amazon for order processing.

Cart functionality is still part of the Amazon E-Commerce Service, so the Service parameter will still be passed with the value AWSECommerceService.

■**Note** The parameter AssociateTag can be passed with all of the requests in this section. If you are an Amazon affiliate, set the value of this parameter to your associate ID. This makes sure that items are identified as having originated from your Web site and makes sure you are credited for traffic and/or sales.

Creating and Retrieving a Cart

Unless you have an existing cart, which must have been accessed within the past 90 days, you will need to create a new shopping cart. To do this, you must add at least one item to the cart during its creation. Items are referenced by an Amazon Standard Item Number (ASIN). You can find these numbers within the product Web pages as well as within the results from other searches. If you look at one of the items in Listing 17-8, you will notice that each item has an ASIN element. For instance, the last Item has the ASIN B0007MGG2M. In the case of books, the ASIN is the same as the ISBN.

So, already aware that this book has the ASIN 1590596331, I could decide to purchase a copy:

```php
<?php
$access_key = '&AWSAccessKeyId=<your Access Key ID>';

$query = 'http://webservices.amazon.com/onca/xml?Service=AWSECommerceService';
$query .= $access_key;
$query .= '&Operation=CartCreate&Item.1.ASIN=1590596331&Item.1.Quantity=1';
$query .= '&MergeCart=True';

$dom = new DOMDocument();
$dom->formatOutput = TRUE;
$dom->load($query);
print $dom->saveXML();
?>
```

The important line in this code is the last $query line. It passes the value CartCreate as the Operation parameter and adds one copy of the book to the cart. You can pass multiple items at a time, which is the reason for Item.1.ASIN and Item.1.Quantity. You supply additional items by incrementing the number 1 for each additional item. A quantity for an item is always required, and unless using an OfferListingId attribute for an Item, which is not covered here, the ASIN is also required. So, adding items take this form:

```
$query .= '&Item.2.ASIN=X&Item.2.Quantity=X&Item.3.ASIN=X&Item.3.Quantity=X';
```

where X represents either a valid ASIN or a quantity.

Note The MergeCart parameter determines how the cart is handled when the purchase is being handed over to Amazon to process. The value False sends the shopper directly to the Amazon checkout system. The value True merges the contents of this cart with anything they may have in a cart on the Amazon system. The shopper is sent to the shopping cart screen. For the United States, False can be used and is the default value for this parameter. All other locales must set this parameter to True. The example in this section uses the value True for the greatest compatibility among readers.

Excluding this additional query, the resulting XML document looks like the one in Listing 17-9.

Listing 17-9. *Response from Creating a New Cart*

```xml
<?xml version="1.0" encoding="UTF-8"?>
<CartCreateResponse xmlns="http://webservices.amazon.com/AWSECommerceService/200
5-10-05">
  <OperationRequest>
    <HTTPHeaders>
      <Header Name="UserAgent"/>
    </HTTPHeaders>
    <RequestId>1058AHG20CGW011JKHFF</RequestId>
    <Arguments>
      <Argument Name="Item.1.ASIN" Value="1590596331"/>
      <Argument Name="ResponseGroup" Value="Cart"/>
      <Argument Name="Operation" Value="CartCreate"/>
      <Argument Name="Service" Value="AWSECommerceService"/>
      <Argument Name="AWSAccessKeyId" Value="XXXXXXXXXXXX"/>
      <Argument Name="Item.1.Quantity" Value="1"/>
    </Arguments>
    <RequestProcessingTime>0.139086008071899</RequestProcessingTime>
  </OperationRequest>
  <Cart>
    <Request>
      <IsValid>True</IsValid>
      <CartCreateRequest>
        <Items>
          <Item>
            <ASIN>1590596331</ASIN>
            <Quantity>1</Quantity>
```

```
      </Item>
    </Items>
    <ResponseGroup>Cart</ResponseGroup>
  </CartCreateRequest>
</Request>
<CartId>102-9876508-1043332</CartId>
<HMAC>JCRKSBLOcCtdVdfK/dAabEwVYkE=</HMAC>
<URLEncodedHMAC>JCRKSBLOcCtdVdfK/dAabEwVYkE=</URLEncodedHMAC>
<PurchaseURL>https://www.amazon.com/gp/cart/aws-merge.html?cart-id=102-98765
08-1043332%26associate-id=ws%26hmac=JCRKSBLOcCtdVdfK/dAabEwVYkE=%26SubscriptionI
d=XXXXXXXXXXX%26MergeCart=False</PurchaseURL>
<SubTotal>
  <Amount>4499</Amount>
  <CurrencyCode>USD</CurrencyCode>
  <FormattedPrice>$44.99</FormattedPrice>
</SubTotal>
<CartItems>
  <SubTotal>
    <Amount>4499</Amount>
    <CurrencyCode>USD</CurrencyCode>
    <FormattedPrice>$44.99</FormattedPrice>
  </SubTotal>
  <CartItem>
    <CartItemId>UH08ZJLDTKO45</CartItemId>
    <ASIN>1590596331</ASIN>
    <MerchantId>ATVPDKIKX0DER</MerchantId>
    <SellerId>A2R2RITDJNW1Q6</SellerId>
    <SellerNickname>Amazon.com, LLC</SellerNickname>
    <Quantity>1</Quantity>
    <Title>Pro PHP XML and Web services</Title>
    <ProductGroup>Book</ProductGroup>
    <Price>
      <Amount>4499</Amount>
      <CurrencyCode>USD</CurrencyCode>
      <FormattedPrice>$44.99</FormattedPrice>
    </Price>
    <ItemTotal>
      <Amount>4499</Amount>
      <CurrencyCode>USD</CurrencyCode>
      <FormattedPrice>$44.99</FormattedPrice>
    </ItemTotal>
  </CartItem>
</CartItems>
  </Cart>
</CartCreateResponse>
```

This has two important pieces of information. The CartId element contains the unique identifier, 102-9876508-1043332, for this cart. The HMAC element contains a security token,

JCRKSBLOcCtdVdfK/dAabEwVYkE=, which must be used with the corresponding CartId in order to access and modify the cart contents. So, if you left your cart today and returned tomorrow, using those values you could retrieve the cart and its contents. The PurchaseURL is also another important element but, unlike the other two, is not needed to access the cart. It, rather, is the URL to send a shopper once they are ready to purchase the contents of the cart. It is not important to capture this value initially because it is accessible when you retrieve the cart or when the cart structure is returned from other operations.

```
/* Cart Id from Listing 17-9 */
$cart_id = '102-9876508-1043332';

/* HMAC from Listing 17-9 */
$hmac = 'JCRKSBLOcCtdVdfK/dAabEwVYkE=';

$query = 'http://webservices.amazon.com/onca/xml?Service=AWSECommerceService';
$query .= $access_key;
$query .= '&Operation=CartGet&CartId='.$cart_id;
$query .= '&HMAC='.$hmac;
```

Calling the query built in to the $query string will return the same document as shown in Listing 17-9. To be clear, the cart is available to be retrieved and modified up to 90 days from the last time it was accessed.

Modifying the Cart

You can modify a cart using the CartAdd, CartModify, and CartClear operations. The easiest of these functions is CartClear. This operation removes all items from the cart. The cart still remains available and can even be retrieved at a later date, but it is empty. You do need to see the contents of an empty cart, and it is assumed the operation is not going to fail, so the following uses a simple file_get_contents to make the request:

```
<?php
$access_key = '&AWSAccessKeyId=<your Access Key ID>';

$query = 'http://webservices.amazon.com/onca/xml?Service=AWSECommerceService';
$query .= $access_key;
$query .= '&Operation=CartClear&CartId=102-9876508-1043332';
$query .= '&HMAC=JCRKSBLOcCtdVdfK/dAabEwVYkE=';

file_get_contents($query);
?>
```

Adding items is also quite simple. You add them in the same fashion as when the cart was created. In fact, the only differences here are that the value of the Operation parameter is CartAdd and that the CartId and HMAC parameters must be passed:

```php
<?php
$access_key = '&AWSAccessKeyId=<your Access Key ID>';

$query = 'http://webservices.amazon.com/onca/xml?Service=AWSECommerceService';
$query .= $access_key;
$query .= '&Operation=CartAdd&CartId=102-9876508-1043332';
$query .= '&HMAC=JCRKSBLOcCtdVdfK/dAabEwVYkE=';
$query .= '&Item.1.ASIN=1590596331&Item.1.Quantity=1';

$dom = new DOMDocument();
$dom->formatOutput = TRUE;
$dom->load($query);
print $dom->saveXML();
?>
```

Again, the cart is back to the same state as that in Listing 17-9, containing one book.

The last operation is to modify the cart contents, which is handled by CartModify. This operation modifies item quantities as well as moves items between the active cart and the "save for later" area. Let's say I want to give some copies of this book away to family members. I will need another five copies. Items within the cart are identified by their CartItemId elements. Because the cart was cleared and the item re-added, the CartItemId has a different value than in the original document from Listing 17-9. In this case, the value is U2TU24TAYQ6N18. The query is almost the same as the CartAdd operation, except in this case the item is identified by the value of the CartItemId element and not by an ASIN. For example:

```php
<?php
$access_key = '&AWSAccessKeyId=<your Access Key ID>';

$query = 'http://webservices.amazon.com/onca/xml?Service=AWSECommerceService';
$query .= $access_key;
$query .= '&Operation=CartModify&CartId=102-9876508-1043332';
$query .= '&HMAC=JCRKSBLOcCtdVdfK/dAabEwVYkE=';
$query .= '&Item.1.CartItemId=U2TU24TAYQ6N18&Item.1.Quantity=6';

$dom = new DOMDocument();
$dom->formatOutput = TRUE;
$dom->load($query);
print $dom->saveXML();
?>
```

The quantity passed is the final quantity you want the item in the cart and not the number to add or subtract. Setting the value to 0 effectively removes the item from the cart. Looking at just a small subset of the resulting document, you can see it has been properly updated:

```xml
<!-- Fragment of Result Document -->
<CartItemId>U2TU24TAYQ6N18</CartItemId>
<ASIN>1590596331</ASIN>
<MerchantId>ATVPDKIKX0DER</MerchantId>
<SellerId>A2R2RITDJNW1Q6</SellerId>
```

```
<SellerNickname>Amazon.com, LLC</SellerNickname>
<Quantity>6</Quantity>
<Title>Pro PHP XML and Web services</Title>
<ProductGroup>Book</ProductGroup>
```

Handing Off the Order

Once the shopper is ready to purchase, all you need to do is send them to the URL identified by the PurchaseURL element. It is not necessary to check for this element every time a response is returned because it is easily retrievable. Simply retrieve the cart, locate the element, and retrieve its contents. For example:

```php
<?php
$access_key = '&AWSAccessKeyId=<your Access Key ID>';

$query = 'http://webservices.amazon.com/onca/xml?Service=AWSECommerceService';
$query .= $access_key;
$query .= '&Operation=CartGet&CartId=102-9876508-1043332';
$query .= '&HMAC=JCRKSBLOcCtdVdfK/dAabEwVYkE=';

$dom = new DOMDocument();
$dom->load($query);

$xpath = new DOMXPath($dom);
$purchase_url = $xpath->evaluate('string(//*[local-name()="PurchaseURL"])');

/* Send shopper to Amazon for fulfillment */
header('Location: '.$purchase_url);
?>
```

Conclusion

REST is an architectural style and not any specific standard. This chapter focused on using REST as applied to Web services. As you may have noticed, you can implement REST in a few ways, though the material presented here pertains more to what you mostly find used in the real world than what a purist view of REST is. Just like the arguments between the SOAP and REST groups about what constitutes a Web service, just as many arguments take place within the REST group about what constitutes a REST-based Web service.

Using REST tends to be easier than dealing with SOAP. You do not have to be concerned with all the complexities, like you do with WSDL. The downside is that SOAP has much more exposure than REST. It's one of those buzzwords that almost every executive knows but probably doesn't understand.

As you will see in the next chapter, SOAP does work well because it was designed explicitly for Web services, but when possible I prefer using REST to avoid having to deal with any additional complexities.

■■■

CHAPTER 18

SOAP

The introduction of PHP 5 brought forth vast improvements in XML support for developers and opened the door to numerous XML technologies. Native support for SOAP was one of these improvements. With the recent upswing in Web service usage, the two major technologies are REST-based services, which you read about in the previous chapter, and SOAP, which is what this chapter will cover. Understanding SOAP is a bit more complex than understanding REST, especially when writing servers, because you need to master several technologies. From the consumer perspective, SOAP can be easy to use.

   This chapter will explain and demonstrate how you can implement SOAP clients and SOAP servers in PHP. To do so, you will be introduced to WSDL and SOAP 1.1. By the end of this chapter, you should understand these technologies enough to consume a SOAP service as well as to write your own SOAP server.

■**Note** Much of the information for the SOAP extension in PHP is based on the extension from PHP 5.1.0. Many changes and additions have been made to the extension over the course of the different releases. Although I do my best to indicate the differences and availability of functionality in the different versions, I recommend you use the latest stable PHP release if you are implementing the SOAP extension in a production environment. This not only will give you the latest functionality but also a more stable version of the extension.

Introducing the Web Services Description Language (WSDL)

WSDL is an XML grammar used to describe a Web service. It defines how the Web service is accessed, the operations it performs, how messages are passed, and the structure of the messages. Although WSDL is not required to work with SOAP, it is an integral part of the WS-I Basic Profile from the Web Services Interoperability Organization (http://www.ws-i.org/), and it makes working with SOAP much easier. The good thing about working with WSDL is that on the consumer side, you do not need to know any details about an API. In fact, you do not even need to understand WSDL to consume the service. However, this has a downside. When the service belongs to you and you are the one who has to create the WSDL document, it can be a bit difficult. In my opinion, writing WSDL documents is like dabbling in the black arts.

Caution Although the material presented here for WSDL is according to the WSDL 1.1 documentation, not everything is considered to be a valid way of doing things when following the WS-I Basic Profile (WS-I BP). Your Web service does not have to conform to the WS-I BP, but certain companies do require this conformance. Covering the actual contents of the WS-I BP is out of the scope of this chapter, but once you have a working knowledge of WSDL and SOAP, it is not difficult to read the documentation if you have a need for conformance.

You might run into various versions of WSDL when working with SOAP. Currently, WSDL 2.0 is the latest W3C working draft (http://www.w3.org/TR/wsdl20/). It is an evolution of WSDL 1.2, which was also a working draft but never officially released (although you may run into its usage in the real world with SOAP 1.2). The structure explained in this chapter, however, will deal with WSDL 1.1 (http://www.w3.org/TR/wsdl), because it is still widely used in conjunction with SOAP 1.1 and is also a bit easier to understand, especially if this is your first time working with WSDL.

Note WSDL and SOAP are complex topics and not easily summarized. To ensure you have a good understanding of each of these topics so you can effectively use SOAP in PHP, this chapter limits WSDL use to version 1.1, covering areas specific to usage with SOAP version 1.1.

This section will explain the structure of a WSDL document and use XML Schemas (covered in Chapter 3) to define the data types, and it will explain how to manually build a WSDL document using a fictional PHP Web service as an example. Although XML Schema is not the only schema language you can use when creating a WSDL document (you can also use RELAX NG), it is the most common and preferential language for maximum interoperability. Before jumping right into the structure, you should know that I will use a few namespaces in this chapter, as shown in Table 18-1. These come from the W3C WSDL 1.1 note, but in this case, contrary to their documentations, the current XML Schema namespace is being used.

Table 18-1. *Common Prefixes Used in WSDL*

Prefix	Namespace URI	Description
wsdl	http://schemas.xmlsoap.org/wsdl/	WSDL namespace for the WSDL framework.
soap	http://schemas.xmlsoap.org/wsdl/soap/	WSDL namespace for the WSDL SOAP binding.
http	http://schemas.xmlsoap.org/wsdl/http/	WSDL namespace for the WSDL HTTP GET and POST binding.
mime	http://schemas.xmlsoap.org/wsdl/mime/	WSDL namespace for the WSDL MIME binding.
soapenc	http://schemas.xmlsoap.org/soap/encoding/	Encoding namespace as defined by SOAP 1.1.
soapenv	http://schemas.xmlsoap.org/soap/envelope/	Envelope namespace as defined by SOAP 1.1.
xsd	http://www.w3.org/2001/XMLSchema	Schema namespace as defined by XSD.
tns	Various	The "this namespace" (tns) prefix is used as a convention to refer to the current document.

The XML document in Listing 18-1, exampleapi.wsdl, is an example of a WSDL document; I will explain its construction in this section. The funny thing about this WSDL document is that for how long it is, only a single function is defined for the Web service it is describing. It may seem complex at first, but I will explain each area in detail. This document should serve as a reference as I cover each area in its own section, making it easier to understand the specifics of the key points. Referring to this document will allow you to see how all the areas fit into the large schema of the WSDL document.

Listing 18-1. *Example WSDL Document for* exampleapi.wsdl

```
<?xml version="1.0"?>
<definitions targetNamespace="urn:ExampleAPI" xmlns:tns="urn:ExampleAPI"
             xmlns:xsd="http://www.w3.org/2001/XMLSchema"
             xmlns:soap="http://schemas.xmlsoap.org/wsdl/soap/"
             xmlns:soapenc="http://schemas.xmlsoap.org/soap/encoding/"
             xmlns:wsdl="http://schemas.xmlsoap.org/wsdl/"
             xmlns="http://schemas.xmlsoap.org/wsdl/">
   <types>
      <xsd:schema xmlns="http://www.w3.org/2001/XMLSchema"
                  targetNamespace="urn:ExampleAPI">
         <xsd:element name="getPeopleByFirstLastName">
            <xsd:complexType>
               <xsd:sequence>
                  <xsd:element name="first" type="xsd:string"/>
                  <xsd:element name="last" type="xsd:string"/>
               </xsd:sequence>
            </xsd:complexType>
         </xsd:element>

         <xsd:complexType name="Person">
            <xsd:all>
               <xsd:element name="id" type="xsd:int"/>
               <xsd:element name="lastName" type="xsd:string"/>
               <xsd:element name="firstName" type="xsd:string"/>
            </xsd:all>
         </xsd:complexType>

         <xsd:complexType name="ArrayOfPerson">
            <xsd:complexContent>
               <xsd:restriction base="soapenc:Array">
                  <xsd:attribute ref="soapenc:arrayType"
                                 wsdl:arrayType="tns:Person[]"/>
               </xsd:restriction>
            </xsd:complexContent>
         </xsd:complexType>

         <xsd:element name="getPeopleByFirstLastNameResponse"
                      type="tns:ArrayOfPerson"/>
```

```xml
        <xsd:element name="DBUnavailableFault">
           <xsd:complexType>
              <xsd:sequence>
                 <xsd:element name="DBMessage" type="xsd:string"/>
                 <xsd:element name="RetryInMinutes" type="xsd:int"/>
              </xsd:sequence>
           </xsd:complexType>
        </xsd:element>

        <xsd:element name="SystemMaintenance">
           <xsd:complexType>
              <xsd:sequence>
                 <xsd:element name="SysMessage" type="xsd:string"/>
                 <xsd:element name="RetryInMinutes" type="xsd:int"/>
              </xsd:sequence>
           </xsd:complexType>
        </xsd:element>
     </xsd:schema>
  </types>

  <!-- Input message -->
  <message name="getPeopleByFirstLastName">
     <part name="parameters" element="tns:getPeopleByFirstLastName"/>
  </message>
  <!-- Output Message -->
  <message name="getPeopleByFirstLastNameResponse">
     <part name="result" element="tns:getPeopleByFirstLastNameResponse"/>
  </message>
  <!-- Fault Messages -->
  <message name="DBUnavailableFault">
     <part name="DBUnavailableFault" element="tns:DBUnavailableFault"/>
  </message>
  <message name="SystemMaintenance">
     <part name="SystemMaintenance" element="tns:SystemMaintenance"/>
  </message>

  <!-- Port for Example API -->
  <portType name="ExamplePortType">
     <operation name="getPeopleByFirstLastName">
        <input message="tns:getPeopleByFirstLastName"/>
        <output message="tns:getPeopleByFirstLastNameResponse"/>
        <fault name="nodb" message="tns:DBUnavailableFault"/>
        <fault name="sysmaint" message="tns:SystemMaintenance"/>
     </operation>
     <!-- Other operations -->
  </portType>
```

```
<!-- Binding for Example API - Document/literal, SOAP over HTTP -->
<binding name="ExampleBinding" type="tns:ExamplePortType">
    <soap:binding transport="http://schemas.xmlsoap.org/soap/http"/>
    <operation name="getPeopleByFirstLastName">
        <soap:operation soapAction="getPeopleByFirstLastName"/>
        <input>
            <soap:body use="literal"/>
        </input>
        <output>
            <soap:body use="literal"/>
        </output>
        <fault name="nodb">
            <soap:fault name="nodb" use="literal"/>
        </fault>
        <fault name="sysmaint">
            <soap:fault name="sysmaint" use="literal"/>
        </fault>
    </operation>
    <!-- Other operations -->
</binding>

<!-- Endpoint for Example API -->
<service name="ExampleService">
    <port name="ExamplePort" binding="tns:ExampleBinding">
        <soap:address location="http://www.example.com/ExampleService"/>
    </port>
</service>
</definitions>
```

Understanding the Document Structure

In this section, I will break a WSDL document down into a simplistic view that takes into account only the most important elements. This document does not take into account namespaces other than the WSDL namespace to which the elements belong. Based upon this breakdown, a WSDL document has the following structure:

```
<definitions xmlns="http://schemas.xmlsoap.org/wsdl/">
    <types>
        <!-- definition of types used in WSDL -->
    </types>

    <message>
        <!-- abstract definition of the data being transmitted -->
    </message>

    <portType>
        <!-- a set of abstract operations referring to input and output messages -->
    </portType>
```

```
<binding>
    <!-- concrete protocol and data format specs -->
</binding>

<service>
    <!-- specifies locations and bindings for a service -->
</service>
</definitions>
```

■**Note** I am using the WSDL elements in this section without prefixes to make them easier to read. These elements, however, belong to the `http://schemas.xmlsoap.org/wsdl/` namespace. Because they are used as fragments from a complete WSDL document, assume that the `wsdl` namespace has been defined as the default namespace.

Types

The `types` element encapsulates the data type definitions used when messages are exchanged. Although you can use any schema language to define these types, XML Schema is the preferred language, as well as what is used in this chapter, because of its maximum interoperability. Here is the syntax:

```
<types>
    <xsd:schema xmlns:xsd="http://www.w3.org/2001/XMLSchema">
        <!-- complexType definitions -->
    </xsd:schema>
</types>
```

Using this element really depends upon the type of data being exchanged. For example, if you are simply passing simple strings or numerics back and forth, then you can handle them using a simple `xsd:string` type, which does not get defined here. Objects and arrays, on the other hand, need to have a type defined.

■**Note** The examples in this section, unless otherwise noted, are smaller fragments from a larger WSDL document. You may not see the actual definition of all namespaces, and in these cases you should assume the namespace has been defined higher in the hierarchy using the prefix/namespace mappings from Table 18-1.

Arrays

Arrays have no native built-in type under XML Schemas. One defined in the SOAP 1.1 encoding schema, however, corresponds to the `soapenc` prefix from Table 18-1. When defining an array in WSDL, you use the soapenc:Array type but not directly. You create a custom complex type by extending the soapenc:Array type and must follow some rules specified in WSDL 1.1:

- The name of the array types should be ArrayOfXXXX, where XXXX is the type of items contained in the array.

- You specify the type of items contained in the array and its dimensions using a default value for the soapenc:arrayType attribute.

- The default value is currently provided using an arrayType attribute from the namespace associated with the wsdl prefix in Table 18-1.

If these rules are making your head spin, don't fret. It is much easier to see how this works in practice than in theory. For example, starting with a simple array on integers:

```
array(1,2,3,4);
```

the actual values within the array do not matter when creating the type definition. All you are concerned with is that it is an array and it contains only integers. For example:

```
<xsd:complexType name="ArrayOfint">
   <xsd:complexContent>
     <xsd:restriction base="soapenc:Array">
       <xsd:attribute ref="soapenc:arrayType" wsdl:arrayType="xsd:int[]"/>
     </xsd:restriction>
   </xsd:complexContent>
</xsd:complexType>
```

Following the WSDL rules, you define a complex type having the name ArrayOfint. As you know from Chapter 3, you create types through the further restriction of base types. In this case, you use the soapenc:Array type as the base type to be restricted. You then specify the types of items using the soapenc:arrayType attribute. The type of these is xsd:int; however, this is an array where multiple integers can be returned, so using the wsdl:arrayType attribute, the item type is finally specified using xsd:int[].

Using arrays of simple types is fairly straightforward. To return an array containing strings, the only parts you need to change in the example are the name of the complexType to ArrayOfstring and the value of wsdl:arrayType to xsd:string[]. Returning arrays of other complex types is also just as straightforward, but many people still have problems when working with them. For this reason, I wrote a separate section about this topic; see the "Complex Type Containing Complex Type" section. The next section will cover what I mean by a complex data type. I will use a PHP object in this case.

Objects

Objects are another type (using the *type* word loosely) you will probably want to be passing back and forth. In all actuality, it is not any specific object that is getting defined but rather the class. When trying to think of this conceptually, however, most people find it easier to think of an object, since that is what is actually being passed. With this in mind, I will use the class definition shown in Listing 18-2 to demonstrate how to write the structure within WSDL using XML Schema.

Listing 18-2. Person *Class Definition*

```
class Person {
    public $id;
    public $lastName;
    public $firstName;

    /* Class methods Here */
}
```

The Person class in Listing 18-2 defines three public properties. Although both the lastName and firstName properties are strings, id is an integer. The types of these need to be known so that you can define them correctly and enforce them using an XML Schema:

```
<xsd:complexType name="Person">
    <xsd:all>
        <xsd:element name="id" type="xsd:int"/>
        <xsd:element name="lastName" type="xsd:string"/>
        <xsd:element name="firstName" type="xsd:string"/>
    </xsd:all>
</xsd:complexType>
```

The first step is to name the complexType. In this example, it is called Person to reflect the name of the class it represents. The name can be anything you want, but it is much easier to figure out its use and debug down the line when the name is the same as or is similar to the class it represents. After naming the type, you define the properties. You do this in the same manner as writing an XML Schema for an XML document, and here the properties are simply considered as the elements in a document.

Complex Type Containing Complex Type

A complex type that contains a complex type is not defined any differently than what you have done so far. In fact, you may already have an idea of how you build such a structure. If you are unsure about building the structure, then you are not alone. The reason for a section dedicated to this topic is that this area is often a point of confusion for many developers just starting out writing WSDL. The easiest way to demonstrate and understand this is through an example.

You already know how to define both an array and a class. Putting these two concepts together, you can define an array containing Person objects, whose class is defined in Listing 18-2. To start, you simply begin by creating the definition for the array type where the tns prefix is associated with the same namespace as a defined targetNamespace:

```
<xsd:complexType name="ArrayOfPerson">
    <xsd:complexContent>
        <xsd:restriction base="soapenc:Array">
            <xsd:attribute ref="soapenc:arrayType" wsdl:arrayType="tns:Person[]"/>
        </xsd:restriction>
    </xsd:complexContent>
</xsd:complexType>
```

There is no difference, besides the value of wsdl:arrayType, between creating an array that holds objects and creating an array that holds integers, as shown earlier. If you are wondering why Person[] is prefixed with tns in this example, you may want to return to Chapter 3 and review the section that covers complex types and targetNamespace. Using the techniques you have learned, including the XML Schema information from Chapter 3, you should easily be able to build even more complex types than shown here, such as objects that have properties that contain objects or arrays.

Messages

According to the WSDL documentation, a *message* is an abstract definition of the data being transmitted. In simple terms, messages define input and output parameters. Do not take this statement as a cold, hard fact. It really depends upon the bindings used, which are covered later in the "Bindings" section, but conceptually this explanation is the easiest way to grasp the concept of a message without already having to understand every technical detail about WSDL and SOAP. Using this simplistic view, however, the client needs to know the types that are expected when a message is sent, which is equivalent to calling to a function, and the type expected in return from the function. The server also needs to know this information, but this time it needs to know what types are expected when a function is called and what type it is supposed to return.

Two binding styles exist, RPC and Document; each can use one of two different bindings, encoded or literal. The style and use of the binding chosen drives how you write a message element. Although I will discuss these binding styles later in the "Bindings" section, it is difficult to understand the forms a message element takes depending upon these. The following code breaks down the message format and what it means when a SOAP message is created (though Document/encoded is omitted). This format is not WS-I conformant and not used, so you can basically forget that it exists.

In all cases, a message element takes the following basic form:

```
<message name="nmtoken">
    <part name="nmtoken" element="qname"? type="qname"?/> *
</message>
```

Every message element has a name that must be unique among all message elements. Each message element also contains zero or more part element children, which represent the parameters or response for a function. Each part element also contains a name. This time the name must be unique among all part elements contained within a single message element. The element and type attributes are exclusive. When using RPC style, you must use the type attribute, but when using Document style, you must use the element attribute instead. This may seem a bit confusing, so the following breaks down the different styles and see how the message is constructed based on a function that retrieves an array of Person objects based on passing first and last name parameters:

```
function getPeopleByFirstLastName($last, $first) {
    /* Function returns an $retVal that contains an array of People objects
       i.e. - $retVal = array(newPerson(xx), new Person(yy)); */
    $retVal = array(
    return $retVal;
}
```

RPC/encoded

RPC/encoded is considered the easiest method to work with in terms of both writing a WSDL and using a client with the WSDL. You write the `input` message for the function as shown in Listing 18-3.

Listing 18-3. RPC/encoded *Message Definition*

```
<!-- Input message -->
<message name="getPeopleByFirstLastName">
   <part name="first" type="xsd:string"/>
   <part name="last" type="xsd:string"/>
</message>
```

What this means is that the function needs two parameters, `first` and `last`, each of which are `string` types. When the actual SOAP message is created, the XML created for the message itself uses the names of the parameters as the element names that wrap the passed values. Because RPC is being used, these elements are wrapped within a single element whose name is determined by the binding, explained later in the "Bindings" section of this chapter. Extracting just this message from a SOAP call, where the first parameter contains the value `John` and the last parameter contains the value `Smith`, would look like the following:

```
<getPeopleByFirstLastName>
   <first xsi:type="xsd:string">John</first>
   <last xsi:type="xsd:string">Smith</last>
</getPeopleByFirstLastName>
```

■**Note** The containing element here, `getPeopleByFirstLastName`, has nothing to do with the name of the message. It comes from the binding, which has not yet been introduced. The name of the message can be anything you like, though it is easier to keep it the same or similar to the function it represents or as a common name if shared by multiple functions.

The message format to be used to return the result from the function takes the following form:

```
<!-- Output message -->
<message name="getPeopleByFirstLastNameResponse">
   <part name="result" type="tns:ArrayOfPerson"/>
</message>
```

Here, a single result of the `ArrayOfPerson` type defined earlier is returned.

RPC/literal

A message written for an RPC/literal WSDL takes the same form as that for RPC/encoded and is just as simple as well. The difference is that the XML created just for the message does not contain the type information. For instance, using the message in Listing 18-3, the XML fragment for the message alone would look like this:

```
<getPeopleByFirstLastName>
    <first>John</first>
    <last>Smith</last>
</getPeopleByFirstLastName>
```

You may wonder then how and why you would choose one of these over the other. For those following standards, RPC/literal is WS-I compliant, and RPC/encoded is not.

Note When using the RPC style, RPC/literal offers the same benefits as RPC/encoded yet does not share its drawbacks. RPC/literal eliminates the overhead of carrying type information when the message is being passed, and the biggest benefit, especially with those concerned with standards and maximum interoperability, is that RPC/literal is WS-I compliant while RPC/encoded is not.

Document/literal

This document style is similar to RPC style when defining the message element, except the part element uses the element attribute rather than a type attribute. This means elements must be defined within the types section of the WSDL document. In most cases, you will see WSDL that uses Document/literal and contains only a single part element within the message, regardless of the number of parameters a function requires. The reason for this is because of how parameters are wrapped. The Document/literal style does not wrap these within an operation name like RPC does. Instead, for each part element, the value is wrapped in an XML element named by the value of the element attribute. Instead of the message within the SOAP call having a single element that contains the values and also names the operation, you'll see an element for each of the part elements in the message definition.

Consider the following types fragment in Listing 18-4. Two elements, first and last, have been defined as string types. The elements getPeopleByFirstLastName and getPeopleByFirstLastNameResponse have also been defined as complex types.

Listing 18-4. *Document-Defined Types*

```
<types>
    <xsd:schema xmlns:xsd="http://www.w3.org/2001/XMLSchema">
        <xsd:element name="first" type="xsd:string"/>
        <xsd:element name="last" type="xsd:string"/>

        <xsd:element name="getPeopleByFirstLastName">
            <xsd:complexType>
                <xsd:sequence>
                    <xsd:element minOccurs="1" maxOccurs="1" name="first"
                                 type="xsd:string"/>
```

```
            <xsd:element minOccurs="1" maxOccurs="1" name="last"
                         type="xsd:string"/>
         </xsd:sequence>
      </xsd:complexType>
    </xsd:element>

    <xsd:element name="getPeopleByFirstLastNameResponse" type="tns:ArrayOfPerson"/>

    <!-- Remainder to type definitions -->

  </xsd:schema>
</types>
```

If the message were defined using a part for each of the first and last parameters, it would look like the following:

```
<message name="getPeopleByFirstLastName">
   <part name="first" element="tns:first"/>
   <part name="last" element="tns:last"/>
</message>
```

Using the same first and last values as before (John and Smith) within a SOAP call, you would construct the extracted message as follows:

```
<first>John</first>
<last>Smith</last>
```

Although complete valid, the WS-I standard allows for only a single child element within the SOAP body from which this message was extracted. Because of this drawback, only a single part element is used within a message definition. The element for the part points to either an element with a simple type or an element with a complex type. For example, using the type definitions from Listing 18-5, you can reconstruct the message using a single part element.

Listing 18-5. Document/literal *Message Format*

```
<!-- Input message -->
<message name="getPeopleByFirstLastName">
   <part name="parameters" element="tns:getPeopleByFirstLastName"/>
</message>

<!-- Output Message -->
<message name="getPeopleByFirstLastNameResponse">
   <part name="result" element="tns: getPeopleByFirstLastNameResponse"/>
</message>
```

Extracting the message from a SOAP message based on this message definition appears like the following:

```
<getPeopleByFirstLastName>
    <first>John</first>
    <last>Smith</last>
</getPeopleByFirstLastName>
```

This result looks the same as that from the RPC/literal example. The parameters are both wrapped within a getPeopleByFirstLastName element, but the reason why is this is done is different. RPC gets this name from the binding, and the Document/literal style gets its name from the name of the referenced element. They just happen to be named the same in each WSDL in this case. Writing a WSDL in this manner is referred to as "Document/literal wrapped." There is no official specification for this. It is just a style that that also happens to conform to the WS-I standard.

Port Types

Using the definition from the WSDL documentation, a *port type* is a named set of abstract operations and the abstract messages involved. In simple terms, a portType element contains a collection of operations (think of these in terms of PHP functions) and associates the messages used with them:

```
<portType name="nmtoken">
    <operation name="nmtoken" .... /> *
</portType>
```

A portType element must have a name that uniquely identifies it among any other portType elements. It contains any number of child operation elements. An operation element exists for each operation (think: PHP function) that will be exposed by the Web service named through its name attribute. When writing a WSDL document, the value of the name attribute is the name of the corresponding PHP function. Working from the client side, the name attribute is the name of the function you will be calling. Four types of operations are supported, though in the majority of cases you will run into only a single one—two if you are lucky. The type of operation defines the structure the operation element will take. For example, using the name ExamplePortType, you create the element as follows:

```
<portType name="ExamplePortType">
    <!-- Operation Elements -->
</portType>
```

■**Note** For services designed based on the WS-I Basic Profile guidelines, only a one-way operation or request-response operation can be used. Both the solicit-response and notification operations are not acceptable to be used under those guidelines.

One-Way Operation

A *one-way* operation involves a service receiving a message without returning a response. This type of operation allows for asynchronous calls where the client can send a message and does not wait for any type of response from the Web service. Take logging data using a remote service, for example. This data is not critical, and you do not care whether it actually gets logged. It is assumed that the service is working well enough that the majority of data is being logged. A message element named dataLogger, whose structure is not important for this example, has been already defined. The operation element for this would appear as the following:

```
<operation name="dataLogger">
    <input message="tns:dataLogger"/>
</operation>
```

Request-Response Operation

The *request-response* operation is probably the most frequently encountered type of operation. A client makes a request and then waits for the response. Because messages are bidirectional in this type of operation, they contain both an input message and an output message. You can also set an additional type, a fault element, which occurs when an error is encountered and is returned to the requestor. The basic structure of the operation element for this type is as follows:

```
<operation name="nmtoken" parameterOrder="nmtokens">
    <input name="nmtoken"? message="qname"/>
    <output name="nmtoken"? message="qname"/>
    <fault name="nmtoken" message="qname"/>*
</operation>
```

The operation element is defined in a similar manner as a one-way operation, except in this case the message format is specified for the incoming parameters (the input element) and the outgoing response (the output element). Optionally, this element can also define the message formats for any faults, outside of those already defined by SOAP, using fault elements.

You can specify a name for each of the child elements (input, output, and fault) using the name attribute. The only uniqueness that applies here is that no two fault elements can have the same name. Using a name is not required unless you need to reference one of the elements elsewhere. This applies when using the parameterOrder attribute or, as you will see when working with the SOAP extension, when returning a specific SOAP fault that has been defined in the WSDL document for an operation.

parameterOrder Attribute The parameterOrder attribute really pertains only when the operation is bound using RPC. By using a list of message part names, separated by a space, it allows the signature of an RPC function to be captured. This parameter serves only as a hint for how the parameters are ordered and can be ignored when the operation is not bound using RPC. In any case, no matter which type of binding is used, this attribute is not required. If you decide to add this attribute, however, you must follow a number of rules. The following is a list of these rules as specified in the WSDL 1.1 documentation:

- The part name order reflects the order of the parameters in the RPC signature.

- The return value part is not present in the list.

- If a part name appears in both the input and output messages, it is an in/out parameter.

- If a part name appears in only the `input` message, it is an in parameter.

- If a part name appears in only the `output` message, it is an out parameter.

fault Element You can use a `fault` element when you encounter an error within the operation being executed. Not only is it considered good practice to declare these, it also allows complex types to easily be used in a fault, which then can easily be handled by the calling client. A `fault` element takes a name, specified by the value of the `name` attribute, and must be unique among any other `fault` element within the scope of the `operation`. Just like the `input` and `output` elements, it also must specify a message using the `message` attribute. The message it refers to, which was covered earlier, is written exactly as every other message is written. Because only a single fault can be returned by an operation per call, it is best to follow the convention you used when writing the message for the response.

Example The request-response is the most often encountered type of operation, so I will show a concrete example; I will use the `getPeopleByFirstLastName()` function, which many of the previous examples were based on, as a reference. The function took the following form:

```
function getPeopleByFirstLastName($last, $first) {
    /* Function returns an $retVal that contains an array of People objects
       i.e. - $retVal = array(newPerson(xx), new Person(yy)); */
    $retVal = array(
    return $retVal;
}
```

The message definitions I will use are from Listing 18-5. In that particular example, the WSDL is being written using the `Document/literal` style, so you do not need to use the `parameterOrder` attribute:

```
<operation name="getPeopleByFirstLastName">
    <input message="tns:getPeopleByFirstLastName"/>
    <output message="tns:getPeopleByFirstLastNameResponse"/>
</operation>
```

This example also does not illustrate the use of the `fault` element. Because it is easier to understand when actually working with SOAP, you will see it in action in conjunction with the SOAP extension. For the syntax, though, you can expand this example to include some faults you may want to return in a specific format.

Two faults will be declared here. One is used in the event the database on the server is unavailable. In the event this happens, the fault will return the specific database error as well as a numeric value indicating the number of minutes to wait until the operation should be tried again. The other fault is similar except it is issued if the system is down for maintenance. It also returns a numeric value with the number of minutes to wait. Although these are generic faults, the operation they are being used with does not have many other cases where a fault would be appropriate. The example in the "Using the SOAP Extension" section has much better examples of fault usage.

Returning to the extended example, you need to define types for the fault messages:

```
<types>
    <xsd:schema xmlns:xsd="http://www.w3.org/2001/XMLSchema">

        <!-- Previous defined types here -->

        <xsd:element name="DBUnavailableFault">
            <xsd:complexType>
                <xsd:sequence>
                    <xsd:element minOccurs="1" maxOccurs="1" name="DBMessage"
                                 type="xsd:string"/>
                    <xsd:element minOccurs="1" maxOccurs="1" name="RetryInMinutes"
                                 type="xsd:int"/>
                </xsd:sequence>
            </xsd:complexType>
        </xsd:element>

        <xsd:element name="SystemMaintenance">
            <xsd:complexType>
                <xsd:sequence>
                    <xsd:element minOccurs="1" maxOccurs="1" name="SysMessage"
                                 type="xsd:string"/>
                    <xsd:element minOccurs="1" maxOccurs="1" name="RetryInMinutes"
                                 type="xsd:int"/>
                </xsd:sequence>
            </xsd:complexType>
        </xsd:element>
    </xsd:schema>
</types>
```

Using these types, you can construct the message formats used by the faults:

```
<message name="DBUnavailableFault">
    <part name="DBUnavailableFault" element="tns:DBUnavailableFault"/>
</message>

<message name="SystemMaintenance">
    <part name="SystemMaintenance" element="tns:SystemMaintenance"/>
</message>
```

So far, nothing is different from what you saw earlier in this chapter. The last step is to add them to the operation:

```
<operation name="getPeopleByFirstLastName">
    <input message="tns:getPeopleByFirstLastName"/>
    <output message="tns:getPeopleByFirstLastNameResponse"/>
    <fault name="nodb" message="tns:DBUnavailableFault"/>
    <fault name="sysmaint" message="tns:SystemMaintenance"/>
</operation>
```

The `fault` elements have been specifically named. Unlike the `input` and `output` elements, it is mandatory that the `name` attribute be specified with a `fault` element. Again, once you see how they are used in the SOAP extension, you will fully understand why they must be named even when only a single `fault` element is present.

Solicit-Response Operation

A *solicit-response* type of operation is the opposite of a request-response. Rather than a client making a request and waiting for a response, a solicit-response occurs when a server solicits a response from a client. The format for an `operation` element in this case is the reverse of a request-response type. The `output` element, which can be considered as a request (or technically a solicitation), is used for the initial message from the server followed by an `input` element, which is the response from the client. This type can also contain `fault` elements just like the request-response. A simple example of this is a client that has registered with a server for some type of subscription-based service. The server can periodically solicit a response from the client, inquiring if they would like to update their subscription. For example:

```
<message name="UpdateSubscriptionRequest">
   <part name="UpdateSubscriptionRequest" type="xsd:string"/>
</message>

<message name="UpdateSubscriptionResponse">
   <part name="UpdateSubscriptionResponse" type="xsd:string"/>
</message>
```

Using these two simple message formats, you write the operation as follows:

```
<operation name="UpdateSubscription">
   <output message="tns:UpdateSubscriptionRequest"/>
   <input message="tns:UpdateSubscriptionResponse"/>
</operation>
```

Of course, this is an oversimplified example and is used only to illustrate the structure in this particular case. You will rarely encounter a solicit-response operation, especially used with WSDL 1.1, because any service designed to the WS-I Basic Profile guidelines will never implement this operation type.

Notification Operation

A *notification* operation is the opposite of a one-way operation. Instead of the client making the request to the server and not waiting for a response, the server is sending a message to the client and not waiting for a response. Accordingly, the format of the `operation` element is the same as that of a one-way operation, except instead of having an `input` element, an `output` element is used. It is also invalid to use a `fault` element in this case. An example of this scenario is a client that has subscribed to a service. The server can send notifications to the clients when updates are available. This would allow the client to go and retrieve updates at its leisure. For example:

```
<message name="UpdateNotification">
   <part name="UpdateNotification" type="xsd:int"/>
</message>
```

Here a simple message format is declared that specifies an integer value in the message. This value could simply take the form of a 1 for updates available or a 0 if no updates are available (in the event the client expects notifications at set times whether or not updates are available). The following operation declares this notification using only the child output element:

```
<operation name="UpdateNotification">
    <output message="tns:UpdateNotification"/>
</operation>
```

This again is an operation type you will rarely encounter, at least at this point in time. It is not supported by the WS-I Basic Profile and thus would most likely appear only in possibly some private Web service implementations.

Bindings

If you have looked at the WSDL 1.1 documentation, you may have seen the terms *abstract* and *concrete* thrown around a lot for the elements covered so far. I have intentionally omitted the *abstract* and *concrete* terms when describing a WSDL document, because they often lead to more confusion than necessary. Everything up until this point has been abstract. A binding specifies concrete details about a portType and a protocol. In simpler terms, for operations from a specific portType, bindings provide the information for the type of transport protocol used and the format of the messages.

You can use three types of bindings in WSDL 1.1. They are SOAP, HTTP, and MIME. Because this chapter deals specifically with SOAP, I will show how to use only SOAP bindings. Listing 18-6 shows the basic structure of a binding element.

Listing 18-6. *WSDL Binding*

```
<wsdl:definitions .... >
    <wsdl:binding name="nmtoken" type="qname"> *
        <-- extensibility element (1) --> *
        <wsdl:operation name="nmtoken"> *
            <-- extensibility element (2) --> *
            <wsdl:input name="nmtoken"? > ?
                <-- extensibility element (3) -->
            </wsdl:input>
            <wsdl:output name="nmtoken"? > ?
                <-- extensibility element (4) --> *
            </wsdl:output>
            <wsdl:fault name="nmtoken"> *
                <-- extensibility element (5) --> *
            </wsdl:fault>
        </wsdl:operation>
    </wsdl:binding>
</wsdl:definitions>
```

When defining bindings, each binding must have a unique name, specified by the value of the name attribute. Typically, unless writing some complex WSDL documents, you will have only a single binding element. The value of the type attribute specifies the portType for which this binding is used. Using the `portType` defined in the previous section, which was named `ExamplePortType`, you can begin constructing the binding:

```
<binding name="ExampleBinding" type="tns:ExamplePortType">
  <!-- Currently Empty -->
</binding>
```

Notice that the `binding` element just performs some simple mappings. The actual details for the binding are defined by the extensibility elements.

▪**Note** When working with a WSDL `binding` element, because of the extensibility, many elements have the same local name but reside in different namespaces. As you continue reading, the element name will be referenced by its `localname` and either WSDL (for the `wsdl` namespace from Table 18-1) or SOAP (for the `soap` namespace from Table 18-1). For example, the top-level `binding` element is the WSDL binding, and the child `soap:binding` element will be referred to as the SOAP binding.

SOAP Binding

This chapter concerns SOAP, so I will use SOAP bindings here. WSDL provides a `binding` element in the `http://schemas.xmlsoap.org/wsdl/soap/` namespace for this purpose. Using this specific element also indicates that this is a SOAP 1.1 binding:

```
<soap:binding transport="uri" style="rpc|document"?>
```

The `soap:binding` element lives as a child of the WSDL `binding` element and refers to extensibility element (1) in Listing 18-6.

The `transport` attribute indicates the SOAP transport used by the binding. In most cases, it will probably be the HTTP transport protocol, specified by a value of `http://schemas.xmlsoap.org/soap/http`, for this attribute. It is possible that something else, such as SMTP or FTP, will be used, in which case the value will be some other URI; however, this is usually unlikely. The `style` attribute sets the default style for each operation contained within the WSDL binding. It can take the value `rpc` or `document` and refers to the style of the service as discussed in the section "Messages." This attribute is optional and defaults to the value of `document` when omitted. The binding used, encoded or literal (which I will get to shortly), is specified further within the WSDL binding structure. Because Document/literal is considered the most widely acceptable style and use combination, I will define the SOAP binding using the document style and will use HTTP for the transport protocol, which can take either of the following forms since the `style` attribute has a default value:

```
<soap:binding transport="http://schemas.xmlsoap.org/soap/http" style="document" />
<soap:binding transport="http://schemas.xmlsoap.org/soap/http" />
```

WSDL operation

The WSDL `operation` element within the WSDL `binding` structure simply specifies binding information for the same named `operation` element within the `portType` structure. If you happen to glance at the WSDL 1.1 documentation, you may notice that it indicates that operations are not required to be named, thus allowing for overloaded method names. In those cases, the input and output elements must be named. Although this is technically true, it is not recommended to write WSDL in this manner. Overloaded method names are not allowed by the WS-I Basic Profile, which possibly may interfere with the interoperability of your Web service, so using distinct names is the easiest way to ensure that all the mappings are performed correctly. For example:

```
<operation name="getPeopleByFirstLastName">
  <!-- Currently Empty -->
</operation>
```

SOAP operation

The SOAP operation element works with the WSDL operation element in a similar fashion as the SOAP binding element does with the WSDL binding element. It provides some concrete information for the specific WSDL operation. It lives as a child of the WSDL operation element and refers to extensibility element (2) in Listing 18-6. For example:

```
<soap:operation soapAction="uri"? style="rpc|document"?>?
```

You may notice a few things about this element right off the bat. Its signature says it is optional. Its use is optional only when *not* using HTTP for SOAP. This is because of the soapAction attribute. When using any other transport protocol than HTTP, you cannot use the soapAction attribute, leaving only the style attribute, which I will get to in a moment.

When using HTTP, the soapAction attribute specifies the value of the SOAPAction header. Now, you probably have no idea what this is used for. It indicates the purpose of the SOAP request and is required to be sent by a client. Without having to read the entire SOAP message, a server such as a firewall could read this header, allowing it to perform filtering on SOAP requests. The value of this attribute is a URI and typically set to the value of the WSDL operation name or the WSDL targetNamespace and some identifier for the operation (though it can be any distinguishable URI you like). The value does need not to be unique, because if you had multiple operations that performed similar functionality, you may want to use a common URI for these. Remember, this is used to allow some sort of header filtering to be performed on the receiving end.

The style attribute allows the style to be set on a per-operation basis. When this attribute is not used, the style attribute set on the SOAP binding element is used for the operation; or in the event the SOAP binding element did not define it, the defaulting document value is used. Now, this should answer an earlier question about why the SOAP operation element is optional when not using HTTP. Because a soapAction attribute is never used in those cases, you do not need to include this element in the WSDL document when there is no need to override the style from the SOAP binding. This does not apply in this case, however, because the chapter strictly deals with HTTP and SOAP, which means every WSDL operation element will have a SOAP operation child element.

Using the WSDL operation defined in the previous section, you can create the SOAP operation element:

```
<soap:operation soapAction="getPeopleByFirstLastName" />
```

The WSDL operation name is simply being used as the SOAPAction in this example. Because no style attribute has been defined, it is using the value from the SOAP binding element. It does not matter which form of the binding example you decide to use. In both cases, the value ends up being document.

WSDL input/output/fault

Within the WSDL operation here, you also define WSDL input, output, and fault elements. The elements you need to use depend upon the type of WSDL operation you defined earlier in this chapter. The WSDL operations I am talking about are the ones you defined within the portType. The input, output, and fault elements within the scope of the binding simply take an optional name attribute. The use of the attribute is determined by the corresponding element within the scope of the portType element. When used within the portType, the same name should be applied to the element within the scope of the binding. This may sound extremely confusing but is easy to understand when looking at an example. If you look at the getPeopleByFirstLastName operation within the ExamplePortType portType using the request-response format, you will notice the following input element being used:

```
<input message="tns:getPeopleByFirstLastName"/>
```

This element does not contain a name attribute, so writing it within the binding scope is easily done using the following:

```
<input>
  <!-- content here -->
</input>
```

The same thing will be done for any output and fault elements, except you will always have a name when writing a fault element. If you recall from the portType section, you *must* specify a name for fault elements.

Note Not every SOAP element is covered in this chapter, because additional ones are defined in WSDL. Many of these are not commonly used or beyond the scope of this book. You can find information about these elements in the WSDL 1.1 documentation.

Both input and output elements generally will contain a soap:body element:

```
<soap:body parts="nmtokens"? use="literal|encoded"? encodingStyle="uri-list"?
        namespace="uri"?>
```

The parts attribute specifies which message parts will appear within the SOAP body of the message. Usually all message parts are included, and this attribute is not used. In the cases I have actually seen it used, the message contained only a single named part, which was also identified by the part attribute.

The use attribute determines whether the message parts are encoded or whether the parts determine the schema of the message. As mentioned in the "Messages" section, which explained the WSDL type and use, this attribute determines whether it is encoded or literal. When the value literal is used, no other attribute is required, although you can optionally use encodingStyle. When the value encoded is used, both the encodingStyle and namespace attributes are used. Using SOAP, the value for the encodingStyle will be http://schemas. xmlsoap.org/soap/encoding/. The value for the namespace attribute is usually the targetNamespace, also referred to by the tns prefix in these examples. Assuming the namespace is urn:ExampleAPI, the value for the this attribute will also be urn:ExampleAPI.

A fault element contains a soap:fault element rather than a soap:body element. It works like a soap:body element, except it has a name attribute and no part attribute. For example:

```
<soap:fault name="nmtoken" use="literal|encoded" encodingStyle="uri-list"?
         namespace="uri"?>
```

The value of the name attribute must be the same as the name of the WSDL fault element so that they can be properly related. It is also required that a fault message have a single part, which if you refer to the messages created for the fault elements in the request-response example, you will see that each has only a single part defined.

Soap:header and Soap:headerfault

The soap:header and soap:headerfault elements define headers transmitted within a soapenv:Header element. This concept may not be completely clear at this moment but will become more evident once you understand the structure of a SOAP message. These elements are valid to use within the scope of the input and output elements within a binding. Their definitions closely resemble and are defined in the same manner as the soap:body element with only a few exceptions. For example:

```
<soap:header message="qname" part="nmtoken" use="literal|encoded"
         encodingStyle="uri-list"? namespace="uri"?>*

<soap:headerfault message="qname" part="nmtoken" use="literal|encoded"
         encodingStyle="uri-list"? namespace="uri"?/>*
```

The value of the message attribute is that of a defined message within the WSDL document. The part attribute defines the single part from within the message specified by the message attribute. The remaining attributes are defined in the same manner as the soap:body and soap:fault elements.

Example Binding

If you remember what I said earlier about writing WSDL being like dabbling in the black arts, you might now start realizing why. It is sometimes enough to make your head spin. Not only is the documentation confusing to wade through, but also there is so much reference to SOAP, and you haven't even been exposed to SOAP yet. As usual, it is often easier to learn by example. The following structure is the portType described in the request-response section:

```
<portType name="ExamplePortType">
   <operation name="getPeopleByFirstLastName">
      <input message="tns:getPeopleByFirstLastName"/>
      <output message="tns:getPeopleByFirstLastNameResponse"/>
```

```
        <fault name="nodb" message="tns:DBUnavailableFault"/>
        <fault name="sysmaint" message="tns:SystemMaintenance"/>
    </operation>

    <!-- Other operations -->

</portType>
```

Using everything I have covered for bindings, write the binding structure for this portType using the Document/literal style:

```
<binding name="ExampleBinding" type="tns:ExamplePortType">
    <soap:binding transport="http://schemas.xmlsoap.org/soap/http" />
    <operation name="getPeopleByFirstLastName">
        <soap:operation soapAction="getPeopleByFirstLastName" />
        <input>
            <soap:body use="literal"/>
        </input>
        <output>
            <soap:body use="literal"/>
        </output>
        <fault name="nodb">
            <soap:fault name="nodb" use="literal"/>
        </fault>
        <fault name="sysmaint">
            <soap:fault name="sysmaint" use="literal"/>
        </fault>
    </operation>

    <!-- Other operations -->

</binding>
```

Service

The service element describes a particular Web service by providing a name and the location and associates a binding to a particular port. It is a collection of ports, referred to as *end points*, exposing a binding. For example:

```
<service name="nmtoken">*
    <port name="nmtoken" binding="qname">*
        <-- extensibility element (1) -->
    </port>
</service>
```

A WSDL document can contain multiple services, but in actuality it is common to find only a single service element. In any event, each service is named using the name attribute. When multiple services are specified, each service must be uniquely named.

Within a `service` element is the collection of uniquely named ports for the service. The number of ports found varies depending upon usage. For example, it is possible that the same binding, where the `binding` attribute specifies the name of a `binding` element that it is referencing, be specified for a number of ports, but the extensibility element is referencing different locations. These allow the service to provide alternate access locations for a binding. It is also possible that other ports can provide services for bindings other than SOAP, such as HTTP GET and POST operations. For example, a REST-based Web service could be described here as well. Again, this chapter uses SOAP, so I will keep it simple and use only a single port for the service.

The only real rules for the `port` element, other than making sure the `name` and `binding` attributes are correctly set, are that a port must specify only address locations and no more than one address. Under SOAP, you do this using the `soap:address` element:

```
<soap:address location="uri"/>
```

This is an empty element where the address is specified by the `location` attribute.

Using the `service` element, you can complete the WSDL document. Assuming the service is located at the address `http://www.example.com/ExampleService`, you can link the rules defined by the `ExampleBinding` binding to the port:

```
<service name="ExampleService">
  <port name="ExamplePort" binding="tns:ExampleBinding">
    <soap:address location="http://www.example.com/ExampleService"/>
  </port>
</service>
```

You have now completed the entire WSDL document from Listing 18-1 along with some additional pieces that are not even part of the original file. You will put many of these, however, to use when working with the SOAP extension and with PEAR SOAP through examples.

Introducing SOAP

Now that you have an understanding of how to write WSDL documents for a SOAP service, or at least can decipher one if needed to when working with a SOAP service, it's time to learn what SOAP actually is. SOAP originally stood for the Simple Object Access Protocol in version 1.1, but with version 1.2, it no longer stands for anything and is now simply called SOAP. The standard simplified definition of SOAP is that it is a lightweight protocol for exchanging information in a decentralized, distributed environment. Although SOAP 1.2 is the latest version, this chapter covers SOAP 1.1. It is still the most widely used version and also allows a SOAP service to conform to the WS-I Basic Profile.

Many finer intricacies of SOAP may be pertinent when creating messages by hand, but in reality most developers use an API that constructs messages for them. Within PHP, this would be the SOAP extension. It is, however, good to understand at least the basic structure of a SOAP message; this will not only help you understand what areas of the message certain API calls affect, but you also may run into times that it is necessary to use a lower-level API call and manually create certain portions of the message. This section will deal with more of the basic structure of a SOAP message and intentionally skips over some of the extensibility aspects and transport details. You can find additional information about these subjects and other topics not covered in this chapter within the SOAP specification.

In the previous section, you learned how to create a WSDL document. The SOAP messages in Listing 18-7 and Listing 18-8 are examples of messages based on the request and response of calling the getPeopleByFirstLastName method using SOAP.

Listing 18-7. *Example SOAP Request Structure Using WSDL in Listing 18-1*

```
<?xml version="1.0" encoding="UTF-8"?>
<SOAP-ENV:Envelope xmlns:SOAP-ENV="http://schemas.xmlsoap.org/soap/envelope/"
                   xmlns:ns1="urn:ExampleAPI">
   <SOAP-ENV:Body>
      <ns1:getPeopleByFirstLastName>
         <first>j*</first>
         <last>*</last>
      </ns1:getPeopleByFirstLastName>
   </SOAP-ENV:Body>
</SOAP-ENV:Envelope>
```

Listing 18-8. *Example SOAP Response Structure Using WSDL in Listing 18-1*

```
<?xml version="1.0" encoding="UTF-8"?>
<SOAP-ENV:Envelope xmlns:SOAP-ENV="http://schemas.xmlsoap.org/soap/envelope/"
                   xmlns:SOAP-ENC="http://schemas.xmlsoap.org/soap/encoding/">
   <SOAP-ENV:Body>
      <result>
         <SOAP-ENC:Struct>
            <id>1</id>
            <firstName>John</firstName>
            <lastName>Smith</lastName>
         </SOAP-ENC:Struct>
         <SOAP-ENC:Struct>
            <id>2</id>
            <firstName>Jane</firstName>
            <lastName>Doe</lastName>
         </SOAP-ENC:Struct>
      </result>
   </SOAP-ENV:Body>
</SOAP-ENV:Envelope>
```

Understanding the SOAP Message Structure

The basic structure of a SOAP message is simple. First, a SOAP message cannot contain a DTD or PIs. A skeleton structure of a message, containing only the main SOAP elements, looks like the following:

```
<Envelope>
   <Header>...</Header>?
   <Body>...</Body>
</Envelope>
```

This is only a simple representation because it also precludes some mandatory namespaces. The prefixes and namespaces in Table 18-2 are the few you may encounter in SOAP messages. The ns* prefix is a generic prefix that could be any prefix you like.

Table 18-2. *Namespaces You May See Using SOAP*

Prefix	Description
SOAP-ENV	http://schemas.xmlsoap.org/soap/envelope/
SOAP-ENC	http://schemas.xmlsoap.org/soap/encoding/
xsd	http://www.w3.org/2001/XMLSchema
ns*	The prefix and namespace URIs are application independent.

Encoding Style

The following text comes directly from the SOAP 1.1 documentation:

The SOAP encodingStyle global attribute can be used to indicate the serialization rules used in a SOAP message. This attribute MAY appear on any element and is scoped to that element's contents and all child elements not themselves containing such an attribute, much as an XML namespace declaration is scoped. There is no default encoding defined for a SOAP message.

—Simple Object Access Protocol (SOAP) 1.1, W3C Note; May 8, 2000

Rather than go into details about this attribute, you should just be aware of its existence. This is another one of those cases where following the documentation goes against the WS-I Basic Profile, and in fact its use is no longer recommended. The only reason why I have mentioned this attribute at all is that if you examine a SOAP message, you may see this attribute being used. When used, this attribute is associated with the SOAP-ENV namespace and normally takes the value of the SOAP encoding namespace:

```
SOAP:encodingStyle="http://schemas.xmlsoap.org/soap/encoding/"
```

SOAP Envelope

Every SOAP message must contain an Envelope document element, which lives within the SOAP-ENV namespace. This namespace identifies the message as a SOAP 1.1 message. This element can contain any number of namespace declarations and attributes. As you can see in Listing 18-7, the urn:ExampleAPI namespace with the ns1 prefix has been declared. Within the message, it is used from the WSDL document where the message was defined. Here the prefix has been changed, but the namespace has been kept intact.

Two others you may see are the declaration of the SOAP-ENC namespace and the encodingStyle attribute. As you already know, using the encodingStyle attribute is discouraged. The SOAP-ENC namespace, when trying to conform to the WS-I Basic Profile, also falls into this same category. You might be thinking at this point, why is it shown in the SOAP response message in Listing 18-8? The answer lies in WSDL. In WSDL, a soapenc:Array was used, causing the SOAP server to automatically add this namespace in order to create the proper output types in the SOAP response message. Although a perfectly valid WSDL document and service, it fails to conform to the WS-I Basic Profile.

You might now understand my initial rant about this in Chapter 1. The WS-I is trying to dictate what constitutes a Web service. It includes a limited amount of technologies and specifications. It adds fuel to the fire by then limiting what is considered correct and incorrect within those specifications. Of course, their goal is to provide maximum interoperability, but why can't they just write their own specs using only those things that are considered conformant rather than leaving it up to the developer to learn all the specs and then having to forget many of the things they were required to learn in the first place? It's enough to make your head spin . . . again.

I have gotten a little sidetracked while covering the structure of a SOAP message, but before I move on I will touch upon the subject of the WSDL document again, because this is important to understand. The soapenc:Array was used because it is part of creating WSDL. It is not required that you conform to the WS-I Basic Profile. If you are looking for conformance for your Web service, then you would need to modify the layout of the WSDL document. As you will see later in this chapter when you actually create a working SOAP server with the SOAP extension, using XML Schema alone it is possible to accomplish the same task as having used soapenc:Array without using SOAP encoding. As I have said all along, writing WSDL is a black art. It does take some practice and patience, especially when trying to follow the documentation and specifications and when what is actually valid is limited in use by other specifications or recommendations.

Getting back on topic here, in its simplest form, a SOAP Envelope element takes the following form:

```
<SOAP-ENV:Envelope xmlns:SOAP-ENV="http://schemas.xmlsoap.org/soap/envelope/">
    <!-- child elements -->
</SOAP-ENV:Envelope>
```

SOAP Header

A SOAP Header element is an optional element. It provides the ability to extend messages in a modular way. For instance, you can implement transaction management or Web services security within a Header element. When used, this element *must* be the first child element of the SOAP Envelope element. The extended modules, referred to as *header entries*, live as children of the Header element, and each must be namespace qualified. For example:

```
<SOAP-ENV:Header>
    <t:Transaction xmlns:t="http://www.example.com">
          <!-- data to be processed -->
    </t:Transaction>
</SOAP-ENV:Header>
```

Two attributes, mustUnderstand and actor, can indicate how the entry is processed and by whom.

SOAP actor

It is not always the case that a SOAP message goes from point A to point B, where point B is the final destination. Any number of SOAP intermediaries could appear along the way before the message reaches its final destination. To clarify the term SOAP *intermediary*, it is an application that can receive and forward SOAP messages. A SOAP message can contain portions that are specific only to certain intermediaries rather than for the final destination.

The `actor` attribute specifies the recipient of a `header` entry. It resides within the SOAP-ENV namespace and specifies a namespace as its value, which identifies the recipient of the entry. When the value is empty or the attribute is not used, the entry is considered to be destined for the final recipient. Once an entry has been processed, it is removed from the `Header` before the message is forwarded. The reason for this is that an entry for a specified recipient is considered to be a contract between the originator and the recipient and is not valid beyond the recipient. It is perfectly fine, however, that intermediaries add header entries before forwarding, so simply modifying any header entries it has processed would be equivalent to having removed and added a new entry. A modified entry, however, sets up a new contract, which would be between the intermediary that added or modified the entry and the specified recipient.

To illustrate this, consider the following path a SOAP message takes:

```
Server A => Server B => Server C
```

Server A is the origination point so needs no further identification. Server B is identified by the namespace urn:ServerB, and Server C is identified by the namespace urn:ServerC:

```
<SOAP-ENV:Header>
    <t:Transaction xmlns:t="http://www.example.com" SOAP-ENV:actor="urn:ServerB">
        <!-- data to be processed -->
    </t:Transaction>
</SOAP-ENV:Header>
```

Upon Server B receiving a SOAP message with this `Header`, it knows it needs to do something with it because it is the receiver. The actual operation is not important right now, but in any event it removes this entry. In this case, it does not add a new entry, so the message is then forwarded to Server C within an empty `Header`.

The `actor` attribute can specify a special value of http://schemas.xmlsoap.org/soap/actor/next. This indicates that the entry is to be handled by the next application processing the message. Rather than having to specify a recipient, it blindly instructs the application, whether it is an intermediary or final destination, to handle the entry.

SOAP mustUnderstand

The `mustUnderstand` attribute provides some direction to the recipient of a `header` entry about what to do if it does not understand or cannot fully and correctly process the entry. This attribute takes the value 0, which is the default when not specified, or 1. When the value 1 is used and the recipient is unable to fully process the header, it is instructed to fail processing the message and issue a SOAP `fault`. When the attribute is omitted or its value is set to 0, the application can ignore the processing failure for the entry and continue processing the message:

```
<SOAP-ENV:Header>
    <t:Transaction xmlns:t="urn:ServerB"  SOAP-ENV:actor="urn:ServerB"
                                           SOAP-ENC:mustUnderstand="1">
          <!-- data to be processed -->
    </t:Transaction>
</SOAP-ENV:Header>
```

SOAP Body

The Body element is the container for the information for the final recipient. The structure of the information depends upon the message structure chosen when creating the WSDL document. This of course assumes you are using WSDL with SOAP. If you recall from the WSDL section, you can choose RPC/encoded, RPC/literal, or Document/literal. The method used determines the structure of the contents of the Body element. Rather than rehash the same information, I will refer you to the "Messages" section for additional information and examples.

The Body element must be the next child element of the Envelope. When a Header is used, it comes directly after the Header element; otherwise, it is the first child element of the Envelope. For example:

```
<!-- BODY with Header -->
<SOAP-ENV:Envelope xmlns:SOAP-ENV="http://schemas.xmlsoap.org/soap/envelope/">
    <SOAP-ENV:Header>
        <!-- Data -->
    </SOAP-ENV:Header>
    <SOAP-ENV:Body>
        <!-- Data -->
    </SOAP-ENV:Body>
</SOAP-ENV:Envelope>

<!-- BODY Without Header -->
<SOAP-ENV:Envelope xmlns:SOAP-ENV="http://schemas.xmlsoap.org/soap/envelope/">
    <SOAP-ENV:Body>
        <!-- Data -->
    </SOAP-ENV:Body>
</SOAP-ENV:Envelope>
```

Header entries and the Body element work in a similar fashion. The difference between them is that the Body element does not use actor or mustUnderstand attributes. Its recipient is the final recipient, and its contents must be fully understood by the application. It is equivocal to having a Header entry that does not use the actor attribute and has a mustUnderstand attribute with the value 1. However, one element, defined by SOAP, does make the Body unique. This is the SOAP Fault element.

SOAP Fault

A SOAP Fault issues an error to the caller. It resides within the content of the Body element and can appear only once. A SOAP Fault element defines four child elements, although you can add elements provided they are properly namespace qualified.

faultcode

The faultcode element allows an application to identify the fault issued. It is a required element within a SOAP Fault, and its value must be a qualified name. Although not explicitly stated, I believe the reason behind a qualified name for the value is that this allows an application to determine from where the fault originated and to be able to distinguish between various fault codes. For example, not only does SOAP include some built-in fault codes, listed in Table 18-3, but imagine a system where SOAP messages pass through intermediaries. It is quite possible that each intermediary uses the same fault code but for different reasons. With each intermediary using a unique namespace, the recipient of the fault is able to properly identify the correct type of fault and handle it.

Table 18-3. *SOAP Fault Codes*

Code	Description
VersionMismatch	The processing party found an invalid namespace for the SOAP Envelope element.
MustUnderstand	A SOAP header entry that contained a mustUnderstand attribute with the value 1 was unable to be properly understood or processed.
Client	The SOAP message was incorrectly formed or did not contain the appropriate information in order to succeed.
Server	The SOAP message could not be processed for reasons not directly attributable to the contents of the message itself but, rather, to the processing of the message.

Each of the fault codes in Table 18-3 is defined by SOAP and resides in the http:// schemas.xmlsoap.org/soap/envelope/ namespace:

```
<SOAP-ENV:Fault>
    <faultcode>SOAP-ENV:Client</faultcode>
    <!-- Additional Fault child elements -->
</SOAP-ENV:Fault>
```

The Fault in this case indicates that there was a problem with the SOAP message sent from the client. Fault codes can also be granular. Using the . character as a separator, you can pass multiple related codes. For example, suppose you need to perform authentication; you can pass this information in a SOAP header entity. An application receiving a message without this entity may want to return an authentication error. This could be considered related to a SOAP Client fault because the client did not pass the proper structure:

```
<SOAP-ENV:Fault>
    <faultcode>SOAP-ENV:Client.Authentication</faultcode>
    <!-- Additional Fault child elements -->
</SOAP-ENV:Fault>
```

faultstring

The faultstring element is also a required element within a Fault. It provides a human-readable explanation of the error that occurred. For example:

```
<SOAP-ENV:Fault>
    <faultstring>Authentication information is missing</faultstring>
    <!-- Additional Fault child elements -->
</SOAP-ENV:Fault>
```

faultactor

The faultactor element indicates who caused the fault to occur. In a simple scenario where there is a client and a single server, this element is not required, but you can use it. You can determine the cause of the fault easily from the fault message. In a scenario where the message is passing through intermediaries, using this element is required, so the proper application can be identified by the receiver of the message as the cause of the fault. This element is similar to using the actor attribute within a SOAP header entry. The value is a URI identifying an application. The difference is that instead of specifying the intended recipient, it identifies the source of the fault. For example:

```
<SOAP-ENV:Fault>
    <faultactor>urn:ServerB</faultstring>
    <!-- Additional Fault child elements -->
</SOAP-ENV:Fault>
```

detail

The detail element contains application-specific information related to the Body of a SOAP message. If there is an error processing the Body element, the use of the detail element is required to provide information about the specifics of the processing error. If the error does not pertain to the processing of the Body element, then the detail element must not be present within the Fault structure.

The detail element contains child elements, called *detail entries*. The structure of the detail element is application dependant but can be described when using a WSDL document. Referring to Listing 18-1, the getPeopleByFirstLastName operation within the ExampleBinding binding defines a Fault named nodb. This fault uses a message composed of the DBUnavailableFault element, which is a complex type containing a DBMessage element, and of the RetryInMinutes element. If during the execution of the getPeopleByFirstLastName function a database error occurs, then the server will issue a nodb fault. The details of the database error will be contained with a DBMessage element, and some value for a time to retry will be contained with the RetryInMinutes element. Assuming the ns1 prefix used by the server is associated with the urn:ExampleAPI namespace and the server is using the WSDL document from Listing 18-1, the Fault produced may look like the following if the server was unable to connect to the database during the execution of the getPeopleByFirstLastName function:

```
<SOAP-ENV:Fault>
    <faultcode>ns1:DBError</faultcode>
    <faultstring>A database error has occurred</faultstring>
    <detail>
        <ns1:DBUnavailableFault>
            <DBMessage>Unable to connect to database</DBMessage>
            <RetryInMinutes>60</RetryInMinutes>
```

```
        </ns1:DBUnavailableFault>
    </detail>
</SOAP-ENV:Fault>
```

Using SOAP in HTTP

You can use SOAP within HTTP with or without the HTTP Extension Framework (http://www.ietf.org/rfc/rfc2774.txt). This framework, though out of the scope of this chapter, defines a generic mechanism to extend HTTP. Whether or not you use this framework, some common aspects exist for both of these when using SOAP in HTTP. When working with SOAP APIs such as the SOAP extension, these are usually automatically handled for you; however, some people like to try to send SOAP messages directly without the use of a SOAP API, so the HTTP request and response are worth mentioning.

SOAP HTTP Request

The first thing to always remember is that you must set the Content-Type header accordingly. When working with SOAP 1.1, as you are doing in this chapter, you must set the type to text/xml. SOAP 1.2 has its own type defined, application/soap+xml, so you would use this instead when working with that version of SOAP. It is always a good idea to include the character set of the XML document as well. For example, a document using UTF-8 encoding would issue the following Content-Type header under SOAP 1.1:

```
Content-Type: text/xml; charset="utf-8"
```

When sending a SOAP request, clients must include a SOAPAction header. This header indicates the intent of the request being made and can be used by servers, such as a firewall, to be able to filter SOAP requests. The value of this header corresponds to the value of the soapAction attribute defined on soap:operation elements within a binding when working with WSDL. For example, using the getPeopleByFirstLastName operation from the WSDL document in Listing 18-1, the SOAPAction header is sent like the following:

```
SOAPAction: "getPeopleByFirstLastName"
```

Putting this all together, the entire request for calling the getPeopleByFirstLastName function using the WSDL in Listing 18-1 would look like the following code. Note that this is an actual request made using the PHP SOAP extension, though I have edited certain headers to change the service location for consistency with the WSDL document shown in this chapter.

```
POST /ExampleService HTTP/1.1
Host: example.com
Connection: Keep-Alive
User-Agent: PHP SOAP 0.1
Content-Type: text/xml; charset=utf-8
SOAPAction: "getPeopleByFirstLastName"
Content-Length: xxx
```

```
<?xml version="1.0" encoding="UTF-8"?>
<SOAP-ENV:Envelope xmlns:SOAP-ENV="http://schemas.xmlsoap.org/soap/envelope/"
                   xmlns:ns1="urn:ExampleAPI">
   <SOAP-ENV:Body>
      <ns1:getPeopleByFirstLastName>
         <first>j*</first>
         <last>*</last>
      </ns1:getPeopleByFirstLastName>
   </SOAP-ENV:Body>
</SOAP-ENV:Envelope>
```

SOAP HTTP Response

SOAP HTTP uses HTTP status codes (found in section 10 of RFC 2616, which is located at
http://www.ietf.org/rfc/rfc2616.txt) when sending a response. For example, a SOAP
request that has been properly received and understood by the server results in the return
of a 2xx status code, which means the request was successful. In the event the server fails to
process a request, an HTTP 500 "Internal Server Error" is returned with a SOAP message containing the appropriate Fault. The following is an example of a response returning a SOAP
message containing a Fault:

```
HTTP/1.1 500 Internal Server Error
Content-Type: text/xml; charset="utf-8"
Content-Length: xxxx

<?xml version="1.0" encoding="UTF-8"?>
<SOAP-ENV:Envelope xmlns:SOAP-ENV="http://schemas.xmlsoap.org/soap/envelope/"
                   xmlns:ns1="urn:ExampleAPI">
   <SOAP-ENV:Body>
      <SOAP-ENV:Fault>
         <faultcode>ns1:DBError</faultcode>
         <faultstring>Test Fault String</faultstring>
         <faultactor>Fault Actor</faultactor>
         <detail>
            <ns1:DBUnavailableFault>
               <DBMessage>DB Error</DBMessage>
               <RetryInMinutes>60</RetryInMinutes>
            </ns1:DBUnavailableFault>
         </detail>
      </SOAP-ENV:Fault>
   </SOAP-ENV:Body>
</SOAP-ENV:Envelope>
```

Using the SOAP Extension

You can use the SOAP extension (ext/soap) to write SOAP servers and clients. It supports subsets of the SOAP 1.1, SOAP 1.2, and WSDL 1.1 specifications. The extension provides some php.ini configuration options, listed in Table 18-4, that you can use to control caching behavior.

Table 18-4. *SOAP INI Options*

Option	Type	Default	Changeable	Description
soap.wsdl_cache_enabled	Boolean	1	PHP_INI_ALL	Determines whether a WSDL document is cached or if a new one must be fetched each time a SoapClient or SoapServer object is instantiated.
soap.wsdl_cache_dir	String	/tmp	PHP_INI_ALL	The directory to cache the WSDL documents.
soap.wsdl_cache_ttl	Integer	86400	PHP_INI_ALL	Amount of time in seconds from when a WSDL document is cached until a fresh copy must be retrieved.

You can enable the SOAP extension by building PHP with the following configure flag:

```
./configure --enable-soap
```

Under a Windows environment, this extension is built as a shared library and must be loaded through the php.ini file. Once you have placed the library php_soap.dll in your PHP library directory, make sure it is enabled in the php.ini file:

```
extension=php_soap.dll
```

With the extension now loaded properly in PHP, you can move on to actually using the SOAP API.

Common SOAP Classes

You use classes in the SOAP extension both when writing a SOAP client and when writing a SOAP server. It is a good idea to understand these classes, including what they do and how they are created, before attempting to work with SOAP. Although you may not need every class, a few of them will come in handy when you are having problems returning or sending data either to or from a SOAP server.

SoapVar

The SoapVar class creates encoded variables. When working without WSDL, it is a bit more difficult to use SOAP. Clients and servers are unable to automatically determine the proper data types like those using WSDL can, though they can make some guesses. Through the use of a SoapVar object, you can specify the data type as well as optionally specify the element name to be used when creating a message. The SoapVar class also comes in handy when working with different aspects of a SOAP message, such as the SOAP Header, regardless of whether WSDL is being used. The SoapVar class is a simple class consisting solely of a constructor:

```
__construct(mixed data, int encoding [, string type_name [, string type_namespace [,
         string node_name [, string node_namespace]]]])
```

The constructor takes a number of parameters, each of which affects how the data will be serialized when the SOAP message is created (see Table 18-5).

Table 18-5. SoapVar *Parameters*

Parameter	Description
data	The data to be serialized in the SOAP message is passed as the data parameter.
encoding	The encoding parameter indicates the data type. The value of this parameter is one of the SOAP encoding constants, which can be found in Appendix B.
type_name	The data type name. When using RPC/encoded, the type_name is the value for the xsi:type attribute in the SOAP message for the data being passed.
type_namespace	The namespace from which the type specified by the type_name parameter resides.
node_name	The name of the element to be used in the SOAP message data.
node_namespace	The namespace in which the element named by the node_name parameter resides.

An example use of the SoapVar class is creating the SOAP Body when working without a WSDL document. The structure needs to be defined somehow, but there is no schema a client or server could use to create it. The following code creates a SoapVar that follows the definitions from the WSDL document in Listing 18-1:

```
/* Define the structure of the getPeopleByFirstLastName types */
class getPeopleByFirstLastName {
    public $first = 'j*';
    public $last = '*';
}

$PeopleStruct = new getPeopleByFirstLastName();

/*
    Create new SoapVar using the types defined in the WSDL from Listing 18-1 and
    causing the element named getPeopleByFirstLastName within the urn:ExampleAPI as
    the containing element
*/
$PeopleVar = new SoapVar($PeopleStruct, SOAP_ENC_OBJECT, "getPeopleByFirstLastName",
                    "urn:ExampleAPI", "getPeopleByFirstLastName",
                    "urn:ExampleAPI");
```

The data used is a getPeopleByFirstLastName object, and in sync with the WSDL document it has first and last members. The object is encoded as a SOAP_ENC_OBJECT. Its type is getPeopleByFirstLastName, which resides in the urn:ExampleAPI namespace, and it conforms to the complex type defined within the WSDL document. Last, the members need to be wrapped within a getPeopleByFirstLastName element that resides in the urn:ExampleAPI within the SOAP message, so these are passed using the node_name and node_namespace parameters.

You may wonder why you went through all this trouble if the WSDL is right there in front of you. This example does not directly use the WSDL document. Its only purpose is to allow you to reference WSDL to understand how the SoapVar parameters relate to WSDL definitions. If the WSDL were being used, none of this would have been necessary because you could have used the $PeopleStruct object directly.

SoapHeader

The SoapHeader class provides the ability to create SOAP header entities, covered in the earlier "SOAP Header" section. SOAP headers simply provide the ability to modularly extend a SOAP message. The class is used both when using a WSDL and when not using WSDL so is a class common to both methods. This class is also a simple class consisting solely of a constructor:

```
__construct(string namespace, string name [, mixed data [, bool mustUnderstand [,
            mixed actor]]])
```

This constructor also takes a number of parameters; they are not difficult to understand because they almost directly map to the structure of a SOAP header entity. The namespace and name parameters go hand in hand. These parameters define the element created for the header entity. The data parameter, which is optional, is what is used as the contents of the header entity. It can be a PHP type or a complex defined type created using a SoapVar object. The mustUnderstand parameter, also optional, sets the mustUnderstand attribute on the header entity. When omitted or FALSE is passed, an attribute is not added. The actor parameter is an optional parameter that sets the value of the actor attribute on the header entity. When used, it must be either a string containing the URI for the actor or one of the SOAP ACTOR constants listed in Appendix B.

For example, you can easily create a similar header to that shown in the "SOAP Header" section using the SoapHeader class. An element with the local name Transaction residing in the namespace http://www.example.com will be created with the contents dummy content. It will specify the mustUnderstand attribute as well as set the actor to the next receiver of the SOAP message. For example:

```
$soapHeader = new SoapHeader("http://www.example.com", "Transaction",
                        "dummy content", TRUE, SOAP_ACTOR_NEXT);
```

Once the message is serialized, the SOAP Header will look similar to the following fragment:

```
<SOAP-ENV:Header>
    <ns2:Transaction SOAP-ENV:mustUnderstand="1"
                    SOAP-ENV:actor="http://schemas.xmlsoap.org/soap/actor/next">
        dummy content
    </ns2:Transaction>
</SOAP-ENV:Header>
```

This is only a fragment, so the missing namespace declarations have not been included. They were defined on the SOAP-ENV:Envelope element where the namespace http://www.example.com was associated with the ns2 prefix.

SoapParam

The SoapParam class provides the ability to create named parameters. Like the other common classes, the SoapParam class only has a constructor that simply takes the data to be associated with a name:

```
__construct (mixed data, string name)
```

The data parameter accepts a value containing either a native PHP type or a SoapVar. The name parameter accepts a string containing the name to be used for the parameter.

Using the $PeopleStruct object, created earlier in the "SoapVar" section, you can create a parameter named getPeopleByFirstLastName that contains the object. You can then pass this parameter to a SoapClient method in order to make a remote call. For example:

```
$PeopleVar = new SoapVar($PeopleStruct, SOAP_ENC_OBJECT, "getPeopleByFirstLastName",
                    "urn:ExampleAPI", "getPeopleByFirstLastName",
                    "urn:ExampleAPI");

$PeopleParam = new SoapParam($PeopleVar, 'getPeopleByFirstLastName');
```

SoapFault

In the respect of commonality, a client uses the SoapFault class when a SOAP Fault is received, and a server uses the class to create a SOAP Fault to return to a client. On the client side, the structure of a SoapFault object is important. Depending upon the SOAP error handling, a SoapFault either is handled as an Exception, which is the default, or is returned as the return value when calling a function. In both cases, the structure of the object is the same. It contains a number of properties, as follows, that provide details of the error:

faultcode: A string an application can use to identify the type of fault issued. Refer to Listing 18-3 for SOAP-defined fault codes.

faultstring: A human-readable error description.

faultactor: The URI for the server responsible for issuing the fault.

detail: Application-specific information related to the Body of a SOAP message. Not all SoapFaults provide information for this property. Its use depends upon the type of fault and the application.

From a server perspective, the SoapFault class creates SOAP faults rather than handling them. A fault is created by instantiating a SoapFault object and returning it from a function. For example:

```
__construct(string faultcode, string faultstring [, string faultactor [,
        mixed detail [, string faultname [, SoapHeader headerfault]]]])
```

You can create a fault through simple instantiation, passing the required information to the constructor. From what you have read earlier in this chapter concerning a SOAP Fault and the properties described previously, the first three parameters should be evident. The detail parameter, however, needs some additional explanation.

The detail parameter can take data of any type. When a fault is defined in WSDL in the output section, the structure of the detail can be defined. It does not need to be a simple type. This portion of a SOAP Fault is application dependant, so you can pass a complex structure in the detail section of a fault to provide extended information the client might need.

When defined in a WSDL document, a fault is named. The faultname parameter maps the SoapFault to the named fault. By passing this parameter, not only does the client know what to expect, but also any data passed in the detail parameter can be properly encoded. This alleviates the need to use SoapVar objects for the detail data.

The headerfault parameter is used when the fault is being issued during the processing of a SOAP header entity. It offers the ability to return a soap:headerfault, which is a fault message in the SOAP Header of the response message. I will provide detailed information about issuing faults from a server later in this chapter in the section "The Soap Server." The following is a quick example of creating a new SoapFault:

```
new SoapFault("DBError", "Error in the header", "urn:ExampleAPI",
            "Fault: Simple String Details", "nodb");
```

The SOAP Client

The SoapClient class is the workhorse for consuming a SOAP service. It can make the requests to a SOAP server. In WSDL mode, which is the recommended mode for working with SOAP, it also performs the majority of data type conversions and encoding you will need to create SOAP messages from PHP variables and types. Working in non-WSDL mode is often a bit more difficult, and this is where a few of the previously discussed common classes come in handy. The following sections will explain the different functionality of the SoapClient class and take you through the creation of a SOAP client to access the services. You can find additional examples of accessing services in the "Seeing Some Examples in Action" section where I show how to create clients to access both eBay and Google using SOAP.

Creating the Client

Create a SOAP client by instantiating a SoapClient object. It is at this point you can set a number of options as well as whether WSDL will be used:

```
__construct (mixed wsdl [, array options])
```

The wsdl parameter is an important parameter. It determines whether the client will use WSDL; if so, it specifies the location of the WSDL document. When using the client in non-WSDL mode, you must pass NULL. You can pass options, listed in Table 18-6, as an associative array. When working in non-WSDL mode, this parameter is required along with the use of the location and uri options. Unlike using WSDL, these two options cannot be automatically determined and must be set in order to access the service.

Table 18-6. SoapClient *Options*

Option	Description
location	Defines the URL to which calls are made to the Web service. When used in WSDL mode, this option will override the default address defined in the WSDL.
uri	Defines the target namespace of the SOAP server.
style	Defines the style of SOAP message structures. This option can have the value SOAP_DOCUMENT or SOAP_RPC.
use	Defines the encoding to use. This option can have the value SOAP_ENCODED or SOAP_LITERAL.
soap_version	Specifies whether to use SOAP 1.1 or SOAP 1.2. This option can have the value SOAP_1_1 or SOAP_1_2.
connection_timeout	The maximum number of seconds to wait to connect to the server. This option is available in PHP 5.0.4 and newer.
stream_context	A stream context to use during requests. This option is available in PHP 5.0.5 and newer.
login	The username to use when HTTP authentication is being used.
password	The password for HTTP authentication.
authentication	Sets the authentication type. The value SOAP_AUTHENTICATION_DIGEST sets the client to use Digest authentication. Any other value sets the client to use Basic authentication. This is available in PHP 5.0.4 and newer.
proxy_host	The proxy server host when making connections through a proxy server.
proxy_login	The username to authenticate with the proxy server.
proxy_password	The password to authenticate with the proxy server.
local_cert	The certificate to use with HTTPS client certificate authentication. This is available in PHP 5.0.4 and newer.
passphrase	The passphrase to use with HTTPS client certificate authentication. This is available in PHP 5.0.4 and newer.
compression	Compression options to use. The value is any combination of SOAP_COMPRESSION_ACCEPT, SOAP_COMPRESSION_GZIP, and SOAP_COMPRESSION_DEFLATE combined using a bitwise "or." For example: SOAP_COMPRESSION_ACCEPT I SOAP_COMPRESSION_GZIP.
encoding	Defines the encoding to use when returning strings. This is available in PHP 5.0.1 and newer.
classmap	Allows some WSDL types to be mapped to PHP classes. The value is an associative array using WSDL types as keys and the names of PHP classes as values. This is available in PHP 5.0.3 and newer.
trace	Enables debugging. Setting this option to 1 allows the use of the __getLastXXX methods.
exceptions	By default, SOAP Faults are thrown as exceptions. Setting the value of this option to 0 disables Fault exceptions and results in an error instead.

The numerous options in Table 18-6 should provide you with plenty of flexibility to control many different aspects of the client. To ensure that you understand how a SoapClient object is instantiated and various are options used, Listing 18-9 demonstrates various configurations used when creating a SoapClient object.

Listing 18-9. *Examples Creating* SoapClient *Objects*

```
$client = new SoapClient("http://www.example.com/example.wsdl");

$client = new SoapClient("http://www.example.com/example.wsdl",
                         array('login'=>"username", 'password'=>"password"));

$client = new SoapClient("http://www.example.com/example.wsdl",
                         array('proxy_host'=>"localhost",'proxy_port'=> 8080));

$client = new SoapClient(null, array('location'=>"http://www.example.com/soap.php",
                                     'uri'=>"http://www.example.com/"));

$client = new SoapClient(null, array('location'=>"http://www.example.com/soap.php",
                                     'uri'=>"urn:ExampleAPI",
                                     'style'=>SOAP_DOCUMENT,
                                     'use'=>SOAP_LITERAL));

class cPerson {
   public $first;
   public $last;
}

$client = new SoapClient("http://www.example.com/example.wsdl",
                         array('classmap' => array('Person' => "cPerson")));
```

■**Note** When working in exception mode, which is the default mode, all SOAP Faults cause a SoapFault exception to be thrown. You should always use try/catch blocks so you can properly handle the fault.

Inspecting a Service

One of the benefits of SOAP, when using a WSDL document, is that it is easy to inspect the data types and function signatures. You do not need to wade through excess documentation or physically read a WSDL document and try to decipher it. They are accessible directly from the SOAP client via the __getTypes() and __getFunctions() methods.

The following example consumes a Conversions service that provides functions to convert numbers into English words, numbers into dollar amounts, and text into title-cased text:

```
<?php
/* Set the location of the WSDL document */
$wsdl = 'http://www.dataaccess.com/webservicesserver/conversions.wso?WSDL';
```

```
try {
    $xConverter = new SoapClient($wsdl);
    echo "Types:\n";
    if ($xTypes = $xConverter->__getTypes()) {
        foreach ($xTypes AS $type) {
            echo $type."\n\n";
        }
    }

    echo "Functions:\n";
    if ($xTypes = $xConverter->__getFunctions()) {
        foreach ($xTypes AS $type) {
            echo $type."\n\n";
        }
    }

} catch (SoapFault $e) {
    var_dump($e);
}
?>
```

Each of the methods returns an array of strings containing either a type or a function signature based upon the method called. In the example, a SoapClient is created, $xConverter, using the WSDL for this service. The client then makes a call to each of the functions and loops through the returned arrays, outputting the contents. Listing 18-10 shows the output from executing this code.

Listing 18-10. *Conversions Service Types and Functions*

```
Types:
struct NumberToWords {
 unsignedLong ubiNum;
}

struct NumberToWordsResponse {
 string NumberToWordsResult;
}

struct NumberToDollars {
 decimal dNum;
}

struct NumberToDollarsResponse {
 string NumberToDollarsResult;
}
```

```
struct TitleCaseWords {
 string sText;
 string sToken;
}

struct TitleCaseWordsResponse {
 string TitleCaseWordsResult;
}

Functions:
NumberToWordsResponse NumberToWords(NumberToWords $parameters)

NumberToDollarsResponse NumberToDollars(NumberToDollars $parameters)

TitleCaseWordsResponse TitleCaseWords(TitleCaseWords $parameters)
```

When a service does not provide WSDL, this introspection cannot be done. The only way you can find out what the service provides is through some sort of documentation.

Location, Location, Location

So far you have seen that the address for a service is either taken from a WSDL document or specified using the location option when a SoapClient is instantiated. It is quite possible that a service is unavailable because of the server being down. When making client calls, this results in a SOAP Fault and 404 error in the HTTP response headers. The service, however, may be provided at other addresses. For example, in a WSDL document, a service may have multiple ports sharing the same port type. The only difference is the soap:address. This indicates that alternative addresses are available for the service. Unfortunately, when listed, a SoapClient does not automatically fall back to these addresses when it is unable to connect. In non-WSDL mode, documentation may provide addresses for a service.

To change the location, you could always create a new SoapClient using an alternate address specified by through the location option. This can become a hassle. It requires you to set up all the options you were previously using again with only a modification to the location option. To avoid this hassle, you can reuse the existing SoapClient object and simply change the location by calling the __setLocation() method.

Caution This method is available only in PHP 5.0.4 and newer.

This method takes one optional parameter. Passing a string containing a URL changes the location to the new URL. Passing in NULL or omitting this parameter reverts the location to the address specified in the WSDL document. In non-WSDL mode, you should not be passing NULL or omitting this parameter because there is no address to fall back on. The return value from this method is the value of any previously defined location option or NULL if not previously specified. In WSDL mode only, a location previously set through the location option or this method will be returned. In the case, no location option has been previously set, and the method does not return the address from the WSDL. For example:

```
/* address is defined as http://www.example.com/example/ in WSDL */
$sClient = new SoapClient('example.wsdl');

/* Override the location from the WSDL */
$location = $sClient->__setLocation('http://www.example.com/alternate/');
```

Making Client Calls

You can use many techniques to make client calls. Much of this depends upon whether WSDL is being used as well as the style and use (that is, Document/literal or RPC/encoded). In this section, I will cover how to make calls using some of these techniques.

I live in the United States, but many of the people I talk with on a regular basis are located all over the world. It's common that someone eventually starts talking about their local weather. Unfortunately, the last time I had to deal with the metric system was long ago in school, so when I hear that the current temperature is 5° Celsius, I really have no idea if that is cold. To me, 5° is cold, but then again I know temperatures in terms of Fahrenheit, not Celsius.

Simple Type RPC-Encoded Call

While searching XMethods one day, I came across a temperature conversion Web service. XMethods (http://www.xmethods.com/) lists a number of publicly accessible Web services. The conversion service provides a number of functions to convert to and from different temperature measurements. The information provided for the server was that it was RPC style and gave the location of the WSDL document. After creating a client using the WSDL document for the service (http://java.hpcc.nectec.or.th:1978/axis/TemperatureConvert.jws?wsdl), I queried it for the types and functions. A quick scan through the list revealed the exact functionality I needed, whose signatures are as follows:

```
/* Convert Fahrenheit to Celsius */
float FahrenheitTOCelsius(float $temp)

/* Convert Celsius to Fahrenheit */
float CelsiusTOFahrenheit(float $temp)
```

Based on the signatures, accessing the functions is simple. Both the input parameter, $temp, and the return value are simple floats. Based on this, the following script demonstrates how the temperature 5° Celsius, defined by the variable $temp_celsius, is converted to Fahrenheit:

```php
<?php
/* Temperature in Celsius */
$temp_celsius = 5;

/* Location of WSDL */
$wsdl = 'http://java.hpcc.nectec.or.th:1978/axis/TemperatureConvert.jws?wsdl';

$sClient = new SoapClient($wsdl1);
```

```
/* Output the temperature in Fahrenheit*/
print $sClient->CelsiusTOFahrenheit($temp_celsius)
?>
```

In only a few lines of code, you are able to access the service and find out that the temperature equates to 41° Fahrenheit.

One thing you can see from this example is that a remote function can be called as a native method of a SoapClient object. The function CelsiusTOFahrenheit() is called from $sClient as if it were a real method of the SoapClient class. This type of calling convention is available whether or not you are using WSDL. What you do get using WSDL in this case is type conversion. To illustrate what I mean, let's try using this service without WSDL:

```
<?php
$temp_celsius = 5;

try {
    /* Location and URI both provided in Web service summary */
    $location='http://java.hpcc.nectec.or.th:1978/axis/TemperatureConvert.jws';
    $uri = 'http://java.hpcc.nectec.or.th:1978/axis/TemperatureConvert.jws';

    /* Create client without using WSDL
        set style to RPC, which was also provided in service summary */
    $sClient = new SoapClient(NULL,
                            array('location' => $location,
                                  'uri'      => $uri,
                                  'style'    => SOAP_RPC));


print $sClient->CelsiusTOFahrenheit($temp_celsius)."\n";
} catch (SoapFault $e) {
    echo $e->faultstring;
}
?>
```

Upon executing this code, a SoapFault is thrown, producing the following output:

```
org.xml.sax.SAXException: Bad types (int -> float)
```

Without using a WSDL document, the client took its best guess at converting the parameter to a type. In this case, the parameter was a PHP integer that translated to an xsd:int. The function on the server is expecting a float.

Note Even though you are making a client call without using the WSDL, the server is using the WSDL document, allowing it to enforce the data types, as well as using RPC/encoded, so it is expecting the data types to be passed in the message.

You can ensure the data is typed correctly in a couple of ways depending upon the data type it needs to be. In this case, the parameter must be a float. Being a simple type as well as having a corresponding PHP type, you can modify the call using PHP casting:

```
/* Cast PHP type */
$tempVar = (float)5;

print $sClient->CelsiusTOFahrenheit($tempVar)."\n";
```

This works fine assuming there is a corresponding PHP type, but when there is not, such as using complex types, you can use a SoapVar object:

```
/* Use SoapVar */
$tempVar = new SoapVar($temp_celsius, XSD_FLOAT);

print $sClient->CelsiusTOFahrenheit($tempVar)."\n";
```

A SoapVar object is created of the xsd:float type using $temp_celsius as its data. This object is then passed as the function parameter, satisfying the required data type constraint.

Complex Type Document Literal Call

If you refer to the Conversions service, whose types and functions are shown in Listing 18-10, you will notice that all the functions take complex types for parameters. You can create these complex types in a variety of ways. For example, the following functions take complex types as parameters and return a complex type as the result:

```
NumberToDollarsResponse NumberToDollars(NumberToDollars $parameters)

TitleCaseWordsResponse TitleCaseWords(TitleCaseWords $parameters)
```

All of these types are structs. In PHP terms, this relates to either associative arrays or objects. Suppose you want to call the NumberToDollars() function. The first thing to do is examine the NumberToDollars struct so that the correct parameter can be created:

```
struct NumberToDollars {
 decimal dNum;
}
```

Using objects, you can define a class for this structure:

```
class NumberToDollars {
    public $dNum;
}
```

You can then use this class to call the function:

```
$wsdl = 'http://www.dataaccess.com/webservicesserver/conversions.wso?WSDL';

try {
    $xConverter = new SoapClient($wsdl);
```

```
$param = new NumberToDollars();
$param->dNum = 123456;

$retVal = $xConverter->NumberToDollars($param);

print $retVal->NumberToDollarsResult."\n";
} catch (SoapFault $e) {
  var_dump($e);
}
```

Upon execution of this code, you would see the following result:

```
one hundred and twenty three thousand four hundred and fifty six dollars
```

The name of the class is unimportant here. You could name it anything you like, although naming it the same or similar to the structure makes it easier to identify and compare to the structure definition. What are important are the class properties. The properties must use the same names as the structure members. When the SoapClient creates the SOAP message, the property names are used as the element names.

The return value in this example is also a complex type. Complex types are returned as objects based on the stdClass class, although later in this chapter you will see how you can map specific classes to data types. Based on the function signature from Listing 18-10, the function returns a NumberToDollarsResponse type, which is structured as follows:

```
struct NumberToDollarsResponse {
 string NumberToDollarsResult;
}
```

Now that you know structures and PHP objects map to each other, you can say that the returned object contains the property NumberToDollarsResult and that the property is a string. Based on this, the example simply outputs the value of this property.

You could also have used an array just as easily for the input parameter. The keys of an associative array work the same way the properties of an object do. For example, you could obtain the same results as before using an array in the following manner:

```
$param = array('dNum'=>123456);

$retVal = $xConverter->NumberToDollars($param);
```

Although an array is used for input, an object is still returned as in the previous example.

Adding SOAP Headers

The SOAP extension added a simple method to add SOAP header entities in PHP 5.0.5. If you're running any version prior to this, you must set headers using other mechanisms described in the section "Low-Level Calls." In all likelihood, you are probably running a newer version of PHP, which means you have access to the __setSoapHeaders() method. This method sets headers for the lifetime of a client, which means once set using this method, subsequent calls made by the client will add the headers to the SOAP message. For example:

```
__setSoapHeaders(array SoapHeaders)
```

The method accepts either an array of SoapHeader objects or NULL. The reason for allowing NULL is that all headers currently set on the client are replaced by the headers passed in, and using NULL allows all headers to simply be deleted.

The following example demonstrates how to add some basic authentication to the SOAP message. A username and password are placed into a header entity for processing by the receiver:

```
/* Create and authentication object with username/password */
class authentication {
  public $username;
  public $password;
}

$auth = new authentication();
$auth->username = 'username';
$auth->password = 'password';

/* You MUST encode the object */
$authVar = new SoapVar($auth, SOAP_ENC_OBJECT);

$header =  new SoapHeader('urn:ExampleAPI', "Authentication",
                          $authVar, TRUE, SOAP_ACTOR_NEXT);

/* Set the new headers to use when creating SOAP messages */
$sClient->__setSoapHeaders(array($header));
```

When the message is sent, the first receiver of the message (in the event the message is going to be forwarded) is required to process the Authentication header entity containing the login credentials. Failure to do so results in a SoapFault being returned. The reason for this is that the mustUnderstand attribute has been set and the actor identified as the next receiver of the message. If you require subsequent client calls that do not require this header, you must remove it by calling __setSoapHeaders with a NULL:

```
$sClient->__setSoapHeaders(NULL);
```

Low-Level Calls

Older versions of the SOAP extension limited what you could perform. For instance, older versions did not have a method to set header entities. You may want to use different options for a specific call than what you had set on the SoapClient. You could always change the options directly from a SoapClient, but then you would have to revert them once the call was made.

In cases like these, you can use the __soapCall() method:

```
__soapCall(string function_name [, array arguments [, array options [,
                                mixed input_headers [, array &output_headers]]]])
```

■**Note** In PHP 5.0.0 and 5.0.1, this method was named __call(). It was depreciated as of 5.0.2 in favor of __soapCall().

Table 18-7 describes the various parameters for this method.

Table 18-7. __soapCall *Parameters*

Parameter	Description
function_name	The name of the function to call.
arguments	An array of arguments to be passed to the function.
options	An array of options. The only options that can be set through this parameter are location, uri, and soapaction.
input_headers	Sets the SOAP Header. The parameter value can be either an array of SoapHeader objects or a single SoapHeader object.
output_headers	A variable to which any headers received in the response will be stored.

The following example demonstrates how to use the various parameters for this method. Once the parameters have been assembled, the SoapClient makes a request to execute the doSearch function from the service.

```
$xConverter = new SoapClient(NULL,
                        array('location'=>'http://www.example.com/exampleAPI',
                            'uri'=>'urn:ExampleAPI'));


/* create a SoapParam */
$param = array(new SoapParam('PHP XML', 'search_term'));

/* Create an options array */
$options = array('location'=>'http://www.example.com/alternateExampleAPI',
                'uri'=>'urn:AlternateExampleAPI');

/* Create SoapHeader */
$soapHeader = new SoapHeader("http://www.example.com", "Transaction",
                            "dummy content", TRUE, SOAP_ACTOR_NEXT);

/* Call remote function and retrieve any response headers */
$ret = $xConverter->__soapCall('doSearch', $param, $options, $header,
                            $response_headers);
```

Message Modification

Not everything is perfect in this world. The SOAP extension may not be doing exactly what you want it to when creating a SOAP message. The specifications are also just like all other XML specifications, and they leave many things up to interpretation. This might result in a service expecting something different in terms of what is contained in the message. Luckily for you, you can modify a message prior to being sent. Using a subclass, the doRequest() method can be overridden.

The doRequest() method is called by a SoapClient object when a function call is made. It first assembles the SOAP messages and then makes a call to this method to actually send the message. By subclassing the SoapClient class, it is possible that this method be intercepted, allowing modifications to a message as well as altering how the message is sent. For example:

```
__doRequest(string request, string location, string action, int version)
```

The request parameter is the serialized SOAP message. Using one of the XML extensions, like DOM, the message can be loaded into a tree and modified. The location parameter is the URL being called for the service. Using this value, you could possibly change the location being called. The action parameter is the SOAP action being taken. This is the value used for the SOAPAction header in the HTTP request. The version parameter identifies the SOAP version being used. Its value is the constant SOAP_1_1 or SOAP_1_2.

Using this method is not difficult at all. You must first create a class extending the SoapClient class. This class will be specifically to modify requests made when calling the CelsiusTOFahrenheit() function used in the "Simple Type RPC-Encoded Call" section.

```
Class mySoapClient extends SoapClient {
    function __doRequest($request, $location, $action, $version) {
        /* Load the request into a DOMDocument */
        $dom = new DOMDocument();
        $dom->loadXML($request);

        /* Find the temp element and set temp to 20C */
        $nodeList = $dom->getElementsByTagName('temp');
        if ($nodeList->length == 1) {
            $nodeList->item(0)->firstChild->nodeValue = "20";
        }

        /* Serialize the tree and send modified request to parent method */
        $request = $dom->saveXML();
        return parent::__doRequest($request, $location, $action, $version);
    }
}
```

The __doRequest() method has been added to the class. When called, it loads the request into a DOMDocument object, searches for the temp element, changes the value to 20, and then sends the modified request to the parent to be handled.

Once the class has been defined, you create a client based on this new class:

```
$wsdl = "http://java.hpcc.nectec.or.th:1978/axis/TemperatureConvert.jws?wsdl";
$sClient = new mySoapClient($wsdl);
```

Next, set the original temperature to be converted:

```
$temp_celsius = 5;
$tempVar = new SoapVar($temp_celsius, XSD_FLOAT);
```

Finally, make the request:

```
print  $sClient->CelsiusTOFahrenheit($tempVar)."\n";
```

The output is much different from the previous results. Instead of the value 41 being printed, the result is not 68. In this version of the __doRequest() method, you modified the SOAP message before it was sent out and changed the value of the temperature to be converted to 20 instead of the original value of 5.

This is just a simple example of modifying a SOAP message prior to sending it out. This method, however, provides great potential for employing a good number of technologies. For example, the SOAP extension does not have any native abilities for performing security for Web services (WS-Security). Imagine what it would take to add XML digital signatures and XML encryption to a SOAP message. These require canonicalization so must be performed on the raw SOAP message. Using the __doRequest() method, it is possible to intercept the message and add this type of functionality from what you learned in Chapter 12. This is only one area where you could take advantage of this functionality, because you could do plenty of other things with the raw message.

Debugging Client Calls

Debugging SOAP can often be tricky. SOAP faults provide only so much information. With this information, you still need to figure out why the error occurred. When a SoapClient is created using the trace option with a value of 1, four methods are available that allow you to inspect different parts of SOAP messages. Without the trace option, these methods are still present, but they return empty strings. The methods being described are __getLastRequest(), which returns a string containing the serialized SOAP-ENV:Envelope document sent by the client; __getLastRequestHeaders(), which returns a string containing the HTTP Request headers; __getLastResponse(), which returns a string containing the serialized SOAP-ENV:Envelope document from the server; and __getLastResponseHeaders(), which returns a string containing the HTTP Response headers.

The debugging calls are not difficult to utilize. Simply call the appropriate method, passing no arguments, and the string returned contains the information you want. The following is a simple example of calling a function that you know is going to cause a SOAP fault. When the SoapFault is caught, the faultstring and request message are output along with the HTTP headers from the response.

```
try {
    $response = $sPublish->getPeopleByFirstLastName(1,2, 3);
} catch (SoapFault $e) {
    echo "Fault: ".$e->faultstring."\n\n";
    echo $sPublish->__getLastRequest()."\n\n";
    echo $sPublish->__getLastResponseHeaders();
}
```

```
Fault: Error cannot find parameter

<SOAP-ENV:Envelope xmlns:SOAP-ENV="http://schemas.xmlsoap.org/soap/envelope/"
                   xmlns:ns1="urn:ExampleAPI">
    <SOAP-ENV:Body>
        <ns1:getPeopleByFirstLastName/>
        <param1>2</param1>
        <param2>3</param2>
```

```
    </SOAP-ENV:Body>
</SOAP-ENV:Envelope>


HTTP/1.1 500 Internal Service Error
Date: Fri, 02 Dec 2005 08:29:32 GMT
Server: Apache/2.0.53 (Win32) PHP/6.0.0-dev
X-Powered-By: PHP/6.0.0-dev
Content-Length: 294
Connection: close
Content-Type: text/xml; charset=utf-8
```

From the faultstring, you can tell there is something wrong with the parameters being passed to the server. The response header in this example does not offer any additional information about the specifics of the error. The request SOAP message is a different story. The structure is completely wrong. The Body should contain a single ns1:getPeopleByFirstLastName element that further contains a first and last element. Instead of this, the Body contains three child elements, which does not match the input message defined in the WSDL document. Without having had access to the raw SOAP message, you probably would have a lot of trial and error with code changes until you found the exact cause and resolution.

The SOAP Server

Have you written some functionality you would like to share with the world? Do you have an application that you would like to open up access to remotely in a universal fashion? If you have answered "yes" to any of these questions, the SOAP extension can be the answer to your dilemma. Not only can you use it to consume Web services, but its API provides the ability to create SOAP servers as well. In the following section, I will cover how you can do this by building a fully functional Web service of your own.

The server is based on the WSDL document in Listing 18-1. It provides a single function that allows a client to search for people's records based on first and last name. Partial names are allowed by using the * wildcard. For example, looking for people whose first name starts with *j* is written as j*. This can also be combined with a last name qualifier, so using s* for the last name searches all people whose first name starts with *j* and whose last name starts with *s*.

Do You Need to Write WSDL?

Once finding out what it takes to write a WSDL document, many developers feel a bit overwhelmed and wonder if they can get away with writing a service without a WSDL document. Not creating a WSDL document for a SOAP server defeats many of the benefits you get from using SOAP compared to creating a REST-based service, explained in Chapter 17.

Looking at it strictly from the client point of view, using a WSDL document allows developers to inspect an API without having to read any documentation. They just need to load a WSDL document into a SoapClient and call the methods to list the types and functions available. From this, a service can quickly be consumed without having to spend large amounts of time sorting through abundant amounts of documentation.

From both the client and server perspectives, end points, bindings, operations, and data types are automatically set up when a WSDL document is loaded. Each knows the encoding to use as well as how message structures should be formatted. Another beneficial aspect is that in both cases data can usually be automatically converted to the needed data type.

Returning to the original question, the answer depends upon how the service will be used as well as by whom. My take on this, however, is that if a WSDL document is not going to be written for a service and made public to the consumers of the service, you are probably better off writing a REST-based service. This type of service is much easier to create and consume, especially when the major benefit of SOAP is not leveraged. If you absolutely do not want to write WSDL, you may be able to find some tools to automatically generate WSDL documents from PHP code. Zend Studio 5 mentions it has this ability. For those unfamiliar with Zend Studio, it is a PHP IDE, developed by Zend (http://www.zend.com), that provides a number of features for developing PHP applications. No, this is not an advertisement for the product, as I have not tried it for several years. How well these work I am unable to say, but they may provide at least enough capability for you to get over the WSDL hump.

Creating the SOAP Server

The hardest part of writing a SOAP server, in my opinion, is the WSDL document itself. Once you get over that hurdle, it is smooth sailing. As I clearly believe that WSDL should be written for a SOAP server, everything discussed during the creation of the service is based upon a SoapServer using WSDL. I cannot stress enough that if you do not want to write WSDL, write a REST-based service. In any event, the service you will be creating is based on the WSDL document, exampleapi.wsdl, from Listing 18-1:

```
__construct(mixed wsdl [, array options])
```

The wsdl parameter specifies the URI for the WSDL document to be used by the server. When working in non-WSDL modes, this parameter must be set to NULL. The options parameter specifies the options to be used for the server. This parameter is optional when working in WSDL mode but is required when working in non-WSDL mode, because the uri option, which specifies the target namespace of the server, must be set. Table 18-8 shows the full list of possible options.

Table 18-8. SoapServer *Options Parameters*

Parameter	Description
actor	The actor URI for the SOAP server.
classmap	An associative array mapping WSDL types to PHP classes. The keys of the array are the WSDL types for the classes, which are the values.
encoding	Defines the encoding to use when returning strings. This is available in PHP 5.0.1 and newer.
soap_version	Specifies whether to use SOAP 1.1 or SOAP 1.2. This option can have the value SOAP_1_1 or SOAP_1_2.
uri	The target namespace of the SOAP server.

Before creating the server for the service, which is not using options, you might like to see how some other servers are created, shown in Listing 18-11.

Listing 18-11. *Various Combinations for Creating a* SoapServer

```
/* Create server using WSDL and specifying Soap version and Actor URI */
$server = new SoapServer("mywsdl.wsdl",
                         array('soap_version' => SOAP_1_2,
                               'actor' => "http://www.example.com/actorA"));

/* Create server using WSDL and mapping a Person Class */
class Person {
    public $id;
    public $firstName;
    public $lastName;

}

$server = new SoapServer("mywsdl.wsdl",
                         array('classmap' => array('book' => "Person")));

/* Create server in non-WSDL mode and setting URI */
$server = new SoapServer(null, array('uri' => "urn:ExampleAPI"));
```

The server you are creating is using a WSDL document, exampleapi.wsdl, and does not need any options. It is simply created by the following:

```
$sServer = new SoapServer("exampleapi.wsdl");
```

Creating Function Handlers

Once you have created a SoapServer, you now need to define functionality to handle the incoming requests. You can write handlers as regular PHP functions or as methods with a class. How they are associated with SOAP actions, which are remote function calls, depends upon the approach taken, and only a single approach can be used when writing a server. What differentiates the two is that a class can be made persistent between SOAP requests as long as the client handles session cookies correctly.

Using PHP Functions

There is little difference between writing handlers using PHP functions and writing regular PHP functions. You just need to make sure the data being returned is of the correct type. Using WSDL makes this easy because in most cases the data is typed and encoded correctly. I say *most cases* because sometimes some unpredictable instances means it does not make this easy. When this happens, the first thing to check is the WSDL document itself, making sure all types and messages are correct. You can perform a quick check using a client and having it list all types and functions. Compare the output with what you thought it should be.

Defining the Function Functions must be named the same as the operation name. Using the WSDL document from Listing 18-1, only one operation is defined, getPeopleByFirstLastName. It takes a single parameter that is a getPeopleByFirstLastName structure and that contains a string for the first name (first) and a string for the last name (last). This is determined by the parts defined for the getPeopleByFirstLastName message. Each part of a message becomes a function parameter. The WSDL document in this example uses Document/literal for the SOAP messages, so a single message part is usually used. When using RPC/encoded, quite often a message contains multiple parts, which means the server function would take multiple parameters—one parameter for each of the parts.

Returning to the function you are creating, you begin by defining the function with the name getPeopleByFirstLastName and by accepting one parameter, which will also be called getPeopleByFirstLastName:

```
function getPeopleByFirstLastName($getPeopleByFirstLastName) {}
```

Although it is required that the function is named the same as the operation in the WSDL, the parameter can be named anything you like. It is easier, however, if you keep the names the same as the WSDL document so that mapping parameters and structures is easier to do when developing the service.

Input Parameters and Return Data Based on the WSDL document, the input parameter is a getPeopleByFirstLastName structure. This equates to a PHP stdClass object with the properties first and last. Because of how the WSDL document was written, the return type, when using the __getFunctions() method from a SoapClient object, is shown as the ArrayOfPerson type rather than the getPeopleByFirstLastNameResponse type. The reason for this is that the getPeopleByFirstLastNameResponse element refers to the ArrayOfPerson type rather than defining the complex type within the scope of its element. In either case, the data returned from this function is created in the same way.

The following code demonstrates how the input parameters are used within this function:

```
$people = array(array('id'=>1, 'firstName'=>'John', 'lastName'=>'Smith'),
                array('id'=>2, 'firstName'=>'Jane', 'lastName'=>'Doe'));

/* Get the first and last values passed from the client */
$firstSearch = str_replace('*', '([a-z]*)', $getPeopleByFirstLastName->first);
$lastSearch = str_replace('*', '([a-z]*)', $getPeopleByFirstLastName->last);

$matching = array();

/* Find all matching records */
foreach($people AS $person) {
    if (empty($firstSearch) || preg_match('/^'.$firstSearch.'$/i',
                                    $person['firstName'])) {
        if (empty($lastSearch) || preg_match('/^'.$lastSearch.'$/i',
                                    $person['lastName'])) {
            /* Match found - Add the record to our return list */
            $matching[] = $person;
        }
    }
}
```

The search is very primitive. This creates an array containing records for two people. The code converts the user's query into regular expressions. It then loops through each person in the array and, based upon the user input for the first and last properties, then either adds the person to the result list or skips it and moves to the next person in the array.

■**Note** Both arrays and objects map to a WSDL structure. Rather than an array containing arrays holding a person's information, you could also write $people as an array of objects. The object would be based on a class, like the class in Listing 18-2, that contains the id, first, and last properties.

Once all matching records have been found, identified by $matching, they must be returned to the client. You can do this in a few ways. The most straightforward method is simply returning the array:

```
return $matching;
```

Using WSDL, the server properly encodes the return value in the SOAP message. This does not always work correctly. For instance, you might not be using a WSDL document, for some reason the client might not be using a WSDL, or possibly the WSDL contains a typographical error. In this case, you might want to think about typing the return data using a SoapVar object. The following example is based on the people records having been built from arrays:

```
/* Initialize the return array */
$retval = array();

/* Loop through the array of people to be return and create a SoapVar
   for each person. The SoapVar is then added to the return array. */
foreach ($matching as $person) {
    $retval[] = new SoapVar($person, SOAP_ENC_ARRAY, "Person", "urn:ExampleAPI");
}

/* Return the final data */
return $retval;
```

As you can see, it's a little more involved to manually type data, but it is much safer. This guarantees that the data is encoded in the exact manner you want it to be in the SOAP message. If you decided to use an array of objects for the people records, the only change would be to the encoding in the SoapVar constructor. SOAP_ENC_OBJECT would be the type of encoding you would want.

Registering the Functions Once you have all the functions defined, you must register them with the SoapServer. You can use the addFunction() method for this purpose. You can add functions in a variety of ways. You can add a single function at a time by calling this method and passing a string containing the function name. This method also accepts an array of strings where each string is the name of a function. The last way to register functions is to call the method and pass the constant SOAP_FUNCTIONS_ALL. This constant instructs the SoapServer to add every function defined in the script. This is handy when the script only contains functions to handle SOAP requests. If the script is large and contains numerous unrelated functions, it is safer to register the functions by name, either one at a time or using an array. This server consists of only one callable function, so it will be added by name:

```
$sServer->addFunction('getPeopleByFirstLastName');
```

Using a Class

Rather than having to register a number of functions, you can use a class that contains all the methods to handle SOAP requests. This not only keeps the handlers contained in a single location, but using a class allows persistence to be handled by the SOAP server. You write a class method the same way you write a function for handling SOAP requests.

Setting the Class The difference between function handlers and method handlers is in how they are registered. Unlike the functions, which must explicitly be registered using the addFunction() method, you register class methods by registering the class in its entirety using the setClass() method:

```
setClass(string class_name [, mixed args [, mixed ...]])
```

The class_name parameter is the name of the class to register with the SoapServer. Only one class can be used, so calling this method again with a different class replaces the original class being used with the new one. The remaining arguments to this method are the arguments to pass to the class when it is instantiated:

```
class mySoapHandler {
    function getPeopleByFirstLastName($getPeopleByFirstLastName) {
        /* same code as previously defined for this function */
    }
}
```

```
$sServer->setClass('mySoapHandler');
```

Persistence The lifetime of the object instantiated by the server is the life of the request. This means that each time a client makes a call to the server, the server must instantiate a new instance of the registered class. It is possible for a client to keep state and make the object persistent through the use of the setPersistence() method. The method takes a single parameter that can be SOAP_PERSISTENCE_REQUEST, which is the default indicating not to maintain state, or SOAP_PERSISTENCE_SESSION, which allows the object to persist between requests in a PHP session.

Once the class has been registered with the server, simply call this:

```
$sServer->setPersistence(SOAP_PERSISTENCE_SESSION);
```

The object will be instantiated on the first request from a client and then saved in session. On subsequent calls, the object is retrieved from session rather than a new instance being created. This not only allows you to save session data for a client, but using constructor arguments with the setClass() method, you are able to create functionality that is executed upon the first request from a client, such as some initialization routines.

Handling the Client Request

Once you have set up the SoapServer, including registering any function handlers or setting a class and persistence, you need to handle the request from the client. Aptly named, the handle() method does this:

```
handle([string soap_request])
```

In most cases, this method is called without any arguments. Services typically run within a Web server, and the SoapServer retrieves the SOAP message from within this context, processes it, and then returns the data to the client.

This is not always the case, because you may have written a daemon, something out of the scope of this book, to listen on some arbitrary port and handle SOAP requests. After setting up the SoapServer, you can pass the SOAP message directly to the handle() method for processing. This ability also comes in handy when developing or debugging a service. Within a single script, you can create a SoapClient, overriding the __doRequest() method. The message contained in the request parameter from this method can then be sent to and handled by a SOAP server running within the same script.

■**Tip** When implementing a SOAP server not running within the context of a Web server, you can leverage the PHP output control functions to retrieve the resulting SOAP message so that it can be sent out in a custom fashion.

The service you are creating in this chapter is to be executed within the context of a Web server, so no special handling of the SOAP message is needed. The server just makes the following call that processes and returns the resulting message to the client:

```
$sServer->handle();
```

Returning SOAP Faults

Operations do not also work flawlessly. For example, if the requested function needs to access a database and the database happens to be down or the query failed for some other unforeseen reason, you want to let the client know that some type of error occurred. Earlier in this chapter, in the section "Common SOAP Classes," you were introduced to the SoapFault class and learned the syntax of creating an object of this type.

A fault is returned to the client simply by having the function being called either throw or return a new SoapFault object. It is created as you saw earlier in this chapter. The server you are creating here contains two named faults defined in the WSDL document for the getPeopleByFirstLastName operation. They are named nodb and sysmaint. This example is not using a database, so the only relevant fault would be sysmaint.

The service should never be shut down completely. The Web server will always be running, and the service should always be accepting requests. Sometimes, however, changes need to be made, so some type of system maintenance may be taking place. A system-wide variable, $SYS_STATUS, is used and set to FALSE to indicate when this is taking place. When this is taking place, the service should return a sysmaint fault to the client. This provides the client with some information about what is going on, as well as the number of minutes it should wait until trying to make another call. For example:

```
function getPeopleByFirstLastName($getPeopleByFirstLastName) {
    if (isset($GLOBALS['SYS_STATUS']) && $GLOBALS['SYS_STATUS'] == FALSE) {

        /* Set the details structure */
        $details = array("SysMessage"=>"System Maintenance", "RetryInMinutes"=>60);

        /* Throw new SoapFault Exception */
        throw new SoapFault("SYSError", "System Unavailable", "urn:ExampleAPI",
                            $details, "sysmaint");
    }

    /* Function Code Here */
}
```

The $details variable in the code is used as the details parameter. The faultcode name sysmaint, passed to the SoapFault constructor, maps the SystemMaintenance structure defined in the WSDL document for this fault with the details data. When this is returned to the client, assuming the client is a PHP SoapClient, a SoapFault exception is returned. An inspection of the exception, looking at only the relevant SOAP parts, appears as shown in Listing 18-12 when var_dump() is called on SoapFault.

Listing 18-12. Var_dump *of* SoapFault *Returned to* SoapClient

```
["faultstring"]=>
string(18) "System Unavailable"
["faultcode"]=>
string(12) "ns1:SYSError"
["faultactor"]=>
string(14) "urn:ExampleAPI"
["detail"]=>
object(stdClass)#2 (1) {
  ["SystemMaintenance"]=>
  object(stdClass)#3 (2) {
    ["SysMessage"]=>
    string(8) "DB Error"
    ["RetryInMinutes"]=>
    string(2) "60"
  }
}
```

Processing SOAP Headers

To properly process SOAP headers, you must specify the soap:header element for a wsdl:operation within a wsdl:binding. If the soap:header element is not included in the WSDL and the client sends a header with the mustUnderstand attribute, the SoapServer will return a fault, even if the header handler is properly set up on the server. Before I get ahead of myself, you first need to see how a header is defined.

Handling a header is implemented the same way a function handler is implemented. It is written as either a PHP function or a class method depending upon which method of handling you have chosen. The important aspects are the name of the function or method and the actor defined for the SoapServer. The following shows the SoapHeader constructor, which is used by a SoapClient to set a SOAP header:

```
__construct(string namespace, string name [, mixed data [, bool mustUnderstand [,
            mixed actor]]])
```

Using the Correct Actor

The actor parameter specifies the actor URI (namely, the URI of the server) that is to handle the header. If this parameter is not specified or is equal to the SOAP_ACTOR_NEXT constant, then the PHP SoapServer will attempt to handle the header. When it is specified, the SoapServer will attempt to handle the header only if it has not specified an actor or the value it specified is equal to the one defined by the client. For example, if the client set the actor of the header to urn:ExampleAPI, then in order for the SoapServer to handle the header, it either must not specify an actor or should be instantiated using the actor option, like the following:

```
$sServer = new SoapServer("exampleapi.wsdl", array('actor'=>'urn:ExampleAPI'));
```

The actor URI is not taken from the WSDL, and if expecting headers, defining the actor is a good idea in the event the client defines a header that is not intended for your service.

Function/Method Naming

The function or method for the header handler is named based on the part element of the message used by the soap:header. The value depends upon whether RPC/encoded or Document/literal is being used in the WSDL document. For an RPC/encoded soap:header, the function is named based on the value of the name attribute of the part element. For a Document/literal soap:header, the name is based on the value of the element attribute of the part element. No matter which value is used, the function is named by the localname, omitting any prefixes of the value. The parameters that are passed are based on the data type of the element (Document/literal) or the data type of the part (RPC/encoded). This is much easier to understand when looking at a WSDL document. For example, you are using Document/literal, so given the following document fragments from a WSDL document, you can determine the function names that must be implemented:

```
<definitions ....>
   <types>        ·
      <xsd:schema ...>
         <!- other types -->
         <xsd:element name="headerfunc" type="xsd:string"/>
      </xsd:schema>
   </types>
```

```
    <message name="headermsg">
        <part name="param1" element="tns:headerfunc"/>
    </message>

    <binding ...>
        <operation ...>
            <soap:operation .../>
            <input>
                <soap:header message="tns:headermsg" part="param1" use="literal"/>
                <soap:body .... />
            </input>
        </operation>
        <!-- Other operations -->
    </binding>
</definitions>
```

Starting with the soap:header element for the operation, you see that the message is tns:headermsg, and the part is param1. Once you locate the specific part for that message in the WSDL, you find the element is tns:headerfunc. Using the localname of this, the function to be implemented must be called headerfunc(). This element is a simple xsd:string data type, so a single string parameter is accepted by this function. The final prototype for the function or method that should be implemented looks like the following:

```
headerfunc(string $param)
```

Completed Server Example

Throughout the "SOAP Server" section, you examined various aspects of writing a SOAP server in PHP. In this section, you will put all the pieces together to create a fully functional SOAP server, shown in Listing 18-13. It is based on the WSDL document from Listing 18-1. The portion of the code not dealing with SOAP makes many assumptions. How it is implemented in the real world is not important here, because you will most likely be working with databases or other data storage mechanisms. What is important is how SOAP is used to glue the pieces together, because a rich backend could easily be added within the framework of this example.

Listing 18-13. *Completed Server Example for WSDL from Listing 18-1*

```php
<?php
/* System status - TRUE indicates normal operation /
                   FALSE indicates down for maintenance */
$SYS_STATUS = TRUE;

function getPeopleByFirstLastName($getPeopleByFirstLastName) {
    /* If system is down throw SOAP fault */
    if (isset($GLOBALS['SYS_STATUS']) && $GLOBALS['SYS_STATUS'] == FALSE) {
        $details = array("SysMessage"=>"Sys Error", "RetryInMinutes"=>60);
        throw new SoapFault("SYSError", "System Unavailable", "urn:ExampleAPI",
                            $details, "sysmaint");
    }
```

```php
    /* Initialize the Person Records */
    $people = array(array('id'=>1, 'firstName'=>'John', 'lastName'=>'Smith'),
                    array('id'=>2, 'firstName'=>'Jane', 'lastName'=>'Doe'));

    $firstSearch = str_replace('*', '([a-z]*)', $getPeopleByFirstLastName->first);
    $lastSearch = str_replace('*', '([a-z]*)', $getPeopleByFirstLastName->last);

    $retval = array();

    foreach($people AS $person) {
        /* Check if match on first name */
        if (empty($firstSearch) || preg_match('/^'.$firstSearch.'$/i',
                                               $person['firstName']))
        {
            /* Check if match on last name */
            if (empty($lastSearch) || preg_match('/^'.$lastSearch.'$/i',
                                                 $person['lastName']))
            {
                /* Add matching records as an encoded SoapVar */
                $retval[] = new SoapVar($person, SOAP_ENC_ARRAY, "Person",
                                        "urn:ExampleAPI");
            }
        }
    }

    return $retval;
}

/* Create the server using WSDL and specify the actor URI */
$sServer = new SoapServer("exampleapi.wsdl", array('actor'=>'urn:ExampleAPI'));

/* Register the getPeopleByFirstLastName function */
$sServer->addFunction("getPeopleByFirstLastName");

/* Handle the SOAP request */
$sServer->handle();
?>
```

To test the server, you need to make requests using a client. The following is a small example of code that can make requests against the server:

```php
<?php
try {
    $sClient = new SoapClient('exampleapi.wsdl');

    /* Set search parameters */
    $params = array('first'=>'jo*', 'last'=>'*');
```

```
    /* Make request and dump response */
    $response = $sClient->getPeopleByFirstLastName($params);
    var_dump($response);
} catch (SoapFault $e) {
    /* Dump any caught SoapFault exceptions */
    var_dump($e);
}
?>
```

Using PEAR SOAP

The PEAR SOAP package is a SOAP client and server implementation written entirely in PHP. It has been around for a number of years, but it is still in beta status and was written to provide SOAP support under PHP 4. If you happen to have an existing implementation based on this package, you will be happy to know that PEAR SOAP works using PHP 5 and newer. If you are looking to implement a new SOAP service, I suggest looking at the native PHP SOAP extension, because PEAR SOAP does have some limitations, which I will get to shortly.

You install the package like all other PEAR packages. It is in beta status, so do not forget to indicate that when installing:

```
pear install SOAP-beta
```

Unfortunately, I cannot say for sure what dependencies this package has, because the documentation is sparse. After a quick look through the source code, it appears that the xml extension (ext/xml) is required, which is not surprising, and the PEAR HTTP_Request package is needed when working with WSDL. Various other optional dependencies also seem to be present, such as PEAR's MAIL_Mime and Net_DIME packages, though are not required to use the SOAP package.

The biggest limitation I ran into playing with the SOAP package was its inability to create Document/literal messages. From the client side, you can work around this, though I cannot say how reliably. Writing a Document/literal server is completely out of the question. This presents a bit of a problem; Document/literal is being used more often now than RPC/encoded, although still RPC/encoded services are being rolled out. Just compare the difference between the number of Document/literal services to those of RPC/encoded at XMethods (http://www.xmethods.net). Document/literal is a newer format than RPC/encoded, yet approximately 65 percent of the services listed at XMethods use it. Just look at two of the larger SOAP services available. Google AdWords and eBay both provide SOAP access, and both require that Document/literal-style messages be supported.

Because of these limitations, I will go into great detail about the PEAR SOAP package. It provides some good functionality and supports PHP 4 and 5, thus allowing you to upgrade to PHP 5 without having to rewrite your code. However, in my opinion, new projects should look at leveraging the PHP 5 SOAP extension. It has some decent documentation, and though certainly lacking in some areas, it is actively maintained. In addition, being written in C, it provides better performance.

Listing 18-14 gives you a quick look at writing a SOAP client with this package. It connects to the service created in Listing 18-13. This demonstrates that even though the server uses Document/literal, you can still use the SOAP package to create a client. Again, I am not saying that it will work in every case, but after a few modifications to calling styles, I have successfully consumed some of the simpler Document/literal services found on the Internet.

Listing 18-14. *PEAR SOAP Client Consuming Service in Listing 18-13*

```php
<?php
include("SOAP/Client.php");

/* Create client using WSDL */
$wsdl = new SOAP_WSDL("exampleapi.wsdl");
$sClient = $wsdl->getProxy();

/* Make request and dump response */
$response = $sClient->getPeopleByFirstLastName('jo*', '*');
var_dump($response);
?>
```

You should note a few things about this example. You can instantiate the SOAP_Client class and pass a WSDL document to the constructor. For some reason, the data typing was not working properly and required the SOAP_WSDL class to be instantiated directly and the service to be accessed through the retrieved proxy. The other notable difference is in the style; the function call is made. Although nothing appears to be wrong with it, the call is using the RPC/encoded style of calling. The function should take a single parameter containing a getPeopleByFirstLastName structure, but instead the components of the structure are passed as arguments.

It is completely your decision to use this package when running PHP 5 or higher. Be warned that unless you are already familiar with it, this package has little to no documentation. Unless you are lucky enough to find something by searching the Internet, the best option you have is the automatically generated PEAR documentation for the package, which lays out the API but offers no other information about what certain functions and properties do. The code is quite complex, and looking at the code for some of its examples may be your best shot. I am not trying to say this package is bad, but after having used both the PHP SOAP extension and the PEAR SOAP package, I found the extension much easier to use. The extension also provides the Document/literal support, which in my mind is important to have.

Seeing Some Examples in Action

Throughout this chapter, you have seen and maybe tried some of the examples of interacting with Web services. A few of them are actual live Web services on the Internet. The ones chosen in the chapter do not provide any real applicable use other than just as demonstration pieces. For this reason, I have chosen to demonstrate how to work with two real-world Web services from some well-known companies: eBay and Google. The eBay example is more of an instructional piece for getting set up and for understanding the different aspects that you must deal with to interface with its Web service. The Google example demonstrates how to use its publicly accessible services to perform searches, spell checks, and cached page retrieval. Google also provides a service to its AdWords system, but the audience for that would be limited to only those with an AdWords account. For this reason, I chose not to demonstrate that service.

Introducing the eBay Web Services

Unless you are living under a rock, you have heard of eBay. eBay is an online marketplace where you can buy, sell, and auction off goods. With so much functionality, it is often difficult to keep track of everything. You might be working for a company whose business is merchandise sales. The company may already have a complete internal system for inventory, sales, and tracking and is branching out to selling on eBay. With a system already in place, the company does not want the hassle of having to manage its internal systems as well as its eBay account. Using eBay Web services can solve this. SOAP is but one of the possible methods that can be used to integrate with eBay, because it also provides REST support.

The eBay example that is provided shows how to get your SOAP environment set up and enables you to understand what it is doing; it isn't a run-through of the API. The reason those who use SOAP like it is because SOAP is supposed to be simple. You load a WSDL document, examine the available functionality, and begin consuming the service. After a good amount of time spent trying to get my first successful connection to the eBay SOAP server, I was wishing I had written about eBay's REST implementation instead. Once over the initial hurdle, accessing the rest of the API was not as difficult. The material I will present in this example should help you avoid all of the issues I personally ran into, decreasing the amount of your development time significantly. If you prefer to get straight to working with the eBay Web service, you should follow the steps and tips provided in the following steps and then skip to the section "Setting Up the Environment." However, be forewarned that some of the information in the following sections may be useful in answering some questions you may have.

1. Sign up for the developer program at http://developer.ebay.com/join to receive your keys (DevID, AppID, and CertID).

2. Sign up for a sandbox user ID at http://developer.ebay.com/DevZone/ sandboxuser.asp. This ID allows you to access the sandbox (test) system just like accessing the live eBay system.

3. Generate a sandbox authentication token at http://developer.ebay.com/tokentool/, using the sandbox user ID.

4. Download the PHP 5 sample code from https://codesamples.codebase.ebay.com/ files/documents/14/74/php5_eBay_codesamples.zip.

5. Use the included ebay.ini file to set up your IDs and authentication token.

Setting Up with eBay

My experience began with the initial registration. You must register for the developer program at http://developer.ebay.com/join to use the Web services. Once you have registered, you will receive three keys: DevID, AppID, and CertID. You will need all three during this exercise. The next step is to get a copy of the documentation. I highly suggest you download the PDF version, because it's a bit slow trying to access the online HTML version. Even if you are on a dial-up connection, it is well worth the wait in the long run to download the 16MB PDF file, because you will most likely need it.

I personally thought the reason people liked SOAP was that it didn't require you to have to read every piece of documentation because WSDL was considered the Holy Grail. Under that assumption, I created a SoapClient and passed in the location of the WSDL, http://developer.ebay.com/webservices/latest/eBaySvc.wsdl. I wasn't expecting everything to work right out of the box, but I at least wanted to see the function list and data types I would be using. After a few minutes, I finally got some output. I found out the WSDL document is more than 2MB in size. If you don't end up saving a copy of the WSDL document locally, make sure the SOAP caching directives in the php.ini file are set properly:

```
soap.wsdl_cache_enabled = 1
soap.wsdl_cache_ttl = (some large value)
```

The default is to enable the WSDL cache for 86,400 seconds, which equates to one day. I couldn't see downloading this large of a file every day and because other applications using SOAP could not increase the wsdl_cache_ttl. For this reason, I decided to store and read the WSDL document on the local file system. Although doing this requires that I must periodically check for an updated WSDL document manually, it saved greatly on bandwidth usage because I could check it every couple of weeks or so rather than every single day.

Having seen some previous code using the SOAP extension, I knew additional authentication than the keys received upon registration were needed. Here the documentation is lacking. It talks about programmatically retrieving this, but after a few unsuccessful tries, I resorted to searching the Web for the answer. Had I read the section "Executing Your First C# Call," I would have found this out immediately, but for some reason logic got the best of me, and I was looking in the "Authentication & Authorization" section. A helpful page on the developer site is the Developer Tools page at http://developer.ebay.com/help/tools. From here you can create eBay test users, test the API, and create an authentication token (http://developer.ebay.com/tokentool/). This will require you to register for an eBay account, but the account is within the sandbox system, so a normal eBay account login will not work here.

Now with the token, I thought I was ready. I fired up the SOAP client again, loaded the WSDL document, and generated the authentication, and of course it didn't work. A WSDL file is supposed to define the end point to access a service. The eBay WSDL does, but only if you are accessing the production system. After reading the documentation more, I come to find out, when working in the sandbox, you need to change the location for the SoapClient to https://api.sandbox.ebay.com/wsapi. On top of that, and it doesn't matter whether running in a production environment or the sandbox, the URL needs to take parameters, and to top it off they must be built dynamically because the function name must be passed. These parameters are required for proper routing, which is something I thought the HTTP SOAPAction was for, but alas it's not used, so it's more like working with a REST/SOAP hybrid. By now, you should have the initial keys, authentication token, WSDL, and documentation as you move toward getting a PHP SoapClient to connect and make its first call.

Setting Up the Environment

Now that you have an idea of what to expect when working the SoapClient to access the eBay service, you need to decide how you want to go about your implementation. You can do this in two ways. The first is to create a bunch of functionality to build the location string, which of course is determined by the function you are calling. This would be required to be duplicated within any scripts you write accessing the eBay service. Of course, this was my first course of action. I just wanted to get something to work. The alternative is to create a custom class by subclassing the SoapClient and to provide the special functionality within the custom class. By doing this, you are able to use your custom class exactly as you have used the SoapClient throughout the rest of this chapter. You do not need to play around with the URL or deal with setting the authentication headers.

Note You can find some sample code for an eBay `SoapClient` wrapper at `https://codesamples.codebase.ebay.com/files/documents/14/74/php5_eBay_codesamples.zip`. It is not required you use the same configuration methods as in the provided code, although until you understand how the calls are made to the service and have made a few successful requests, it is in your best interest to leave any changes there until later.

To get you quickly interfacing with eBay, you will use this code base to make a couple of API calls. Rather than explaining the API to you (since you can find the functions and types in the documentation as well as from using the `__getTypes()` and `__getFunctions()` methods from the object), I will cover what the provided code does. You may wonder why this is necessary. In the event something is not working or new parameters or SOAP headers are ever required, you may need to change the base code yourself. It will also give you better insight into how PHP SOAP interacts with eBay, making understanding the eBay documentation much easier.

The provided code uses the following: an INI file for your keys, the authentication token, the eBay system to connect with, and the API version. Each of your keys and token has two sets of entries. One section, labeled `production`, is used when you are ready to access the live eBay system with your client. The other section, labeled `sandbox`, contains the values when accessing the test system. The only setting in each of these sections you should not change is `gatewaySOAP`. This should already contain the correct locations for each of the two systems. The remaining section, labeled `settings`, has two entries. The `site` entry specifies whether you are working in the `sandbox` or `production` environment. The `compatibilityLevel` entry specifies the eBay API version you are using. This can be located at the top of the WSDL document within the comments. This is also another reason why you may want to keep the WSDL local. Always grabbing the latest WSDL from the eBay site is a sure way to get the version level out of sync. This is not something that is guaranteed to break your application, but there is always the possibility. After adding your entries and verifying the other settings, your `ebay.ini` should end up looking like the following:

```
[production]
authToken = "Your Auth & Auth Token"

devId = "Your DevID"
appId = "Your AppID"
cert = "Your CertID"
gatewaySOAP = "https://api.ebay.com/wsapi"

[sandbox]
authToken = "Your Auth & Auth Token"
```

```
devId = "Your DevID"
appId = "Your AppID"
cert = "Your CertID"
gatewaySOAP = "https://api.sandbox.ebay.com/wsapi"

[settings]
site = "sandbox"
compatibilityLevel = 437
```

If you open one of the example files, such as GetUser.php, you should notice the following code at the top of the file:

```
require_once 'eBaySOAP.php';

// Load developer-specific configuration data from ini file
$config = parse_ini_file('ebay.ini', true);
$site = $config['settings']['site'];
$version = $config['settings']['compatibilityLevel'];


$dev = $config[$site]['devId'];
$app = $config[$site]['appId'];
$cert = $config[$site]['cert'];
$token = $config[$site]['authToken'];
$location = $config[$site]['gatewaySOAP'];


// Create and configure session
$session = new eBaySession($dev, $app, $cert);
$session->token = $token;
$session->location = $location;
$session->site = 0; // 0 = US;
```

This loads and parses the ebay.ini file and loads the settings into an eBaySession object, which is defined in the eBaySOAP.php file. The one property you may have to change, depending upon your location, is site. The eBay documentation defines site as "This is the site that item of interest is (or will be) listed on or (for requests that get/set user information) that the requesting or target user is registered on." The value is a numeric site ID found within the documentation. I have provided them here for easy reference in Table 18-9. For the course of this chapter, the code will be using the site ID of 0, for the United States, but you can change this to a more appropriate site based on your needs.

Table 18-9. *eBay Site IDs and Codes by Name*

Site Name	Site ID	Site Code
Australia	15	AU
Austria	16	AT
Belgium (Dutch)	123	BENL

Continued

Table 18-9. *Continued*

Site Name	Site ID	Site Code
Belgium (French)	23	BEFR
Canada	2	CA
China	223	CN
France	71	FR
Germany	77	DE
Hong Kong	201	HK
Ireland	205	IE
India	203	IN
Italy	101	IT
Malaysia	207	MY
Netherlands	146	NL
Philippines	211	PH
Poland	212	PL
Singapore	216	SG
Spain	186	ES
Sweden	218	SE
Switzerland	193	CH
Taiwan	196	TW
United Kingdom	3	UK
United States	0	US
US eBay Motors	100	—

By default, the eBaySession object is set to disable exceptions and use the remote WSDL document. If you are fine with just using the WSDL cache settings from the php.ini file to handle this, then you should have no problem; otherwise, you should use a local copy requiring you to set the location using the wsdl property:

```
$session->wsdl = 'eBaySvc.wsdl';
```

Whether or not you want to work with exceptions or have functions return SoapFault objects is up to you. The example code has exceptions disabled yet is using try/catch blocks and not testing for a SoapFault return value. For the sake of this chapter, you will use exceptions, so they must be reenabled. The eBaySession object has an options property. The value is an array of options that are to be passed to the SoapClient constructor. You simply need to enable exceptions within the array:

```
$session->options['exceptions'] = 1;
```

With the eBaySession object, $session, finally initialized correctly and the site property properly set, you are now ready to make your first SOAP call to eBay.

Interacting with the eBay Service

Using the eBaySession object previously created, you need to instantiate a new eBaySOAP object. The eBaySOAP class, being a subclass of the SoapClient class, takes an eBaySession object as its constructor parameter and uses the wsdl and options properties to call the parent SoapClient constructor:

```
try {
   $client = new eBaySOAP($session);
   ...
```

All that is left is to create any parameters that are to be passed to an eBay function and then call the function. Before the call can be made, however, it has a catch. All request types are based upon the AbstractRequestType type, and the version, being part of base type, must be passed within the SOAP body with every request. This means with every function call you make, you must pass the Version parameter as part of the structure.

To demonstrate this additional parameter requirement, you will make a call to the GetUser() function. Looking at its signature using the __getFunctions() method, you can see that it takes a single parameter:

```
GetUserResponseType GetUser(GetUserRequestType $GetUserRequest)
```

The GetUserRequestType parameter is a structure that takes the following form:

```
struct GetUserRequestType {
 ItemIDType ItemID;
 string UserID;
}
```

Both members of the structure are optional, but within the WSDL, they are defined as minOccurs="0". The ItemID member is in all fairness a string but is defined in the structure as an ItemIDType. A search through the types (__getTypes()) will show you exactly this. The GetUserRequestType structure, however, extends the AbstractRequestType from which the Version member comes. When called with only the Version parameter, the function returns data for the user identified by the authentication token used to make the request:

```
$response = $client->GetUser(array('Version'=>$version));
```

When called with a UserID parameter, data pertinent to the specified user is returned. The amount of data depends upon the UserID requested. When requesting information on any user other than yourself, the returned structure omits certain information:

```
$response = $client->GetUser(array('Version'=>$version, 'UserID'=>'pierre'));
```

This is where the ItemID comes into play. If you are a seller and need to look up information for a user who has successfully purchased an item from you, you can include the ItemID in the request to retrieve the previously omitted information:

```
$params = array('Version'=>$version, 'UserID'=>'pierre', 'ItemID'=>'1');
$response = $client->GetUser($params);
```

Of course, if the specified user has no association with the specified item, the data is returned in a limited fashion.

Just like the request types, the response types also extend a base type. In this case, the AbstractResponseType type can provide additional information such as a time stamp from when the request was processed or possibly messages from eBay. The type you are concerned with is the GetUserResponseType. In addition to members from the AbstractResponseType type, the GetUserResponseType adds a single User member of the UserType type and appears as the following:

```
struct UserType {
 boolean AboutMePage;
 string EIASToken;
 string RESTToken;
 string Email;
 int FeedbackScore;
 int UniqueNegativeFeedbackCount;
 int UniquePositiveFeedbackCount;
 float PositiveFeedbackPercent;
 boolean FeedbackPrivate;
 FeedbackRatingStarCodeType FeedbackRatingStar;
 boolean IDVerified;
 boolean eBayGoodStanding;
 boolean NewUser;
 AddressType RegistrationAddress;
 dateTime RegistrationDate;
 SiteCodeType Site;
 UserStatusCodeType Status;
 UserIDType UserID;
 boolean UserIDChanged;
 dateTime UserIDLastChanged;
 VATStatusCodeType VATStatus;
 BuyerType BuyerInfo;
 SellerType SellerInfo;
 CharityAffiliationsType CharityAffiliations;
 CharitySellerType CharitySeller;
 boolean SiteVerified;
 <anyXML> any;
}
```

Assuming no exceptions were thrown and you have successfully retrieved a GetUserResponseType structure, you simply access information as properties from the returned object:

```
print $results->User->Status."\n";
print $results->User->Email."\n";
```

```
Confirmed
Invalid Request
```

Here is a case where information is unavailable to you. The email address is not given out unless you retrieve your own user record or the user is associated to you through an ItemID.

Looking Under the Hood

Now that you can at least make calls to the eBay service, you should understand what is going on behind the scenes in PHP. Unlike many of the services you have seen and maybe tried in this chapter, much more is required to make a SOAP call than when simply calling a function. For starters, you need to add the authentication information to the SOAP message.

Authentication Structure

If you look within the eBaySOAP.php file, you will notice the eBayCredentials and eBayAuth classes. The eBayAuth class is the container for all authentication data. Upon creation, the eBaySession object, $session, is passed to the constructor. Using the keys and token that were added to $session at the beginning of the script, the proper structure is created using the correct data types. It is important that SoapVar objects are created because the data must not only be properly typed but also properly namespaced. Incorrect namespacing will result in a SoapFault being issued.

The authentication information is not passed within the body of the message, but rather, it is set in the SOAP Header. When the eBaySOAP object, $client, is instantiated, the constructor makes a call to the __setHeaders() method, which is not part of the SOAP API but rather a custom method that instantiates the eBayAuth object, creates a SoapVar for the object, and then creates a SoapHeader object using the resulting SoapVar. This is a bit confusing I know, but again, data typing and namespacing is essential when working with the eBay service. An array containing this header is then set as a property of $client because it will be used later when a function call is made.

Remote Calls

When calls are made to the eBay service, not only does the SOAP message need to be properly created, but also the URL being called must be dynamically created. The eBay system uses URL parameters to properly route and filter a SOAP request. It is possible to do this without resorting to method overloading, but you need to consider what has to occur to perform this.

One of the required parameters is the name of the function being called. Without using overloading, you could hard-code the function name into the URL and call the function like a normal SOAP call. This presents a problem in reusability. The next time you need to call a different function, you need to also change the value of the URL parameter. You could use a variable to set the URL and call the function. For example:

```
$function = 'GetUser';

/*
  Code to build URL using $function variable
*/


$client->$function($params);
```

Although this works, it is not all that intuitive. You would always have to find what the value of $function was to know what function you were actually calling using the SoapClient. The example code from eBay uses a different technique. Within the eBaySOAP class method, overloading is employed through the use of the __call() method. When you make the call $client->GetUser($params), the call is routed through the __call() method. The name of the method, equating to an eBay function, is passed as the first parameter. The URL can now be dynamically created without having to change the calling convention you have grown accustomed to in SOAP. The method then calls the `__soapCall()` method, passing the name of the function to call, the new location as an input option, and lastly the authentication header that was created earlier.

This example demonstrated only a single function call, but you should have a better understanding of the interaction between the PHP SOAP extension and the eBay service. Using a combination of the documentation and the type and using function information retrievable from a `SoapClient`, you should be able to move on to more complex calls and data structures. The most difficult parts should be behind you. Whether or not you decide to use the example code as the basis for your application is entirely up to you. It definitely is a good starting point to say the least. If you do plan on using the code, it is to your advantage to check on the eBay site itself because the example code is not static. Even as I wrote this chapter, new updates were made available on the site.

Introducing the Google Web Services

Google provides Web services to perform searches, do spell checks, and retrieve cached Web pages, all of which make up its search service. You even have access to manage AdWords accounts, using the AdWords API service. AdWords is an advertisement system where you can purchase cost-per-click or cost-per-impression ads to be displayed on Google search result pages. Both of these services are currently in beta status and provide SOAP-only access.

The AdWords API service requires an AdWords account. Using your account credentials, you can register at `https://adwords.google.com/select/ApiWelcome` to receive your developer token. This token is required to access the service. Not everyone reading this has an AdWords account, so rather covering an API that only a few readers will benefit from, I will use the search service as the example. If you care to find out more about the AdWords API service, including the API documentation, you should browse to `http://www.google.com/apis/adwords/`.

The search service is a free service for noncommercial use. The only restriction is that you are limited to 1,000 queries per day. Registration is required to access the service, because you need to obtain a license key. You will also need to download the developer's kit, which includes the WSDL document you will be using to access the service. You can find registration and the developer's kit at `http://www.google.com/apis/`.

Once you have downloaded the developer's kit, extract the contents, and either note the location of the WSDL file or copy it to another accessible location. The kit actually contains three WSDL files, but the one you need to use is located within the root `googleapi` directory from the package. At this point, it is not required that you have your license key because all you want to do is load the WSDL file into a `SOAPClient` and inspect the API. The first step is to examine the types used within the WSDL file. This will give you an idea of the type of return data you should expect when making calls to the service. For example:

```php
<?php
try {
    $GoogleClient = new SoapClient('GoogleSearch.wsdl');
    $types = $GoogleClient->__getTypes();
    foreach($types AS $type) {
        echo $type."\n\n";
    }
```

```
} catch (SoapFault $e) {
    var_dump($e);
}
?>
```

```
struct GoogleSearchResult {
 boolean documentFiltering;
 string searchComments;
 int estimatedTotalResultsCount;
 boolean estimateIsExact;
 ResultElementArray resultElements;
 string searchQuery;
 int startIndex;
 int endIndex;
 string searchTips;
 DirectoryCategoryArray directoryCategories;
 double searchTime;
}

struct ResultElement {
 string summary;
 string URL;
 string snippet;
 string title;
 string cachedSize;
 boolean relatedInformationPresent;
 string hostName;
 DirectoryCategory directoryCategory;
 string directoryTitle;
}

ResultElement ResultElementArray[]

DirectoryCategory DirectoryCategoryArray[]

struct DirectoryCategory {
 string fullViewableName;
 string specialEncoding;
}
```

As you can see, few types are defined. Only three structures exist, and they are not overly complex. Now that you have an idea of what the types look like, you can then use the SoapClient to examine the callable operations from the service:

```php
<?php
try{
   $GoogleClient = new SoapClient('GoogleSearch.wsdl');
   $google_funcs = $GoogleClient->__getFunctions();
   foreach($google_funcs AS $function) {
      echo $function."\n\n";
   }
} catch (SoapFault $e) {
   var_dump($e);
}
?>
```

```
base64Binary doGetCachedPage(string $key, string $url)

string doSpellingSuggestion(string $key, string $phrase)

GoogleSearchResult doGoogleSearch(string $key, string $q, int $start,
                                  int $maxResults, boolean $filter,
                                  string $restrict, boolean $safeSearch, string $lr,
                                  string $ie, string $oe)
```

This service is compact and to the point. It contains only three operations, and only one, doGoogleSearch(), takes a good number of parameters and returns complex results. If you haven't yet already registered and received your license key and would like to follow along with the examples, now is the time to do so. Notice the $key parameter in all of the operations. This parameter is your license key, and without it, the only result you can expect is a SOAP Fault telling you that your key is invalid.

The first two operations, doGetCachedPage() and doSpellingSuggestion(), are simple functions. The doGetCachedPage() function takes your license key and the URL to retrieve from Google's cache as parameters and returns the cached page. The SOAP extension automatically performs the Base64 decoding, so the value returned from the function can be used immediately. The doSpellingSuggestion() function takes your key and the phrase to spell check and returns a string containing the suggested spelling of the phrase. In the event no acceptable spellings are found, an empty string is returned. Because of the simplicity of these functions, I will demonstrate only a short example of calling them. The location of the Google WSDL file is assumed to be in the same directory of the script. If you happen to have it located elsewhere, modify the constructor call for the SoapClient to reflect this location:

```php
<?php
$key = "<insert license key here>";

try {
   $GoogleClient = new SoapClient('GoogleSearch.wsdl');

   /* Retrieve cached page for http://www.php.net/ and display first 500 chars */
   $cached = $GoogleClient->doGetCachedPage($key, 'http://www.php.net/');
```

```
    echo "Cache Retrieval Results: \n";
    if ($cached) {
        echo substr($cached, 0 , 500);
    } else {
        echo "No Cached Page Found";
    }
    echo "\n\n";

    /* Perform Spelling Suggestion */
    $orig = 'Pleeze Ceck my speling';
    $spelling = $GoogleClient->doSpellingSuggestion($key, $orig);

    echo "Spelling Suggestion Results: \n";
    if ($spelling) {
        echo "   Original Spelling: ".$orig."\n";
        echo "   Suggested Spelling: ".$spelling."\n";
    } else {
        echo "   No Suggested Alternatives Found\n";
    }
} catch (SOAPFault $e) {
    var_dump($e);
}
?>
```

```
Cache Retrieval Results:
<meta http-equiv="Content-Type" content="text/html; charset=ISO-8859-1">
<BASE HREF="http://www.php.net/"><table border=1 width=100%><tr><td>
<table border=1 bgcolor=#ffffff cellpadding=10 cellspacing=0 width=100%
 color=#ffffff>
   <tr><td><font face=arial,sans-serif color=black size=-1>This is <b>
       <font color=#0039b6>G</font> <font color=#c41200>o</font>
       <font color=#f3c518>o</font> <font color=#0039b6>g</font>
       <font color=#30a72f>l</font> <font color=#c41200>e</font></b>'s
 <a href="http://www.google

Spelling Suggestion Results:
   Original Spelling: Pleeze Ceck my speling
   Suggested Spelling: Please Check my spelling
```

The doGoogleSearch() function is a bit more complicated than the previous two functions. Not only does it take a fair number of parameters, described in Table 18-10, but it also returns a GoogleSearchResult structure, which is a complex type containing additional complex types.

Table 18-10. doGoogleSearch *Function Parameters*

Parameter	Description
key	License key provided by Google upon registration.
q	Query terms. Queries can contain the same syntax as allowed when using the Google Web interface to perform a search. You can find additional details about syntax at http://www.google.com/apis/reference.html#2_2.
start	Zero-based index of the first desired result.
maxResults	Maximum number of results to return per query. This value cannot exceed 10.
filter	Activates or deactivates automatic results filtering, which hides similar results and results that all come from the same Web host. Filtering tends to improve the end user experience on Google, but for your application you may prefer to turn it off.
restricts	Restricts the search to a subset of the Google Web index, such as a country like Ukraine or a topic like Linux. See http://www.google.com/apis/reference.html#2_4 for more details.
safeSearch	A Boolean value that enables you to filter adult content in the search results.
lr	Restricts the search to documents within one or more languages. See http://www.google.com/apis/reference.html#2_4 for more details.
ie	This parameter has been deprecated and is ignored.
oe	This parameter has been deprecated and is ignored.

The good thing about the SOAP extension is that it makes it simple to work with complex types. The resulting GoogleSearchResult structure is accessed like an object, which you are probably comfortable using. The following example searches Google using the query *PHP 5 SOAP*, starting at the first record designated by position 0 and returning a maximum of 5 records. Each of these parameters is easily changed at the beginning of the script. The script could also be integrated into a Web page, allowing the parameters to be passed in from a form. No matter how you go about the input, the basic logic remains the same:

```php
<?php
/* Values to pass as parameters */
$key = "<insert license key here>";
$query = 'PHP 5 SOAP';
$startrec = 0;
$maxResults = 5;
$filter = FALSE;

try {
    $GoogleClient = new SoapClient('GoogleSearch.wsdl');

    $searchResults = $GoogleClient->doGoogleSearch($key, $query, $startrec,
                                        $maxResults, $filter, '', FALSE,
                                        '', '', '');
```

```
    if ($searchResults) {
        echo "Search Time: ".$searchResults->searchTime."\n\n";
        foreach ($searchResults->resultElements AS $result) {
            echo "Title: ".$result->title."\n";
            echo "URL: ".$result->URL."\n";
            echo "Summary: ".$result->snippet."\n";
            echo "Cache Size: ".$result->cachedSize."\n\n";
        }
    }
} catch (SOAPFault $e) {
    var_dump($e);
}
?>
```

Once the query has been executed, the script outputs the amount of time in seconds it took Google to perform the query. It then loops through each of the resultElements from the GoogleSearchResult structure and displays the title, URL, snippet, and cachedSize for each of the ResultElement structures.

```
Search Time: 0.074399


Title: Zend Technologies - <b>PHP 5</b> In Depth - <b>PHP SOAP</b> Extension
URL: http://www.zend.com/php5/articles/php5-SOAP.php
Summary: <b>PHP 5&#39;s SOAP</b> extension is the first attempt to implement the
<b>SOAP</b> protocol for<br>  <b>PHP</b> in C. It has some advantages over the
existing implementations written in <b>...</b>
Cache Size: 101k


Title: Zend Technologies - <b>PHP 5</b> In Depth - <b>PHP SOAP</b> Extension
URL: http://www.zend.com/php5/articles/php5-SOAP.php?article=php5-
SOAP&kind=php5&id=6460&open=1&anc=0&view=1
Summary: <b>PHP 5&#39;s SOAP</b> extension is the first attempt to implement the
<b>SOAP</b> protocol <b>...</b><br>  Hi I couldn&#39;t find the answer May be some
problem with <b>Php5 Soap</b> extensions <b>...</b>
Cache Size: 101k


Title: Using the <b>PHP 5 SOAP</b> extension
URL: http://rootprompt.org/article.php3?article=8520
Summary: Using the <b>PHP 5 SOAP</b> extension. <b>...</b> In this article and
through code examples,<br>  learn how to use the new <b>SOAP</b> extension in <b>PHP
5</b> to access a J2EE application <b>...</b>
Cache Size: 5k
```

Title: php tutorials - A Clean Start: The New PHP 5 SOAP Extension
...
URL: http://www.communitymx.com/abstract.cfm?cid=DF35C
Summary: Flash, Dreamweaver, Fireworks, ColdFusion, Freehand and
Studio MX tutorials,
  articles and extensions.
Cache Size: 19k

Title: Access an enterprise application from a PHP script
URL: http://www-128.ibm.com/developerworks/library/os-phpws/?ca=dgr-phpw11PHP5soap
Summary: Using the PHP 5 SOAP extension to consume a WebSphere Web service
... New in PHP
  5 is a built-in SOAP extension,
which we'll refer to as ext/soap. ...
Cache Size: 81k

Conclusion

Depending upon whether you are a consumer of a SOAP service or the developer, SOAP is not always for the weak of heart. WSDL is a language that can take some practice to write correctly. This chapter introduced you to many of the components that make up WSDL using a step-by-step examination of the different areas of functionality and their relation to each other. For a consumer of a SOAP service, this may not have been an area you were too interested in, but it is good information to know. Being able to read a WSDL document often helps when the documentation just won't do. From WSDL, the chapter moved on to SOAP, discussing its relation to WSDL and providing a deep look at the structure of SOAP messages. Again, this may not be something you want to know, but it's helpful to understand during SOAP debugging sessions.

You put these technologies to some use as you looked at the PHP SOAP extension. Not only did you learn about the API and some functionality not even documented, but also you saw how some of the methods relate to the parts of a SOAP message. SOAP, in general, is not difficult to use, until you run into problems. The more you understand the different aspects, the easier and faster it becomes to resolve the issues. The information and examples in this chapter should provide you with enough knowledge of SOAP to create some powerful Web services. Whether or not it is more difficult than doing the same using REST is another story. It all depends upon your preference, who will be consuming the service, and how complex the application is. No matter which technology you choose, you are now well prepared to take on the task at hand.

■ ■ ■

Universal Description, Discovery, and Integration (UDDI)

Armed with the knowledge of consuming and creating Web services, you set off to create the next killer application. No matter how great the application might be, the question becomes, how do you go about finding or advertising this Web service? Of course, getting it listed in the popular search engines is one of the first steps you should take, but wouldn't it be great if you could easily discover and integrate with Web services without having to wade through all the nonrelevant information returned from search engines and then having to find documentation for a particular service? This is where Universal Description, Discovery, and Integration (UDDI) plays a role. This chapter will introduce many of the concepts behind UDDI and show how you can leverage UDDI registries by using PHP.

Caution As of January 16, 2006, the Universal Business Registry (UBR) mentioned throughout this chapter has been shut down. Registries have been privatized, so it is possible that some of the examples presented in this chapter will not work.

Introducing UDDI

In 2000, Microsoft, IBM, and Ariba collaborated on a project to create standards for describing, discovering, and consuming Web services. The idea was for registries, known as *UDDI registries*, to be set up to manage information about service providers, service implementations, and service metadata. Providers, typically businesses, could then publish and maintain their information while giving consumers, consisting of anyone needing to consume a service, the ability to query the information to find services they needed and to query the information about how the services are consumed. UDDI performed this interaction. After the release of the UDDI 1.0 specification, UDDI was moved under the control of OASIS in 2002; you can find additional information about UDDI at http://www.uddi.org.

UDDI Registries

When UDDI was first conceived, the idea was that a master directory (the UBR) of publicly available services would be made available and serve as the central repository for all businesses to register their services for consumption. The UBR was operated by four companies: IBM, Microsoft, SAP, and NTT Communications. The UBR is split into nodes, similar to the Domain Name System (DNS). When information is published to one node, it is replicated as read-only data to the other nodes; therefore, when a query is made, it does not matter which node is used to retrieve the data. Because of the read-only replication, it does mean that updating data must be performed at the node with which the data was first registered. This does not mean that you are locked into a node once registered, because you have methods to transfer to another node. For more information about the different nodes, the following are the UDDI home pages for each company:

IBM: http://www-306.ibm.com/software/solutions/webservices/uddi/

Microsoft: http://uddi.microsoft.com/

SAP: http://uddi.sap.com/

NTT Communications: http://www.ntt.com/uddi/

The adoption of UDDI never reached the scale originally intended. If you looked at the number of services registered in the UBR, you might have been surprised how few businesses have registered services. From what I can tell, proponents of UDDI claim that although the listings in the UBR are sparse, UDDI is more often used in a private environment, such as an intranet or extranet. Because these are private, I have no way to verify or dismiss these claims. In private environments, the UBR does not play a role. These environments have their own private registries.

UDDI Usage

Depending upon which point of view you believe, it is unclear whether UDDI was a success or failure. Certainly in the public space, it is not living up to the original vision, which is a bit funny if you think about it. UDDI is listed as one of the factors for being considered a *true* Web service in a purist's view. With so little external usage, it makes one wonder why UDDI is one of the technologies that defines a Web service. Does this mean that even if you are using SOAP for a Web service, it's not really a Web service? In my opinion, it comes back to who created and who is pushing the technology. The same companies that created SOAP and UDDI are the ones who defined what a supposed Web service is.

You might be wondering then why you should even bother with UDDI. With the usage of Web services on the rise, UDDI and the UBR could still gain momentum. It's also a possibility that one day you might need to work with a company that has employed it internally. Supposedly most of the Web services in use today are not meant for public accessibility but are used internally within organizations. This again is something that I cannot really verify or dismiss. Of course, you could also be one of the Web service purists, which in that case you don't have a doubt in your mind about UDDI usage. In any case, understanding what UDDI is and how to interface with registries is one of those nice topics to discuss during those company parties when you can't get rid of that person who just won't stop talking.

UDDI Specifications

No matter what you think after reading the previous sections, UDDI is not dead. It took only about three-and-a-half years, but UDDI 3.0 was finally approved in February 2005. Because I will use the UBR to demonstrate how to access a registry using UDDI, I will use and reference UDDI 2.0 in this chapter. If you happen to glance at the IBM 3.0 registry (https://uddi.ibm.com/ beta/registry.html), you will understand why. UDDI 3.0 is still in beta status. So, what exactly does the specification define?

- SOAP APIs that applications use to query and to publish information to a UDDI registry

- XML Schema schemata of the registry data model and the SOAP message formats

- WSDL definitions of the SOAP APIs

- UDDI registry definitions (technical models, or tModels) of various identifier and category systems that can be used to identify and categorize UDDI registrations

Because you should already be familiar with SOAP and WSDL from Chapter 18 and XML Schemas from Chapter 3, this chapter focuses on the data structures in UDDI as well as the SOAP API used to query and publish information to a registry.

Introducing Data Structures

UDDI 2.0 contains five data structure types that make up a registration:

- businessEntity

- businessService

- bindingTemplate

- tModel

- publisherAssertion

These structures form a hierarchy, as shown in Figure 19-1. No structure can have more than one parent, but the parent can have multiple child structures. You will see this in more detail in the "Accessing the SAP UDDI Registry via SOAP" section.

The data structures are defined in terms of XML Schemas, which for version 2 can be found at http://www.uddi.org/schema/uddi_v2.xsd. The schemas and structure breakdowns in the following sections come from the UDDI Version 2.03 Data Structure Reference (http:// uddi.org/pubs/DataStructure_v2.htm). Not only does this inclusion allow for quick reference, but you also need to understand the structures to properly access and utilize a UDDI registry.

■**Note** Throughout the UDDI data structure definitions, you will encounter the term *universally unique ID* (UUID). UUIDs serve as the keys for the UDDI data, similar to how you would use database keys, both unique and foreign, in a database.

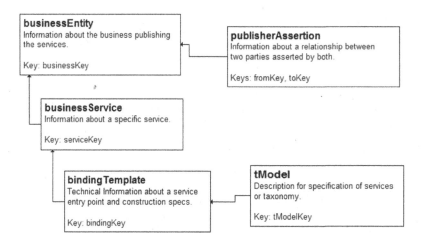

Figure 19-1. *UDDI data structure relationship*

The businessEntity Structure

The businessEntity structure is the top-level structure containing all the information about a business. It not only contains the business information, but it also serves as the container for the information regarding the services the business offers. A businessEntity element is defined within the UDDI XML Schema by the following:

```
<element name="businessEntity" type="uddi:businessEntity" />

<complexType name="businessEntity">
    <sequence>
        <element ref="uddi:discoveryURLs" minOccurs="0" />
        <element ref="uddi:name" maxOccurs="unbounded" />
        <element ref="uddi:description" minOccurs="0" maxOccurs="unbounded" />
        <element ref="uddi:contacts" minOccurs="0" />
        <element ref="uddi:businessServices" minOccurs="0" />
        <element ref="uddi:identifierBag" minOccurs="0" />
        <element ref="uddi:categoryBag" minOccurs="0" />
    </sequence>
    <attribute name="businessKey" type="uddi:businessKey" use="required" />
    <attribute name="operator" type="string" use="optional" />
    <attribute name="authorizedName" type="string" use="optional" />
</complexType>
```

Table 19-1, Table 19-2, and Table 19-3 further break down this schema by describing the elements, attributes, and substructures found within a businessEntity element.

Table 19-1. businessEntity *Structure*

Field	Description	Data Type	Length
businessKey	Required attribute. This is the unique identifier for a given instance of a businessEntity structure.	UUID	41
authorizedName	Attribute. This is the recorded name of the individual who published the businessEntity data. This data is generated by the controlling operator and should not be supplied within save_business operations.	string	255
operator	Attribute. This is the certified name of the UDDI registry site operator who manages the master copy of the businessEntity data. The controlling operator records this data at the time data is saved. This data is generated and should not be supplied within save_business operations.	string	255
discoveryURLs	Optional element. This is a list of URLs that point to alternate, file-based service discovery mechanisms. Each recorded businessEntity structure is automatically assigned a URL that returns the individual businessEntity structure. A URL search is provided via find_business calls.	structure	
name	Required repeating element. These are the human-readable names recorded for the businessEntity, adorned with a unique xml:lang value to signify the language in which they are expressed. A name search is provided via find_business calls. Names cannot be blank.	string	255
description	Optional repeating element. This is one or more short business descriptions. One description is allowed per national language code supplied.	string	255
contacts	Optional element. This is an optional list of contact information.	structure	
businessServices	Optional element. This element serves as a container for businessService elements.	structure	
identifierBag	Optional element. This is an optional list of name/value pairs that can be used to record identifiers for a businessEntity. These can be used during a search via find_business.	structure	
categoryBag	Optional element. This is an optional list of name/value pairs that are used to tag a businessEntity with specific taxonomy information (for example, industry, product, or geographic codes). You can use this element during a search via find_business.	structure	

As you can see from Table 19-1, additional structures can reside within the businessEntity structure.

discoveryURLs

A discoveryURLs element is a container for discoveryURL elements, because you can use multiple discoveryURL elements. A discoveryURL element points to URL-addressable discovery documents with the attribute useType, whose value can be businessEntity or businessEntityExt, and with content, which is a URL that points an instance of the type of structure specified by the useType attribute. For example, a businessEntity record with the businessKey of ABCDE might also have the following discoveryURL within the XML document:

```
<discoveryURLs>
    <discoveryURL useType="businessEntity">
        http://uddi.example.com/?businessKey=ABCDE
    </discoveryURL>
</discoveryURLs>
```

Navigating to the URL would basically return the entire businessEntity record again.

Contact Structure

Contact structures are contained within a contacts element. These serve to provide contact information for a business. Table 19-2 shows this structure.

Table 19-2. *Contact Structure*

Field	Description	Data Type	Length
useType	Optional attribute that is used to describe the type of contact in free-form text. Suggested examples include technical questions, technical contact, establish account, sales contact, and so on.	string	255
description	Optional element. This is zero or more language-qualified descriptions of the reason why the contact should be used.	string	255
personName	Required element. Contacts should list the name of the person or name of the job role that will be available behind the contact. Examples of roles include administrator and webmaster.	string	255
phone	Optional repeating element. This holds telephone numbers for the contact. You can adorn this element with an optional useType attribute for descriptive purposes.	string with attributes	50 50
email	Optional repeating element. This holds email addresses for the contact. You can adorn this element with an optional useType attribute for descriptive purposes.	string with attributes	255
address	Optional repeating element. This structure represents the printable lines suitable for addressing an envelope.	structure	

A contacts element can have multiple contacts as well as identify the type of contact by using a useType attribute. It is not required that a business even define a contact.

Address Structure

When adding an address to a contact, you use the address structure. Zero or more address elements, using the useType attribute to differentiate the type of address, can exist within a contact element. The address structure consists of the attributes and elements shown in Table 19-3.

Table 19-3. *Address Structure*

Field	Description	Data Type	Length
useType	Optional attribute that describes the type of address in free-form text. Suggested examples include headquarters, sales office, billing department, and so on.	string	255
sortCode	Optional attribute that can drive the behavior of external display mechanisms that sort addresses. The suggested values for sortCode include numeric ordering values (for example, 1, 2, 3), alphabetic character ordering values (for example, a, b, c), or the first n positions of relevant data within the address.	string	10
tModelKey	Optional attribute. This is the unique key reference that implies that the keyName/keyValue pairs given by subsequent addressLine elements are to be interpreted by the taxonomy associated with the tModel that is referenced.	string	255
addressLine	Optional repeating element containing the actual address in free-form text. If the address element contains a tModelKey, these addressLine elements are to be adorned each with an optional keyName/keyValue attribute pair. Together with the tModelKey, keyName and keyValue qualify the addressLine in order to describe its meaning.	string with attributes	80

The businessService Structure

A businessService structure describes an available service in generalized business terms:

```
<element name="businessService" type="uddi:businessService" />

<complexType name="businessService">
   <sequence>
      <element ref="uddi:name" minOccurs="0" maxOccurs="unbounded" />
      <element ref="uddi:description" minOccurs="0" maxOccurs="unbounded" />
      <element ref="uddi:bindingTemplates" minOccurs="0" />
      <element ref="uddi:categoryBag" minOccurs="0" />
   </sequence>
   <attribute name="serviceKey" type="uddi:serviceKey" use="required" />
   <attribute name="businessKey" type="uddi:businessKey" use="optional" />
</complexType>
```

The businessService structure is linked to the parent businessEntity structure by the businessKey element in a similar fashion to how foreign keys in a database work. When returned within a businessEntity, the businessService elements are contained within a businessServices element and are structured according to the layout described in Table 19-4. I say *when* here because using the UDDI API, it is possible to query for a single businessService record.

Table 19-4. businessService *Structure*

Field	Description	Data Type	Length
businessKey	This attribute is optional when the businessService data is contained within a fully expressed parent that already contains a businessKey value. If the businessService data is rendered into XML and has no containing parent that has within its data a businessKey, the value of the businessKey that is the parent of the businessService is required to be provided. This behavior supports the ability to browse through the parent-child relationships given any of the core elements as a starting point. The businessKey may differ from the publishing businessEntity's businessKey to allow service projections.	UUID	41
serviceKey	Required attribute. This is the unique key for a given businessService. When saving a new businessService structure, pass an empty serviceKey value. This signifies that a UUID value is to be generated. To update an existing businessService structure, pass the UUID value that corresponds to the existing service. If this data is received via an inquiry operation, the serviceKey values may not be blank. When saving a new or updated service projection, pass the serviceKey of the referenced businessService structure.	UUID	41
name	Optional repeating element. These are the human-readable names recorded for the businessService, adorned with a unique xml:lang value to signify the language in which they are expressed. A name search is provided via find_service calls. Names cannot be blank. When saving a new or updated service projection, pass the exact name of the referenced businessService here.	string	255
description	Optional element. This is zero or more language-qualified text descriptions of the logical service family.	string	255
bindingTemplates	This structure holds the technical service description information related to a given business service family.	structure	
categoryBag	Optional element. This is an optional list of name/value pairs that are used to tag a businessService with specific taxonomy information (for example, industry, product, or geographic codes). You can use the categoryBag element during search via find_service.	structure	

The bindingTemplate Structure

A bindingTemplate structure provides technical descriptions of a Web service:

```
<element name="bindingTemplate" type="uddi:bindingTemplate" />

<complexType name="bindingTemplate">
    <sequence>
        <element ref="uddi:description" minOccurs="0" maxOccurs="unbounded" />
            <choice>
                <element ref="uddi:accessPoint" />
```

```
            <element ref="uddi:hostingRedirector" />
        </choice>
    <element ref="uddi:tModelInstanceDetails" />
</sequence>
<attribute name="serviceKey" type="uddi:serviceKey" use="optional" />
<attribute name="bindingKey" type="uddi:bindingKey" use="required" />
</complexType>
```

As shown by the fields in Table 19-5, the bindingTemplate structure allows for a description as well as technical entry points or, optionally, remotely hosted services. This structure is one of the most important structures in UDDI. If you recall the purpose of UDDI (to allow the description and discovery of Web services), this structure contains exactly that information. This structure is linked to a parent businessService structure through the serviceKey attribute. Although this structure is contained within a bindingTemplates element when returned in the scope of a businessService, it can also be returned as a stand-alone structure when requested from the UDDI API.

Table 19-5. bindingTemplate *Structure*

Field	Description	Data Type	Length
bindingKey	Required attribute. This is the unique key for a given bindingTemplate. When saving a new bindingTemplate structure, pass an empty bindingKey value. This signifies that a UUID value is to be generated. To update an existing bindingTemplate structure, pass the UUID value that corresponds to the existing bindingTemplate instance. If this data is received via an inquiry operation, the bindingKey values cannot be blank.	UUID	41
serviceKey	This attribute is optional when the bindingTemplate data is contained within a fully expressed parent that already contains a serviceKey value. If the bindingTemplate data is rendered into XML and has no containing parent that has within its data a serviceKey, the value of the serviceKey that is the ultimate containing parent of the bindingTemplate is required to be provided. This behavior supports the ability to browse through the parent-child relationships given any of the core elements as a starting point.	UUID	41
description	Optional repeating element. This is zero or more language-qualified text descriptions of the technical service entry point.	string	255
accessPoint	Required attribute qualified element. This element is a text field that conveys the entry point address suitable for calling a particular Web service. This can be a URL, an email address, or even a telephone number. You cannot make any assumptions about the type of data in this field without first understanding the technical requirements associated with the Web service.	string with attributes	255

Continued

Table 19-5. *Continued*

Field	Description	Data Type	Length
hostingRedirector	Required element if accessPoint is not provided. This element is adorned with a bindingKey attribute, giving the redirected reference to a different bindingTemplate. If you query a bindingTemplate and find a hostingRedirector value, you should retrieve that bindingTemplate and use it in place of the one containing the hostingRedirector data.	Empty with attributes	
tModelInstanceDetails	This structure is a list of zero or more tModelInstanceInfo elements. This data, taken in total, should form a distinct fingerprint that can identify compatible services. Refer to the "The tModel Structure" section for additional information.	structure	

The accessPoint element provides the location of a Web service. A required URLType attribute identifies the type of content within the accessPoint element. It is limited to only the following values:

mailto: Designates that the accessPoint string is formatted as an email address reference (for example, mailto:purch@example.com).

http: Designates that the accessPoint string is formatted as an HTTP-compatible URL (for example, http://www.example/purchasing).

https: Designates that the accessPoint string is formatted as a secure HTTP-compatible URL (for example, https://www.example.com/purchasing).

ftp: Designates that the accessPoint string is formatted as a FTP directory address (for example, ftp://ftp.example.com/public).

fax: Designates that the accessPoint string is formatted as a telephone number that will connect to a fax machine (for example, 1 234 567 8901).

phone: Designates that the accessPoint string is formatted as a telephone number that will connect to human or suitable voice or tone response–based system (for example, 1 234 567 8901).

other: Designates that the accessPoint string is formatted as some other address format. When this value is used, one or more of the tModel signatures found in the tModelInstanceInfo collection must imply that a particular format or transport type is required.

The hostingRedirector element refers to another bindingTemplate entry. This allows a service to be described and queried based on the description yet refers to a service that has been described in a separate bindingTemplate record. When you use this element, it must be an empty element with a bindingKey attribute that points to another bindingTemplate structure. Also, you must not use the accessPoint element when using a hostingRedirector element.

The tModel Structure

Unlike the other structures you have seen, tModel structures have no owner; rather, they are just referenced from other structures. In fact, you should not be surprised to find multiple businessEntity structures referencing the same tModel structure. The reason for this is that in most cases, the tModel represents some common technical interface, business relationship, or categorization scheme. UDDI provides a number of predefined tModels, which you will see in the "Creating a tModel" section later in this chapter. A tModel structure, shown in the following XML Schema form and broken out in Table 19-6, allows for a description of a description, basically acting as metadata:

```
<element name="tModel" type="uddi:tModel" />

<complexType name="tModel">
   <sequence>
      <element ref="uddi:name" />
      <element ref="uddi:description" minOccurs="0" maxOccurs="unbounded" />
      <element ref="uddi:overviewDoc" minOccurs="0" />
      <element ref="uddi:identifierBag" minOccurs="0" />
      <element ref="uddi:categoryBag" minOccurs="0" />
   </sequence>
   <attribute name="tModelKey" type="uddi:tModelKey" use="required" />
   <attribute name="operator" type="string" use="optional" />
   <attribute name="authorizedName" type="string" use="optional" />
</complexType>
```

Table 19-6. tModel *Structure*

Field	Description	Data Type	Length
tModelKey	Required attribute. This is the unique key for a given tModel structure. When saving a new tModel structure, pass an empty tModelKey value. This signifies that a UUID value is to be generated. To update an existing tModel structure, pass the tModelKey value that corresponds to an existing tModel instance.	string	255
authorizedName	Attribute. This is the recorded name of the individual who published the tModel data. This data is calculated by the controlling operator and should not be supplied within save_tModel operations.	string	255
operator	Attribute. This is the certified name of the UDDI registry site operator who manages the master copy of the tModel data. The controlling operator records this data at the time data is saved. This data is calculated and should not be supplied within save_tModel operations.	string	255
name	Required element. This is the name recorded for the tModel. A name search is provided via find_tModel calls. Names cannot be blank and should be meaningful to someone who looks at the tModel. The name should be formatted as a URI, and as a consequence, the xml:lang attribute of the name element should not be used.	string	255

Continued

Table 19-6. *Continued*

Field	Description	Data Type	Length
description	Optional repeating element. This contains one or more short language-qualified descriptions. One description is allowed per national language code supplied.	string	255
overviewDoc	Optional element. This houses references to remote descriptive information or instructions related to the tModel.	structure	
identifierBag	Optional element. This is an optional list of name/value pairs that can record identification numbers for a tModel. You can use these pairs during searches via find_tModel.	structure	
categoryBag	Optional element. This is an optional list of name/value pairs that are used to tag a tModel with specific taxonomy information (for example, industry, product, or geographic codes). You can use these during searches via find_tModel.	structure	

The tModel structure has two main uses. Its primary use is representing a technical specification. For example, you might use a tModel to describe an Open Financial Exchange (OFX)[1] specification (http://www.ofx.net/). This tModel structure then might be referenced by various bindingTemplate structures. When performing a search for services, in particular those that conform to OFX, the tModel for OFX could be located; then, using its key, services that reference the particular tModel could be queried.

The other use for a tModel structure is to define organizational identity and various classifications. For example, many companies register themselves with Dun & Bradstreet and receive a D-U-N-S number. A tModel representing the D-U-N-S number identifier system could be used to identity a businessEntity with a D-U-N-S number. The following is the tModel record for the D-U-N-S number identifier system taken from the SAP test registry (it has been formatted for easier readability):

```
<tModel tModelKey="UUID:8609c81e-ee1f-4d5a-b202-3eb13ad01823"
        operator="uddi:replicationtest:node1" authorizedName="uddi.org">
  <name>dnb-com:D-U-N-S</name>
  <description xml:lang="en">Dun &amp; Bradstreet D-U-N-S Number.</description>
  <overviewDoc>

    <overviewURL>
        http://uddi.org/pubs/tModels/UBR_Taxonomy_tmodels.htm#D-U-N-S
    </overviewURL>
  </overviewDoc>
  <categoryBag>
```

---

1. OFX is a specification for the electronic exchange of financial data between financial institutions, businesses, and consumers via the Internet. CheckFree, Intuit, and Microsoft created it in early 1997, and it is currently used by many banks, brokerages, and major payroll-processing companies.

```
<keyedReference tModelKey="uuid:c1acf26d-9672-4404-9d70-39b756e62ab4"
                keyName="uddi-org:types:identifier" keyValue="identifier" />
<keyedReference tModelKey="uuid:c1acf26d-9672-4404-9d70-39b756e62ab4"
                keyName="uddi-org:types:unchecked" keyValue="unchecked" />
    </categoryBag>
</tModel>
```

Within a bindingTemplate structure, you may have noticed the tModelInstanceDetails element. That element acts as a container for tModelInstanceInfo elements that are used to reference a tModel. For example:

```
<tModelInstanceDetails>
    <tModelInstanceInfo tModelKey="uuid:5FCF5CD0-629A-4C50-8B16-F94E9CF2A674">
        <instanceDetails>
            <overviewDoc>
                <overviewURL>http://www.example.com/ftp</overviewURL>
            </overviewDoc>
            <instanceParms/>
        </instanceDetails>
    </tModelInstanceInfo>
</tModelInstanceDetails>
```

The tModel in this case indicates that the service is compliant with the FTP specification referenced by the tModel, http://uddi.org/taxonomies/UDDI_CoreOther_tModels.htm#_ Toc25463130. When searching for a binding, you can use these as digital fingerprints returning only those services matching the specified fingerprint. Other places where you might see tModel being used, though not covered in this chapter, are within the identifierBag, categoryBag, and address structures. The tModel works in a similar fashion though it is used in different contexts.

The publisherAssertion Structure

The publisherAssertion structure, added in UDDI 2.0, creates relationships between businessEntity records. For example, a company may have multiple subsidiaries where each subsidiary has its own businessEntity record. Relationships between these records are then created using publisherAssertion structures. For example:

```
<element name="publisherAssertion" type="uddi:publisherAssertion" />

<complexType name="publisherAssertion">
    <sequence>
        <element ref="uddi:fromKey" />
        <element ref="uddi:toKey" />
        <element ref="uddi:keyedReference" />
    </sequence>
</complexType>
```

Table 19-7 breaks down the publisherAssertion structure.

Table 19-7. publisherAssertion *Structure*

Field	Description	Data Type	Length
fromKey	Required element. This is the unique key reference to the first businessEntity for which the assertion is made.	UUID	41
toKey	Required element. This is the unique key reference to the second businessEntity for which the assertion is made.	UUID	41
keyedReference	Required element. This designates the relationship type for which the assertion is made, represented by the included tModelKey and described by the included keyName/keyValue pair.	Empty with attributes	

For a valid relationship to be made, each businessEntity in the relationship must create a publisherAssertion. It is not considered valid if only one of the parties does this, because the other party in the relationship must acknowledge the relationship by means of an identical assertion. For example, if an entity with a businessKey of 0D28A920-ABCD-11D7-813C-➥ 000621DC0A23 were to create a relationship with an entity that happens to be one of its child subsidiary companies and that has a businessKey of 3604E5F0-DCBA-11D6-83CD-000C0E00230A, the relationship would look like the following:

```
<publisherAssertion>
    <fromKey>0D28A920-ABCD-11D7-813C-000621DC0A23</fromKey>
    <toKey>3604E5F0-DCBA-11D6-83CD-000C0E00230A</toKey>
    <keyedReference keyName="subsidiary" keyValue="parent-child"
                    tModelKey="uuid:807A2C62-EE22-470D-ADC7-E0424A337C03"/>
</publisherAssertion>
```

For this relationship to be considered valid, the other child entity must also assert the same relationship.

The keyedReference element specifies the type of relationship between the entities. The relationship is defined in terms of a tModel. In this case, the tModel specified by the value of the tModelKey attribute references the uddi-org:relationships tModel, which is a classification of businessEntity relationships. You can find additional information about this tModel at http://www.uddi.org/taxonomies/UDDI_Taxonomy_tModels.htm#Relationships. The keyName qualifies the relationship specified by the keyValue attribute. So, reading this assertion, the entity identified by the fromKey, 0D28A920-ABCD-11D7-813C-000621DC0A23, is the parent of the subsidy entity identified by the toKey, 3604E5F0-DCBA-11D6-83CD-000C0E00230A.

Introducing the SOAP API

UDDI uses SOAP to access the two APIs. The inquiry API is a publicly accessible API to query a registry for information accessed over HTTP and requiring no authentication. The publisher API, on the other hand, allows information to be created, updated, and deleted. It uses HTTPS and an authentication scheme that depends upon the registry's implementation being accessed. Although neither API has a large number of functions, some of the structures can become quite complex. The following sections deal with these in simple terms, because you can find more detailed information in the API documentation at http://uddi.org/pubs/ ProgrammersAPI_v2.htm.

■**Note** Most of the response message structures have not been described in much detail in this chapter. In most cases, they are not overly complex and can easily be broken down by examining the return data in PHP, by reading the UDDI 2.0 WSDL documents, or by referencing the sample response messages in Appendix C of the UDDI 2.0 specification (`http://uddi.org/pubs/DataStructure_v2.htm#_Toc25130791`).

Inquiry

The inquiry API searches and retrieves information from UDDI registries. This API is described in the following WSDL document:

`http://uddi.org/wsdl/inquire_v2.wsdl`

Although you are free to not use the WSDL, it makes it much easier to work with SOAP. The WSDL is generic and does not contain any service information, but you can easily add it. For example, save the WSDL file locally and open it in an editor. After the closing `binding` element, add the following fragment:

```
<service name="InquireSoap">
  <port name="InquireSoap" binding="tns:InquireSoap">
    <soap:address location="http://udditest.sap.com/uddi/api/inquiry" />
  </port>
</service>
```

This `service` element ends up being the last child element of the `definitions` element. Once you have saved the WSDL, you can then use it to connect to the SAP test registry. Loading this WSDL into a `SoapClient` and using the SOAP extension, a call to the `__getFunctions()` method will return the functions in Table 19-8 as well as the return types. A call to `__getTypes()` will return all types defined in the WSDL, which includes the arguments taken by the functions and all the UDDI structures.

Table 19-8. *UDDI Inquiry Functions*

Name	Description
find_binding	Searches for bindings based on a serviceKey. This function returns a bindingDetail element that encapsulates all matching bindingTemplate records.
find_business	Searches for entity records. This function returns a businessList element that contains a businessInfos element that contains the matching businessInfo records. Each of these elements contains the businessKey attribute that can retrieve a specific businessEntity record as well as a summary of the entity and services.
find_relatedBusinesses	Searches for business entities that have a defined relationship, using publisherAssertions, to the supplied businessKey. This function returns a relatedBusinessesList, which is documentated at http://uddi.org/pubs/DataStructure-V2.03-Published-20020719.htm#_Toc25130808.

Continued

Table 19-8. *Continued*

Name	Description
find_service	Searches for a service within a registered businessEntity. This function returns a serviceList.
find_tModel	Searches for tModel information structures. This function returns a tModelList.
get_bindingDetail	Retrieves specific bindingTemplate records, contained within a bindingDetail element, based on one or more bindingKey values.
get_businessDetail	Retrieves specific businessEntity records, contained within a businessDetail element, based on one or more businessKey values.
get_businessDetailExt	Retrieves extended information for specific businessEntity records based on one or more businessKey values.
get_serviceDetail	Retrieves specific businessService records, contained within a serviceDetail element, based on one or more serviceKey values.
get_tModelDetail	Retrieves specific tModel records, contained within a tModelDetail element, based on one or more tModelKey values.

If you tried calling __getTypes(), you might have noticed that many of the find_xxx() functions accept an optional findQualifiers. These qualifiers allow you to refine your search results by specifying aspects such as name matching and sorting. Table 19-9 shows the full list of available qualifiers, and I will demonstrate many of them later in the "Accessing the SAP UDDI Registry via SOAP" section.

Table 19-9. *UDDI* findQualifiers

Name	Description
exactNameMatch	This qualifier causes only entries that exactly match the value of the name argument to be returned.
caseSensitiveMatch	This qualifier results in a case-sensitive search based on the value of the name argument.
sortByNameAsc	Returns the results sorted on the name field in ascending order.
sortByNameDesc	Returns the results sorted on the name field in descending order.
sortByDateAsc	This qualifier returns the data sorted on the date last updated in ascending order. Sort qualifiers involving dates are secondary in precedence to the sortByName qualifiers.
sortByDateDesc	This qualifier returns the data sorted on the date last updated in descending order. Sort qualifiers involving dates are secondary in precedence to the sortByName qualifiers.
orLikeKeys	When a bag container contains multiple keyedReference elements, any keyedReference filters that come from the same namespace are OR'd together rather than AND'd. This allows one to say "any of these four values from this namespace and any of these two values from this namespace."
orAllKeys	This qualifier changes the behavior for tModelBag and categoryBag to OR keys rather than AND. It negates any AND treatment as well as the effect of orLikeKeys and applies to find_binding, find_business, find_service, and find_tModel.

Name	Description
combineCategoryBags	This qualifier is used by the find_business function. It makes the categoryBag entries for the full businessEntity element behave as though all categoryBag elements found at the businessEntity level and in all contained or referenced businessService elements were combined. Searching for a category will yield a positive match on a registered business if any of the categoryBag elements contained within the full businessEntity element (including the categoryBag elements within contained or referenced businessService elements) contains the filter criteria.
serviceSubset	The find_business function uses this function. It is used only in conjunction with a passed categoryBag argument and causes the component of the search that involves categorization to use only the categoryBag elements from contained or referenced businessService elements within the registered data and ignores any entries found in the categoryBag direct descendent element of registered businessEntity elements. The resulting businessList message will return those businesses that match based on this modified behavior, in conjunction with any other search arguments provided.
andAllKeys	This qualifier is used with find_business and findtModel functions and changes the behavior for identifierBag to AND keys rather than OR.

Publisher

The publisher API creates, updates, and edits information within a registry. It also has a WSDL describing the API, whose functions are listed in Table 19-10, and is located at the following site:

```
http://uddi.org/wsdl/publish_v2.wsdl
```

Again, using the WSDL makes things a bit easier when working with the SOAP extension. You access the service for the publisher API, though, through a different URL than the inquiry API. The following is the fragment to add to the WSDL to access the SAP publisher service for the test registry. You could use other registries, such as any of the UBRs where each also has two different locations for the APIs. You can find a list of these locations at `http://uddi.org/find.html`.

Just insert the following fragment as the next sibling of the binding element, which would make it the last child of the definitions element, to use the WSDL to connect to the SAP test registry in order to access the publisher interface:

```
<service name="PublishSoap">
  <port name="PublishSoap" binding="tns:PublishSoap">
    <soap:address location="https://udditest.sap.com/uddi/api/publish/" />
  </port>
</service>
```

Table 19-10. *UDDI Publisher Functions*

Name	Description
add_publisherAssertions	Adds relationship assertions to the assertion collection.
delete_binding	Removes one or more instances of the bindingTemplate data from the registry.
delete_business	Deletes one or more registered businessEntity records and the contents from the registry.
delete_publisherAssertions	Deletes one or more assertions from the assertion collection. Any relationships based on this assertion will become invalid.
delete_service	Deletes one or more businessService records from a registry.
delete_tModel	Hides registered information about a tModel. Any tModel hidden in this way is still usable for reference purposes and accessible via the get_tModelDetail message but is simply hidden from find_tModel result sets. There is no way to actually cause a tModel to be deleted, except by administrative petition.
discard_authToken	Informs an operator site that a previously provided authentication token is no longer valid and should be considered invalid if used after this message is received.
get_assertionStatusReport	Gets a status report containing publisher assertions and status information. Returns an assertionStatusReport that includes the status of all assertions made involving any businessEntity controlled by the requesting publisher account.
get_authToken	Gets an authentication token, which is required for all other publisher API calls. This is equivalent to a logon.
get_publisherAssertions	Retrieves list of all active publisher assertions.
get_registeredInfo	Retrieves an abbreviated list of all businessEntity and tModel data managed by a given individual.
save_binding	Saves a new or updates an existing bindingTemplates. You can save multiple bindingTemplates at once.
save_business	Saves or updates a complete businessEntity element. You must use this function carefully because it also performs deletions on contained structures when the businessEntity element being saved differs, such as not including a substructure, from the data in the registry.
save_service	Creates or updates one or more businessService elements.
save_tModel	Creates or updates one or more tModel elements.
set_publisherAssertions	Saves the complete set of publisher assertions for an individual publisher account. Replaces any existing assertions and causes any old assertions that are not reasserted to be removed from the registry.

Accessing the SAP UDDI Registry via SOAP

If you have been following along to this point, you should already have two WSDL files configured to access the SAP test registry for the inquiry functions (http://udditest.sap.com/uddi/api/inquiry) and for the publisher functions (https://udditest.sap.com/uddi/api/publish/).

In the following sections, you will use the SOAP extension to create, update, and delete information from the registry as well as to perform queries.

■**Note** Performing inquiries against the UBRs is open to the public and does not require any authentication. To access the publisher API against the SAP registries, you must be authenticated by a user ID and password. If you are going to follow along with the publishing examples in this section, you need to register for your own logon at `http://udditest.sap.com/`.

Performing Inquiries

If you have not already done so, retrieve a copy of the UDDI inquiry API WSDL located at `http://uddi.org/wsdl/inquire_v2.wsdl`. Add the `service` element as the last child element of the `definitions` element, so the end of the file looks like the following:

```
<service name="InquireSoap">
   <port name="InquireSoap" binding="tns:InquireSoap">
      <soap:address location="http://udditest.sap.com/uddi/api/inquiry" />
   </port>
</service>
</definitions>
```

Although the order of this element does not matter as long as it is a child of the `definitions` element, this placement makes it easier to insert and locate in the event you decide to change to a different registry for primary use. Once you have the WSDL correctly set up, you can easily create the client. Use the name of the downloaded WSDL file, `inquire_v2.wsdl`, as the name for the local modified WSDL that will be used in the example. For example:

```
$sClient = new SoapClient('inquire_v2.wsdl');
```

Now say Mr. Wile E. Coyote is trying to find some of his old friends to help him finally catch that old roadrunner. Being now tech savvy, rather than calling his favorite company Acme, he decides to see whether any other companies offer Web services that will let him find the telephone numbers for his friends. He decides to tap into the IBM UBR to see what he can locate:

```
function outputBusiness($bizInfo) {
   print "Name: ".$bizInfo->name->_."\n";
   print "Business Key: ".$bizInfo->businessKey."\n";
   if (isset($bizInfo->description)) {
      print "Desc: ".$bizInfo->description->_."\n";
   }
```

```
    /* Output serviceInfo information only if one serviceInfo element is present */
    if (isset($bizInfo->serviceInfos->serviceInfo) &&
        ! is_array($bizInfo->serviceInfos->serviceInfo)) {
        print "Service Name: ".$bizInfo->serviceInfos->serviceInfo->name->_."\n";
        print "Service Key: ".$bizInfo->serviceInfos->serviceInfo->serviceKey."\n";
    }
    print "\n";
}
```

The outputBusiness() function outputs some pertinent information from a businessInfo response message. This example is using WSDL and not performing any class mappings. All complex types are returned as stdClass objects. Most of this you are already familiar with from Chapter 18, which covered SOAP. I will point out in this function the output for the serviceInfo information. Based on the data from the test registry, only a few of the returned records contained serviceInfo. To shorten the code, it outputs serviceInfo for a businessInfo only as long as one and only one serviceInfo element is present in the response. From the records returned, they have either one or zero serviceInfo elements, but this is something you should be aware of if looking to model your code after this example. For example:

```
try {
    $bizList = $sClient->find_business(array("generic"=>"2.0", "name"=>"Acme%",
                                "maxRows"=>5,
                                "findQualifiers"=>"sortByNameAsc,sortByDateAsc"));
    if ($bizInfos = $bizList->businessInfos) {
        if (isset($bizInfos->businessInfo)) {
            if (is_array($bizInfos->businessInfo)) {
                foreach($bizInfos->businessInfo AS $bizInfo) {
                    outputBusiness($bizInfo);
                }
            } else {
                outputBusiness($bizInfos->businessInfo);
            }
        } else {
            print "No Records Found";
        }
    }
} catch (SoapFault $e) {
    var_dump($e);
}
```

As you can see, there is not much to this code. The main block simply calls the find_business() method. The arguments being passed are what are important here. The first argument, generic, comes from the UDDI 2.0 API. This argument is used for every API call and indicates the UDDI version to which it is conforming. In this case, 2.0 is the value used throughout the examples. The maxRows argument indicates the maximum number of records to retrieve. This argument is optional and, when omitted, will return all of the matching records.

The name argument is the name of the business being searched for. You probably notice the % at the end of the name. This acts as a wildcard, just like when used in SQL. Based on the value Acme%, all records whose businessEntity name begins with Acme will be returned in the response message. This search is also being performed using case-insensitive matching, as you can see by the findQualifiers. The reason for this is that a case-insensitive search is the default type of search and is not being overridden by the qualifiers being passed in. When the response message is returned, the records will be ordered based on the businessEntity name, in ascending order, and further sorted based on the last updated date and time in ascending order. This is not because of the order the qualifiers were specified but because of the rules, which are included in the descriptions of the qualifiers in Table 19-9, of how the qualifiers passed to the method are handled.

Our dear friend Wile executes the code and gets the following output:

```
Name: Acme Business
Business Key: 0cb8b470-52c4-11da-98fc-0002a58b4eaf
Service Name: Acme Open Service
Service Key: 639d6ce0-52c4-11da-90ff-0002a58b4eaf
```

This is where it is sometimes hard to be from the instant gratification generation. Either because of the slowness of the test registry or because of the amount of data being returned in the response (or possibly both), it takes a little bit of time to get the results. When they do finally appear, a quick check of the results shows there is an Acme Web service for Acme Business . . . eureka! The Acme Business company with a businessKey of 0cb8b470-52c4-11da-➥ 98fc-0002a58b4eaf has an Acme telephone directory Web service with a serviceKey of 639d6ce0-52c4-11da-90ff-0002a58b4eaf. Using this serviceKey, Wile can now get the needed information on how to access the Web service:

```
function outputTemplate($bindingTemplate) {
   if (isset($bindingTemplate->description)) {
      print "Desc: ".$bindingTemplate->description->_."\n";
   }
   if (isset($bindingTemplate->accessPoint)) {
      print "Access Point: ".$bindingTemplate->accessPoint->_."\n";
      print "Access Point Type: ".$bindingTemplate->accessPoint->URLType."\n";
   } else {
      print "Hosting Redirector Binding Key: ".
            $bindingTemplate->hostingRedirector->bindingKey."\n";
   }
   if (isset($bindingTemplate->tModelInstanceDetails)&&
       isset($bindingTemplate->tModelInstanceDetails->tModelInstanceInfo)) {
      $modelDetails = $bindingTemplate->tModelInstanceDetails;
      print "tModel Key: ".$modelDetails->tModelInstanceInfo->tModelKey."\n";
   }
   print "\n";
}
```

This function works in the same manner as the previous output function. In this case, a bindingTemplate is passed in, and the select data is output. This includes any description it may have, a tModelKey if present (which can be used to look up the tModel information using the get_tModelDetail() method), and the information from either an accessPoint or a hostingRedirector. If you recall from the bindingTemplate structure, it must have one, but not both, of these structures. For example:

```
try {
    $serviceDetail = $sClient->get_serviceDetail(array("generic"=>"2.0",
                        "serviceKey"=>"639d6ce0-52c4-11da-90ff-0002a58b4eaf"));
    if (isset($serviceDetail->businessService)) {
        $bizService = $serviceDetail->businessService;
        if (isset($bizService->bindingTemplates)) {
            if (isset($bizService->bindingTemplates->bindingTemplate)) {
                if (is_array($bizService->bindingTemplates->bindingTemplate)) {
                    $bindingTemplates = $bizService->bindingTemplates;
                    foreach ($bindingTemplates->bindingTemplate AS $bindingTemplate) {
                        outputTemplate($bindingTemplate);
                    }
                } else {
                    outputTemplate($bizService->bindingTemplates->bindingTemplate);
                }
            } else {
                print "No bindingTemplate elements found\n";
            }
        } else {
            print "bindingTemplates element not found\n";
        }
    }
} catch (SoapFault $e) {
    var_dump($e);
}
```

Again, the bulk of the work takes place in the first call. The get_serviceDetail() method retrieves the service information for the Web service identified by the previous example. The generic argument is required to be passed, and because you are using UDDI 2.0, you supply the value 2.0. The only other argument you need is the serviceKey of 639d6ce0-52c4-11da-➡ 90ff-0002a58b4eaf, which was obtained from the previous example using the find_business() method.

Upon execution of the code, Wile finally has all the information he needs to access the Web service and make his calls (the following results have been modified because of the length of URL present in the results):

```
Access Point: http://localhost:38080/axis/EchoService1.jws
Access Point Type: other
```

Based on this information, he now knows that the Web service is located at the URL shown for the value of Access Point in the previous results.

Note This Web service is not physically accessible. The test registry is for testing purposes only, and much of the data you will find there does not point to any publicly accessible, or even real for that matter, service.

Publishing to the Registry

The easiest way to publish information is using SOAP with a WSDL. Just as was done in the "Performing Inquiries" section, retrieve a copy of the publishing WSDL from http://uddi.org/wsdl/publish_v2.wsdl. Using this local copy, add the following fragment just before the closing definitions element:

```
<service name="PublishSoap">
   <port name="PublishSoap" binding="tns:PublishSoap">
      <soap:address location="https://udditest.sap.com/uddi/api/publish/ " />
   </port>
</service>
```

Using this new local publish_v2.wsdl file, instantiate the client:

```
$sPublish = new SoapClient('publish_v2.wsdl');
```

Note To execute any of the remaining code in this example, you need to use your credentials from the IBM UDDI registration. If you have not yet registered, you can do so at http://udditest.sap.com.

Authenticating with the Registry

The first step you need to take once you have instantiated your client is to authenticate. This is critical because without a valid authInfo structure, you will unable to perform any publishing operations against the registry. You can handle authentication simply by calling the get_authToken() method and passing in your userID and cred, which is your password in this case. Like all the methods that have been called using UDDI, the generic parameter must also be supplied. For example:

```
/* UserID and Password */
$userID = <userID for registry>;
$cred = <password for registry>;

try {
   $authToken = $sPublish->get_authToken(array("generic"=>"2.0", "userID"=>$userID,
                                                "cred"=>$cred));
   $authInfo = $authToken->authInfo;
} catch (SoapFault $e) {
   var_dump($e);
}
```

Unless you encountered an error here, the variable $authInfo now contains your authentication information, which is a UUID, that is needed for the other publisher functionality. The rest of the example will use this variable.

Although an authToken (identified by the authInfo) eventually will expire, a hard logoff, destroying the authToken, is often a good idea. You do this using the discard_authToken() method. This is a safe method to call even if the authToken has expired because it will still return a success message. For example:

```
try {
    $response = $sPublish->discard_authToken(array("generic"=>"2.0",
                                            "authInfo"=>$authInfo));
} catch (SoapFault $e) {
    var_dump($e);
}
```

Creating an Entity

Now that you have the logon/logoff basics behind you, let's create the first entry in the registry. The fictitious company Acme XML will be created. You never know when Wile might need Acme's help in this area. For example:

```
try {
    /* Create the businessEntity structure */
    $businessEntity = array("businessKey"=>"",
                        "name"=>'Acme XML',
                        "description"=>"Acme's XML wing");

    /* Save the businessEntity structure */
    $bizDetail = $sPublish->save_business(array("generic"=>"2.0",
                                        "authInfo"=>$authInfo,
                                        "businessEntity"=>$businessEntity));
    var_dump($bizDetail);

} catch (SoapFault $e) {
    var_dump($e);
}
```

In this example, you create a simple businessEntity structure. The businessKey is set to empty. This indicates to the registry that the businessEntity being passed in is new and that a new record and businessKey are to be created. A name is required, and the value Acme XML is used. An optional description (Acme's XML Wing) is also supplied for the structure. For now, only the initial entity information is to be saved, and this is done by calling the save_business() method.

This method not only serves to create new entities but also updates them when a valid businessKey is supplied. Because it takes a complete businessEntity structure, you must be careful when performing updates this way. If you are updating an entity record that contains services and accidentally forget to include all the service information, the registry service thinks you meant to remove the service information and will delete it. Once you see how to add service information, you can address this issue. Returning to the entity creation, upon execution of this code, a businessDetail message is returned. Calling var_dump() on this returned data outputs the following:

```
object(stdClass)#2 (3) {
  ["businessEntity"]=>
  object(stdClass)#3 (6) {
    ["discoveryURLs"]=>
    object(stdClass)#4 (1) {
      ["discoveryURL"]=>
      object(stdClass)#5 (2) {
        ["_"]=>
        string(89) "http://udditest.sap.com/uddi/discovery/businessEntity/e1a5c990-
6e3d-11da-c5d9-0002a58b4eaf "
        ["useType"]=>
        string(14) "businessEntity"
      }
    }
    ["name"]=>
    object(stdClass)#6 (2) {
      ["_"]=>
      string(8) "Acme XML"
      ["lang"]=>
      string(2) "en"
    }
    ["description"]=>
    object(stdClass)#7 (2) {
      ["_"]=>
      string(20) "Acme's XML wing"
      ["lang"]=>
      string(2) "en"
    }
    ["businessKey"]=>
    string(36) "e1a5c990-6e3d-11da-c5d9-0002a58b4eaf"
    ["operator"]=>
    string(25) "uddi:udditest.sap.com"
    ["authorizedName"]=>
    string(10) "95f36a40-6da5-11da-c273-0002a58b4eaf"
  }
  ["generic"]=>
  string(3) "2.0"
  ["operator"]=>
  string(25) "uddi:udditest.sap.com"
}
```

As you can see, a businessKey of e1a5c990-6e3d-11da-c5d9-0002a58b4eaf has been assigned to this new record. The registry has also automatically created the following discoveryURL, which is wrapped across two lines here:

http://udditest.sap.com/uddi/discovery/businessEntity/e1a5c990-6e3d-11da-c5d9-
0002a58b4eaf

Navigating to this URL in a browser returns an XML document of the businessDetail
record.

■**Caution** The keys you see in these examples are used only for demonstration purposes. They are likely
to be different throughout this chapter because the same data is consistently deleted and re-created by
myself while I write the examples.

Creating a Service

The next step you might want to take is setting up the first service for the entity. You can accomplish this using the save_service() method. It works in a similar manner to the save_business()
method except this method takes a businessService structure. For example:

```
try {
    /* Create the businessService structure */
    $businessService = array("name"=>"Test Web Service",
                        "description"=>"Acme XML's First Web Service",
                        "businessKey"=>"e1a5c990-6e3d-11da-c5d9-0002a58b4eaf",
                        "serviceKey"=>"");

    /* Save the businessEntity structure */
    $svcDetail = $sPublish->save_service(array("generic"=>"2.0",
                                        "authInfo"=>$authInfo,
                                        "businessService"=>$businessService));
    var_dump($svcDetail);

} catch (SoapFault $e) {
    var_dump($e);
}
```

The businessService being created consists of just a name, Test Web Service, and
a description, as shown previously. The businessKey is required here. The businessService
must provide the key so it is properly linked to the businessEntity. The key—in this case
e1a5c990-6e3d-11da-c5d9-0002a58b4eaf—comes from the businessDetail response from
the previous example when the entity was created. Because this is a new service, the supplied
serviceKey must be empty.

Upon calling the save_service() method with all of the required data and assuming
a SoapFault is not thrown, a serviceDetail message is returned containing the information,
including the assigned serviceKey, for this new service. Rather than wading through the information from a var_dump(), navigate to the discoveryURL created when the entity was created.
The entire entity record as an XML document, including the newly added service, is returned.
It should look similar to the following, although the following output has been modified for
presentation:

```xml
<?xml version="1.0" encoding="UTF-8" ?>
<businessEntity xmlns="urn:uddi-org:api_v3"
                businessKey="uddi:e1a5c990-6e3d-11da-c5d9-0002a58b4eaf">
   <discoveryURLs>
      <discoveryURL useType="businessEntity">
         http://udditest.sap.com/uddi/discovery/businessEntity/e1a5c990-6e3d-11da-
c5d9-0002a58b4eaf
      </discoveryURL>
   </discoveryURLs>
   <name xml:lang="en">Acme XML</name>
   <description xml:lang="en">Acme's XML wing</description>
   <businessServices>
      <businessService serviceKey="uddi:e31278f0-6e3d-11da-a644-0002a58b4eaf"
                       businessKey="uddi:e1a5c990-6e3d-11da-c5d9-0002a58b4eaf">
         <name xml:lang="en">Test Web Service</name>
         <description xml:lang="en">Acme XML's First Web Service</description>
      </businessService>
   </businessServices>
</businessEntity>
```

Creating a Binding

The last piece to complete the entity record is creating a binding for the new service, identified by a serviceKey of e31278f0-6e3d-11da-a644-0002a58b4eaf. For this nonexistent service, I will use the location http://www.example.com/acmexml as the accessPoint. Here's the code:

```php
try {
   /* Create the tModelInstanceDetail structure */
   $tModelInstanceDetails = array("tModelInstanceInfo"=>
                  array("tModelKey"=>"UUID:68DE9E80-AD09-469D-8A37-088422BFBC36"));

   /* Create the bindingTemplate structure */
   $bindingTemplate = array("description"=>"Acme XML's Web Service",
      "accessPoint"=>array("_"=>"http://www.example.com/acmexml","URLType"=>"http"),
      "tModelInstanceDetails"=>$tModelInstanceDetails,
      "serviceKey"=>"e31278f0-6e3d-11da-a644-0002a58b4eaf",
      "bindingKey"=>"");

   /* Save the bindingTemplate structure */
   $bindDetl = $sPublish->save_binding(array("generic"=>"2.0",
                                       "authInfo"=>$authInfo,
                                       "bindingTemplate"=>$bindingTemplate));
   var_dump($bindDetl);

} catch (SoapFault $e) {
   var_dump($e);
}
```

This is an HTTP service, so HTTP's tModel is used, identified by a tModelKey of UUID:68DE9E80-AD09-469D-8A37-088422BFBC36. Once the tModelInstanceDetails structure has been set up, which is required to save the bindingTemplate, the bindingTemplate structure itself is established. It is given the description (Acme XML's Web service), and the accessPoint and tModelInstanceDetails are established. The required serviceKey of e31278f0-6e3d-➡ 11da-a644-0002a58b4eaf comes from the businessService previously created. This is used to link the binding to the service when the binding is saved. Finally, the save_binding() method is called, passing in the structure you built in $bindingTemplate. If you navigate to the discoveryURL, you will now see the businessEntity record that also contains the following fragment:

```
<bindingTemplates>
    <bindingTemplate bindingKey="e4782370-6e3d-11da-954b-0002a58b4eaf"
                     serviceKey="e31278f0-6e3d-11da-a644-0002a58b4eaf">
        <description xml:lang="en">Acme XML's Web Service</description>
        <accessPoint URLType="http">http://www.example.com/acmexml</accessPoint>
        <tModelInstanceDetails>
            <tModelInstanceInfo tModelKey=" uddi:uddi.org:transport:http"/>
        </tModelInstanceDetails>
    </bindingTemplate>
</bindingTemplates>
```

Creating a tModel

This chapter did not cover how to create a tModel. It is not complicated to do, because it follows the same pattern as you saw when saving other structures. Calling the save_tModel() method with the appropriate parameters and structures is all you need to do. Using the tModelKey from the tModelDetail response, you can then easily reference the tModel from your data. In most cases, however, you will use precreated tModels when needed. For example, when saving the binding in the previous example, you used the tModel for HTTP. tModels already defined for use include the following:

UDDI registry tModels: Represents UDDI programming interfaces. You can find the documentation at http://uddi.org/taxonomies/UDDI_Registry_tModels.htm.

UDDI other core tModels: Various tModels defining technical definitions. You can find the documentation at http://uddi.org/taxonomies/UDDI_CoreOther_tModels.htm.

Replication tModels: Represents the programming interface for replication between UDDI instances. You can find the documentation at http://uddi.org/taxonomies/UDDI_Replication_tModels.htm.

Taxonomy tModels: Represents categorization schemes, such as taxonomies, identifier systems, and relationships. You can find the documentation at http://uddi.org/taxonomies/UDDI_Taxonomy_tModels.htm.

Updating Data

As I mentioned before, updating data is the same as adding new data to the registry. The same method calls as you saw demonstrated in the "Publishing to the Registry" section are used.

The only difference is that the value of the key for the specific structure is supplied rather than passed as an empty value. The one thing you need to watch out for is ensuring that the structure being updated contains all substructure information as well. Take, for example, a change in the business name.

Suppose you wanted to change the name of the businessEntity from Acme XML to Acme XML, Inc. Imagine what would happen if you made the following calls:

```
/* Modify the businessEntity structure */
$businessEntity = array("businessKey"=>" e1a5c990-6e3d-11da-c5d9-0002a58b4eaf",
                        "name"=>'Acme XML Inc.',
                        "description"=>"Acme's XML wing");

/* Save the businessEntity structure */
$bizDetail = $sPublish->save_business(array("generic"=>"2.0",
                                            "authInfo"=>$authInfo,
                                            "businessEntity"=>$businessEntity));
```

If this were actually executed, all the previous service information that was added would be lost. This is probably not something you want to do. The question is then how to perform updates without losing existing data. For example:

```
try {
    /* Connect to the inquiry service */
    $sClient = new SoapClient('inquire_v2.wsdl');
    /* Retrieve the businessDetail record for the entity */
    $bizDetail = $sClient->get_businessDetail(array("generic"=>"2.0",
                        "businessKey"=>" e1a5c990-6e3d-11da-c5d9-0002a58b4eaf"));

    /* Get the businessEntity from the response */
    $businessEntity = $bizDetail->businessEntity;

    /* Change the name of the businessEntity */
    $businessEntity->name->_ = 'Acme XML Inc.';

    /* Save the updated businessEntity using the publisher service */
    $bizDetail = $sPublish->save_business(array("generic"=>"2.0",
                                            "authInfo"=>$authInfo,
                                            "businessEntity"=>$businessEntity));
} catch (SoapFault $e) {
    var_dump($e);
}
```

As you can see, this is actually quite simple. Using a combination of functions from the inquiry service, the current businessEntity record is retrieved. Modifications are then made to this structure and saved to the registry using the publisher service. You can use this technique to update each UDDI structure.

Deleting Data

You have already seen one way to delete data. Not including data when updating a structure causes the missing data to be removed from the registry. Unless doing some major updates, this is not a safe method of performing a delete. It becomes quite easy to accidentally make a mistake. A more controlled way to delete information is to use the delete_xxx() methods. These methods take keys for arguments, so you can safely delete specific structures. For example, if the businessEntity had a bindingTemplate with a bindingKey and value of e4782370-6e3d-11da-954b-0002a58b4eaf, to safely delete this binding, you would execute the following code:

```
$response = $sPublish->delete_binding(array("generic"=>"2.0", "authInfo"=>$authInfo,
                          "bindingKey"=>" e4782370-6e3d-11da-954b-
0002a58b4eaf"));
```

Assuming no SoapFault was thrown from this method, the binding would be successfully removed. You can handle the remaining structures in the same way, using their specific delete methods, so I won't demonstrate any further examples.

Conclusion

The goal of UDDI was to provide a universal registry, the UBR, where businesses could register their Web services and where those searching for Web services could locate them. In a sense, the UBR is similar to a specialized search engine. UDDI goes a bit beyond that because not only can Web services be located but also it provides the technical information about how they are to be consumed. Whether this will ever come to realization is another matter. UDDI in the public sense never gained much momentum, and data is sparse. Supposedly on private networks, either intranets or extranets, UDDI has found its place. Companies and the businesses they have relationships with are able to publish and locate the services they need in order to work together. Personally I cannot comment on this.

This chapter showed how simple working with UDDI is, especially by means of the PHP SOAP extension. Being this simple, it is almost worth understanding how UDDI works and how to interface with it because for all you know, one day it may move more mainstream. I haven't covered every aspect of UDDI, but I have covered the most important portions you need to understand and work with when interfacing with a registry. Using what you have learned in this chapter, it should not be difficult to understand other concepts presented in the UDDI specification. UDDI is the last of the prominent Web service technologies covered in this book.

The next chapter provides an overview of the Web service extensions found in the PEAR repository that you can use to work with specific services.

■ ■ ■

PEAR and Web Services

By now you should understand how to implement and access Web services using technologies such as REST and SOAP. Through examples, you have seen how to use these technologies to interface with some real-world Web services. This chapter will cover some of the PEAR packages that have already been written to access other specific Web services found on the Internet. By the end of this chapter, you may not completely understand how to use every Web service package in the PEAR repository, but you should have at least an idea of what each one does.

As mentioned in Chapter 13, PEAR (http://pear.php.net/) is a centralized location for open source libraries, known as *packages*, that developers can leverage within their applications. Not only does PEAR contain a number of XML packages, but it also includes a few packages specifically written for Web services. You can find additional information about PEAR and how to install packages in Chapter 13.

■**Caution** When using many of the PEAR packages in a system with E_STRICT enabled in error_reporting, be prepared for an abundant amount of "deprecated" messages. You can ignore these messages, which stem from packages using syntax compatible with that of PHP 4.

Currently, 16 PEAR packages are designed specifically for Web services. In PHP 4, where XML support was slim, the packages filled a great need. With the advances made in XML support in PHP 5, you will have little need to use the majority of them, unless your Web site is hosted on a server that does not include the vast XML support of PHP 5. I will present about half of the existing packages in this chapter and provide examples for a few of them. In most cases, using SimpleXML alone to access a service will be enough to understand the package. In addition, only a couple of the Web service packages have reached a release state; the rest have little to no development currently taking place. The choice to use any of these packages is completely up to you, but in the majority of cases you simply will not need them.

Using Services_Amazon

In Chapter 17, I showed you how to access some of the functionality using REST that Amazon exposes via its Web services. As you may have noticed, the Amazon E-Commerce Service (ECS) contains a good amount of functionality for interfacing with Amazon. Rather than having to manually build the URLs yourself, you can use the Services_Amazon package, which allows you to call the ECS operations as object methods. Along with this, the package also provides caching capabilities.

Note Accessing the Amazon Web services requires an access key ID, which you can obtain from http://www.amazon.com/gp/aws/registration/registration-form.html.

After installing the package, you will have access to both the Services_Amazon class, which is used to access the ECS 3.0 API, and the Services_AmazonECS4 class, which is used to access the ECS 4.0 API. The examples in this section will use the Services_AmazonECS4 class. Even though Amazon does not have plans to eliminate the ECS 3.0 API in the near future, the ECS 4.0 API is more extensible and thus is the preferred API for any new development. Once you have included the correct file, you can instantiate the object:

```
require_once 'Services/AmazonECS4.php';
```

The constructor takes the required access key ID you received when you registered, as well as an optional associate ID. If you are a registered associate, by passing your associate ID you will ensure that any purchase made, if using such functionality, will be credited to your account. For example:

```
$accesskey = '<insert your Access Key ID>';

/* If not using an associate ID, you should either set this variable to NULL
   or not pass it to the constructor */
$associd = '<insert your Asscoiate ID>';

$amazon = new Services_AmazonECS4($accesskey, $associd);
```

A nice feature of this class is the ability to set the locale. As you probably recall from Chapter 17 (specifically Table 17-8), the URL for the Web service depends upon your locale. Using the setLocale() method, you do not need to remember the URL to which you should be connecting. The method takes any of the two-letter codes from Table 17-8, which consist of US, UK, DE, JP, FR, and CA. By default, Amazon US is the service Services_AmazonECS4 will connect to, but you can easily change this to Amazon CA by calling the following:

```
$amazon->setLocale('CA');
```

Any interaction with the Web service from this point in the chapter will be interfacing with http://webservices.amazon.ca/onca/xml?Service=AWSECommerceService.

The names of the methods are the same as the names of the operations defined in the API. I have not included the complete list here, but you can find it in the Amazon Web services documentation. You can't really get around reading the documentation, because most of the parameters for the methods are passed in an array where the parameter name is the key for the value. The following example performs the same item search as in Chapter 17. Table 17-9 showed the list of options that can be passed, though Operation and SearchIndex should not be passed as options since Operation is dictated by the method being called and SearchIndex is passed as the first argument to the ItemSearch method.

```php
<?php
require_once 'Services/AmazonECS4.php';

/* Your Amazon access key */
$accesskey = '<insert your Access Key ID>';

/* Create the object without an associate ID */
$amazon = new Services_AmazonECS4($accesskey);

$options = array();
$options['Keywords'] = 'linksys';

/* array()Services_AmazonECS4::ItemSearch(string SearchIndex, [array() $options]) */
$result = $amazon->ItemSearch('Electronics', $options);

var_dump($result);
?>
```

The response is returned from the method as an array. The following is an abbreviated version of the output. Only one item is shown, although the method did return ten items. This output is equivalent to that shown in Listing 17-8.

```
array(4) {
  ["Request"]=>
  array(2) {
    ["IsValid"]=>
    string(4) "True"
    ["ItemSearchRequest"]=>
    array(2) {
      ["Keywords"]=>
      string(7) "linksys"
      ["SearchIndex"]=>
      string(11) "Electronics"
    }
  }
  ["TotalResults"]=>
  string(3) "488"
  ["TotalPages"]=>
  string(2) "49"
  ["Item"]=>
  array(10) {
    [0]=>
    array(3) {
      ["ASIN"]=>
      string(10) "B00007KDVI"
```

```
      ["DetailPageURL"]=>
      string(290) "http://www.amazon.com/exec/obidos/redirect?tag=ws%26link_code=
xm2%26camp=2025%26creative=165953%26path=http://www.amazon.com/gp/redirect.html
%253fASIN=B00007KDVI%2526tag=ws%2526lcode=xm2%2526cID=2025%2526ccmID=165953%2526
location=/o/ASIN/B00007KDVI%25253FSubscriptionId=0MWT9W26N2NFGGJZ33R2"
      ["ItemAttributes"]=>
      array(3) {
        ["Manufacturer"]=>
        string(7) "Linksys"
        ["ProductGroup"]=>
        string(2) "CE"
        ["Title"]=>
        string(32) "Linksys WRT54G Wireless-G Router"
      }
    }
    /* Additional nine items omitted */
  }
}
```

The following example demonstrates how to use the shopping cart. It performs similar functionality as shown in Chapter 17. This code creates a new cart, and using `CartId` and `HMAC` (which is the security token needed to access and modify the newly created cart returned from the Web service), it locates the `CartItemId` for this newly added item and updates it to have a quantity of 6.

```php
<?php
require_once 'Services/AmazonECS4.php';

/* Your Amazon access key */
$accesskey = '<insert your Access Key ID>';

/* Create the object without an associate ID */
$amazon = new Services_AmazonECS4($accesskey);

/* Create a new cart, adding one item */
$items = array(array('ASIN'=>'1590596331', 'Quantity'=>1));
$result = $amazon->CartCreate($items);

/* Retrieve the CartId and HMAC from the results */
$cartid = $result["CartId"];
$hmac = $result["HMAC"];

/* Find the CartItemId for the item just added to the cart */
$cart_item_id = NULL;
foreach ($result['CartItems'] AS $key=>$value) {
   var_dump($key);
```

```php
    if ($key == 'CartItem' && $value['ASIN'] == '1590596331') {
        $cart_item_id = $value['CartItemId'];
    }
}

/* If CartItemId is found, then modify the quantity to 6 */
if (! is_null($cart_item_id)) {
    $items = array(array('CartItemId'=>$cart_item_id, 'Quantity'=>6));
    $result = $amazon->CartModify($cartid, $hmac, $items);
}

var_dump($result);

$purchase_url = $result['PurchaseURL'];

/* Send user to this URL to make purchase */
print $purchase_url;
?>
```

Other than the results being in array format, the output should be similar to the output shown in Chapter 17. Although this has only been a short introduction to the Services_Amazon package, it should give you an idea of how to use the rest of the functionality provided by Services_Amazon. Other than using a predefined class, using Services_Amazon is no different from performing it all yourself using only an XML-based extension such as SimpleXML.

Using Services_Delicious

Services_Delicious provides access to the del.icio.us Web service (http://del.icio.us/), which offers the capability to use online bookmarks that you can access from anywhere you have Internet access. You can then share these bookmarks with others in the community. Using tags, you can categorize the bookmarks, allowing them to be easily searched using keywords. Because it is currently in beta status, this package can be installed using the following command:

```
pear install Services_Delicious-beta
```

■**Note** This package is currently missing a few important method parameters for some of the del.icio.us API calls. Therefore, I will provide only a brief description and example of this package. You can find additional information for this package at http://pear.php.net/package/Services_Delicious.

Accessing del.icio.us and using this package requires a valid login, which you can obtain at http://del.icio.us/register. The following is a short example of how to create a Services_Delicious object, pass the user ID and password to the constructor, and return the 25 most recent posts with the tag *php*:

```php
<?php
require_once 'Services/Delicious.php';

$userid = '<your del.icio.us userid>';
$password = '<your del.icio.us password>';

$svcDelicious = new Services_Delicious($userid, $password);

$posts = $svcDelicious->getRecentPosts('php', 25);
var_dump($posts);
?>
```

Using Services_Ebay

The Services_Ebay package was developed to create a simple interface for integrating applications with eBay. The current version of this package is 0.12.0-alpha and is based upon eBay's Legacy XML API. As of June 1, 2006, eBay will be dropping support for the legacy schema in favor of the New XML API that was released in early 2004. You can find additional information about this at http://developer.ebay.com/migration. Unless this package is updated to support the New XML API, you should refrain from developing any new applications using this package.

■**Caution** Because of the discontinuation of eBay's Legacy XML API on June 1, 2006, which this package is currently based upon, you should perform any new development interfacing with eBay using REST, SOAP, or some other library compatible with PHP 5 that provides access to the eBay Web services.

Using Services_Google

The Services_Google package is simply a wrapper around the SOAP extension and is used to access the Google Web APIs (http://www.google.com/apis/reference.html) for the search engine, spelling suggestions, and cache. To access any of these services, you must obtain a license key by registering for an account. A link to the registration page is available from the previously mentioned URL. Because this package is a wrapper for SOAP, both PHP 5 and the SOAP extension are prerequisites for installing and using this package. Having met these conditions, and because the package is currently in alpha status, you install it using the following:

```
pear install Services_Google-alpha
```

Once you have installed it, you add support for the package to a script by calling the following:

```
require_once "Services/Google.php";
```

■**Note** Google limits you to 1,000 automated queries per day based upon your license key.

This package consists of a single class, Services_Google, that is instantiated by passing your license key as the only argument to the constructor:

```
$google = new Services_Google($key);
```

Checking Spelling

You can perform a spell check by calling the spellingSuggestion() method. This method takes a string containing the phrase to be checked as its only parameter, and it simply returns a string containing the suggested spelling for the supplied phrase. For example, the following example performs a spell check on the phrase *PHP xnl*, and it is followed by the resulting phrase suggested by Google's spell-checking engine:

```php
<?php
require_once "Services/Google.php";

/* Google license key */
$key = '<your Google license key>';

/* Create instance, passing license key as argument */
$google = new Services_Google($key);

/* Output the resulting suggested spelling */
echo $google->spellingSuggestion('PHP xnl')."\n";
?>
```

```
PHP xml
```

Retrieving Cached Pages

You can retrieve cached pages from Google by calling the getCachedPage() method from an instantiated Services_Google object. The object takes a single parameter, which is a string containing the URL to retrieve the cached page for, and it returns a string containing the cached page.

■**Caution** As of version 0.1.1 of this package, this method is incompatible with PHP 5.1 and does not return any valid data.

Searching the Web

You can perform Web searches via a Web service just like using Google from a browser by calling the search() method. Once you have an instantiated the Services_Google object, you can use a number of options, listed in Table 20-1, to control various aspects of the search.

■**Caution** When running the alpha version 0.1.1 of this package with a Web search, you must always set the limit option, and the start option has no bearing on the results returned.

Table 20-1. *Query Options*

Option	Default Value	Description
start	0	Zero-based index of the first desired result.
maxResults	10	Maximum number of results to return for the query. The maximum value per query is 10.
limit	FALSE	Although Google limits the maximum number of results for a query, the Services_Google class uses this option to make multiple requests as you move through the returned results, retrieving up to a maximum number of records specified by this option. It is currently mandatory that you use this option, or no results will be returned.
filter	TRUE	Activates or deactivates automatic results filtering, which hides similar results and results that all come from the same Web host.
restricts	empty	Restricts results to certain countries and/or topics. You can find additional information about using this parameter at http://www.google.ca/apis/reference.html#2_4.
safeSearch	TRUE	A Boolean used to filter adult content from the results.
language	empty	Restricts the search to documents within one or more languages. Refer to http://www.google.ca/apis/reference.html#2_4 for additional information.

You set these options using the queryOptions property, which is in fact an array where the keys consist of the options from Table 20-1. For example, using $google as the object, you can limit the results to those that are in the French language by using the following convention:

```
$google->queryOptions['language'] = 'lang_fr';
$google->queryOptions['limit'] = 3; /* Set to make the search work */
```

Once you have set any and all options, the search() method is called, passing the query string as the argument, as shown here. The query string can contain any type of query that is valid to be used on the Google search page itself.

```
$google->search("PHP XML");

foreach($google as $key => $result) {
   echo $result->title."\n";
}
```

You can find additional information about writing advanced queries at `http://www.google.ca/apis/reference.html#2_2`. The actual results when this is executed look like the following:

```
PHPIndex : <b>PHP</b>, <b>XML</b> et XSLT
PHPIndex : <b>PHP</b>, <b>XML</b> et XSLT : point de situation
<b>XML</b> parsing avec <b>PHP</b>
```

Using Services_Technorati

Technorati (`http://www.technorati.com/`) is a search engine for locating information from weblogs. Rather than a traditional search engine that searches the entire Internet, usually without concern of the source of the content, searches performed using Technorati are limited to content coming from weblogs. The Services_Technorati package is an interface for accessing their services.

Note To access the Technorati Web service, you must register for an API key at `http://www.technorati.com/developers/signup.html`.

Once you have installed the package, you must include the required file and instantiate the class:

```
require_once 'Services/Technorati.php';
$key = '<your API key here>';

$technorati = new Services_Technorati($key);
```

The constructor for the class also accepts an optional Cache object from the Cache_Lite package, but this is not required to utilize the class. An optional method for creating a Services_Technorati object is using the factory() method. This method is meant to be called statically and takes the API key, an optional Cache object, and an optional version number:

```
$technorati = Services_Technorati::factory($key);
```

I did not use this when the object was initially instantiated because it produces E_STRICT messages when they are enabled on the server. The method, however, allows the package to provide additional and extended behavior in the future, where the class used for the object is based on the version number passed as an argument. Currently, no additional interfaces exist, so you can ignore this for the time being.

This class supports a number of methods. Table 20-2 lists the stable ones. By *stable*, I do not mean that those not listed are not implemented properly in the package but, rather, that the functionality itself is either disabled or considered experimental by Technorati.

Table 20-2. Services_Technorati *Methods*

Method	Prototype	Description
cosmos	array cosmos(string $url, [array $options = null])	Returns the blogs that link to a specific URL.
search	array search(string $query, [array $options = null])	Returns the blogs that contain a given search string.
outbound	array outbound(string $url, [array $options = null])	The outbound query lets you see what blogs are linked to on a given blog, including their associated information.
blogInfo	array blogInfo(string $url)	The bloginfo query provides information about what blog, if any, is associated with a given URL. It also returns additional information such as cosmos stats or RSS feeds.
getInfo	array getInfo(string $username)	The getinfo query tells you the information that Technorati knows about a user.
keyInfo	array keyInfo()	The keyinfo query provides information about the daily usage of an API key. Key info queries do not count against a key's daily query limit, where a day is defined as 00:00–23:59 Pacific time.
topTags	array topTags([array $options = null])	The toptags query allows you to get a list of the most popular post-tags tracked by Technorati.
blogPostTags	array blogPostTags(string $url, [array $options = array()])	The blogposttags query returns the top tags for a given blog URL.

The majority of these methods also can take a number of options. You can find the available options for the methods in the Technorati documentation at http://developers. technorati.com/wiki/TechnoratiApi.

Note Not every option has been implemented within the Services_Technorati class. Some are marked as experimental or have been recently added and have yet to make their way into the package.

You pass options as an array where the keys are the names of the options for each value. For example, the cosmos() method is able to accept the type, limit, start, current, claim, and highlight options. To limit the number of results returned to five and add highlighted, linked text, you initialize and pass the options in the following manner:

```
$options = array('limit'=>5, 'highlight'=>1);
$technorati->cosmos($url, $options);
```

The API is actually quite simple to use. The following example demonstrates how to call each of the methods from Table 20-2 and calls var_dump() on each of the returned arrays:

```php
<?php
require_once 'Services/Technorati.php';

$key = '<your API key here>';

/* Instantiating object rather than static call to avoid E_STRICT message */
$technorati = new Services_Technorati($key);

/* Check the stats on our API Key usage */
$keyinfo = $technorati->keyInfo();
var_dump($keyinfo);

/* Set limit of results to a max of 2 */
$options = array('limit'=>2);

$cosmos = $technorati->cosmos('www.php.net', $options);
var_dump($cosmos);

$search = $technorati->search('PHP 5 XML', $options);
var_dump($search);

$outbound = $technorati->outbound('www.planet-php.org');
var_dump($outbound);

$blogInfo = $technorati->blogInfo('www.planet-php.org');
var_dump($blogInfo);

$topTags = $technorati->topTags($options);
var_dump($topTags);

$options = array('limit'=>3);
$blogPostTags = $technorati->blogPostTags('http://blog.bitflux.ch/', $options);
var_dump($blogPostTags);
?>
```

Because of the amount of information this example outputs, I will show only a couple of the results here. The following is the result from calling var_dump() on the array returned from calling the blogInfo() method:

```
array(2) {
  ["version"]=>
  string(3) "1.0"
  ["document"]=>
  array(1) {
    ["result"]=>
    array(4) {
      ["url"]=>
      string(25) "http://www.planet-php.org"
```

```
    ["weblog"]=>
    array(11) {
      ["name"]=>
      string(10) "Planet PHP"
      ["url"]=>
      string(25) "http://www.planet-php.org"
      ["rssurl"]=>
      string(30) "http://www.planet-php.org/rss/"
      ["atomurl"]=>
      string(31) "http://www.planet-php.org/atom/"
      ["inboundblogs"]=>
      string(2) "16"
      ["inboundlinks"]=>
      string(2) "17"
      ["lastupdate"]=>
      string(23) "2005-06-16 11:05:04 GMT"
      ["rank"]=>
      string(6) "153696"
      ["lat"]=>
      string(1) "0"
      ["lon"]=>
      string(1) "0"
      ["lang"]=>
      string(2) "18"
    }
    ["inboundblogs"]=>
    string(2) "16"
    ["inboundlinks"]=>
    string(2) "17"
  }
 }
}
```

As you can see, this output provides some basic information about the weblog (including the link), provides links to RSS and Atom feeds, and summarizes the number of inbound and outbound links.

The `blogPostTags()` method returns the tags based on the most popular topics referenced on the weblog. In this case, I chose Christian Stocker's blog (`http://blog.bitflux.ch`); Stocker is one of the PHP XML developers. To reduce the length of the output, only the top three tags were selected, by means of the `limit` option. The following is the result of the corresponding call to `var_dump()` on the resulting array:

```
array(2) {
  ["version"]=>
  string(3) "1.0"
  ["document"]=>
```

```
array(2) {
  ["result"]=>
  array(1) {
    ["querycount"]=>
    string(1) "3"
  }
  ["item"]=>
  array(3) {
    [0]=>
    array(2) {
      ["tag"]=>
      string(3) "PHP"
      ["posts"]=> *
      string(2) "65"
    }
    [1]=>
    array(2) {
      ["tag"]=>
      string(5) "Trips"
      ["posts"]=>
      string(2) "48"
    }
    [2]=>
    array(2) {
      ["tag"]=>
      string(11) "Switzerland"
      ["posts"]=>
      string(2) "45"
    }
  }
}
```

Based on these results, you can clearly see that the most referenced items on his weblog pertain to PHP, trips, and Switzerland, in that order.

Using Services_Weather

The Services_Weather package is one of the more interesting Web services packages. It provides a simple interface to gather weather information from a number of sources. These sources include Weather.com (http://www.weather.com/services/xmloap.html), GlobalWeather (http://www.capescience.com/webservices/globalweather/index.shtml), the National Weather Service (http://weather.noaa.gov/weather/metar.shtml), and EJSE (http://www.ejse.com/weather_data.htm).

Although this package provides a good amount of functionality, I will demonstrate only a simple example using Weather.com. It is the only service that does not require the PEAR SOAP package and does not require the DB package. Registration, however, is required to access this service. The first step you should take before proceeding, assuming you would like to try the code, is to register at http://www.weather.com/services/xmloap.html and obtain a partner ID and license key. Once you have these, you can begin using the package, as follows:

```
require_once "Services/Weather.php";
$partner_id = '<your partner id>';
$license_key = '<your license key>';

$weather = Services_Weather::service("WeatherDotCom");
$weather->setAccountData($partner_id, $license_key);
```

The services() method is a factory method used to create the object with the correct class type to connect to the correct weather service. In this case, WeatherDotCom is passed, resulting in a Services_Weather_Weatherdotcom object being returned. Other available parameter values are Globalweather, Metar, and Ejse. Because this is connecting to Weather.com, the account data must be set prior to making any remote calls.

The next step is to retrieve the ID for the location from which to retrieve the specific weather information. You do this by using the searchLocation() method. It takes a string that identifies the location. For example, to specify the city of Portland in the state of Maine, you would make the following call:

```
$location_id = $weather->searchLocation("Portland, Maine");
```

This location ID, $location_id, then retrieves the information about the location, the current weather, and even the upcoming forecast.

Retrieving Location Information

The following shows how to retrieve location information:

```
$locInfo = $weather->getLocation($location_id);
var_dump($locInfo);
```

```
array(8) {
  ["cache"]=>
  string(4) "MISS"
  ["name"]=>
  string(12) "Portland, ME"
  ["time"]=>
  string(8) "15:46 PM"
  ["latitude"]=>
  string(5) "43.65"
  ["longitude"]=>
  string(6) "-70.31"
  ["sunrise"]=>
  string(7) "6:39 AM"
  ["sunset"]=>
  string(8) "16:13 PM"
```

```
  ["timezone"]=>
  string(2) "-5"
}
```

Retrieving Current Weather Conditions

The following shows how to retrieve the current weather conditions:

```
$weatherInfo = $weather->getWeather($location_id);
var_dump($weatherInfo);
```

```
array(19) {
  ["cache"]=>
  string(4) "MISS"
  ["update"]=>
  string(17) "11/18/05 19:51 PM"
  ["updateRaw"]=>
  string(20) "11/18/05 2:51 PM EST"
  ["station"]=>
  string(12) "Portland, ME"
  ["temperature"]=>
  float(37)
  ["feltTemperature"]=>
  float(33)
  ["condition"]=>
  string(4) "Fair"
  ["conditionIcon"]=>
  string(2) "34"
  ["pressure"]=>
  float(30.19)
  ["pressureTrend"]=>
  string(6) "steady"
  ["wind"]=>
  float(5)
  ["windGust"]=>
  float(0)
  ["windDegrees"]=>
  string(1) "0"
  ["windDirection"]=>
  string(3) "VAR"
  ["humidity"]=>
  string(2) "33"
  ["visibility"]=>
  float(10)
  ["uvIndex"]=>
  string(1) "0"
```

```
    ["uvText"]=>
    string(3) "Low"
    ["dewPoint"]=>
    float(10)
}
```

Retrieving the Forecast

The following shows how to retrieve the forecast:

```
$forecastInfo = $weather->getForecast($location_id);
var_dump($forecastInfo);
```

I have altered the following results for brevity by omitting the actual weather conditions:

```
array(4) {
  ["cache"]=>
  string(4) "MISS"
  ["update"]=>
  string(17) "11/18/05 20:05 PM"
  ["updateRaw"]=>
  string(20) "11/18/05 3:05 PM EST"
  ["days"]=>
  array(2) {
    [0]=>
    array(6) {
      ["temperatureHigh"]=>
      float(0)
      ["temperatureLow"]=>
      float(23)
      ["sunrise"]=>
      string(7) "6:39 AM"
      ["sunset"]=>
      string(8) "16:13 PM"
      ["day"]=>
      array(8) {
        /* Weather conditions */
      }
      ["night"]=>
      array(8) {
        /* Weather conditions */
      }
    }
    [1]=>
    array(6) {
      ["temperatureHigh"]=>
      float(40)
```

```
        ["temperatureLow"]=>
        float(30)
        ["sunrise"]=>
        string(7) "6:41 AM"
        ["sunset"]=>
        string(8) "16:12 PM"
        ["day"]=>
        array(8) {
          /* Weather conditions */
        }
        ["night"]=>
        array(8) {
          /* Weather conditions */
        }
      }
    }
  }
}
```

The example shown here is specific to the Services_Weather_Weatherdotcom class. The methods differ based upon the weather data provider you are accessing. You can find additional information about this package and the other classes at http://pear.php.net/package/Services_Weather.

Using Services_Webservice

The Services_Webservice package is one of the more interesting Web services packages, although it is not ready to be rolled out in a production environment. It requires you to be running PHP 5.1+, and both the DOM and SOAP extensions are available. Services_Webservice offers the capability to quickly and easily create a Web service exposing the functionality of a class's methods simply by having the class extend the Services_Webservice class. Doing so also provides automatic WSDL creation as well as Discovery of Web Services (DISCO), which provides a means to discover and retrieve the WSDL description of services on remote machines.

For example, the following is the skeleton code:

```
function people_search($id, $lastName=NULL) {
   /* Functionality Here */
}

class Person {
    public $id;
    public $firstName;
    public $lastName;
```

```php
    /* Constructor to build the Person object based on ID */
    public function __construct($id) {
        /* Functionality Here */
    }
}

class People {
    /* Method to search for people based on last name returns an array */
    public function search($lastName){
        /* functionality here */
    }

    /* Return a Person object based on ID */
    public function getPerson($id) {
        /* Functionality here */
    }
}
```

The main class is People, which searches for IDs and retrieves specific Person records.
This is easily converted into a Web service using the Services_Webservice class. For this to
work properly, the first step is to document the code using Docblock. If you are unfamiliar
with documenting PHP code using this syntax, you can find additional information at the
phpDocumentor project (http://www.phpdoc.org/index.php). This documentation is required
in order for your service to be able to automatically generate a WSDL document and provide
an information page for your Web service.

The last change to make is to have the main class that will be used for the Web service
(in this case the People class) extend the Services_Webservice class. The following code
demonstrates these changes as well as fully implements the previous skeleton code:

```php
<?php
include_once('Services/Webservice.php');

/* Generic function to provide search and record retrieval functionality */
function people_search($id, $lastName=NULL) {
    $arPeople = array(1=>array('lastName'=>'Doe', 'firstName'=>'Jane'),
                      2=>array('lastName'=>'Doe', 'firstName'=>'John'),
                      3=>array('lastName'=>'Smith', 'firstName'=>'Joe'));

    if (is_null($id)) {
        if (! empty($lastName)) {
            $retval = array();
            foreach ($arPeople AS $key=>$value) {
                if (stripos($value['lastName'], $lastName) !== false) {
                    $retval[] = $key;
                }
            }
            return $retval;
        }
```

```php
    } else if (is_numeric($id) && array_key_exists($id, $arPeople)) {
        return $arPeople[$id];
    }
    return NULL;
}


/* A specific record for a Person */
class Person
{
    public function __construct($id)
    {
        $retval =  people_search($id);
        if (! is_null($retval)) {
            $this->id = $id;
            $this->firstName = $retval['firstName'];
            $this->lastName = $retval['lastName'];
        } else {
            throw new Exception("Not Found");
        }
    }

    /**
     * @var int
     */
    public $id;
    /**
     * @var string
     */
    public $firstName;
    /**
     * @var string
     */
    public $lastName;
}


/* The class being exposed for the Web service */
class People extends Services_Webservice
{
    /**
     * Says "Locate IDS by Last Name"
     *
     * @param string
     * @return int[]
     */
    public function search($lastName)
```

```
    {
        $retval =  people_search(NULL, $lastName);
        if (! is_null($retval)) {
            return $retval;
        }
        return new SoapFault("404", "No people found");
    }

    /**
     * Says "Get a Person object based on ID"
     *
     * @param int
     * @return Person
     */
    public function getPerson($id)
    {
        try {
            $person = new Person($id);
            return new SoapVar($person, SOAP_ENC_OBJECT, 'Person', 'urn:People');
        } catch (Exception $e) {
            return new SoapFault("404", "Invalid ID");
        }
    }
}

$People = new People('People',
    'Find People',
    array('uri'=>'People', 'encoding'=>SOAP_ENCODED,'soap_version'=>SOAP_1_2));

$People->handle();
?>
```

The last two calls in this example instantiate the new People object and prepare it to accept incoming SOAP requests. The first argument defines the namespace. In this case, People is used. The second argument is the description of the service. This value displays the description of the service on the informational page. The last parameter is a list of options to send to the SoapServer when it is created. Because this package uses the SOAP extension, this argument is the same argument as documented for the SoapServer __construct() method in the SOAP extension.

Once the People object, $People, has been instantiated, a simple call to the handle() method is executed. This method appropriately handles the incoming request based on the parameters sent in. For example, a SOAP request is handled by the SoapServer to execute functionality. When accessed directly from the Web, such as from a browser, passing no arguments returns the informational page, which provides documentation, to the browser. For instance, suppose this Web service were located at http://www.example.org/PeopleSearch. Navigating to that URL with a browser would produce the output shown in Figure 20-1.

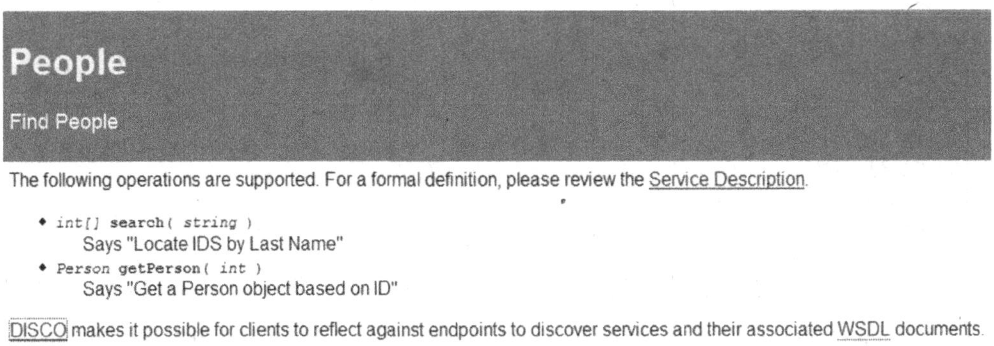

People

Find People

The following operations are supported. For a formal definition, please review the Service Description.

- `int[] search( string )`
  Says "Locate IDS by Last Name"
- `Person getPerson( int )`
  Says "Get a Person object based on ID"

DISCO makes it possible for clients to reflect against endpoints to discover services and their associated WSDL documents.

Figure 20-1. *People Web service information page*

Passing the parameter DISCO, as in http://www.example.org/PeopleSearch?DISCO, returns discovery information for the service, like the following:

```
<?xml version="1.0" encoding="utf-8"?>
<discovery xmlns:xsi="http://www.w3.org/2001/XMLSchema-instance"
           xmlns:xsd="http://www.w3.org/2001/XMLSchema"
           xmlns="http://schemas.xmlsoap.org/disco/">
   <contractRef ref="http://www.example.org/PeopleSearch?wsdl"
                docRef="http://www.example.org/PeopleSearch"
                xmlns="http://schemas.xmlsoap.org/disco/scl/">
      <soap address="http://www.example.org/PeopleSearch"
            xmlns:q1="People" binding="q1:People"
            xmlns="http://schemas.xmlsoap.org/disco/scl/"/>
   </contractRef>
</discovery>
```

Passing the parameter WSDL in the URL returns the WSDL document for the service, which a client can use to access the service. The following code demonstrates how to access this service, using the SOAP extension's SoapClient while also using the WSDL document from the service:

```php
<?php
try {
    $sClient = new SoapClient('http://www.example.org/PeopleSearch?WSDL');
    $response = $sClient->search('smi');
    foreach ($response AS $key=>$value) {
        $person = $sClient->getPerson($value);
        var_dump($person);
    }
} catch (SoapFault $e) {
    var_dump($e);
}
?>
```

```
object(stdClass)#2 (3) {
  ["id"]=>
  int(3)
  ["firstName"]=>
  string(3) "Joe"
  ["lastName"]=>
  string(5) "Smith"
}
```

You might now see why this package is interesting. With little coding and absolutely no knowledge of Web services, SOAP, or WSDL, you can quickly create a Web service.

■**Caution** Again, at this time, Services_Webservice is at version 0.4.0 and is in an alpha state. Be cautious if considering using this package on a production server.

Using Services_Yahoo

Services_Yahoo provides an object-oriented approach to interfacing with the Yahoo Web Search service (http://developer.yahoo.net/search/index.html) and Yahoo Maps. The Yahoo Web Search service includes audio, content analysis, image, local search, news, video, and Web services. It depends upon the HTTP_Request package, and although the Yahoo Web Search service requires the SimpleXML extension, working with Yahoo Maps requires DOM. The package currently consists of a number of classes, although the classes pertaining to searching share a good amount of functionality and can be created through a common factory method.

■**Note** At this time, the Services_Yahoo package is at version 0.1.1 and is in an alpha state. To install this package, you should use the command `pear install Services_Yahoo-alpha`. I won't demonstrate Yahoo Maps in this section, because currently neither documentation nor examples exist for using the class. I have mentioned it, however, because by the time of this book's publication, you might be able to find either updated documentation or examples for this package.

Using Services_Yahoo_Search

The Services_Yahoo_Search class is simply a central point used to create the appropriate class based on the type of search to be performed. To use the search capabilities of this package, first load the class:

```
require_once "Services/Yahoo/Search.php";
```

Once included in a script, only a single function named factory() can be called. This function takes a single argument, which is a string identifying the type of search to be executed. The value can be any of the following:

web: Searches the Internet for Web pages. You can find additional information at http:// developer.yahoo.net/search/web/V1/webSearch.html.

image: Searches the Internet for images. You can find additional information at http:// developer.yahoo.net/search/image/V1/imageSearch.html.

news: Searches the Internet for news stories. You can find additional information at http://developer.yahoo.net/search/news/V1/newsSearch.html.

video: Searches the Internet for video clips. You can find additional information at http://developer.yahoo.net/search/video/V1/videoSearch.html.

local: Searches the Internet for a business near a specified location. You can find additional information at http://developer.yahoo.net/search/local/V1/localSearch.html. (Note: Currently only version 1 of the API is implemented in PEAR.)

In many examples, you may see the factory() method called statically. This is one of the areas where doing so will result in a PHP Strict Standards message when running with the E_STRICT notices enabled.

Note You can find additional documentation for the searches that can be performed with this class at http://developer.yahoo.net/search/index.html as well as in Chapter 17, where you can find examples accessing some of the Yahoo Web services using REST.

Classes returned from this function are based upon a common class and thus share a good number of methods, shown in Table 20-3. However, the classes returned for web, news, and local add a couple of specific methods for those particular searches.

Table 20-3. *Public Search Methods*

Method	Prototype	Description
setAdultOK	void setAdultOK()	Allows adult content to be returned in results. This is not used in all searches.
setAppID	void setAppID(string $id)	Sets the application ID, which is an ID that has been registered with Yahoo. The default value when not used is PEAR_Services_Yahoo.
setFormat	void setFormat(string $format)	This method sets the format parameter for a search. This method does not pertain to all search types, and the acceptable values depend upon the type of search being performed. You can find additional information within the Yahoo documentation for the specific search type.

Continued

Table 20-3. *Public Search Methods*

Method	Prototype	Description
setQuery	void setQuery(string $query)	Sets the query for the search.
setResultNumber	void setResultNumber(int $count)	Sets the number of results to return from a search. The use of this method depends upon the type of search being performed.
setStart	void setStart(int $start)	Sets the starting position for the first result returned. The use of this method depends upon the type of search being performed.
setType	void setType(string $type)	Sets the kind of search to be performed. This method does not pertain to all search types, and the acceptable values depend upon the type of search being performed. You can find additional information within the Yahoo documentation for the specific search type.
submit	(object)Services_Yahoo_Response submit()	Submits the search and returns a Services_Yahoo_Response object used to handle the results.

The following example performs a Web search using the query *php5 xml*. This is the same query performed in Chapter 17 in Listing 17-5:

```php
<?php
require_once "Services/Yahoo/Search.php";

try {
    /* Instantiating object rather than static call to avoid E_STRICT message */
    $service_yahoo = new Services_Yahoo_Search();
    $search = $service_yahoo->factory("web");

    $search->setQuery("php5 xml");
    $search->setResultNumber(5);

    $results = $search->submit();

    if ($results->getTotalResultsReturned() > 0) {
        foreach ($results AS $info) {
            print 'Title: '.$info['Title']."\n";
            print 'Url: '.$info['Url']."\n";
            print 'Mod Date: '.date ('M d Y', (int)$info['ModificationDate'])."\n\n";
        }
    }
```

```
} catch (Services_Yahoo_Exception $e) {
    echo "Error: " . $e->getMessage() . "\n";
    foreach ($e->getErrors() as $error) {
        echo "    " . $error . "\n";
    }
}
?>
```

If you compare this code to that used in Chapter 17 with the code written using the Services_Yahoo_Search class, the biggest difference is that you do not need to manually create the query. Working with the results is not too much different. Rather than using SimpleXML to navigate the results, like in Chapter 17, you can use a mixture of a Services_Yahoo_Search_Response object and arrays.

I don't know about you, but in my opinion working with SimpleXML natively to parse a response from Yahoo is much simpler and cleaner than working with these classes; however, you may find that not having to deal with manually creating a query outweighs this. Your decision should be based on personal preference. In any event, the resulting output looks the same as that from Chapter 17, although the individual results will vary since the scripts were not run on the same day:

```
Title: Zend Technologies - PHP 5 In Depth - XML in PHP 5 - What's New?
Url: http://www.zend.com/php5/articles/php5-xmlphp.php
Mod Date: Nov 02 2005

Title: XML with PHP5 - encoding
Url: http://www.topxml.com/forum/m_1470/printable.htm
Mod Date: Oct 18 2005

Title: Zend Technologies - PHP 5 In Depth - SimpleXML
Url: http://www.zend.com/php5/articles/php5-simplexml.php
Mod Date: Nov 13 2005

Title: ONLamp.com: Using PHP 5's SimpleXML
Url: http://www.onlamp.com/pub/a/php/2004/01/15/simplexml.html
Mod Date: Nov 13 2005

Title: PHPBuilder.com - [Resolved] PHP5 xml_set_default_handler
Url: http://www.phpbuilder.com/board/showthread.php?s=&threadid=10272891
Mod Date: Oct 29 2005
```

Using Services_Yahoo_ContentAnalysis

The Services_Yahoo_ContentAnalysis class is also a central point to create the correct object needed to perform spelling suggestions and term extractions. You can include this class like so:

```
require_once "Services/Yahoo/ContentAnalysis.php";
```

Just like with the `Services_Yahoo_Search` class, you use the factory method to create the appropriate class for the Web service. The acceptable values that can be passed in this case are as follows:

`termExtraction`: Accesses the Spelling Suggestion service to get a suggested spelling correction for a given term. You can find additional information at `http://developer.yahoo.net/search/web/V1/spellingSuggestion.html`.

`spellingSuggestion`: Accesses the Term Extraction Web service to get a list of significant words or phrases extracted from a larger content. You can find additional information at `http://developer.yahoo.net/search/content/V1/termExtraction.html`.

The number of methods for either of these is quite small. They both have `setAppID()`, `setQuery()`, and `submit()` methods, which are the same as those shown in Table 20-3. When performing a term extraction, you also have a `setContext()` method that does not return a value and simply takes a single string argument from which to extract terms. Because neither of these is a complex service, the following simple example demonstrates the Spelling Suggestion Web service along with its result:

```php
<?php
require_once "Services/Yahoo/ContentAnalysis.php";

try {
    /* Instantiating object rather than static call to avoid E_STRICT message */
    $service_yahoo = new Services_Yahoo_ContentAnalysis();
    $search = $service_yahoo->factory("spellingSuggestion");

    $search->setQuery("PHP 5 XnL");

    $results = $search->submit();

    foreach ($results as $result) {
        echo $result . "\n";
    }
} catch (Services_Yahoo_Exception $e) {
    echo "Error: " . $e->getMessage() . "\n";
    foreach ($e->getErrors() as $error) {
        echo "    " . $error . "\n";
    }
}
?>
```

PHP 5 Xml

Using SOAP

The PEAR SOAP package provides all the functionality to create and consume Web services based on SOAP. You can install the package, just like other PEAR packages you have encountered so far, using the PEAR installer. It is currently in beta status but can be used if the PHP 5

SOAP extension is unavailable to you. You can find additional information about this package and its usage in Chapter 18, which covers SOAP and WSDL in detail.

Using UDDI

As explained in detail in Chapter 19, UDDI provides the means to publish and maintain information about Web services in a centralized location called the UBR. This registry can then be searched by anyone needing a specific service from which even details of how the service is to be consumed can be retrieved. The UDDI package provides a means of querying a registry in an easy fashion, although the returned data is in XML format, which means you still need to parse it by some means. Although it also provides mechanisms for publishing data, using the SOAP extension along with WSDL binding is a much easier method for accessing a registry. Because of these limitations, I will provide just a short example of querying the UBR.

The first step, like all other PEAR packages, is to include the required file and instantiate the object. The constructor takes two optional parameters. The first is the registry to use. It can be a full URL, the value IBM (which is the default) to connect to the test registry, or Microsoft to connect to Microsoft's test registry. The second optional parameter is the version of UDDI to use. Although the default version is 1, you are probably better off using version 2. For example:

```
require_once 'UDDI/UDDI.php';
$uddi = new UDDI('IBM', 2);
```

The following is the only demonstration that I will provide for this package; it queries the registry for the business Acme XML that you created in Chapter 19. Once you see the data that is returned, you will understand why using SOAP as shown in the previous chapter is actually much easier than using the UDDI package.

```
<?php
require_once 'UDDI/UDDI.php';
$uddi = new UDDI('IBM', 2);

$params = array("generic"=>"2.0", "name"=>"Acme XML%",
                                "maxRows"=>5,
                                "findQualifiers"=>"sortByNameAsc,sortByDateAsc");

$result = $uddi->find_business($params);
var_dump($result);
?>
```

The call does not look much different from the one using SOAP. In fact, the find_business() call made in Chapter 19 could have been cut and pasted here. All that would be different is the name of the variable to match the one used when the UDDI class was instantiated. The output, on the other hand, is much different, as shown here. You do not get a nicely nested structure. Instead, the raw XML is returned, which means more work for you because it now needs to be parsed.

```
HTTP/1.1 200 OK
Via: HTTP/1.1 www-3.ibm.com (IBM-PROXY-WTE)
Date: Fri, 18 Nov 2005 06:54:00 GMT
Server: IBM_HTTP_SERVER/1.3.28  Apache/1.3.28 (Unix)
Content-Length: 681
Content-Type: text/xml
Content-Language: en-US

<?xml version="1.0" encoding="UTF-8" ?>
<SOAP:Envelope xmlns:SOAP="http://schemas.xmlsoap.org/soap/envelope/">
<SOAP:Body>
<businessList generic="2.0" xmlns="urn:uddi-org:api_v2"
 operator="www.ibm.com/services/uddi" truncated="false">
<businessInfos>
<businessInfo businessKey="68676670-5163-11DA-8A45-000629DC0A53">
<name xml:lang="en">Acme XML Inc.</name>
<description xml:lang="en">Acme's XML wing</description>
<serviceInfos>
<serviceInfo serviceKey="914B4F30-517B-11DA-8A45-000629DC0A53"
 businessKey="68676670-5163-11DA-8A45-000629DC0A53">
<name xml:lang="en">Test Web Service</name>
</serviceInfo>
</serviceInfos>
</businessInfo>
</businessInfos>
</businessList>
</SOAP:Body>
</SOAP:Envelope>
```

What's worse is that not only do you get the raw XML, but you also get the entire response. So because the XML needs to be parsed, you first need to remove the rest of the response information before parsing can even take place. Therefore, even if you are one who despises working with SOAP, it clearly is easier to work with and performs a much better job when interfacing with a UDDI registry.

Using XML_RPC

The XML_RPC package from PEAR provides an object-oriented API for creating XML-RPC clients and servers. It also provides the mechanisms for transporting the data between the client and the server. The only requirement for using this package is that the xml extension in PHP be installed. You install the package, just like other PEAR packages you have encountered so far, using the PEAR installer. In many cases, this package may have already been installed by default. Chapter 16 explained this package.

Conclusion

The purpose of PEAR is to eliminate having to reinvent the wheel every time you need some specific functionality. By using any of the packages, you have an instant solution to your problem. In the area of Web services, PEAR falls short of fulfilling this need when using PHP 5. Systems running PHP 4 and those running PHP 5 without all of the new XML features can still benefit from the use of these packages, though. Trying to build and manipulate XML documents, as well as implement or consume a Web service, is often difficult to do manually. A system running PHP 5 with the new XML features, however, makes obsolete the need to use PEAR for any Web services. You can access a service requiring REST in a number of ways, such as using DOM or SimpleXML. SimpleXML provides one of the easiest interfaces for working with REST-based services. The SOAP extension also provides an abundant amount of functionality, and when used with WSDL, it is actually pretty simple for you to interact with a service.

Web services implemented in REST are already simple to use. The hardest part is having to build the query string, which means you need to know the API of the Web service being accessed. In most cases when using PEAR, you still need to know the API as well. Of course, the location of the service and the name of the method are already provided, but a majority of the packages require you to know the possible parameters that can be passed and force you to supply them as an associative array. The return data from PEAR also ends up as arrays. I don't know about you, but in my opinion reading XML data using SimpleXML is *much* easier than dealing with multidimensional arrays.

If you look at services that require SOAP to access them, it is not that difficult to use the SOAP extension, especially in the case of working with WSDL. Using the PEAR packages still has the same issues as using REST, such as having to know the API and returning the data as arrays. With SOAP and WSDL, you can work directly with objects, calling the Web service functions as an object method and dealing with returned data as objects. Now don't get me wrong; PEAR does have its place, but Web services just aren't one of them in PHP 5. In prior versions of PHP, I might not have said this because XML had very little support, but times have changed.

■ ■ ■

Other XML Technologies
and Extensions

Throughout this book, you have seen the numerous XML-based extensions and technologies that you can use with PHP. This does not mean you are limited to only those I have covered. Using the extensions and techniques demonstrated in this book, you should be able to leverage virtually any XML technology you encounter. Originally this chapter was going to provide only descriptions of other XML technologies you may run into, but during the course of my writing, some new developments in PHP in relation to XML have come about and are what I consider to be valuable information.

As of PHP 5.1.2, the XMLWriter extension, originally a PECL extension, has been included in the core PHP distribution, making it available to a much wider audience. In addition, SDO, particularly the SDO_XML_DAS portion of it, has been released into the PECL. Although not ready for production use, it is possibly a technology to keep on your radar. This chapter will provide more information about these two technologies than I had planned to include. In addition, Ajax has started causing quite a stir in the developer community, so it is only natural that I demonstrate this technology and its interaction with PHP. Lastly, I could never leave out the Wireless Application Protocol (WAP). Mobile devices accessing the Internet seem to be making a comeback, so this is another area you should understand.

Using XMLWriter

The XMLWriter extension provides a lightweight way to generate XML, streaming the output directly to disk or memory. Rather than creating in-memory XML trees that can be navigated and edited, XMLWriter creates serialized documents that do not necessarily live in memory because the document can be streamed to a URI or even flushed from memory as portions of the document are no longer needed.

■**Note** The XMLWriter extension was included with the core PHP distribution and enabled by default in PHP 5.1.2. By the time this decision was made, it was too late to dedicate a chapter in this book to the extension. Though not an in-depth examination of this extension, this section has been expanded from more than a summary of XMLWriter, and its API is documented in Appendix B. This is not to say that PECL extensions do not deserve the same attention as those distributed with PHP. It is just that the audience is much wider because those using hosting services are not always able to control the inclusion of extensions from the PECL.

The XMLWriter extension is modeled upon the C# implementation of the XMLWriter and XmlTextWriter classes and, like the other extensions you have read about in this book, is built upon the libxml2 library. This means it follows the same rules as the other XML extensions with respect to PHP stream usage and any error handling configured in the libxml extension. It happens to also be one of the only XML-based extensions that provides both an object-oriented interface and a procedural interface. Because the other extensions are object oriented, the material presented here will be within the object-oriented context as well. If you happen to prefer procedural functions, after reading about how to use XMLWriter, make sure you read the section "Introducing the Procedural Interface."

Compared to building XML using the DOM extension, XMLWriter uses fewer system resources. The API is also simple and straightforward, which means it can create an XML document faster, and with the simple API, writing code with it is much faster than writing code using DOM. Of course, this is applies only when creating straightforward documents and not requiring the use of XPath or XInclude to create the documents.

Another advantage of the extension is its handling of special XML characters. If you were writing a Web service using REST and needed to return data coming from a database, you could build the resulting XML using DOM or even manually build the XML response document using strings. In both cases, you need to pay careful attention to the data that is going into the document. To ensure no invalid characters are used in spots where they cannot be used, such as for the ampersand (&), you need to use a function such as htmlspecialchars() to make sure the data is encoded correctly. This is not the case with XMLWriter. XMLWriter automatically handles these conversions for you, allowing the raw data to be directly passed to its methods. Although not foolproof, the extension makes its best effort to ensure the XML document you are creating is well-formed and conforms to the W3C XML and namespace specifications.

Enabling the XMLWriter Extension

As of PHP 5.1.2, XMLWriter is included with the core PHP distribution and enabled by default. Prior to this version, XMLWriter was available only through the PECL at http://pecl.php.net/package/xmlwriter. I will explain both types of installation.

XMLWriter from PECL

PECL is similar to PEAR, explained in Chapter 13, except rather than a collection of software and classes written in PHP, PECL is a collection of extensions to PHP written in C. These extensions work in the same manner as those you already use when working in PHP. The only difference is that they are not included in the default distribution, so you must install them separately.

Windows users can simply get precompiled binaries at http://pecl4win.php.net/index.php for the current version they are running. You place the dll in the same location you have placed the other PHP extension libraries based on your installation. The last step, which is often overlooked, is to enable the extension in your php.ini file:

```
extension=php_xmlwriter.dll
```

Users running non-Windows environments have two methods to install the extension. The first method is to use the PEAR/PECL installer. The installer used depends upon the version of PEAR installed on your system. As of PEAR 1.4.0, PECL extensions are installed using the pecl command rather than the pear command. Every option that you normally would pass to pear, you pass to pecl:

```
/* Install with PEAR 1.4.0+ */
pecl install XMLWriter

/* Install with PEAR pre-1.4.0 */
pear install XMLWriter
```

In the event the installer did not work or you want to install it yourself, simply download the package, extract it, build it using phpize, and add the extension to php.ini. You may also need to make note of the location it gets installed to and set extension_dir appropriately in php.ini.

XMLWriter in PHP Distribution

If you are running PHP 5.1.2, the XMLWriter extension is already included in the build and enabled by default. If for some reason the source you are building from has it disabled, add the following flag to your configure directives to include the extension in your build:

```
--enable-xmlwriter
```

Note I will use the term *writer* throughout the following sections to refer to an XMLWriter object.

Initializing the Writer

To use the writer, you must first instantiate it and then set it up for the appropriate output. Its constructor does not take any arguments, and upon instantiation, it is pretty much just an empty shell until initialized:

```
$writer = new XMLWriter();
```

The method used for initialization depends upon how you want to output the data. To use a file or URI, call the openUri() method. This method takes a single parameter, which is the URL to which the data is sent:

```
$writer->openURI('somefile.xml');
```

If you want the data to remain in memory, thus making it available to be returned as a string, you use the openMemory() method, which takes no parameters, to initialize the writer:

```
$writer->openMemory();
```

Both methods return TRUE on success and FALSE on failure when using the object-oriented interface. These two functions are the only exception cases where the object-oriented interface returns different values than the procedural functions. I will explain this further in the "Introducing the Procedural Interface" section later in the chapter.

Creating the XML Document

Since this is the last chapter of the book, you should be comfortable with the different node types, such as element nodes, attribute nodes, comment nodes, and PI nodes. XMLWriter is an API that lets you create an XML document in almost the same manner that you would verbally describe the construction. Before I elaborate on this, just refer to a few of the writer methods in Table 21-1. You can find a complete list of XMLWriter methods, along with their prototypes, in Appendix B.

Table 21-1. *XMLWriter Methods*

Method	Description
startDocument	Creates the XML declaration specifying the version at a minimum.
startElement	Creates an element start tag.
writeAttribute	Creates an entire attribute that includes a name and value.
writeElement	Creates an entire element that includes a name and value. This method will output the start and end tag for an element.
endElement	Creates an element end tag for the currently open element.
endDocument	Closes off the document. This method closes all open tags in the proper order.
flush	Flushes the contents of the buffer to the URI or a string. The destination is determined by the method used to initialize the writer.

If you look at the methods in Table 21-1 in the order they are listed, you might be able to visualize a document being created. The sample code in Listing 21-1 demonstrates this point. Other than two methods used for formatting (explained in the "Formatting the Document" section), this listing creates an XML document using only the methods from Table 21-1 in the exact order in which they appear.

Listing 21-1. *Creating Your First Document*

```php
<?php
/* Create a new XMLWriter object, buffering output to memory for string access */
$writer = new XMLWriter();
$writer->openMemory();
```

```
/* Set indenting using three spaces, so output is formatted */
$writer->setIndent(TRUE);
$writer->setIndentString('   ');

/* Create the XML document */
$writer->startDocument();
$writer->startElement('root');
$writer->writeAttribute('att1', 'first');
$writer->writeElement('child1', 'some "random" content & text');
$writer->endElement();
$writer->endDocument();

/* Retrieve the current contents of the buffer */
$output = $writer->flush();

print $output;
?>
```

```
<?xml version="1.0"?>
<root att1="first">
   <child1>some &quot;random&quot; content &amp; text</child1>
</root>
```

Although not tested within the example, each of the methods creating components of the document returns a Boolean that indicates success or failure. A typical usage of the return value is to test whether the component was successfully created. If the piece of the document being written at the time results in invalid XML, the writer will not send it to the output. Instead, it will silently fail, returning FALSE as the result of the method call. In all other cases, the method will return TRUE, indicating the data was successfully written to the buffer.

Comparing the output from the example and the code used, located below the /* Create the XML document */ comment, you should get an idea of what I meant by visualizing the document being created. You can describe the resulting document as follows in respect to the associated method used to create the different components:

1. *Create the XML declaration:* Call the startDocument() method.

2. *Create the start tag for the root element:* Call startElement(), passing in the element name. The writer maintains the element context.

3. *Create an attribute for the currently open element in context:* Call writeAttribute(), setting the attribute name and value.

4. *Create a new child element named child1 with some content:* The writer is still in the context of the root element, so upon the call to writeElement(), the start tag for root is closed, meaning the > character is added to the tag, the writer context changes to the content of the root element, and a complete element named child1 with the content some "random" content & text is written.

5. *Close the root element:* The writer context is still the content of the root element, so calling endElement() creates a closing root tag. The context now becomes that of the XML document itself.

6. *Complete the document:* Call the endDocument() method. This method ensures that the writer context is properly cleaned up. In the event the context is not the XML document at this point, the writer will close any open tags starting at its current context and moving up in the hierarchy of the document until the XML document context is reached.

Dealing with Character Encoding

The example in Listing 21-1 demonstrates the automatic character encoding mentioned in the introduction to the XMLWriter extension. When creating the element child1, the string some "random" content & text is passed for the content. Immediately you should notice the problem with this data. The ampersand character (&) must be escaped within XML, and in most cases, the double quotes (") should be as well.

The usage of the ampersand character has to be one of the most common problems I see people encounter when working with XML. Most often, when a developer encounters an issue with an ampersand, it is either because they forget it is a special character or because the data they are using to create the XML with is being dynamically generated and they do not even realize the data needs additional handling.

Using XMLWriter, you no longer need to be concerned about this. Content being written to the document is automatically encoded for you. This makes working with dynamic data, such as that being retrieved from a database, simple. You would use the same data to write to the document as you would to read and write from the database.

Formatting the Document

Two methods used in Listing 21-1 that I have yet to explain are setIndent() and setIndentString(). Besides four other methods (two handle the writer initialization, which you have seen, and two manipulate the buffer, which is demonstrated in Listing 21-1 and covered in detail in the "Handling the Buffer" section), the indenting methods are the only other ones explicitly used to create the document. They are used for formatting. Like the DOM formatOutput property from Chapter 6, the setIndent() method instructs the writer to add line feeds and indentation at the appropriate places in the document.

The default formatting used when the document is created is none. Unless manually added within the document, such as by calling $writer->text("\n");, no line feeds or indentation is automatically added. You can toggle automatic formatting on and off by passing a Boolean to the setIndent() method:

```
/* Turn on formatting */
$writer->setIndent(TRUE);

/* Turn off formatting */
$writer->setIndent(FALSE);
```

What sets this formatting apart from that used in the DOM extension is that the writer allows the formatting to be changed as the document is being created. This means you could have a document where some parts are automatically formatted and some parts are not.

Although XMLWriter controls the insertion of line feeds, you have control over the string used for the actual indents when indentation is enabled. By default, a single space is used for indenting. You can change this by calling setIndentString(), passing in a string to be used instead of the one currently in use:

```
/* Set indenting to use a tab instead of a space */
$writer->setIndentString("\t");
```

You can use this method at any time during the creation of the document to change the indenting string as needed.

Handling the Buffer

You can send output from the writer to a URI or hold it in memory and retrieve it into strings. You set this up during the initialization phase of the writer, explained in the "Initializing the Writer" section. For example, Listing 21-1 is holding the output in memory. To retrieve the contents, you must call the method flush(). This method performs dual functionality. When working with memory, it returns a string containing the contents. When working with a URI, it flushes any data that may be sitting in the buffer to the output.

When working with a buffer in memory, the flush() method is able to return a string in one of two ways. The first way, which is also the default behavior, simply returns the contents of the buffer to a string, clearing the content in the buffer. This is performed by the call $writer->flush();. The next time flush() is called, only content added after the previous $writer->flush(); call is returned.

One of the advantages of working with the writer is that you can keep memory usage to a minimum, but sometimes you will want to leave the contents in the buffer after retrieval. The flush() method accepts a parameter named empty, which is applicable only when working with the memory buffer, that can control what happens with the data in the buffer when it is being retrieved. For example, passing the value FALSE simply returns the contents of the buffer, leaving the buffer intact. Passing the value TRUE or omitting the option not only returns the current contents but also clears the contents of the buffer. This means the next time the method is called, only content added after the previous $writer->flush(); call is returned. For example:

```
<?php
$writer = new XMLWriter();
$writer->openMemory();
$writer->setIndent(TRUE);
$writer->startDocument();
$writer->startElement('root');

/* output buffer contents */
echo 'Data: '.$writer->flush(FALSE)."\n\n";

$writer->writeElement('child1', 'content');
```

```
/* output buffer contents, and clear buffer */
echo 'Data: '.$writer->flush()."\n\n";
$writer->endElement();
$writer->endDocument();

/* output buffer contents, and clear buffer */
echo 'Data: '.$writer->flush()."\n";
?>
```

```
Data: <?xml version="1.0"?>
<root

Data: <?xml version="1.0"?>
<root>
 <child1>content</child1>


Data: </root>
```

When working with a URI or PHP streams, you do not need to do much with the buffer. The buffer simply holds data until it is ready to send it to the output channel. You can use the flush() method to force whatever contents the buffer is holding to be sent to the output channel. The only time you usually need to do this is when you are done creating the document to make sure all data has been written to the destination.

■ **Tip** When working with URIs, the stream is not closed until the writer is destroyed. There is currently no method that can be called to close the stream. You can use the unset() method to destroy the object, assuming it is not referenced elsewhere, causing the stream to close.

Creating Namespaced Documents

Creating a document containing namespaces is similar to creating any other document. The only components' namespaces that affect documents are elements and attributes, and some methods exist to handle these:

```
/* Methods for creating elements */
startElementNS(string prefix, string name, string namespaceURI)
writeElementNS(string prefix, string name, string namespaceURI, string content)

/* Methods for creating attributes */
startAttributeNS(string prefix, string name, string namespaceURI)
writeAttributeNS(string prefix, string name, string namespaceURI, string content)
```

Caution Creating documents with complex namespace usage may not produce the expected output. Although the document will be well-formed, namespace declarations can be repeated throughout the final document rather than using a namespace that would otherwise already be in scope. Certain issues may be resolved in the libxml2 library by the time you read this.

Here's the code:

```php
<?php
$writer = new XMLWriter();
$writer->openMemory();
$writer->setIndent(TRUE);
$writer->startDocument();
$writer->startElement('root');

/* Create a namespaced Element */
$writer->startElementNS('ns1', 'child1', 'urn:ns1');
$writer->writeElementNS('ns2', 'child2', 'urn:ns2', 'child2 contents');
$writer->endDocument();

print $writer->flush();
?>
```

```xml
<?xml version="1.0"?>
<root>
 <ns1:child1 xmlns:ns1="urn:ns1">
  <ns2:child2 xmlns:ns12="urn:ns2">child2 contents</ns2:child2>
 </ns1:child1>
</root>
```

Introducing the Procedural Interface

Not everyone is a fan of object-oriented programming. If you happen to be one of these people, then you are in luck with XMLWriter. It was originally developed to run under PHP 4.3 and was designed with a procedural-style interface. This interface is still available under PHP 5. Only two functions work a little differently than the corresponding methods, and these pertain to the initialization of the writer. Using procedural style, there is no such thing as the new keyword. The writer is created and initialized by a single function call, like so:

```php
/* Create procedural-style writer with memory buffer */
$writer = xmlwriter_open_memory();

/* Create procedural-style writer with uri */
$writer = xmlwriter_open_uri('somefile.xml');
```

Looking at these function names should give you an idea of what the rest of them look like. Based on the object-oriented method name, simply append xmlwriter_ to the beginning of the method, add an underscore (_) between a lowercase character and an uppercase character, and finally convert the uppercase character to lowercase. For example, following these rules, you would write the method startElementNS() as xmlwriter_start_element_ns(). When calling the function, the first parameter is always the writer, and the remaining parameters are the same as those used by the method. The example in Listing 21-2 is the code from Listing 21-1 written using the procedural style, and it produces identical output.

Listing 21-2. *XMLWriter Using Procedural Style*

```php
<?php
/* Create a new writer, buffering output to memory for string access */
$writer = xmlwriter_open_memory();

/* Set indenting using three spaces, so output is formatted */
xmlwriter_set_indent($writer, TRUE);
xmlwriter_set_indent_string($writer, '   ');

/* Create the XML document */
xmlwriter_start_document($writer);
xmlwriter_start_element($writer, 'root');
xmlwriter_write_attribute($writer, 'att1', 'first');
xmlwriter_write_element($writer, 'child1', 'some "random" content & text');
xmlwriter_end_element($writer);
xmlwriter_end_document($writer);

/* Retrieve the current contents of the buffer */
print xmlwriter_flush($writer);
?>
```

Using SDO XML Data Access Service

Service Data Objects (SDO) provide a means to access various data sources in a unified manner. The SDO specification (http://www-128.ibm.com/developerworks/java/library/j-commonj-sdowmt/) is a joint collaboration between IBM and BEA. Originally available only for Java, the SDO package in PECL (http://pecl.php.net/package/sdo) brings SDO to the PHP world. The package provides two data access services (DAS): SDO_DAS_Relational for reading/writing SDO from/to relational data sources and SDO_DAS_XML for reading/writing SDO as XML documents. Because XML is the data you are accessing, the following sections deal strictly with the SDO_DAS_XML service.

■**Caution** The SDO package is currently marked as *experimental*. It is possible that changes to the API and/or behavior have been made since the time of this writing. For this reason, the following sections on SDO and XML usage in PHP will cover how to use the extension using simplistic examples.

Installing SDO

Installing SDO is similar to installing XMLWriter from the PECL. You need to pay attention, however, when editing the php.ini file. The package is split between modules requiring the base SDO module, php_sdo, to be loaded and modules requiring the data service module, php_sdo_xml, to be loaded. Those running Windows should grab the prebuilt binaries from PECL4Win (http://pecl4win.php.net/index.php), place them in the directory containing your extensions, and enable them in the php.ini file:

```
extension=php_sdo.dll
extension=php_sdo_das_xml.dll
```

On other platforms, you can use the PEAR/PECL installer with the package name SDO. The version depends upon the current release of the package. At this time, it is in beta, so for the following installations, you replace <version> with beta:

```
/* PEAR 1.4.0+ */
pecl install SDO-<version>

/* PEAR pre-1.4.0 */
pear install SDO-<version>
```

Once you've installed SDO, you must load the modules through the php.ini file:

```
extension=sdo.so
extension=sdo_das_xml.so
```

Working with XML

To work with SDO, it is required that the data be modeled. In simpler terms, you must define the structure the data can take. When working with XML data, XML Schemas is the language used to do this. As you recall from Chapter 3, I used an XML document containing course information to validate against an XML Schema. The schema in Listing 21-3, referred to in the examples as sdoschema.xsd, is a simplified version of the original schema from Chapter 3; I will use this schema in this chapter's examples to demonstrate SDO.

Listing 21-3. *XML Schema (*sdoschema.xsd*) for the Course Document*

```xml
<?xml version="1.0"?>
<xsd:schema xmlns:xsd="http://www.w3.org/2001/XMLSchema">
    <xsd:element name="courses">
        <xsd:complexType>
            <xsd:sequence>
                <xsd:element name="course" minOccurs="0" maxOccurs="unbounded">
                    <xsd:complexType>
                        <xsd:sequence>
                            <xsd:element name="title" type="xsd:string"/>
                            <xsd:element name="description" type="xsd:string"/>
                            <xsd:element name="credits" type="xsd:decimal"/>
                            <xsd:element name="lastmodified" type="xsd:dateTime"/>
                        </xsd:sequence>
                        <xsd:attribute name="cid" type="xsd:ID"/>
                    </xsd:complexType>
                </xsd:element>
            </xsd:sequence>
        </xsd:complexType>
    </xsd:element>
</xsd:schema>
```

SDO does not require an existing XML document. Using only the schema, you can create documents from scratch. Some of the API that is required to do this is currently in a state of flux, so I will limit the discussion to reading and writing XML using the existing XML document shown in Listing 21-4.

Listing 21-4. *XML Course Document (*courses.xml*)*

```xml
<?xml version="1.0" encoding="UTF-8"?>
<courses>
    <course cid="c1">
        <title>Basic Languages</title>
        <description>Introduction to Languages</description>
        <credits>1.5</credits>
        <lastmodified>2004-09-01T11:13:01</lastmodified>
    </course>
    <course cid="c2">
        <title>French I</title>
        <description>Introduction to French</description>
        <credits>3.0</credits>
        <lastmodified>2005-06-01T14:21:37</lastmodified>
    </course>
</courses>
```

> ■**Note** SDO issues exceptions upon errors. You should use `try/catch` blocks when writing code with the extension in order to properly handle errors.

To work with XML data, you must first load the schema and create an SDO_DAS_XML object:

```
$xmldas = SDO_DAS_XML::create("sdoschema.xsd");
```

Using the $xmldas object, you then load the course data from the `courses.xml` file into an SDO_DAS_XML_Document, called $xmldo:

```
$xmldo = $xmldas->loadFromFile("courses.xml");
```

The next step in preparing to manipulate the XML is that you need to get a handle on the document element, in the form of a data object:

```
$courses = $xmldo->getRootDataObject();
```

Reading XML Data

Navigating XML using SDO is similar to doing it using SimpleXML, except when using SDO, both elements and attributes are accessed as object properties. SDO, however, does not seem to be concerned with namespaces, whereas within SimpleXML, you must specify from which namespace you want to retrieve elements and attributes. Each of these methods has its merits, and which is better is a matter of personal opinion. You also need to take into account the type of functionality you need to perform with the XML.

Getting back to reading XML data with SDO, the following example demonstrates how to iterate through the `course` elements and print the content of the `title` element and the `cid` attribute:

```
foreach ($courses->course AS $course) {
    print "Title: ".$course->title."\n";
    print "Course ID: ".$course->cid."\n\n";
}
```

```
Title: Basic Languages
Course ID: c1

Title: French I
Course ID: c2
```

Other than the `cid` attribute being accessed by a property from $course, you wouldn't be able to tell this code apart from SimpleXML. You can also access specific elements by offset:

```
print $courses->course[1]->title."\n";
```

This piece of code outputs the contents of the `title` element from the second `course` element that is a child of the `courses` element so would result in the output French I.

Accessing an element or attribute not specified in the XML Schema for an element results in much different behavior than that of SimpleXML. Within SimpleXML, trying to read an element that does not exist simply returns an empty string. Doing the same in SDO causes an exception to be thrown:

```
try {
    print $courses->course[1]->notinschema."\n";
} catch (Exception $e) {
    var_dump($e);
}
```

The structure of a course element, defined in the XML Schema, does not include an element or attribute named notinschema. When accessed, SDO throws an exception that indicates it is not found.

Writing XML Data

Modifying existing data is as easy as setting the value on a property; again, this is something you are already familiar with from using SimpleXML. For example, you can change the title of the second course element from French I to Intro to French simply by setting the value for the title property for the specific course:

```
$courses->course[1]->title = 'Intro to French';
```

Creating new XML data is a bit different. Using the data object for the specific element for which the new data should be created, the createDataObject() method is called, passing in the type of object to create. The type of object when using SDO and XML is the name of the element from the schema. For example, to create a new course element within the courses element structure, you make the following call:

```
$course = $courses->createDataObject('course');
```

This creates a new data object, $course, that corresponds to the course element from the schema in Listing 21-3. Calling this method also inserts a new empty course element into the XML document that is loaded in memory.

Once you have created the new object, then you can add the data, just like if you were modifying an existing element. One thing to note is that properties not set are not created in the resulting XML. For example:

```
$course->cid = 'c3';
$course->title = 'French II';
$course->description = 'Intermediate French';
$course->credits = '3.0';
```

As you can see, all the elements specified in the schema for a course element have been defined except for the lastmodified element. To see what the resulting XML document looks like, you can save it to a file and output it using file_get_contents():

```
$xmldas->saveDocumentToFile($xmldo, 'courses.xml');

print file_get_contents('courses.xml');
```

■ **Note** You can send the output directly to a string using a couple of different SDO methods. The version of the SDO package used for this example is an unpublished, still-in-development version. The functionality is in the process of changing but the `saveDocumentToFile()` method is stable, so this is the only method I will demonstrate here.

The `saveDocumentToFile()` method takes as parameters the initial `SDO_DAS_XML_Document` object, `$xmldo`, and the file to save the XML document. The following shows what the resulting document looks like (note that I have formatted this for readability by adding line feeds and spaces):

```xml
<?xml version="1.0" encoding="UTF-8"?>
<courses xmlns="" xsi:type="courses"
        xmlns:xsi="http://www.w3.org/2001/XMLSchema-instance">
   <course cid="c1">
      <title>Basic Languages</title>
      <description>Introduction to Languages</description>
      <credits>1.5</credits>
      <lastmodified>2004-09-01T11:13:01</lastmodified>
   </course>
   <course cid="c2">
      <title>Intro to French</title>
      <description>Introduction to French</description>
      <credits>3.0</credits>
      <lastmodified>2005-06-01T14:21:37</lastmodified>
   </course>
   <course cid="c3">
      <title>French II</title>
      <description>Intermediate French</description>
      <credits>3.0</credits>
   </course>
</courses>
```

Summarizing SDO_XML_DAS

The goal of the project in PECL is to bring the SDO technology to PHP, providing a unified means of accessing data. It is still in the development stage, so SDO_XML_DAS is currently in a state of flux. As far as I can tell—purely through my own personal testing—SDO_XML_DAS works in a similar fashion to SimpleXML. The only current differential is the ability to create new data. For many, this may not be a necessary feature because the XML interoperability in PHP allows you to read with the SimpleXML extension and to write XML using the DOM extension.

A feature that would set SDO_XML_DAS apart, in my mind, would be if it were to respect and enforce the XML Schema in regard to data typing as well as the overall schema of data. For instance, in the section "Writing XML Data," you were able to create a course element without the required lastmodified element. As you probably recall from Chapter 3, the default value for the `minOccurs` attribute is 1, so in order for the resulting XML document to be valid, the `lastmodified` element is required. The same goes for data typing; because during my testing, I was able to set a text value for the `credits` element, which is defined as an `xsd:decimal` type.

These are just a few of the features that would make this extension much more usable. Again, this extension is still under development, so new features may already planned for the extension. For now, the package is not ready to be used in a production environment but is something you may want to keep your eye on in the future.

Introducing Asynchronous JavaScript Technology and XML (Ajax)

I understand that Ajax is not really a PHP-centric XML technology and is more UI related than anything else, so you may be wondering why it is mentioned in a PHP and XML book. Formerly known as the acronym for Asynchronous JavaScript Technology and XML, Ajax has gained much attention and popularity among developers and is something you might need to implement one day with a PHP backend. For this reason, it may be worthwhile for you to at least understand the basics and see an example of Ajax interfacing with PHP.

What Is Ajax?

In a typical Web environment, a user might fill out information contained in a form and then submit the data to the server. The server processes this data and then might send an error page if any data is invalid or might send a page indicating that everything was filled out correctly. During this time, the user is sitting there idle waiting for the response. When it does return, the entire page reloads with the new data. To get around this idle period (as you know, the Web is a fast-paced environment, and users do not have long attention spans), some developers use JavaScript to validate form elements immediately on the user side as they are filled out. This works well as long as no data in the form needs to be validated against information located where the server resides. For example, you cannot test whether a username is already in use without having the server check its database for you. This is where Ajax comes in.

Ajax allows for asynchronous requests, which means that request and response handling can take place in the background and be sent to a server while the user is still interacting with the UI. The response from these requests can then update portions of the UI without interrupting the user. This is handled through *callbacks*, which are registered functions that are called based on events that may occur. In the scenario of entering form data, as a user moves to the next field in the form, Ajax could be used to make a request to the server to validate the data just entered in the form field. This does not interrupt the user from completing other form entries. Once the response is received, an event is triggered that may execute some functionality that causes the page to display some indication that the field is not valid. Again, this all happens without the user being interrupted. When the user is finally finished with the form, then they can submit the entire page to the server. Of course, on the server side, data still needs to be validated again, but the chances of it being invalid are much slimmer. As a user, when filling out forms on a Web site, are you more upset at having to wait for the next page to load or more upset having to wait just to find out that the data you entered is invalid for some of the fields? I know the latter usually gets under my skin.

Working with Ajax

Implementing a solution using Ajax is similar to implementing a REST-based Web service, explained in Chapter 17. The difference here is that the client is an object embedded in a Web page manipulated using JavaScript. Based on some event within the page, such as an `onclick` or `onblur` event, a URL is built with all the appropriate parameters, and then the request is made to the server. All this happens without the user ever leaving the page. As far as the server side goes, there is absolutely no difference when working with Ajax than the REST services you saw in Chapter 17. The server parses the incoming request parameters, performs whatever logic it needs to do, and then returns its response in XML format. The bottom line is that Ajax is just a REST-based client that can be used to make asynchronous calls from a Web page to your REST-based Web service.

Rather than duplicating much of the information from Chapter 17, I will demonstrate only a simple example of working with Ajax and PHP here. All of the new material you will see in the example is based on JavaScript and therefore not directly related to PHP. This material is described only in terms of its functionality and how it relates to the interaction with the PHP-based Web service. Information pertaining to writing code using JavaScript is out of the scope of this book; you can obtain the specification directly from Ecma International:

```
http://www.ecma-international.org/publications/standards/Ecma-262.htm
```

Listing 21-5 contains an HTML page with embedded JavaScript that will be used to interact with a PHP script on the server. The HTML page contains a simplistic registration form requesting the user to input a username, a password, and their first and last names. Once a user has entered the username they would like to register with and has moved the cursor out of the form field, Ajax checks its availability without interrupting the user, who is completing the rest of the requested information.

Upon receiving a response from the server, one of two actions can take place. If the username is available, the previously disabled submit button is enabled, allowing the user to submit their data. If the username has already been taken, an alert pops up on the screen, indicating that the user must choose another username. An alert may not be the best choice, because it is intrusive, but this clearly illustrates the Ajax functionality. In a real-world scenario, CSS would probably better serve the purpose of allowing some text to be displayed on the Web page rather than a pop-up window appearing.

Listing 21-5. *Client HTML Page*

```
<html>
<head>
<meta http-equiv="Content-Type" content="text/html; charset=iso-8859-1">
<title>Untitled Document</title>
<script language="javascript">
var httpreq;

// Change the location to point to your server script
var server = 'http://www.example.com/ajax.php';
```

```
// function called by onblur in form
function checkusername(input) {
    url  = server + '?uname=' + input;

    // native XMLHttpRequest
    if (window.XMLHttpRequest) {
        httpreq = new XMLHttpRequest();

        // Register the response callback
        httpreq.onreadystatechange = processReqChange;
        httpreq.open("GET", url, true);
        httpreq.send(null);
    // Windows/IE
    } else if (window.ActiveXObject) {
        httpreq = new ActiveXObject("Microsoft.XMLHTTP");
        if (httpreq) {
            // Register the response callback
            httpreq.onreadystatechange = processReqChange;
            httpreq.open("GET", url, true);
            httpreq.send();
        }
    }
}

// response handler function
function processReqChange()  {
    if (httpreq.readyState == 4) {
        if (httpreq.status == 200) {
            response  = httpreq.responseXML.documentElement;
            result    = response.getElementsByTagName('result')[0].firstChild.data;
            if (result == 1) {
                alert('Username already taken');
            } else {
                document.form1.submitinfo.disabled = false;
            }
        } else {
            alert("Unable to retrieve Data:\n" + httpreq.statusText);
        }
    }
}
</script>
</head>
<body>
    <form name="form1" id="form1">
        Username: <input id="username" name="username" type="text"
                        onblur="checkusername(this.value)" /><br>
```

```
        Password: <input id="password" name="password" type="password" /><br>
        First Name: <input id="firstname" name="firstname" type="text" /><br>
        Last Name: <input id="firstname" name="firstname" type="text" /><br>
        <input type="submit" name="submitinfo" id="submit" disabled /><br>
    </form>
</body>
</html>
```

Once the user enters a username in the username form field in Listing 21-5 and the focus moves outside the field, the onblur event is triggered. This calls the JavaScript function checkusername() with the value entered in the field. This function builds a request URL using the server variable defined at the beginning of the JavaScript and then instantiates an XMLHttpRequest object. When using Internet Explorer in a Windows environment, the object needed is actually an ActiveX object, so the code makes sure the correct object is used.

Using the newly created object, you need to set up the function to be called when the server returns a response. The processReqChange() function contains the code to handle the server response, so in the previous code you set it on the object using the onreadystatechange property. The object then opens the URL that was built in the script and sends the request to the server. All this time the user is continuing to enter data in the other form fields.

When the server finally sends the response, the processReqChange() function gets executed. The response is in XML format, and using properties of the object, the document element of the data is accessed. Using the JavaScript DOM, the specific information from the response the application is interested in is then retrieved. In this case, it is the value of a result element. Based on the value, the script either enables the submit button if the requested username is available or pops up an alert indicating that the name is taken.

Listing 21-6 shows the script used on the server to process the request. It is basic and simply checks the value of an array containing existing usernames. The content of the result element is then populated based on the return value of the checkname() function. The functionality and data returned from the server can be as complex as it needs to be to fulfill the needs of the client. You can find additional information about creating more advanced server responses in Chapter 17.

Listing 21-6. *Server-Side Ajax Processing Script*

```php
<?php
header('Content-Type: text/xml');
print '<?xml version="1.0" encoding="UTF-8"?>';

$current_users = array('rob', 'john', 'joe');
function checkname($username) {
   if (in_array($username, $GLOBALS['current_users'])) {
      return 1;
   }
   return 0;
}
?>
<response>
  <result><?php echo checkname((string)$_GET['uname']) ?></result>
</response>
```

Because of the nature of Ajax and because its actions are based upon events, it is impossible to include any figures that clearly demonstrate its functionality. To get an idea of how Ajax works, you might want to try the code in Listing 21-5 and Listing 21-6. The HTML page in Listing 21-5 is the UI portion. Simply copy the code into a file, such as `ajax.html`, and save it within a directory served up by a Web server. You should then change the `server` variable within the JavaScript code to point to your Web server. Also, copy the code in Listing 21-6, which is the backend logic called by the Ajax request, into a file, such as `ajax.php`, that is located within the same Web server. Once you have done this, simply navigate to the `ajax.html` page, enter the name **joe** in the Username field, and move to another field. This should cause a JavaScript alert to appear with the message "Username already taken." Performing the same action using the name **Mike**, on the other hand, will cause the submit button to be come enabled.

Note It is important that the `ajax.html` and `ajax.php` pages reside within the same Web site. Because of the default security settings for the `XMLHttpRequest` object, access to a location different from the page the object is being used on is normally denied.

Introducing Wireless Application Protocol (WAP)

WAP is a standard allowing wireless devices, such as mobile phones, to access information. It is quite likely that you have a mobile phone that allows you to connect to the Internet and access pages just like the browser on your computer. The phone actually has a built-in browser; unlike your typical Web browser, though, it does not deal with HTML pages. Instead, it deals with pages built using one of the WAP-supported languages: Wireless Markup Language (WML) or XHTML Mobile Profile (XHTML MP), which is a mobile version of XHTML.

WAP was first introduced around 1997, give or take a year. At that time, WML was the language to write applications for wireless devices. The technology was pretty much considered a failure. To name a few of the issues, browsing was slow, sites offering WAP services were far and few between, and the amount of data that could be passed in a page was often very limited.

Toward the end of 2001, WAP 2.0 was released. To make the language easier to work with and closer to what was used to create regular pages, a stripped-down version of XHTML 1.1 was devised specifically for use with mobile phones. This subset, which is also an extension of XHTML Basic, is XHTML MP.

Times seem to be changing. Wireless computing in general is commonplace; even within households, high-speed networks are considered the norm, and leveraging much of this, mobile phone companies have been marketing phones with a wide range of multimedia capabilities. The younger generation seems to be more plugged in than any previous generation. It is no longer enough to be able to simply talk on the phone while on the go. They need text messaging, MP3s, and Internet access around the clock wherever they are. This might possibly produce a big turnaround for WAP usage.

▬**Tip** Testing WAP is often difficult to do because development is usually performed on networks inaccessible to mobile phone access. Phone emulators are usually used during the development stages to test mobile documents, because they allow access to any IP address and even flat files. From personal experience, I know how difficult it is to find a good emulator. If you need a good Windows-based emulator, you should try the one from Openwave, a company that provides products and services to the communications industry. The emulator is available from the developer section at `http://developer.openwave.com/dvl/tools_and_sdk/openwave_mobile_sdk/phone_simulator/`.

Introducing Wireless Markup Language (WML)

WML was the original WAP language and is synonymous with WAP 1.0. With how quickly technology changes and how fast new mobile phones are pushed to the market, no mobile phones in use today are unable to support XHTML or WAP 2.0, although they are still backward compatible with WAP 1.0. In fact, many companies have started completely abandoning WAP 1.0 in favor of WAP 2.0, which is XHTML MP, so deciding whether you want to support WML in your mobile application is completely up to you.

WML works with the concepts of decks and cards. A *deck* is a document that can be broken up into smaller pieces. A *card* is one of these smaller pieces of the document that is displayed on the mobile device. If you think of it in terms of Web pages, a deck is a collection of Web pages (the cards). A mobile device requests access to a WML document, which returns this collection (the deck), all at once. Rather than having to make multiple requests to the server for individual pages (the cards), navigation among the cards in the deck is done using the deck it already has in memory. WML also possesses the ability to pass variables between cards in a deck based on selections made within cards.

This does not mean additional decks cannot be requested. A card can contain links to resources outside the current deck. When navigating to these links, the mobile device retrieves the WML and loads the new deck. Remember, back in the day, wireless connections were very slow. The goal was to send as much data to the device at once to reduce the number of times a remote connection needed to be made.

WML Structure

WML documents require the use of a DTD, which identifies the structure and version of WML used within the document. You can use four different XML versions, ranging from WML 1.0 to WML 1.3. To support the lowest common denominator, I will describe WML 1.1 in this section. I did not choose WML 1.0, because the DTD was not available from the older specification list:

`http://www.openmobilealliance.org/tech/affiliates/wap/wapindex.html#previous`

WML is based on XML, so a document should always include an XML declaration. WML needs to include the DTD, and in this case WML 1.1 is being used, so the document would use the following:

```
<!DOCTYPE wml PUBLIC "-//WAPFORUM//DTD WML 1.1//EN"
                "http://www.wapforum.org/DTD/wml_1.1.xml">
```

The document begins with a wml element, which serves as the document element and defines the deck. The cards are defined within card elements that live only as children of the wml element. Within a card element, the rules are strict about which elements can appear in certain contexts. WAP browsers are not as forgiving as Web browsers usually are. A tag appearing where it is not supposed to be will often cause the document not to render.

This section on WML serves only to provide some general information about the language, because XHTML is the technology you most likely will want to be using for new wireless applications. Instead of looking at all the different pieces of WML, the following list just points out some of the more common mistakes made when writing WML that cause documents not to render. The complete rules and available tags for creating a WML document are available by reading the DTD. You may want to refer to Chapter 3 if you need help dissecting the contents.

- You can use paragraph tags, p, only as direct children of a card element.

- The contents of anchor tags, or a tags, cannot contain text formatting elements such as bold (b) or strong tags.

- WML must be XML compliant, so br tags must be closed, as in <br />.

- Tables do not have header elements (TH) like they do in HTML.

- Fonts are not changeable in WML, so the font tag does not exist.

WML Example

The following example uses only some of the basic features of WML. It contains two cards that can be navigated between. On the initial card, identified by the id with the value main, an additional anchor tag demonstrates how to link to another external deck. If you decide to try this example, you can load it directly from the file system by placing the contents into a file and giving it a .wml file extension. To use it within a Web server environment, make sure the correct MIME type, text/vnd.wap.wml, is sent by the server when the file is requested. Figure 21-1 shows the resulting document, as rendered by an emulator.

```
<?xml version="1.0"?>
<!DOCTYPE wml PUBLIC "-//WAPFORUM//DTD WML 1.1//EN"
                    "http://www.wapforum.org/DTD/wml_1.1.xml">
<wml>
    <card id="main" title="Index" newcontext="true">
        <p><a href="http://www.example.com/deck2.wml">Next Deck</a></p>
        <p>Welcome! <br/>
           Go to next card <a href="#card2">next card</a>.
        </p>
        <p>Another way to navigate: <br />
           <anchor title="See Card 2">
              next card <go method="get" href="#card2" />
           </anchor>
        </p>
    </card>
```

```
  <card id="card2" title="Card 2" newcontext="false">
    <p>This is the 2nd card in the deck<p>
      <a href="#main" title="back to index">Done</a>
    </p>
  </card>
</wml>
```

Figure 21-1. *WML rendered by emulator*

Introducing XHTML

A number of XHTML specifications exist. You have XHTML Basic, which is the base implementation of XHTML with a minimal set of XHTML features and which is geared toward
mobile applications. You have XHTML MP, also known as WAP 2.0, which is an extension of
XHTML Basic that adds a few components. Lastly, you have XHTML 1.1, which contains the
full set of XHTML features. You would think that WAP 2.0 is the logical choice that phone vendors would all agree upon. Looking at all the different phones available, however, this is not
the case. Many support WAP 2.0, and others support just XHTML Basic. Others even support
the full XHTML 1.1 feature set. As a developer, what are you supposed to do?

■**Caution** There is no definite agreement on the use of XHTML MP vs. XHTML Basic. Some groups believe
WAP 2.0 should always be used, some stick to XHTML Basic, and others implement features found in any of
the different XHTML versions. The problem is with vendor support. Mobile phone vendors have no set standard they all use, so determining which type of XHTML to serve up is not an exact science.

I have had to deal with this issue. After plenty of research, I decided to serve XHTML using
syntax from XHTML Basic (http://www.w3.org/TR/xhtml-basic/) and a few presentational

elements from XHTML MP, so the XHTML MP DTD is specified in the XHTML document being served by the server. Because both WAP 2.0 and XHTML 1.1 are supersets of it, XHTML Basic provides the greatest range of operability. You need to consider the limitations of mobile applications. The user is on a mobile device, so the screen is smaller; navigating is more difficult; and bandwidth is still not close to that when browsing from a desktop. Mobile applications should be lean and mean. Flashy applications might look nice at first, but if they slow the user down from getting to where they want to go, then users will just stop using those applications.

WAP 2.0 uses the MIME type `application/vnd.wap.xhtml+xml`, defined by the Open Mobile Alliance (`http://www.openmobilealliance.org/`), but not every phone fully supports the WAP 2.0 feature set. Many developers, including myself, often use the `application/xhtml+xml` type instead. This type encompasses the entire XHTML family, so with XHTML MP being a member of this family, WAP 2.0–enabled devices should in most cases accept this type. There is no guarantee, though, that this type will be accepted, but it seems that—and I say this from experience—virtually all do. I have heard reports that specific models of phones do not work with this type but have yet to run into this myself.

Document Structure

The first part of the document is the XML declaration and the doctype. The following example is using the XHTML Mobile 1.0 DTD:

```
<?xml version="1.0" encoding="UTF-8"?>
<!DOCTYPE html PUBLIC "-//WAPFORUM//DTD XHTML Mobile 1.0//EN"
                  "http://www.wapforum.org/DTD/xhtml-mobile10.dtd">
```

If you have written XHTML documents before, then you already understand the structure. If you have worked only with HTML documents, you will be happily surprised that the markup is almost identical. You could consider XHTML to be HTML written using proper XML syntax. For example, every tag you open must have an associated closing tag. In some cases, this means an element will simply be an empty element tag. Take the `<BR>` tag, for example. It is common for HTML developers to use this tag as written. In XHTML, this is not valid because the tag is never closed, so you must write it as `<br />`.

Not only do you need to take care that the document is well-formed but also of the characters you use within the document. Have you ever written content that used the ampersand, as in `<title>This & That</title>`? In XHTML you cannot do this because the ampersand must be properly escaped, as in `<title>This &amp; That</title>`.

A minimal XHTML document must have an `html` element, a `head` element, a `title` element, and a `body` element. They are laid out in the same format as an HTML document. The difference between these elements used within XHTML, though, is that they live within the XHTML namespace, `http://www.w3.org/1999/xhtml`. For example:

```
<?xml version="1.0" encoding="UTF-8"?>
<!DOCTYPE html PUBLIC "-//WAPFORUM//DTD XHTML Mobile 1.0//EN"
                  "http://www.wapforum.org/DTD/xhtml-mobile10.dtd">
<html xmlns="http://www.w3.org/1999/xhtml">
   <head>
      <title>Example WAP 2.0 document</title>
   </head>
```

```
<body>
    <p>This is an XHTML MP document</p>
</body>
</html>
```

WAP Cascading Style Sheets (WCSS)

WAP Cascading Style Sheets (WCSS) are a simplified version of CSS where features not appropriate or not necessary for mobile devices have been removed. Style sheets are normally included using `link` elements:

```
<link rel="stylesheet" type="text/css" href="mobilestyle.css" />
```

Supposedly mobile browsers cache content including CSS files; however, some UI developers I have talked to have mentioned that they prefer inline CSS when dealing with mobile devices because they are finding that this is just not true. When the files are not cached, the CSS must be retrieved for every page accessed. Not only does this slow things down for the user, but it also increases the amount of bandwidth they require for every page access.

XHTML 1.0, XHTML 1.1, and Mobile MP support inline CSS. The `style` element is not part of the XHTML Basic specification. As mentioned earlier, this is one of those features outside of XHTML Basic that I use. For example:

```
<style type="text/css">
h1 {text-align: right; color: blue}
</style>
```

This style used within the document sets the h1 tags to use the right alignment and to be blue.

Another potential issue to be aware of is that some mobile browsers do not even recognize CSS or will ignore it. The good news is that unrecognized tags are simply ignored, so the page will render, but it may not look exactly how you expect it to look. For this reason when using CSS, it is wise not to rely on CSS for the entire formatting of the rendered page. The page should look decent even if you removed the CSS.

XHTML Example

Here's an XHTML example:

```
<?php
header('Content-type: application/xhtml+xml');
echo '<?xml version="1.0"?>';
?>
<!DOCTYPE html PUBLIC "-//WAPFORUM//DTD XHTML Mobile 1.0//EN"
                      "http://www.wapforum.org/DTD/xhtml-mobile10.dtd">
<html xmlns="http://www.w3.org/1999/xhtml" lang="en" xml:lang="en">
<head>
    <title>XHTML Mobile Example</title>
</head>
```

```
<body>
    <p>Select a category from the pull-down or an anchor link.</p>
    <form action="catselect.php" method="POST">
    Select a category:
        <select name="category">
            <option value="1">Audio &amp; Video</option>
            <option value="2">Camera &amp; Photo</option>
            <option value="3">Computers</option>
        </select>
        <input type="submit" value="Go" />
    </form>
    <br /><br />
    <a href="catsel.php?category=4&amp;subcat=1">Electronics/Phones</a>
    <br /><br />
</body>
</html>
```

As you can see, this example looks similar to plain HTML. Some PHP code has been included at the top of this file, assuming it is saved as a .php file to modify the Content-type header and produce the application/xhtml+xml MIME type, as well as the XML declaration. The doctype has been set to the XHTML Mobile 1.0 DTD, and the elements have been placed in the proper namespace, http://www.w3.org/1999/xhtml. The other changes from HTML you may have also noticed are that all elements are now in proper XML format and all ampersands (&) have been escaped using the entity &. When viewed on a mobile device, the page renders similar to that shown in Figure 21-2.

Figure 21-2. *WAP 2.0 rendered by emulator*

Performing WAP Detection Using PHP

When a mobile user comes to visit your site, more often than not the user will navigate directly to your main site page. This page, however, is typically written for access from a Web browser. Mobile-enabled pages usually are kept within a subdirectory of the main site or have their own tertiary domain. For example:

```
/* Example tertiary domain names */
mobile.example.com
wml.example.com
wap.example.com
```

If you have mobile-enabled content on your site, you probably don't want the user's mobile device to either not be able to render anything or try rendering a page designed for an HTML browser. What you can do in a case like this is to automatically redirect the device to the appropriate location on your Web site.

How fancy you want to or need to get with the detection is really up to you and what your application does. If determining the client type down to the make and model of their phone is what your application requires, then most likely you or your company is in the mobile device business, and you probably already know all about WAP and the various languages and specifications. For all other developers, usually they just want to know whether it is a mobile device; if so, does it require WML, WAP 1.x enabled, or does it support XHTML, WAP 2.0 enabled?

The following piece of code is similar to the tests I use for mobile detection. I place this code at the top of all my Web site files. Once it is executed, you end up with the constant WAP_TYPE having one of three values. You can then use the value where necessary to perform some type of action depending upon the type of client it is.

```
define('TYPE_BROWSER', 0);
define('TYPE_WAP_1', 1);
define('TYPE_WAP_2', 2);

/* Check whether client is a mobile device - does it support WAP? */
if (strpos($_SERVER['HTTP_ACCEPT'], 'vnd.wap.wml')) {
    /* Does this WAP device also support XHTML/WAP 2.0? */
    if (strpos($_SERVER['HTTP_ACCEPT'], 'xhtml+xml')) {
        define('WAP_TYPE', TYPE_WAP_2);
    } else {
        define('WAP_TYPE', TYPE_WAP_1);
    }
} else {
    /* Client is not a mobile device, so handle as a regular browser */
    define('WAP_TYPE', TYPE_BROWSER);
}
```

For example, if you place this code in your index file, you can then test the value of the WAP_TYPE client and redirect any mobile devices to another page or even another site:

```
If (WAP_TYPE != TYPE_BROWSER) {
    header("Location: http://mobile.example.com/index.php");
    exit;
}
```

You can also use the code within the `mobile.example.com` site if you want to support both WML and XHTML. Rather than having two separate sites or the clients accessing two different pages on the same site, you can use wrapper pages, where the wrapper page includes or generates the correct content type based on the `WAP_TYPE` constant. For example:

```
if (WAP_TYPE == TYPE_WAP_1) {
    include ('content.wml');
} else {
    include ('content.xhtml');
}
```

Although nothing fancy, these checks provide a simple manner of determining the functionality supported by the client. If you really need to start getting into the details of the actual device, you can also start inspecting the `HTTP_USER_AGENT` value. In most cases, though, the code shown in this section is more than adequate to handle various mobile devices.

Conclusion

Wrapping up the coverage of PHP and XML, I introduced two additional PHP extensions, XMLWriter and SDO, and a couple of XML technologies, Ajax and WAP, that you can work with using PHP. XMLWriter provides a simple yet powerful interface for creating well-formed XML documents without having to build them in memory or worry about character encoding. When combined with PHP streams, you can create some complex and interesting applications.

The SDO extension is a recent addition to the PECL library and is still in the development phase. It is uncertain the direction this technology is going to go in PHP, but it has potential for providing an interesting manner of working with XML data. Currently, data is accessed similarly to when using the SimpleXML extension. SDO adds the capability of being able to create new data within XML data. If taken in the direction suggested by my feature requests, it would allow you to work with XML in the same way as working with a database. Using XML Schema, it would be equivalent to XML data integrity through the enforcement of data types and structure.

Ajax is currently a hot technology. It allows for asynchronous interaction between a Web page and a server using a REST-style Web service. Requests can be sent and responses can be received without interrupting the user. Ajax opens up the potential for a new way to write Web applications.

In addition, WAP, although not a new technology, is starting to creep back into the mainstream. Mobile devices nowadays contain features never seen before. Whether it is because people have grown accustomed to accessing the Internet using more than just a browser or that hardware has finally caught up with the technology, interest in WAP is finally starting to get off the ground. Whether every Web site will eventually have a mobile-enabled site is a completely different animal, but in any event you are now ready if you ever have to tackle that problem.

Advances in technology never stop, and new ones are born every day. Even PHP continues to evolve on a daily basis. During the course of my writing, new features have been added and changes have been made in the area of XML alone. Some of these changes have made it into PHP 5.1.2, and others are scheduled to be released with PHP 6. It's worth your time to read Appendix C, which covers the changes and upcoming XML features that have taken place since the time I wrote the earlier chapters.

■ ■ ■

XML Schema Built-in Data Types Reference

XML Schemas provide a number of built-in data types. You can use these types directly as types or use them as base types to create new and complex data types. The built-in types presented in this appendix are broken down into primitive and derived types and further grouped by area of functionality for easier reference.

Type Definition

XML Schema data types are built upon relationships where every type definition is either an extension or a restriction to another type definition. This relationship is called the *type definition hierarchy*. The topmost definition, serving as the root of the hierarchy, is the ur-type definition, named anyType. It is the only definition that does not have a basis in any other type. Using this data type is similar to using ANY within a DTD. It effectively means that the data has no constraints. Take the following element declaration, for example:

```
<xsd:element name="anything" type="xsd:anyType" />
```

An element based on this declaration can contain any type of data. It can be any of the built-in types as well as any user-derived type.

The simple ur-type definition, named anySimpleType, is a special restriction on the ur-type definition. It constrains the anyType definition by limiting data to only the built-in data types, shown in the following sections. For example, the following element declaration defines an element that can be any built-in type but cannot be a complex type, which is simply an element that can contain subelements or attributes, as explained in Chapter 3:

```
<xsd:element name="simplelement" type="xsd:anySimpleType" />
```

The built-in types are divided into two varieties: primitive types and derived types.

Primitive Types

Primitive data types are those that are not defined in terms of another type. For easy reference, the following tables group the primitive types together based on general, non-schema-specific data types. Table A-1 shows the logical types, Table A-2 shows the numeric types, Table A-3 shows the textual types, Table A-4 shows the date/time types, Table A-5 shows the binary types, and Table A-6 shows the XML types.

Table A-1. *Logical Types*

Type	Description	Example
boolean	Represents the binary-valued logic literals	true, false, 1, 0

Table A-2. *Numeric Types*

Type	Description	Example
decimal	Arbitrary-precision decimal numbers. The sign is optional, and when omitted, + is assumed.	1.0, 1.00, -1, 01.1230, 1.123
double	Real numbers with a double-precision, 64-bit, floating-point type.	INF, -INF, NaN (Not a Number), 1.234, 1.2e3, 7E-10
float	Real numbers with a double-precision, 32-bit, floating-point type.	INF, -INF, NaN (Not a Number), 1.234, 1.2e3, 7E-10

Table A-3. *Textual Types*

Type	Description	Example
string	Any legal XML character string according to the XML 1.0 specification. Special characters such as <, >, &, ', and " should be escaped.	This is a string, This & that are strings
AnyURI	A URI. It can be absolute or relative and can contain a fragment identifier.	http://www.example.com

Table A-4. *Date/Time Types*

Type	Description	Example
dateTime	A date and time in the format CCYY-MM-DDTHH:MM:SS.	October 31, 2005, at 2:30 p.m. Coordinated Universal Time (UTC) time is written as 2005-10-31T14:30:00. The same date and time written in Eastern Standard Time (EST) is 2005-10-31T14:30:00-5:00.
date	A calendar date in the format CCYY-MM-DD with an optional time zone.	October 31, 2005, is written as 2005-10-31.
time	An instance of time during a day in the format HH:MM:SS.	So, 2:30 p.m. UTC time is 14:30:00; the same time written in EST is 140:30:00-5:00.
duration	A duration of time in the format PnYnMnDTnHnMnS. If the number of years, months, days, hours, minutes, or seconds in any expression is zero, the number and its corresponding designator can be omitted, but at least one designator and the *P* designator must always be present.	A duration of 1 year, 2 months, 3 days, 10 hours, and 30 minutes is written as P1Y2M3DT10H30M, while a duration of 1 year is written as P1Y.

Type	Description	Example
gMonth	Two-digit Gregorian month in the format —MM with an optional time zone.	October is written as —10, and April is written as —04.
gDay	Two-digit Gregorian day in the format —DD with an optional time zone.	The 22nd day of the month is written as —22.
gYear	Four-digit Gregorian year in the format CCYY with an optional time zone.	The year 2005 is written as 2005.
gMonthDay	Combination of the Gregorian month and day in the format —MM-DD with an optional time zone.	October 31 is written as —10-31.
gYearMonth	Combination of the Gregorian year and month in the format CCYY-MM with an optional time zone.	October 2005 is written as 2005-10.

Table A-5. *Binary Types*

Type	Description	Example
base64Binary	Base64-encoded arbitrary binary data	See base64_decode() in the PHP manual.
hexBinary	Arbitrary hex-encoded binary data	See bin2hex() in the PHP manual.

Table A-6. *XML Types*

Type	Description	Example
QName	Represents an XML qualified name.	prefix:name, xsd:attribute
NOTATION	Represents an XML NOTATION attribute. This type must *not* be used in an XML Schema. You can use it only to derive types that can be used in an XML Schema.	

Derived Types

Derived types are data types that are defined in terms of other types, called *base types*. As you will see in the following tables, a base type for a derived type can be a primitive data type or even another derived type. These types also have been grouped into generalized, non-schema-specific data types. Table A-7 shows the numeric types, Table A-8 shows the textual types, and Table A-9 shows the XML types.

Table A-7. *Numeric Types*

Type	Base Type	Description	Example
integer	decimal	The mathematical concept of integer numbers	1, 0, -1, 12345
nonPositiveInteger	integer	Any integer less than or equal to 0	0, -1, -12345
negativeInteger	nonPositiveInteger	Any integer less than 0	-1, -12345, -23456
long	integer	Any integer less than or equal to 9,223,372,036,854,775,807 and greater or equal to -9,223,372,036,854,775,808	-100000, 0, 10000
int	long	Any integer less than or equal to 2,147,483,647 and greater or equal to -2,147,483,648	-2147483648
short	integer	Any integer less than or equal to 32,767 and greater or equal to -32,768	12345, -12345
byte	short	Any integer less than or equal to 127 and greater or equal to -128	-123, 0, 123
nonNegativeInteger	integer	Any integer greater than or equal to 0	0, 1, 12345
positiveInteger	nonNegativeInteger	Any integer greater than 0	1, 12345, 123456
unsignedLong	nonNegativeInteger	Any integer greater than or equal to 0 and less than or equal to 18,446,744,073,709,551,615	0, 12345, 1234567
unsignedInt	unsignedLong	Any integer greater than or equal to 0 and less than or equal to 4,294,967,295	0, 12345, 1234567
unsignedShort	unsignedInt	Any integer greater than or equal to 0 and less than or equal to 65,535	0, 1234, 65535
unsignedByte	unsignedShort	Any integer greater than or equal to 0 and less than or equal to 255	0, 100, 126

Table A-8. *Textual Types*

Type	Base Type	Description	Example
normalizedString	string	A whitespace-normalized string. This means it does not contain carriage returns, line feeds, or tab characters.	Example normalized string
token	normalizedString	A tokenized string. This means it does not contain carriage returns, line feeds, or tab characters. It also does not have leading or trailing spaces, and any two consecutive characters in the string are spaces.	A B C
language	token	Language identifiers as defined by RFC 3066 (http://www.ietf.org/rfc/rfc3066.txt).	en-US

Table A-9. *XML Types*

Type	Base Type	Description	Example
Name	token	Represents an XML name as defined in the XML 1.0 specification	
NCName	Name	Represents XML "noncolonized" names, which are simply QNames without the prefix and colon	element
ID	NCName	Represents the ID attribute type from the XML 1.0 specification	
IDREF	NCName	Represents the IDREF attribute type from the XML 1.0 specification	
IDREFS	IDREF	Represents the IDREFS attribute type from the XML 1.0 specification	
ENTITY	NCName	Represents the ENTITY attribute type from the XML 1.0 specification	
ENTITIES	ENTITY	Represents the ENTITIES attribute type from the XML 1.0 specification	
NMTOKEN	token	Represents the NMTOKEN attribute type from the XML 1.0 specification	
NMTOKENS	NMTOKEN	Represents the NMTOKENS attribute type from the XML 1.0 specification	

■■■

Extension APIs

This appendix is a quick reference for the XML parser extensions in PHP. You can find usage examples and more detailed information in each parser's respective chapter. The information provided for the APIs covers functionality found in PHP 5.1.2, as well as a few new methods that will be released with PHP 6.

libxml

The libxml extension, described in Chapter 5, is the foundation for all the XML-based extensions in PHP. As of PHP 5.1, the extension defines common constants and functionality used by a majority of the other related extensions. Table B-1 lists the general constants. Note that some constants are defined only when using certain versions of the libxml2 library.

Table B-1. *libxml General Constants*

Name	Description
LIBXML_VERSION	The numeric value of the libxml2 version being used by PHP. You can use this value to test the version number for functionality that depends upon certain versions of libxml2.
LIBXML_DOTTED_VERSION	The string value using dotted notation of the libxml2 version being used. This value is primarily used for display purposes.

The extensions, such as DOM and SimpleXML, allow parser options to be passed to functions and methods that are loading XML documents (see Table B-2).

Table B-2. *libxml Constants for Loading Documents*

Name	Description
LIBXML_NOENT	Substitutes entities found within the document with their replacement content.
LIBXML_DTDLOAD	Loads any external subsets but does not perform validation. This flag also ensures that IDs set in a DTD are created within the document.
LIBXML_DTDATTR	Creates attributes within the document for any attributes defaulted through a DTD.
LIBXML_DTDVALID	Loads subsets and validates a document while parsing.

Continued

Table B-2. *Continued*

Name	Description
LIBXML_NOERROR	Suppresses errors from libxml2 that may occur while parsing.
LIBXML_NOWARNING	Suppresses warnings from libxml2 that may occur while parsing.
LIBXML_NOBLANKS	Removes all insignificant whitespace within the document.
LIBXML_XINCLUDE	Performs all XIncludes found within the document.
LIBXML_NSCLEAN	Removes redundant namespace declarations found while parsing the document.
LIBXML_NOCDATA	Merges CDATA nodes into text nodes. A document using CDATA sections will be created with no CDATA nodes, as these will now be converted into plain-text nodes. This flag is useful when loading a document to be used for an XSL transformation.
LIBXML_NONET	Disables network access when loading documents. You can use this flag to increase security from untrusted documents so resources cannot be fetched from the network.
LIBXML_COMPACT	Enables some memory optimizations that may help speed up an application using XML. This constant is available only when using libxml2 2.6.21 or higher.

Several constants are also defined that can be used in the context of serializing an XML document (see Table B-3). These are available only when using libxml2 2.6.21 and higher.

Table B-3. *libxml Constants for Saving Documents*

Name	Description
LIBXML_NOXMLDECL	Does not produce an XML declaration when saving the document
LIBXML_NOEMPTYTAG	Does not output empty tags; rather, always outputs an opening and closing element tag with no content between

Table B-4 lists libxml's functions.

Table B-4. *libxml Functions*

Function	Description
libxml_clear_errors(void)	Clears libxml error buffer.
libxml_get_errors(void)	Retrieves an array of errors.
libxml_get_last_error(void)	Retrieves the last error from libxml.
libxml_set_streams_context (resource streams_context)	Sets the stream's context for the next libxml document load or write.
libxml_use_internal_errors ([bool use_errors])	Disables libxml errors and allows the user to fetch error information as needed. This returns a Boolean of the previous state.

The LibXMLError class was introduced in PHP 5.1. Objects of this type are returned from the libxml error-handling functions. A few constants are defined explicitly for use with this object (see Table B-5). Table B-6 lists the LibXMLError class properties.

Table B-5. *libxml Error-Level Constants*

Name	Description
LIBXML_ERR_NONE	No error has been detected.
LIBXML_ERR_WARNING	This is a simple warning that the XML document may have problems.
LIBXML_ERR_ERROR	This is a recoverable error. The XML document contains errors, but the parser was able to continue processing.
LIBXML_ERR_FATAL	This means a fatal error was detected, and the parser is unable to continue processing the document.

Table B-6. LibXMLError *Class Properties*

Property	Type	Description
level	integer	Indicates the severity of the error using one of the error-level constants as its value
code	integer	Indicates the error code from libxml2
column	integer	Indicates the column number, if available, from within the document where the error occurred
line	integer	Indicates the line number, if available, from within the document where the error occurred
message	string	Indicates the textual representation of the error
file	string	Indicates the filename of the XML document containing the error

xml

The xml extension, covered in Chapter 8, provides a SAX parser to process XML based on events using handlers. Because this extension maintains compatibility and also can be built using expat rather than libxml2, it defines its own set of parser option constants. Table B-7 lists the xml parser's options constants, Table B-8 lists the xml parser's error code constants, and Table B-9 lists the xml parser's XML functions.

Table B-7. *XML Parser Options Constants*

Option	Description
XML_OPTION_TARGET_ENCODING	Sets the encoding to use when the parser passes the XML information to the function handlers. The available encodings are US-ASCII, ISO-8859-1, and UTF-8. The default is either the course encoding set when the parser was created or UTF-8 when not specified.
XML_OPTION_SKIP_WHITE	Skips values that are entirely ignorable whitespaces. These values will not be passed to your function handlers. The default value is 0, meaning to pass whitespaces to the functions.
XML_OPTION_SKIP_TAGSTART	Skips a certain number of characters from the beginning of a start tag. The default value is 0 to not skip any characters.
XML_OPTION_CASE_FOLDING	Determines whether element tag names are passed all uppercase or left as is. The default value is 1 to uppercase all tag names. The default setting tends to be a bit controversial. XML is case-sensitive, and the default setting is to case fold characters. For example, an element named FOO is not the same as an element named Foo.

Table B-8. *XML Error Code Constants*

Name
XML_ERROR_NONE
XML_ERROR_NO_MEMORY
XML_ERROR_SYNTAX
XML_ERROR_NO_ELEMENTS
XML_ERROR_INVALID_TOKEN
XML_ERROR_UNCLOSED_TOKEN
XML_ERROR_PARTIAL_CHAR
XML_ERROR_TAG_MISMATCH
XML_ERROR_DUPLICATE_ATTRIBUTE
XML_ERROR_JUNK_AFTER_DOC_ELEMENT
XML_ERROR_PARAM_ENTITY_REF
XML_ERROR_UNDEFINED_ENTITY
XML_ERROR_RECURSIVE_ENTITY_REF
XML_ERROR_ASYNC_ENTITY
XML_ERROR_BAD_CHAR_REF
XML_ERROR_BINARY_ENTITY_REF
XML_ERROR_ATTRIBUTE_EXTERNAL_ENTITY_REF
XML_ERROR_MISPLACED_XML_PI
XML_ERROR_UNKNOWN_ENCODING
XML_ERROR_INCORRECT_ENCODING
XML_ERROR_UNCLOSED_CDATA_SECTION
XML_ERROR_EXTERNAL_ENTITY_HANDLING

Table B-9. *XML Functions*

Function	Description
xml_parser_create([string encoding])	Creates and returns an XML parser. You can specify an optional encoding for output.
xml_parser_create_ns([string encoding [, string sep]])	Creates and returns an XML parser. You can specify an optional encoding for output, and you can use an optional separator to separate the namespace with the local name. If not specified, a colon is used as the default separator.
xml_set_object(resource parser, object obj)	Associates a parser with an object so callback functions will use the object's methods as handlers. This returns a Boolean indicating success or failure.
xml_set_element_handler(resource parser, string shdl, string ehdl)	Sets start and end element handlers for the parser. This returns a Boolean indicating success or failure.
xml_set_character_data_handler(resource parser, string hdl)	Sets a character data handler for the parser. This returns a Boolean indicating success or failure.

Function	Description
xml_set_processing_instruction_handler (resource parser, string hdl)	Sets a PI handler for the parser. This returns a Boolean indicating success or failure.
xml_set_default_handler(resource parser, string hdl)	Sets the default handler for a parser. This functionality is now working as of PHP 5.1. This returns a Boolean indicating success or failure.
xml_set_unparsed_entity_decl_handler (resource parser, string hdl)	Sets unparsed entity declaration handler for the parser. This returns a Boolean indicating success or failure.
xml_set_notation_decl_handler(resource parser, string hdl)	Sets the notation declaration handler for the parser. This returns a Boolean indicating success or failure.
xml_set_external_entity_ref_handler (resource parser, string hdl)	Sets the external entity reference handler for the parser. This returns a Boolean indicating success or failure.
xml_set_start_namespace_decl_handler (resource parser, string hdl)	Sets the start namespace declaration handler for the parser. This returns a Boolean indicating success or failure.
xml_set_end_namespace_decl_handler (resource parser, string hdl)	Sets the end namespace declaration handler for the parser. This returns a Boolean indicating success or failure.
xml_parse(resource parser, string data [, integer isFinal])	Parses the XML sent in the data parameter. Parsing can be performed in chunks, and the isFinal parameter identifies whether the chunk being passed is the end of the XML document.
xml_parse_into_struct(resource parser, string data, array &values[, array &index])	Parses the XML into an array, values, and optionally an array, index, containing pointers to values in the values array.
xml_get_error_code(resource parser)	Returns the XML parser error code. This code is a constant defined by the XML extension.
xml_error_string(integer code)	Returns the error string for the code.
xml_get_current_line_number(resource parser)	Returns the line number the parser is currently processing.
xml_get_current_column_number(resource parser)	Returns the column number the parser is currently processing.
xml_get_current_byte_index(resource parser)	Returns the byte index the parser is currently processing.
xml_parser_free(resource parser)	Frees the reference to the XML parser.
xml_parser_set_option(resource parser, integer option, mixed value)	Sets the value for one of the XML parser options. This returns a Boolean indicating success or failure.
xml_parser_get_option(resource parser, integer option)	Retrieves current value for an option.
utf8_encode(string data)	Encodes an ISO-8859-1 string to UTF-8.
utf8_decode(string data)	Converts a UTF-8 encoded string to ISO-8859-1.

XMLReader

XMLReader, covered in Chapter 9, is a stream-based, lightweight, and simple-to-use parser. This extension is written specifically for PHP 5 and newer. It originated as a PECL extension but was not added to the main distribution until PHP 5.1. For PHP 5.1, all constants have been moved to the XMLReader class rather than to global constants. Table B-10 lists the XMLReader node type constants, Table B-11 lists the options class constants, and Table B-12 lists the XMLReader properties, which are read-only.

Table B-10. *XMLReader Node Type Constants*

Name	Description
NONE	No current node
ELEMENT	Element node
ATTRIBUTE	Attribute node
TEXT	Text node
CDATA	CDATA node
ENTITY_REF	Entity reference node
ENTITY	Entity node
PI	PI node
COMMENT	Comment node
DOC	Document node
DOC_TYPE	Doctype node
DOC_FRAGMENT	Document fragment node
NOTATION	Notation node
WHITESPACE	Whitespace
SIGNIFICANT_WHITESPACE	Significant whitespace
END_ELEMENT	End element
END_ENTITY	End entity
XML_DECLARATION	XML declaration

Table B-11. *XMLReader Parser Options Class Constants*

Name	Description
LOADDTD	Loads DTD while parsing
DEFAULTATTRS	Indicates the default attributes defined in the DTD while parsing
VALIDATE	Validates the document while parsing
SUBST_ENTITIES	Substitutes entities while parsing

Table B-12. *XMLReader Properties (Read-Only)*

Property	Type	Description
attributeCount	integer	Returns the number of attributes on the current element
baseURI	string	Returns the base URI for the current node
depth	integer	Returns the depth of the node within the tree using a zero-based starting point
hasAttributes	Boolean	Indicates whether the element has any attributes
hasValue	Boolean	Indicates whether the node has a child text node
isDefault	Boolean	Indicates whether the attribute is defaulted from the DTD
isEmptyElement	Boolean	Indicates whether the element is an empty element tag
localName	string	Returns the local name of the node
name	string	Returns the full qualified name of the node
namespaceURI	string	Returns the namespace URI for the node
nodeType	integer	Returns an XMLReader node type constant for the current node
prefix	string	Returns the prefix of the current node
value	string	Returns the text value of the node
xmlLang	string	Returns the xml:lang scope for which the node resides

The majority of methods from the XMLReader class return a Boolean that indicates the success or failure of the operation. Unless otherwise indicated in the method description, you should assume a Boolean as the return type. Table B-13 lists the XMLReader class methods.

Table B-13. XMLReader *Class Methods*

Method	Description
close()	Closes the XMLReader parser and returns a Boolean indicating success or failure.
getAttribute(string name)	Returns the value of the attribute specified by name.
getAttributeNo(integer index)	Returns the value of the attribute specified by index.
getAttributeNs(string name, string namespaceURI)	Returns the value of the attribute specified by name and namespace.
getParserProperty(integer property)	Returns a Boolean for the value of the specified property. The property is identified by one of the XMLReader parser option class constants.
isValid	Boolean isValid() When in validating mode, returns Boolean indicating whether parsed document is valid.
lookupNamespace(string prefix)	Returns the namespace URI in scope for the given prefix.
moveToAttribute(string name)	Positions the reader on the attribute specified by name.
moveToAttributeNo(integer index)	Positions the reader on the attribute specified by index.
moveToAttributeNs(string name, string namespaceURI)	Positions the reader on the attribute identified by the name and namespace.

Continued

Table B-13. *Continued*

Method	Description
moveToElement()	When positioned on an attribute, this method positions the reader back on the containing element.
moveToFirstAttribute()	Positions the reader on the first attribute.
moveToNextAttribute()	Positions the reader on the next attribute.
open(string URI [, string encoding [, integer options]])	Sets the URI to be opened by the reader. The optional parameters are currently available only in CVS for the upcoming PHP 6. You can specify the encoding of the document within the file and parser options.
read()	Positions the reader to the next node in the stream.
next([string localname])	Moves the reader to the next node in the stream, skipping over any subtrees. Optionally, you can specify a local name, causing the reader to continually call the next method until it either has found a node with the specified name or has reached the end of the stream.
setParserProperty(integer property, Boolean value)	Sets the value for a specified property, which is one of the parser options.
setRelaxNGSchemaSource(string filename)	Sets the URI of a RELAX NG schema to be used for validation.
setRelaxNGSchemaSource(string source)	Provides a string containing a RELAX NG schema to be used for validation.
XML(string source [, string encoding [, integer options]])	Sets data, contained in the string parameter, to be processed by the reader. The optional parameters are currently available only in CVS for the upcoming PHP 6. You can specify the encoding of the document within the file and parser options.
expand()	Creates a copy of the node the reader is currently positioned on and returns it as the appropriate DOM class. This function is available in PHP 5.1 and newer.
readInnerXml()	Returns a string containing the contents of the current node, including child nodes and markup. This method is currently available only in CVS for the upcoming PHP 6. libxml2 version 2.6.20 or newer is also required for this functionality.
readOuterXml()	Returns a string containing current node, including its contents, child nodes, and markup. This method is currently available only in CVS for the upcoming PHP 6. libxml2 version 2.6.20 or newer is also required for this functionality.
readString()	Reads the contents of an element or a text node as a string. This method is currently available only in CVS for the upcoming PHP 6. libxml2 version 2.6.20 or newer is also required for this functionality.

SimpleXML

The SimpleXML extension, covered in Chapter 7, provides a tree-based parser that allows an XML document to be manipulated as an object. Other than a few functions used to load XML data and create a SimpleXMLElement object, you perform all functionality using the

SimpleXMLElement class. Table B-14 lists the SimpleXML functions, and Table B-15 lists the SimpleXMLElement methods.

Table B-14. SimpleXML *Functions*

Function	Description
simplexml_import_dom(DOMNode node [, string class_name])	Performs a zero-copy import from a DOMNode. This function either returns a SimpleXMLElement object or returns an object from the class specified by the class_name parameter. When this parameter is used, the class must inherit from the SimpleXMLElement class.
simplexml_load_file(string uri [, string class_name [, integer options]])	Loads the data from the location specified by the uri parameter. The class_name parameter allows the returned object to be instantiated as the specified class rather than a SimpleXMLElement, as long as the class inherits from SimpleXMLElement. The options parameter, added in PHP 5.1, allows the use of LIBXML constants appropriate when loading a document.
simplexml_load_string(string data [, string class_name [, integer options]])	Loads the data contained in the data parameter. The class_name parameter allows the returned object to be instantiated as the specified class rather than a SimpleXMLElement, as long as the class inherits from SimpleXMLElement. The options parameter, added in PHP 5.1, allows the use of LIBXML constants appropriate when loading a document.

Table B-15. SimpleXMLElement *Methods*

Name	Description
__construct(string data)	Constructor for SimpleXMLElement. The data parameter is a string containing an XML document and is used to create the XML tree within the returned object.
asXML([string uri])	Returns a well-formed XML string based on the SimpleXMLElement.
attributes([string ns])	Returns a SimpleXMLElement for the attributes of an element. The ns parameter specifies a namespace for the attributes to be retrieved.
children([string ns])	Returns a SimpleXMLElement for the children of an element. The ns parameter specifies a namespace for the children to be retrieved.
xpath(string path)	Runs XPath query on XML data returning the results in an array.
registerXPathNamespace(string prefix, string namespace)	Registers a namespace and associated prefix that can be used when performing XPath queries. This method was added in PHP 5.1.

Continued

Table B-15. *Continued*

Name	Description
getDocNamespaces([bool recursive])	Returns an array containing all namespace declarations defined on the document element. When recursive is passed as TRUE, all namespace declarations in the entire document are returned. The array is an associative array using the namespace prefix as the key. Any redefined prefixes further in the tree when using this method recursively are not returned in the array, because their first definition takes precedence. Default namespace declarations do not have a prefix, so an empty string is used as the key in the array. This method was added in PHP 5.1.2.
getNamespaces([bool recursive])	Returns an array containing all namespaces in use for the current element or attribute. When the recursive parameter is set to TRUE, all namespaces for child nodes are returned as well. The array is an associative array using the namespace prefix as the key. Any redefined prefixes further in the tree when using this method recursively are not returned in the array, because their first definition takes precedence. Default namespaces do not have a prefix, so an empty string is used as the key in the array. This method was added in PHP 5.1.2.

DOM

The DOM extension, covered in Chapter 6, is a tree-based parser that offers the most flexibility and functionality to manipulate an XML document. As you can see from its API, it is also the most complex extension to use. Table B-16 lists the DOM node type constants, Table B-17 lists the DOM exception code constants, and Table B-18 lists the DOM functions.

Table B-16. *DOM Node Type Constants*

Name	Description
XML_ELEMENT_NODE	The node is a DOMElement.
XML_ATTRIBUTE_NODE	The node is a DOMAttr.
XML_TEXT_NODE	The node is a DOMText.
XML_CDATA_SECTION_NODE	The node is a DOMCharacterData.
XML_ENTITY_REF_NODE	The node is a DOMEntityReference.
XML_ENTITY_NODE	The node is a DOMEntity.
XML_PI_NODE	The node is a DOMProcessingInstruction.
XML_COMMENT_NODE	The node is a DOMComment.
XML_DOCUMENT_NODE	The node is a DOMDocument.
XML_DOCUMENT_TYPE_NODE	The node is a DOMDocumentType.
XML_DOCUMENT_FRAG_NODE	The node is a DOMDocumentFragment.
XML_NOTATION_NODE	The node is a DOMNotation.
XML_HTML_DOCUMENT_NODE	The node is a DOMDocument containing an HTML document.

Table B-17. *DOM Exception Code Constants*

Name	Description
DOM_INDEX_SIZE_ERR	Indicates whether the index or size is negative or greater than the allowed value.
DOMSTRING_SIZE_ERR	Indicates whether the specified range of text does not fit into a DOMString.
DOM_HIERARCHY_REQUEST_ERR	Indicates whether any node is inserted where it doesn't belong.
DOM_WRONG_DOCUMENT_ERR	Indicates whether a node is used in a different document than the one that created it.
DOM_INVALID_CHARACTER_ERR	Indicates whether an invalid or illegal character is specified, such as in a name.
DOM_NO_DATA_ALLOWED_ERR	Indicates whether data is specified for a node that does not support data.
DOM_NO_MODIFICATION_ALLOWED_ERR	Indicates whether an attempt is made to modify an object where modifications are not allowed.
DOM_NOT_FOUND_ERR	Indicates whether an attempt is made to reference a node in a context where it does not exist.
DOM_NOT_SUPPORTED_ERR	Indicates whether the implementation does not support the requested type of object or operation.
DOM_INUSE_ATTRIBUTE_ERR	Indicates whether an attempt is made to add an attribute that is already in use elsewhere.
DOM_INVALID_STATE_ERR	Indicates whether an attempt is made to use an object that is not, or is no longer, usable.
DOM_SYNTAX_ERR	Indicates whether an invalid or illegal string is specified.
DOM_INVALID_MODIFICATION_ERR	Indicates whether an attempt is made to modify the type of the underlying object.
DOM_NAMESPACE_ERR	Indicates whether an attempt is made to create or change an object in a way that is incorrect with regard to namespaces.
DOM_INVALID_ACCESS_ERR	Indicates whether a parameter or an operation is not supported by the underlying object.
DOM_VALIDATION_ERR	Indicates whether a call to a method such as insertBefore or removeChild would make the node invalid with respect to "partial validity." This exception would be raised, and the operation would not be done.

Table B-18. *DOM Functions*

Function	Description
dom_import_simplexml(SimpleXMLElement node)	Imports a SimpleXMLElement and returns the corresponding DOMNode. This function performs a zero-copy import.

DOMException

The DOMException class inherits from the built-in Exception class. When an exception error occurs, according to the DOM specifications, DOM throws a DOMException, unless error handling has been changed using the DOMDocument strictErrorChecking property. This allows a developer to explicitly catch and handle a DOMException. The value of the code property corresponds to one of the DOMException code constants.

DOMImplementation

Table B-19 lists the DOMImplementation methods.

Table B-19. DOMImplementation *Methods*

Method	Description
createDocument([string namespaceURI[, string qualifiedName[, DOMDocumentType doctype]]])	Creates a new DOMDocument object. This method is typically used to create a document containing a doctype.
createDocumentType(string qualifiedName, string publicId, string systemId)	Creates an empty DOMDocumentType object that can be used with the createDocument() method.
hasFeature(string feature, string version)	Tests whether the DOM implementation implements a specific feature for a specified version.

DOMXPath

Table B-20 lists the DOMXPath methods.

Table B-20. DOMXPath *Methods*

Method	Description
__construct(DOMDocument doc)	Constructs a new DOMXPath object for the given DOMDocument.
registerNamespace(string prefix, string uri)	Registers a prefix and namespace that can be used in the XPath expressions.
query(string expr [,DOMNode context])	Evaluates the given XPath expression and returns a DOMNodeList containing the resulting nodes. A DOMNode can be passed to set the initial context.
evaluate(string expr [,DOMNode context])	Evaluates the given XPath expression and returns a typed result if possible. A DOMNode can be passed to set the initial context. This method was added in PHP 5.1.

DOMNodeList

The DOMNodeList class has a single read-only property called length. It returns the number of nodes contained within the list. Nodes are accessed using the item(integer index) method. The index parameter specifies the zero-based index of the node to retrieve from the list.

DOMNamedNodeMap

The DOMNamedNodeMap class has a single read-only property called length. It returns the number of nodes contained within the map. This class defines three methods to retrieve nodes (see Table B-21).

Table B-21. DOMNamedNodeMap *Methods*

Method	Description
getNamedItem(string name)	Retrieves a node specified by name.
getNamedItemNS(string namespaceURI, string localName)	Retrieves a node specified by local name and namespace URI.
item(integer index)	The index parameter specifies the zero-based index of the node to retrieve from the list.

DOMNode

The DOMNode class is the base class for the majority of the rest of the DOM classes. Table B-22 lists its properties, and Table B-23 lists its methods.

Table B-22. DOMNode *Properties*

Name	Type	Read-Only?	Description
nodeName	string	Yes	Returns the more accurate name for the current node type.
nodeValue	string	No	The value of this node, depending on its type.
nodeType	integer	Yes	Gets the type of the node. This is one of the predefined XML_xxx_NODE constants.
parentNode	DOMNode	Yes	The parent of this node.
childNodes	DOMNodeList	Yes	A DOMNodeList that contains all children of this node. If there are no children, this is an empty DOMNodeList.
firstChild	DOMNode	Yes	The first child of this node. If there is no such node, this returns NULL.
lastChild	DOMNode	Yes	The last child of this node. If there is no such node, this returns NULL.
previousSibling	DOMNode	Yes	The node immediately preceding this node. If there is no such node, this returns NULL.
nextSibling	DOMNode	Yes	The node immediately following this node. If there is no such node, this returns NULL.
attributes	DOMNamedNodeMap	Yes	A DOMNamedNodeMap containing the attributes of this node (if it is a DOMElement) or NULL otherwise.
ownerDocument	DOMDocument	Yes	The DOMDocument object associated with this node.

Continued

Table B-22. *Continued*

Name	Type	Read-Only?	Description
namespaceURI	string	Yes	The namespace URI of this node or NULL if it is unspecified.
prefix	string	No	The namespace prefix of this node or NULL if it is unspecified.
localName	string	Yes	Returns the local part of the qualified name of this node.
baseURI	string	Yes	The absolute base URI of this node or NULL if the implementation wasn't able to obtain an absolute URI.
textContent	string	No	This attribute returns the text content of this node and its descendants.

Table B-23. DOMNode *Methods*

Method	Description
appendChild(DomNode newChild)	Adds the newChild node to the end of the children.
cloneNode(Boolean deep)	Clones a node. If deep is specified, then all child nodes are also cloned.
hasAttributes()	Returns a Boolean indicating whether the node has attributes.
hasChildNodes()	Returns a Boolean indicating whether the node has children.
isDefaultNamespace(string namespaceURI)	Returns a Boolean indicating whether the supplied namespaceURI is the default namespace in scope for the node.
insertBefore(DomNode newChild, DomNode refChild)	Adds a new child node before a reference node.
isSameNode(DomNode other)	Indicates whether the current node is the same node being passed to method.
isSupported(string feature, string version)	Checks whether the feature is supported for specified version.
lookupNamespaceURI(string prefix)	Returns the namespace URI currently associated with the supplied prefix.
lookupPrefix(string namespaceURI)	Gets the namespace prefix of the node based on the namespace URI.
normalize()	Normalizes the node.
removeChild(DomNode oldChild)	Removes the child node from list of children.
replaceChild(DomNode newChild, DomNode oldChild)	Replaces a child node with a different node. This method returns the node that was replaced.

DOMDocumentFragment

DOMDocumentFragment extends DOMNode (see Table B-24).

Table B-24. DOMDocumentFragment *Methods*

Method	Description
__construct()	Constructs a new DOMDocumentFragment element that is not associated with a document.
appendXML(string data)	Builds an XML tree based on the input data within a DOMDocument➡ Fragment. This function was added in PHP 5.1.

DOMDocument

DOMDocument extends DOMNode. Table B-25 lists the DOMDocument properties, and Table B-26 lists the DOMDocument methods.

Table B-25. DOMDocument *Properties*

Name	Type	Read-Only?	Description
actualEncoding	string	Yes	Indicates the encoding of the document.
doctype	DOMDocumentType	Yes	Indicates the document type declaration associated with this document.
documentElement	DOMElement	Yes	This is a convenience attribute that allows direct access to the child node that is the document element of the document.
documentURI	string	No	Indicates the location of the document or NULL if undefined.
encoding	string	No	Indicates the current encoding of the document.
formatOutput	bool	No	During serialization, this property specifies whether line feeds and indentation should be added. The default value is FALSE.
implementation	DOMImplementation	Yes	Indicates that the DOMImplementation object handles this document.
preserveWhiteSpace	bool	No	Does not remove redundant whitespace. The default is TRUE.
recover	bool	No	Indicates the parser recover on a fatal error while loading the document. The default is FALSE.
resolveExternals	bool	No	Loads external entities from a doctype declaration. This is useful for including character entities in your XML document.
standalone	bool	No	Indicates the value of the standalone attribute from the XML declaration.
strictErrorChecking	bool	No	Throws DOMException on errors. The default is TRUE.

Continued

Table B-25. *Continued*

Name	Type	Read-Only?	Description
substituteEntities	bool	No	Determines whether the parser should substitute entities with their content when loading a document.
validateOnParse	bool	No	Loads and validates against the DTD. The default is FALSE.
version	string	No	Indicates the XML version being used in the document.
xmlEncoding	string	Yes	Specifies, as part of the XML declaration, the encoding of this document. This is NULL when unspecified or when it is not known, such as when the document was created in memory.
xmlStandalone	bool	No	Specifies, as part of the XML declaration, whether this document is stand-alone. This is FALSE when unspecified.
xmlVersion	string	No	Specifies, as part of the XML declaration, the version number of this document. If there is no declaration and if this document supports the XML feature, the value is 1.0.

Table B-26. DOMDocument *Methods*

Method	Description
__construct([string version[, string encoding]])	Creates a new DOMDocument object.
createAttribute(string name)	Creates a new attribute associated with the DOMDocument.
createAttributeNS(string namespaceURI, string qualifiedName)	Creates a new attribute node with an associated namespace associated with the DOMDocument.
createCDATASection(string data)	Creates a new CDATA node associated with the DOMDocument.
createComment(string data)	Creates a new comment node associated with the DOMDocument.
createDocumentFragment()	Creates a new document fragment associated with the DOMDocument.
createElement(string tagName [, string value])	Creates a new element node associated with the DOMDocument.
createElementNS(string namespaceURI, string qualifiedName [,string value])	Creates a new element node with an associated namespace associated with the DOMDocument.
createEntityReference(string name)	Creates a new entity reference node associated with the DOMDocument.
createProcessingInstruction(string target[, string data])	Creates a new PI node associated with the DOMDocument.
createTextNode(string data)	Creates a new text node associated with the DOMDocument.
getElementById(string elementId)	Searches for an element with a certain ID.

Method	Description
getElementsByTagName(string tagname)	Searches for all elements with the given tag name.
getElementsByTagNameNS(string namespaceURI, string localName)	Searches for all elements with given tag name in specified namespace.
importNode(DOMNode importedNode, Boolean deep)	Imports a node into current document.
load(string URI [, integer options])	Loads XML from a file.
loadHTML(string source)	Loads HTML from a string.
loadHTMLFile(string URI)	Loads HTML from a file.
loadXML(string data [, integer options])	Loads XML from a string.
normalizeDocument()	Normalizes the document.
relaxNGValidate(string filename)	Performs RELAX NG validation on the document loading the schema from a URI.
relaxNGValidateSource(string data)	Performs RELAX NG validation on the document loading the schema from a string.
save(string URI[, integer options])	Dumps the internal XML tree back into a file.
saveHTML(string source)	Dumps the internal document into a string using HTML formatting.
saveHTMLFile(string URI)	Dumps the internal document into a file using HTML formatting.
saveXML([node n [, integer options]])	Dumps the internal XML tree back into a string.
schemaValidate(string filename)	Validates a document based on a schema loaded from a URI.
schemaValidateSource(string data)	Validates a document based on a schema.
validate()	Validates the document based on its DTD.
xinclude([integer options])	Substitutes XIncludes in a DOMDocument object.
registerNodeClass(string baseclass, string extendedclass)	Registers classes that will be used to create DOM objects rather than the internal ones. This method is in CVS for the upcoming PHP 6.

DOMAttr

DOMAttr extends DOMNode. Table B-27 lists the DOMAttr properties, and Table B-28 lists the DOMAttr methods.

Table B-27. DOMAttr *Properties*

Name	Type	Read-Only?	Description
name	string	Yes	The name of the attribute
ownerElement	DOMElement	Yes	The element that contains the attribute
value	string	No	The value of the attribute

Table B-28. DOMAttr *Methods*

Method	Description
__construct(string name, [string value])	Creates a DOMAttr with a specified name and optional value
isId()	Returns a Boolean indicating whether the attribute is an ID

DOMElement

DOMElement extends DOMNode. Table B-29 lists the DOMElement methods, and Table B-30 lists the DOMElement methods.

Table B-29. DOMElement *Properties*

Name	Type	Read-Only?	Description
tagName	string	Yes	The element name

Table B-30. DOMElement *Methods*

Method	Description
__construct(string name, [string value [, string uri]])	Creates a DOMElement object with a specified name and optionally a value and namespace URI.
getAttribute(string name)	Returns the value of the attribute based on the name.
getAttributeNode(string name)	Returns the attribute node with the specified name.
getAttributeNodeNS(string namespaceURI, string localName)	Returns the attribute node with given namespace and name.
getAttributeNS(string namespaceURI, string localName)	Returns the value of the attribute based on namespace URI and name.
getElementsByTagName(string name)	Gets elements by tag name.
getElementsByTagNameNS(string namespaceURI, string localName)	Gets elements by namespaceURI and localName.
hasAttribute(string name)	Indicates whether the specified attribute exists.
hasAttributeNS(string namespaceURI, string localName)	Indicates whether the specified attribute exists within a namespace.
removeAttribute(string name)	Removes the attribute by name.
removeAttributeNode(DOMAttr oldAttr)	Removes the attribute from the element.
removeAttributeNS(string namespaceURI, string localName)	Removes the attribute by name and namespace.
setAttribute(string name, string value)	Adds a new attribute with the specified name and value.
setAttributeNode(DOMAttr newAttr)	Adds a new attribute node to the element.
setAttributeNodeNS(DOMAttr newAttr)	Adds a new attribute node to the element.

Method	Description
setAttributeNS(string namespaceURI, string qualifiedName, string value)	Adds a new attribute in the specified namespace with fully qualified name and value.
setIdAttribute(string name, Boolean isId)	Sets IDness of an attribute by name. This method is implemented only in CVS for upcoming PHP 6.
setIdAttributeNS(string namespaceURI, string localName, Boolean isId)	Sets IDness of an attribute by name and namespace. This method is implemented only in CVS for upcoming PHP 6.
setIdAttributeNode(attr idAttr, Boolean isId)	Set IDness of an attribute node. This method is implemented only in CVS for upcoming PHP 6.

DOMCharacterData

DOMCharacterData extends DOMNode. Table B-31 lists DOMCharacterData properties, and Table B-32 lists DOMCharacterData methods.

Table B-31. DOMCharacterData *Properties*

Name	Type	Read-Only?	Description
data	string	No	The contents of the node
length	integer	Yes	The length of the contents

Table B-32. DOMCharacterData *Methods*

Method	Description
appendData(string arg)	Appends a string to the end of the character data of the node
deleteData(integer offset, integer count)	Removes a range of characters from the node starting at the offset
insertData(integer offset, string arg)	Inserts a string at the specified 16-bit unit offset
replaceData(integer offset, integer count, string arg)	Replaces a substring within the DOMCharacterData node
substringData(integer offset, integer count)	Extracts a range of data from the node

DOMComment

DOMComment extends DOMCharacterData. Table B-33 lists the DOMComment method.

Table B-33. DOMComment *Methods*

Method	Description
__construct([string value])	Creates a DOMComment object with the specified value

DOMText

DOMText extends DOMCharacterData. Table B-34 lists the DOMText properties, and Table B-35 lists the DOMText methods.

Table B-34. DOMText *Properties*

Name	Type	Read-Only?	Description
wholeText	string	Yes	Returns all text of text nodes logically adjacent to this node, concatenated in document order

Table B-35. DOMText *Methods*

Method	Description
__construct([string value])	Creates a DOMText object with specified value.
splitText(integer offset)	Splits the text of a DOMText node at offset, creating an adjacent DOMText node.
isWhitespaceInElementContent()	Returns a Boolean indicating whether the node contains only whitespace.
isElementContentWhitespace()	This method is depreciated by isWhitespaceInElement➡Content().

DOMCdataSection

DOMCdataSection extends DOMText. Table B-36 lists the DOMCdataSection method.

Table B-36. DOMCdataSection *Methods*

Method	Description
__construct([string value])	Creates a DOMCdataSection object with the specified value

DOMDocumentType

DOMDocumentType extends DOMNode. Table B-37 lists the DOMDocumentType properties.

Table B-37. DOMDocumentType *Properties*

Name	Type	Read-Only?	Description
publicId	string	Yes	The public identifier of the external subset.
systemId	string	Yes	The system identifier of the external subset. This can be an absolute or relative URI.
name	string	Yes	The name of DTD, that is, the name immediately following the DOCTYPE keyword.
entities	DOMNamedNodeMap	Yes	A DOMNamedNodeMap containing the general entities, both external and internal, declared in the DTD.

Name	Type	Read-Only?	Description
notations	DOMNamedNodeMap	Yes	A DOMNamedNodeMap containing the notations declared in the DTD.
internalSubset	string	Yes	The internal subset as a string, or NULL if there is none. This does not contain the delimiting square brackets.

DOMNotation

DOMNotation extends DOMNode. Table B-38 lists the DOMNotation properties.

Table B-38. DOMNotation *Properties*

Name	Type	Read-Only?	Description
publicId	string	Yes	The public identifier of the DOMNotation
systemId	string	Yes	The system identifier of the DOMNotation

DOMEntity

DOMEntity extends DOMNode. Table B-39 lists the DOMEntity properties.

Table B-39. DOMEntity *Properties*

Name	Type	Read-Only?	Description
publicId	string	Yes	The public identifier associated with the entity if specified and NULL otherwise.
systemId	string	Yes	The system identifier associated with the entity if specified and NULL otherwise. This can be an absolute URI or relative.
notationName	string	Yes	For unparsed entities, the name of the notation for the entity. For parsed entities, this is NULL.

DOMEntityReference

DOMEntityReference extends DOMNode. Table B-40 lists the DOMEntityReference method.

Table B-40. DOMEntityReference *Methods*

Method	Description
__construct([string name])	Creates a DOMEntityReference object with specified name

DOMProcessingInstruction

DOMProcessingInstruction extends DOMNode. Table B-41 lists the DOMProcessingInstruction properties, and Table B-42 lists the DOMProcessingInstruction method.

Table B-41. DOMProcessingInstruction *Properties*

Name	Type	Read-Only?	Description
target	string	Yes	The target name of the PI
data	string	No	The content of the PI

Table B-42. DOMProcessingInstruction *Methods*

Method	Description
__construct(string name [, string value])	Creates a DOMProcessingInstruction object with the specified target name and optionally specifies the value

XSL

The XSL extension, detailed in Chapter 10, implements the XSL standard and performs XSL transformations. The functionality of this extension is provided through the XSLTProcessor class. Table B-43 lists the XSL constants, Table B-44 lists the XSLTProcessor properties, and Table B-45 lists the XSLTProcessor methods.

Table B-43. *XSL Constants*

Name	Value	Description
XSL_CLONE_AUTO	0	Allows XSL to determine whether document passed to importStylesheet() needs to be cloned
XSL_CLONE_NEVER	-1	Never clones document passed to importStylesheet()
XSL_CLONE_ALWAYS	1	Always clones document passed to importStylesheet()

Table B-44. XSLTProcessor *Properties*

Name	Default Value	Description
cloneDocument	XSL_CLONE_AUTO	This property determines how the cloning of a document is handled when passed to the importStylesheet. It may take any of the values from Table B-43.

Table B-45. XSLTProcessor *Methods*

Name	Description
getParameter(string namespace, string name)	Returns the value of the parameter specified by name. The namespace parameter is currently unused.
hasExsltSupport()	Returns a Boolean indicating whether PHP has EXSLT support.
importStylesheet(DOMDocument doc)	Imports a style sheet from a DOMDocument object.

Name	Description
registerPHPFunctions([mixed function])	Enables the ability to use PHP functions as XSLT functions. The function parameter was added in PHP 5.1 and allows the available functions to be called to be limited to those specified in the function parameter. It can be a string to set a single function at a time or an array to set multiple functions at once.
removeParameter(string namespace, string name)	Removes a parameter. Returns a Boolean indicating success or failure.
setParameter(string namespace, mixed name [, string value])	Sets value for a parameter. In PHP 5.0 parameters must be passed one at a time passing the namespace: a string containing the name of the parameter and a string containing the value. In PHP 5.1 it is possible to set multiple parameters at once by passing the namespace and an associative array containing the parameter names, where the names are the keys and their corresponding values. Returns a Boolean indicating success or failure.
transformToDoc(DOMDocument doc)	Transforms the input DOMDocument containing the XML data to a resulting DOMDocument.
transformToURI(DOMDocument doc, string uri)	Transforms the input DOMDocument containing the XML data to URI and returning the number of bytes written to the URI.
transformToXML(DOMDocument doc)	Transforms the input DOMDocument containing the XML data to a resulting string.

SOAP

The SOAP extension, covered in Chapter 18, provides functionality allowing for the consumption and creation of SOAP-based Web services. Table B-46 lists the SOAP options constants, Table B-47 lists the SOAP encoding constants, and Table B-48 lists the SOAP functions.

Table B-46. *SOAP Options Constants*

Name	Name
SOAP_1_1	SOAP_ACTOR_NEXT
SOAP_1_2	SOAP_ACTOR_NONE
SOAP_PERSISTENCE_SESSION	SOAP_ACTOR_UNLIMATERECEIVER
SOAP_PERSISTENCE_REQUEST	SOAP_COMPRESSION_ACCEPT
SOAP_FUNCTIONS_ALL	SOAP_COMPRESSION_GZIP
SOAP_ENCODED	SOAP_COMPRESSION_DEFLATE
SOAP_LITERAL	SOAP_AUTHENTICATION_BASIC
SOAP_RPC	SOAP_AUTHENTICATION_DIGEST
SOAP_DOCUMENT	

Table B-47. *SOAP Encoding Constants*

Name	Name	Name
UNKNOWN_TYPE	XSD_GMONTHDAY	XSD_NONPOSITIVEINTEGER
XSD_ANYTYPE	XSD_GYEAR	XSD_NORMALIZEDSTRING
XSD_ANYURI	XSD_GYEARMONTH	XSD_NOTATION
XSD_ANYXML	XSD_HEXBINARY	XSD_POSITIVEINTEGER
XSD_BASE64BINARY	XSD_ID	XSD_QNAME
XSD_BOOLEAN	XSD_IDREF	XSD_SHORT
XSD_BYTE	XSD_IDREFS	XSD_STRING
XSD_DATE	XSD_INT	XSD_TIME XSD_TOKEN
XSD_DATETIME	XSD_INTEGER	XSD_UNSIGNEDBYTE
XSD_DECIMAL	XSD_LANGUAGE	XSD_UNSIGNEDINT
XSD_DOUBLE	XSD_LONG	XSD_UNSIGNEDLONG
XSD_DURATION	XSD_NAME	XSD_UNSIGNEDSHORT
XSD_ENTITY	XSD_NCNAME	SOAP_ENC_OBJECT
XSD_ENTITIES	XSD_NEGATIVEINTEGER	SOAP_ENC_ARRAY
XSD_FLOAT	XSD_NMTOKEN	XSD_1999_TIMEINSTANT
XSD_GDAY	XSD_NMTOKENS	XSD_NAMESPACE
XSD_GMONTH	XSD_NONNEGATIVEINTEGER	XSD_1999_NAMESPACE

Table B-48. *SOAP Functions*

Function	Description
use_soap_error_handler([bool handler])	This function disables SOAP error handling and uses the current PHP error handler. The SOAP error handler is enabled by default when working with a SoapClient or SoapServer.
is_soap_fault(zval data)	Returns a Boolean indicating whether data is a SoapFault.

SoapVar

The SoapVar class defines only a constructor and is used to type and encode data:

```
__construct(mixed data, int encoding [, string type_name [,
        string type_namespace [, string node_name [, string node_namespace]]]])
```

Table B-49 lists the SoapVar constructor parameters.

Table B-49. SoapVar *Constructor Parameters*

Parameter	Description
data	The data to pass or return
encoding	The encoding ID, one of the SOAP encoding constants
type_name	The type name
type_namespace	The type namespace
node_name	The XML node name
node_namespace	The XML node namespace

SoapParam

The SoapParam class creates a name-based parameter. This class implements only a constructor:

__construct(mixed data, string name)

Table B-50 lists the SoapParam constructor parameters.

Table B-50. SoapParam *Constructor Parameters*

Parameter	Description
data	The data to pass or return. Typically this is a SoapVar object.
name	The name of the parameter.

SoapHeader

The SoapHeader class creates SOAP header entities to be added to the SOAP message within the SOAP header:

__construct(string namespace, string name [, mixed data [, bool mustUnderstand [, mixed actor]]])

Table B-51 lists the SoapHeader constructor parameters.

Table B-51. SoapHeader *Constructor Parameters*

Parameter	Description
namespace	The namespace of the SOAP header element.
name	The name of the SOAP header element.
data	A SOAP header's content. It can be a PHP value or a SoapVar object.
mustUnderstand	Value of the mustUnderstand attribute of the SOAP header element.
actor	Value of the actor attribute of the SOAP header element. This is the URI of the recipient or one of the SOAP_ACTOR_ ... constants.

SoapFault

The SoapFault class creates SOAP faults from a server that are returned to the calling client to be handled:

```
__construct(string faultcode, string faultstring [, string faultactor [,
        mixed detail [, string faultname [, SoapHeader headerfault]]]])
```

Table B-52 lists the SoapFault constructor parameters.

Table B-52. SoapFault *Constructor Parameters*

Parameter	Description
faultcode	The error code of the SoapFault
faultstring	The error message of the SoapFault
faultactor	A string identifying the actor that caused the error
detail	A PHP variable or SoapVar object to pass in the SOAP fault detail
faultname	Can be used to select the proper fault encoding from WSDL
headerfault	Can be used during SOAP header handling to report an error in the response header

SoapClient

The SoapClient class creates SOAP messages and makes SOAP requests. Table B-53 lists the SoapClient methods.

Table B-53. SoapClient *Methods*

Method	Description
__construct(mixed wsdl [, array options])	Constructor for SoapClient.
__getLastRequest()	Returns a string containing the last SOAP message request when the trace option is enabled.
__getLastResponse()	Returns a string containing the last SOAP message response when the trace option is enabled.
__getLastRequestHeaders()	Returns a string containing the last request headers when the trace option is enabled.
__getLastResponseHeaders()	Returns a string containing the last response headers when the trace option is enabled.
__getFunctions()	Returns an array of functions extracted from the WSDL.
__getTypes()	Returns an array of types extracted from the WSDL.
__doRequest(string request, string location, string action, int version)	This method is called by the SoapClient class when a request is made. Implementing this method in a subclassed SoapClient object allows access and modification to the SOAP message prior to the request being sent to a SOAP server. When implemented, it is required that the parent's __doRequest method be called for the request to be made.

Method	Description
__soapCall (string function_name [, array arguments [, array options [, mixed input_headers [, array &output_headers]]]])	Calls a function by name and returns appropriate typed data. This method depreciated __call() in PHP 5.0.2.
__setCookie(string name [, string value])	Sets a cookie that is sent with the request. This method was added in PHP 5.0.4.
__setLocation([string new_location])	Sets a new URL (endpoint) for the SoapClient. This method was added in PHP 5.0.4.
__setSoapHeaders(array SoapHeaders)	Sets SOAP headers by passing an array of SoapHeader objects, replacing any previously set headers. This method was added in PHP 5.0.5.

SoapServer

Table B-54 calls the SoapClient methods.

Table B-54. SoapClient *Methods*

Method	Description
__construct(mixed wsdl [, array options])	Constructor for SoapServer.
setClass(string class_name [, mixed args])	Sets the class and its constructor arguments that will handle SOAP requests.
addFunction(mixed functions)	Registers function handlers either one at a time, by array, or all at once using SOAP_FUNCTIONS_ALL constant.
getFunctions()	Returns an array of functions registered with the server.
handle([string soap_request])	Handles a SOAP request. A SOAP message can be passed directly rather than retrieved automatically.
setPersistence(int mode)	Sets the persistence mode of SoapServer using one of the persistence constants.
fault(string code, string string [, string actor [, mixed details [, string name]]])	Issues a SOAP fault.

XMLWriter

The XMLWriter extension, mentioned in Chapter 21, is an API to create XML-serialized XML documents using a simple interface. It was added to the default PHP distribution in PHP 5.1.2. It originally was a PECL extension developed for PHP 4.3 using procedural calls, but an object-oriented interface was added for PHP 5. The API documented here is for the object-oriented interface using the XMLWriter class. Table B-55 lists the XMLWriter class methods.

Table B-55. *XMLWriter Class Methods*

Method	Description
openUri(string source)	Initializes the writer and sets the URI to which the data will be written.
openMemory()	Initializes the writer using memory to provide string output.
outputMemory([bool flush])	Returns the current data in the memory buffer as a string. The memory buffer can be cleared when flush is passed as TRUE.
flush([bool empty])	Sends the writer buffer to the output. The return type depends upon the output method being used (memory or URI). The empty parameter, default FALSE, determines whether the writer buffer is cleared when data is sent to output.
setIndent(bool indent)	Turns indenting on/off. The default setting is off.
setIndentString(string indentString)	Sets string to use for indenting.
startComment()	Starts a comment.
endComment()	Closes an open comment.
writeComment(string content)	Creates a complete comment tag.
StartAttribute(string name)	Starts an attribute.
endAttribute()	Closes an open attribute.
writeAttribute(string name, string content)	Creates a complete attribute with a name and content.
startAttributeNs(string prefix, string name, string uri)	Starts a namespaced attribute. libxml 2.6.17 and newer is required for this method.
startElement(string name)	Starts an element.
endElement()	Closes an open element.
startElementNs(string prefix, string name, string uri)	Starts a namespaced element tag.
writeElement(string name, string content)	Creates a complete element tag.
writeElementNs(string prefix, string name, string uri, string content)	Creates a complete namespace element tag.
startPi(string target)	Starts a PI tag.
endPi()	Closes an open PI.
writePi(string target, string content)	Creates a complete PI tag.
startCdata()	Starts a CDATA section.
endCdata()	Closes an open CDATA section.
writeCdata(string content)	Creates a complete CDATA section.
text(string content)	Writes some text within current context.
startDocument([string version[, string encoding[, string standalone]]])	Starts a document setting as version, encoding, and standalone.

Method	Description
endDocument()	Closes an open document.
startDtd(string name[, string pubid[, string sysid]])	Starts a DTD tag.
endDtd()	Closes an open DTD tag.
writeDtd(string name[, string pubid[, string sysid[, string subset]]])	Creates a complete DTD tag.
startDtdElement(string name)	Starts a DTD element.
endDtdElement()	Closes an open DTD element.

▪▪▪
Features and Changes
in PHP 6

Technology is in a continual state of perpetual motion. It is nearly impossible to keep up with all the changes and new features. This also holds true within PHP. During the time it took to write the chapters in this book, PHP has added new functionality and has fixed or changed some behavior. This appendix addresses some of these changes and introduces some new functionality that will be released with PHP 6.

▌Note Although most of the new features mentioned in this chapter are currently planned to be released in PHP 6, it is possible they may be introduced in an earlier version depending upon the PHP release schedule.

---

xml Extension

Chapter 8 pointed out the problems of using default handlers. When using the xml extension under PHP 4 and implementing a default handler, any data not handled by any other handler will use the default handler. Under PHP 5, when defined, the default handler will process only comments and entities. With the release of PHP 5.1, this has changed. Although XML declarations and DTDs are still not handled, other types of data, otherwise unhandled in PHP 5.0, are now processed by the default handler. Listing C-1 demonstrates how to parse a document containing various node types using only a default handler. The results shown in Listings C-2 and C-3 demonstrate the difference in output when the code is executed in PHP 5.0 and in PHP 5.1.

Listing C-1. *Parsing XML Using Default Handler*

```php
<?php
function defaultData($parser, $data) {
    print "$data";
}
```

```
$xmldata = '<?xml version="1.0"?>
<root att1="attval">
    <e1>some content</e1>
    <!-- A comment -->
    <?php echo "Processing Instruction"; ?>
    <e2/>
</root>';
$xml_parser = xml_parser_create();
xml_parser_set_option ($xml_parser, XML_OPTION_CASE_FOLDING, 0);
xml_set_default_handler($xml_parser, "defaultData");
xml_parse($xml_parser, $xmldata, true);
?>
```

Listing C-2. *Results Under PHP 5.0*

```
<!-- A comment -->
```

Listing C-3. *Results Under PHP 5.1*

```
<root att1="attval">
    <e1>some content</e1>
    <!-- A comment -->
    <?php echo "Processing Instruction"; ?>
    <e2></e2>
</root>
```

XMLReader Extension

Once PHP 6 is released, XMLReader will provide some new functionality. Probably the most notable feature is the ability to specify the encoding of the XML and parser options from the libxml extension. For example:

```
boolean open(string URI [, string encoding [, int options]])
boolean XML(string source [, string encoding [, int options]])
```

The ability to specify an encoding might not seem all that exciting, but being able to specify parser options now means that XMLReader can perform an XInclude as it processes a document. For example, Listing C-5 shows how to process a document that contains an xinclude call to retrieve only a specific course element from the document in Listing C-4. When the first XML document contained in Listing C-5 is loaded into the XMLReader object, the LIBXML_XINCLUDE parser option is specified, resulting in the XMLReader object also processing the specified course element, shown by the results in Listing C-5.

Listing C-4. *External Document* courses.xml

```
<courses>
    <course cid="c1">
        <title>Basic Languages</title>
        <description>Introduction to Languages</description>
        <credits>1.5</credits>
        <lastmodified>2004-09-01T11:13:01</lastmodified>
    </course>
    <course cid="c2">
        <title>French I</title>
        <description>Introduction to French</description>
        <credits>3.0</credits>
        <lastmodified>2005-06-01T14:21:37</lastmodified>
    </course>
</courses>
```

Listing C-5. *XMLReader Using XInclude and Resulting Output*

```php
<?php
$xincdata = '<?xml version="1.0" ?>
<academic xmlns:xi="http://www.w3.org/2001/XInclude">
   <xi:include href="courses.xml" parse="xml"
               xpointer="xpointer(/courses/course[@cid='.'"'c1'".'])">
      <xi:fallback>Element not found</xi:fallback>
   </xi:include>
</academic>';

$reader = new XMLReader();

/* Load the XML document, and pass the LIBXML_XINCLUDE parser option */
$reader->XML($xincdata, NULL, LIBXML_XINCLUDE);
while ($reader->read()) {
   if ($reader->nodeType == XMLReader::ELEMENT) {
      print $reader->localName;
      /* If element is named title, move to text node and output contents */
      if ($reader->localName == 'title') {
         $reader->read();
         print ": ".$reader->value;
      }
   print "\n";
   }
}
?>
```

```
academic
course
title: Basic Languages
description
credits
lastmodified
```

Three other new methods allow for text content to be accessed in a simpler manner. These new methods, shown in Table C-1, are available only when PHP is built with libxml2-2.6.20 and higher. None of the methods take any parameters, and all return a string.

Table C-1. *New XMLReader Methods for PHP 6*

Method	Description
readInnerXml()	Returns a string containing the contents of the current node, which includes child nodes and markup.
readOuterXml()	Returns a string containing the current node and all of its contents, which includes child nodes and markup.
readString()	Returns a string containing the contents an element or text node. When positioned on an element, the content of all text and CDATA nodes within the subtree of the element are concatenated together in the resulting string.

The example in Listing C-6 uses XMLReader to process a document containing various node types. I have not modified the results in order to demonstrate that all text nodes, including the whitespaces, are returned in the resulting string from each of the method calls.

Listing C-6. *Example Calling* readString(), readInnerXml(), *and* readOuterXml()

```php
<?php
$xmldata = '<?xml version="1.0"?>
<root att1="attval">
    <e1>some content</e1>
    <!-- A comment -->
    <?php echo "Processing Instruction"; ?>
    <e2/>
    <![CDATA[ more content ]]>
</root>';

$reader = new XMLReader();
$reader->XML($xmldata);
while ($reader->read()) {
    if ($reader->nodeType == XMLReader::ELEMENT) {
        switch ($reader->localName) {
            case 'root':
                print "readInnerXML():\n";
                print $reader->readInnerXml()."\n";
                print "readString():\n";
```

```
            print $reader->readString()."\n";
            break;
        case 'e1':
            print "readOuterXML():\n";
            print $reader->readOuterXML()."\n";
    }
  }
}
?>
```

readInnerXML():

```
  <e1>some content</e1>
  <!-- A comment -->
  <?php echo "Processing Instruction"; ?>
  <e2/>
  <![CDATA[ more content ]]>
```

readString():

```
  some content


  more content
```

readOuterXML():
<e1>some content</e1>

SimpleXML Extension

No time has been wasted with the SimpleXML extension. As of PHP 5.1.2, two new methods have been introduced, getNamespaces() and getDocNamespaces(), and the resulting structure from calling var_dump() with a SimpleXMLElement has changed for the better.

Working with namespaced documents is probably the area that causes the most problems for developers working with SimpleXML. To access an element or attribute within a namespace, and not the default namespace, you must specify the namespace URI. The issue faced is that it is up to the developer to remember all the namespaces used throughout the document. The only way to introspect the document for namespaces is to import it into DOM and use XPath to locate namespaces. That is, that was the only way until now.

The getNamespaces() and getDocNamespaces() methods return an associative array of namespaces where the prefix is the key and the namespace URI is the value. The difference between the two methods is the scope of the document that is searched and the type of namespace returned in the array. The getNamespaces() method operates on the current element. The namespace URI for which the element resides in, if any, is added in the returned array. The getDocNamespaces() method uses the document element as the starting point rather than the element from which it is called. This method not only adds the namespace of the document element but also any namespaces that have been declared on the document element.

■**Note** Prefixes are not used with default namespaces. If a default namespace is added to the return array by either of these functions, the key for the item is an empty string.

These methods also take an optional Boolean parameter, recursive. When passed as TRUE, both methods will also add namespaces found within the starting element's subtree to the array as well. The use of the recursive parameter might give you pause. It is perfectly legal for prefixes to change their namespace associations within a document. Even default namespaces can be changed for different scopes. Then how do you deal with the issue of using prefixes for the array keys?

When working with SimpleXML, it naturally would be more important to know about namespaces within an element that are closer to the element rather than ones that have been redefined and reside further down in the subtree. The returned array, when called recursively, returns the first namespace URIs encountered that have their prefixes redefined further within the tree. This may be a bit hard to visualize, so the example in Listing C-7 should clarify this.

Listing C-7. *Retrieving Namespace URIs with SimpleXML*

```php
<?php
$xmldata = '<?xml version="1.0" ?>
<root xmlns:a="urn:namespace:A" xmlns:b="urn:namespace:B">
    <a:node_1 xmlns="urn:newns:C" xmlns:b="urn:newns:B">
        <a:node xmlns:a="urn:newns:A" />
    </a:node_1>
</root>';

$sxe = simplexml_load_string($xmldata);

/* getDocNamespaces() call */
$arnames = $sxe->getDocNamespaces();
print "Doc Namespaces: \n";
foreach ($arnames AS $prefix=>$namespace) {
    print "  Prefix: $prefix URI: $namespace \n";
}

/* Recursive getDocNamespaces() call */
$arnames = $sxe->getDocNamespaces(TRUE);
print "\nDoc Namespaces Recursive: \n";
foreach ($arnames AS $prefix=>$namespace) {
    print "  Prefix: $prefix URI: $namespace \n";
}
```

```
/* getNamespace() call */
$a_ns = $sxe->children('urn:namespace:A');
$node_1 = $a_ns->node_1;
$arnames = $node_1->getNamespaces();
print "\nElement a:node_1 Namespaces: \n";
foreach ($arnames AS $prefix=>$namespace) {
   print "   Prefix: $prefix URI: $namespace \n";
}

/* Recursive getNamespace() call */
$arnames = $node_1->getNamespaces(TRUE);
print "\nElement a:node_1 Recursive: \n";
foreach ($arnames AS $prefix=>$namespace) {
   print "   Prefix: $prefix URI: $namespace \n";
}
?>
```

```
Doc Namespaces:
   Prefix: a URI: urn:namespace:A
   Prefix: b URI: urn:namespace:B

Doc Namespaces Recursive:
   Prefix: a URI: urn:namespace:A
   Prefix: b URI: urn:namespace:B
   Prefix:   URI: urn:newns:C

Element a:node_1 Namespaces:
   Prefix: a URI: urn:namespace:A

Element a:node_1 Recursive:
   Prefix: a URI: urn:namespace:A
```

As you can see by the results, the first call to getDocNamespaces() returns the two namespaces, urn:namespace:A and urn:namespace:B, that are declared on the document element, root. The next call to the method is performed recursively by passing TRUE as the parameter. In this case, not only the two namespaces from the previous method call are returned but also the urn:newns:C namespace is returned. The namespace urn:newns:A, from the a:node element, is not returned in this case because the prefix a has already been mapped from the declaration of the urn:namespace:A namespace on the document element. The last two getNamespaces() method calls return namespaces that are actually used and not only declared within the scope of the element from which the method is called. From the code in Listing C-7, the method is called using the a:node_1 element as the starting point. The first call to getNamespaces() simply returns the namespace urn:namespace:A, which is the namespace in which the element resides. The second call to the method is performed recursively. Because the prefix a has already been added to the array being returned, the urn:newns:A namespace is not added to the returned array.

Besides the addition of these two methods, the data returned by calling var_dump()
on a SimpleXMLElement has also changed. First, attributes are now included in the output.
SimpleXMLElement objects containing attributes will be output, with this function containing
an additional property named @attributes. The value of this property is an array containing
its attributes. Second, how objects deal with namespaces has changed. The var_dump() function now also respects the namespace of the object, meaning that any child elements included
in the output are within the same namespace of the object with which the function was called.
Prior to this change, namespaces were not respected, and all elements within the objects subtree were output.

Listing C-8 uses a document where one of the child course elements resides in a prefixed
namespace. Each of the course elements also contains a cid attribute. You will notice the difference between the output when the script is executed using PHP 5.0, shown in Listing C-9,
and the output when executed using PHP 5.1.2, shown in Listing C-10. Not only do you see the
attributes in Listing C-10, but only the first course element is contained in the output. The
object being passed to var_dump() has not had any namespace specified, such as creating an
object using the children(namespaceURI) method, so only children not within a namespace
or within the default namespace will be included.

Listing C-8. *Using* var_dump() *with* SimpleXMLElement

```php
<?php
$xmldata = '<?xml version="1.0" ?>
<courses>
    <course cid="c1">
        <title>Basic Languages</title>
    </course>
    <a:course cid="c2" xmlns:a="urn:namespace:A">
        <!-- this course element is within prefixed namespace -->
        <title>French I</title>
    </a:course>
</courses>';
$sxe = simplexml_load_string($xmldata);
var_dump($sxe);
?>
```

Listing C-9. *PHP 5.0 Results from Listing C-8*

```
object(SimpleXMLElement)#1 (1) {
  ["course"]=>
  array(2) {
    [0]=>
    object(SimpleXMLElement)#2 (1) {
      ["title"]=>
      string(15) "Basic Languages"
    }
```

```
   [1]=>
   object(SimpleXMLElement)#3 (2) {
     ["comment"]=>
     object(SimpleXMLElement)#4 (0) {
     }
     ["title"]=>
     string(8) "French I"
   }
 }
}
```

Listing C-10. *PHP 5.1.2 Results from Listing C-8*

```
object(SimpleXMLElement)#1 (1) {
  ["course"]=>
  object(SimpleXMLElement)#2 (2) {
    ["@attributes"]=>
    array(1) {
      ["cid"]=>
      string(2) "c1"
    }
    ["title"]=>
    string(15) "Basic Languages"
  }
}
```

DOM Extension

Not to be left out, the DOM extension contains new functionality for PHP 6. Developers who regularly use this extension will be excited to know that one of the most requested features has finally been implemented—the ability to have DOM return nodes using extended classes rather than the built-in ones. Before going into more details on this, I will mention the other new functionality that has been implemented, because it is now possible to add and remove IDs using any attribute.

The DOM specification defines the setIdAttribute(), setIdAttributeNS(), and setIdAttributeNode() methods on a DOMElement object. Until now, these have not been implemented in the DOM extension. The methods do not create new attributes in a document. The parameters passed are used to locate a specific attribute and indicate whether it should be an ID. For example:

```
setIdAttribute(string name, boolean isId)
setIdAttributeNS(string namespaceURI, string localName, boolean isId)
setIdAttributeNode(DOMAttr idAttr, boolean isId)
```

Prior to these methods, the only way to create the attribute ID in a document was to use a DTD to specify an attribute is of the ID type or use the xml:id attribute. This was limiting because the DTD cannot be changed after the document has been loaded, so attributes not specified in the DTD could not be made into an ID. Also, once an attribute was made into an ID, you had no way to remove the ID other than to physically remove the entire attribute from the document. Listing C-11 demonstrates how to set and remove an ID on a document not containing a DTD and use only these new methods.

Listing C-11. *Setting Attribute IDs Using* DOMElement *Methods*

```php
<?php
$xmldata = '<?xml version="1.0" ?>
<courses>
    <course cid="c1">
        <title>Basic Languages</title>
    </course>
</courses>';

$dom = new DOMDocument();
$dom->loadXML($xmldata);
$root = $dom->documentElement;
$node = $root->firstChild;
$course = $node->nextSibling;

$course->setIDAttribute('cid', TRUE);
print "setIDAttribute - TRUE\n   ";
if ($element = $dom->getElementByID('c1')) {
   print $element->nodeName;
} else {
   print "ID Does not exist";
}

$attr = $course->getAttributeNode('cid');
$course->setIDAttributeNode($attr, FALSE);
print "\n\nsetIDAttributeNode - FALSE\n   ";
if ($element = $dom->getElementByID('c1')) {
   print $element->nodeName;
} else {
   print "ID Does not exist";
}
?>
```

```
setIDAttribute - TRUE
   course

setIDAttributeNode - FALSE
   ID Does not exist
```

Finally, I will now cover probably one of the most requested features for DOM. The normal method for creating objects based on a class that extends one of the DOM classes and inserting it into the tree was to create the node using the new keyword to instantiate an object of the extended class type. This node was then inserted into the tree using any of the various DOM methods applicable for this action. This method had a few drawbacks. Probably the most important one was that you should use the createXXXX() methods from DOMDocument when creating a new node to properly create it with a document association. The other big drawback, which mostly affected developers, was that once the newly created object fell out of scope and no longer had any references, the next time the node was accessed, the object returned would be based on one of the internal DOM classes and no longer the extended class type.

The good news is that you can finally do this—or at least once PHP 6 rolls around, you will be able to do this. The registerNodeClass() method has been added to the DOMDocument class. This method allows a user class that extends any of the DOM classes based on DOMNode to be registered with a document and cause the extended class to be instantiated when needed rather than the internal DOM class. Every method within DOM will respect the class registration:

```
registerNodeClass(string baseclass, string extendedclass)
```

This method takes two parameters and returns a Boolean indicating whether registration was successful. The first parameter, baseclass, is the name of the DOM class that the user class is replacing. The extendedclass parameter is either the name of the user class to register, which must inherit from baseclass, or NULL. When NULL is passed, any class that may have previously been registered for the baseclass will unregister itself, causing the baseclass to once again be used as the class type when objects are created.

■**Note** Classes are registered per document and not per request. This also means that reusing a DOMDocument object for multiple XML documents will reset the registered classes to the original empty state each time a new document is loaded.

As mentioned in the previous note, classes are registered per document. This means every time a new document is created, you must register your classes. For example, each of the following calls creates a new document:

```
/* Create a new empty document */
$dom = new DOMdocument();

/* Load a string creating a new document */
$dom->loadXML(...);

/* Load a URI creating a new document */
$dom->load(...);
```

Based on this, unless you are creating a new document from scratch, you would not register any classes until after having called one of the load methods. A benefit of this being based on a document, however, is that if you are working on two or more documents simultaneously, each document can use a different class for a node type, rather than only a single class per node type for every document. This may sound more complex than it really is. Listing C-12 should make things much clearer.

Listing C-12. *Registering Extended Classes in DOM*

```php
<?php
class userElement extends DOMElement {
    function customFunction() {
        print "Node Name: ".$this->nodeName."\n";
        print "Node Contents: ".$this->nodeValue."\n";
    }
}


$xmldata = '<?xml version="1.0" ?>
<courses>
    <course cid="c1">
        <title>Basic Languages</title>
    </course>
</courses>';

$dom = new DOMDocument();
/* Load the XML, and remove blanks for simplicity */
$dom->loadXML($xmldata, LIBXML_NOBLANKS);

/* Register the userElement class */
print "Register userElement class\n\n";
$dom->registerNodeClass('DOMElement', 'userElement');
$root = $dom->documentElement;
$course = $root->firstChild;
$title = $course->firstChild;
$title->customFunction();

/* Unregister our custom class */
print "Unregister Custom Class\n\n";
$dom->registerNodeClass('DOMElement', NULL);
print "Remove reference to title node using unset()\n\n";
/* Call unset() to remove reference to title node */
unset($title);
?>
```

```
Register userElement class

Node Name: title
Node Contents: Basic Languages
Unregister Custom Class
```

```
Remove reference to title node using unset()

course element is of the userElement class

title element is of the DOMElement class
```

No longer do you need to use the new keyword. The ability to register classes with a document solves many of the issues developers have had when a subclassed object loses scope. Even when a class was unregistered, objects in scope that were created based on the extended class remain the extended class type until they also lose scope. Listing C-12 demonstrated this with the course element. This still does not provide persistence; when an object goes out of scope, it is re-created when the node is accessed again. Therefore, property values will be reset, but all the functions of the class are available.

Index

Find it faster at http://superindex.apress.com/

Find it faster at http://superindex.apress.com/

Find it faster at http://superindex.apress.com/

Find it faster at http://superindex.apress.com/

Find it faster at http://superindex.apress.com/

Find it faster at http://superindex.apress.com/

Find it faster at http://superindex.apress.com/

Find it faster at http://superindex.apress.com/

Find it faster at http://superindex.apress.com/

Find it faster at http://superindex.apress.com/

Find it faster at http://superindex.apress.com/

Find it faster at http://superindex.apress.com/

Find it faster at http://superindex.apress.com/

Find it faster at http://superindex.apress.com/

You Need the Companion eBook

Your purchase of this book entitles you to its companion eBook for only $10.

We believe this Apress title will prove so indispensable that you'll want to carry it with you everywhere, which is why we are offering the companion eBook for $10 to customers who purchase this book now. Convenient and fully searchable, the eBook version of any content-rich, page-heavy Apress book makes a valuable addition to your programming library. You can easily find, copy, and apply code—and then perform examples by quickly toggling between instructions and the application. Even simultaneously tackling a donut, diet soda, and complex code becomes simplified with hands-free eBooks!

Once you purchase this book, getting the $10 companion eBook is simple:

❶ Visit **www.apress.com/promo/tendollars/**.

❷ Complete a basic registration form to receive a randomly generated question about this title.

❸ Answer the question correctly in 60 seconds and you will receive a promotional code to redeem for the $10 eBook.

2560 Ninth Street • Suite 219 • Berkeley, CA 94710

All Apress eBooks subject to copyright protection. No part may be reproduced or transmitted in any form or by any means, electronic or mechanical, including photocopying, recording, or by any information storage or retrieval system, without the prior written permission of the copyright owner and the publisher. The purchaser may print the work in full or in part for their own non-commercial use. The purchaser may place the eBook title on any of their personal computers for their own personal reading and reference.

Offer valid through 08/06.

Printed in the United States
By Bookmasters